MEDIEVAL FOUNDATIONS

OF

WESTERN CIVILIZATION

MEDIEVAL FOUNDATIONS

OF

WESTERN CIVILIZATION

By GEORGE C. SELLERY, *Dean of the*
College of Letters and Science, Professor of History
University of Wisconsin, and A. C. KREY
Professor of History, University of Minnesota

WITH MAPS

HARPER & BROTHERS PUBLISHERS
NEW YORK AND LONDON MCMXXIX

CONTENTS

CONTENTS

MAPS

EDITORIAL FOREWORD

THERE was a time when a goodly part of the period covered by this volume was called the Dark Ages. The title was justified by the way in which the age was treated by most of the writers who dealt with it. Any reader who came out at the far end of their accounts freely accepted the designation. Happily, the clouds of dust have cleared from the pages of modern writers and we see now the works and worth of the centuries between Romulus Augustulus and Richelieu. Despite all our modernity, we betray our medieval origins and we know ourselves better the more we know of our heritage from the Europe this book reconstructs.

The American who looks in reverence at the cathedrals and monuments of European civilization thinks of the thousand years that are looking down upon him. But behind the eyes that look up are the cultural traces of institutional attitudes of just as many centuries. Whatever the New World may have added to us, we are yet basically the heirs of European peoples and the modified products of European history. So much of what seems essentially European in this our heritage took shape in the ages covered by this volume, that the thoughtful student will have a growing sense that its pages are in a real sense an introduction to American history. The last chapter fairly carries him past the threshold of his own nation's history.

As I have read the manuscript, I have found pleasure in the skill with which the authors drew upon their own and all scholarship for fresh views and transferred to the printed page the skillful presentation that has hitherto been shared only by the students in their classrooms. As an editor, I have contributed little to the text. The book is wholly the work of Professors Sellery and Krey. I only helped contribute the "and."

GUY STANTON FORD

PREFACE

THIS book is intended to give the modern reader a background of familiarity with the medieval foundations of our contemporary Western civilization. For we of the Americas and of other lands settled by Europeans share Western civilization with Europe. This Western civilization has a varying color from country to country; but it is the variation of identical flora growing under different skies. It is one civilization. And it is one largely because we share a common heritage with Western Europe.

No one disputes the reality or importance of the contributions of the ancient Orient, Greece, and Rome to our civilization; and fortunate is he who knows, with some intimacy, what they have given to the common store. But it is to be remembered that their contributions, by and large, were made via the Middle Ages. We moderns are the immediate heirs of the Middle Ages. It is the conviction of the writers of this book that a fruitful understanding of our contemporary civilization demands the study of the temper, achievements, successes, failures, prejudices, and aspirations of our medieval ancestors.

For convenience of exposition the written record of medieval times is usually broken up into such fragments as politics, religion, economics, art, letters, and social institutions. Such a scheme carries with it the danger that the reader may fail to realize that these separate aspects of past civilization are knit together inextricably; that, for example, the economic life of the age affects political policies, and that both in turn shape and are shaped by social organization and the productions of art and literature.

And as their civilization was really a single fabric, although of many hues, so the medieval peoples, in spite of localism and the poorness of their roads, were intimately bound together in the common adventure of life. No major discovery, no major disturbance left any part of Western Europe unaffected. The history of medieval Europe is more than the history of each of the countries composing it.

The authors of this work have endeavored to show the unity of medieval history and the interdependence of the various aspects of medieval civilization. They have centered attention upon the particular region of greatest activity for the time being, have shifted from one country to another as it has taken over the leadership, and have caught up the subordinate strands of national history at convenient and logical intervals. An enhanced sense of variety and unity in medieval development should result from this method of presentation. In their consideration of such topics as education, literature, art, and economics, they have likewise striven to illuminate the path traveled by our medieval ancestors, and have not been content merely to assert the progress of the important arts we inherited from them.

The annexation of an additional century and a half (1500 to 1660) to the medieval story is not intended to indicate a willful indifference to the customary periodization. It was carried out, *ad hoc,* because the authors were impelled to round out their survey with a study of the working out of some of the most significant and influential results of medieval effort. The era from 1500 to 1660 belongs as much to medieval as to modern times.

The authors are under heavy obligations to historical specialists. The footnotes and the bibliographies at the end give some general clues to their indebtedness to others. The text itself, in several places, will tell the historical scholar the sources to which the authors have gone for guidance. For bibliographical and kindred aid they gladly acknowledge their debt to Mrs. A. C. Krey and to Miss Faith Thompson and Mrs. Alice Felt Tyler of the University of Minnesota.

G. C. S.
A. C. K.

MEDIEVAL FOUNDATIONS

OF

WESTERN CIVILIZATION

CHAPTER I

THE BACKGROUND OF MEDIEVAL HISTORY

THE ancient history of European peoples was centered in the Mediterranean basin. Other parts of Europe and adjacent lands were populated throughout antiquity, but the inhabitants were not sufficiently civilized to leave a written record of their activities. Mention is found only of those tribes which moved southward and invaded the Mediterranean circle. As the countries of the south developed, enterprising traders ventured into the northern regions and their observations ultimately found some space in the writings of the time. For all practical purposes, however, recorded ancient history was confined within the boundaries of the Roman Empire. One of the facts, therefore, which sets off medieval from ancient history is the breaking of that line and the inclusion of northern, especially western, Europe within the scope of history.

In general, historians have recognized a great difference between the life of man in ancient times and in the subsequent period to which the term medieval has been applied. They have likewise made efforts to fix a definite date before which society was ancient and after which it was medieval. They have not been able to agree, however, and their dates cover a range of five centuries. They do agree in regarding as ancient history events before 312 A.D., when Christianity was recognized by the Roman emperors as a legal religion, and as medieval history events since the coronation of Charlemagne in 800. But none of the suggested intermediate divisions has won general acceptance without qualifications.

Purely for the sake of convenience, therefore, we begin the narrative of medieval history toward the end of the fourth century A.D.   Certainly the persons then living were conscious of no radical change in their lives, and there was none.   Christianity was gaining more adherents; there were more Teutons [1] within the Roman Empire; there were fewer people engaged in writing literature, or reading it; the Roman imperial officials had less power than formerly: all this is certainly true.   But these changes did not take place all at once, and in some of the generations of the fifth century and in some localities the reverse was more nearly true.   To the people then living there was no apparent break between what we call the old and the new; it required centuries to reveal the alterations that had actually occurred in the political and the social life of the people.

The complete description of affairs before the end of the fourth century belongs properly to ancient history, and we must here content ourselves with a brief survey of those conditions without which the events of the later fourth century cannot be well understood.   Among these conditions and circumstances must be considered both the character of the population and the geography of Europe.   It is essential also to understand something of the life of the uncivilized peoples of Europe before the beginning of the fifth century and the gradual transformation of the Roman Empire up to that time.

THE PEOPLES AND THE GEOGRAPHY OF EUROPE

Most of the peoples of Europe were similar in racial characteristics.   Various methods of race classification have been urged, but none has found universal acceptance.   One method, based upon a study of physical measurements and peculiarities, recognizes three distinct types in Europe—the Mediterranean, the Alpine and the Nordic.   The members of the first group are relatively short in stature, with swarthy skins and dark hair and eyes.   The second, or Alpine group, includes persons with larger frames, clearer skins and short skulls.   The people in the third, or Nordic group, are long-headed, tall and blond.   Under this

---

[1] The terms Teuton and German are frequently used as synonymous.   In this book the term *Teuton* is used to designate the race, while the term *German* is used to designate that portion of the race which lived east of the Rhine, a territory covered by modern Germany.

scheme of classification the Teutonic peoples would be classed as Nordics, the Celts and Slavs as Alpine, and the majority of the Mediterranean population would fall in the first division.

An older classification has considered the peoples of Europe as belonging to four different branches of the Aryan, or Indo-European, race. This system is based upon similarities in language. According to it, most of the inhabitants of the Greek and Italian peninsulas are known as the Græco-Latin branch of the Aryan race; the people of northern Italy, Gaul, Spain and the British Isles as the Celtic branch; the people north and east of the Rhine, including the Scandinavian peninsulas, as the Teutonic branch; and the inhabitants of the interior of the continent, to the east of the Teutonic peoples, as the Slavic branch.

By the end of the fourth century A.D. these peoples occupied most of Europe, but the more remote regions of the north and the less accessible mountain regions of the south were inhabited by unrelated peoples of different races. This fact indicates that important racial movements had taken place in prehistoric times. One of the most extensive of these alien groups still existent is that of the Finns who occupy the frozen northland. Racially they are connected with the Turanian peoples of central and northern Asia. The Basques, inhabitants of the Pyrenees, and the Albanians, dwellers among the more rugged mountains in the western Balkans, appear also to be survivors of earlier races which once occupied more extensive territory.

In addition to these fairly distinct types of people, there were large numbers, especially in the Mediterranean lands, who represented the intermixture of many racial strains. This was most true of the servile population, but there had doubtless been some degree of intermingling among all classes and all peoples. Despite minor variations, however, the similarity of most of the peoples of Europe held a promise that, under favorable conditions, they might all develop a civilization as high as that of the Greeks and Romans.

The influence of geography has played an important part in determining the density of population and manner of life in the various parts of the continent. In the Mediterranean lands, where water, warmth and vegetation were abundant, it was natural that population should increase rapidly and people develop the arts of civilization early. Farther north, where the climate was more severe and the soil more stubborn, the struggle for existence was so hard that population grew but slowly and people had but little leisure to devise elaborate means of comfort and well-being. In the south the Mediterranean, with its numerous arms and tributaries, furnished a natural route dotted with chains of islands to lure the more timid to commercial, social and political intercourse. In the north, on the other hand, rugged hills, forests and forbidding swamps interposed many obstacles to easy movement and so delayed the union of little settlements into large states. Streams, of course, afforded avenues of travel in both regions, but even these were more inviting in the south than in the north. As a result, the people in the south had developed large states and a highly cultivated life centuries before the people of the north had been able even to develop large tribes.

There were two areas in the region outside the Mediterranean circle where conditions changed rapidly and with important consequences for the inhabitants. One of these was in central Asia in the region of the grassy steppes. When rainfall was abundant this region was well suited to grazing, and the nomadic tribes which lived by grazing increased in size. When rain failed, as it did at intervals, much of this land became desert and the struggle for existence sharpened. At such times the herdsmen developed more warlike characteristics and, once started upon a career of warfare, they usually swept over the whole of the steppes country, which extended westward into central Europe. Their expansion was then felt east and west and south, though the mountains furnished some obstacle on the east and south.

The other of these regions was located in northwestern Europe around the western end of the Baltic Sea. The juxtaposition of two seas and numerous inlets combined to moderate the climate there. Fertile lands and convenient waterways favored not only the growth of population but also more extensive coöperation than was usual among northern peoples at the time.   Here too, however, seasons varied abruptly and on such occasions the population had the choice of battle, starvation, or migration.   Probably in times past the inhabitants had tried all of these methods, but when they come within the range of history we find them usually choosing systematic migration.   The direction of such migration was almost necessarily toward the south or southeast, preferably up the river valleys which flowed into the Baltic. These two centers, the one in Asia, the other on the Baltic, may be likened to ethnic volcanoes whose periodic outbursts caused disturbances from time to time affecting all the peoples who dwelt between them and the Mediterranean lands.

Such upheavals did occur in force in the first century A. D., again in the third, and, again, toward the end of the fourth century.   In all, the migrations from the Baltic penetrated as far southeast as the Black Sea, causing turmoil among the peoples all along the route.   The combined effect of these circumstances was pressure upon the Roman frontier.   For nearly four centuries the Roman Empire resisted the farther advance of these people southward.   The Romans fortified their northern frontier, using the Rhine and Danube rivers as natural barriers and strengthening the gap between them by a wall.[1]   The northern part of Great Britain, which they had also included in their Empire, was strengthened against attack from the north by a series of walls. Along these fortifications were stationed garrisons of Roman soldiers, and, as a further protection, retired veterans were settled on these frontier lands.   In a sense this frontier line acted as a dam against the pressure of tribes from the north, but it served also as a means of civilizing them, for peace was more common than warfare along its front.   At any rate it furnished a line of constant contact between Roman and barbarian which could not fail to influence both.

[1] The completed wall was rather a boundary mark than a formidable military barrier.   In part it consisted of a ditch and mound of earth, the Pfalgraben, whose remains can still be seen in parts of southern Germany. Another portion of it was in the form of a low wall, the famous Teufelsmauer, much of which can still be traced.   Military garrisons erected fortifications some distance back from this wall.

THE BARBARIANS BEFORE THE INVASIONS

As a result of this contact the Romans learned much about these people who were pressing on their border. Roman writers from the time of Julius Cæsar, who had actually invaded the land beyond the Rhine, had something to say about them. The most systematic attempt to describe them was made by Tacitus, who wrote more than a century after Cæsar. Thereafter the Romans seem to have felt so well informed that, though references to the barbarian tribes became more and more numerous, few writers felt it necessary to describe them. From the earlier accounts it may be gathered that these northern neighbors of the Romans were a people physically larger than the average Romans, larger even than the Gauls. Their manner of life was semi-nomadic, and included some practice of agriculture and grazing with a great deal of hunting and fishing. The chief occupations of the men were fighting and hunting, domestic economy (generously interpreted) being left largely to the women and some slaves. Their organization was simple. Resting upon blood-kinship, it extended little beyond the limits at which such kinship was recognized. They had a religion which reflected a high degree of enslavement to nature, for they deified the forests, swamps and ocean mists, as well as the more striking phenomena of sun, moon and lightning. Their language was well developed, but the art of writing was still in a very rudimentary stage, consisting of simple runic inscription. Their weapons, cooking utensils and other implements unearthed in recent archeological explorations indicate a degree of advance considerably beyond that of the North American Indians of our colonial period. From the investigations of philologists it appears that there were two large groups of these people—the West Teutons who occupied the regions on the other side of the Rhine, and the East Teutons who lived along the Baltic. Philological evidence also points to the existence of amphictyonies, or confederations of tribes for religious purposes, especially among the East Teutons. So much may be said with a fair degree of certainty about these people when the Romans first encountered them.

PHYSICAL EURASIA

Scale of Miles

PHYSICAL EURASIA

Scale of Miles

0   200   400   600

KEY TO VEGETATION

Grasslands and Steppes

Forest Regions

Desert and Arctic Tundra

Alpine or Montane

ATLANTIC OCEAN

ICELAND

ARCTIC

FAROE IS.

SHETLAND IS.

ORKNEY IS.

BRITISH ISLES

NORTH SEA

Irish Sea

JUTLAND PEN.

SCANDINAVIAN HIGHLANDS

SCANDINAVIAN PENINSULA

G. of Bothnia

BALTIC SEA

Loire

Rhine

Rhône

Rhine

Danube

Seine

PYRENEES

IBERIAN PENINSULA

Douro

Tagus

Ebro

ALPS

APENNINES

CORSICA

SARDINIA

Tiber

ITALIAN PENINSULA

ADRIATIC SEA

CARPATHIAN MTS.

Danube

BALKAN MTS.

BALKAN PENINSULA

GREEK PEN.

Aegean Sea

SICILY

CRETE

MEDITERRANEAN

ATLAS MOUNTAINS

A F R I C A

Many changes, however, took place among them in the four centuries during which the Roman frontier barred their progress southward. The most apparent change was that, toward the middle of the fourth century, these Teutonic tribes extended all the way along the Roman frontier from the mouth of the Rhine to the eastern end of the Black Sea, instead of merely along the Rhine and around the Baltic. Another noticeable change was in their organization. In place of the many small tribes indicated by Cæsar and more fully mentioned by Tacitus later, they were now grouped in large confederations, six of these holding the immense stretch of territory north of the Roman frontier, in place of the thirty or more small tribes which, in the time of Tacitus, had clustered around the Rhine alone. This consolidation arose doubtless from their experience in fighting the Roman Empire as well as each other and was likewise incidental to their migration. Some of the small tribes along the lower Rhine did not consolidate into a large confederation until the end of the fifth century.

During this period, too, the tribes along the border learned much of Roman ways of living. This result came about in many ways. Not only did Roman traders visit them and refugees from Roman justice seek asylum among them, but government officials were constantly going back and forth between them. In the earlier days many Teutonic tribesmen paid for their rashness in making raids into the Empire by being captured and sold into slavery, from which state they sometimes returned. Sometimes small tribes, fearing famine or their more powerful neighbors, were permitted to settle within the Roman frontier as agricultural laborers. This had happened frequently during the four centuries of contact, so that by 400 A.D. a belt from fifty to a hundred miles in width inside the frontier was dotted with such settlements. Then, too, the long-continued Roman policy of divide and conquer—*divide et impera*—had brought, at one time or another, nearly all the frontier tribes into alliance with the Romans against other tribes. During the third century, when many of the tribes had united against the Romans, the barbarian fighters had penetrated southward to the Mediterranean, even across the Pyrenees, and had returned to tell about their travels. More important, however, than any of these methods of contact was the practice of enrolling Teutonic warriors in the Roman legions. As soldiers of the Empire they saw service in all its provinces and were finally rewarded with the same allotments of land on the border as other Roman veterans. Frequently they returned to their own tribes. From the end of the third century the Roman emperors enlisted more and more of these tribesmen in their armies, in the course of time recruiting not merely individuals, but whole bands, under their own leaders. By this time, when the Roman army was chiefly composed of former tribesmen and commanded by men of similar origin, Teutons were no longer strangers to Romans, nor Romans to Teutons. The women and children, of course, had still to learn Roman ways from the men.

Perhaps the most convincing evidence of the spread of Roman civilization among the barbarians was their widespread adoption of Christianity. According to legend, a Roman family captured on a raid in the Black Sea country by a band of Visigoths was adopted into the tribe. The family was Christian, and a grandson determined to convert the tribe. To this end he went to Constantinople to study theology, and returned with several other priests to carry on the work of conversion. He was very successful in his mission, and Christianity spread from the Visigoths to the neighboring tribes so rapidly that practically all the Teutonic border tribes, except those at the mouth of the Rhine, were converted before the fifth century. Ulfilas or Wulfilas, as this first missionary is named, not only converted many of the Visigoths, but he also undertook to translate the Bible into their Gothic tongue. A copy of his Gothic version of the Bible is preserved today at Upsala, Sweden, as practically the first important example of the Teutonic language. Unfortunately for later events, the type of Christianity which Ulfilas taught the Visigoths was the Arian.[1] This type had been declared heretical at the Council of Nicæa in 325, but its adherents main-

[1] See pages 16, 31.

tained their faith for many years. This Arianism of the Teutons was to cause trouble later.

The degree of Roman civilization acquired by the tribes varied greatly, being dependent chiefly upon the amount of friendly contact which each tribe had had with the Empire. The tribes immediately on the border were more civilized than those farther away. In general it may be said that they had learned to respect the Roman name. They had learned, too, the value of concerted action. Their life was more settled and agriculture played a larger part in it than formerly. Tribal ideas of relationship in blood were broken down and, though the theory was maintained, adoptions into the tribe were made quite easily. As a matter of fact, the confederations into which they were now organized were so large that blood kinship had to be rather loosely interpreted. With their young men constantly going away to serve in the Roman armies and frequently returning with wives from distant lands, it could not be otherwise. They had, however, not yet learned the Roman principle of regarding all dwellers on their lands as subjects of their law and in a sense members of their state. Warfare was still their chief interest and they were always capable of reverting to their former ways of life. Their acquired Roman civilization was as yet only skin deep.

During the first three and a half centuries of the Christian era the chief ethnic disturbances in Europe had come from the Baltic region. In the third quarter of the fourth century, however, Europe received the full shock of an Asiatic disturbance caused by the advance of the Huns. These were a people quite unlike the Teutons or any of the European peoples thus far mentioned. Short in stature, swarthy in complexion, with eyes wide apart and somewhat slanted, with noses upturned so that the nostrils seemed like mere holes in their faces, they made a very unpleasant impression upon the Europeans with whom they met. This impression was accentuated by the swiftness and unexpectedness of their movements. They seemed always on horseback, and, when on foot, their bow-legs only added to the superstitious dread which their military success had already aroused. From the somewhat distorted descriptions given by contemporary writers, it seems safe to identify them with the Turanian stock of central Asia, to which the modern Turks, Bulgars and Finns are distantly related. The people of western China probably exhibit the racial characteristics in purer form. In the later fourth century the Huns galloped across the steppes westward between the Caspian Sea and the Ural Mountains, where they fell upon the easternmost of the Teutonic tribes. These they quickly conquered and added to their already long list of subject peoples, bound to do the will of their conquerors.

The Visigoths, whose neighbors had already succumbed, sought to avoid a similar fate and asked permission to enter the Roman Empire. This permission was granted in 376. According to the somewhat confused account which has come down, the imperial commissioners entrusted with the task of admitting them were more interested in lining their own pockets than in serving the Empire. Gothic warriors were allowed to retain their arms if they had anything of value to offer in return for this privilege. The commissioners sold food to them at starvation rates, took their children as slaves in payment, and mistreated the elders with a reckless disregard of consequences. The result was a rising on the part of the outraged Goths. The emperor in the East, Valens, was engaged in a war in Mesopotamia at the time, but he hurried back at the news of the Gothic disturbance. Without pausing either for accurate information or for adequate troops, he rushed out of Constantinople to suppress the rising. In 378 he encountered the Goths at Adrianople, where they outnumbered and outfought him. Valens himself was slain, and the Visigoths in their wrath were free to do as they pleased. They moved southward into the Greek peninsula, ravaging the country as they went.

This was a new development in the relations of Roman and Teuton. Here was a tribe, or rather a whole confederation, with its women and children, making its permanent home within the Roman Empire, with or without permission. Perhaps they felt that they had permission and were merely executing justice, as they understood it, for the outrages which the imperial commissioners had perpetrated upon them. But a whole confederation with all its permanent equipment making a home on Roman soil! The Rhine-Danube frontier had been maintained to prevent just that. True, small tribes had been settled on Roman soil in the past, but as agricultural laborers, subject to strict conditions as well as to Roman law. True, also, that large confederations had entered the Empire with their fighting forces, but that was war and they had been driven back. What would the Roman Empire do in this emergency? The outcome was not of interest to Visigoth and Roman alone. Other large tribes were also in the dilemma of the Visigoths, uncertain whether to submit to the Huns or to seek some other way out.

THE ROMAN EMPIRE BEFORE THE INVASIONS

The Roman Empire, which had to decide this momentous question, had itself changed greatly since the days when it first came into contact with the Teutonic tribes. It is a common failing to think of the Roman world as it was in the days of Cæsar, Cicero, Virgil, or Augustus, and then to assume that it remained just so for the next four hundred years. Those golden days when the Roman senate sat in dignity and power, ruling the destinies of the civilized world; when every Roman citizen was thrilled with patriotic pride and stood ready to lead or be led to the outermost edges of civilization; when Virgil's poems and Livy's prose first glorified Rome's greatness—those days had passed long since. Another picture frequently drawn is that of a somewhat later time when the senate no longer wielded the power, though it still had the dignity; when each city in the provinces of the West was a miniature Rome with consuls, magistrates and a curial class as proud of the Empire as though they themselves had created it, as well versed in the literature of Rome as the inhabitants of the capital itself, and as ready to contribute to that literature, to the Roman army, and even to the imperial throne. But that time, the silver age of Roman culture, which could boast the spread of Roman civilization through the western provinces, also had passed, and decline had advanced much further.

The most pronounced change had occurred in the relative position of emperor and senate. The emperors had made themselves
absolute largely through their control of the army. They had
succeeded also in obtaining control of the civil service, whereupon governors, vicars and prefects owed their appointments to
the emperor. Their edicts became the law for the Empire and
their decisions final. The majesty of the Empire was revered
in them, and their statues, set up at all governmental centers, were
regarded in much the same fashion as statues of the gods. The
Roman senate was thus left little but its dignity which reached
back to the days when there was no emperor. It cannot be said
that the senate ever entirely forgot its inheritance or was unready
to assume power whenever opportunity arose; but it lacked command of the army, and its prestige had waned before that of the
emperor. Opportunities for its exercise of power were few.
This development reached its culmination when Diocletian (285-
303) not only assumed all power, but surrounded himself with
a magnificence of courtiers and ceremonial.

Closely related to this transformation was the change in the
character of the army. The proud Roman citizenry no longer
predominated in its ranks. The Roman state no longer had a
civilized enemy of consequence, and perhaps civic pride did not
therefore feel challenged to the patriotic sacrifice of military
service. Doubtless, also, routine garrison duty on the northern
frontier failed to attract the inhabitants of the balmier southland,
and the emperors may have preferred men without Roman ancestry for use against Roman citizens. At all events, the composition
of the army was changed. With Constantine (311-330) the
movement toward a mercenary army composed chiefly of barbarians was well under way, and by the end of the fourth century
the chief commanders were often men of the same kind. Perhaps
the emperors felt safer thus, for the army and its commanders
were the only persons in a position to overthrow them. Men of
Roman ancestry might well have found it hard to resist the
temptation to do so, especially when the emperors were dissolute
or weak. As it was, the emperors were none too safe, for, unless
they controlled the army beyond disaffection and intrigue, they

were only too liable to lose their thrones and their lives. Clearly the Empire was in jeopardy when the only check on the throne was in the possession of such men.

The problem of succession to the throne had been most difficult. There were no other imperial or royal families with which to intermarry, thereby creating a special class from which successors might be drawn. Despite the elaborate ceremonial and religious character with which the office was surrounded, the man who occupied it came from the same stock as thousands of his fellow citizens, who were not apt to forget that fact. Military commanders of no exalted birth had sought and gained the office by force. Why should other officers of equal rank not aspire to it—and by the same means? To guard against this danger and to develop a substitute for the more modern royal caste, Diocletian gave his final approval to a plan by which there were to be two emperors, *Augusti,* and two understudies, *Cæsars.* Each had a separate portion of the Empire under his immediate charge, and together they formed a select group through which was attained the position of senior emperor. The plan thus provided for a trained successor to the imperial throne. In practice, however, this scheme worked no better than the former. The junior emperors were too strongly tempted to hasten their succession, and ambitious military commanders or nobles were not prevented from seeking the office by force or intrigue.

In the reign of Constantine another change was accomplished. A new capital was established on the Bosporus and named after its founder, Constantinople. This was henceforth the preferred seat of the emperors, the real capital of the Empire. The junior emperor ruled in the West and was usually, though not necessarily, in Italy—more often at Ravenna or Milan than at Rome. Several explanations have been advanced for this important change, one being that the frontier problems were now so pressing that the emperors had to be near the scene of danger, and Constantinople was strategically located with reference to both the northern and the eastern frontier. Another explanation is that Constantinople was a much better economic center than any place in Italy. Still another is that at Constantinople the emperors would enjoy freedom from the annoying claims of the Roman senate to a share in the government. There were at Constantinople no embarrassing traditions; the place had been founded by an emperor, and the East, where it was situated, was much more congenial to the semi-Oriental despotism which the imperial office now resembled. There was no open opposition in Rome to this transfer of the capital, for the senate was powerless, but there was much resentment. Covert allusions to the "Greek" emperor in western writings of the period indicate that loyalty to a government definitely established in the East was cooling in the West. For all practical purposes Rome and Italy, after Constantine, were no longer the center of the Empire, but provinces of Constantinople, much as Gaul was a province.

These were the chief outward changes which had taken place in the Empire, but there were others of spirit no less important. The most prominent of these, the acceptance of Christianity by the imperial government, was also associated with the name of Constantine. As late as the reign of Diocletian, and, in fact, until Constantine himself became emperor, the Christian religion had been actively persecuted by the Roman government. Deriving its impulse from the doctrine of the Messiah so tenaciously held by much-abused Hebrews and its vitality and universal appeal from the life, death and teachings of Jesus of Nazareth, Christianity had won many converts. It taught a broad humanity in the idea of universal brotherhood and the equal importance of all souls in the eyes of God. Its cheering message of hope for eternal happiness appealed strongly to the imagination of the down-trodden. For these reasons it spread rapidly among the lower classes in the Empire. The upper classes, especially the slave-holding nobility, viewed it with suspicion as fraught with dangerous possibilities of social revolution. Its Jewish origin and its greater prevalence in the East also made it less welcome to the ruling classes of the West. The refusal of the Christians to make sacrifices to the image of the emperor and their habit of meeting secretly had led the government to suspect them of political revolutionary designs. For all of these reasons the government had opposed the spread of this religion with increasing severity, as the thousands of martyrs attest. Nevertheless, it spread. A religion for which people were willing to give up their lives must have exerted a powerful fascination even upon the very crowds which thronged to see the spectacles of martyrdom. Despite, or because of, the persecutions, it made converts even among the upper classes, especially among the women. At length the attitude of the government changed. Christianity became legally recognized as early as 311, definitely in 312, and before his death in 337 Constantine himself was baptized into that faith.

During the next century much of the intellectual, most of the literary, a great deal of the social and a not inconsiderable amount of the political energy of the Empire was spent on the problem of religion. The cultured nobility, particularly in the West, despised the literature of Christianity as crude in comparison with the pagan philosophies which they read and studied. Their criticisms were met, in turn, by Christian scholars who wrote in reply. The debate raged on throughout the century, and its course was dramatically reflected in the frequent removal of the statue of the Winged Victory from the senate chamber in Rome, and its subsequent restoration. Happily, only ink, not blood, was shed in this particular debate. The victory was finally won for Christianity when such able scholars as Jerome and Augustine had rewritten Christian theology in the language of the philosophers. This rationalization afforded a bridge by which the proud Roman nobility could safely pass from their pagan philosophy to Christianity.

The debate between pagan and Christian was only a phase of the religious discussion that was going on. Much more bitter were the disputes which arose among the Christians themselves as to the meaning of certain doctrines. One of these concerned the relative position of the three members of the Trinity and caused such serious division that Constantine called a council of all leading churchmen in the Empire at Nicæa in 325 A.D. To insure the success of the council, and to maintain the unity of the faith, Constantine placed the imperial post chariots at the disposal of the churchmen. The council decided in favor of the view upheld by Athanasius, which is that still held by most Christians today, and against that of Arius, whose followers were denounced as heretics. The Arian view held the Son somewhat inferior to the Father, denying Him co-eternity and equality in the Trinity. Arianism continued to have followers in the East throughout the century and at times threatened to gain the upper hand. The Teutonic tribes along the Danube were converted by Arian missionaries. Other points of difference arose to divide the Christians into opposing camps, some of which, like Arianism, required the intervention of governmental officials. Unlike the debate between paganism and Christianity during the fourth century, these differences in doctrine within the religion frequently led to blows and even bloodshed. Most of the controversy, however, was confined to writings. Only one of the emperors during this century went back to paganism, but several of them entertained one or another divergent view on Christian doctrine. One fortunate result of this varied and free discussion was to fortify Christian doctrine on nearly all questions of religion which were apt to occur to the mind of man. There were few centuries so important as the fourth in the construction of Christian theology.

It was perhaps inevitable that, in the midst of all this discussion of religion, the thoughts of many should be directed toward extreme forms of religious life. In the East this tendency had already developed on a large scale before the fourth century. It now affected all parts of the Roman world. The eastern practice set the example. Men decided for themselves that the only goal worth striving for was eternal happiness. To them life on earth seemed only a brief span between two eternities, a time which could be best employed in preparation for eternal bliss. They felt that the best assurance lay in uncompromising self-denial of the pleasures of this world. Many went to live as hermits in the desert or out-of-the-way places. Others, more courageous, perhaps, practiced their asceticism at home, but thousands left their customary occupations to become monks or nuns devoted to the quest for eternal happiness. These thousands upon thousands included in the fourth century many scholars, former government officials, business men and people of the better classes generally, both men and women, as well as many less desirable persons who could be more easily dispensed with. Such people were completely lost to the world themselves, and they left no children after them, which was especially regrettable, for the qualities of character which enabled them to carry out successfully a life of such self-denial are always much needed in the world. Many others who did not go to the extreme of retirement from the world, nevertheless felt the ascetic spirit to the extent of refusing to enter occupations which involved the killing or ruling of their fellow men. They were willing to become officials of the Church, but not of the Empire. It is difficult to measure the amount of change in Roman society and government which was caused by the spread of the ascetic spirit. The evidence of the known thousands who abandoned life in society for solitary existence indicates that it was very great.

No less important was the economic transformation of society during the two centuries before the migrations. The citizen farmers who owned small tracts which they themselves cultivated had almost disappeared. Agricultural land not only in Italy, but throughout the western provinces, was held by nobles and cultivated by dependents who were bound to the soil. Large landed estates were the rule, small estates the rare exception. The agricultural population was now almost entirely of the class of *coloni,* a semi-free group to which slaves had risen and freemen sunk. These workers had some freedom and legal rights in their dealings with one another, but they were bound to the soil, and their children after them. They received a living, but little else. Food, fuel and clothing were secured on the estate. All surplus not required by the inhabitants of the estate was marketed by the owner, the proceeds belonging entirely to him. Such laborers were not allowed to enlist in the army, nor were they free to seek a career in industry or trade. Disputes which arose among them were settled by the owner of the estate, who was not only landlord, but also legislator, administrator and supreme judge over them. The Roman Empire meant almost nothing to them. If they were well treated by the landowner, well and good; if not, they doubtless wished that something unpleasant might happen to the government which made such conditions possible.

The towns, too, had been much modified. The *curiales,* as the upper class of the provincial towns was called, had dwindled in number. Trade had declined, especially in the West. The great nobles of the countryside either needed nothing from the towns or obtained what little they needed to import from the greater centers. The agricultural laborers had little or no money with which to buy articles of commerce. This condition sapped the vitality of the towns from the bottom, while from the top they were afflicted with an increasing burden of taxation. This the landed nobility were able to escape, exemption from taxation being frequently a privilege of their class. With most of the land in the hands of the nobles, and without any decrease in the expenses of imperial government, the burden on the towns increased. Members of the curial class were appointed tax-collectors and were held accountable for definite sums of money which they must either collect from their fellows or pay out of their own possessions. Little wonder, then, that these men frequently disposed of their property as best they could and fled to live among the barbarians, rather than hold office in the towns. The wealthier among them frequently acquired country estates and lived as nobles; the poorer sank to a condition little better than that of agricultural laborers. It became the common practice for even tradesmen to attach themselves as clients to some noble, in order thus to gain protection from taxation and other burdens. Throughout the West, toward the end of the fourth and the beginning of the fifth century, there was a marked tendency toward the formation of a two-class society of nobles and dependents.

The nobility belonged chiefly to the senatorial class, whose dignity bore little relation to the Roman senate, but marked its possessors as the privileged class of the Empire. It was a dignity obtained through specific imperial favor or usurped through the power of wealth. Distinguished service for the emperor, whether military, political, or merely financial, usually won such recognition. This senatorial nobility was wealthy and tended to become more so. Its members usually had numerous estates over the countryside, and homes in the leading towns as well. Their rural homes, called villas, were usually lavish in appointment

and equipped with sumptuous baths, private libraries, lounging
and recreation rooms. The extensive grounds included groves
and gardens and provided opportunity for outdoor sports. On
their estates and also in their town houses the nobility had large
retinues of servants who were either slaves or very close dependents. Among themselves they led very pleasant lives, visiting
each other frequently and entertaining on a generous scale. They
tended to form a caste, confining their marriages to their own
class and aiding each other against any calamities. Toward the
Empire their attitude varied. They were ready to enter the imperial service as administrators; in fact, they expected to have
all the administrative offices in their own provinces, and were
quite willing to take lucrative or important positions nearer the
imperial throne. They did not, as a rule, enter the military
service, even as officers, though there were important exceptions
to this rule. They expected exemption from taxes, and, when a
niggardly, hostile, or reforming emperor sought to compel them
to pay taxes, they protested loudly. If possible, they entertained
the tax-collectors lavishly and thus bribed them either to forego
collection entirely or to keep it down to a minimum. Sometimes
when the imperial troops were far away they had their men beat
off the tax-collectors. In one way or another they managed to
avoid the burden of tax-paying. On their estates and toward their
own people they practiced all the duties and rights of government.
They represented all of their dependents as well as themselves
before the imperial courts. They were interested in the Empire
and made it their duty to keep informed on imperial politics.
To have a friend as emperor was fortunate, and under such circumstances they were very patriotic. If the emperor was a
stranger or hostile, they desired as little connection as possible
with imperial affairs. Upon them, however, the inner strength
or weakness of the Empire was largely dependent.

These variations in the social and political structure of the
Roman Empire were not everywhere equally apparent. It would
have been possible to find in the fourth and even in the fifth
century towns in sheltered spots which were just as flourishing
and whose inhabitants were just as contented and as patriotic as

they had ever been. Such areas could have been found even in the West. All of the changes mentioned had not taken place everywhere and to the same degree. There were always some nobles who paid taxes more or less cheerfully, who expected to serve in the Roman imperial administration and who welcomed careers as soldiers. There were places in which Roman citizens still farmed their own land and there were towns in which business flourished and the Empire was regarded with reverence and pride. Generalizations about the tendency of the times in the fourth century must be accepted with such reservations in mind.

The Empire which had to solve the problem presented by the Visigoths in 378 was therefore a very different Empire from that which had built up the Roman state. The emperor had absolute power, so far as the law was concerned, but he was actually dependent upon the support of the army. The Empire was nominally one, but was actually divided between East and West, the two parts coöperating none too harmoniously. The army, upon which so much depended, was composed chiefly of barbarians and officered from the same non-Roman stock. The responsible citizenry of the Empire was made up almost exclusively of the upper class, the great bulk of the population having sunk to a dependent condition. The interest of the population as a whole was not in imperial affairs. The problem of the Visigoths was not one that stirred the Roman world from end to end. It was serious enough to the people of the Greek peninsula whose possessions had been ravaged, and probably of concern to others in the immediate neighborhood whose belongings were endangered. But the Empire as a whole felt it not at all.

CHAPTER II

ROMAN OR TEUTON
376-565

FOR the moment, the Visigoths were free to pillage and plunder the Balkan peninsula, which they did with considerable ruthlessness. When Gratian, emperor in the West and brother of Valens, heard of these events, he sent his general, Theodosius, to deal with the situation. By a judicious mingling of force and diplomacy, by striking at scattered bands of marauders and by discussing terms of peace with the leaders of the tribes, Theodosius managed, four years later, to quiet the Visigoths. He granted them, as *fœderati,* certain lands in the Balkan peninsula and subjected them to definite military obligations. Apparently he had settled the problem.

For these services and in recognition of his great ability, Theodosius was made ruler of the East and later became virtual ruler of the whole Empire. His reign was characterized by military successes and by his support of the orthodox Church. All risings were put down with dispatch, and the establishment of the Christian religion as the only religion of the Empire may be dated from his reign. His temper is very clearly revealed by an incident which occurred in 390. The people of Thessalonica arose in revolt against the excesses of the soldiers garrisoned there. Theodosius promptly ordered the citizens to be massacred. Doubtless he won the gratitude of his soldiers by the rigor of his treatment, but the affair brought him into conflict with Ambrose, bishop of Milan. Ambrose was one of the Roman nobles who had given up the idea of service in the imperial administration for a career in the Church. He had already risen to the office of governor of a province in northern Italy when the people of Milan chose him for their bishop. He accepted and turned his remarkable administrative ability to the service of the Church.

When the news of the wholesale slaughter of men, women and children reached him, he determined to punish the emperor by excluding him from the sacrament of communion. Such an act was inconceivable under the old pagan religion, in which the emperor had figured as one of the deities. Possibly it might have seemed inconceivable also to a bishop of humbler origin, but Ambrose, with the tradition of a distinguished senatorial ancestry behind him, dared to apply the judgment of a higher law even to an emperor. Ambrose persisted in his resolve and at length Theodosius accepted his judgment and did penance.

As he neared his end, Theodosius sought to provide for the succession by placing one of his sons at Constantinople and the other in the West. Realizing the need for further military support for his two sons, he recommended to each a master of soldiers, chosen from his most loyal lieutenants. That one of these was a man of barbarian origin only serves to illustrate the extent of the change which had occurred in the army. Theodosius died a peaceful death in 395, probably happy in the thought that he had provided amply both for his sons and the Empire. Unfortunately, his sons failed to exhibit the ability of their father, and the masters of soldiers with whom he had provided them were more intent in looking after their own interests and those of their respective charges than in caring for the Empire as a whole.

This short-sighted policy was illustrated in the treatment of the Visigoths, who again became a problem. By 395 a new generation had grown up among them, eager for the practice of arms. Until the death of Theodosius, the experience of the older men had restrained them. Now, however, under the leadership of a young chieftain, Alaric, they prepared for warlike deeds. There seems to be some ground for the story that Alaric, their leader, sought to become master of the soldiers in the West and that he was angered at the emperor's refusal to bestow this office upon him. At any rate, Alaric complained that the lands allotted to his tribe were inadequate and demanded more. He invited adventurous warriors from across the border to join him, and in his army were not only Visigoths and kindred peoples, but even Huns.

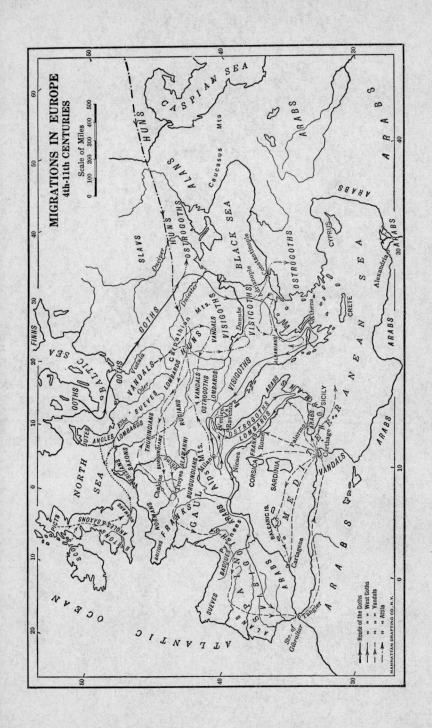

MIGRATIONS IN EUROPE
4th-11th CENTURIES

Scale of Miles
0   100 200 300 400 500

Route of the Goths
"   "   West Goths
"   "   Vandals
"   "   Attila

MANHATTAN DRAFTING CO., N.Y.

A danger of such magnitude required joint action from the emperors, particularly as the Visigoths occupied the territory where the two portions of the Empire met. But the emperor of the East made an arrangement with Alaric which induced him to spare the East and turn toward the West. For nearly ten years, Stilicho, master of soldiers in the West, held the Visigoths back, but at great cost. In order to procure sufficient forces, he found it necessary to strip the frontier of its garrisons. This was at once a signal for other tribes on the border to enter the Empire and for ambitious provincial leaders to set up independent states, and the two frequently made common cause. Finally, in 408, Stilicho was murdered by some of his household, which made matters all the worse, for now many of Stilicho's soldiers went over to Alaric, and the road to Italy lay open before him.

What happened then throws an interesting light upon the attitude of the tribesmen toward the Roman Empire. With apparently nothing to prevent his advance, Alaric yet remained in northern Italy for two years. During this time he thrice demanded of the emperor, who was shut up in Ravenna, a further allotment of lands for himself and his people. He threatened to sack Rome if the emperor refused and, upon his third refusal, in 410 he actually carried out his threat. Some restraint was observed in the sack of the city, Alaric's main purpose being still to force from the emperor further grants of lands. But he remained stubborn, and Alaric started southward with his army, as if to cross to Africa, the granary of Italy. Death overtook him in southern Italy, and his successor changed the plan by marching northward once more. This time the emperor was more compliant, for he agreed to let the Visigoths settle in southern Gaul as *fœderati,* protectors, of the Empire. Their leader married the sister of the emperor, who had been captured by them, and established his followers in southwestern Gaul.

This attitude of forbearance on the part of the Visigoths was shared by other tribes which entered the Empire at this time. It was not a desire to overthrow the Roman Empire which prompted their advance; it was, rather, a desire to obtain better lands as compensation for their services as *fœderati.* The attitude was similar to that of men striking for higher wages. This may have been the logical outcome of the military policies of the emperors since the time of Constantine. A citizen army replaced by mercenaries, the mercenaries drawn more and more from Teutonic tribes, and, finally, the enrollment of whole tribal contingents in the Roman army, formed a chain of development which could easily lead to such a result. Certain it was that nearly all the tribal warriors who now entered the Empire had been employed at one time or another by the Roman emperors. The lands which they now held were wrested from their Roman employers, to be sure, but, on the whole, the intruders seem to have respected their obligations as *fœderati* of the Empire.

But if such was, indeed, the feeling of the Teutonic tribes within the Empire, it was not shared by all the Romans. The sack of Rome in 410 made a profound impression upon the whole Roman world. Jerome, a provincial Roman who had started on a career of learning, but had concluded instead to become a Christian monk on the waste lands of Palestine, felt that the Roman Empire had come to an end when he heard of it. He prepared to write its funeral dirge, but he was deterred from this task by the return of Rome to the possession of the Romans. He did, however, urge them to take warning and, like himself, turn their thoughts to the preparation of their souls for eternity. Thousands followed his example, and the desert lands around Palestine became crowded with Romans, men and matrons, who imitated the ascetic life of Jerome.

In northern Africa, Augustine, who had also given up a scholar's career to devote himself to Christianity, was equally moved by the sack of Rome, though in a different way. The thousands of refugees who had fled to Africa before the advance of Alaric's army contained many nobles of secret pagan leanings. These complained bitterly, ascribing the disasters of Rome to the neglect of the old pagan gods. In answer to them, Augustine wrote a book arguing that Christianity had nothing to do with the calamities of the time, that Rome had suffered in the days of the old gods, and that, if anything, Christianity had mitigated the misfortunes of Rome since Alaric had spared

Christian churches and shrines. This work, *The City of God,* was one of the greatest writings of the period, and it has exerted a powerful influence upon the thoughts of men down to our own day. Its composition occupied Augustine during his closing years and was brought to an end in 429, just as Hippo, the city in which he dwelt, was about to be taken by another of the Teutonic tribes, the Vandals.

At Constantinople there was no great expression of concern at the sack of Rome. Whether this was due to a secret feeling of relief that Rome and not Constantinople had suffered, or to a conviction that the Eastern Empire, too, had its hands full in checking invasions and repressing revolts, cannot be said. At any rate, the Eastern Empire did nothing to assist in the emergency.

By 415 the Visigoths were again quiet, but the questions raised by their entrance into the Empire were not yet answered. The problem had indeed been magnified at least fivefold by the number of additional tribes that were now located in Gaul, Spain and northern Africa. It is idle to speculate on what a series of strong emperors might have accomplished. There was not even one strong emperor until 518, and meanwhile the presence of these tribes within the Empire afforded almost endless opportunities for designing politicians to advance their own interests and private ambitions. A certain Count Boniface, who hoped to make himself ruler of northern Africa, at least, invited—if indeed he had any choice in the matter—the Vandals to help him carry out his purpose. Boniface failed, but the Vandals were in northern Africa. Likewise, Avitus, who was very friendly with the Visigoths, was made emperor in 455 because it was thought that he could count on their support, and such examples continued to recur throughout the century.

ROMANS AND TEUTONS WITHIN THE EMPIRE

From the Roman point of view, the most hopeful incident during this time was the way in which these tribes rallied to the support of the Empire against the invasion of Attila. This new leader of the Huns seemed fired with the same spirit which first brought his people into Europe in the fourth century. He organized a large army, composed chiefly of the Teutonic tribes which his people had subjected. With this army he planned a great invasion of the West, which was to include the taking of Rome. Proceeding up the Danube and across the Rhine, he burst upon Gaul. Here he was confronted by Aëtius, master of soldiers in the West. Aëtius was probably a Roman himself, but he had married a Gothic princess and understood the tribesmen very well. He rallied the Visigoths, Burgundians and Franks to his aid, and, with this combined force, he more than held his own against Attila on the Mauriac plains near Chalôns in 451. Attila, the Scourge of God, was no longer to be feared. He did make an incursion into Italy in the following year, which is chiefly memorable for the legend of his interview with Pope Leo and the founding of Venice.[1] But his force was spent, and, when he died the next year, the Huns whom he had commanded disappeared from European history, and the people over whom he had ruled separated to follow their individual destinies. Aëtius, who was chiefly responsible for the defeat of Attila, was murdered by palace politicians in 454.

The death of Valentinian III in 455 marked the end of the dynasty of Theodosius in the West. Ambitious Romans fought one another for the succession, seeking support from the mercenary army in Italy or from tribes in other parts of the West. It was in 455, early in the course of these rivalries, that the Vandals came over to take Rome. After thoroughly sacking the city, they returned to Africa. Other tribes now took advantage of the general disorder to extend their holdings in their own neighborhoods. In Italy, control of affairs soon fell into the hands of mercenary leaders, who set up and pulled down emperors in rapid succession. Finally, they dispensed with these puppets, and from 476 to 493 Odoacer, master of soldiers, ruled in Italy. At length the emperor at Constantinople found an opportunity to interfere. The tribe of the Ostrogoths, who had

---

[1] It is said that the people on the mainland sought refuge on the islands as Attila approached, and remained on those islands, their settlement becoming the nucleus of later Venice. It is probable, however, that these islands and sandbars were already occupied by fishermen.

been released from subjection to the Huns by the death of Attila, had become dangerously close neighbors. Their chieftain, Theodoric, had spent a part of his boyhood in Constantinople as a hostage and had also served in the army of the emperor. Fearing lest he might become a dangerous foe, the Eastern emperor, Zeno, commissioned Theodoric to depose Odoacer and rule Italy for the Empire. He succeeded rather better than Zeno had hoped, and by 493 was firmly established with his Ostrogoths in Italy. Thus, at the end of the century all of the West was under the rule of these *fœderati*.

Theodoric, the Ostrogoth, set a standard of correct conduct toward the imperial court which was probably higher than that of his fellow kings and not without some influence upon them. For thirty years he gave to Italy good government such as had not been known there since the days of Theodosius. In addition, he tried to maintain peace among the other Teutonic kingdoms, as though he were empowered by the emperor to govern not only Italy, but the whole of the West. Though not always successful, he did check much disorder and pointed a way to the solution of the problems created by the entrance of the tribes into the Empire.

An examination of the way in which these people were living among the Romans is made difficult by lack of adequate sources of information. The few accounts which have come down to the present furnish but a fragmentary description and leave much to the imagination. The best of these sources are the letters of two men, both of the Roman nobility. One, Apollinaris Sidonius (431-490) lived in Gaul; the other, Marcus Aurelius Cassiodorus (480-575), senator, in Italy. Both came from families accustomed to holding office in the imperial administration, and both were trained for such careers. Sidonius had risen to a position very close to the emperor at Rome, but the very uncertainty of the emperor's tenure of office at that time made advancement in such service very dubious. So he retired to Gaul, where he soon appeared as bishop of Clermont, an office in which he used his ability to help his flock in their dealings with Burgundians and Visigoths. Cassiodorous began his official career about the time that Theodoric came to power in Italy. He soon attracted the notice of the Ostrogoth and became his secretary and most intimate adviser, a position which he held under several of Theodoric's successors as well. Books of letters of both Sidonius and Cassiodorus have been preserved.

The first question which naturally arises in any consideration of this problem of the invasions is the actual number of Teutons in the Empire by the end of the fifth century. On this question Sidonius and Cassiodorus afford only impressions, and the few writers who do employ figures use them in an extravagant and unreliable fashion. The census taken by the Vandal king after his people had settled in northern Africa offers some standard of measurement. There were then in his tribe about 80,000 men, women and children, or about 16,000 fighting men. Comparing the relative strengths of the other tribes, modern historians have reached the conclusion that none of the tribes had more than 200,000 members, and that most of them were nearer the size of the Vandals. These numbers seem insignificant when compared with the Roman population, for the city of Rome in its heyday had a larger population than the sum of all the Teutonic tribes in the Empire. Such figures are deceptive, however, for they only take into account the tribes as they were when they entered the Empire. They embrace neither the many tribesmen already in the Empire nor the smaller bands which came in later unnoticed. Nor do such estimates represent even all of a single tribe. The Ostrogoths may be taken as an example. At the time Theodoric established his people in Italy, there was a large colony of Ostrogoths in Asia Minor, a large contingent of Ostrogothic soldiers at Constantinople, another colony in the Balkans, and still another on the Danube. In addition, bands of Ostrogoths had gone to join the Visigoths in Gaul and Spain. A close examination of other tribes that had made extensive migrations would reveal similar dispersion. Another factor apt to cause confusion was the flexibility of tribal membership. Blood relationship was only a theory among the tribes in the fifth century. Not one of the greater tribes was composed entirely of its own blood members. The army of Theodoric, like that of other tribal leaders, included elements as diverse as refugee Romans, adventurous Saxons, and even Huns. Taking all available considerations into account, however, the total number of Teutons within the Empire at the close of the fifth century was still but a fraction of the Roman population.

The manner of settlement adopted by the tribes, on which point the testimony of Sidonius and Cassiodorus is more helpful, varied somewhat in different portions of the West. When the Visigoths settled in southern Gaul, they received two-thirds of the lands, animals and property, rent free. This involved but a small portion of Gaul, chiefly in the Garonne Valley. The same principle was followed more or less fully in the case of nearly all the other tribes within the Empire. Whether the division was literally carried out, or merely served as a basis of computation, cannot be determined. As a rule, the Teutons preferred the country districts for themselves and their families, though their kings held their courts in towns and maintained fairly large garrisons. When the kings began to extend their power over the surrounding country, they used their mobile forces and left garrisons at convenient points. It may be safely assumed that the broad valleys and the regions along the main highways received many Teutons who were interspersed among the Romans. Away from these spots, the Romans continued to live their lives much as before, molested rarely or not at all. From the letters in which Sidonius describes villas of Gaul, it would be difficult to understand that Burgundians, Visigoths, Franks and Alamanni were already established there. Life was, apparently, just as luxurious, servants just as numerous, and diversions just as gentle as they had been before the entrance of the tribes.

Some degree of friction between Romans and Teutons was inevitable under the circumstances, but this varied greatly. It was worst, perhaps, in Britain, where the Angles, Saxons and Jutes were establishing themselves. These people were more primitive and more savage than the other tribes which had lived long beside the Romans. They acknowledged no obligation toward the Roman emperor and showed little respect for Roman civilization, of which there was considerable evidence around

them. The other tribes, in Gaul, Spain and Africa, all maintained
the relationship of *fœderati* with more or less fidelity. Their
kings acted as protectors of the Roman population within their
respective areas, employed Roman advisers, and even had codes
of law drawn up for the benefit of their Roman subjects.
Sidonius, whose ancestral estate at Lyons had been taken by the
Burgundians, while his episcopal city had been captured by the
Visigoths, still found it possible to carry on dealings with both
peoples. His descriptions of the royal courts of these tribes
reveal great numbers of Romans swarming about the Teutonic
kings. Not only did the kings seem to know some Latin, but
many of the Romans set themselves to master the Teutonic languages. Sidonius speaks of his friend, Syagrius, as one before
whom even the leading tribesmen feared to make mistakes in
their own speech. While peaceful relations were the rule, the
Teutons raged savagely when thwarted in their purposes. On
such occasions, villas were burned and even towns destroyed,
though few of the large towns suffered. The experience of Rome,
while typical, was not universal.

It might seem that, in living so closely together, the two peoples would fuse into one, and this did, indeed, occur to a very
considerable extent. The example of Aëtius, who married a
Gothic woman, was not isolated. Even more numerous examples
of the marriage of Roman women to Teutons could be cited.
Furthermore, leading Teutons were rapidly taking on the gentler
manners and more refined customs of the Romans with whom
they daily associated. There were, however, very important
obstacles to the complete amalgamation of the two races.

One of these obstacles lay in the fact that cultured Romans
had difficulty in hiding their contempt for the rude manners of
the tribesmen. In the letters of Sidonius are to be found several
lampoons directed against the Teutons for the private amusement
of his friends. And even Cassiodorus, though he tried diligently
to make the Ostrogoths acceptable to the Romans by tracing their
lineage back to the siege of Troy, was not always able to conceal
his feelings of cultural superiority. On the other hand, there
were among the Teutons many who looked with foreboding upon

the intimacy of their leaders and fellows with the Romans. They regarded the abandonment of stern and simple ways as a form of degeneracy, and Witigis, who became leader of the Ostrogoths in 536, proudly proclaimed that, according to the old tribal custom, he had been elevated on a shield.

A more serious obstacle to amalgamation arose from religious differences. All of the East Teutons had become converted to Arian Christianity before entering the Empire, whereas the Romans were practically all orthodox Christians. The old bitterness between the two forms of Christianity was continually in danger of being revived, and did, in fact, lead to serious outbreaks from time to time, especially in Africa among the Vandals. As a rule, the Teutons were tolerant, though they viewed with disapproval the efforts of the orthodox to convert their people. Many conversions did, of course, occur, especially among those Teutons who had become enamoured of Roman ways of life. But few were converted to Arianism. The religious differences were all the more serious since the Roman nobility, like Sidonius, filled leading positions in the Church, and cultural prejudice thus combined with religious prejudice against the Teutons. Likewise, the conservative elements among the tribesmen clung to their Arianism as a sort of racial rallying-point. Between the two there could be no compromise. The weight of numbers was in favor of the Romans. All they needed was some military aid and direction.

This help appeared first from an unexpected quarter. The confederation of the Franks, which had spread southward into Gaul during the fifth century, was still heathen. Under an unscrupulous but very able leader, Clovis, who disposed of many petty chieftains by the process of guile and murder, they became a very powerful fighting force. He extended their power to the Loire by 486, when he defeated Syagrius, "King of the Romans." Ten years later he was struggling with the Alamanni for control of northeastern Gaul. According to legend, it was in the course of this war that he became a Christian. His wife, Clotilda, a Burgundian princess whose family had given up Arianism for orthodox Christianity, was perhaps chiefly responsible for his conversion.   At any rate, he was baptized, and his warriors with him.   The Roman Christians in the West now looked to him as their deliverer, and their assistance made easy the conquest of the Visigoths and Burgundians in Gaul.   The Romans, however, were to find Clovis no less Teutonic than the others, even if orthodox in his Christianity.

A more favorable answer to Roman hopes appeared in 518 with the rise of a strong emperor at Constantinople.   This was Justin, by birth a humble Illyrian peasant, but an excellent soldier, who had risen to the command of the imperial bodyguard before he was made emperor.   Without education himself, he sought to repair this defect by having a young nephew, named Justinian, trained in the best schools of the time.   He soon associated Justinian with himself in the rule of the Empire.   Both uncle and nephew were staunch adherents of the orthodox faith, which some of the previous emperors had neglected, and they were therefore doubly agreeable to the Romans of the West.   Close relations were established between the imperial court and the bishop of Rome, who, in 519, made a formal visit of reconciliation to Constantinople.

Four years later, Justin began to persecute the Arian Christians in the East.   The meaning of this move was soon clear to Theodoric, who was still ruling in Italy, and its effect upon him was tragic.   He had regarded toleration of the Arians somewhat as a deserved reward for his considerate government of Italy. In almost frenzied despair, he arbitrarily condemned to death two leading Romans and practically forced the bishop of Rome to go to Constantinople in behalf of the Arians.   When this effort failed, as it was bound to do, he threw the pope into prison as a traitor.   He even meditated a general persecution of orthodox Christians, but his death in 526 prevented the execution of the plan.   The issue was now clear, and these final high-handed acts of Theodoric only served to alienate much of the good will which his otherwise truly remarkable reign had won from the Romans.

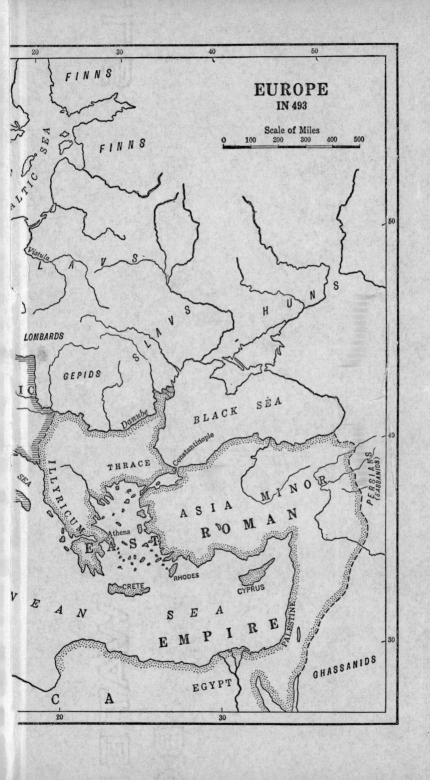

EUROPE
IN 493

Scale of Miles

0   100   200   300   400   500

FINNS

FINNS

BALTIC SEA

Vistula

S L A V S

SLAVS

HUNS

LOMBARDS

GEPIDS

DANUBE

BLACK SEA

ILLYRICUM

THRACE

Constantinople

SEA

ASIA MINOR

ROMAN

PERSIANS
(SASSANIDS)

Athens

E A S T

RHODES

CRETE

CYPRUS

PALESTINE

SEA

EMPIRE

GHASSANIDS

EGYPT

CA

With the Teutons themselves divided into pro-Roman and anti-Roman parties, the united orthodox Christians now looked confidently to the East for deliverance and for the restoration of the Roman Empire as it was before the entrance of the Visigoths.

Patience and caution were yet necessary. Justin had died in 527, and Justinian, who succeeded him, had some work to do at home before he could devote himself to the West. The Persians began a war which lasted five years, being ended by the death of the Persian king and the willingness of his successor to compound a peace. In the same year that ended this war, Justinian nearly lost his life in a riot, known as the Nika Riot, which broke out in the Hippodrome. From this he was rescued by the skill of a military commander named Belisarius, and by the cool courage of his wife, Theodora. She had been an actress when Justinian fell in love with her, and it required an act of the senate to enable him to marry her. From the time of her marriage her conduct was above reproach, and in the Nika Riot her courageous example kept Justinian from attempting flight. The uprising was soon quelled and Justinian fixed upon his throne. With peace at home and on his eastern border, he was now free to carry out his ambitious plans regarding the West.

The situation there first reached a climax in northern Africa, where the anti-Roman party drove out the pro-Roman ruler. Justinian sent a fleet and army under the command of Belisarius to espouse the cause of the ousted Vandal king. The war was very short (533-534) and at the end of it nearly all of northern Africa was again administered by officials appointed by the emperor.

The opportunity for intervention in Italy came the next year when Theodoric's daughter appealed for help against the anti-Roman party which had dethroned her. Greater precautions were taken in dealing with the Ostrogoths, however, and arrangements were made to attack them simultaneously on three fronts. The orthodox Franks, who had already overcome the Arian Burgundians and Visigoths in Gaul, were persuaded to attack from the northwest, while an imperial army from Constantinople attacked on the east. Meanwhile Belisarius in 535 crossed to Sicily, of which he made himself master in very short order. He then moved on southern Italy, where he encountered almost no resistance. Before the end of 536 he had established himself in Rome. At this juncture difficulties arose. The Franks made peace with the Ostrogoths when the latter gave them southeastern Gaul. With this danger removed, the Ostrogoths marched on Rome and besieged Belisarius for a year. They were forced to raise the siege when the imperial army, under the eunuch Narses, penetrated into northern Italy from the East. Thus placed between two imperial armies, the Ostrogoths were forced to give up the struggle, and with the surrender of Ravenna in 540, the war came to an end. Italy, like northern Africa, was again a Roman province, administered by the emperor's appointees.

This victory proved more apparent than real for, upon the recall of Belisarius to oppose the Persians who had begun another war in the East, the Ostrogoths rose under a new leader. Within three years they were again masters of Italy and continued so until 552, when Narses, with a large army composed chiefly of Lombards, overcame the remainder of the Ostrogoths. Before this conquest was assured, Narses had to repel an invasion of the Franks. Apparently the Franks had concluded that they had more in common with the Teutonic Ostrogoths, Arian though they were in religion, than with the Romans, however orthodox. They came too late to save the Ostrogoths, and their army of invasion was too small to regain Italy.

Thus assured of Italy, Justinian began a similar conquest of Spain. Party strife among the Visigoths there was used as an entering wedge, and once more an imperial army advanced as a friend of one Teutonic faction against another. The Visigoths managed to reunite, however, before Justinian's army had made much advance, so that only the cities along the southeastern coast were gained for the emperor.

From these victories over Vandal, Ostrogoth and Visigoth, Justinian might well have believed that the Empire was restored as it had been by Diocletian after the disorders of the third century, or by Theodosius after those of the fourth century. The

Roman nobility and others who had suffered keenly from the rudeness of the Teutonic kingdoms again had the pleasure of living under a government that was directly Roman. The church-men of the orthodox faith rejoiced in the overthrow of the Arian heretics and found the task of converting the remainder of the heretics much facilitated. The formal conversion of the Visi-gothic king, Reccared, in 588 was probably due in no small meas-ure to the conquests of Justinian.

Justinian's effort to restore the Roman Empire to its former grandeur, the imperial office to its former power, was not con-fined to military conquest. Under his patronage, schools flour-ished and scholars were encouraged to restore learning, which had declined in the preceding period. In his zeal for the Christian religion, Justinian devoted much money to the building of churches. The great church in Constantinople, St. Sophia, was the chief example of this new interest in religious architecture and soon became the model for other buildings of a distinct style, the Byzantine. Equally remarkable and no less enduring was Justinian's work in the field of law. He realized, as some earlier emperors had done, the need for a systematic statement of the Roman law. The vast accumulation of imperial edicts and the much larger accumulation of decisions by jurists through the centuries of Rome's existence had made the determination of justice exceedingly difficult. Many of the edicts and decisions, when brought together, proved contradictory to a confusing degree. To correct this state of affairs, Justinian appointed a commission of lawyers under the leadership of Tribonian, one of the ablest lawyers in Roman history. After years of labor, this commission presented a systematic statement of Roman law known as the *corpus iuris civilis*. This included not only the edicts of the emperors, or statutory law known as the *Code,* but also the *Pandects,* or decisions of jurists, together with a brief statement of the principles of Roman Law, called the *Institutes,* for the law student. To this Justinian added new laws, or *Novellæ,* designed to remedy the defects discovered by the com-missioners in their work, or to meet new problems which had arisen in his own time. In these four parts Justinian's *Corpus* of

Roman Law was complete, and he ordered that henceforth it should stand, without addition or modification, as the final statement of the law of the Empire, all previous laws being abrogated. This work still stands as one of the greatest and most influential achievements in the field of law, and Justinian deserves a large measure of credit for its completion.

The last years of Justinian's reign were not so happy. The West, which he had seemingly redeemed for the Empire, proved to be a heavy drain on the resources of the East. In all of the conquered region it was necessary to maintain strong armies, and the people of the West, whose prosperity had suffered during the period of warfare, were unable or unwilling to defray the cost. The military policy that his generals had followed in Italy finally proved a boomerang, as it had done before. In the East, the Lombards came back and the Persians continued to endanger the Empire up to 562, when they agreed to a fifty years' truce. At home, in Constantinople, the people groaned under the heavy burden of taxes which these great projects had involved. As Justinian went to his grave in 565, a feeble old man, it was without any assurance that his successors would, or could, carry out his plans.

Civilization now centered in Constantinople, as it formerly had in Rome. In appearance the Roman Empire was again in control of the civilized world, somewhat smaller than before and with its center shifted, but thoroughly active. In reality, there were other more important points of difference. Justinian was the last Latin ruler at Constantinople. After him, even the emperors used Greek as the official language. The Romans of the West, who had expected so much from the restoration of the Empire, soon felt themselves subjects of an alien power. Differences of religion which the orthodoxy of Justinian had erased reappeared more strongly than ever, and Roman churchmen went very reluctantly to Constantinople for approval of their elections. The estrangement felt by the Roman was experienced more keenly by the Teutonic tribes now settled in the former Roman regions. Justinian's wars, especially his last campaigns in Italy, had made it clear that their status as *fœderati,* protectors of their

respective regions for the Empire, was only a fiction. Most of
them had been very scrupulous in maintaining the Roman law
for the benefit of their Roman subjects, coining money with the
emperor's image upon it, and, in general, trying to uphold the
Roman system. That attitude was now rapidly changing to one
of complete independence. The continuance of the imperial hold
upon Italy and the towns of southeastern Spain depended henceforth upon the military strength of the garrisons which occupied
them. The Romans regarded the representatives of the East as
strangers interested only in extracting taxes from them, and the
Teutons began to look upon them as actual enemies. The Lombards, who had replaced the Goths in Italy, kept up an almost
constant warfare with the imperial garrisons in the Italian towns.
The Franks, now in control of all Gaul, ceased to concern themselves about the separate rights of the Romans dwelling there,
and the Visigothic kings felt themselves qualified to rule both
Romans and Teutons. All this meant that Justinian's work, to
be effective, must be followed up by his successors with skill
and vigor.

CHAPTER III

THE SEPARATION OF EAST AND WEST:
THE EAST TO 718. MOHAMMED

PERSIA AND THE EASTERN EMPIRE

THE immediate successors of Justinian were weaklings comparable to the predecessors of Justin I. On the other hand, their Persian neighbors were much more fortunate in the possession of strong rulers. Chosroes I, whose rule began in 531, centered his energies upon the task of building up a great Persian empire. He profited from Justinian's consuming ambitions in the West, receiving annual subsidies as the price of peace. In the half century of his reign, which outlasted that of Justinian by nearly twenty years, he succeeded in his task and left to his successor an empire nearly as strong as that of Constantinople.

The war which appeared inevitable broke out in 572 and continued until 591. The Empire at Constantinople was forced to use all its resources. The garrisons on the European frontiers were drawn upon so heavily that only a screen of troops remained, which offered very inadequate resistance to the tribesmen in the Balkan country and in Italy. The peace which was concluded with Persia in 591, though advantageous to Constantinople, was only a truce which was needed by the latter to drive back the invaders from the Balkan peninsula. Persia used the interval to rebuild its strength, and in 610 was ready to renew the war. This war lasted as long as the former and was much more exhausting. Chosroes II, who now led the Persians, seemed at one time about to overthrow the Empire. His armies had conquered Syria, Palestine and Egypt. His allies, the Hun-like Avars, appeared before the gates of Constantinople, and Heraclius, the emperor, thought seriously of transferring his court to northern Africa. Only the coöperation of the Church and merchants enabled him to maintain his resistance. At length, in 622, the tide turned. Chosroes found that his great effort had exhausted Persia. His armies were driven back from place to place. By 628 Heraclius marshaled his army before the gates of Ctesiphon. The people in the city rose in revolt against Chosroes, killed him, and sued for peace. Heraclius was able to impose a very humiliating peace upon the Persians and to return to Constantinople as a glorified hero celebrating his triumph.

How little that triumph meant! Persia was beaten and exhausted, to be sure. But the Empire at Constantinople was almost as exhausted as if it, too, had been beaten. Little of the Balkan peninsula remained to it, and only a few fortified cities in Italy. The clergy and the merchants had used up nearly all their wealth to supply money for the army, which had been weakened by heavy losses. The domains of the Empire in the war zone had been swept over, first by the Persians, and then by the imperial armies, with heavy losses both times. They were scarcely in a position to refill the depleted treasury of the Empire. At best, it would require at least a generation of healing, constructive work to restore the Empire. But there was to be no respite, for a new enemy had arisen.

THE RISE OF MOHAMMED

The most important event which happened about this time was neither the triumphant return of Heraclius to Constantinople nor the overthrow of the Persian Empire. Little more than a year later the Arab preacher, Mohammed, returned to Mecca, from which he had been forced to flee eight years before. Mecca was the religious center of all Arabia, and its acceptance of Mohammed insured his success among the Arabs. Probably no one at the time foresaw the future importance of this event, but conditions, geographical and political as well as religious, were peculiarly propitious.

Arabia, the country of Mohammed's life work, formed a wedge between the Persian and Byzantine empires. Altogether, it had an area larger than the part of the United States east of the Mississippi, but it did not sustain a very large population.   High, rocky and barren, much of it sandy desert with very little rainfall, it possessed few fertile areas.   Only along the seacoast, particularly on the west, were regions suitable for settled life.   The country was fit only for sporadic grazing, except where oases in the desert afforded limited opportunity for agriculture.   It was not inviting to outsiders, and, though all the great empires of ancient history had expanded around its edges, none of them had made any prolonged efforts to acquire it.   It did, however, lie between India and Asia Minor, and two of the great trade routes between the Mediterranean and the far East ran along its borders.

The character of the country was such that only the hardy could survive.   The people who inhabited it were of the Semitic race, like the Jews.   They were organized in tribes around a family nucleus, and most of them led a nomadic, or semi-nomadic, life. They grazed their herds of camels, horses, sheep and goats along the edge of the desert, or carried on a certain amount of agriculture in the scattered oases.   Some degree of unity was maintained among the tribes by the annual rendezvous at certain favored spots such as Mecca.   Here they kept the tribal idols by the side of the revered black stone of meteoric origin.   The Kaaba, in which these religious objects were stored, may be regarded as the religious center of Arabia.   In the spring of the year as many of the tribesmen as could gathered about Mecca.   Along with the religious ceremonies, they engaged in trade or courting, and listened to the efforts of orators and poets.   Poetry appears to have been a national passion with them and was highly cultivated.   After these meetings, the tribes departed for their accustomed grazing grounds.   When the grass was poor, they often resorted to plunder and warfare.   Their great hardihood and love of fighting made them desirable soldiers, and as such they were hired by both the Persians and the Eastern Empire.   Many of the tribes took part in the last great struggle between the two and were therefore aware of the condition in which their powerful neighbors had been left at the end of it.

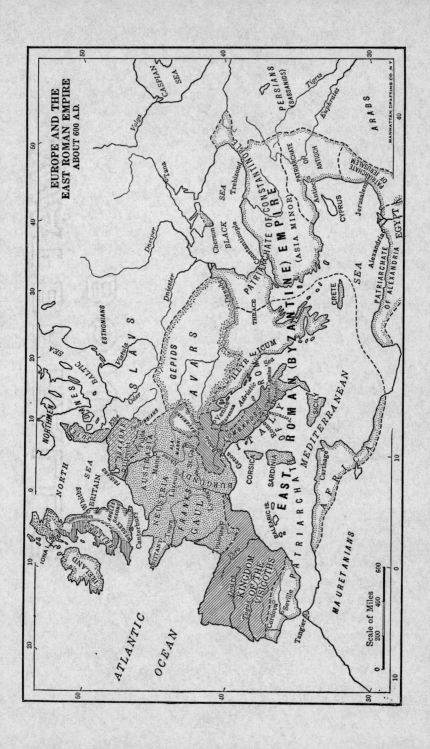

EUROPE AND THE
EAST ROMAN EMPIRE
ABOUT 600 A.D.

ATLANTIC
OCEAN

NORTH
SEA

BRITAIN

IRELAND

IONA

BALTIC
SEA

NORTHMEN

ESTHONIANS

SLAVS

GEPIDS

AVARS

CASPIAN
SEA

PERSIANS
(SASSANIDS)

ARABS

Volga

Tigris

Euphrates

Don

Dnieper

Dniester

Danube

BLACK SEA

Cherson

Trebizond

Constantinople

PATRIARCHATE OF CONSTANTINOPLE

PATRIARCHATE

(BYZANTINE) EMPIRE
(ASIA MINOR)

CYPRUS

Antioch
ANTIOCH

Jerusalem
PATRIARCHATE
OF JERUSALEM

Alexandria
PATRIARCHATE
OF ALEXANDRIA

EGYPT

CRETE

MEDITERRANEAN
SEA

SICILY

SARDINIA

CORSICA

BALEARIC IS.

EAST
ROMAN PATRIARCHATE
OF ITALY

Rome
ILLYRICUM

Ravenna

Venice
Adriatic Sea

Genoa

ITALY

AFRICA

Carthage

Tangier

MAURETANIANS

KINGDOM
OF THE
VISIGOTHS

Seville
Cordova

Ebro

Tagus

Douro

GAUL

NEUSTRIA

AUSTRASIA

BURGUNDY

TRANS-
JURANE

THURINGIANS

BAVARIANS

ALEMANNI

BRITTANY

Canterbury

Whitby

ANGLES

SAXONS

JUTES

FRISIANS

Toulouse

Lyons

Tours

THRACE

Scale of Miles
0   200   400   600

MANHATTAN DRAFTING CO. N.Y.

Mohammed (570-632), whose teaching was destined to influence these people so profoundly, was a member of that important tribe which held the lands around Mecca and acted as guardian of the Kaaba. His early life was one of hardship, for the death of his parents left him an orphan in the care of an uncle with a large family and small means. When he had grown to early manhood, he obtained employment with a wealthy widow, Kadija, to whom he was related. In her employ he engaged in commerce, chiefly at Mecca, though he made journeys as far as Syria. His circumstances became easier still when the widow Kadija married him.

He is described at this time as a man "of middle height, bluish-colored, with hair that was neither straight nor curly, with a large head, large eyes, heavy eyelashes, a reddish tint in his eyes, thick bearded, broad-shouldered, with thick hands and feet." Another description adds that he had "a large mouth, eyes horizontally long, hands abnormally soft, and with little flesh on his heels." More importance, perhaps, can be attached to what is said of his character. He was very gentle, loved children and hated the sight of blood. Evil odors were offensive to him and he abhorred garlic and onions. He dressed plainly but neatly, for he disliked untidy clothes. Abstemious in both food and drink, he particularly loathed drunkenness, which was only too common among the Arabs of his tribe. Among his more positive traits are to be counted business ability, skill as an orator, though not as a debater, and confidence in himself, or in his inspiration, which amounted to the same result. Though a member of the leading tribe, his humble beginning had kept him from attaining a position of importance among his fellows. His unfailing sympathy for slaves and outcasts was doubtless a reflection of his own early difficulties.

With his marriage to Kadija, however, his social position was much improved, and he obtained the leisure and dignity to pursue his personal inclination toward religious speculation. In the market place at Mecca he had conversed with Jews and Persians as well as Christians on this favorite theme and had reached the decision that the primitive idol-worship of his people was wrong.

He sought some better solution and finally concluded that it was his mission to bring a new religion. Frequent visions came to him, revealing the principles of this new faith. An affliction, diagnosed as epilepsy, probably accentuated his natural tendency toward abnormal imaginings. It became his habit to withdraw from all society for periods of several weeks, which he spent in a cave outside of Mecca. Visions commonly came to him at these intervals. His wife encouraged his belief in his mission and he began to seek converts. The authorities of Mecca became angry at his attack upon the popular religion which meant so much to the prestige and prosperity of their town. When Kadija died and her powerful influence was removed, Mohammed was forced in 622 to flee for his life. This flight is known as the *hegira,* and from it the Mohammedans date their calendar. He found an asylum at Medina, which was a trade rival of Mecca, and here his converts increased rapidly in number and his religion assumed its final form.

This religion has many points of similarity with Judaism and Christianity. Some of its features, too, reflect the influence of Persian Zoroastrianism. It contains also many precepts derived from the folk-lore of the Arabs or from Mohammed's own experience. The fundamental doctrine is that there is one God, Allah, and Mohammed is his prophet. Every pious Mohammedan is expected to pray five times each day facing toward Mecca, to make a pilgrimage to Mecca at least once during his lifetime, to contribute a fifth of his income to charity, and otherwise to conduct himself in accord with the utterances of Mohammed. If he does so, he will go to Paradise when he dies— a Paradise filled with all the delights of this world in unwearying measure. Among other regulations, Mohammed prescribed cleanliness of person, abstinence from wine and intoxicating liquor, forbade pictures or images, and permitted polygamy. During his exile from Mecca, Mohammed enunciated the further doctrine that any of his followers who died fighting for their faith would be immediately transported to Paradise.

His firm belief in his mission, his willingness to share misfortune, his tact and his fair administration of justice won and held his followers. All were treated alike and all shared equally in the spoils of plundering expeditions. In order to protect their caravans, the people of Mecca made several efforts to destroy Mohammed's growing army, but without success. At length, in 630, when it appeared that Mohammed was willing to respect the Kaaba and to make Mecca the center of his faith, that city surrendered without a struggle.

SPREAD OF MOHAMMEDANISM

Mohammed died in 632, knowing only that Arabia had acknowledged him as Allah's prophet. He left no son to carry on his mission, but several widows and collateral relatives claimed position in his name. He had made no provision for succession. At his death some of his immediate followers chose to regard his oldest friend and follower, Abu-Bekr, as caliph, or successor.

The descriptive term, caliph, soon became adopted as the title of the head of the Mohammedan world. The caliph exercised all the functions which Mohammed had practiced except that of prophetic utterance. All political as well as religious powers were theoretically held by him. In practice, however, the caliph's position tended finally to become honorary rather than actual, religious rather than political.

Abu-Bekr held the office until his death in 634. Omar (634-644) and Othman (644-656), who followed as caliphs, were likewise chosen in a rather informal manner. Discord broke out upon the death of Othman, Mohammed's son-in-law Ali being the leader in the opposition. By 655 the family of Othman succeeded in gaining the command and held it in their possession until 750. This *Ommiad* dynasty, as it is called, had its capital at Damascus. It was overthrown after a century by the descendants of Ali's family, known as the *Abbasids*. The latter established the capital at Bagdad, where it was to remain for several centuries.

One of the achievements of the first three caliphs was the compilation of Mohammed's utterances, which constituted at once the religion and law of his followers. Mohammed himself had left no writings, his knowledge of writing being very limited, if, indeed, he was not wholly illiterate. His utterances had been preserved in part by devoted followers, who had written them on palm leaves, stone tablets, or shells, or had merely retained them in memory. The collection and arrangement of this material, so vital to the unity and continued existence of the faith, was carried out by these caliphs.

This collection is known as the *Koran* and remains to this day the Law and the Bible of the Mohammedan world. The arrangement of the material is in part chronological, in part according to the length of the separate items. There is considerable repetition and not a little contradiction within the book. Mohammed's last statement is, therefore, regarded by the disciples as the Law. Like the Christian Bible, the Koran calls for commentaries and elaborations by scholars. The most important of these are the six collections of traditions about Mohammed made at Bagdad and regarded as authentic by orthodox Moslems ever since. The effect of the traditions and other commentaries was to enlarge the relatively simple precepts of the prophet to meet the more complex problems which expansion beyond the tribal life of Arabia had brought about.

The first wave of expansion was checked when discord broke out between the Ommiads and Ali in 655. It was renewed again after the Ommiad dynasty became established at Damascus. It reached a climax with the siege of Constantinople (678-683), which was saved by most heroic resistance as well as by the discovery of the unquenchable Greek fire. Constantinople was besieged a second time in 717-718, to be saved again by the same means. The advance to the northeast was but a symptom of the general advance on all fronts. In the West the Ommiads swept over northern Africa and in 711 began their advance northward into and across Spain. Within a century after the death of Mohammed, his followers were to be found as far northwest as the Pyrenees and as far southeast as the Indus river. This was the high tide of their expansion.

The Mohammedan faith continued to be held by most of the people throughout the region.   Non-Moslems were tolerated, being allowed to practice their own religion, subject only to higher taxes than were paid by the faithful.   Thus many Jews and not a few Christians remained in Mohammedan lands.   The great majority of people, however, held to the Moslem faith, which satisfied them better than any other religion.   The religious bond was more lasting and stronger than any of the political bonds and herein lay the strength of the Mohammedan world.   There was always the possibility that some rising power within the Mohammedan world might rally the whole by proclaiming a *Jehad,* or holy war, either for an attack upon infidel lands or in defense against encroachments from such foes.   In practice this possibility seldom operated as an aggressive force, but its passive power has continued to exert tremendous influence down to the present time.

Within the boundaries of their military advance, the Arabs had to deal with the exacting problem of government.   Here they showed some ability, but a lack of the genius which characterized the Romans.   Politically, one part and another fell away and refused to pay tribute to the caliph of Bagdad.   Even in religion minor differences were enough to bring about separation.

THE CULTURE OF THE ARABS

As the Arabs swept outward over the adjoining territory, their life was greatly modified.   They mingled with the people whom they conquered or converted.   They learned from them the art of government and the arts of leisure.   As they became more firmly settled in the conquered regions, their connections with their homeland gradually ceased.   Subject natives rose to high place in government, and, in return for the Arab religion and language, they taught their conquerors much about life.   The result was a new period of culture in Egypt and in the regions of Mesopotamia, especially under the caliph Haroun al Raschid (786-809), the influence of which was felt throughout the Mohammedan world.   The fundamentals of this culture were bor-

rowed from antiquity or Byzantium. Their buildings, their
philosophy, their learning and their art revealed this debt in convincing manner, but to the borrowed foundation they added a distinctive touch. This difference is revealed most clearly, perhaps,
in their imaginative literature, as any reader of the *Arabian
Nights* can testify. It is apparent also in their architecture with
its arabesques and twisted domes and minarets. Likewise in
philosophy, where Plato and Aristotle served as chief patrons, the
writings of such men as Avicenna (d.1038) exhibit both the debt
and the difference. The best of the culture developed at the Mohammedan centers compared very favorably with that to be found
at Constantinople at the same time. For the world at large, this
development had chiefly the effect of extending the life of ancient
learning and of preserving it, but some of the contributions which
the Arabs made are still of use in modern life.

BYZANTINE EMPIRE IN THE EIGHTH CENTURY

For the Byzantine Empire the growth of Mohammedanism
created a menace which was to last as long as that Empire. From
678 to 683 it had withstood a fearful Moslem attack, and again
from 717 to 718. Thereafter the fighting was chiefly along the
mountain line of the Taurus and Armenian mountains in Asia
Minor. Sometimes the pressure was light, at other times heavy,
but the danger was never gone. The lands that had been lost east
and south of the line were never to be recovered by Constantinople. The men and money which those regions had formerly
contributed to the strength of the Empire were no longer available. Nor was the situation to the north and west much happier.
The Danube River and the mountain chains of the Balkan
peninsula were called upon to play much the same rôle there as the
Taurus range and the uplands of Asia Minor played on the east.
Successive invasions of barbarous tribes, chiefly from Asia, like
the Avars, Bulgarians, Petcheneks, or the Slavs from central
Europe, continued to encroach upon this area and to endanger the
existence of the Empire. From 600 onward the political

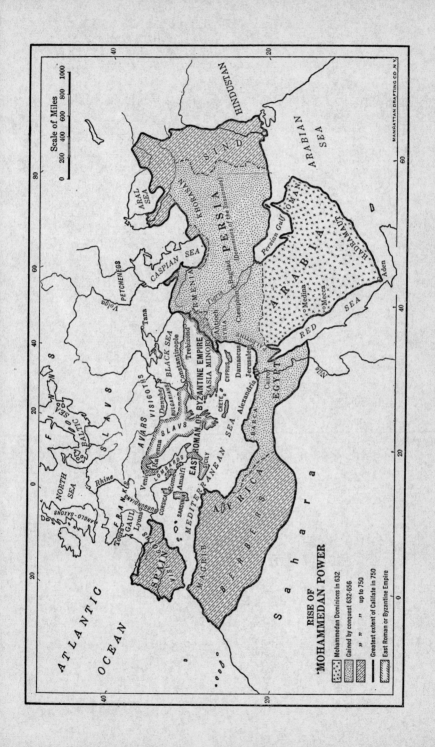

RISE OF
MOHAMMEDAN POWER

Scale of Miles
0 200 400 600 800 1000

Mohammedan Dominions in 632
Gained by conquest 632-656
"   "   "   up to 750
Greatest extent of Califate in 750
East Roman or Byzantine Empire

MANHATTAN DRAFTING CO. N.Y.

Byzantine Empire led a purely defensive existence. Any attempt to regain control of the West was practically out of the question.

The wonder is not, therefore, that Constantinople made no further serious efforts to regain the West, but rather that it continued to exist at all. The strategic location of its capital saved it from conquest on two occasions and always afforded it an economic advantage. With Trebizond and Tana on the Black Sea and Venice and Amalfi on the Mediterranean as its outposts, the main stream of commerce from two continents continued to flow through Constantinople. This yielded a golden harvest with which the citizens of the capital were able not only to provide themselves with the necessaries of life, but also to buy off the less insistent of their enemies. It enabled them also to maintain a high state of civilization which had an unbroken connection with that of Rome and Greece and a strength and beauty peculiar to itself. Barbarians were attracted into the military service of Constantinople by the luxury which they knew it possessed. Emperors came and went in bewildering succession, as they had in fifth-century Italy, without seriously disturbing the existence of the state. Their function in practice was largely military, to hold back the invaders on either side, and to keep open the sea roads to the commercial outposts. In this task, the nature of the country aided them, as did also the rugged qualities of the provincials who occupied these regions. The organization of the army provided a steady stream of officials from which the imperial office could readily be filled, if the incumbent fell a victim to luxurious living, assassination, or death without heir. Dynastic changes and rapid succession of rulers, therefore, had less bearing on the fate of the state than was usually the case. The Byzantine Empire is to be viewed henceforth rather as a commercial organization with a military cover than as an empire in the old Roman sense.

This change was fully apparent by 600. By that time the court as well as the scholars had given up the Latin language of the Roman Empire and all used the Greek tongue which was more natural to them. With the abandonment of the Latin language went also the abandonment of the Roman genius for war and imperial organization. A high degree of civilization, however, was maintained, not always with great vigor, to be sure, but always with enough reserve to insure its revival when conditions should be favorable. Henceforth Constantinople played practically no part in the affairs of the West, but in it existed a reservoir of civilization destined in time to serve western Europe.

CHAPTER IV

SEPARATION OF EAST AND WEST: THE WEST
TO 700. THE MONKS

WHETHER the Teutonic tribal kingdoms in the West understood the full meaning of events in the East mattered little. They did realize that the emperors were no longer able to send armies to the West and they therefore became careless about their obligations as "protectors" of Rome. Disputes arose between brothers or more distant relatives for possession of the kingship. Such disputes had not been unknown in earlier times, but now the warriors who had formerly been mindful of the dangers of dissension no longer felt any restraint. Expecting greater favors from one side or the other, they joined passionately in the strife. The Romans among whom they lived were drawn into the struggles, some willingly, more perhaps unwillingly, and the distinction between Roman and Teuton tended to disappear more rapidly than before. No pains were taken to preserve separate law for the two peoples; little effort was made to prevent intermarriages. In fact, little attention was paid to public law of any kind, so busy was most of the population in warlike support of one or another faction. Warfare between rival claimants for the position of king, or between different chieftains for power, became the rule in every one of the Teutonic kingdoms on Roman soil. It was true of the Lombards in Italy, the Visigoths in Spain, the Franks in Gaul and the Anglo-Saxons in Britain. A lull would occur in one region when a chieftain had succeeded in beating down all his rivals, but this truce usually ended upon his death, when factional strife would again appear. Such, in brief, for more than a century after the death of Justinian, was the history of what had once been the Roman West.

Such a condition of chronic strife was perhaps a more natural state for the Teutons than the relatively orderly life which they had led since 378. Their natural outlook was essentially warlike. A man's standing among them depended largely upon his ability as a warrior. This was regarded as the highest profession of the freeman, almost the only respectable occupation which he could follow. He was trained to it from earliest boyhood and expected to follow it throughout his active life. Formal learning such as the Romans used to give their children seemed effeminate to them and they scorned it accordingly. During all the years that they had been on Roman soil they had maintained their warlike tradition and their organization. They chafed during the intervals of enforced peace and they viewed with disapproval the imitation of Roman civilization which had crept in among their people during that time. Only their awe of the Empire had restrained them. Now that those invisible bonds were snapped by the failure of the Roman Empire to reëstablish its authority, the Teutons again felt their natural instincts coming to the front.

The Roman population of the West found adjustment to such life more difficult. It probably mattered but little to the servile group, some of whom may even have found in the disturbed conditions of the time an opportunity for the improvement of their lot. The middle class, however, of which there were still some representatives in the towns, and the upper class suffered. That life of cultured ease which the latter had lived even in the fifth century was no longer possible. It was no longer sufficient for them to be on good terms with a king; it was now necessary to give armed assistance or to lose their possessions, possibly also their lives. Those who could equip themselves for fighting enjoyed the hazards of the game of war and made the transition well enough. But those who scorned to fight and counted upon the arts of persuasion alone to save them from spoliation were less fortunate. At the worst they lost their lives, but at best they lost their leisure and the pleasures that come from the reading of books and from cultivated conversation. This was in many ways the greatest danger which the times held, namely, that in the constant strife and training for war the knowledge of books should disappear and, with it, the fruits of all the learning of centuries.

THE CHURCH BECOMES A FORCE IN AFFAIRS

The chief safeguard against such a calamity lay in the Church. But how strong was it, and could it survive in such troubled times? It had some organization, we know. Its foundations had been laid in the period of the persecutions and there remained a heritage of independence possible not only without governmental support, but in opposition to it. On those foundations the rapid spread of Christianity after the persecutions had built a super-structure of organization modeled upon that of the Roman Empire at its best. A well-organized priesthood ministered directly to the people. There were priests wherever the religion was established. Over each considerable town and its adjacent country-side there was an official called a bishop. His duties were partly religious and partly administrative, in a broad sense. He not only looked after the priests and provided for their training, but he also served the people at large as a leader. Some of the emperors had entrusted not a little governmental service to them, and often during periods of unrest able bishops had been virtual governors of their communities, or dioceses, as they were regularly called. In the larger towns, especially in the chief towns of a province, the bishop occupied a somewhat superior position over the other bishops of the province. He was known as the metropolitan, or chief bishop. The term archbishop came to be generally applied to such officers. All of these bishops were elected by the priests and the people of their dioceses. The metropolitan, or archbishop, merely had superior dignity. Jerusalem, Antioch, Alexandria in the East, and Rome in the West had long held such pre-eminence. These patriarchates might almost be likened to the four prefectures of the Empire. After the capital was established at Constantinople, the leading bishop of the city was likewise recognized as of patriarchal dignity.

The actual headship of the Church had not become fixed without dispute for the whole of Christendom. In the West this position was accorded to the bishop of Rome and was recognized in the imperial legislation of Valentinian III, in 445. The title of *papa,* or father, commonly applied to any priest, was accorded to the bishop of Rome by the whole Church, at least in the West. Thus the bishop of Rome came to be known as the *papa,* or pope, of the Church, whose position might be likened to that of the emperor in the State. His power over the lower clergy, however, had not become fully defined before there ceased to be emperors in the West. His superior dignity was unquestioned. On matters of Church doctrine, too, the lesser clergy of the West had come to follow his decision. To what extent they would keep in constant touch with him, submit their disputes to him, or rely upon him for aid in their administrative problems was not settled. It was here that the greatest danger lay, for there was now great likelihood that, in the disturbed conditions of the time, the bishoprics would become as separate as the political areas already were. The fact that Rome was one of the few places still held by the Eastern Empire in the seventh century militated against, rather than for, the pope's continued preëminence. Fortunately, however, Christianity had been so long established in the Roman world that the Latin language in which it was known to the West had come to be almost a part of the faith itself. This was the language of Rome, and its continued use was bound to keep alive the memory of Rome's greatness. All these matters, however, were fraught with uncertainty in western Europe at the opening of the sixth century.

It was indeed a critical period, but the crisis ultimately brought forth a great man. This was Gregory I, known in history as "the Great," and the last of the four great Latin Church fathers. He was descended from one of the proudest families of imperial Rome. His parents left him great wealth, but, instead of following a secular career, he early decided to lead the life of a monk. To this end, he gave his lands to monastic communities and converted his own house in Rome into a monastery. There he lived as a simple monk, following the rule which had been formulated by St. Benedict at Monte Cassino some fifty years before. The seclusion which he so much desired was interrupted when the pope sent him to Constantinople as his representative. Here Gregory learned imperial ways and also conditions in the East. He did not like his situation there and appears not even to have learned the Greek language. When he was at length allowed to return to

Rome and his monastery, he resumed his monastic ways. Very shortly thereafter he was chosen abbot of his community and was thus again brought into contact with active life. In 589 occurred a devastating overflow of the Tiber, which was followed by an even more devastating plague. The reigning pope fell victim to the plague, as did also thousands of more humble Romans. To fill the vacancy in the papal office, clergy and people acclaimed Gregory as their choice, and his name was sent to the emperor for approval. Gregory sought to avoid this office, but in vain.

As pope, Gregory displayed all the administrative genius for which his family had long been noted. He quieted the people, panic-stricken by the plague. When the Lombards again threatened Rome, Gregory undertook negotiations with them and secured the safety of the city and ultimately a truce between Lombards and Romans. In doing this he was transgressing the authority of the exarch, who, in the name of the Eastern emperor, held several small districts in Italy, including that around Rome.[1] He realized, however, that something must be done to save the people, whether the dignity of the powerless exarch were saved or not. His personal attitude was always humble, and but few people in history have displayed greater courage in their official conduct. Realizing the helplessness of the East, he sought to build up power in the West. He worked energetically to convert the Teutons to orthodox Christianity. He was intensely interested in the work of the Spanish Christians who were converting the Visigoths. Similar work was going on among the Lombards. But perhaps his greatest achievement in this field was in the conversion of the Anglo-Saxons. In 597 he dispatched an embassy of Benedictine monks to England. Their leader, St. Augustine, was successful in his mission and became the first archbishop of Canterbury, the founder of the Church of England. In addition to all this, Gregory busied himself in writing. He was anxious to bind all the clergy of the West to Rome and to improve the standard of their work. His little book of instruction for priests and bishops is still read with approval today. This, the *Pastoral Care,* was

[1] Exarchate of Ravenna was the name applied to the territory in Italy held by the Eastern Empire. The imperial representative was known by the Greek title, exarch, and ruled from Ravenna.

one of the books which King Alfred of England translated into English. He also wrote edifying stories of the lives of Italian saints in a style which the world of that time could appreciate and a commentary on the Book of Job which was to have great influence on Western Christians. At the same time he indicated that, however the patriarch of Constantinople and even the emperor might feel about the orthodox teaching, he would adhere to it.

MISSIONARY ACTIVITIES

None of the many important activities of Gregory's career had more lasting influence than his promotion of Benedictine monasticism. Gregory wrote the life story of Benedict and probably modeled his own life upon that of his hero. Benedict, too, had been of the Roman nobility and had early forsaken the world for a monastic life. Monasticism had not yet been very well organized when he embarked upon that life, and it was at the cost of much bitter experience that he finally formulated a rule which he put into practice at Monte Cassino in the hills to the south of Rome. His rule differed from previous regulations in its eminently practical wisdom. Men were not allowed to become monks until they had gone through a trial period of a year. This period of the novitiate was a protection both to the candidate and to the monastery. When properly observed, it saved the candidate from following a career for which he was not fitted, and protected the monastery against undesirable members. At the end of the year the novice could take the irrevocable vows of poverty, chastity and obedience. The life of the monks was carefully regulated. Religious observances and devotions were judiciously varied by a certain amount of manual labor, and provision was made for adequate food and clothing. The government of the community may be described as an elective monarchy. The power of the abbot was absolute, but Benedict carefully admonished him to consult the elder brethren in all important matters. Though the rule was made for the monastery at Monte Cassino, Benedict's wisdom made it so flexible that it could be readily adapted to conditions anywhere. It was perhaps a defect of the rule that no provision was made for a common organization of many monasteries, so that each could help the other to maintain the spirit of the rule to the full. As it was, each monastery was a unit by itself, subject to the bishop of the diocese in which it was located.

Three names may properly be added to that of Benedict in the shaping of the Benedictine rule to the great social usefulness which it served. The first is that of Scholastica, Benedict's sister, who presided over the first female community under the rule. The second is that of Cassiodorus, the long-lived secretary of Theodoric, king of the Ostrogoths. It was the example of Cassiodorus after his retirement from public life which led to the recognition of teaching and copying of books as legitimate forms of labor in the meaning of the rule. The third is that of Pope Gregory, who appreciated the practical value of the rule as a model for monastic communities anywhere, and who was probably the first to appreciate the full value of the energy which it contained. When he sent Augustine with his band of monks to convert England he established a practice of far-reaching consequences. The monks were to take the lead in missionary work among the heathen Teutons. As missionaries, they carried with them not only the Roman Catholic religion, but the Latin language and many of the practical arts of civilization as well. The monasteries which they built in the forests among the heathen became the schools through which the elements of ancient civilization were imparted to the people of the North.

The great fruits of Gregory's very active career appeared after his time. He knew of the success of Augustine's mission before he died, but he did not know that the English monasteries were to send out missionaries, in turn, to preach the Roman religion and to win new lands to the allegiance of Rome. He had displayed indefatigable energy in keeping in touch with the secular clergy everywhere. He had sent them presents of books or relics, had advised them in matters of doctrine, and had judged their disputes, thus strengthening their tendency to look to Rome for guidance. The missionary monks far away on the frontier kept this habit alive as they wandered through the intervening lands on their way back and forth to Rome. Like other Romans, he desired both political and religious unity, nor did he give up altogether the idea that the emperors at Constantinople might bring about this concord. As long as an exarch remained at Ravenna, even though he had no more than a corporal's guard to protect it, the Romans cherished this hope.

LEARNING AND EDUCATION IN THE SIXTH CENTURY

It was indeed fortunate that Gregory lived when he did and accomplished all that he did accomplish, for even in his writings the decline of learning is painfully evident. The writings of the great Church fathers of the later fourth and the early fifth centuries do not reveal so polished a style as that of the previous literary age, but their authors at least were still in touch with the best of ancient learning. That had not since been true. Boethius (480-527), virtually the last writer seriously considered in the history of Latin literature, had spent much of his time in translating the leading Greek text-books of the liberal arts, because his fellow Romans were no longer able to read them in the original language. After him, Cassiodorus (480-575), who had postponed most of his literary work until he retired from the Ostrogothic court about 543, seems childish in comparison. Gregory's own literary contemporaries were still less accomplished. Isidore, (d.636), bishop of Seville in Spain, was urged by some former pupils to compile a collection of all that a man of learning needed to know. He therefore wrote an encyclopedia which would scarcely fill the space of an ordinary text-book today. For centuries to come, even that was more than sufficient for the needs of the time. Gregory of Tours (d.594), in Gaul, though he prided himself upon his Roman nobility and was conscious of better style than his own, wrote his *Ecclesiastical History of the Franks* because "liberal culture was on the wane or rapidly perishing in the Gallic cities and no grammarian skilled in the dialectic art could be found to describe these matters either in prose or in verse." Modestly, he justified his unclassical language "because, to my surprise, it has often been said by men of our day that few understand the learned words of the rhetorician, but many the rude language of the people."

The continued use of the learned language, the key to the books of the past, depended then, as now, upon the work of the schools. Gregory's statement may be interpreted as a confession that schools were practically nonexistent in his day. This conclusion is reinforced by other evidence. The flourishing schools which were to be found, as late as the fourth century, in every town of the Empire, had begun even then to decline. Support from the imperial treasury had become very fitful during stormy times. The more able emperors, looking to the future, had striven to maintain the schools even in seasons of trouble, but the weaker emperors looked with disfavor upon the expenditure for education of large sums which could be used for more immediate purposes. Local communities bore the steady burden of school support, but, as their prosperity declined under unfavorable political conditions and heavy imperial taxes, they, too, were forced to abandon their schools. As early as the fifth century, Roman nobles were complaining of the difficulty of getting competent teachers for their children. Some of them were driven to do their own teaching or to go without. One such noble, Martianus Capella, whose villa was in northern Africa, composed an elementary text of the seven liberal arts in story form for his children. The fact that in the West this book continued to be used for centuries is less a tribute to its excellence than a reflection upon the period that could not devise a better text. The situation of the schools grew even worse. When the Teuton kings were ruling the Empire, some of them, like Theodoric the Ostrogoth, allowed government funds to be used for the support of teachers, and a temporary revival took place. But in the period of civil wars this practice was no longer followed and the state of education soon reached the point described by Gregory of Tours.

SPREAD OF LEARNING BY THE MISSIONARIES

The age of Gregory of Tours, however, witnessed a development which was to prevent the schools from disappearing altogether. This was the assumption by the Church of the elementary education of prospective priests. Until the sixth century, churchmen apparently had given little thought to the construction of a complete scheme of education for their officials. They had been content to furnish training in theology and Church law, leaving the fundamental education to the government schools. Cassiodorus was one of the first to realize that this practice could not continue, and when he retired from active life his chief interest seems to have been the training of churchmen in elementary subjects. Several treatises written by him on this subject are still extant. Others, like Isidore of Seville in Spain and Pope Gregory, helped to further the work, though Gregory is sometimes blamed because he chided one of the bishops for spending too much time in teaching and study. The work of these men took on a more permanent form when the Benedictine monasteries made teaching and the copying of books recognized forms of labor in the meaning of their rule. By the beginning of the seventh century the Church schools were practically the only formal schools, and education had become primarily ecclesiastical. Fortunately, the Latin language was by this time so firmly associated with the Catholic religion as to seem almost a part of it, and thus was preserved the key to the great storehouses of past experience which the libraries contained. As long as this religion continued, there was hope for the preservation of ancient civilization.

But even the persistence of the Roman Catholic religion in a unified Church seemed none too certain in the early seventh century. Nominally, all of the Teutons on former Roman territory were adherents of this faith, but under the stress of civil wars there was little coöperation among the clergy, a condition which might have led to complete separation. This misfortune was prevented, however, from a strange quarter.

It was in Britain, where Roman civilization had been least thoroughly established and where the Teutonic invaders had had but little contact with the Roman Empire before they entered it, that the chief impulse for its preservation now arose. The Benedictine monasteries established in the land of the Anglo-Saxons through St. Augustine, whom Pope Gregory had sent there in

597, now took the lead in the missionary work of the seventh and eighth centuries. Many Saxon lads chose to become monks. At Canterbury, and later at other centers, they studied the Latin necessary for the priesthood. Some of them became teachers and scholars, mastering the learning of the time so thoroughly that one of them, the Venerable Bede (d.732), was soon recognized as the greatest scholar of his day. Possibly more important, however, was the missionary work which these newly won Catholics carried on in Britain and elsewhere. They spread out among their own people north and westward, where they achieved a notable victory over another form of Christianity which had its center in Ireland, not in Rome.

The Irish faith had arisen when the Romans were still in Britain. This form of Christianity was highly ascetic and varied in organization and in several of its practices from the Roman Catholic faith, but the chief point of difference was that its center lay outside the lands of ancient civilization. At the synod of Whitby, in 664, the king of Northumbria decided, after hearing representatives of both faiths, to accept the Roman, rather than the Irish, form of Christianity.

The first great figure of the Irish faith was St. Patrick, still the patron saint of Irish Catholics, whose work extended from 432 until his death in 461. He had received his instruction in Christianity in Gaul and his desire to convert the Irish followed some years of captivity among them. His labors as a missionary were brilliantly successful, and within little more than a half century after his death the Irish were sending out missionaries to other lands. St. Columba (Collumkille) established himself with twelve companions on the island of Iona about the year 563. From here as a base he carried on work among the Highland Scots. Another Irish missionary of importance was Columbanus, who worked on the Continent from 585 to 615. His journeys took him to the heathen Hessians, the Alamanni and, finally, to the Arian Lombards. The monasteries of Luxeuil, in Gaul, and Bobbio, in northern Italy, as well as St. Gall, in Switzerland, long commemorated his work. The debate at Whitby was followed by the gradual conversion of the Irish to Roman allegiance, and the work which they had begun was taken over by the Roman Church.

It was shortly after Whitby that the English began their great missionary work on the Continent. Willibrod, a Northumbrian, who had studied both with the Irish churchmen and with those from Canterbury, carried on missionary work among the heathen Frisians. His church at Utrecht became the nucleus around which Christianity developed among these people and he himself received recognition for his success when, in 695, the pope consecrated him at Rome as archbishop. Even more important was the work of Winfrith, a Saxon noble from Wessex, better known as Boniface. He worked as a missionary among the Hessians, Thuringians and the Franks who dwelt on the Saxon border. He also labored among the Bavarians and finally met a martyr's death among the unconverted Frisians. Like Willibrod and the other English missionaries, he kept in close touch with Rome. He, too, was made an archbishop, with his see at Mainz, and is known to this day as the Apostle of the Germans.

While winning new converts for Christianity and thereby linking up new peoples with the ancient Roman civilization, Boniface helped to assure the success of his work by gaining the confidence of the Frankish rulers. They aided him in many ways. In a letter to a friend at home Boniface wrote: "Without the patronage of the prince of the Franks, I am able neither to rule the people of the Church nor to defend the priests or deacons, the monks or nuns; and I am not powerful enough to hinder the very rites of the pagans and the sacrilege of idols in Germany without his order and dread of him." Impressed with the work of Boniface among the heathen, the "prince of the Franks" asked him to undertake the reform of the Church in Gaul. Boniface began his labors there with energy and success. By holding frequent Church councils, at which all the prominent churchmen of the region met, he was able to establish a common standard of conduct and practice which the long period of civil wars had almost destroyed. Men unqualified to hold Church office were dismissed, and provision was made for the proper training of priests. In addition, he taught the clergy of Gaul to look again to Rome for leadership.

And thus it came about that the missionary venture of Pope Gregory in sending the Benedictine monks to Britain now brought to his successors the allegiance of a vast region, including much territory never before under the authority of Rome. The Latin language and many of the arts of Rome were being taught to a hitherto barbarous people.

Through the work of these churchmen, bishops and monks, a path was kept open to the learning of the past. The Roman Catholic faith had now a sufficient hold upon the Teutonic peoples to prevent their return to heathenism. With that faith went the Latin language, which was in turn the key to the storehouse of ancient civilization as preserved in Latin literature. True, only the clergy possessed the key, and their concern might have ended in the Christian literature alone. Fortunately, however, the text-books in the liberal arts which had to be mastered as the introduction to theology led back to classical times. The writings of the fathers, too, led back in the same way, for Gregory the Great went back to Augustine, and Augustine, in turn, drew from Plato and Aristotle as well as the Scriptures. Doubtless considerable purely pagan literature was lost through neglect, some perhaps destroyed because of its paganism, but surprisingly much of it was preserved. Christian and pagan literature thus combined to hasten the civilization of the Teutonic peoples, and to preserve that of Greece and Rome.

CHAPTER V

THE RISE OF THE FRANKISH EMPIRE TO 850

THE "prince of the Franks" who aided Boniface both in his missionary work among the heathen Germans and in his reform of the Church in Gaul was probably Charles Martel. Charles was mayor of the palace, not king of Frankland. His position of authority requires some explanation.

When Clovis died in 511, his kingdom was divided among his sons. Thereafter the Franks were involved in civil wars like those which afflicted the other Teutonic kingdoms on Roman soil. The kingdoms into which Frankland was divided seemed destined to fare even worse than the others, for the later descendants of Clovis underwent a physical degeneracy. Feeble in body and short-lived, these Merovingians were incapable of ruling. At this juncture, the actual management of their kingdoms was left to the members of the royal household. In Austrasia, the north-eastern division of the Frankish kingdom, there arose a family which succeeded in making this service hereditary in the office of mayor of the palace. This office at first had been largely domestic in nature, consisting of such menial duties about the royal household as only nobles were allowed to perform, but in the hands of a strong alert noble it became the means of actual rule. By 687, Pepin of Heristal, a member of this family, seized an opportunity to make himself mayor of the palace for two of the Frankish kingdoms. He defeated the army of Neustria at Testry and thereby extended his power over West Frankland as well. An illegitimate son, Charles, gained possession of the office and power after him, and held it until his death in 741. He was a vigorous and able military commander. Efforts of nobles in Neustria, Swabia, Bavaria and Aquitaine to gain independence were quickly put down, but the achievement for which he is best remembered is the repulse of the Moors in 732.

The Mohammedan caliphate, whose progress had been halted by civil discord, was brought under control by the Ommiad dynasty, and at the end of the seventh century it was again ready to advance. Its armies moved north and east and west. The last remnant of Byzantine power in northern Africa fell before the close of the century. The Berbers and the Moorish kingdoms which had successfully resisted Justinian also succumbed. Constantinople itself was placed under siege once more, but in 718 it was saved a second time by its superior sea power. Its hold on southeastern Spain was lost in 711, and the Moslems, finding the Visigothic kingdoms broken up by civil wars, advanced rapidly over the whole peninsula. By 718 they held all of Spain and were ready to cross the Pyrenees. At first Gaul promised to fall as easily as Spain. The semi-independent regions of southern Gaul were quickly overpowered. By 732 the Moslems had advanced as far as Lyons in the east and Tours in the west. Here it was that they encountered Charles, mayor of the palace, thereafter dubbed Martel (the Hammer). Franks and Moors faced each other for seven days and then engaged in furious battle. When it ended, the Moorish leader was dead and his army withdrew, realizing that further progress could not be made without reënforcements. Owing to civil war in Africa, these reënforcements did not arrive for many years, and in the meantime the Franks were not idle.

Perhaps this narrow escape from Moslem conquest taught the people of the West the necessity of greater unity. Possibly, also, the great military ability of the Carolingian family and the missionary genius of Boniface and his helpers made the lesson fruitful. Fortunately, all three were operating at the same time. Charles Martel aided Boniface in his missionary endeavors, and Boniface aided Charles in unifying the clergy of Gaul. Charles had his sons educated in a Benedictine monastery, thus promoting the coöperation of Church and State after his death. When these sons succeeded him in 741, it was to carry on the work of their father. The danger of strife between them was happily eliminated when one of the brothers chose to enter monastic life, leaving command of the whole kingdom to the other, Pepin the Short. This Pepin lived up to the traditions of his grandfather and father, in both military and political ability. Like them, he was still only mayor of the palace.

Circumstances had already arisen, however, which were destined to change his title. The further weakening of the Byzantine Empire through the attacks of the Ommiads at the beginning of the eighth century had encouraged the Lombards to renew their assaults upon the cities of central Italy. The popes at Rome, after calling in vain for aid from Constantinople, turned their attention westward, as Gregory I had done, and begged Charles Martel to come to their aid. But Charles felt under obligations to the Lombards for the help which they had given against the Moors and refused to fight against them. With Pepin, however, this obligation was not so strong, and with the renewal of the Lombard attack on Rome there was possibility of help from him. Pepin, as it happened, was in need of spiritual assistance. For three generations his family had discharged all the duties of kings without the title, which continued to be held by weak, wretched, almost imbecile Merovingians. Once an earlier Carolingian had made an attempt to displace the king, but the people rose in revolt and he was forced to pay for his rashness with his life. Pepin was just as anxious for the crown, but he realized that he must convince his subjects that such a step had the sanction of religion. This assurance the pope was able to give, and Boniface, who knew both pope and Pepin, may have suggested the means. At any rate, in 751 the pope received personal envoys from Pepin, who submitted to him the hypothetical question whether the man who reigned or the man who ruled should be king. The pope answered with full understanding, and his reply in favor of Pepin was put into writing and carried to Gaul. A great council was then held at which the leading churchmen and nobles were present. The pope's letter was read and the assembly elected Pepin king, after which Boniface placed the crown upon his head. Thus peacefully was accomplished the revolution by which the Carolingian dynasty displaced the Merovingian. The coronation of Pepin was

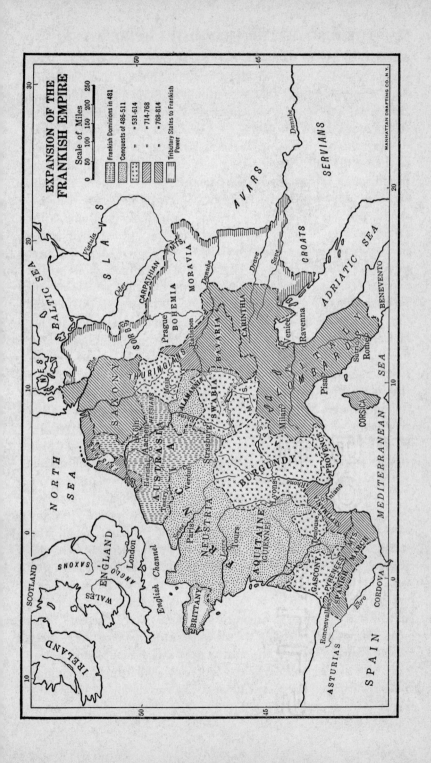

EXPANSION OF THE
FRANKISH EMPIRE

Scale of Miles
0   50 100 150 200 250

Frankish Dominions in 481
Conquests of 486-511
" " 531-614
" " 714-768
" " 768-814
Tributary States to Frankish
Power

MANHATTAN CRAFTING CO. N.Y.

almost the last important act of Boniface.   His martyrdom by the
Frisians in 754 brought his life to a close.

The service which the pope had rendered to Pepin was soon repeated and rewarded.   Frankish envoys went down to Italy the
next year and the pope accompanied them back to Gaul, where he
himself recrowned Pepin.   Doubtless many matters were discussed
between them in the several months of the pope's stay in Gaul.   At
any rate, when the pope returned to Italy in the spring, it was
with a Frankish army.   The Lombards were defeated and agreed
to give up many of the towns which they had captured.   Pepin
then made a grant to the pope of most of the exarchate of Ravenna, which had been completely overrun by the Lombards in 751,
when Ravenna itself was taken.   This was, in a way, the beginning
of the Papal States, which were to remain under papal rule until
1870.   But the promise of the Lombards to acquiesce was not
carried out after the Franks had left Italy, and it was necessary
for Pepin to return in 756.   This time the transfer was accomplished, though the Lombards yielded grudgingly and were
certain to cause trouble again.   Pepin, however, never returned to
Italy.   The remainder of his life was spent in strengthening his
control over outlying portions of the kingdom and in regaining
Aquitaine down to the Pyrenees.   Throughout these years he
continued that close coöperation with the Church which had already meant so much to his family.

THE REIGN OF CHARLES THE GREAT (CHARLEMAGNE)

Two sons succeeded Pepin in 768.   Again an incident occurred
to save the Carolingian line from the baneful effects of the Teutonic principle of succession.   One of the brothers died in 771 and
the other, named Charles, took over the whole kingdom, disregarding the claims of his nephew.   Charles had inherited all the
ability of his father and grandfather and, because he was able to
begin his reign with the accumulated achievements of his three
great ancestors, that reign was a most brilliant one.   He is known
to history as Charles the Great, or Charlemagne.

From 771 until 814 Charles was undisputed master in Frankland, and yet there was scarcely a year of that time in which he was not engaged in wars, usually as a personal participant. These wars were nearly all of his own choosing, and in no case did he have to meet the attack of an equally powerful foe. Almost all these wars added territory to his kingdom. Among the first of his conquests was the overthrow of the Lombard kingdom, of which he himself took the crown in 774. From it he added portions to the lands which his father had given the pope and he confirmed his father's donation. He also led his armies beyond the Pyrenees and, though these expeditions were only partly successful, they did yield a small district extending almost to the Ebro, which was included in his kingdom as the Spanish March.[1] His first Spanish campaign has been immortalized by the *Song of Roland,* which grew up about a rear-guard fight in the Pass of Roncesvalles during the return from Spain. Extensions on the eastern frontier included territory to the northeast of Italy and a march established on the Danube after several punitive expeditions against the Avars. The most troublesome enterprise which he undertook was the conquest of the Saxons. About thirty-two campaigns were required to accomplish this, and he experienced great difficulty in holding them subject. He succeeded finally in incorporating their lands and in making some additional gains toward Denmark, to the north, and toward the Elbe, on the east. The Slav states lying just beyond this region deemed it wise to pay tribute, and Charles never made a serious effort to conquer them. This widening frontier brought together under one rule most of the western portion of the former Roman Empire and almost as much territory which had never been a part of that Empire.

The four able Carolingians whose successive efforts had brought together this growing state had also been strong enough to maintain peace within it, and civilization, which had been seriously endangered by the preceding civil wars, was again given opportunity for development. By the time of Charles the Great numerous scholars were engaged in writings of a considerable

[1] The term *March,* or *Mark,* was used to designate a district governed as a military frontier. The official in charge was known as the *Mark-Graf* or *Margrave.* The more modern title, *Marquis,* is a derivation.

variety, from which a fairly detailed understanding of the time
can be obtained. These writings reveal the intermingling of
Teutonic and Roman ways of living and conducting affairs. The
writers were nearly all of Teutonic blood, but the language in
which they wrote was Latin. Charles drew around him many men
interested in learning. At one time or another there appeared at
his court Peter of Pisa, who taught Charles grammar; Alcuin,
from northern England, who was master of the Palace School;
Paul the Deacon, a Lombard, who wrote a history of the Lombards; Theodolphus, a Visigoth from Aquitaine, who was a poet
of considerable skill; Angilbert, a Frank, also a poet; Clement, an
Irishman, who was a teacher and philosopher; and Einhard, another Frank, who wrote a biography of Charles. The quality of
Latin which these men wrote compares very favorably with that
of Gregory of Tours. These men were all churchmen, to a
greater or less extent, and all had been trained in Church schools,
but their services were not confined to the work of the Church.

Charles, like his father, had received some education. He
could understand and read Latin, though "he understood Greek
better than he spoke it," and he began his study of writing
too late to master it. The scholars whom he had at court, especially Alcuin, were frequently interrogated by him for knowledge
about the universe. Under Alcuin's leadership an academy was
formed for the discussion of intellectual matters, and in this
exchange Charles and most of his family, as well as the scholars,
took part. Its sessions were usually held around the king's din-
ner table and the members were known by names borrowed from
ancient literature or the Scriptures. The actual discussions were
not impressive. Much more serious was the use Charles made of
these men as advisers and even as representatives in matters of
government. In the Palace School the children of Charles and of
his court nobles were educated for positions of trust in the kingdom. The size of the kingdom was so great, however, that the
need for educated men to hold governmental positions could not
be filled from this source alone. Charles issued several edicts,
or capitularies, requiring both monasteries and bishoprics to provide schools for laymen as well as for prospective churchmen.

So impressed was he with the need of education that one of his capitularies suggests that he even considered a plan for having the sons of all freemen educated. It was never carried out, but excellent schools were established at monasteries and bishoprics throughout his kingdoms, even among the turbulent Saxons. Thus Latin, the language of ancient civilization, tended to become the official tongue of this state as well as of the clergy. Certainly ancient civilization was not doomed to pass away altogether when Saxon lads could be seen reading the poetry of Virgil in the shade of their native forests.

In the affairs of government the same intermingling of Teutonic and Roman institutions was evident. The practice of swearing allegiance to the king was doubtless Teutonic. So, too, was the system of military service according to which the warriors were expected to assemble each spring, and the idea that fighting was the regular and noblest occupation of freemen was maintained. In time this custom was modified, because of the size of the kingdom. Only a portion of the fighting men were called out and the proportions varied with the distance from the proposed battle-ground. Fewer men were called out from the more distant regions, more from those nearest the scene of the fighting. This practice tended to make the business of fighting a representative, rather than a universal, affair, even for the freemen. The spring assembly became less and less a democratic meeting for the consideration of new laws. In Charles's day such assemblies were still used somewhat for advice, but the king made the laws much as the Roman emperors had done. More of the Roman practice appeared in local government, which was organized by districts, not by peoples. Over the district was a count appointed by the king; his tenure was usually for life. In some of the districts the duties of counts were exercised by bishops or abbots, a practice which had arisen in the days of the migrations. Charles extended this system of local government into the more purely Germanic portions of his kingdom, like Bavaria and the land of the Saxons, where tribal organization was still very strong. On the frontier, where the danger of sudden attack was greatest, a different type of government was used. At these points, Charles established marks, or marches, known as the Spanish March, the March against the Avars, the March against the Danes, and the March against the Slavs. Here trusted military commanders were stationed, with large bodies of fighting men who could be summoned quickly to arms. Over all the kingdom Charles tried to keep a personal supervision, and, since it was too large for regular personal visits, he resorted to the practice of sending out representatives called *missi dominici*. These usually went out in pairs, a bishop and a noble, and visited districts comprising a number of counties. They held court, heard complaints against misgovernment, made known the king's commands, and audited the accounts of the king's estates, which were scattered all over the realm. This inspection was annual, but Charles guarded against collusion on the part of his *missi* by sending them out to different districts and in different pairs each year.

Such a scheme of government marked a great advance over the old tribal arrangement which depended so largely upon personal contact between ruler and ruled. On the other hand, it had some defects when compared with the more elaborate system of the Roman Empire. The personal ability and activity of the ruler were still too essential. If his judgment of men was unerring, his alertness unwavering, the kingdom prospered. The four great Carolingians measured up to this standard remarkably well. A little carelessness in permitting sons of counts to step into their father's positions, as though the office were hereditary, and an occasional display of extravagant trust in allowing some officials, especially churchmen, immunity from royal supervision, might be charged against them, but during the lifetime of Charles the Great these practices did no real harm.

In matters of trade, agriculture and building the Teutons had little to contribute of their own and much to borrow from the Romans. Under Charles, commerce again developed to very considerable proportions. His regulations concerning the coinage, which he made a function of the government, concerning roads and bridges, canals and coastwise trading, all bear evidence of real revival. Towns grew up even in the regions of the Saxons and Thuringians. Agriculture received considerable attention, as the capitularies regarding Charles's own estates testify. The yearly gathering of men from all parts of the kingdom for military campaigns now in Spain, now in Italy, more frequently in Saxony or to the East, afforded opportunity for the exchange of ideas from which the men of the north doubtless gained most. The more constant work of the Benedictine monasteries established over all this area was probably even more important in spreading knowledge of improved methods of living. In them were cultivated many of the finer arts such as calligraphy, metal work and the manufacture of ornate vestments. Even architecture received attention. The art of building in stone, though not elaborate, was effectively introduced into the more northern regions. Most famous of the buildings erected during this time was the chapel of Charlemagne at Aachen, for which, however, the columns had to be brought up from Ravenna. According to one tradition, the plans for the building were devised by Einhard from a study of Vitruvius's work on architecture.

The broad development of power and civilization under the Carolingian rulers, especially in the time of Charles the Great, led to the revival in strange form of the idea that the Roman Empire might be restored in the West. This idea was held chiefly by the clergy, influenced by ancient learning as well as by the traditions of the Church. The popes at Rome had been brought into closer touch with the churchmen of all the West through the support which the Carolingians, from Charles Martel to Charles the Great, had given. The overthrow of the exarchate of Ravenna by the Lombards had practically cut communication between Rome and Constantinople, unsatisfactory as that communication had been for more than a century past. The extension of the Carolingian kingdom into Italy almost made the papacy part of that state, though its separate dignity was preserved by the donations of Pepin and Charles. Everything pointed to a closer relationship of the papacy with the fortunes of the West. The great friendship of the popes with the Carolingians had been attested by numerous acts on the part of both. In connection with Pepin's journey to Italy in 754, the pope had granted him the title, "Patrician of the Romans," a title which, generations before, had been conferred by Roman emperors and which was passed on to Charles. The imagination of Charles's many friends among the clergy was stirred by the vast extent of his kingdom as well as by his great power and ability. The title of king seemed inadequate to describe him. And these friends were, of course, in close touch with the papacy. In 799 Leo III, then pope, appeared at the king's court as a refugee from enemies in the city of Rome. Charles sent him back under escort, and, after investigating matters, went to Rome himself.

At Christmas time in the year 800 he attended divine services, and, as he arose from his prayers, Pope Leo placed a crown upon his head and proclaimed him Emperor of the Romans. This title was taken up with a shout by the assembled people. According to Einhard, although the opinion is not easy to accept, this occurrence was an unwelcome surprise to Charles. At any rate, he accepted the title and had his subjects take a new oath of allegiance to him as emperor.

Just what this title meant, aside from the gratitude of the churchmen for Charles's constant help, or what it involved, was not clear. Some writers of the time regarded it as a grant of title not only to the western half, but to the whole of the Roman Empire, on the ground that the Empress Irene, then ruling at Constantinople, was not legally qualified to rule. Others suggested that Charles marry her, or, at least, that a marriage be arranged between their respective families. Negotiations seem actually to have been undertaken toward some such end, involving recognition of Charles as emperor, but the attitude of the Byzantine authorities was highly scornful. They neither recognized Charles as emperor nor acquiesced altogether in his possession of Italy. So far as they were concerned, the coronation of Charles only widened the breach between Constantinople and Rome. Later writers in the West looked upon the coronation as indicating a desire on the part of the pope to claim authority over the rulers of the West. There was little in the attitude of either pope or Charles to justify such a view. In Charles's opinion, there had never been a division of authority. In his own kingdom he had

ruled both Church and State.   His capitularies frequently dealt
with matters usually regarded as purely ecclesiastical. He had pronounced upon education, the proper conduct of services, the quality
of sermons, and, in one instance at least, upon a matter of
Church doctrine.   Doubtless the capitularies dealing with these
matters were drawn up by the clergy at his court, but they were
issued by him with the full weight of his authority.   There was
nothing to indicate that his attitude was other than that ascribed
to his grandfather, the "prince of the Franks," by St. Boniface.
His dealings with the popes had been of the same nature—the
arm of his might had protected them and supported them in
their work.   Pope Leo III, who crowned Charles, had just been
restored to Rome through his help.   Charles was reasonably devout and faithful in his attendance upon divine service, but he
seems to have behaved in rather dubious ways at times, not
always in accord with the teachings of his faith.   Apparently
there is no good reason for regarding the coronation as anything
but the payment of a very high compliment by a grateful clergy.
The changes which that title later underwent properly belong
to later times and will be considered in due course.

Charles continued to rule his empire for nearly fourteen
years.   His total reign lasted forty-six years, and he outlived
all but one of his sons.   In his reign were brought to flower the
seeds of progress planted by his ancestors.   To later ages that
looked back upon him across the misrule of many less able successors, he seemed an heroic figure, without equal since the last
days of the Roman Empire.   We have a description of him by
Einhard, who was his secretary during his last years.   Though
his picture of Charles is clearly touched with some degree of over-
admiration, the outlines may be regarded as real.   He "was
large and strong and of lofty stature . . . (his height is known
to have been seven times the length of his foot), the upper part
of his head was round, his eyes were very large and animated,
nose a little long, hair fair, and face laughing and merry. . . .
His neck was thick and somewhat short and his belly rather
prominent, but the symmetry of the rest of his body concealed
these defects. . . . His voice was clear, but not so strong as his

size led one to expect. In accordance with the national [Frankish] custom, he took frequent exercise on horseback and in the chase . . . and often practiced swimming, in which he was such an adept that none could surpass him. Charles was temperate in eating and particularly so in drinking, for he abominated drunkenness in anybody. . . . While at table he listened to reading or music. The subjects of the readings were the stories and deeds of olden times; he was fond, too, of St. Augustine's books, and especially of the one entitled *The City of God*. . . . While he was dressing and putting on his shoes, he not only gave audience to his friends, but, if the count of the palace told him of any suit in which his judgment was necessary, he had the parties brought before him forthwith, took cognizance of the case, and gave his decision just as if he were sitting on the judgment seat. . . . He used to wear the national, that is to say, the Frankish, dress. . . . He despised foreign costumes, however handsome, and never allowed himself to be robed in them except twice in Rome. . . . On great feast days he made use of embroidered clothes . . . but on other days his dress varied little from the common dress of the people. . . . He caused the unwritten laws of all the tribes that came under his rule to be modified and reduced to writing. He also had written out for transmission to posterity the old crude songs that celebrate the deeds and wars of the ancient kings. He began a grammar of his native language. He gave the months names in his own tongue in place of the Latin and barbarous names by which they were known." This picture leaves no doubt that we are not dealing with a Diocletian or a Constantine, nor yet with a Louis XIV. But with all the informality of this monarch, the description reveals a man greatly in advance of an Alaric or a Clovis.

The importance of Charles has been well summarized by D. C. Munro. "In spite of his enthusiasm for the Roman education, Charles was a thorough German. His greatness was due largely to his keen appreciation of the actual conditions and of what it was possible to accomplish. His aim was to graft upon the German stock and the German customs all that was best in the older civilization. He seems to have realized the strength which would result from the union of the best qualities in both societies. That is why men have agreed to call him great, so that his name is usually written Charlemagne, Charles the Great."

SUCCESSORS OF CHARLEMAGNE

The beneficent fate which had followed the Carolingian family through four generations still seemed to operate in the succession of a single heir to Charles. The old principle of succession, equal division among all legitimate sons, had not been abandoned, but, to the profit of the kingdom, circumstances had determined otherwise. The heir to the empire of Charles seemed destined to a reign even more glorious than that of his father, for there was no one to dispute his rule or to divide it. But this bright outlook was soon overcast with forebodings. Louis, the Pious as he has been correctly surnamed, inherited the empire but not the ability of his father. He was physically strong and his formal education had been better than that of any of his predecessors, but he lacked the force which had characterized them, and lacked, too, something of the mental alertness which they had all possessed. In his early career he had become much attached to a saintly monk, Benedict of Aniane, who exerted great influence over him. The stern moral views of the monk were shared by the new emperor, and one of the first acts of his reign was to rid the imperial court of those whose conduct was too easy and loose. Unfortunately, political wisdom and unblemished conduct are not always combined, and this step not only deprived Louis of a number of his father's most able counselors, but made enemies of them as well. Opposition became widespread as Louis gave evidence of a determination to extend his moral reforms throughout the empire. An equally serious mistake or weakness appeared when Louis was called upon to put down a rebellion in Italy. The rising was easily suppressed, but, when the leaders were condemned to death by a court of the realm, Louis modified the sentence to blinding. Even this troubled his conscience and he later underwent a public penance, allowing himself to be flogged by a monk. Such an act might have appealed to some of his contemporaries as comparable to the penance inflicted upon Theodosius by Ambrose, but to most of his people it seemed an indication of unpardonable weakness.

The cares of government did, in fact, weigh heavily upon Louis, and upon his wife's death he thought seriously of withdrawing to a monastery. At a meeting of the nobles and ecclesiastical leaders in the previous year, he had already apportioned the empire among his three sons. His advisers, however, urged him strongly against carrying out this division, for they feared the outbreak of civil wars if these unseasoned youths were entrusted with the government. They persuaded Louis to choose a beautiful maiden for his second wife and hoped thereby to maintain peace and unity in the empire. The result proved otherwise, however. When a son was born to this second marriage, the mother determined that he should receive at least an equal share with his stepbrothers. These, for their part, having been allotted the whole of the empire, were unwilling to yield any of it. What began as family bickering finally broke out in civil war, for the disgruntled stepbrothers found ample support among the disaffected or self-interested nobility. Louis was incapable of taking drastic steps to quell the disorder.

It is unnecessary to follow the turns which this disgraceful family quarrel took. In vain did clergy and pope seek to intervene in the interests of peace. Neither the death of one of the older brothers in 838 nor the death of Louis himself in 840 accomplished this end. Finally, after a campaign in which the two younger brothers united against the elder and defeated him, a treaty was drawn up which promised to end the war. This was the Treaty of Verdun in 843. According to its terms, Lothair, the eldest of the three, was given the title of emperor and a strip of territory which included both the capital of their grandfather at Aachen and the seat of the empire at Rome. Louis, or Ludwig, the second son, was given the more compact territory to the east, while the stepbrother, Charles the Bald, whose birth had occasioned the trouble, received the territory to the west.

Perhaps the strange elongated state accorded Lothair implied that the imperial title also carried with it the right to a general supervision of the other kingdoms and thereby a maintenance of the unity of Charlemagne's empire. But an opposite tendency was revealed in the famous Strassburg Oaths of 841, by which the two younger brothers bound themselves to help each other against Lothair. This oath, in order to be properly understood by the respective adherents of the two brothers, was written in two languages, the one Germanic, the other a primitive Romance, neither of them in Latin. Which of these tendencies, centripetal and centrifugal, would prevail, only the future could determine. In the meantime, the twenty years of almost unbroken civil war had destroyed much of the unity which the predecessors of Louis the Pious had brought about in western Europe.

CHAPTER VI

THE BEGINNINGS OF FEUDALISM
EUROPE 850–1050

THE division of the Carolingian Empire at this time was a misfortune, for the task of building a common state of civilization within its borders was only well started. The newer northern and eastern portions had accepted Christianity, had acquired a Church organization which included everyone, and had learned to respect the monasteries spreading through their territories. But the soldiers of the annual muster now went no farther south or west than the Rhine, if indeed so far. The journeys across Gaul into Italy or Spain, which had been so instructive, ceased for the time being, at least. The people, instead of having a growing sense of union within the empire, began to regard one another with suspicion and distrust. The mere fact that they were no longer in steady touch with one another made them all the readier to accept reports of malevolence on the part of their neighbors. Commerce was hindered by this growing distrust, and with the differentiation of language and custom came increasing difficulties in the conduct of affairs. That the division should result in slowing down the spread of civilization was inevitable, but it carried with it, also, grave danger of civil wars which might destroy the gains already made.

The phase of civilization most directly imperiled in the division of the empire was the control and direction of the central government. The imperial power of Lothair was not the imperial power of Charles the Great. From the events which preceded the Treaty of Verdun it was quite clear that the younger brothers would not permit from him such visits as Charles the Great had been accustomed to make either in person or through *missi dominici*. Lothair had no real authority within the other kingdoms. At best, the title of emperor gave him only an added dignity and a precedence in any joint activity.   When Lothair died in 858, leaving his portion of the empire to be divided among his three sons, the title of emperor, which went to his son Louis, had no meaning at all for the two uncles in their kingdoms.   It had almost none for the brothers of Louis.   Thereafter the imperial crown and title had only a traditional and sentimental value, which could be translated into authority only under rare conditions.

The breakdown of the imperial government did not stop, however, with the disembodiment of the imperial title and power. The kings did not have within their own territories the degree of power which Charles had had over his whole empire.   It will be recalled that the Carolingians, before the time of Louis the Pious, had sometimes allowed sons of counts to succeed their father, and that especially trusted officials, usually bishops and abbots, had been allowed to administer their districts, undisturbed by visits from the king's officials.   When the sons of Louis engaged in warfare against their father or one another, they sought all possible military support.   This rivalry placed many of the counts and other officials in a position to bargain with the princes and to demand or receive various privileges in return for support.   In some cases the bargain was for specific grants of money or property, but it usually included recognition of the son's right to succeed the father as count, and also immunity from royal supervision in the administration of the county. The practice of bargaining spread, and, as the wars continued, there were very few counts who by 850 had not made themselves practically independent rulers of their districts.   The degrees of independence, the amount of privilege held by the different counts and local officials, varied according to circumstances.

THE COMING OF THE VIKINGS

With the restoration of peace among the brothers, the progress of decentralization would probably have been overcome, had not a new factor entered in.   This was the coming of the Northmen, or Vikings, from the Scandinavian peninsulas.   The later eighth and early ninth century witnessed another ethnic upheaval from that area which so often before had sent forth its surplus population. This time the migration was preceded by innumerable small raiding expeditions which went by sea southward and westward. The Northmen had already raided the western islands before the close of the eighth century. Year after year the Viking bands had appeared at the inlets of the Irish, Scottish and English coasts, to make sudden and daring raids over the countryside. Success had emboldened them to come down in greater numbers, to penetrate the countries more deeply, and, finally, to stay longer. By the opening of the ninth century they had established themselves at numerous points on those islands. Their forays proved to be highly destructive to the growth of civilization, for they early discovered that the richest booty was to be taken in the churches and monasteries, which they looted and burned. Many of the monks fled to the Continent, which, as long as the Carolingian Empire remained strong, was reasonably safe from these raiders. During the last days of Charles the Great the Vikings had made occasional forays on his territories, but they usually met with adequate resistance. After the outbreak of the civil wars, however, the percentage of successful attacks on the Carolingian coast increased.

The manner of the raids was the same on the Continent as it had been on the islands. Year after year the Viking long open boats appeared at the river mouths. These boats were propelled by oars and sails and the shields of the crew of warriors were set up along the sides. They beached their ships upon the little islands and dashed out over the countryside in search of plunder. Sometimes they stole horses and thereby increased the range of their depredations. When they had gathered sufficient loot, they returned to their ships and sailed back home, to return the following year in greater numbers.

They extended their cruises southward, especially after 840, venturing as far as northern Africa and even into the Mediterranean. Every river valley emptying into the western seas saw their raids. The Seine, Loire and Garonne, however, opened up the most tempting regions, and from these rivers they raided far inland.   Paris was attacked several times, and in 845 was destroyed by a fleet of over a hundred ships.   In the next forty years they established settlements at various points near the coast, from the mouth of the Elbe to that of the Garonne.   The most lasting and important of their settlements were around the mouth of the Seine, and in northern England, of which more will be said later.

The Viking raids continued until the end of the ninth century and their influence was in many ways permanent.   Despite all the harm and destruction which they wrought, their story has evoked a secret admiration from the adventurously inclined ever since.   In the course of the two centuries of their activity they performed almost incredible feats of navigation and heroism. Their little boats followed the western coast of Europe around Spain and up the mouth of the Rhone.   Some went westward across the Atlantic to the continent of America; others went overland through the Slavic regions to the Black Sea, from which they attacked Constantinople.   For a long period they maintained a kingdom which included the islands north of Britain and much of the western coast of Scotland and the eastern coast of Ireland. Their settlements in England, France and Russia contributed permanent and important elements to the development of those countries.   Their civilization was like that of the other Teutonic tribes when they came into contact with the Romans, though somewhat advanced.   Even so, their use of writing was still rudimentary, and, notwithstanding their wide travels and astounding exploits, the history of their achievements was not preserved in any accurate form.   Wherever they settled down they soon gave up their connection with the homeland, and assimilated the ways of the people among whom they dwelt.   In these particular regions they showed great ability to take on civilization and, within a century after their settlement in France, England and Russia, their descendants were among the leaders in religion, art, learning and government.   Their coming stirred all Europe to greater activity, for better and for worse.   Ireland, for instance, has little to thank them for, yet the Continent profited from the many Irish scholars who sought occupation there.

THE BREAK UP
OF THE
FRANKISH EMPIRE

Scale of Miles

0   50 100 150 200 250

Greatest extent of Frankish
Empire in 843

Tributary Slavic States in 843

To Moravia in 888

To Burgundy in 888

Boundary between East &
West Frankish Kingdoms
in 870

Territory to Louis in 843

    "   " Charles in 843

MANHATTAN DRAFTING CO. N.Y.

The political and social effects of the descent of these Northmen upon the Carolingian kingdoms require attention here. Their raids were swift and unexpected. It was almost impossible for any royal army to be ready to meet them, for they were gone again before such an army could arrive. Each locality was perforce compelled to look after itself. In 859, in the region between the Seine and the Loire, the peasants rose up in an effort to drive off the Northmen. Elsewhere heroic acts of resistance by purely local forces have been recorded. The constant menace of the Viking raids made the local fighting men all the more unwilling to leave home to serve the king elsewhere. This reluctance tended still further to reduce the king's power.

THE BREAKDOWN OF ROYAL POWER

The temporary reunion of the whole Carolingian Empire under Charles the Fat only emphasized the king's impotence. Charles was the son of Ludwig, the German, whom he had succeeded on the throne of East Frankland. The death of Lothair's sons gave him their lands. In 884 the grandson of Charles the Bald was an infant, and the much harassed people of West Frankland invited Charles the Fat to rule over them also. They expected him to defend them against the Northmen. Two years later the test came when the Northmen again attacked Paris, which had been rebuilt on the island in the Seine. Charles appeared with an army, but decided that his forces were not strong enough to offer battle and proceeded to negotiate with the invaders, granting them a sum of money and persuading or permitting them to depart and to ravage Burgundy. Such weakness emboldened the nobles to depose him the following spring. Count Odo, who had distinguished himself in the defense of Paris, was chosen king in West Frankland, and, similarly, Arnulf of Carinthia, who had fought successfully against the Northmen, was chosen king in East Frankland. Neither had the allegiance of all the nobles in his titular kingdom.

Before the kingship had reached quite the stage of weakness indicated in the deposition of Charles the Fat, the nobles had taken the precaution to strengthen their own power.   In 847 a capitulary was issued at Meersen by Charles the Bald requiring every freeman to choose a lord.   This measure was primarily in the interest of the nobles.   Apparently some of the free fighting men were dealing with their counts in much the same manner as those counts had dealt with the king, making their military sup-͗ port conditional upon a recognition of their practical independence. To some extent the measure was directed also against roving fighters, who were a source of danger to the nobles.   The capitulary makes clear two significant points.   One is that the nobles, though they had gained their own privileges individually or in small groups, were now class conscious, and were working jointly for their class interest.   The other is that their power in their own localities was none too secure.   In obtaining such a capitulary from the king, the nobles probably expected rather to secure common agreement among themselves than enforcement of the law by the king.   They doubtless imagined that the ordinary freeman might respect the king's authority more highly than they themselves did.

As a result of the warfare among the Carolingian kings, the ambitions of the nobles, and the coming of the Northmen, the political organization of the kingdom of Charles the Great was thoroughly shattered.   Each locality had now to build its own governmental machinery, which varied with the nature of the country and the local traditions of the people.   In general, West Frankland was inclined to continue the arrangement of counties which had prevailed in most of that region for several centuries. East Frankland, on the other hand, where tribal organization had existed until the time of Charles the Great, tended to return to its duchies, to tribal units ruled over by dukes.   This reaction, quite natural for the Saxons and Bavarians, brought about a similar development in the Rhine country, where for centuries county divisions had been the rule.   The Rhineland duchies of Lorraine, Franconia and Swabia, however, never went back fully to the tribal form.   Rather, their dukes ruled over counts, instead of over a people who cherished strongly a belief in a common ancestry.   In Italy there was a marked tendency to revert to the city-state idea, with counts in control of the towns. In that portion of Italy which included few or only small towns the ducal type of government prevailed, but these Italian duchies were quite different in spirit from true tribal duchies like Saxony and Bavaria. In none of the parts of the former Carolingian Empire was there uniformity or a common system. Each locality developed its own peculiarities and no two were governed exactly alike.

This condition of local separation and independence was at best not a very happy one for the development of civilization. It did afford a larger measure of protection against the raids of Northmen and others than the weakened kings could give, and this is probably the most that can be said for it. At worst, it led to anarchy, from which all suffered. Even during the wars of rivalry between the kings, the fighting was confined to but a small fraction of the whole region. Now, however, fighting might go on everywhere at the same time. For the century following the deposition of Charles the Fat this latter extreme was almost reached, and in much of the region actually prevailed. No divine sanction hallowed or facilitated the rule of a noble over his territory. All depended upon his ability to enforce his claims with his sword. If he showed signs of weakness, he might find his territory filched by ambitious neighbors, or his power challenged by his own subjects. Whether he felt well disposed toward humanity or not, his situation was much the same. In the one case, he would be compelled to defend his possessions; in the other, he would probably seek to acquire those of his neighbor. Any attempt to depict accurately the political boundaries during this time would involve the representation of innumerable small principalities, with the borders of each constantly changing—a baffling task for even modern art.

EFFECTS OF POLITICAL DISORDER ON THE CHURCH

The political prop to civilization built up by the Carolingian family was thus torn down in much less time than it had taken to build it up. To a large extent the other elements of civilization depended upon government. This was true even of the Church, which had an organization of its own going back to Roman days. When the sons of Louis the Pious first began their wars, the clergy maintained their organization quite firmly. For a while it seemed that they might be able to check the worst consequences of this warfare. They held councils and sought to bring the brothers into accord. A series of strong popes at Rome gave them a leadership which promised success.

One of these, Nicholas I (858-870), acted with unusual force and ability. He urged an uncompromising battle against the danger of a separatist movement within the Church whereby the archbishops of the different kingdoms might become practically separate from Rome. The able Hincmar, archbishop of Rheims, no mean antagonist, was compelled to acknowledge the pope's authority. Nicholas not only claimed, but, through force of circumstances, was able to exercise, control over kings in matters connected with the Church sacraments. Lothair II, after whom the lower Rhine region (Lorraine, originally *Lothari regnum*) was named, had become involved in a breach of his marriage vows. Lothair's uncles, between whom his kingdom lay, needed but little excuse to take it away from their nephew. Lothair's hold upon his kingdom depended upon his satisfying the demands of Nicholas. The erring king was forced to make a journey to Rome to seek the pope's absolution, and the fact that he died on his return journey was regarded as a just judgment of God which later kings would do well to remember. The full range of the pope's ambition and his conception of his office were indicated by his interference in a dispute between the emperor and the patriarch of Constantinople. One more pope of high aims succeeded Nicholas, but after him the office unfortunately became immersed in the whirl of local Italian politics.

In this immersion the papal office merely succumbed to the forces which had engulfed many bishops and abbots, and its submersion only hastened the extension of the calamity to most of the other clergy. Their holdings were coveted by the nobility of the neighborhood, who, even though they bore no ill will toward the churchmen as such, still desired to attach to themselves the support of the fighting men who lived on their lands. Pangs of conscience were forgotten in the fierce competitive strife of the age, and almost no property was regarded by these struggling noblemen as too small to attack. Their opportunity to interfere lay in the method of succession employed in Church offices. The old canonical formula of election by the clergy with the approval of the people of the diocese (*clero populoque*), was still almost literally followed for all episcopal offices from the bishop of Rome to the humblest bishop of the provinces. Abbots, of course, were elected by their monks. It was not a difficult matter for a designing noble to interfere in these elections, so as to gain a candidate favorable to his plans. Sometimes the mere indication of preference was sufficient, sometimes bribery was employed, at other times intimidation and force were required. All these methods were more or less commonly applied. In a short time interference by neighboring nobles at episcopal elections became so well established that it grew to be customary for the new official to receive both the Church lands and the symbols of his spiritual office from the hands of the noble. This practice, called lay investiture, was widespread throughout Europe before the end of the tenth century, and it held for both bishops and abbots.

Needless to say, churchmen whose first qualification for office was their willingness to obey the wishes of a warlike noble were not apt to be conscientious spiritual guides or able scholars. Often, in fact, they were less skillful in carrying a crozier than in wielding a lance. Some were so talented in this respect that they actually led bands of fighters themselves. Such men had little in common with genuine churchmen, they had less understanding yet of theology and Church practice, and the priests whom they ordained could not be expected to excel their superiors. They formed poor links in the chain that extended from Rome to the outermost reaches of Christendom. Moreover, the conditions at Rome, where the bulk of the papal lands lay, furnished still greater temptation to the ambitious nobles, and were frequently as bad as in any of the scattered bishoprics. The breakdown of the Carolingian Empire thus involved the Church as well.

Learning, which had been revived and spread by the clergy under Charles the Great, was seriously endangered by these dis-

turbances.   Oddly enough, that learning had been carried to a
higher level in the generation after Charles by the pupils of his
scholars.   The greatest of these, Rabanus Maurus (d. 856), had
been a pupil of Alcuin.   His home was in the region of the
missionary activities of Boniface, and he became, in turn, the
abbot of Fulda and the archbishop of Mayence.   His great interest was in scholarship.   His writings were more voluminous
than those of the Venerable Bede and show a greater advance in
knowledge.   In fact, Rabanus Maurus came to occupy much the
same position in German scholarship as that held by Bede in
England.   The difficulties under which learning labored at this
time, however, are graphically revealed in the resolutions of a
council held in 844: "We have found in the holy places that some
from choice, . . . and many from sheer need of food and clothing are leaving the monastic profession."   The plundering of
monastic possessions here indicated was only too common during
these wars, and only the more sheltered spots could afford sufficient protection to these centers of learning.   Fortunately, there
were a number of such sheltered places.   The most famous was
the monastery of St. Gall in Switzerland where, toward the end
of the ninth century, Notker the German was composing his
stories of Charlemagne and laying the foundations of modern
music.

The other arts of peace also were interrupted in this era of
neighborhood warfare.   Commerce, even when not actually exposed to pillage, was discouraged from venturing very far abroad
by the great tolls levied upon it in every little principality through
which it passed.   The result was frequently disastrous, for when
a district suffered a crop failure, there was no regular channel
through which to obtain needed supplies, even though another
district fairly close by might be enjoying plenty.   The local
famines which are chronicled so frequently during this period
were often due to such conditions as these.   For most of the
Carolingian Empire, civilization sank within less than a century
after the death of Charles the Great to a point lower than it had
been when his dynasty began.

EMERGENCE OF EAST FRANKLAND, OR GERMANY

Strangely enough, it was the newer, more recently civilized portion of the empire, the East Frankish kingdom, which suffered least from these troubles. This kingdom, which may henceforth be called Germany, did not split into so many small principalities as the other regions had done. Saxony and Bavaria quickly emerged as united duchies. Thuringia and Franconia also formed fairly solid states. Swabia and as much of Lorraine as belonged to this kingdom tended to do likewise, though their county organization did not entirely disappear. These larger divisions were not too large to deal effectively with raiders, or to be controlled by a single head. As a consequence, warfare was usually confined to the borders of these divisions, leaving large regions in each which were usually free from disturbance. Here churches and monasteries continued to thrive. The Northmen, who had made some raids up the Elbe and the Rhine, did not penetrate very far, and, after a stinging defeat on the Dyle in 891, they ceased to be a serious factor in German affairs. The enemies on the east were of a different kind. The Hungarians, another Turanian host from central Asia who had become masters of the central Danube, moved onward in a solid mass, demanding concerted, rather than scattered, resistance. The Slavs to the north were less dangerous, but also required united opposition.

For nearly forty years after the deposition of Charles the Fat, Germany did not show much interest in any unity which might involve real control over the dukes. Kings were elected, but any attempt to make the kingship real led to serious trouble. In 918, however, at least two of the duchies were convinced of the necessity of common action, and Henry, duke of Saxony, was chosen king. Henry did not attempt to interfere within the other duchies, but performed the common tasks with singular success. He drove back the Slavs and established marches on their territory. He also put up a stout resistance to the Hungarians. When the question of Lorraine, which had been divided in 870 between East and West Frankland, arose, he acted vigorously, and in 925 added the whole of it as a duchy to Germany.

These events gave him prestige, if not also power, so that he had little difficulty in having his second son, Otto, elected as his successor. He wisely held the election before his death. The son proved to be as able as his father and ruled nearly twice as long. Through the work of these two the Saxon dynasty was firmly established, but, after four reigns, the line failed in 1002.

For nearly a century, therefore, Germany had an undisputed succession of kings. Henry I had established the dynasty; Otto I, or the Great, laid the foundations of a strong central power. Charlemagne's policy apparently did not appeal to him. Instead of trying to eliminate the dukes, he placed members of his family in the ducal positions. Practically the only effective step taken by him toward lessening the power of the dukes was to gain control over the appointment to important Church offices. He was successful also in dealing with the enemies on the frontier. The Hungarians were finally defeated at Lechfeld in 955, and a march was established against them. He extended the marches on the Slav frontier farther eastward and compelled the Bohemians, who had the strongest of the Slav states, to pay tribute. Like Charlemagne, Otto aided the missionaries in spreading Christianity to the heathen people on his border. On his northern frontier he came into contact with the Danes. Here missionary work was more important than conquest, and the western frontier required neither. West Frankland, or France, was so thoroughly involved in the throes of domestic warfare that, by the use of diplomacy among the warring factions, Otto was able to devote all his energies to other problems.

Otto I was distracted from the salutary work of establishing a strong centralized monarchy by the temptation to interfere in Italy and gain the imperial crown. He married the widow of a claimant to the kingdom of Italy, and, with the aid of an army, succeeded in making himself king there. In 962 he was crowned emperor by the pope at Rome. During the last ten years of his life his attention was chiefly on his Italian and imperial ambitions. He arranged a marriage for his son with Theophano, a princess of the imperial family at Constantinople. Her influence helped to keep her husband and her son, the successors of Otto I, equally engrossed in Italian affairs, so that the useful work of centralizing Germany was halted. Otto II ruled only ten years, leaving his son, Otto III, a minor, in his mother's charge. Meanwhile, the dukes in Germany began to regain a large measure of their former power. In Italy, where Otto II spent much of his time and where Otto III sought to establish his capital, they were regarded as foreigners, to be respected only so long as they were accompanied by strong armies from outside of Italy. As a result, Otto III was driven out of Rome, contracted smallpox while a fugitive, and died in 1002 without an heir.

This left the German kingship again to free election by the nobles of Germany. The imperial crown had been worn by three successive kings of Germany and had, therefore, come to be identified with that kingdom. The papacy felt free to grant or withhold the title, but the candidate who obtained the German crown expected likewise to obtain the imperial title.

If the net achievements of the Saxon dynasty were not so large as they might have been, yet its services to civilization in general were highly important. The association with Italy and the marriage connection with the Byzantine court were both helpful in the restoration of commerce. Venice became a mart for German merchants, who found there the products of China and India, as well as those of the eastern Mediterranean. The Byzantine merchants had maintained trade with Venice from the days of Justinian, and in a very real sense that city may be regarded as an outpost of the Byzantine Empire. The amount of trade which centered there had swelled or contracted as conditions changed in the West. The connection with Germany caused it greatly to increase. Silks and spices from the far East as well as colored textiles from Constantinople came to be quite common throughout Germany. These products were exchanged for the coarser materials of the north. Along the main trade routes, over the passes of the Alps, and along the important rivers like the Danube, Rhine and Main, commerce and some manufacturing arose at favored spots and led to the growth of towns. Some of these places had become prominent in the time of Charles the Great, but their prosperity had dwindled, and, under the discouragement of neighborhood warfare, their population had shrunk. Ratisbon, Augsburg, Frankfort and Mayence recovered to a marked degree during the Saxon period, as did also the towns along the lower Rhine. The demand for the goods of commerce and industry was now so thoroughly established that only a very protracted and devastating period of warfare could seriously endanger it. New impulses to the development of civilization arose from exchange of ideas as well as of wares, and the growth of industry led to an improvement in the manner of living.

LEARNING IN THE NINTH AND TENTH CENTURIES

The period of the Saxon dynasty is likewise distinguished for a renewal of intellectual interest. Each of the kings had been friendly to the work of the Church, had protected the clergy and supported their missionary activities. This fact led not only to the firm establishment of Christianity and Latin learning in northern Germany, which had only recently been converted, but also to their extension to northern and eastern lands as yet unconverted. With all of Germany under Saxon sway, it became again possible for monks and churchmen interested in learning to circulate freely and exchange their ideas. As a result, the learning of the Carolingian period was preserved and advanced. Books of ancient authors were extensively copied in the leading monasteries and episcopal schools. Large libraries grew up in many places, and scholars studied diligently the style, as well as the content, of classic models. It was in this period that Hrotswitha, the nun of Gandersheim, composed her plays on the model of Terence. Hrotswitha was not an isolated phenomenon. It was customary for nobles to send their daughters to convent schools, though few of them attained literary distinction. This period is also marked by the appearance of a poem in which the form and language of Virgil were used to relate a pre-Christian tale. It was composed by Ekkehard, a pupil at St. Gall, and was the first important work of its kind. The impulse to learning was also strengthened by the addition of Italy to the Saxon realm. German clergy went to Italy in greater numbers, many of them became established there, and thus made available the ancient writings there preserved. Incidentally, their acquaintance with other scholars was widened, and the introduction of Gerbert into the learned circles of Germany can be ascribed directly to the presence of the Germans in Italy.

The career of Gerbert casts an interesting light upon the opportunities which clever boys enjoyed in the Middle Ages. He was born in Aquitaine. His parents were humble people, and the boy was taken into a monastery at Aurillac, where he soon displayed great aptitude for learning. The abbot seized upon the first opportunity to further his education. A nobleman from the Christian part of Spain returning from a pilgrimage received the hospitality of the monastery and, in return, offered to do a favor for the abbot. The abbot, discovering that there were opportunities for study in Spain, sent Gerbert along in the noble's protection. After several years there, Gerbert went to Rome with his patron and the bishop under whom he had studied in Spain. At Rome he continued his studies and made so favorable an impression that the pope recommended him to the attention of Otto I, who took him into his court circles as a teacher for his children, and after some time sent him to Rheims for further study. He was soon placed in charge of the school and gained great fame as a teacher. All this while he maintained his connection with the Saxon court and rendered valuable service to the Ottos in their political plans concerning Lorraine and northern France. His political genius was as marked as his scholarship and teaching ability. In 983 Otto II had him appointed abbot of Bobbio, in northern Italy. This position proved so dangerous and so distasteful that he shortly gave it up. For a time he was archbishop of Rheims, but a political upheaval forced him out and he again appeared at the court of the Ottos. In 999 he occupied the second most important church office of Italy, as archbishop of Ravenna. A vacancy in the papacy at this time enabled Otto III to have his old teacher made pope (999-1003).

As a scholar, Gerbert stands out above his age. His interest lay more in secular than in theological subjects. His wide experience in the schools of Christian Spain, Italy, Germany and France gave him opportunities such as no other scholar at that time possessed. He seems to have known the writings of Boethius in mathematics, astronomy, music and philosophy, as well as many classical authors in more purely literary fields. In his mastery of these subjects he far excelled any scholar at Charlemagne's court, any scholars, in fact, since the sixth century. His royal pupils, Otto II and Otto III, were devoted to him all their lives, as were many students of more humble origin.

His close association with the ill-fated Otto III lent to him an evil reputation among succeeding generations. A story that he had sold his soul to the devil for the possession of knowledge was long current. To what extent his influence over Otto III was responsible for the visionary government which the latter attempted to establish in Italy cannot be determined. Certainly Theophano, the mother of the young emperor, had much to do with it. On the other hand, Gerbert, as Sylvester II, cherished dreams of papal power beyond the conception of any pope since Nicholas I. As the older man and an intimate adviser of the young emperor, he had opportunity for guidance which later ages were to interpret as control. Sylvester II was involved in the same disturbances as Otto III, whom he survived less than a year. His influence as a scholar and teacher was more enduring than his activities as pope, for he set a new standard of scholarly achievement inspiring to coming generations.

THE MONASTIC REFORM MOVEMENT OF THE TENTH AND ELEVENTH CENTURIES

The character of the new king would reveal to what extent the growth of civilization was imperiled by the failure of the Saxon dynasty. In the struggles which ensued over the selection of a successor to Otto III, Henry, duke of Bavaria, managed to gain the support of enough princes to win the crown. But the accompanying disorders gave opportunity for successful revolts on the borders. Once crowned, Henry II (1002-1024) recognized as his life work the reëstablishment of law and order. This process was necessarily dangerous and slow. In it, however, he found that the clergy could be very helpful, and he worked with them throughout his life. His close association with them led people to apply the term, the Pious, to him, but his was a piety tempered with calculation. He did not overlook the fact that the Church had ready access to the confidence of the people upon whom his rivals must depend for successful opposition to himself. The favorable policy of the Saxon kings had led to the strengthening of many bishoprics and monasteries. Henry gained the good will of the clergy also by his constant interest in their welfare and his aid to them in their disputes with the dukes. Above all, he respected the cause of monastic and religious reform in his own as well as other duchies. Such an attitude made it easier for him to gain for himself the virtual appointment of most of the high Church officials throughout Germany. Though he was careful to favor genuine churchmen, he was, nevertheless, certain of their support. In this way he built up a fair measure of power during his reign, but, unfortunately, died without providing a successor.

The reign of Henry II revealed a new force in European affairs. This was a growing reform party of churchmen who were beginning to show definite political force. The need of reform in the Church had been periodic, and reform movements had frequently occurred. The greatest of these, the one in which St. Boniface had figured, owed much of its effectiveness to the support of a single strong ruler. This new movement, however, drew its strength not from a strong ruler, but from the efforts of high-minded men who had learned that, by combining the little strength which each possessed, they could overcome formidable opposition. The movement was strong in Germany, where Henry II made use of it, but its greatest center lay just outside the boundaries of that kingdom, in Burgundy.

Here was the monastery of Cluny. As early as 910, a little band of monks was given a grant of land by Duke William of Aquitaine under a charter in which the dukes guaranteed their possession of it against all interference, whether from neighboring nobles, the king, or even the pope. The importance of this foundation resided not so much in the sweeping and highly optimistic guaranty of Duke William as in the character of the men who composed the community of monks. They were imbued with deep religious fervor and had the strength of character to adhere strictly to the Benedictine rule. Under a series of remarkably long-lived abbots, this tradition was maintained and deepened. The monastery was early granted exemption from control by the local bishop and placed directly under the authority of the papacy. Its high standard of conduct won the respect and admiration of all who came into contact with it. In view of the prevalent disorder which characterized so much of the life of the time, even of churchmen, the conduct of the monks of Cluny must have appeared saintly indeed. At any rate, people in the neighboring regions were soon asking the abbot of Cluny to reform the monasteries in their localities, or to erect in their midst new communities like that of Cluny. In meeting these requests, the abbots wisely stipulated that such reformed centers should be connected with Cluny and subject to the supervision of its abbots. This arrangement led to the formation of a group of monasteries called the Congregation of Cluny.

The mere fact that Cluny could grow and prosper was of itself evidence of improvement in the disordered conditions of the time. Only a year or two after its foundation the Northmen accepted from the king of West Frankland, or France, a grant of land around the lower Seine. This marked the founding of Normandy, which was to be so important in later history. A marked decline in the depredations of the Northmen on the Continent followed thereafter. People in other localities, once relieved of the constant danger of Viking incursions, began forthwith to form more permanent organizations. Strong nobles were able to pass on their possessions to their sons, and, where such succession occurred for two or three generations, the process became easier and was attended with less warfare. Indeed, certain of the nobles succeeded in making their authority recognized over definite areas of considerable size. By the end of the tenth century, Brittany, Normandy, Flanders, Guienne, Toulouse and Burgundy were already outstanding divisions of West Frankland, wherein it was

possible for members of the ruling family to succeed one another
with reasonable prospect of success. Geographical unity or peculiarities of racial mixture in these regions were probably in part
responsible for this stability. In the areas where the Franks had
settled most thickly, the establishment of strong principalities was
more difficult. Even here, however, some improvement was visible. A strong series of counts in Champagne had succeeded in
amassing a very generous parcel of adjacent bits of territory
which they ruled generation after generation. Another series of
counts, made famous by their heroic struggles against the Northmen, had maintained a principality of some size around Paris,
and after the deposition of Charles the Fat in 887, a member of
this family had been chosen king of France, or West Frankland.
For a hundred years the crown passed back and forth between
these counts of Paris and feeble Carolingians. Finally, in 987,
Hugh Capet, another member of this same family of counts, was
chosen king, and thereafter the crown continued in his family.

Conditions were still far from peaceful, even within the regions enumerated above, and there was a large area between
them which was in a relatively fluid state. It was amid such conditions that the Congregation of Cluny began to expand. The
great nobles were in general very friendly to it, and many of
them aided in the founding of similar monasteries in their territories. As a result, Cluniac monasteries were spread out over
all of France and even beyond its borders. It was not long before the organization was drawn into political affairs, for it
formed a connecting link between the forces of law and disorder, almost the only one. The first interest of these monks
lay, naturally, in the affairs of the Church, which were seriously
disturbed by neighborhood warfare. Accordingly, they lent their
aid to a measure favored by all right-minded churchmen, which
was called the *Peace of God*. This provided that churches,
churchmen, women, children and peasants should be immune from
attack. To this was added another provision called the *Truce of
God*, which set aside the period from Saturday noon to Monday,
and Church festivals generally, as sacred from the violence of
such warfare. These measures were first enacted at church

councils in southern Gaul before the end of the tenth century, but they were soon taken up by other church councils and expanded.   The most flagrant offenders against the Truce of God were, of course, the petty nobles, who were also thorns in the sides of the greater nobles.   The coöperation of this latter class with the clergy in support of these measures helped to quell the prevalent disorder.   This work, preached by the clergy and reinforced by the greater nobility, went on in the eleventh century with increasing effectiveness.

It would, however, be an injustice to assign to the Congregation of Cluny the sole credit for the promotion of these measures. The example of Cluny was taken up by monasteries in other lands, especially in Germany, but also in Italy and Spain, sometimes under the direction of Cluny, but often quite independently. Nor were the monasteries alone interested.   Priests and bishops, more naturally involved in secular affairs, were likewise leaders in the movement.   This was especially true in the western part of Germany and in the lower and upper Rhine country.   It was true, also, of southern Germany, the home of Henry II.   Germany, in fact, was to be the scene of the greatest triumphs of this reform party.   Party it truly was, for the clergy was now of two kinds—those who were the obedient creatures of neighboring nobles, and those whose chief interest was in the welfare of the Church.   The strength of the latter group lay in their command of the respect of their people and in the close coöperation existing among themselves.

THE EMPERORS AND THE REFORM MOVEMENT

Henry II was wise in attaching to himself the support of the reform party among the clergy.   He aided them in their efforts to place trained men in the more important Church offices, and their gratitude was worth more to his royal power than the support of any of his dukes.   They were an important element in the election which followed the death of Henry II.   Of the leading two candidates for the office, one had been friendly, the other opposed, to the reform party.   The latter was chosen, but what had seemed to some of the reformers a defeat was turned into victory when the abbot of Cluny and the archbishop of Cologne (Köln) appeared prominently in his councils, for these were the leaders of the reform party.

The new king, Conrad II (1024-1039), was a man who relied upon force rather than influence. He did not depend upon the support of the reformers, as Henry II had done, but neither did he oppose them. His acquisition of the kingdom of Burgundy served to increase their influence in Germany, for Cluny was powerful there. He kept the virtual appointment to important Church offices in his own hands and expected substantial gifts from his appointees, but they were, as a rule, true churchmen. His many victories on the field of battle established peace on the border as well as in Germany itself. On his journeys he dispensed justice freely, and with a high degree of impartiality. Altogether, his rule was a very able one, and, had he not been forced to undertake the task of reëstablishing a central government, he might be ranked as one of the greatest figures in German history. His work, however, helped to earn that honor for his son.

Conrad's son, Henry III (1039-1054), succeeded him without any trouble, because of the father's wise precaution in having Henry elected during his own lifetime. Conrad had also been careful of his son's training, neglecting neither the arts of peace nor those of war. Henry III had great ability and was able, therefore, to profit by his father's work. Under him Germany reached its widest extent. The kingdom of Bohemia was thoroughly knit to the kingdom of Germany. The larger kingdom of Poland was made tributary, and Henry exercised overlordship in Hungary in a very real sense. Throughout his reign he was a consistent friend of the reform party in the Church, and the abbot of Cluny was his intimate friend and official adviser. His famous indulgence, which granted forgiveness to all his former enemies and invited his subjects to do the same, was in the spirit of the Peace and Truce of God.

Possibly the most important act of Henry's life was his journey to Italy in 1046. In preparation for this, he gathered together not only his army, but many important churchmen as well. The presence of a powerful king in Italy at the invitation of the Church was not new, but never before had the papacy required spiritual aid from a ruler. Such, however, was now the case, and the invitation had come not so much from the pope as from the reform party of clergy north of the Alps. Roman factional strife had placed on the papal throne a youth whom even the office could not dignify. His conduct had become so scandalous that the Romans had driven him out of the city and replaced him with a less objectionable candidate. Meanwhile, the outcast had sold to another aspirant his claim on the office, and then had finally decided that he could not be deprived of it either by violence or by sale. There were thus three claimants to the office, and this was the situation that Henry sought to correct. At a synod held at Sutri, December 20, 1046, the purchaser of the office voluntarily gave up his claim, and the other two were deposed. At another synod held in Rome a new pope was elected from among Henry's followers, and the Roman people agreed henceforth not to elect a pope without the approval of Henry. On Christmas day the new pope was consecrated, and Henry was crowned emperor by him. In the remaining ten years of Henry's reign, four German churchmen successively became pope. All were members of the reform party.

Thanks largely to Henry III, the well-organized reform party in the church now had the support of the papacy. In its growth of more than a century it had acquired much political experience and knowledge. This experience was preserved and exchanged among the leaders of the party by means of letters and books as well as by frequent visits and meetings. Each advance was made a source of additional strength, and the party was now well organized in all of western Europe. In the pope they now had a leader who could bring them all into united action. The ten years in which Henry III lent his strength to maintaining reform leaders on the papal throne enabled them to acquire a firm hold on the office. Even before his death, there were indications that, though the reformers appreciated Henry's help, they were unwilling for him to control the papal office. That question, however, was to be decided later. Henry III died in 1056, leaving a son too young to rule. But the principle of heredity was sufficiently strong to secure his succession and to provide a regency during his minority.

The death of Henry III marks the close of a period in the history of western Europe. There had been little unity in the two centuries since the permanent division of the Carolingian Empire. Disorder was the prevailing characteristic of the age. The invasions of Northmen, Slavs, Hungarians and Saracens had lent a certain variety—from our standpoint—to the otherwise monotonous civil strife. Out of all this confusion, however, some progress appeared. Tribal government had practically disappeared, and western Europe was working on a political basis which involved a settled life. Military service no longer rested upon personal or tribal loyalty. It was conditioned upon the possession of a fief, usually land or profitable privilege from which the possessor derived his living without manual labor of his own. Society was becoming clearly differentiated into three classes: the bulk of the population which performed the labor, the nobles who only fought and ruled, and the clergy. The movement had proceeded so far that by this time the civilization of western Europe may be described as that of a feudal society. Learning had survived, and in certain centers had maintained the level reached in the time of Charles the Great; in a few it had even made appreciable advance. The circle of Latin civilization had widened to include the lands of the Northmen, Slavs and Hungarians. And a new organization had arisen based on the confidence of the people in spiritual leadership of a very fine quality.

CHAPTER VII

THE RISING POWER OF THE CHURCH
EUROPE 1050–1150

THE career of one of the popes designated by Henry III marks a change in the papal attitude toward the imperial throne. Leo IX, a German from the upper Rhine country, was nominated as pope by the emperor, but he nevertheless presented himself for election to the clergy and people of Rome and did not take office until elected by them. The activities of his five years as pope (1049-1054) laid the foundations of a papal policy that was to endure for more than a century. He had belonged to the reform party before he became pope, and in his new office he saw great possibilities for the spread of that movement. Three times he journeyed across the Alps to hold synods in France and Germany as well as in Italy. At all of these assemblies he inveighed against abuses within the Church, especially against simony [1] and marriage of the clergy. At one of them he went further and attacked lay investiture as the root of the other evils. In Lorraine he had an opportunity to display his attitude toward neighborhood warfare. Godfrey the Bearded, duke of Lorraine, had carried on a war with Henry III which involved the plunder and burning of churches. Leo compelled Godfrey to come as a humble suppliant before him at Aachen and imposed a severe penance upon him. Shortly afterward Leo sought to make peace between Henry III and the king of Hungary, but neither would accept his mediation. In the following year, with a band of German soldiers and some mercenaries from Italy, Leo marched against the Normans, who had been causing trouble in southern Italy. He was defeated and taken captive, but his captors bowed

[1] Simony, a term derived from Simon the Magician's offer to buy the peculiar power of the apostles, was used at this time to describe various efforts to gain Church office other than by merit and regular election.

down in reverence before him. The hardships which he endured doubtless hastened his death. Reformer, peacemaker and warrior, his career was prophetic.

Once more the Romans sent to Henry III for advice regarding the choice of a successor, but when the time of election came they adopted a different course. Most of the clergy of Rome were now of the reform party and ready to resist simoniacal influences of any kind. These men elected the next pope without consulting the imperial court, for Henry IV was too young to rule. In 1058 another election was necessary. This time the Roman nobility, emboldened by disturbances in Germany, sought to put in one of their own adherents. The reform party withdrew from Rome and held an election of their own. In 1059 their pope, Nicholas II, issued a decree declaring that only cardinal clergy, or those designated by the pope, were qualified to vote at the election of a new pope. In this way the reform party could hope to perpetuate its control of the papal office. The very Normans with whom Leo IX had fought now furnished the necessary support against the Roman nobility. The Norman right to hold territory in the south of Italy had at length been recognized by Leo IX, and now Nicholas II reaped the reward of their gratitude. Germany was so disturbed by the uprisings of its dukes and other troubles during the minority of Henry IV that the regency was powerless to interfere in Italy. The reform party was both physically and spiritually in control at Rome.

The Normans, who now figured as a prop to the reform papacy, had come from Normandy in northern France, and were the offspring of the union of the Northmen with the native French. They were apparently Christianized and somewhat civilized, but the descendants of this union had not lost all the traits of their Viking ancestors. In 1017 a band of them, returning from a pilgrimage to Jerusalem, stopped in southern Italy and found the disturbed conditions there very inviting to their adventurous souls. They passed the news to their friends back home, and, from that time on, bands of Normans continued to seek their fortunes in southern Italy. The most famous of them were the sons of Tancred of Hauteville, whose estate was quite inadequate

to provide for his twelve lusty heirs. Most of them found their
way down to southern Italy, and all of them proved themselves
highly resourceful fighters, gifted with the strength, cunning
and shrewdness so frequently found among the Vikings. Two of
them were leaders of the band which took Leo IX captive in 1053.
Two others in 1059 supported Nicholas II against the Roman
nobles. The help of these Normans probably made it easier for
the papacy to approve the invasion of England in 1066 by the
duke of Normandy. Another of these Normans, Robert Guiscard, led his motley following of Normans, Lombards and
Saracens to the rescue of Pope Gregory VII, who in 1084 was
besieged by Henry IV. This last incident was highly typical of
the methods used by the Normans. Their own numbers were not
very large, but they succeeded in dominating and in using the
various conflicting elements to be found in southern Italy. To
them, apparently, there was nothing incongruous in obeying the
pope and at the same time taking his lands, or in rescuing him
with an army of Saracens. Personally, they were respectful and
loyal to the popes.

STRUGGLE OF GREGORY VII AND HENRY IV

Gregory VII, who in 1084 was in such dire straits, had become pope eleven years earlier. He was of relatively humble
Italian origin, and had been educated for the priesthood. As
Hildebrand, his name until he became pope, he figured in many
of the incidents of papal history just recounted. He was appointed to office in Rome by Leo IX, who had met him in Germany
among the Roman envoys sent to request the aid of Henry III
in choosing a new pope. On several later occasions, likewise, he had
gone to Germany on missions for the popes. He was among
those who supported Nicholas II. In all of these experiences he
was thoroughly schooled for the office which in 1073 he was
called upon to fill. He knew the situation in Germany, he appreciated the strength and ramifications of the reform party in the
Church, and he understood Roman and Italian affairs as a
birthright. The confidence which successive popes had reposed

in him was sufficient evidence of his ability, and his career as pope was to show that he possessed courage equal to his ability.

The regency for Henry IV had been weak. The greater nobles had asserted almost complete independence and Henry's education had been woefully neglected. When Henry became of age and tried to follow in his father's footsteps, he found difficulties on every side. The dukes and greater nobles refused to yield the independence which they had temporarily enjoyed; the people on the borders were causing trouble; and Henry was surrounded by advisers of doubtful judgment. Gradually he succeeded in making headway against these difficulties and in regaining some of the loyalty which his father and grandfather had won. He was still far from that goal, however, when his trouble with Gregory intervened.

Gregory's determined opposition to lay investiture and his stand for reform precipitated the controversy. He insisted that laymen, whether ordinary feudal nobles, or kings, or emperors, should not control the selection of the clergy. The emperor and several of the kings had been willing to coöperate with the reform party in getting appointments out of the control of the nobles, but they were scarcely willing to take the next logical step in that direction. The control of Church offices furnished so useful a means for undermining the power of the nobles that rulers would not readily relinquish it. Gregory was insistent. He repeatedly urged upon all monarchs the abolition of lay investiture, but conditions in Germany enabled him to press his demand there.

The occasion for the outbreak was Henry's appointment of men to fill important Church offices in Italy as well as in Germany. Henry had befriended a number of bishops and other prelates in Germany whose attitude toward simony and marriage had incurred Gregory's opposition. A series of letters and envoys passed back and forth between Gregory and Henry. The tone of the papal letters was at first quite paternal, but, as Henry persisted in harboring the offending bishops and in filling vacancies in the Church, it became threatening. If Henry had in mind his father's patronage of the papal office, Gregory's demands must have seemed impertinent and insubordinate. However that may be, he felt it unwise to become involved in a conflict with the pope while his nobles were still causing him serious difficulty.

A favorable turn in his war with the duke of Saxony, combined with unusually provoking remarks from the pope's envoys, led him to assemble his bishops at Worms on January 24, 1076. He had a formidable document drawn up declaring that Gregory was unfit for the office of pope, had not been regularly elected, and therefore had never been pope. This was signed by nearly all the bishops present and sent to Gregory. Whether it represented the real views of many of these bishops or their concession to Henry's wrath can scarcely be determined. In Henry's thought, certainly, it amounted to the deposition of Gregory.

Henry's messengers presented this document to Gregory as he was presiding at a synod in Rome. When its meaning became clear to the assembly, the messengers barely escaped with their lives. What Gregory's feelings were can only be imagined. There was no course for him to take except to carry out his threat of excommunication against Henry. He declared Henry guilty of many moral wrongs, and unfit to rule over Christian people; he was therefore denied communion in the Church. All Christians were forbidden to have any dealings with him, under pain of eternal damnation.

News of his excommunication reached Henry at Easter time and he replied by making public announcement of Gregory's deposition and by calling a council to meet at Worms on Ascension Day. It was a test of strength between pope and king, each having deposed the other. The probable outcome was soon revealed by the scanty attendance at Worms. The assembly was adjourned, to meet again at Mainz on the 29th of June, but with no better result. The great nobles seized upon the embarrassment of the king to clothe their own ambitions in the mantle of righteousness. Even those bishops who had originally supported Henry found it difficult to continue on his side. Before the summer was over, Henry was almost without any friends whatever, not to mention subjects. Gregory was in touch with the German nobles, and plans were well under way for the election of a successor to Henry. A meeting was arranged to take place at Augsburg early in 1077, at which the pope would be present to counsel with the princes concerning the kingship. Even Gregory could not have foreseen such a complete and speedy victory as this course indicated.

Among the people of importance who still befriended Henry was Hugh, abbot of Cluny. Possibly Hugh was moved by the recollection of the many favors which Henry's father had bestowed upon Cluny and the cause of reform. Perhaps, too, he felt personally drawn to the young king, whose godfather he was. At any rate, Hugh now appeared as Henry's friend and counselor. It was probably at his suggestion that Henry undertook his penitential journey to Italy. This journey has been described with dramatic detail by numerous writers of that time and since. It involved crossing the Alps in the dead of winter, at great risk and with bitter hardship, but it was successfully accomplished. Henry appeared in northern Italy just as Gregory was starting on his way to Germany. Gregory had many enemies in Lombardy, and these rallied to the cause of Henry. For safety Gregory retired to Canossa, a castle in the Apennines, which his friend, the Countess Matilda of Tuscany, had placed at his disposal. Abbot Hugh and several others acted as intermediaries. Henry wisely refused military support from the Lombards, and appeared as a suppliant at Canossa. After spending three days outside the castle, he was admitted to the pope's presence and, under promise of correct conduct in the future, was again allowed to partake of Christian communion.

The humiliation of Henry IV at Canossa constitutes one of the most dramatic events in the history of Europe. The spectacle of Gregory presiding at Augsburg over the election of Henry's successor would have afforded a much greater display of worldly power. In admitting Henry to communion at Canossa Gregory won a spiritual victory and gave up the political triumph which he might have enjoyed at Augsburg. On the other hand, Henry gained a point by going to Canossa, for he would probably have fared worse at Augsburg. As it was, the people of Germany who had abandoned Henry on purely religious grounds could now conscientiously return to his support. The greater nobles who had sought to make capital out of Henry's difficulty with the pope now found their personal ambitions clearly exposed. In a sense, they felt that Gregory, by pardoning Henry, had betrayed them, and they would be less ready in future to respond to a papal appeal.

Henry soon reverted to his former practices, and the struggle was renewed. Gregory again excommunicated him, and Henry replied in 1084 by putting up an anti-pope, Wibert, archbishop of Ravenna, and by leading an armed force to Rome. It was then that the Norman, Robert Guiscard, came to the rescue of Gregory and carried the pope safely down into southern Italy. Here Gregory died in exile the next year, because, as he said, he had "loved justice and hated iniquity." His cause, however, was not lost.

The reform party of which Gregory had been the great leader persisted in its stand. The abbot of Monte Cassino was reluctantly dragged from his monastery to act as pope after Gregory, and his early death was probably a relief from the cares of an office which he had never desired. The next pope of the reform party was Urban II. He, too, had been a close friend of Gregory VII and a staunch partisan of reform. Despite the disorder in Rome, where he was able to remain only for short intervals, and despite the beggary to which he was frequently reduced, he maintained the reform policy. These three popes paid a heavy price in human suffering for their devotion to their ideas and ideals. Their goal was a united church, free from outside control, in which the attention of all churchmen should be centered on the work of the Church, and obedience should be rendered only to Rome. Much of the advance of the reform party thus far had been due to the help of sympathetic rulers, from William of Aquitaine to Henry III. The reformers were now attempting to maintain their organization and their ideals independently, and, if need be, in defiance of secular rulers. The outlook was not promising. They had lost possession of Rome, and that the popes had not also lost their lives was due largely to the protection of the Normans.

THE PAPACY IN COMMAND OF ARMIES. THE FIRST CRUSADE

In 1093 their prospects brightened. Henry IV's son, Conrad, sided with the reform party and led a revolt against his father in Italy. North of the Alps the reform party continued strong both in Germany and in the regions of France. Urban II, who came from the neighborhood of Rheims and had himself been a monk and prior of Cluny, received reassuring reports from the north. A generous gift from the abbot of Cluny about this time was of great assistance to the pope. Toward the end of the year he succeeded in getting control of most of Rome, and in the following year he felt it safe to undertake a journey across the Alps. On his way he held a council at Piacenza, which was very well attended. Envoys from the Byzantine court were present at this council and were received by the pope. From there Urban went across the Alps into France, where in November of the year 1095 he presided over the momentous Council of Clermont.

The Council of Clermont was attended by most of the leading churchmen of France. The matters considered at this council were chiefly those which had formed the program of the reform party, the Peace of God, and the reform of the Church. But the memorable event of the council was the oration delivered by Urban urging the fighting men to rescue the Holy Sepulcher from the hands of the Infidel. The exact report of the speech has not been preserved, but its chief points can be fairly well established from several accounts of it written later by men who were there. Urban deplored the disorders which prevailed among Christians in the West, where eternal damnation was so frequently incurred by the shedding of Christian blood, where famine so often occurred, and where human misery was great. He pictured the Holy Land as desecrated by the control of the Infidel, who maltreated the pilgrims and endangered the welfare of Christian countries. There was a land flowing with milk and honey, here was poverty and overpopulation. If Christians must fight, let them gain salvation by fighting the Infidel, rather than damnation by killing each other. He appealed to their piety, their pride, their valor and their love of adventure. The effect of his oration

was astounding. Almost with one voice the audience shouted:
"God wills it. It is the will of God!" The enthusiasm aroused
proved contagious, and men went from that council to fire their
people with the same religious zeal. Urban continued his journey through northern France, holding councils as he went, and
the next year he returned to Rome. Meanwhile, preparations were
going on throughout France, in western Germany, in England,
and also in Italy for the journey of the Cross, the First Crusade.

Urban II had warned those who planned to go on the crusade
to make adequate preparations and not to depart till after the
harvest of 1096. But the enthusiasm he had aroused was too
great to countenance such delay. A monk called Peter the Hermit
went through the regions of northern France and the Rhineland
preaching the crusade. Everywhere he went he was regarded as
a prophet and the lesser folk were especially influenced. These
peasants, in the main, would not wait, but started out in several
bands, early in 1096. They followed the Danube as far as
Belgrade and then turned southeastward toward Constantinople.
Their journey through Hungary, Servia and Bulgaria was attended with great disorder, for they were ill provided with
means, and their frequent foraging expeditions aroused the wrath
of the natives. At Constantinople they were, on the whole, well
received by the emperor, who advised them to wait there until
other bands should arrive to reënforce them. Their disorder,
however, proved so annoying that he was obliged to ship them
across the strait to Asia Minor. Here they soon became involved
with the Turks, who caught them in ambush and destroyed the
whole ill-organized force. Peter the Hermit happened to be in
conference with the emperor at Constantinople and thus managed
to escape the fate of his fellows.

The main body of the crusaders followed the pope's advice
and started their march later in 1096. They moved in four
divisions. The northernmost was led by Godfrey, duke of Lorraine, and Baldwin, his brother. They followed the path of the
Peasants' Crusade to Constantinople, but conducted themselves
in a more orderly fashion. Another large band formed in northwestern France under the leadership of Robert, duke of Nor-

mandy, Robert, count of Flanders, and Stephen, count of Blois, who was the brother-in-law of Robert of Normandy. This group moved southward through France down into Italy. When they reached Rome, they stopped to drive out Wibert, the anti-pope, and to place Urban II once more in power. They wintered in southern Italy, and then crossed over the Adriatic on their way to Constantinople. A third group from southern and south-eastern France marched under the leadership of Raymond, the wealthy count of Toulouse, and of the papal vicar, Adhemar, bishop of Puy. This group crossed northern Italy and followed the Dalmatian coast until near Durazzo, where they turned eastward to Constantinople. A fourth somewhat smaller group formed in southern Italy under Bohemund, the son of Robert Guiscard, and Bohemund's nephew, Tancred. They crossed over to the Balkan peninsula and marched, like the others, to Constantinople.

As these bands converged on Constantinople, the Byzantine emperor, Alexius, was somewhat perplexed about dealing with them. Some historians have seriously questioned the assertion that he had ever called upon the West for help. Twenty-five years before, when the Turks had defeated his predecessor at Manzikert in 1071 and had overrun Asia Minor, such an appeal had, indeed, been made. Alexius had steadily been extending his control, however, and seemed at this time in no need of outside assistance. Furthermore, among the crusading bands was that of the southern Normans, with whom Alexius had had trouble. Bohemund had accompanied his father on an invasion of the Balkan peninsula and had been driven back by Alexius. All in all, Alexius viewed the crusading army with misgiving. The first leader to reach Constantinople was Hugh of Vermandois, brother of the king of France. His small force had been shipwrecked and he came almost alone. Alexius kept him under close watch and made use of him in dealing with the others. As band after band arrived, the emperor tried to get the leaders to agree to return to the Empire any of its former possessions which they might capture. He then wished to ship them as quickly as possible across the strait, where they could not endanger the imperial city. This policy led to frequent misunderstandings and some trouble, but Alexius persisted in his plan and had each band across the strait before the next arrived.

The strength of the Christian army became apparent before Nicæa, where the crusaders came together for the first time. Fulcher of Chartres, who was with the army of Stephen of Blois, fixes the total number of crusaders at six hundred thousand, adding, that if all who had signed had come, there would have been six million. Fulcher was not a military statistician, and his comparison of those who took the vow with those actually present at Nicæa is probably more valuable than his estimate of the strength of the entire force. A careful calculation by modern historians has set the number at a little more than one hundred thousand, including noncombatants, women and children. Many of these were from regions other than those indicated by the homes of the leaders. Southern Germany, Lombardy, England and Ireland were all represented, and there were people from Bohemia and Hungary as well.

At Nicæa the crusaders were reënforced by the Greek army, and, after a siege of six weeks, the place surrendered to Alexius. The crusaders were somewhat dissatisfied at this, for they had expected to plunder the city, but, instead, they had to content themselves with gifts from Alexius.

From Nicæa the crusaders marched across Asia Minor. Much of that territory was barren enough by nature, but the Turks had taken care to make it even more so. As the Christians marched along their way, the Turks, mounted on swift horses, hovered around the rear and flanks of the expedition and picked off stragglers. At Dorylæum, where the army was divided for a time, the Turks attacked the smaller section. When the others arrived, the Turks in their turn were put to flight with heavy losses. After that, the Turks confined their attacks to guerilla warfare, but this accounted for a great many Christians, whose bleaching bones blazed the trail across Asia Minor for years to come.

The march of the crusaders stopped at Antioch, which they besieged from October, 1097, to June, 1098. There were a number of engagements both with the Turks inside the city and with detachments outside, and the crusaders suffered much from hunger. The city was finally betrayed to them on June 5, 1098. The Christians entered and were still engaged in trying to take the citadel, in which the defenders were making a last stand, when Kerbogha came up from Mesopotamia with a large army of Mohammedans and surrounded the city. The plight of the crusaders was now not an enviable one. Stephen of Blois returned from a trip to the coast to find a forest of Moslem tents around the city and concluded that the doom of the Christians was sealed. He rushed back across Asia Minor, met Alexius just coming to the aid of the Westerners, and persuaded him also to retreat. It cannot be said that the Christians inside Antioch felt any more hopeful as to the outcome. Many of them let themselves down over the city walls by ropes and tried to make their escape to the seacoast. Several of these, Peter the Hermit among them, were caught and brought back in disgrace. The rest suffered from hunger as well as despair and conditions within the city became frightful.

Then occurred one of those incidents not unknown even in modern wars. A humble peasant from the army of Raymond of Toulouse had a series of visions in which two of the apostles appeared to him. They directed him to dig in a certain spot under a church in Antioch, where he would find the Holy Lance with which the Saviour's side had been pierced. These visions were now reported to the leaders of the army, who, though somewhat sceptical, decided to dig as directed. Twelve men dug all day long until dusk, when Peter Bartholomew went down into the pit and reappeared shortly afterward with a spear point. The news flew through the crusading host and the men were greatly heartened. According to one chronicler, even the horses, long suffering from hunger and thirst, began to prance about eager for battle. After due ceremony, battle lines were formed, and the crusaders, carrying the Lance, marched out to fight. Apparently the Moslem army was taken by surprise, for they had concluded that the crusaders would be forced to surrender. They outnumbered the Christians, but they were put to flight and their army was cut to pieces. This battle took place on June 28, 1098.

Northern Syria was won and the road to Jerusalem lay open. In the interval of rest and recuperation, however, the leaders began to quarrel among themselves over the possession of Antioch and other towns. The papal vicar died inopportunely on August 1, 1098, and there was no recognized mediator. The leading opponents in the quarrel were Bohemund, who had extracted a promise from the other leaders that Antioch should be his if he found a means of gaining admission to it, and Raymond of Toulouse, who professed to be bound by the agreement with Alexius to turn the city over to the Empire. Finally, the soldiers of Raymond threatened to go on to Jerusalem without him, and Raymond was reluctantly forced to move onward.

Trouble broke out anew near Tripoli, where a strong fortress resisted attack. Raymond wished to remain there until it was captured. The other rulers wanted to accept the tribute of the ruler of Tripoli and go on to Jerusalem. But Raymond had with him Peter Bartholomew, who had had the visions regarding the Lance. Peter now had other visions which favored Raymond's plans. Arnulf, the chaplain of Robert of Normandy, thereupon challenged the validity of the Lance, denouncing its discovery as a fraud. The debate became very bitter, and finally Peter offered to prove the genuineness of the Lance by undergoing the ordeal by fire. Two piles of brush were heaped up, each about four feet high and thirty feet long, with a lane between them about two feet wide. These were then set on fire, and when the flames were at their height, Peter Bartholomew was sent through them, carrying the spear point in his hands. He emerged, but died from the effects of the ordeal shortly afterward. The more zealous proponents of the Lance still insisted upon its validity, claiming that Peter Bartholomew died from the press of relic-hunters who crowded upon him for shreds of his garments, and not from the burns caused by the fire. But the majority viewed the judgment of the ordeal otherwise, and the army moved on to Jerusalem.

Jerusalem was captured on July 15, 1099, after a siege lasting not quite six weeks. The joy of the crusaders was boundless. One writer, describing the slaughter of the Saracens within the city, said the crusaders rode in the blood of the Infidel up to the knees of their horses. Shortly after they had gained possession of the city, the leaders met to choose a ruler. Several were nominated, but the choice finally fell upon Godfrey as a compromise candidate. He had played an eminently respectable, if not distinguished, part in the events of the crusade, and was one of the older leaders. He refused the title of king "where the Saviour had worn a crown of thorns," and ruled under the more humble and pious title, "Defender of the Holy Sepulcher." Meanwhile, the Mohammedans of Egypt had gathered a large force for the recapture of Jerusalem. The Christians met them near Ascalon and put them to rout. After this battle, most of the Christians went to bathe in the Jordan and to gather palm leaves. They then started back home, leaving Godfrey, with about two hundred knights, to hold Jerusalem. With Godfrey remained also Arnulf, the chaplain of Robert of Normandy, who had been chosen ecclesiastical head of Jerusalem.

CONSEQUENCES OF THE FIRST CRUSADE

The First Crusade was thus accomplished. It had been successful beyond all reasonable calculation. Its favorable outcome was due, in part, to bitter factional strife among the Mohammedans and their inability to make common cause against the Christians. To the people of the West at this time, however, the achievements of the crusade marked the triumph of faith, and the stories of miracles wrought on the expedition were embellished with much detail. The returning crusaders were greeted as heroes by admiring thousands. The stories of their exploits echoed throughout Europe and aroused everywhere a desire to go and visit the Holy City. Many who had failed to start with the expedition, others who had started but turned back, and some who had caught the fire for the first time formed a new expedition, to further the conquests of the first. This was the ill-fated crusade of 1101-1102, on which both Stephen of Blois and Hugh of

Vermandois lost their lives, as did thousands of others, most of them in Asia Minor.

Naval expeditions were also formed to aid the Christian armies. Genoese sailors took part in the siege of Antioch and also in that of Jerusalem. A fleet of Angles is said to have reached Antioch in 1098. A Pisan fleet arrived in northern Syria in the fall of 1099, and the first expedition of the Venetians took place in 1100. The most picturesque naval expedition was that from Scandinavia. After two earlier unsuccessful attempts, a fleet left in 1107, under Sigurd, the Crusader. He and his men arrived in the Holy Land two years later, and, after helping to capture the seaport of Sidon, they sailed to Constantinople, sold their ships, and traveled overland through Russia back to their homes. This sweeping journey involved no regions which their Viking ancestors had not already visited.

The First Crusade had important bearings upon the struggle between the reform papacy and Henry IV. Urban II did not preach the crusade in Germany, and Godfrey and Baldwin were the only important leaders from that land. The general feeling there can be well understood from the words of a chronicler of the time: "But for the East Franks, the Saxons, the Thuringians, the Bavarians and the Alamanni this trumpet call sounded only faintly because of the schism between the Empire and the papacy from the time of Pope Alexander even until today. This, alas, has strengthened our hatred and enmity against the Romans, as it has theirs against us. And so it came to pass that almost all the Teutonic race, at first ignorant of the reason for this setting out, laughed to scorn the many legions of knights passing through their land, the many companies of foot soldiers, and the crowds of country people, women and little ones. They regarded them as crazed with unspeakable folly, inasmuch as they were striving after uncertainties in place of certainties, and were leaving for naught the land of their birth, to seek with certain danger the uncertain land of promise; and, while giving up their own possessions, they were yearning after those of strangers. But although our people are more perverse than other races, yet in consideration of the promise of divine pity, the enthusiasm of the Teutons was at last turned to this same proclamation, for they were taught, forsooth, what the thing really meant by the crowds passing through their lands." Thus wrote Ekkehard, abbot of Aura, who himself had shared these changing feelings and who took part in the crusade of 1101.

Henry IV was moved almost as much as the good abbot. The march of the east-bound crusaders impressed him deeply, and in 1097 he felt inclined to make peace with Urban. When the news of the success of the crusade reached the West, Henry thought seriously of going himself. Meanwhile, Urban II had died late in 1099, probably without having heard of the capture of Jerusalem. His successor, Paschal II, though also a former monk of Cluny and a staunch partisan of reform, was not endowed with the superior qualities of either Gregory or Urban. Paschal closed the door to reconciliation by the extreme denunciations which he heaped upon Henry IV. The struggle which his predecessors had waged with Henry was complicated because it included the questions of simony, marriage of the clergy and objectionable conduct, as well as lay investiture. Henry indicated a willingness to yield all points except the last. Paschal, however, refused all compromise, and Henry IV, in despair, surrendered his crown to his son, Henry V, and died a few months later.

Henry V showed his obedience to the papacy even to the extent of avoiding his excommunicated father, but soon found that the surrender of lay investiture would seriously endanger his royal power. In this stand he had the support of many of the clergy, who felt that as long as the king was instrumental in putting good men into office, there might even be an advantage in having his support for these officials. At least they saw no harm in it. Backed by this support, Henry V carried on a vigorous conflict with Paschal II, whom he took prisoner in 1111. Peace was made on more favorable terms than Paschal's earlier attitude seemed to indicate. The question was not settled, however, for the reform party was now too strong to be bound by a forced treaty. The controversy was continued until 1122, when an agreement without duress was reached at Worms. The *Concordat of*

Worms, as the agreement is called, provided that the emperor must yield the right to invest with the symbols of spiritual office, though he might be present at elections, and was conceded the right to invest with the lands which pertained to the office. This was a compromise which left the emperor opportunities for influence and control. The papacy, on the other hand, had won an important principle, namely that the spiritual office should be free from secular control. To what extent the principle could be effective outside, as well as inside, of Germany and Italy, only the future could tell.

THE TRIUMPH OF THE CHURCH. BERNARD OF CLAIRVAUX

The fact that less able successors of Gregory VII and Urban II could gain such a victory was in itself evidence of the power which the reform party had acquired. The movement was further strengthened by the accession of the new monastic orders which sprang up in the wake of the religious zeal aroused by the investiture struggle and the First Crusade. The most important of these was the Cistercian Order, so called from its first monastery, Citeaux in Burgundy, which had been founded in 1098. It did not take on its distinctive character, however, until after 1113, when Bernard, a young noble of Burgundy, entered its ranks.

Bernard was born not far from Cluny in 1091. As a lad he had seen the crusaders leave for the East and, on their return, had listened to the wonderful tales they had to tell. His forefathers had been soldiers, but his ability ran in more peaceful, although not less strenuous, channels. At twenty-two he had already resolved to enter the monastic life. Cluny did not satisfy him; it seemed to him too comfortable, too much immersed in the affairs of the world. He cast in his lot with one of the newly founded orders of a more rigorous kind, the Cistercian, and he helped to establish one of its mother houses, that of Clairvaux. The order was still so young that he was one of its pioneers, and his influence so shaped its course that he has come to be regarded as its chief founder.

The Benedictine rule was followed by the Cistercian Order. The modifications made by the Cistercians consisted chiefly of certain differences in practice. Each monastery had its own abbot, but all were more closely bound together than the Congregation of Cluny. Chapter meetings at which monks from each house were present were held regularly, and a distinct effort was made to visit each member house. As a safeguard against localism, it was also a deliberate policy of the order to have each monastery composed of monks from widely scattered regions. The fact that the order acknowledged obedience to the pope alone was a support to the idea of the universal Church detached from all local connections. Its houses were deliberately placed in out-of-the-way places, often on what had hitherto been regarded as waste land. The Cistercian monks practiced new methods of cultivating such land, and so closely are they identified with the progress of agriculture that they are often referred to as the agricultural monks. They worked with their hands not only in the soil, but also in various forms of handicraft, and they thus became of importance in industrial development generally. Learning was deprecated, if not always opposed in practice. The vow of poverty was more closely adhered to than in the other orders. Social activities were subordinated both outside and inside the monastery. Silence was cultivated as a virtue, and the devil was cheated by the constant occupation of their hands. This order rested its hopes upon the strength of simple faith.

Such was the order which Bernard joined. He passionately espoused the ideals which it represented and as fervently preached them. He was a deeply emotional and gifted speaker whose powers of persuasion were almost irresistible. Under his driving force hundreds entered the Cistercian monasteries. No class of society was outside his reach. Stories were told of a band of noble knights who were all converted by his pleas; of an address which he made to students at Paris, after which some twenty young men renounced their studies and followed him into the monastic life; of the conversion of his whole family through his efforts. He preached by example as well as by precept. He used so little food that he was in a half-starved condition most of the time, and, with rare consistency, he shunned those little concessions to comfort which even monks of the older orders had often made. His fame spread, the stories of his holy life led people everywhere to believe him a saint on earth with power to cure their ailments, and the sick crowded upon him for his touch. Stories of miraculous cures added to the reputation which he had already won and gave his words a weight which even kings and popes were glad to respect. The example of such a personality helped to make the new order popular, so that before his death it numbered more than one hundred and fifty monasteries as compared with the one which it had when he entered. About fifty of these were in Germany, more in the regions of France, and the rest were scattered through Italy, Spain, England and elsewhere.

The peculiar circumstances and spirit of the time, as well as his own remarkable ability and character, made Bernard the dominant figure of his age. He was consulted on nearly all matters of broad importance and his influence was often decisive in shaping their course. In 1128 at the Council of Troyes, a council more general in its composition than any since Carolingian days, he was the outstanding figure. He appeared there as the champion of the new Order of Knights Templars, or Knights of the Temple of Solomon. This order had arisen from the needs of pilgrims in the Holy Land for protection as they went about from shrine to shrine. A band of nine men decided to devote themselves to this task, and their work was so successful that they now applied for a charter to establish a permanent order. Bernard not only wrote their rule, but induced the Council of Troyes to accept it. The Knights of St. John, or the Hospitallers, formed originally to care for sick pilgrims in the Holy Land, received similar recognition not long afterward. Thus were founded the two great orders of soldier monks whose splendid work in the East gained for them substantial gifts from the grateful and the pious throughout Christendom. Bernard took an abiding interest in their work, especially in that of the Templars, and could always be counted upon to lend a willing ear to their pleas for help.

In 1130 occurred a schism in the papacy which aroused discussion and division generally, and Bernard again had an opportunity to make his influence felt. Two factions had formed in the college of cardinals, and each had chosen one of its members as pope. This situation had come about not because of imperial or other outside interference, but from personal ambition among the cardinals themselves. The choice of the majority was Anaclete, the son of a very able Jewish banker in the service of Urban II. His family had adopted Christianity, and he himself had studied in France, had been a monk at Cluny, and had then entered the service of the papal court. In this capacity he expected that the wealth and influence of his family, added to his natural ability, would be of great assistance in forwarding his career. Innocent II, the minority candidate, was a man of less distinction and less personal wealth and power, but he commanded the deeper loyalty of his followers. Both were members of the reform party, which was, to be sure, no longer a party, but rather the entire Church. Both strove to win the support of influential leaders throughout the Church. Bernard gave his allegiance to Innocent II and undertook to lead the campaign for his recognition.

Bernard persuaded the king and nearly all the greater nobles of France to support his candidate. His eloquence likewise won the clergy of France, England and Spain. His personal appeal to the king of Germany was an important factor behind that monarch's espousal of Innocent's cause, and the people in northern Italy were won over by the same means. The military support of the king of Germany was necessary to install Innocent in Rome, where Anaclete's influence was still powerful, and Bernard helped to secure this. When it became necessary to summon aid a second time, Bernard succeeded in healing the factional strife in Germany which threatened to prevent any assistance from that quarter. Through him even the Normans of southern Italy were induced to support Innocent II. In all of this campaign Bernard's influence was not the only factor, nor always the deciding factor, but it was an important one, nevertheless, and Innocent II was under deep obligation to him. Innocent was compelled to acknowledge this indebtedness, at times with embarrassment, for Bernard criticized the pope as freely as he did his other friends, and enemies, too, for deviations from the high standard of conduct which was his passionate ideal.

The first half of the twelfth century saw many other new forces at work in Europe, and nearly all of them received some attention from Bernard. Always suspicious of learning, though a man of no mean learning himself, Bernard was especially opposed to the new development in the study of theology whereby the writings of the Church fathers were subjected to the same rules of logic as were applied to other spheres of learning. The leader of this movement, the brilliant Abélard, was overcome through the influence of Bernard. Hitherto Abélard had been able to confound his lesser opponents by his clear thought and eloquence, but before Bernard he was powerless. At the Council of Sens, in 1141, the appeal to logic of the one succumbed to the passionate appeal to faith of the other. New developments in commerce and industry which were leading to the concentration of population at town centers also claimed Bernard's attention. An uprising of the people of Rheims against their feudal ruler, the archbishop, aroused his wrath, and he denounced them vigorously. To him, the efforts of merchants and craftsmen to govern themselves seemed little short of a subversion of divine law. Arnold of Brescia, a pupil of Abélard's, was engaged in stirring up revolt at Rome, and this fact only confirmed Bernard in his view. The new style of church architecture also drew from him a sharp rebuke. The lofty spires with which new church buildings were being surmounted appeared to him as an unwarranted evidence of human vanity. Later ages did not concur in all these judgments of Bernard's, nor did all men in his day. Peter the Venerable, abbot of Cluny, sheltered the broken Abélard, and Suger, the abbot of St. Denis at Paris, heartily encouraged the rising commercial class. Both of these men were Bernard's friends, and both approved of the new style of architecture, the Gothic, which was to attain full expression in the next half century.

THE SECOND CRUSADE

Another movement with which Bernard's name is connected was the Second Crusade. Edessa, the easternmost principality of the Latins, had been captured by the Moslems in 1144. To the Latins in Syria the loss was a serious one, for Edessa commanded the highways from Mesopotamia into northern Syria. To the uninformed people in the West the fall of Edessa did not seem highly important, for it was not a large city, nor did it contain any very sacred shrines. Bernard, however, saw the danger involved in its capture and tried to arouse a general crusade like the first to go to the help of his friends in the East. He devoted himself to the preaching of the crusade with such zeal and success that his name is usually connected with it almost as closely as is that of Urban with the First Crusade. The military leaders of this expedition were Louis VII, king of France, and Conrad III, king of Germany. The crusading force was better organized than was that of the First Crusade, though it was not so large and certainly not nearly so successful. It followed the land route through Asia Minor, where it suffered great losses. After arriving in Syria, it was hampered by differences in counsel. Each principality there tried to use the crusading army in its own interest. After frittering away many months, the two monarchs finally led their forces against Damascus. This move was ill advised and worse managed, and the Christians were forced to withdraw. In disgust, the leaders returned home after an absence of about two years. The failure of the expedition was a bitter disappointment to Bernard, and he brooded upon it for the remainder of his life.

A political sequel to this crusade was the separation between Louis VII and his wife Eleanor of Aquitaine, who had accompanied him to the East. Earlier evidences of incompatibility between the two were definitely established in the course of the crusade, and scandalous stories about her conduct in the East were circulated in the West. Louis sought to obtain a divorce from her, but Suger, the abbot of St. Denis, who had administered the affairs of France while Louis was on the crusade and who was deeply interested in the growth of royal power there, dissuaded him from carrying out his purpose. He argued that the loss of Aquitaine, which had come to Louis through his marriage, would constitute a serious setback to the king's strength. Bernard of Clairvaux took an opposite view, and, whatever his motives, helped to bring about the separation after the death of Suger, on the ground that the two were within the prohibited degree of relationship. Eleanor promptly married Henry, count of Anjou, who shortly after became Henry II, king of England, and thus the extensive duchy of Aquitaine passed into the possession of the king of England.

Bernard died in 1153 and was canonized as a saint by the Church. No man of his time, whether king or pope, had wielded influence comparable to his. In addition to his many activities, which left their lasting mark on the history of Europe, he found time to do some notable writing. His sermons are models of mystic eloquence, and as such are still read. Much of his work failed to win the approval of the generations which followed. Yet the fact that this Cistercian monk, armed only with piety, unusual eloquence and almost unlimited energy, could dominate so many lands in such an age was evidence of the growth of the spiritual ideal throughout Europe and of the progress which Europe had made.

The growth of the power of the Church from the time of Leo IX (d.1054) to the death of Bernard of Clairvaux has been well characterized by Henry C. Lea: "History records no such triumph of intellect over brute strength as that which in an age of turmoil and battle was wrested from the fierce warriors of the time by priests who had no material force at their command and whose power was based alone on the souls and consciences of men. Over soul and conscience their empire was complete. No Christian could hope for salvation who was not in all things an obedient son of the Church and who was not ready to take up arms in its defense; and, in times when faith was a determining factor of conduct, this belief created a spiritual despotism which placed all things in reach of him who could wield it." To what uses this new-found strength might be put only the future could reveal. That kings and emperors might well quail before it had already been made clear. The Church, headed by the papacy, must now be regarded as a power in Europe independent of, and stronger than, any secular ruler.

CHAPTER VIII

EUROPEAN SOCIETY IN THE TWELFTH CENTURY

I. THE CLERGY

BY THE middle of the twelfth century the society of Europe had assumed a character which can no longer be clearly or fully described in terms of the Roman or Teutonic institutions from which it had developed. In the fluid state of constant change into which nearly all social institutions had been melted by the general disorder following the Carolingian rule considerable crystallization had occurred, especially in the last century. European society was still predominantly agricultural, but within it three classes were clearly recognizable at this time. The clergy formed one, the ruling and fighting nobility another, and the laborers, or peasants, the third. John of Salisbury, who lived at this time, likened them all to the body, and saw in the first the eyes of the mind, in the second the arms, and in the third the feet.

The clergy, not the most numerous class, though probably more numerous now than it had ever been in European history, was divided between regular and secular. The regular clergy (from Latin *regula,* or rule) were those who lived according to monastic rule. The greater monastic orders, Benedictine, Cluniac and Cistercian, have already been described.[1] Their monasteries were scattered throughout Christendom. That modification of the Benedictine rule which the latter two had made, substituting for diocesan direct papal control, suited the spirit of the times and many of the older Benedictine houses were taken over by the newer orders. Some of the more famous old monasteries, like Monte Cassino, Fulda and St. Gall, received exemption from their local bishops and so came directly under the authority of the

---

[1] See pages 54, 94, 117.

pope. The general standard of excellence maintained in these monasteries had probably never been so high as it was at this time. Their buildings were centers of industry as well as of religious devotion. Most of the orders employed peasants to do the agricultural labor, but some, like the Cistercians, did much of this themselves. The lands which they tilled, their gardens, orchards and flocks, were usually models of care. The monks spent most of their time in or about their monasteries, engaged in their prescribed tasks, but not infrequently they were sent on journeys of business for their order. In the middle of the twelfth century the black-robed Benedictines and the white-robed Cistercians were frequently seen on the highways of Europe. This was less true of the Carthusian Order, another new but less popular order of the time, whose members spent most of their time, engaged in devotional exercises, in separate cells within their monasteries.

The religious fervor of the time led people to form or enter new orders quite different in character from the preceding. The Templars and Hospitallers, or soldier monks, have already been mentioned. People formed themselves into religious associations which performed certain tasks, such as the ransoming of Christians from Moslem slavery or the building of churches. Something of the same spirit was manifested at this time in the rapid spread of the Augustinian and Præmonstratensian rules. These were created for the regulation of the canons, or priests, who assisted the bishop, usually in connection with the cathedral church and schools. Under these rules the cathedral canons formed almost monastic communities, but their work was usually of a secular nature. The Augustinian, or Austin, canons derived their name from a similar rule which St. Augustine of Hippo had written for the clergy who assisted him, while the Præmonstratensian canons received their name from the place at which their rule was first used, Prémontré.

As these last groups indicate, the line of separation between the regular and secular clergy was not a very sharp one. The regular clergy shaded gradually from the extremely ascetic Carthusians to orders which were chiefly secular. The two were further confused by the common practice of having monks serve as parish priests or bishops, and most of the popes during the past century had been monks. Even the Cistercian Order, whose aim had been to avoid the worldly entanglements of Cluny, had already furnished a number of bishops and was to furnish several popes also. Usually, however, parishes and dioceses were governed by truly secular clergy, or churchmen who did not live according to a prescribed round of duties, but adjusted themselves more or less to the conditions of the world in which they worked. These men were recruited from various walks of life, trained in schools, ordained by bishops and appointed to hold office as priests. They might then be used in various capacities and many of them were elected to fill bishoprics, archbishoprics, or even the papacy itself. In all of these offices they mingled freely with their fellows, differentiated only by their clerical garb and function.

The official hierarchy of the Church was in form as it had been in the fifth century, leading step by step from parish priest through bishop and archbishop to the pope. As a result of the First Crusade, Latin patriarchates had been established in the East at Jerusalem and Antioch. These were fitted into the hierarchy of the Roman Church as higher archbishoprics with authority only in their respective provinces or patriarchates. There were thus in some regions five steps, instead of four, from parish priest to pope. The college of cardinals established by the decree of Nicholas II did not mark, properly speaking, a change in the hierarchy, though these clergy had a dignity superior to that of archbishops. Each member of the college had an office in the Church of Rome, ranging from deacon to archbishop. As a body, they had only the one function of electing the pope, but they came to be regarded as his official family, assisting him in the manifold duties of his office. In this way they wielded influence which any archbishop might well envy. Their prestige increased along with that of the papacy, and the delegation of power to the cardinals became fixed by custom. The formation of the college of cardinals was typical of the changes which were taking place in the government of the Church.   These changes involved less the creation of new offices than addition to the duties of the old.

The most striking feature of the Church in the middle of the twelfth century, and one in which it differed from all previous periods, was its universal character.   In the territory in which the Roman Church was established everyone except a negligible number of Jews was a member.   Only in the lands conquered from the Mohammedans—in Syria, Sicily and Spain—was there a considerable number of non-Christians.   It was possible for a Christian monk, cleric, or pilgrim to travel from remote Ireland or Scandinavia to Syria in comparative safety and with fair assurance of hospitality at every stage of the journey.   Thanks to the interest which the crusades had aroused, pilgrims were making precisely this journey to an extent never before true.   The establishment of monastic orders directly under the pope made it easier for persons from one region to gain position in a different part of Europe.   This widespread membership was a policy of the Cistercian Order, but it was practiced by other orders also. The military orders especially had foundations over all Christendom.   Among the secular clergy also this unity was true to a remarkable degree at this time.   Nearly every country numbered at least one foreigner among its prominent clergy.   There were Italians in England, France and Germany; Germans, French and Englishmen in Italy.   Many of the popes during the preceding century were men from outside Italy—Leo IX from Germany, Urban II from France and Hadrian IV from England.   The Church likewise embraced all classes of society, and in several instances men had risen from the peasant class to the headship of the Church.   In general, however, there was a marked tendency to fill the higher places in the Church with men from the upper classes of society.

Despite this unity of the Church, its separate branches displayed wide variation in organization.   The divisions established in the beginning in any given region seemed to exercise a permanent influence which neither disorder nor strong government could seriously disarrange.   Thus, Ireland with its four archbishoprics,

and Scotland with none, Germany with its large bishoprics, and
Italy with its minute bishoprics and even archbishoprics, all were
within the same Church.   The lack of uniform organization appeared even within the same countries.   England had two archbishoprics, one of which had seventeen, the other only two, subject bishops.   In France the size of the archbishoprics varied
from the small provinces near the Italian border to the larger
Rheims on the German frontier.   Similar differences appeared
also in the size and character of parishes.   There were differences likewise in the authority exercised by different officials of
the same rank.   The archbishops in the Rhine country were
princes of Germany as well as prelates of the Church and governed their provinces with both swords, the spiritual and the
temporal, while some archbishops in other regions had little
enough power of either kind.   Changes were occurring constantly,
bishoprics were elevated to archbishoprics or divided to form
new bishoprics, and new parishes were formed within the territory of older parishes.   The tendency of each official to insist
upon having all the territory which had formerly belonged to his
office was so strong, however, that sometimes even popes were
constrained to reëstablish former boundaries.

While there were these innumerable differences in the extent
of districts and in the amount of authority which individual
churchmen exercised, the spiritual duties of the clergy were becoming standardized.   This fact was due in large measure to the
insistence of the reform party that all churchmen must be trained
for their work.   It was due also to the advance in the study of
theology which made this subject not an incidental interest in the
career of a practical churchman, but a profession in itself.   The
two causes worked hand in hand.   The first has been dealt with
sufficiently.   As the interest in Church careers grew and as prospective churchmen from all classes of society flocked to the
schools, it was only natural that certain teachers and certain
centers should be singled out as best.   The variety of practices
in territories widely separated led to many questions, and the
need of a common understanding, especially on fundamental matters of doctrine, became quite clear.

This problem was fully revealed in the career of Abélard. He was born in 1079, the son of a Breton nobleman. Instead of a military career, he inclined to one in the Church, as did many a noble youth at this time. For this calling he was especially endowed. With an unusual memory, gifted tongue and attractive personality, he advanced rapidly in learning. He studied first at home and in Normandy and then went to Paris, already famous for its superior teachers. It so happened that his early teachers differed widely on a fundamental question of philosophy, the problem of the universals. Briefly stated, this was the problem of reality on which Plato and Aristotle had differed. His first teacher, like Aristotle, held the view that the individual was the only reality and that classes were names only, not realities. This view was called Nominalism. The great teacher at Paris, William of Champeaux, held, like Plato, the opposite view, that reality resided in the class, of which the individual was only a more or less imperfect example. This view was called Realism. When applied ruthlessly to the doctrine of the Trinity, the Nominalist recognized only the three separate elements, while the Realist stressed the oneness of God. The problem entered into the explanation of other doctrines also, especially those regarding the sacraments. Abélard, who had been taught the Nominalist view, found some difficulty in accepting also the Realist view and soon concluded that the truth lay somewhere between the two positions. He therefore boldly disputed the views of William of Champeaux, and won his fellow students to his position. As a result, he found it necessary to leave Paris, but the students followed after him and he found himself a teacher of philosophy.

It was his ambition, however, to enter upon a career as churchman, and to this end he went to study theology under Anselm of Laon. Here his boldness caused him further difficulties, for he soon concluded that he could teach this subject better than Anselm and so convinced his fellow students there. In theology he laid emphasis on the fact that the great Church fathers whose writings were invariably consulted for explanation of the Scriptures differed among themselves on vital matters. Their work had been interrupted by the migrations, and no systematic attempt had been made since that time to reconcile their differences.   In a little book called *Sic et Non,* Abélard set forth in parallel columns the opposite opinions of different Church fathers on important problems of theology.   He urged that the proper attitude to take was to question, that questioning would lead to investigation, and investigation to the truth.   Out of the varying opinions of the Church fathers reason could arrive at a final answer which would satisfy all needs.   In theology, as in philosophy, Abélard had rendered a real service which his many students were to realize.   But Abélard himself had shocked the established authorities of his day, the teachers and older churchmen who were accustomed to less exact methods.   His unfortunate love affair with Héloïse only added to the circle of his enemies.   He was twice tried, the last time at the Council of Sens at which Bernard of Clairvaux led the attack upon him, and his work was declared heretical.   He died at Cluny before he could carry his appeal to the pope.

Peter Lombard, a pupil of Abélard, applied his method to the fundamental doctrines of the Church.   His *Book of Sentences,* or his conclusions on the articles of the Christian faith, became the recognized text-book in theology and did much to bring about a common understanding and practice regarding spiritual doctrine.   The seven sacraments were treated quite fully and almost finally.   These were baptism, confirmation, penance, the eucharist, ordination for the priests, marriage for the laity and extreme unction.   Five of these could be administered by priests, all of them by bishops.   Ordination and confirmation were reserved to the bishop.   The sacrament of the eucharist was especially important.   According to the doctrine of transubstantiation, the bread and wine of the sacrament became the actual body and blood of Christ.   Priests obtained the power to bring about this change through the sacrament of ordination administered by a bishop to whom the power had come in unbroken succession from the apostles, who had received it directly from the Saviour Himself. For disciplinary purposes the most important sacrament was that of penance, which involved the three steps of contrition on the part of the sinner, confession to a priest and absolution, with some form of penance or satisfaction imposed by the priest. The penances imposed on Louis the Pious, Henry IV and Godfrey the Bearded of Lorraine were typical, if somewhat extreme.[1] Usually fasting and prayers were prescribed, but pilgrimages were imposed for greater crimes. Gifts for worthy causes also might be made as a form of penance. The sacrament of marriage had likewise occasioned periodic discussion. It was held to be binding throughout life. Separations were only possible because of irregularities, such as marriage within prohibited degrees of relationship, which made the original ceremony null.

The administration of the sacramental system became fairly uniform throughout the Church at this time and was regarded as the regular duty of ordained clergy. Attendance at Church service was obligatory upon all Christians, the priests being expected to conduct services on all Church holidays and festivals. Preaching of sermons was peculiarly the duty of bishops, but the preaching of the crusades had given rise to itinerant preachers who made preaching an art. Certain special duties, like prayers for the dead, might be discharged by any of the churchmen. It became a practice, quite widespread at this time, to establish foundations for this purpose with endowments to maintain chaplains. The veneration of relics frequently led to the establishment of special shrines under the care of assigned churchmen. Some of the more famous of these shrines, like that of St. James of Compostella in Spain, and that of Thomas à Becket at Canterbury, became especially revered and were visited by pilgrims from distant lands.

In addition to these spiritual duties, each rank of the clergy had certain other duties as well which became more or less standardized. The parish priest who ministered to the peasants in the rural villages kept the records of the parish, trained his altar boys, looked after the needy and was an important factor in the social life of the community. Frequently he had obligations to the feudal lord of the district as well as to his bishop, for many of the lords exercised the right of patronage which often involved the actual designation of the priest for the parish. Not infre-

[1] See pages 74, 100, 105.

quently these rural parish priests had risen from the servile class, winning freedom for themselves, and usually also for their parents, by this step. This transition required the consent of the lord. Often, too, the lord provided the salary of the priest and usually the lord expected his coöperation in maintaining peace and order among the peasantry. When questions arose which required judicial action in ecclesiastical concerns, such matters were referred to the bishop, under whose supervision the parish priest worked. The parish priest had no land, except perhaps a kitchen garden beside his parish house. All lands belonging to the Church in his neighborhood were administered by the bishop.

The bishops regularly administered all Church lands in their dioceses, were responsible for the training of priests for their parishes and had to supervise the work of all their priests. In addition they had many judicial matters to settle, and at this time the Church courts were especially sought in the settlement of disputes. On matters of grave importance a council of bishops under the archbishop usually sat in judgment. Those duties of the bishop were, as a rule, so heavy that he could not attend to them all in person, and had a staff of assistants attached to his cathedral church. These were usually organized as a cathedral chapter of canons, a miniature college of cardinals, resembling the latter also in that they elected the bishop. The bishop might devote himself to the field of his own personal interest. Some of them with heavy administrative duties did little else; some of them, whose interests were primarily academic, acted as heads of their schools, leaving the administrative and other work to assistants. During this time the inspection of the clergy was usually entrusted to an official known as archdeacon, who was usually also the presiding officer of the cathedral chapter. This separation of duties could, and did, lead to friction which caused further rearrangements in the episcopal household.

The archbishop in earlier times had been merely bishop with added dignity. Now, however, there was a tendency for many of them to exercise authority as well as precedence among their bishops. The archbishops were required to seek the pallium, the distinctive mark of their rank, from the pope at Rome. This gave the papacy some control over the office, for the pope could refuse to confer the pallium, without which the archbishop was not fully established. In addition to their duties as bishops, the archbishops found the judicial work of their provinces very heavy. The guardianship which the Church exercised over the relatives and property of crusaders had increased the judicial business of the Church, as had also the better organized administration of Church sacraments. Learning and politics and business were all becoming organized on a basis wider than the episcopal diocese, and this change threw heavier responsibilities upon the archbishops. In some regions, as in Germany, the archbishops were also rulers of large principalities. The changing conditions in Europe increased the work of the archbishops, for these officials were not only burdened by the expanding needs of society, but were also charged with more duties by the papacy. This fact was especially true of Canterbury in England, of Rouen and Rheims in France, and of Ravenna in Italy.

If the bishops and archbishops were crowded by increasing duties, the papacy was indescribably burdened. Periodic confirmation of all charters and special privileges held by all monastic orders; grants of new charters, confirmation of elections of archbishops; conferences with legates who went to all parts of Christendom on missions for the pope; authentication of relics and canonization of saints; authoritative pronouncement on questions of faith and morals—all these were regular duties requiring the pope's attention. The management of the Papal States and their political relations, the collection of revenues from the whole Church, the preaching of crusades, the support of the Latins in the East, were all duties of the office. In addition there were numerous suitors for papal justice. Disputed elections of churchmen, violations of canon law, disputes over property between Church bodies or with lay rulers, all came before the papal court. The roads to Rome were again thronged as they had not been since the time when the ancient emperors still sat there, and everyone was apparently intent upon a personal interview with the pope. This, of course, was impossible and the popes were occupied with the problem of organizing bureaus to deal with the more common and regular business. The secretariat of the pope and cardinals was sufficient to people a city, and Church business was on the increase. In the time of Innocent III, fifty years later, the problem became yet more urgent, and its detailed discussion will be left until that time.

The expansion of the legal business of the Church had created a need for a more uniform knowledge of law. Much of this judicial work related not to ecclesiastical matters, but to purely secular affairs, like disputes over property. Decisions of popes and councils, often made without regard to each other, led to confusion, and many questions which now arose had not been dealt with before by the Church. In the interest of uniformity a monk named Gratian, who had studied law, applied Abélard's method with excellent results. His *Decretum* became a text-book in canon law and through its study this law was uniformly applied by bishops and archbishops throughout Christendom. The "rediscovery" of the Code of Justinian, brilliantly explained by a certain Irnerius at Bologna, afforded an almost inexhaustible source of help, for the Romans had had experience with almost every type of legal problem which was apt to arise between reasonable men. Priests and even bishops went to Bologna to study law, and it soon became a law school for all Christendom, as Paris had become the leading center for the study of theology. Law, like theology, had become a profession, though perhaps not yet to the same extent. It required the full time of men who taught the subject in the schools or acted as advisers for pope and archbishops and sometimes for kings.

The clergy as a class occupied a privileged position in society. They were subject only to ecclesiastical jurisdiction, they could not be taxed or required to perform any service or be tried for any offense whatsoever by secular authorities. It was the duty and also the practice of society to help them when in need and they were assured of hospitality practically everywhere. As a class, they extended vertically through all society. There was no peasant hovel, however humble, which they might not enter, nor was there any royal court, however proud, which was closed to the lowliest of them. They kept in touch with one another through their excellent organization, through frequent travel and through extensive writings, in all of which they far surpassed any other class of the time. They enjoyed, too, the intimate confidence of all classes as no other class did, and neither battle line nor castle wall was any barrier to them. A class so favored could not fail to arouse the envy of others less privileged, and there never was a time when designing and unscrupulous persons did not seek to gain those privileges. Whether some crafty faker sold horseshoe nails as nails of the true Cross, or some more ambitious person gained priestly ordination in order to use his calling for personal gain, the problem of winnowing the chaff from the wheat faced the Church at all times. In general, the Church as a whole was probably freer from abuse at this time than in any previous period. There was already abundant evidence, however, to indicate that this condition would not long endure.

CHAPTER VIII
(*Continued*)

EUROPEAN SOCIETY IN THE TWELFTH CENTURY

II. THE NOBILITY

BY THE middle of the twelfth century the title of nobility in much of Europe had become hereditary and its bearers class conscious. The line of demarcation between the nobles and the lower classes was knighthood and the possession of a fief. All who possessed these qualifications may be described as nobles, who constituted the ruling class as well as the fighting class. They were not the only fighters, but they were distinguished by the fact that they possessed a complete fighting equipment of horse, armor and weapons and did not engage in manual labor. The class line was not yet very rigid, but as society became more peaceful and orderly the distinction between classes became more marked.

Social stratification had progressed farther in the dominions of France than elsewhere in Europe and was there the product of military and religious forces. Nowhere else in Europe had the central power collapsed so completely. In France it was almost a miracle that the title of king had survived, for from the last quarter of the ninth century to the first quarter of the twelfth there was little evidence of any royal power. The authority which the nobles had usurped from the king seemed at first in danger of being dissipated in general anarchy, for there was nothing to prevent the subjects of the greater nobles from treating them exactly as those nobles had treated the king. There was a time when any man who could acquire equipment in any way and use it effectively might make himself a ruler. Gradually, however, the stronger families, whose sons were able to maintain that strength, succeeded in establishing a recognized authority which could weather the calamity of an occasional weak member in their line of descent.

The natural and widespread desire for peace and order made people prefer almost any ruler to none. This was clearly illustrated in the case of the count of Paris, Hugh Capet, who received the title of King of France in 987. From that time on the Capetian family never failed of an heir, but some of these were men of little ability who required for support all the traditions of their heroic forbears and the active work of the clergy. At times their authority meant little even in the neighborhood of Paris, but time and the Church worked in their favor, so that by the middle of the twelfth century the king of France was actually one of the most powerful nobles in his kingdom. Nearly all of this gain had been made during the twelfth century, and much of it was due to the work of the churchmen, especially to that of Suger, abbot of St. Denis.

Similar forces had operated to establish the greater nobles as hereditary rulers. These were tenants-in-chief, who held title directly from the king, like the count of Flanders, the duke of Normandy, the duke of Burgundy, the count of Champagne, the duke of Aquitaine and the count of Toulouse. How firmly these titles had become established was illustrated by the fact that a woman was allowed to inherit Aquitaine and to transfer it from the king of France to the count of Anjou, later king of England. For all practical purposes these great tenants were independent and did not permit the king to interfere seriously in their affairs. The same condition, however, did not hold for the relation of the great nobles to the nobles within their territories.

The great nobles tried to hold the allegiance of their subject nobles by fiefs, in addition to the personal oath of loyalty. The fief had come to be the standard method of insuring services. Upon receiving the fief, the vassal took the oath of homage and fealty. On bended knee, his hands held between those of the lord, the vassal promised to be the man (*homo*) of the latter, to love what he loved and shun what he shunned. Thereupon the lord bade him rise, they exchanged the kiss of peace, and the lord gave to the vassal some token as a symbol of the fief. The latter ceremony was known as the investiture. A written contract in which the obligations of both parties were set forth usually accompanied this transaction.

The attempt to make these fiefs hereditary was resisted by the greater nobles as long as possible, so as to keep their lesser nobles more fully under their control. In northern Italy Conrad II of Germany had found it a wise move to support such lesser nobles in their efforts to establish heredity by legislation. In France, however, where there was no strong king, the same tendency took form slowly and less definitely. After the hereditary rights of the lesser nobles were fairly established, the lords still claimed the right to invest the vassal's heir with the paternal fief, exacting the usual oath of homage and fealty. If the heir was a minor the lord exercised the right of wardship and controlled the fief during the minority of the vassal.

The military service generally required of a vassal noble varied according to the size of his fief. The length of such service was becoming standardized at forty days a year. The lord could require further service if necessary, but in such cases he had to pay the expenses of his vassals for the additional period. The number of knights which he could require from his vassal was fixed in the original contract, and the vassals resisted strongly any effort to increase the number. The vassal was also expected to assist his lord in trying legal cases, especially when these involved other nobles. Some material return was also expected each year, though this was usually nominal and served chiefly to remind the vassal that the land belonged to the lord. On a few special occasions the vassal was expected to make substantial money payments to his lord; for instance, at the knighting of the lord's eldest son, or at the marriage of the lord's eldest daughter. Ransom was expected if the lord was taken captive, and a contribution if the lord went on a crusade. These were called the *feudal aids* and were generally observed. During the twelfth century these obligations were becoming fixed, but in practice a strong, aggressive lord usually managed to exact from his vassals much more than custom allowed.

In the regions of France the stages from king to knight were numerous and, in theory, each stage dealt only with those next to it. The lesser nobles also had vassals who held fiefs of them. The relationship of these sub-vassals to their superiors was also that of vassal to lord, as described above. To this process of division and subdivision the term sub-infeudation has been applied, and it continued to the lowest point possible at which the retainer could earn his living without actually tilling the soil. This stage was called the knights' fief or fee and was usually reckoned as based upon the work of five servile families. Below this point nobility did not extend. Perhaps there once was a time when the ordinary knights actually lived in the neighborhood of the five families and drew their living directly from the labor of these peasants, but by this time the greater nobles kept a number of knights in constant attendance upon them and furnished them with a living. Such knights were used as a bodyguard or as castle guard and usually aided in policing the highways.

Originally, perhaps, this process of sub-infeudation might have been diagrammed in a fanlike fashion from the king to the ordinary knight. At this time, however, the emphasis had shifted from exclusive military allegiance to the possession of property. The language was still the feudal terminology of fiefs, but the practice was the acquisition of property. Fiefs might be acquired through warfare, marriage, gift and heredity. Exchange and purchase, too, were beginning to be practiced. When this stage was reached the system became hopelessly confused from a military point of view, though clear enough from that of a realtor. It then became possible for a noble to hold fiefs from all of his neighbors and even from his own sub-vassals. He might at the same time be in vassalage to others of the feudal hierarchy. In case of conflict between two of his lords he would have to exercise rare discretion. Among the most successful of these feudal realtors were the counts of Champagne, who for successive generations seem to have inherited the gift. If a map of the holdings of these counts in the later twelfth century were colored to represent the fiefs from different lords, it would much resemble a crazy quilt; but, if left uncolored, the principality would appear fairly compact. However, the very existence of such an assemblage of fiefs indicated a much more peaceful society than that in which feudalism first arose. The restraint of private warfare had advanced to such a point that the undisturbed possession of small fiefs was reasonably assured. Changes were more apt to occur on the outside fringes of the greater fiefs.

The description of noble society thus far set forth applies primarily to the regions of France, but even there important variations occurred in the different localities, especially if Brittany be included. During the eleventh and twelfth centuries many of these practices were introduced into the neighboring countries, especially into Germany and England, likewise into Spain and Italy, as well as into more remote lands. In all of these places, however, there were important differences, and the resemblances were often more superficial than real. Feudalism, as a system of landholding, was well established in England by the Norman Conquest, but as a political system it never obtained any great hold, for the Norman kings insisted upon the direct allegiance of all fighting men. In Germany neither system was accepted to any complete extent, though features of both appeared, especially on the new frontier. The German nobility adopted the practice of dividing their holdings among their sons, a process which in the course of time led to numerous infinitesimal holdings, in each of which the holder ultimately sought to exercise political as well as economic control. This process had not yet gone very far, but great progress was made in this direction during the struggle between the German kings and the popes. In Italy the feudal nobility were superimposed upon the population chiefly through the influence of the German kings, so that there the nobility not only constituted a separate class, but were also of different blood. In all these regions, nevertheless, there was a tendency to establish a common noble class, a movement which was greatly hastened by the intercourse which followed in the wake of the crusades.

Although one may thus speak of general tendencies in the so-called feudal system, and neatly mark off its social frontiers between clergy and peasantry, the scheme defies any neat, simple and universally applicable description. When viewed as a working institution, the regularity of the system lies in its irregularity, and it is uniform in lacking uniformity.

The institution of knighthood, which was the hall-mark of nobility, was undergoing a great transformation and had become nearly fixed at this time. Its origins appeared in the ancient practice of admitting the Teuton lad into the circle of the tribal warriors, but knighthood in the later twelfth century was a much more elaborate affair. The feudal noble probably trained his son in horsemanship and the handling of weapons from the earliest possible age, but it became a custom to recognize three distinct stages in the training of a knight. Until the age of seven the boy was left in his mother's care. Between the age of seven and fourteen he was usually sent to some other noble to serve as a page. If the son of a sub-vassal, he went ordinarily to the court of the overlord; if a son of the latter, to some more distant court. During this period the boy was expected to learn gentle manners by serving about the court, and as a rule at this time he was also given instruction in letters, in music, and in the art of entertaining. During the third period, from fourteen to twenty-one, he became a squire and took up the serious study of the profession of arms. He associated with the knights, looked after horse and armor, and practiced with both. His more gentle training was not entirely neglected at this time, but the emphasis was upon the military side. At twenty-one he was ready to become a knight.

The ceremony by which the squire entered the rank of knighthood had already become quite elaborate. It included prayers and fasting, the blessing of the weapons, a bath of purification, and a vow to live up to certain principles of conduct; in particular, to help the weak, the needy and the Church; and, finally, it included a test of his horsemanship and his skill in handling weapons. The last step in the process was the accolade, in which a knight touched the kneeling candidate on the shoulder with the flat of his sword, saying, "I dub thee knight." The final ceremonies usually lasted several days and were attended by many invited guests and hired entertainers. The cost of this initiation was so heavy that younger sons had frequently to do without it. When the king or great noble chose to knight a warrior for some deed of valor on the battlefield, the accolade alone was sufficient.

This ceremony revealed the operation of several forces which had been at work during the past century. The custom of requiring men to take an oath to observe the Peace of God, with its protection of the weak, the needy and the Church, was clearly in evidence. The crusade, in which fighting men were definitely engaged in the service of God, added further strength to his oath. The literary development of the time also kept such ideas constantly before the fighting men. The epic story of the First Crusade had been written and rewritten, with many embellishments of legend and idealism. In the early twelfth century, too, primitive folk epics, long popular at gatherings of warriors, were finally put into writing and thus given a wider circulation. The most famous of these was the *Nibelungenlied,* which had grown up during the days of the migrations, and even earlier, and the *Chanson de Roland,* which found its origin in Charlemagne's invasion of Spain. These epic poems were filled with the pageantry of tournaments and deeds of arms in behalf of the weak and the Church. Nor can the influence of Bernard of Clairvaux and his efforts in behalf of the Knights Templars be overlooked, for in the military monastic orders the ideals of Christian knighthood reached their highest level in practice. All these forces were even more clearly reflected in the development of a new literature intended for the noble class alone. This was the court epic, or stories of the Knights of the Round Table of King Arthur's Court. Though originating probably in the Celtic lands of Britain and Brittany, these stories were circulated and rewritten in various lands of Europe, some of the finest of them being composed in France and Germany at about this time. The lofty plot which held them together, the quest of the Holy Grail and service to King Arthur, gave inspiration to the fraternity of knighthood everywhere and formed a distinct class literature.

The social life of the nobility centered in the castles, large fortress homes, which, during the twelfth century, were under-going great transformation. Intended originally as shelter in case of attack, they had passed through a steady evolution with the changing methods of warfare. They were now taking on their final form, in which so many of them have been preserved to the present time. The idea of the fortress, impregnable to attack, was still the dominant factor in their construction. But they were larger, of heavier masonry and more skillful construction and were, as a rule, provided with great open courts in which the joy of life as well as its danger could find room for expression. Such castles, however, were beyond the means of a simple knight or even lesser noble. The resources of a small county at least were necessary to build and maintain such structures. Kings and greater nobles usually had several such castles scattered over their domain. In England at this time the kings attempted to keep all the castles under their own control. As the twelfth cen-tury moved on, the passage of time was marked in castle con-struction by an increasing regard for the comfort of its res-idents. The castle afforded room not only for the noble and his family, but also for numerous knights and servants of various kinds, and in emergency the open court became a refuge for the peasantry.

The ménage of the castle usually included, in addition to its military personnel, one chaplain or more, who conducted religious services and taught the elements of liberal arts to the children of the nobility. It frequently included also entertainers, though, as a rule, entertainments were furnished by professional itinerant performers who recited, sang, danced and performed acrobatic feats. Music was much appreciated, and the knowledge of stringed instruments was becoming a knightly accomplishment. Bare walls and floors were softened by tapestries and rugs, often imported from the East. The knights engaged in gentle games, chess coming into vogue at this time, and entertainments were more frequent than in former days. Hospitality to strangers and the exchange of noble gossip occupied a more prominent place than heretofore. The ladies of the castle filled important posi-tions. Much of the management of the household fell to their lot, and when the fighting men were gone on long campaigns the lady managed the whole castle. She took a large part in the social training of the candidates for knighthood and usually kept herself well informed on feudal gossip.

As in the case of the clergy, so also in that of the nobles, extensive travel became very common during this period. The crusades afforded an opportunity for the fighting men of all of Christendom to make the journey to Syria. The necessity of holding the Latin states established in the East offered a constant and urgent invitation for the adventurous to make the same journey. The crusading zeal aroused increased activity in Sicily, Spain and northeastern Germany, where holy wars were likewise carried on at this time. These travels opened up other possibilities for adventure along the way, so that the knight marked with the cross had little need to suffer from the monotony of his journey. Knight-errantry was never more general than in the twelfth century and appealed especially to the younger knights and the younger sons of nobles whose opportunities at home were limited. Knights from western Europe were to be found in almost all parts of eastern and southern Europe, where, like the Normans, many a one established himself in control of principalities and sometimes even of kingdoms. The effect of this extensive travel was to establish a widespread knowledge of various manners and customs which led inevitably to imitation and adaptation of what seemed best in foreign lands. Castles, dress and manners, as well as weapons of war, became more or less standardized and western civilization began its series of fashions which have increased in sweep and change ever since. This cultivation of a common taste was a great help to commerce and industry, as well as an aid to civilization as a whole.

CHAPTER VIII
(Concluded)

EUROPEAN SOCIETY IN THE TWELFTH CENTURY

III. THE CULTIVATORS OF THE SOIL

THE third class of society, the peasantry, was larger and more varied in character than either of the others, or, indeed, than the other two combined. The one trait that its members had in common was that they gained their living by manual labor. They were the workers. In the earlier periods they had not been so sharply differentiated, especially among the tribesmen, though the Romans had had a highly developed caste system. As life became more settled after the centuries of migration and feudal disorder, the gulf between the classes noticeably widened, and in the literature of the twelfth century the workers are either not mentioned at all or are named with scorn. Villain, the class name applied to the partially free, grew to be synonymous with the term rogue. And yet, no class was so differentiated or is so difficult to describe under common characterizations.

Most of the workers were engaged directly or indirectly in agriculture. But the character of their labor varied with the nature of the region in which they lived, whether in rugged country or flat, whether in warm climate or in cold, whether on the seacoast or inland. And few parts of the world possess wider variations of soil, climate and topography in so narrow a space as Europe. The status of the peasants as free or unfree varied even more widely, for their position was affected by the character of their labor and the nature of their homeland, and also by the racial and social traditions of their environment. The proportion of freemen was higher in the more homogeneous countries of the north than in the much mixed regions of the south, higher also in the rugged upland regions and on the edges of a country. In Brittany, for example, which was homogeneous and rugged and in the outlying portion of Europe, serfdom was almost nonexistent, whereas in many other places it was the rule.

The usual rural community consisted of villages of various types. The land of Europe was not yet completely occupied. Deep forests, unoccupied prairies and undrained lowlands were still dominant features in the landscape. Much of this had never been occupied; some of it had once been occupied in Roman days but had reverted to its primitive condition during the centuries of disorder that followed. Such lands were characterized as waste lands, but most of them awaited only a more peaceful age when men could learn to cultivate them. That age was clearly dawning in the twelfth century. As yet, however, the agricultural villages lay mostly in valleys and on edges of waste lands. In some places they were concentrated, the houses forming a central nucleus with the arable lands lying in blocks around the center. In others the houses straggled along a single road, the arable land extending on either side some distance along the road. Sometimes the houses stretched along the road at intervals, as though each house were the center of a separate farm. Combinations of the first and third, more frequently of the second and third, types also occurred. These combinations usually indicated a population of more mixed status, with free farmers on the separate farms and villains of various types in the clustered village center. The settlements reflected the feudal condition of the time, the land being theoretically owned by the ruling class, on which even the free farmer with his fixed piece of land was dependent.

Most of these rural settlements were organized as manors. Their management depended upon a number of circumstances. If the noble had only the one estate, he would manage it himself; if he had several, he would place a bailiff in charge of the separate manors. These were usually freemen. Sometimes there was placed in charge an official called *prévot,* or provost, elected by the villagers themselves. If the lord had extensive holdings, he might entrust the management of a series of manors to a seneschal of free and even noble rank, with many bailiffs and provosts under him. In such cases careful accounts were usually kept, often with the help of clerics. As a rule, the management was divided and a considerable portion left to the peasants themselves, particularly the arrangement of shifting services, such as plowing, haying and harvesting. The oversight of the manorial buildings and their use remained in the hands of the lord's representative. The relation of the peasantry to the managers of the rural estates was not any more harmonious than that existing between vassal and lord. Each class was naturally ready to advance its own interests. The lord's representative was apt to increase the amounts due from the peasants, and the peasants, in their turn, avoided payment. At times, especially when there was crop failure, there was often trouble unless the lord shared the loss. As money came into wider use, the peasants found it easier to improve their condition.

Naturally the system of agriculture varied, but there was usually some rotation of crops and resting of the soil. The constant use of the same piece of land year after year by means of regular fertilizing was not unknown at this time, but the three-field system was the common practice. This meant that all the arable land was treated as a unit, one-third of it being planted in the late fall, another third being sown in the spring, while the remaining third was allowed to rest or lie fallow. The crop on any given piece of land was rotated every three years. Under the three-field system, the lands of lord and peasant, freeman and villain, were pooled. Class rights were maintained, however, by the simple device of dividing the ploughed fields into strips. Each then received as many of these strips as his station required, and the strips were scattered so that no one should have only the choice land or only the poor land. The portion belonging to the lord, usually a generous fraction of the whole, was called domain or demesne land. All the land was worked by the peasants, freemen cultivating their own portions. The partially free divided their labor between the portions allotted to them and those of the lord. As this service was regular, it was sometimes called week work, being reckoned at so many days per week for different degrees of villainage. At the critical periods of the year, such as plowing, haying and harvesting, when the coöperation of many hands was necessary, all the free and unfree were called upon to help on the lord's land. This was called boon-work.

The meadow land and forest were more directly under the lord. Grazing and wood rights were reserved by him, also, but they might be shared by the peasants under conditions which involved a generous payment to the lord. The barns and mill belonged to the lord and might be used by the peasants on similar terms. The flocks and herds were usually tended together by the unfree herdsmen in the employ of the lord. The amount of produce of different kinds which the peasants paid to the lord, in addition to the service which they gave him, was fixed by local custom and varied in different parts of Europe. Payments, as a rule, were in kind, but money was coming into more general use during the twelfth century.

The buildings of the lord were usually grouped together, and if the manor was the permanent home of a great lord, they might all be enclosed within the walls of an imposing castle. Ordinarily, however, this was not the case. The lord's representative or the petty lord himself lived in a more or less imposing stone house called the manor-house. Near by were the barns, some used as granaries and storehouses, others as stables for the different animals. Poultry roosts, a dairy, usually also a brewery or cider-press or wine-press might occupy separate buildings or be scattered through the other buildings. The whole group was regularly inclosed within a wall or hedge of some kind. Here was centered the economic interest of the feudal lord. His crops and herds and flocks were gathered here. The customary dues in kind were delivered here. It was a magazine of foodstuffs and, to a certain extent, it was also a manufacturing establishment. Dairy products, beverages of various kinds and textile materials were prepared in it. The domestic servants and herdsmen who worked and lived there regularly received periodic assistance from the villagers, both men and women. The former were in special demand at threshing time, while the latter were called upon for aid in spinning and weaving the textile materials.

The stores of material, both raw and manufactured, which were accumulated here served either to provide for the itinerant owner and his following or furnished a surplus which was sold at nearby markets.

The buildings of the peasantry were usually a little distance away from the manorial enclosure and composed the village proper. There was usually a village church with its accompanying churchyard and parish house for the priest. There was often a village smithy, and most manors also had mills in which the grain was ground. The mill might be located on a stream and apart from the main cluster of houses. Usually there was a bake-oven, built of brick or stone, near the mills. This served the whole community, the housewives taking turn in preparing their bread supply for two or three weeks. Most of the buildings were houses of villagers, free and unfree. Practically all of the homes had more or less extensive garden plots connected with them. Both homes and gardens varied in size according to the status of the peasant who possessed them. The houses of the peasants were, as a rule, not yet built of stone. Wood, or plastered wattle, or even clay-coated framework usually served for walls, which were covered over with a thatched roof.

The peasant's home often sheltered his livestock and poultry as well as his family and himself. In a certain sense his one house served for all the uses to which the buildings on the manorial inclosure were put. He usually dug pits in which to store his winter supply of grain and vegetables. The rafters of his house were often hung with smoked meats and strings or bags of dry vegetables, fruits and nuts. The furniture was of the simplest and scantiest. A spinning-wheel, some sort of loom, utensils for cooking and a few tools constituted the more complicated furnishings and indicated that the peasant's home was also his workshop, as it was his storehouse and stable, too. All members of the household shared in the labor. The peasant's wife had by no means the lightest lot. She cared for the children, who were usually quite numerous, prepared their food and made their clothing. She assisted her husband in caring for the cattle and poultry, in working the garden, and often at his work in the

field as well.   In addition, she had her own duties to the lady of
the manor.   The children had duties also as soon as they grew
strong enough to be of any help.

The social life of the village revolved chiefly around the church,
whose festivals and sacramental services afforded opportunities
for mental and social diversion.   There was usually merry-making
and exchange of gossip enough to satisfy the simple needs of
young and old.   The gatherings for special work at the manor-
house were likewise often accompanied with feasts and merrymak-
ing.   There was relatively little contact with the outside world.
If the village was not too far from the site of a fair, the villagers
might go to look at the varied goods and entertainment exhibited
there during fair-time.   Periodically, one or another member of
practically every family would visit the nearest market town.
The men, at least, would have some opportunity, more or less
often in their lives, to go considerable distances for special supplies, such as salt or mill-stones and iron.   Aside from such occasions, their contact with the world was usually limited to the
visits of travelers, whose number varied according to the importance of the road which ran through the village.   Such travelers were often churchmen or soldiers, but merchants were
becoming increasingly numerous.   A wayfaring minstrel or a
band of entertainers doubtless was a most welcome, if only occasional, interruption to the routine of life.

The description of the peasantry so far has dealt only with
those in the agricultural communities.   While most of the peasantry were so engaged, there were other types of laboring communities.   The iron and salt so necessary to manorial economy were
mined at various places in Europe.   Other metals, too, were being
mined, and charcoal-burning had come to be a subsidiary industry to the smelting of ores.   Communities engaged in mining were
usually located in remote places in the hills and on the edges of
the forests.   Salt was either mined, as in the Danube and east-
Alpine regions, or obtained along the seacoast.   There were also
villages along the seacoast whose chief occupation was fishing.
The sum total of such communities had not yet reached proportions which seriously modified the economic life of the age, but

signs of expansion were not wanting. For the most part even these communities engaged in enough agriculture to fill their needs. The profits of special industries were usually monopolized by king or great noble.

The twelfth century was, however, an age of economic expansion unlike any previous age in medieval history. The phase of this expansion most immediate to the agricultural peasantry was the invasion of the so-called waste lands. The relative prevalence of peace was perhaps chiefly responsible for this movement. It employed surplus labor hitherto used in war and it gave the nobility an opportunity to vary their preparation for war with interest in the management of their estates. Increased travel furnished ideas and the increased use of money an incentive. Under such a combination of influences, the work of draining lowlands, clearing forests and utilizing prairie land went on with great enthusiasm. The Cistercian Order of monks was a pioneer in this work, but kings and nobles, as well as prelates, were quick to see the opportunities. Many a Villeneuve, or Neuburg, or Newton on the map of Europe today is a living monument to this agricultural expansion of the later twelfth century. The feudal lords drew off the surplus labor from their estates and set them to work on these clearings. The promoters frequently enticed serfs from other holdings with the promise of greater liberties. Owners of established manors had to hold their serfs by improving their condition.

The circumstances which favored the promotion of new agricultural communities likewise favored the growth of towns whose chief occupation was industry. Pilgrim travel to the Holy Land, or Rome, or less distant shrines, crusading troops on their way to or from the East, emissaries of kings and great nobles, or representatives of the Church journeying back and forth on distant business, made necessary the concentration of food and shelter at points along the important highways. At the same time the more general use of money encouraged trade and industry, which tended to develop at these same centers. Once the roads were improved and the practice of carrying foodstuffs and other supplies to consuming centers was established, there was added incentive for the nobility to erect permanent houses, large spacious castles of stone which called loudly for articles of comfort and luxury.   Contact with other peoples, especially with the higher civilizations to the south and east, caused a knowledge of, and a desire for, articles to be made nearer home.   The improved standard of living reflected in the homes of the nobility required more and finer products of industry which could only be met by specially trained laborers.

Rural communities and villages had but little need of such laborers, and the manorial enclosures required very few.   A manor might have a smith who could do all the necessary kinds of welding.   A miller might spend much of his time at the mill, but he doubtless found time for some agriculture as well.   A thatcher and carpenter would probably serve a number of manors. Fullers and dyers doubtless served an even wider community. Masons likewise traveled wide distances in carrying on their work.   Such workmen received their living, and perhaps a money wage in addition.   With the advance in agricultural development during the twelfth century, some of the greater landowners kept a number of special workmen occupied from manor to manor, as occasion demanded.   They added to the number of foresters, vintners, brewers, carters and wagoners.

The town communities which were clustered around bishoprics, monasteries and feudal courts, required other special laborers. There bakers and cooks were in special demand.   Tanners and weavers, saddlers and shoemakers, usually were to be found there also, while hat-makers and milliners could be expected at court towns.   Masons and carpenters had their headquarters in the towns, probably also the fullers and dyers.   The demand for smiths was constant and great enough to permit some of them to specialize in the finer metals alone.   Carters and wagoners were essential, of course.   Before the twelfth century there were few towns where the workers did not largely supplement their special occupations with some agricultural labor.

During the twelfth century, however, there was a marked change.   Many new villages sprang up, old villages grew into towns, and some towns, notably in Italy and in Flanders, became actual cities. A poet of the later decades of that century describes his native village as having only one cart in his grandfather's day, whereas in his own time it contained five hundred carts. Such economic expansion is rivaled only by the town development of the nineteenth century. Agriculture ceased to be an important element in the industry of larger towns. The special occupations increased in number and refinement. Bakers grew in number, and some were able to devote themselves to the baking of pastry alone. The making of leather ranged from tanning to the manufacture of fine leather products, each separate operation becoming a special occupation in itself. Cloth-making and metal-work developed even wider ranges than that of leather. Carpentry and masonry likewise expanded to include artistic effort. Towns which had already developed reputations for excellence in particular products expanded those occupations. This movement continued with greater force in the next century and will be discussed in connection with the development of commerce.

This industrial development had very important consequences for the peasantry. It implied the use of money, which reached out even to remote rural communities. In many places thrifty serfs were able to substitute money payments for service dues and ultimately even to purchase their freedom from all service obligations. This movement was clearly under way in a number of places in the twelfth century. Normandy might be cited as an excellent example. Hand in hand with this development was a movement of the peasants to the towns where they could enjoy greater freedom. Industry had expanded so rapidly that its demands could not be met by the mere increase in the town population. Additional labor was obtained from the rural communities. Freemen, serfs who had purchased their freedom and serfs who ran away were tempted to enter the industrial field in the towns. Many of them came to perform unskilled labor, but, once there, learned some craft or other. Nearly every town charter granted during this period contained a provision that, if a serf had lived a year and a day in the town, he was thereafter immune from seizure and return to serfdom. Nothing could be more eloquent of the effect which the industrial development was having upon serfdom. It both widened and increased the paths to promotion.

Hitherto the chief avenue out of serfdom had been the service of the Church, as the careers of Gerbert and Suger so brilliantly testify. The parish priest in training his altar boys might discover a youth of unusual endowment and obtain permission from the lord of the manor to send the boy on to school. Better still if, as in the case of the two men already mentioned, such youths lived near a monastery. Then the chances of their discovery and also the opportunities for their education were much greater. If the youth became a priest, he was automatically free and in a position to obtain freedom for his immediate relatives as well. Doubtless the devoted servile mother entertained hopes of such careers for her sons. This avenue to freedom and distinction was still open to the peasantry. In fact, the great expansion in the business of the Church which had been going on in the eleventh and twelfth centuries had greatly increased such opportunities, for there were now many more positions for persons of learning. That expansion continued throughout the thirteenth century.

It would be a mistake to assume that the peasantry were altogether discontented with their lot. Among themselves they were not greatly conscious of limitations on their freedom. In fact, there seems reason to believe that they were quite satisfied with their careers, for the oldest son was the one to whom the villain holding of the parent went. There was certainty in such an occupation and probably most of the peasantry preferred certain living as villains to an uncertain venture into unknown careers which might lead to wealth and distinction, but which might also lead to slavery and worse. The more enterprising and venturesome among them, however, could seek advancement, and before the end of the twelfth century the bolder and abler of the peasantry might aspire to wealth, distinction and power. Probably it was from the free peasantry that most of the venturesome came, but the records indicate that the humblest serfs also furnished a large proportion of them.

CERTAIN differences in the period which followed the death of Bernard of Clairvaux mark it off rather sharply from the preceding century. The spirit of the former age was not entirely gone, but instead of the monk, it was the Christian knight who played the leading rôle. It was as if ceremonial knighthood, the crusades, and literature in general had combined to sanctify the profession of arms and to give to its leaders almost a priestly status. The preceding period had witnessed the growth of a fraternity of knighthood which was as wide as the Church, but this fraternity was primarily a servant of the Church and not a separate organization.

The unity of Christendom was now approached in political affairs. Governmental units formerly divided were united under one leader, and these larger groups together covered the width of Latin Christendom. A disturbance in one region was no longer of interest to that locality alone or to the Church, which extended everywhere, but equally concerned political leaders nearly everywhere in Europe.

The most definite expression of this development was to be seen in the increased power of the kings. Political interest concentrated in them as it had not done since Carolingian days. To some extent this was not a new condition in Germany, where the kings since Henry I had always been of general consequence, even though personally weak. In France and England the tide began to turn. A single feudal noble was no longer able to ignore or defy his king with any hope of success. To hold their former independence, it was now necessary for the nobles to make alliances with each other, or, better still, with rival kings. This necessity tended more and more to restrict feudal independence to the border districts, a circumstance curiously reminiscent of the days when the Carolingian kings began to lose their power. The movement now was in the opposite direction. Alliances came to have a paramount interest, and diplomacy, the art of political persuasion, which had hitherto been used almost exclusively by churchmen, was now becoming the province of nobles and kings. In this change may be detected the influence of the Church, of Roman law, of commercial development, and of contact with the more highly advanced countries of the East, especially with the Byzantine Empire. All operated to the same end.

RISE OF THE HOHENSTAUFENS. FREDERICK I, BARBAROSSA

The king of Germany still occupied the most prominent place in political affairs, partly because it had become customary to associate the title of Emperor of the Holy Roman Empire with that office. No ruler of any other region had held that title since 962, and every German king confidently expected to receive it. The nobles who elected him had likewise come to assume that they were electing the emperor as well as the king. Theoretically, the papacy was free to grant the title and crown to anyone, but the German connections were so fully established that custom exercised its imperious sway over both papacy and German nobles. At the most, the popes at times withheld the crown, but it was not given to anyone else, and even under such circumstances the king of Germany was regularly referred to as emperor-elect.

In 1154 Conrad III, whom Bernard of Clairvaux had persuaded to go on the Second Crusade, was succeeded by his young nephew, Frederick of Hohenstaufen. Frederick I, commonly called Frederick Barbarossa, began his reign under more favorable auspices than any German king or emperor since Henry III. The Church for which Conrad III had sacrificed so heavily was very well disposed toward the successor designated by the dying emperor. Furthermore, Frederick was very closely related to the leaders of the rival noble factions in Germany. As a result, he began his reign with a united kingdom such as his predecessors had gained only after a life-long struggle. He was, therefore, free to devote most of his attention to affairs outside Germany, a program which suited his ambition.

During his first five years as emperor Frederick became acquainted with conditions in Italy, where marked changes had taken place. Politically, there were now four forces in operation: the Norman kingdom in the south, the papacy, the nobility, and the towns. The first two were not materially changed. The nobility represented a foreign institution superimposed upon Italy from outside. As a rule, the nobles were opposed to the reform papacy as well as to the rising townsmen. The result was that the nobility sought protection by class alliances among themselves. The broken character of the country in central Italy, especially in the Papal States, was very favorable to feudal control, and here the nobility were numerous. Here, too, they came into conflict with the papacy, which had title to the land. In northern Italy, which was low and fertile and the highway of the most important trade routes of Europe, towns developed to great size. Venice and Milan were foremost in importance. Venice had never afforded a very firm footing for the maneuvering of armored feudal nobles, but its trade routes ran over the mainland, and this fact brought it into contact with the feudal nobility. Milan had been under feudal control, as had also the other lesser towns along the route. The interests of commerce and of feudalism were inevitably in conflict, and as the towns grew they shook themselves free from direct control of the nobles and began to extend their military operations over the surrounding country. In some cases, wars developed between cities, the smaller towns around Milan being especially fearful of their larger neighbor. Frederick's great problem in Italy was to fix upon a policy of dealing with these diverse elements.

He was still young and had exalted notions of his position. He was also a knight and shared the prejudices of his class. An incident in his coronation journey to Rome is indicative of his attitude and character. He refused to hold the pope's stirrup, regarding the implied request as an insult to his dignity, until his advisers convinced him that it was merely an old custom. Even then he performed the task grudgingly. Hadrian IV, the pope at this time, was an Englishman who had risen from very humble station to the highest office in the Church. His conception of his office, however, was quite as lofty as that held by his predecessors, and he was not ready to yield to Frederick's pride. Other differences of more serious nature occurred later between the two, but at this time they were able to treat each other in a friendly fashion. Frederick rendered a service to the pope by turning over to him Arnold of Brescia, the eloquent pupil of Abélard who had led an uprising of the townsmen in Rome against papal control. Hadrian repaid Frederick by crowning him emperor.

On his second journey to Italy Frederick came more fully into contact with the towns. He took with him a large army and marched against Milan, presumably as the champion of the smaller towns which had suffered from her aggressions. A siege of several weeks forced the townsmen to terms, and Frederick had the pleasure of receiving their consuls with swords tied about their throats. Later in the year, Frederick had a commission composed of professors of law from Bologna and representatives of the towns report on the rights and regalia of the emperor. These reported at the Diet of Roncaglia in 1158 in favor of very extensive imperial rights regarding matters of justice, coinage and administration. In accordance with their report, Frederick appointed a representative called *podesta* to exercise these rights in each town. Theoretically, this marked a great advance in the substitution of law for force as the basis of government, and was a triumph of the new study of Roman law. Practically, it meant that the towns were again subject to outside government, from which they had hitherto freed themselves. It meant, also, that they were to be controlled by men who were both foreign and feudal, for Frederick appointed as these officials his own German knights. Friction was bound to occur, and the townsmen forgot their own rivalries in a united opposition to this interference. Had Frederick appointed men of sympathy and understanding through whom the townsmen might have received the blessings of political order and encouragement of trade, the result would probably have been different. As it was, the scheme appeared merely an extension of Frederick's power into Italy and alarmed the papacy as well as the townsmen.

Frederick and Hadrian IV were never truly friends. Under the advice of his chancellor and other men trained in the Church, Frederick found a means of filling important Church offices in Germany without violating the letter of the law. His extension of authority into Italy threatened to bring about a similar situation there. To this Hadrian was decidedly opposed, but there were as yet no overt acts which could be made the basis of a struggle. The feeling had become quite tense when Hadrian died in 1159.

A double election followed, and the majority candidate took the title Alexander III. He had been the adviser of Hadrian IV and was a skilled student of law. The minority candidate was supported by only a few cardinals, but by a powerful group of Roman nobles, and was generally considered the imperial candidate. This view received confirmation from the fact that Frederick almost immediately espoused his cause. It was a sign of the times, however, that Frederick did not violently set up an antipope, as Henry IV had done, but scrupulously followed the forms of law in having some of the cardinals elect him. The election seemed disputed, like that of 1131, and Frederick encouraged this idea by inviting other monarchs and leading men to join him in a council, to determine which was the rightful pope. This move enabled Frederick to retain the support of most of his clergy and nobility, and indicated that the emperor was following very learned and shrewd advisers.

Alexander III found Rome an uncomfortable place of residence and fled to France, where he sought support in his campaign for recognition. There was now no Bernard of Clairvaux to conduct the campaign for him, but Alexander III was a man of greater ability and skill than Innocent II had been. The struggle lasted for eighteen years. Alexander very early gained recognition in France and in the extensive domain of the king of England. He also had the support of Sicily and the towns of northern Italy. He may be regarded, in general, as representing the principles of the reform papacy of earlier days, but the issue was so cleverly confused by Frederick's procedure that, during the whole period, his position was never entirely certain. Frederick's agents were busy throughout this time calling for councils to determine the rightful pope, or seeking recognition for their candidate. In this way there was kept alive the possibility that the countries favoring Alexander might change their allegiance, and this fact weakened the power of the papacy in dealing with undesirable developments.

THE ANGLO-NORMAN EMPIRE. HENRY II

In no part of Europe was this uncertainty as to the rightful pope more consequential than in the Anglo-Norman Empire of Henry II, king of England. This empire had been formed as a result of the conquest of England by William, duke of Normandy, in 1066. The term "conquest" applied to this event has been misleading and has made unintelligible what happened afterward. As Haskins has so clearly pointed out, the Normans and the people of England had much in common. The Scandinavian strain was certainly common to both. Trading relations between Rouen and London were well established and political intercourse had become increasingly intimate. The English king, Æthelred, had married Emma, daughter of the Norman duke, in 1002. She was married a second time to Canute, Æthelred's successor (1017-1035), and her son Edward the Confessor ruled from 1042 to 1066. During all this time the relations between England and Normandy were very intimate. Edward had taken many Normans into his service and both Edward and Harold had given William reason to expect the inheritance of the English crown. The war of 1066 was, therefore, more truly dynastic than many historians have held, and this view is further supported by the relatively brief resistance which was offered to Duke William. Had the war been one of national resistance, the success of the small army which accompanied William could scarcely be explained. As it was, the only portion of the English people seriously displaced by the "conquest" were the nobles, and not all of these. The great majority of the people were practically undisturbed by the victory of the Normans.

The advent of William and his barons was of service to England in several ways. It brought to an end the intermittent struggle which had resulted from the coming of the Vikings nearly three centuries before. It brought England into close touch with the affairs of continental Europe and thus enabled the English to share in the advance of civilization which had there taken place. It also gave to England a strong central government, superior in many respects to any on the Continent, and fundamental to the growth of many of those institutions which characterize the English government of modern times. William, who ruled until 1087, and his third son, Henry I, who ruled from 1100 to 1135, were not only strong rulers, but also remarkable business men, a rare combination at any time. In his *Domesday Book* William made an inventory of the lands of England, which gave his successors a sounder basis for taxation and government than that possessed by any other ruler of their time. The excesses of feudalism, so common on the Continent, were avoided in many ways. It may almost be said that William introduced feudalism only as a means of paying his debts to the men who had served him. He did not depend upon it for military organization, for he very carefully required the direct allegiance of all fighting men to himself, regardless of what other feudal connections they might have. Castles were treated as royal fortresses under the king's appointed custodians, and private castles were forbidden. The finances of the realm were organized under a central exchequer and justice was brought under royal control. The rule of the Norman kings was productive of more good results in England than on the Continent, where old feudal customs interfered with the full exercise of their power.

The twenty years following the death of Henry I were years of unrest, owing to the rival claims of Henry's daughter, Matilda, and of his nephew. The latter, Stephen of Blois, gained the crown, but the disorder which attended his whole reign nearly undid the work of William and Henry. Nobles built castles and usurped jurisdiction after the continental fashion. Meanwhile, Henry's grandson was growing up in Anjou, of which his father was count. At intervals during his youth he had gone to England to keep alive his mother's claim to the crown. His education was excellent, and the youth, also named Henry, proved an unusual pupil. His father succeeded in gaining Normandy for him and, with this in his control, Henry was able to press his claims upon England. Even before Stephen's death he was recognized as the heir to the English throne, to which he succeeded without dispute when Stephen died in 1154. Two years before he had married Eleanor of Aquitaine, who had just been separated from Louis VII of France.

The lands over which Henry II ruled included nearly the whole of western France from the Pyrenees to the Channel, as well as England, an empire nearly as large as that of Frederick. In a certain sense, it was even more compact, for the Channel was less a barrier than the Alps, differences in race and customs less marked than they were in Frederick's empire, and commercial relations just as lively. The problems involved in ruling it were many, but Henry was fully equal to the task. He returned immediately to the practices of his grandfather. Private castles were torn down or taken over by the king's officials. Very few remained in private hands. The exchequer was restored and operated with scrupulous care. Royal officials, called justices, went about to look after the king's lands which were scattered over England, and, incidentally, they kept a close watch upon the nobles. They were also sent around to administer the king's justice in various parts of the realm. Henry's legislation for the improvement of local justice, though little noticed outside of England in his time, has had a lasting effect and has won the admiration of the world. Charters were granted to towns, and merchants were protected by Henry to a degree hitherto unknown. Accounts were strictly kept, and the precision of his chancery has aroused the admiration of scholars ever since. All these measures helped to fill the royal treasury and caused Henry to be regarded as the wealthiest monarch in Europe. Henry also knew how to use this wealth for the increase of his power. Though he was a knight and had received knighthood in approved ceremonial fashion from the king of Scotland, he never allowed himself to be blinded by knightly prejudices, as Stephen had done and as Frederick was doing. He was quite willing to appoint men of common class to his service, and he was more than willing to hire mercenaries as soldiers. In fact, he encouraged his nobles to commute their knights' service for money payments, which he used to maintain his mercenary forces.

Henry was equally successful in managing the border problems. He attacked the Welsh in several campaigns and finally reached an understanding with them which made them friendly neighbors. Welsh troops played an important part in his military operations and Welshmen were prominent among his advisers. He early developed a plan for the invasion of Ireland, for which he received papal approval from Hadrian IV. The Scots were skillfully dealt with and Henry had little trouble from them throughout his reign.

On the Continent his problems were complicated by the fact that he was vassal of the king of France for all his lands there. His attitude toward the king of France was scrupulously correct, according to the best standards of feudal observance, but he did not allow this attitude to interfere with the management of his own lands. He used all the arts of diplomacy to keep the French king from doing him any damage, and he confined his efforts toward expansion on the Continent to those regions in which his direct allegiance to Louis was not involved. Henry was a fighter, but he preferred diplomacy when that could accomplish his purpose. He has been called an inveterate match-maker, and he was a master at this game, but such matches were usually made with a definite political end in view. He betrothed his son Henry to the daughter of Louis VII of France and provided that certain border lands near Normandy should constitute her dowry. When the children were only about five years old, Henry took advantage of the presence of papal legates to have the marriage solemnized, and then seized the dowry as belonging to his son. This act was strictly legal and involved no breach of his feudal bond to Louis, but Louis, nevertheless, felt tricked. In a somewhat similar fashion Henry obtained Brittany, first lower Brittany, and then the whole of it.

HENRY II AND THE CHURCH. THOMAS À BECKET

The problem of the Church was a difficult one for Henry, as it was for other rulers who attempted to cope with it. The Normans of England had generally adopted that independent attitude toward the Church which the Normans of southern Italy had assumed. They were determined to be masters in their own households, professing at the same time the greatest reverence for the papacy. William had sought the pope's sanction for the invasion of England and Henry did likewise for his invasion of Ireland. Both, however, insisted that the clergy within their realm should coöperate with, if not always obey, them. Henry II filled the leading Church offices with his adherents, but he observed the correct forms, as in the case of Thomas à Becket, his chancellor, whom he made archbishop of Canterbury.

Thomas, the son of a tradesman, had been thoroughly trained as a churchman, having studied theology at Paris and law at Bologna. Henry had taken a fancy to him and had made him chancellor, a post which Thomas filled in a most impressive manner. When the archbishopric became vacant, Henry determined to put his friend into that office. He sent word to the monks of Christ Church, with whom the election lay, to proceed with an election, but to choose Thomas. This was done in 1162. Perhaps Henry hoped to control the Church in England more thoroughly by having his chancellor at the head of it. He had designs upon the jurisdiction of the Church courts, which were a source both of income and authority. The extension of royal power had weakened the nobles as well as enriched the treasury, and perhaps a similar extension into the domain of the Church courts might afford even greater gains. The entering wedge lay in the abuse of ecclesiastical justice by criminals who were, or professed to be, clerics and therefore subject only to the Church courts, whose penalties were much milder than those of the secular courts. Unfortunately, few men realized as clearly as Thomas just what this move of the king's meant. Thomas had been reluctant to take the office of archbishop, but upon Henry's insistence he yielded, and almost immediately resigned the office of chancellor. This move was a clear indication that he no longer considered himself the servant of the king. Few knew the workings of Henry's mind better than Thomas, and he was now in a position to thwart Henry's schemes, which he did.

The struggle between Henry and Thomas à Becket was all the more bitter because of their former friendship and because the situation of the papacy was such that Henry had reasonable hopes of avoiding interference from that source. After a few preliminary skirmishes between them, in which Thomas attacked several of Henry's plans for gaining money or privilege at the expense of the clergy, matters came to a head in the council held at Clarendon in 1164. Henry here presented the so-called *Constitutions of Clarendon,* setting forth his view of certain ancient customs of the realm, and requested the clergy to accept them. Henry employed all the pressure that he could, short of physical violence, and finally persuaded Thomas to change his abrupt refusal into a reluctant and cautious acceptance. These Constitutions set down in definite form some rights which kings had occasionally exercised, but which the Church, since the time of Gregory VII, could scarcely have approved. They gave to the king not only extensive jurisdiction over the affairs of the clergy, but also established the right of appeal from the archbishop's court to the king's court and made journeys to Rome conditional upon the king's permission. Trouble followed when Henry tried to put these Constitutions into effect, and Thomas fled to France, where he hoped to escape further pressure. Here he remained in exile for six years. Pope Alexander, who naturally sided with Thomas, was not in a position to force matters, for Henry's representatives at the court of Frederick seriously considered recognition of Alexander's rival. The pope, therefore, had to content himself with remonstrances and efforts at mediation.

Thomas carried on an epistolary campaign of denunciation and wholesale excommunication against his enemies. Henry replied by seizing all of the lands of the archbishop and by beggaring the relatives and loyal friends of Thomas. The men whom Thomas had excommunicated appealed to the pope, a proceeding which suspended the effect of the ban. It was warfare under the form of law and without violence. Many of the clergy and all of the important nobles remained loyal to Henry. Only the king of France, who was glad to see his too powerful vassal and neighbor embarrassed, gave much real encouragement to Thomas. Finally the efforts of the pope brought about a reconciliation and Thomas returned to England in 1170. The peace did not last long, however, for Thomas became involved in a serious quarrel with some of Henry's adherents and excommunicated them. News of this action roused Henry to a furious burst of anger. Four knights thought to gain Henry's favor by ridding him of Thomas, and accordingly they went to Canterbury where they fell upon Thomas and killed him within the church.

All Christendom was horrified at this outrage and Henry's careful work of years seemed shattered by one rash act. King Louis and the leading clergy of France wrote to the pope urging him to excommunicate Henry and even to preach a crusade against him. Henry was equal to the emergency. He dispatched representatives to the pope with generous gifts as evidence of his devotion and disavowed responsibility for the act. The actual murderers were excommunicated, and an interdict laid upon the continental portion of Henry's domain by the archbishop of Sens was confirmed, though Henry was personally exempted. Envoys were sent to fix the terms of absolution. Meanwhile, Henry found the opportunity to go to Ireland, which his forces had invaded, a welcome respite before the arrival of the envoys. In 1172 he was back in Normandy to receive the terms of absolution from the papal legates. These were arranged after some argument, and the final document was a diplomatic achievement. It imposed some penance, including a promise to go on a crusade, but it did not settle the question at issue between Henry and Thomas. However, it did contain Henry's promise not to recognize Alexander's opponent, a concession which somewhat weakened Henry's position.

The difficulties which Henry experienced as a result of the murder of Thomas à Becket aroused high hopes in the breasts of his opponents. The quick action of the French ecclesiastics in writing to the pope was only partially the result of righteous indignation. They were much concerned about the kingdom of France, which was trembling beneath the towering shadows of the two empires which surrounded it. King Louis VII had viewed in helpless alarm the unification of Henry's dominion, but the clever diplomacy of Henry in outwardly observing the forms of vassalage and in arranging marriage alliances with the daughters of Louis quite disarmed the French king. In former years, and under the guidance of his counselor, Suger, Louis had followed a policy of royal aggrandizement similar to that now adopted by Henry, but after Suger's death in 1151 Louis had lost the art. Since 1154 his concern had been largely defensive.

The effort to capitalize Henry's difficulties with the papacy was foiled, but the opposition found another outlet by playing upon the ambitions of Henry's sons. Under the prodding of Louis and his advisers, Henry, the oldest son, already crowned as king to succeed his father, was persuaded to demand the rule of Normandy and other portions of the kingdom. Henry II naturally refused this demand and, as a result, a revolt broke out in which the young Henry obtained the support of two of his brothers. This was in 1172, and during the next four years Henry was engaged in putting down rebellions in which disaffected elements on the Continent, in Scotland, and a few in England joined. King Louis was lending all the support in his power to the rebels and encouraged them to continue the strife whenever they were inclined to make peace. It was a serious test of Henry's strength, but he came through it successfully, and in 1176 seemed stronger

than ever.   His advice and support were sought by the leading
rulers of Europe, and in that year he was easily the most powerful
monarch of them all.

The year 1176 was also important in the career of Frederick I.
His Italian policy had led him to cast his lot definitely with the
nobility against the Normans of Sicily, the papacy and the towns.
As long as his chancellor, Reinald von Dassel, lived, Frederick
was fairly successful in Italy.   His policy of maintaining the
schism in the papacy enabled him to retain his German support,
but after the death of this clever adviser in 1167, matters began
to go awry.   Henry, duke of Saxony, stirred up trouble in Germany, and the towns of northern Italy formed a coalition against
Frederick.   He was in Italy in 1176 and attempted to punish
the townsmen for their arrogance.   Alexander III, who now enjoyed the support of Henry II, made common cause with the
Lombard towns and encouraged them to resistance.   A battle
occurred near Milan at Legnano, between the knightly cavalry
of the emperor and the citizen foot-soldiers of the towns.   Frederick's force was heavily outnumbered and the help which he
had expected from the duke of Saxony failed to arrive.   The
result was a great victory for the townsmen.   It was their first
victory over knights on an open field of battle, and, as such, has
been celebrated in later history.   It was also a victory for Alexander III.   A series of peace negotiations took place from 1176
to 1178 in which all three parties were concerned, and peace was
finally made at Venice.   The schism was ended and, through the
pope's good offices, some of the concessions which Frederick had
made to the towns immediately after the battle of Legnano were
rescinded.   Alexander III returned to Rome with an escort of
Frederick's troops, and there in 1179 presided over a Lateran
Council which gave proof of a reunited Church, for it included
representatives from all parts of Christendom.

Meanwhile, the fortunes of Henry II had altered.   The revolt
of his sons had revealed to his enemies his one vulnerable spot,
an excessive affection for his numerous offspring and an inability to discipline them properly.   As they grew up they clam-

ored for a share of the great empire ruled by their father and were encouraged in this desire by France. Henry allotted them principalities on the Continent, but none of them showed any real ability as statesmen. They misruled their subjects, quarreled among themselves, or joined in revolts against their father. The conduct of his children clouded the last years of Henry's reign and spelled the doom of his empire. Only two of his sons survived him, Richard and John. Their mother, Eleanor of Aquitaine, whose married life with Henry had been no more happy than with Louis VII, also survived. She had spent some years in prison as a result of Henry's displeasure, and in the rebellions of her sons against their father she had uniformly favored the former. Another item of interest in connection with Henry's last years was that, as a loyal vassal, he befriended Philip, the young son and successor of Louis VII, even though Philip supported Richard against his father. Henry died in 1189, in the midst of a war with Philip, who was urged on and aided by Henry's sons.

Frederick, on the other hand, had come out of his defeat by the Lombard townsmen with the friendship of the pope. His position in Germany was regained, and Henry, the Lion of Saxony, was compelled to go into exile. Even in Italy events turned out favorably for him. A final peace was arranged with the Lombard townsmen in 1183 at Constance on terms even more pleasing to Frederick than those at Venice in 1178. Sicily, which had formerly been hostile, was drawn into friendly relations with Frederick by a common opposition to the Byzantine emperor, Manuel. This friendship was cemented in 1186 by the marriage of Constance, heiress of the Norman kingdom, to Henry, the son of Frederick. Thus, nearly all the ambitions which Frederick had cherished in his youth seemed realized in his old age, and in the latter years of his life he occupied a foremost position in Europe. Likewise in contrast to his great contemporary, his death in 1190 occurred while on the Third Crusade, which gave to his memory a heroic glamour absent from the ignominious death of Henry II.

THE THIRD CRUSADE

While the monarchs were engaged in building up their states at the expense of the nobles and the Church, events in the Latin East were taking an ominous turn. As the fall of Edessa in 1144 had already indicated, the Moslems were becoming more united. Saladin finally succeeded in holding under one command Egypt, Damascus and northern Syria, while the royal family at Jerusalem had gone into decline. They were sickly, weak, and died very young. As usual under such conditions, rival leaders struggled for the actual regency, which led to division among the Christians, one faction becoming so embittered as to make an alliance with Saladin. Such was the Eastern situation in 1185. England and France, to whose leaders many of the Latin nobles in the East were related, were disturbed by the struggles between Henry and his sons, and could therefore send little aid. Henry did send some money, but men and leadership were more sorely needed. It was not difficult for Saladin to find the occasion for an attack upon the weakened Christian state. He made his preparations carefully and began his decisive campaign in 1187. The Latin leaders staked all upon one battle, keeping almost no force in reserve, and stupidly permitted Saladin to select the battle-field. The Christian army was almost completely destroyed at Hattin, just west of Tiberias, in July, 1187. In quick succession the important towns of the Kingdom of Jerusalem fell into Saladin's hands, and in September of that year Jerusalem itself. Only Acre, the strongly fortified seaport where the few scattered Christian troops sought refuge, offered any resistance, but it, too, was forced to surrender.

The news of the fall of Jerusalem cast a pall over the West. The papacy, after recovering from the shock, threw all of its energy into the organization of a crusade. Preachers and legates hastened to rouse the people. Richard, Henry II's son, was the first important prince to sign himself with the cross. The aged Frederick followed shortly afterward. Henry II and Philip II were persuaded to take the cross after a stirring appeal by the archbishop of Tyre. Preparations were started almost immediately. Henry issued orders that everyone who did not go on the crusade should contribute a tithe of his goods. This was the *Saladin tithe,* a measure which was to become famous in the history of taxation in England. Similar measures were inaugurated in France and in Germany. The departure of the armies was delayed, however, by the impulsive Richard, who chose to redress a grievance against the count of Toulouse, and by Philip, who saw an opportunity to cause trouble for Henry II. A war followed, in which Philip joined Richard against his father, and it was not until the death of Henry II that the crusade got under way. Even then, Philip was reluctant to go, but the threats of his leading vassals forced him to move. Meanwhile, Frederick had made elaborate preparations which included treaties with the monarchs along the way to insure adequate food supplies for his army. He began his march in 1189, reaching Asia Minor in 1190. Philip and Richard did not start on their way until 1190, fully a year after Frederick's forces had left Ratisbon.

In English and German literature the Third Crusade has been the most celebrated of all these expeditions. This fact is due partly to the higher development of the literary art as revealed in the contemporary court epic, and partly to the brilliant company which took part in the crusade. The preparations showed the advantage gained from previous expeditions. Financial provisions were adequate for the purchase of food and the needs of the army. The personnel of the army was limited almost entirely to fighting men, noncombatants and camp-followers being kept to a minimum. Precautions were taken to have sufficient war material available and the ships which bore the Western armies were provided with double sets of equipment. Even the treasure was carefully divided among the ships, to guard against loss. In addition, detailed regulations were drawn up to insure order within the armies. The thorough discipline of Frederick's army aroused astonishment even among the Saracens.

Yet, despite all these preparations and the impressive array of famous leaders and knights who participated, the crusade, measured by the attainment of its aim, was a failure. After two years of heroic fighting, the recovery of the seaport of Acre was almost the only reward of the crusaders. Many factors contributed to this result. The first and the most serious was the death of Frederick just as he was about to enter Syria. His forces had been dwindling all along the route, due to the secret antagonism of the Byzantine emperor and the Turks of Asia Minor, with whom that emperor made common cause. After Frederick's death, many of his followers returned to Germany, more concerned about the succession there than about the recapture of Jerusalem. The second factor was the remarkable ability of Saladin, who kept the Moslems united and reënforced his military maneuvers with a network of alliances. The third and most important reason, perhaps, was the dissension which arose between Philip and Richard. Philip never forgot that he was king of France and feudal overlord of a large portion of Richard's dominions. The close and constant association with Richard, whose lavish expenditure of funds made Philip seem beggarly, and whose free, impulsive conduct and physical prowess were constantly embarrassing, galled the French king. The strained relation between the rulers was reflected among their followers, and during the siege of Acre it became quite unsafe to send both armies out on the same day. The tension was somewhat relieved when Philip abandoned the crusade on plea of illness and returned to the West. This defection also weakened the Christian army, for it left Richard and his army almost alone, with but a small contingent of Germans and French to assist them. The fact that Richard carried on equal battle with Saladin for nearly a year after Philip's departure was not only a tribute to Richard's quality as a soldier, but indicated what might have been the outcome had the whole Christian army been able to coöperate under a single leader. Richard won from the chivalrous Saladin a truce under which the Christians were permitted to visit Jerusalem. On this expedition he acquired for all time the title of Lion-hearted, which he quite deserved. Returning home, he was shipwrecked and fell into the hands of the duke of Austria, whose overlord, Henry VI, held him for ransom, as much at the behest of Philip as on account of his differences with Richard regarding Sicily.

The failure of the crusade only increased the determination of the papacy to continue its efforts to bring about a successful expedition. The preaching of a new crusade came to be almost a constant concern of the popes. At the same time, the effect of the failure on the laity was one of discouragement, and they responded with apathy. It became far easier to obtain contributions than recruits, though from time to time expeditions were started, some of which will be dealt with later.

Meantime, political conditions in Europe were much disturbed. The absence of Richard gave his brother John an opportunity to gain control of his dominions. He proved an incompetent and unpopular ruler. His position was weakened by the fact that he was only a regent whose acts might be reversed upon Richard's return. But many of his ill-advised acts afforded Philip an effective means for undermining the strength of the Norman-English Empire. When Richard finally returned from captivity he found himself with a war on his hands against Philip and John. He had made considerable headway and seemed about to regain all the authority which his father had held, when a rash military venture led to his death in 1199. This placed John, less popular than ever, on the throne, a situation which Philip knew how to use to the utmost.

In Germany Henry VI succeeded his father. He had much difficulty, however, in establishing himself in his wife's kingdom of Sicily, where trouble brewed up to the time of his death. His effort to establish his authority in southern Italy as well as in the north was naturally viewed with alarm by the papacy. Henry's death in 1197 probably prevented the outbreak of serious difficulties with the pope. Henry's son, Frederick, was but two years old, and the dispute between the Hohenstaufen and Saxon families over the regency and kingship promised to prevent revival of the contest with the pope.

In 1198 the vacancy on the papal throne was filled by the election of Innocent III. He was the youngest of the cardinals, being only thirty-seven years old at the time of his elevation, but few abler men have ever filled the office. He was an Italian of noble family, and had been thoroughly educated, having studied theology at Paris and law at Bologna. In personal habits and inclination he was ascetic, almost as much so as his great forerunners Gregory the Great and Gregory VII. In his official attitude, however, he was imperially minded beyond either of them, and no pope has ever shown greater skill in the exercise of power than Innocent III.

The last five years of the twelfth century witnessed almost as many changes in the four great powers of Europe as had the five years with which the last half of the century had begun. The same four powers still dominated Europe and were still interlocked, but the situation was almost completely reversed. Then the rising tide was with Frederick Barbarossa and Henry II, while Louis VII and the papacy were overshadowed or in difficulties. Now, at the opening of the thirteenth century, England and Germany were in the background, with France and the papacy in control of crafty, able men.

CHAPTER X

THE AGE OF INNOCENT III

1198-1216

THE opening years of the thirteenth century are commonly known as the age of Innocent III, for circumstances, as well as the remarkable ability of the man himself, combined to place him at the center of nearly all the important developments of the period. His personal inclinations were strongly in the direction of legal studies, of which he was a master, and he loved power. Furthermore, he was endowed, like Gregory the Great, with seemingly inexhaustible energy, and he was capable of grasping and understanding the multitudinous and varied affairs of his time.

The first task which the pope undertook was the humble but important one of becoming master in his own household, the Papal States, or the Patrimony of St. Peter. This might seem a simple undertaking for an official accustomed to dominate the affairs of all Europe, and yet it was precisely this task which no pope before him had succeeded in accomplishing. A few popes, rather feudal nobles than spiritual heads of the Church, had exercised a fair degree of control. In the past those who had been primarily spiritual leaders had relied upon the emperors and, later, upon the Normans, to establish order in the Papal States. Control was another matter, which Innocent understood, for he was sprung from one of the noble families accustomed to rule. In attaining his purpose the pope was aided by the general dissatisfaction with the German nobles who had come to dominate so many portions of Italy during the reigns of Frederick Barbarossa and Henry VI. Upon the death of Henry VI, the Italian elements, including both the common people and the lesser nobility, rose in revolt against the German nobles, many of whom were driven out. Innocent utilized this revolt to gain recognition of his rights as lord over the region. He required an oath of allegiance from those who had displaced the German nobles, and, on threat of similar risings, likewise obtained such recognition from the German nobles who retained their places. With the funds at his disposal Innocent was able to provide his lieutenants with troops to reënforce his wishes. Most of these lieutenants were relatives accustomed, like himself, to dealing with the political problems of the region. The result of this policy was that by far the greater portion of the Papal States recognized the right of the pope to rule and kept the peace. The number of feudal nobles who still retained their independence was so small as to be practically negligible. To have accomplished this result without calling in outside help from the Empire or Sicily was a mark of high political ability.

INNOCENT III AND THE CRUSADES

Innocent felt the papal desire for the recovery of Jerusalem as strongly as any of his predecessors. He seems never to have let the thought drop entirely from his mind. Throughout the whole of his reign preachers were commissioned to arouse interest, collect contributions and engage troops. This was the most difficult problem which Innocent faced, for the failure, though a brilliant one, of the Third Crusade in 1192 had been followed by another failure of a German Crusade in 1196. In 1202, however, a large number of knights from France, Germany and northern Italy were persuaded to go on yet another crusade which promised real hope of success. Innocent's plans were thwarted, however, and his high hopes frustrated by the machinations of Venice.

The Venetian authorities invited the crusaders to take ship there, promising to furnish ships for the expedition which was to undertake an attack upon Jerusalem from the south through Egypt. It has been said that the Venetians had very profitable commercial relations with the Moslems there and had even made a treaty with them to prevent the crusaders from molesting Egypt. Also, the trade of Venice had grown to such proportions that the city had come into actual rivalry with Constantinople, of which it had been an outpost through so much of the Middle Ages. The Venetians desired trading privileges at the Byzantine capital beyond any which they had hitherto enjoyed. Whatever the motives, the Venetians lured the crusaders on to the sandbars outside Venice and there entangled them thoroughly in a network of debts, a species of financial enslavement in which the knights had had but little experience. There were also charges of generous bribes to the leaders. At any rate, the crusaders finally promised to perform certain political services for Venice before going on to Jerusalem. They captured Zara, a Christian city, but a commercial rival of Venice on the Adriatic. The Venetians then convinced the crusaders that they were now even more deeply indebted for food and transportation than before, and gained their reluctant consent to join in an attack on Constantinople. A claimant to the Byzantine throne named Alexius was produced by the Venetians, and the story of his mistreatment and the unjust denial of his rights was used to justify the attack. Persuaded, cajoled, or compelled, the crusaders engaged in a siege of Constantinople in 1204. The city fell after a comparatively short time and was then subjected to a most shameful plunder, in which all the Latin Christians joined, for the temptation was too great even for the pious men who had opposed the attack in the first place. Upon the fall of the Byzantine capital, the crusaders erected a Latin Empire of the East in which Venice had the lion's share. This Empire endured until 1261.

The diversion of the Fourth Crusade from its avowed object did not have the approval of the pope. Innocent repeatedly sent legates to interfere, and finally excommunicated the leaders. The Venetians craftily prevented the legates from reaching the crusaders and counted upon removing the ban by presenting to the pope control of the Greek East. In this they succeeded, for the addition of the Byzantine East to Latin Christendom was too dear a wish of the papacy to be refused. On the other hand, Innocent held the crusaders still liable for the discharge of their vow to capture Jerusalem. This was also the feeling of Europe. Many people regarded the fall of Constantinople as a just punishment for what they considered the duplicity of the Byzantine emperors in dealing with the earlier crusaders and pilgrims. Yet it was a Christian city, and in sacking it the crusaders degraded their vow to rescue the Holy City.

In 1212 occurred that strange expedition known as the Children's Crusade. The impression had been widespread that the reason for the failure of the Third and Fourth Crusades was that they were composed of sinful men, and some of the more simple folk believed that God would somehow grant to innocent children what He had withheld from sinful adults. Thousands of children from the Rhine country and from northern France started on this journey. The French king consulted the professors of theology at Paris about the propriety of the expedition and, armed with their condemnation of it, kept most of the French children at home. The rest, however, crossed the Alps and disappeared from history at the ports along the Mediterranean. Many legends arose to explain their disappearance. A few who went down into Italy reached Rome, where Innocent turned them back, to discharge their vow when they should grow up.

The pope's desire to regain Jerusalem persisted, however, and one of the projects discussed at the Lateran Council of 1215 was another great crusade to be led by Frederick II, who had promised at his coronation to go on a crusade. Innocent III did not live to see this plan carried out.

The constant agitation for a crusade tended to involve the papacy in the political affairs of Europe, since countries engaged in warfare would be less likely to furnish soldiers for the reconquest of Jerusalem. But other influences also drew Innocent into politics. The Holy Roman Empire, which under Henry VI had threatened to enclose the Papal States between Sicily and the north as in a vise, was of special concern to him.

PAPAL AUTHORITY AT ITS HEIGHT

Two claimants appeared for the crown of Germany, Philip of Hohenstaufen, the brother of Henry VI, and Otto of Brunswick known as Otto IV, the leader of the Saxon party. Meanwhile, Frederick had been entrusted to Innocent's guardianship when Constance, Henry's widow, died. It was not to the interest of the papacy to have a strong Hohenstaufen rule, and it was probably this motive, as well as reasons of a more personal character, which prompted Innocent to favor Otto. War broke out between Philip and Otto and continued until the former was killed. Much to Innocent's displeasure, Otto soon shared the ambitions of his predecessors for control in Italy. Philip II of France, who had profited from the disturbances in Germany, was dismayed at the prospect of a strong ruler there. Whether it was the suggestion of Philip or the plan of Innocent, the two combined in supporting young Frederick as a rival to Otto. The Hohenstaufen faction could be counted upon to break away from Otto in favor of Frederick. On the other hand, this move had real elements of danger for the papacy, since Frederick was powerful in Sicily. If he should become a power in the north as well, the papacy would again be surrounded. Only the future could reveal the extent of this danger, and for the time being Frederick could be counted upon to weaken Otto's support. Otto found an ally in John of England, who was not only related to him through marriage, but also had many scores to settle with Philip II. The battle of Bouvines in 1214 proved a disastrous defeat for Otto and John, and a victory for young Frederick and Philip II, who espoused his cause. The battle had many far-reaching consequences for all its leading participants, and it is also interesting for the part which the citizen soldiers of Philip's army played. This overthrow of an army of knights on the open battlefield is not so historically important as the victory of the Lombard townsmen at Legnano forty years earlier, but it does indicate the growth of a new spirit in the north as well as in the south. The immediate effect of the battle was to establish Frederick II as king of Germany and to discredit John on the eve of an uprising of the English barons.

It was a different situation which drew Innocent into the affairs of England. A disputed election for the archbishopric of Canterbury, in which the monks of Christ Church supported one candidate and King John another, was appealed to the pope. The contrast of this election with the earlier choice of Thomas à Becket, Henry's candidate, was a fair measure of John's weakness. Innocent chose to disregard both candidates and, instead, appointed an Englishman named Stephen Langton, whom John refused to accept. Such open defiance of the pope even Henry II had been careful to avoid, and John soon learned its futility. Innocent excommunicated John and placed England under an interdict. John, who had already accumulated various enemies, now saw many more arise as the interdict continued year after year. Philip of France more than willingly offered to lead a crusade against John and was engaged in extensive preparations for the expedition when John spoiled his plans by making peace with Innocent. John's surrender was almost abject, for he not only accepted Stephen Langton as archbishop of Canterbury, but in May of 1213 agreed to rule thereafter as a vassal of the pope. As a vassal, John appears not to have been altogether dutiful, for he could scarcely have consulted his papal overlord the next year when he joined Otto IV against Philip and Frederick. He did, however, plead for help when his barons forced him to accept the Great Charter in 1215 and begged Innocent to denounce the document as illegal. Nevertheless, England figured as a fief of the papacy in a very real sense during most of the thirteenth century.

During Innocent's reign, nearly all the Christian rulers in the Spanish peninsula also became vassals of the pope. His power was appreciated there even more than in most parts of Europe, for while Innocent's crusading efforts had met with little success in the East, they were winning great rewards in Spain. Little has been said thus far about the war with the Moslems in this region, but the call for the crusades was attended with important consequences for the war in Spain. The opportunity to gain merit by expelling the hated Infidel so near home was not lost to sight. Toward the end of the First Crusade, many crusaders crossed the Pyrenees to fight in Spain. A fleet of Englishmen on their way to Syria in the Second Crusade stopped to aid in the capture of Lisbon from the Moslems. After the murder of Thomas à Becket, when Henry II was required to promise to go on a crusade, it was expressly stipulated that he might postpone his journey to the East if he went to fight in Spain. These additions to the Christian forces there during the twelfth century resulted in great extension of Christian holdings. Now in the time of Innocent III a new drive was started which did not stop until the Moors had been dislodged from all their possessions except Granada. The battle of Las Navas de Tolosa in 1212 practically decided the issue. Under the circumstances it was extremely unwise for the rulers of the several Christian kingdoms in Spain to alienate the friendship of the pope. Indeed, it was in his power to maintain even a ruler of doubtful title. Peter of Aragon went to Rome to be crowned, accepting his kingdom as a fief of the pope. Sancho of Portugal was forced to acknowledge the pope's overlordship, and several other rulers there had their affairs set in order by Innocent.

Almost all the other rulers of Christian Europe came in some way or other to feel the power of Innocent III. The king of Denmark acknowledged his authority. The rulers of Poland, Bohemia and Hungary gave him their submission, and the Latin emperor of Constantinople sought his aid. The strong hand of the pope was felt even by Philip II of France, who had become the most important political figure north of the Alps. This was in connection with his marriage to Ingeburga, whom, from the day of his marriage, Philip refused to regard as his wife. The matter was already some years old when Innocent began his reign, but the new pope energetically revived the issue by placing France under an interdict. Philip held out for nine months or more and then apparently yielded to the pope's demands. He renounced Agnes of Meran with whom he was living, and went through a formal reconciliation with Ingeburga. The reconciliation was not sincere, for after the interdict was raised Philip resumed his former relationship. The matter came again to the attention of Innocent. Perhaps the many services rendered by Philip kept Innocent from again applying the drastic measure of the interdict, but he seems never to have wholly given up his purpose. In 1213, when Philip was preparing to go on a crusade against John of England, he took back Ingeburga as queen, if not as wife, and in this honorable position she continued during the remainder of Philip's life.

Under Innocent III the Roman Catholic Church reached its widest extent during the Middle Ages. Every region west of a line drawn from the southeastern end of the Baltic Sea to the western end of the Black Sea acknowledged the headship of the pope at Rome. The exceptions were few, Granada in Spain being the most important. The temporary adherence of the Armenians to the Church and the existence of a few Christian strongholds in Syria offset this Moslem stronghold in Spain. The Fourth Lateran Council of 1215, the year before Innocent's death, may almost be regarded as a triumphal celebration of this expansion of Latin Christianity. To insure full representation, Innocent sent out the invitations to this council in 1213, nearly two years before the event. It was the most impressive gathering of churchmen since the Council of Nicæa in 325. The possibility of such a gathering illustrates at once the improved conditions of the time, the wide extent of Latin Christianity, and the great power of the Church, especially of the pope who ruled over it. No matters were discussed, no action taken which had not previously been submitted to and approved by Innocent. He presided, not as the chairman of a legislative body, but like a Roman emperor issuing irrevocable decrees. At this council there passed in review, as it were, most of the important events of Innocent's reign. In addition, there were discussed many questions of moment for the future on which it was desirable to have a common understanding. Such, especially, were the reform of the clergy, the perfecting of Church organization, and the ever-recurring plans for a crusade. Aside from its enactments which epitomized the affairs of all Europe, the council was chiefly important as a concrete demonstration of the pope's power and of the unity and universality of the Church.

HERESY AND REFORM

The question of reform in the Church had assumed a new angle. It was now no longer necessary to repel the high-handed intrusion of unfit men into Church offices. Very few men attained priestly rank in this period without first going through the long training required by the Church. Undesirables did, however, creep in. The offices in the Church, particularly the higher offices, were no less attractive to the nobility now than they had been before. Bishops still had much power and greater influence than ever, and their wealth was much increased. The nobility coveted these offices and, in order to gain them, regularly designated their younger sons for priestly training. This was as true of kings and great nobles as it was of lesser nobles, and it now became a common practice for men of noble birth to hold the higher Church offices. Often this practice led to excellent results, for these men were accustomed from birth to rule, and their relationship with the upper classes of society enabled them to work more effectively there. Unfortunately, however, it sometimes had the opposite effect when these men chose to lead an idle social life, to the neglect of their Church duties. But whether the bishops and archbishops were men of high or low degree by birth, the great wealth and power which their offices entailed proved too tempting for many of them. There were a number of districts in which the leaders of the Church cared but little for the spiritual duties of their offices, seeming to value them, if at all, only because of the money and influence which they could extract from them. This attitude on their part invariably led to discontent, especially in the towns where people came into daily contact with the higher clergy.

In southern France, where the Peace and Truce of God had first been promulgated and where the Congregation of Cluny had first spread, this discontent reached serious proportions in the latter years of the twelfth century. The returning crusaders had brought back some strange religious ideas from the East which took hold and spread rapidly in this region. Here was formed a new religion called the Albigensian, probably from the town of

Albi, where the sect first attained prominence. They believed that the world was governed by a good and an evil spirit. The former they identified with the Jehovah of the Scriptures who was worshiped by the Christian Church. The highest class of this group were known as *Cathari,* or the pure, who abstained from all pleasures of the flesh, leading a life of such extreme asceticism that many of them virtually starved themselves to death. The Cathari were not so very numerous, and much of the spread of Albigensianism was due more to the popular discontent with the lives of the Christian clergy than to genuine conversion to the tenets of this sect.

This fact was brought out clearly in the career of Peter Waldo, a wealthy merchant of Lyons, who decided to give up his wealth and devote himself to religious work among the poor. He sought to win papal sanction for his plan, but he was so critical of the clergy and had so many enemies among them that this sanction was withheld. Failing to obtain approval within the Church, he proceeded to carry on his work without it. He advanced a number of new notions. Anyone who felt called to preach could do so; a barn was as good a meeting-place as a church; women could preach and conduct services as well as men. He worked chiefly among the poor and gained many followers there who were known as *Waldenses.* His sect grew very strong in southern France, that region of religious discontent.

Innocent III, though a reformer himself, was scarcely a pope to view with indifference this breach of the unity of the Church. He commissioned preachers to go among these people to win them by persuasion. In order to recall them to the Church he even authorized a zealous Spaniard, Durand de Huesca, to found the Order of Poor Catholics, much like the Waldenses. He finally endeavored to end these heresies by prevailing upon the count of Toulouse, in whose territory their followers were most numerous, to take action against them. The problem was a difficult one for the count of Toulouse, because the majority of his subjects belonged to these sects and he himself was not altogether without sympathy for them. Matters were brought to a sharp issue in 1208 when a papal emissary was killed by some followers of the count. Innocent thereupon launched actively upon a project for a crusade against Toulouse and the heretics, hoping to achieve by force what persuasion had so far failed to accomplish. Perhaps no single act of the pope has been so severely criticized as this impatient appeal to force. The crusading army, led by Simon de Montfort, broke into the lands of the count of Toulouse with savage fury which left little room for discrimination. Motives of plunder were as strong as those of religion among the followers of Simon, and poets have wept over the destruction wrought in this land of the troubadours. Political motives were not unmixed, and ultimately the king of France became the chief beneficiary of this wasteful and wicked war. Innocent found as much difficulty in restraining the excesses of the crusaders as he had formerly experienced in trying to win back the heretics.

Another measure instituted at this time for dealing with the heretics was the Inquisition. This was a system of courts for determining whether or not persons accused of heresy were guilty. In its inception it was expected to inquire into the heresy, and, if possible, win back the heretics. Under the régime of the crusading army, however, the flood of suspected persons driven before these courts became so voluminous that clemency became almost impossible and justice exceedingly difficult. People were denounced as heretics on slight suspicion and, after trial before the Courts of Inquisition, were turned over to the secular authorities for punishment. This, in its severest form, was death by burning. Both the crusade and the Inquisition set precedents for dealing with heretics in comparison with which the devices of earlier years seemed moderate.

THE FOUNDERS OF THE FRIARS—FRANCIS AND DOMINIC

That every feeling of humanity had not departed from the age received eloquent testimony in the founding of two new orders, the Franciscans and the Dominicans. Francis of Assisi, the son of a merchant in the little town of Assisi in the Papal States, grew up expecting to follow his father's occupation. He had taken part in his father's journeys to southern France and elsewhere, and no doubt had been affected by the state of religious unrest there. Much has been made of his gay life as a youth, but it was probably very much like that of any youth of his station. A change came over him after a very serious illness which he scarcely survived. Thereafter he devoted himself entirely to religion, much to the anger and disgust of his father who finally disowned him. Francis roamed about seeking to do good, and others joined him in his quest. They begged food, for they would not own property of any kind. They tended the sick, especially those outcasts in the leper colonies outside of towns. Where they found poverty, they tried to relieve it by begging from those who had plenty. Francis preached to the people, seeking to turn their thoughts back to simple faith. He exhibited no malice even toward those of the clergy whom his own devotion to poverty put to shame. Few men in history have ever so completely lived with malice toward none and with charity toward all. As his followers increased it became necessary for him to gain the approval of the pope for the continuance of his work. The appearance of Francis before Innocent III has captured the imagination of poets and artists ever since. Innocent was in the midst of his troubles with the Albigenses and Waldenses of France, and the career of Peter Waldo was so fresh in his mind that he received Francis with caution. After an examination by some cardinals, who were very favorably impressed with Francis, Innocent III gave his informal approval to the work of the young ascetic. The formal approval of the rule of St. Francis occurred after Innocent's death.

About the same time a Spanish churchman, Dominic by name, who had done some work in southern France, conceived a similar yet variant plan for the correction of heresy. He believed that the heretics were the victims of erroneous ideas and that they could be converted by convincing argument. To this end he set himself to study theology and its kindred subjects more thoroughly than had usually been the case. Thus equipped, he entered upon his career as a preacher to convince people, especially heretics, of the truth of the Christian faith. Like Francis, he believed in poverty, and like Francis, too, he began to have a following. He prescribed for his adherents the same rigorous training that he himself had undergone. Perhaps it was less difficult for Innocent to give his approval to the Order of St. Dominic than it had been in the case of St. Francis, but he approved both, and later popes, those of the thirteenth century at least, had little cause to regret his action. The Dominicans became known as the "preaching friars" and as the most learned group in the Church. Their numbers grew and they were soon found in all the centers of learning, at the courts of rulers, and on the battle front of the struggle against the heretics. Because of their learning and their chief interests they were soon placed in charge of the Inquisition. They were likewise prominent in Spain, where it was necessary to follow up the advance of the crusading armies with a campaign of conversion. Educated Jews and Moors, so numerous there, afforded occupation for the best efforts of the Dominicans. The "preaching friars" carried on missionary work beyond the boundaries of the Latin Church, seeking converts especially in the East.

In many respects the two orders of friars were much alike, and yet different from previous monastic orders. They were itinerant, and their organization was by districts or provinces. They met at regular intervals and then dispersed to carry on their work. At the head of each order was a master-general who was directly under the authority of the pope. Both orders became extremely popular, and, under a modification of the rule whereby laymen could associate themselves with the labors of the friars, many people of importance identified themselves with one or the other. The two founders admired each other greatly, though they differed diametrically in some of their theories. Francis opposed learning as a form of human vanity, whereas Dominic espoused it as the most effective tool of the Church. Francis and his followers worked chiefly among the lowly, whereas Dominic and his group were found in all centers of importance, especially at the courts and at the schools. Before the thirteenth century had reached its close, however, it was almost impossible to distinguish the two orders, for each numbered leading scholars in its membership, and both were carrying on work among the poor and outcast. They became rivals for merit in any form of Church work. As props to the papacy they were much more efficient than any of the previous orders, for they reached everywhere, were constantly moving about, and could be used wherever needed. At the same time their very flexible nature afforded opportunity for abuse since, under the guise of the friars, many scoundrels practiced fraud.

THE PAPAL CURIA AT THE DEATH OF INNOCENT III

This series of happenings in the reign of Innocent III was but a fraction of the business which the papal court, or *curia,* had to transact. The pope had become almost the supreme executive head in the governmental affairs of Europe, as for some time he had been the supreme judicial authority. In addition, the routine work of confirming charters, conferring the pallium, authenticating relics, canonizing saints, deciding questions of faith and morals, had increased in volume. These matters required careful attention, sometimes extended negotiation, and always involved painstaking search of previous records and multiple legal recording. The papal *curia* expanded to meet this business, and the number of persons directly or indirectly concerned in it was enough to people a fair-sized town. A stranger coming to Rome on business with the pope might well have been bewildered at the prospect of ever reaching his attention. This situation led to a good deal of corruption. Many Romans, whether connected with the *curia* or not, undertook for a consideration to procure a speedy transaction of business. Wealthy suitors for papal justice were usually ready to avail themselves of such aid, and the practice grew until it became almost a recognized custom. Innocent III tried hard to correct this vice and dismissed numerous officials whom he discovered guilty of it, but the problem proved almost insoluble. In several places the counterfeiting of papal documents became a regular business, and forged papal decrees were common enough to receive attention at the Fourth Lateran

Council. Many precautions were devised to guard against this danger, but without success.

Innocent III died in 1216. He brought the temporal power of the papacy to its height. He transformed into power the heritage of organization and influence which his predecessors since Gregory VII had accumulated. In accomplishing his purpose he devised many tools which later popes could use. He not only dominated in his own day, but stored up a reserve of prestige and power upon which his successors could draw for at least a century. The position of the papacy in the thirteenth century was, in large measure, due to his efforts.

CHAPTER XI

FREDERICK II AND THE COLLAPSE OF THE EMPIRE

1215-1273

THE papacy, at the death of Innocent III, was in appearance and largely in fact, the supreme arbiter of Europe; the other powers were, for the time at least, subordinate. England, to which the Anglo-Norman Empire had almost shrunk, was a vassal state. The German Roman Empire was practically in the same position. The two great powers of the later twelfth century had been humbled. France, which had so long shuddered between these two powerful neighbors, had been a constant friend to the papacy. Philip Augustus had served the latter as a dutiful servant against both England and Germany. There seemed no possible challenge to papal authority from France. And yet what had become of the power which these two empires had but recently possessed? Had it all been assumed by the papacy? Had it merely been dissipated? Or had much of it passed to France? Was it the pressure of religious discontent among his subjects or fear of invasion from France which caused John to submit to the pope? Did Frederick II owe his crown more to the will of Innocent or to the victory of Philip at Bouvines? Such questions might easily have been raised by the followers of the French kings. Perhaps it was a mark of the shrewdness of these kings that such questions, if already thought, were not yet voiced. The immediate challenge to papal political supremacy was to come from Frederick II.

THE YOUTH OF FREDERICK II

Frederick II, it will be recalled, was the son of Henry VI and Constance, heiress to Sicily. Frederick Barbarossa of Germany and Roger II of Sicily were his grandfathers—truly a brilliant ancestry. His mother was already over forty years, his father not yet thirty, when Frederick was born, and both died before he was four. Constance, who outlived her husband by a year, designated Innocent III guardian for the infant. Innocent had but just become pope and was occupied with a multitude of other duties, but he was not unmindful of his charge. He saw very little of his ward, but much of the best in Frederick's early training was due to the teachers whom the pope selected. The child was to be brought up as king of Sicily. The empire was to be disposed of otherwise, for the papacy could not view with composure the reunion of these two territories about the Papal States. Accordingly young Frederick was kept in Sicily, to grow up in the land of his maternal ancestors. The plan was clear enough, but circumstances were to alter it radically.

The Sicily of Frederick's youth could scarcely be described as an ideal nursery for an orphan king. It had only recently come into the possession of the Normans. The population consisted of numerous Greeks, many Mohammedans, and a considerable number of Jews. Latin Christians constituted only a dominant minority. One of the secrets of the Norman success had been their ability to adapt themselves to the customs of the people whom they ruled without yielding a fraction of political control. Consequently, these various elements were still very clearly present in the population, though their controlling power was gone. In addition, Sicily was situated at the center of the Mediterranean world, easily accessible to influences from Africa as well as from Italy, and was a port of call for every ship that sailed between the western and eastern Mediterranean. Its location tended to accentuate the diversities among the peoples, or at least to keep them alive. As a result, the young king became the center of the rival ambitions of the different factions on the island and was exposed to a host of conflicting ideas. He was flattered and bullied, indulged and threatened, sometimes kidnapped and at other times forced to seek refuge among his humblest subjects. With Norman dukes and German mercenary captains, Saracen

emirs, papal governors and teachers all struggling to gain possession of the young lad for their own ends, there is little wonder
that, along with more wholesome instruction, he was early and too
well initiated into the secrets of human duplicity and treachery.

The effects of such training depended largely upon the character
of the lad. Two pen pictures of him at this period have been
preserved. One describes him as a boy of seven resisting the
attempt of a mercenary captain to carry him off: "He sought
refuge not in weapons, but in tears. And yet he was not able—
a good omen for the future ruler—to hide his royal spirit . . .
for he sprang . . . upon his captor and sought, so far as he was
able, to maim the arm of him who had laid hands upon the
anointed of the Lord." The other describes him six years after
this: "The king's stature cannot exactly be called small, but it
is not larger than befits his age. Nature has endowed him with
strong limbs and a vigorous body which is capable of enduring
every activity. He is never quiet, but is in motion all day long."
Then, after reciting Frederick's skill and constant practice in
fencing, sword-play, shooting with the bow, and horsemanship,
the account continues: "Moreover, he possesses royal dignity; he
has the mien and commanding majesty of a ruler. His face is
of a gracious beauty with a serene forehead, and his eyes are so
full of joy that it is a pleasure to look at him." The narrator
remarks, however, that he was "headstrong and willful, impatient
of tutelage of any kind, the defects of training rather than of
nature." The description closes with the summary: "But his
talents so far outrun his years that, although he is not a grown
man, he is well equipped with knowledge and learning, and the
shrewdness that one normally acquires only in the course of
years; . . . he is already a man in knowledge and learning, and
in majesty a ruler." His precocity was recognized when he was
declared of age at fourteen. At fifteen Innocent arranged a
marriage for him with a Spanish princess of mature years who
was expected to steady him. Thus his guardianship was discharged with success and the former guardian and ward continued firm friends.

FREDERICK AND THE CRUSADE

The circumstances which led Innocent to change his plans regarding the career of Frederick have already been told. When the pope sent him north to take the kingship of Germany, Frederick was seventeen years old and the father of a son who might succeed him in Sicily. With the support of Philip Augustus and what remained of the Hohenstaufen party in Germany, he gained recognition. His charming personality and the generous grants which he made won him many friends among the nobility, and in 1215 he was crowned at Aachen "king of the Romans and future emperor." Some significance has been attached to the fact that he, like Frederick Barbarossa, opened the tomb of Charles the Great to gaze upon the bones of the great emperor. Was it an indication of dangerous ambition? If so, his other acts indicated deep affection and loyalty to the pope. He promised to protect the Church, to regard himself as the vassal of the pope and not to unite the Empire and Sicily. In the excess of his gratitude he volunteered to lead a crusade to the Holy Land. It gave Innocent great pleasure to make this announcement at the Lateran Council in November of that year. The great pope died without having any cause to regret his services to Frederick.

Frederick remained in Germany four years after this, but his long stay only convinced him that he preferred Sicily. When he returned to Italy in 1220 to receive the imperial crown, he continued on to Sicily where disorders had again arisen. He soon established peace but made no move to return to Germany. Instead he sent his son Henry, duke of Swabia, while he himself remained in Italy. Years passed, but he made no effort to carry out the crusade which he had promised. His activities were directed rather toward bringing northern and southern Italy completely under his control. The immediate successor of Innocent was old and indulgent and accepted the excuses for delay which Frederick offered. The Lombard towns, however, were greatly alarmed at the extension of imperial control and revived their League. In 1227 a new pope, Gregory IX, was elected. He shared the alarm of the Lombard towns at Frederick's encroachments and began immediately to insist that Frederick go on the crusade. Frederick was given until a certain day in 1227 to start, his failure to be punished by excommunication. Frederick actually embarked in September, but an illness from which he was suffering became so serious that he returned after a day at sea. Gregory IX chose to regard this as a pretext and promptly excommunicated the emperor.

Frederick resented Gregory's unreasonable action and, as further evidence of his own sincerity, made renewed preparations to go. After the death of his first wife he had married Isabelle of Brienne, who was heiress to the crown of Jerusalem. She died while Frederick was in the midst of his crusading preparations, but Frederick determined now to regain the kingdom of Jerusalem for their son, Conrad. The expedition finally started in September, 1228. Gregory excommunicated Frederick again for daring to go while unabsolved from the former ban, and he forbade all Christians in the Holy Land to aid the emperor.

Frederick probably had less than a thousand knights with him, but he was fortified with a thorough knowledge of the Eastern situation and counted upon gaining his ends by diplomacy. The sultan of Egypt, whose troops had recently captured Jerusalem, proved amenable to persuasion. A treaty was drawn up declaring a truce of ten years and giving Frederick Jerusalem, Bethlehem, Nazareth and Sidon. Moslems were to be allowed free access to the Temple and to the Mosque of Omar in Jerusalem, and there were certain other reservations. Frederick crowned himself king of Jerusalem and returned home. He had accomplished more than any crusader since the First Crusade and had done so practically without bloodshed. When he reached Italy he found the pope's troops overrunning his southern kingdom. These were quickly driven out, and after negotiations in which Frederick agreed to submit to some of the pope's demands for fuller control of the clergy in Sicily, peace was made between pope and emperor at San Germano in 1230. Christian Europe hailed Frederick as a great hero, but his renown was somewhat tarnished by the unorthodox manner in which the crusade had been conducted.

FREDERICK AS A RULER

The peace of San Germano could only be a truce. For six years Frederick gloried in his position as successful crusader and emperor of the Holy Roman Empire. His Sicilian court was the most brilliant in Europe. Scholars and poets found a ready welcome there. His chancellor, Pierre de Vigne, was one of the keenest lawyers in Europe and something of a poet at the same time. Even Frederick took a turn at composing verse both in the vernacular and in Latin. Dante, writing half a century later, assigned to the circle at Frederick's court a very important place in the development of Italian literature. The scholars who frequented this court were of many different origins. Learned Mohammedans, accomplished Jews, and educated Christians seem to have been equally welcome. Frederick's intellectual curiosity embraced nearly all fields of learning, including astronomy, geography, mathematics, law and medicine. He founded the University of Naples in order to keep his young men from being drawn into the papal service, and there he especially encouraged the study of medicine and law. He grew to be intensely interested in the falcons used in hunting, and determined to find out all he could about these birds. The spirit with which he pursued this study was like that of a modern scientist, and the book which he wrote upon the subject is a model of thoroughness. His menagerie of elephants, camels, lions, leopards and other beasts was the most complete collection of animals which had been brought together in western Europe since ancient times.

This period of Frederick's reign was distinguished also by the enactment of important legislation. His *Sicilian Constitutions* of 1231, which owed much to the practice of his Norman ancestors in Sicily, were the most advanced governmental regulations in Europe. Their fundamental principle was the absolute power of the king, in the spirit of the Roman law. Nobles and churchmen were deprived of many of the governmental functions which they exercised in most of Europe, and towns were not permitted self-government. The administration of law and justice, the collection of taxes, the coining of money, and like duties were entrusted to officials appointed by Frederick himself. These royal officials were men of various races and creeds, whose qualifications for office were but two—ability and loyalty to the ruler. Sicily prospered under this régime. In 1235 Frederick held a Diet, or assembly, of the princes of Germany at Mainz and instituted several important measures for the government of that region also. The spirit of his legislation there was like that in Italy, but not so thorough, and the manner of carrying out its provisions was diametrically opposed to his Sicilian practice. In Germany he left the actual execution of his plans to the nobles, each to do much as he pleased in his own territory. A curious phase of his German legislation was the enactment of measures against heretics, the most drastic and comprehensive set of laws on the subject enacted by any ruler. These regulations were general for his whole empire, but they were carried out in far different ways in Germany and Italy. In the former they led to cruel persecutions. In Italy the popes complained that Frederick was using these laws to punish men whose only crime was fidelity to Rome. It has been suggested that Frederick passed these laws only as a means of justifying himself in the eyes of Europe, without much thought of ever putting them into force. But the fact that a man so notoriously unorthodox as Frederick should have sponsored such laws at all must remain one of the enigmas of his career.

RENEWAL OF TROUBLE WITH THE PAPACY

Peace between papacy and empire, however, could not last. Frederick's progress in Italy again aroused the Lombard towns to action, but they were badly beaten at Cortenuova in 1237. The terms of peace imposed by the emperor were very harsh and afforded the pope an opportunity to intervene on the side of clemency. Frederick would not yield, for he was determined to control Lombardy as he did Sicily, and it was precisely this that Gregory IX was determined to prevent. In the midst of the negotiations Gregory again excommunicated Frederick (1239). Frederick was charged with inciting sedition against the Roman Church, oppression of the clergy in Sicily, obstruction of Christian activities in the Holy Land, and finally with heresy. Nothing was said about Lombardy. Frederick replied to this by a manifesto which he addressed to the leading princes of Europe. He took the view that the Lombard towns had risen in rebellion against their lawful sovereign and that the pope had been an active conspirator in inciting this rebellion. In addition, he recalled the numerous hostile acts of Gregory, including the excommunication of 1229, Gregory's letter to the sultan of Egypt against him, and Gregory's invasion of the Sicilian realm during his absence. He suggested that the pope was a too much interested party to be an impartial judge and that a council should therefore be held to determine between them. Finally, he urged that his cause was that of all rulers and that, if the pope succeeded in undermining him by aiding rebels, it would be only a matter of time before other rulers would be treated in the same way by the pope. The struggle was thus extended to all Christendom.

The war of pamphlets continued. Gregory replied to this manifesto by a circular letter of great length in which he bitterly denounced Frederick as anti-Christ, charging among other things "that that king of pestilence [Frederick] has openly maintained, and here we shall use his own words, 'that the whole world has been deceived by three impostors, namely Jesus Christ, Moses and Mohammed.' . . . Furthermore . . . he has presumed untruthfully to say that all are fools who believe that God, who created all things, could be born of the Virgin." Gregory at length decided to hold a council at Rome to consider the matter, whereupon Frederick announced that he forbade such a council because its only purpose was to interfere with his lawful measures against the Lombard rebels. Gregory directed the clergy to meet at Genoa, with whose government he had made arrangements for a naval escort to Rome. Frederick thereupon gathered the ships of Sicily and Pisa, took the Genoese fleet by surprise, and captured the clergy and Lombard townsmen on their way to the council. Thus the council was broken up. Pope Gregory lived only a few weeks longer and the college of cardinals was deadlocked for nearly two years before a successor was chosen, thus giving Frederick a considerable respite.

In 1243 a new pope of Genoese origin was elected and took the ominous title of Innocent IV. Frederick began negotiations looking toward friendship with the new pope, but Innocent eluded the emperor by going to Genoa and thence to Lyons, whither he summoned a general council. Few clergy from the empire and almost none from Sicily attended, but this only facilitated Innocent's purpose. Frederick was denounced and declared deposed.

This action led to a new war of pamphlets, fiercer and more pointed than before. Frederick urged the rulers to prevent the raising of money in the papal behalf because he was really fighting their battle. He asked Louis IX to mediate between himself and the pope and even offered to go on another crusade with Louis. In another manifesto Frederick called upon all the rulers to aid him in compelling the Church to return to its primitive condition, "leading an apostolic life and imitating the humility of the Lord. In those days the clergy used to see angels, to shine with miracles, to cure the sick and raise the dead and to subjugate kings and princes by sanctity and not by arms." This dangerous proposal drew a lengthy and dignified reply from Innocent, who met all of Frederick's arguments, among other points dryly calling the attention of the world to the condition of the Church in Sicily as an example of what Frederick meant by its primitive simplicity. As for the pope's authority over the emperor, Innocent announced that it had existed "in the very nature of things and potentially from the beginning." This campaign of propaganda had some effect. Both Henry III of England and Louis IX of France urged the pope to leniency at times, though neither made any real effort to intervene on either side. The war continued with varying fortunes. Frederick was actually making gains in Lombardy when, in December of 1250, a severe attack of dysentery carried him off.

OVERTHROW OF THE HOHENSTAUFENS AND THEIR EMPIRE

With Frederick's death his party lost its great leader. His son Conrad was killed in 1254, leaving an infant son also named Conrad, who was too young to rule. This circumstance encouraged civil strife, especially in Germany where rival claimants to the throne arose. The quarrel was embittered by religious complications, for the papacy was determined never to permit the hated Hohenstaufen brood to rule again. Germany was kept in a furor of civil war unparalleled since the days of the Carolingian débâcle. In Sicily where the people were wholeheartedly devoted to the memory of Frederick II, his illegitimate son, Manfred maintained effective resistance to the papal attack and was even making headway in southern Italy until 1268, when the final act of this drama occurred. Young Conrad, Frederick's grandson, was old enough to lay claim to his inheritance and appeared in southern Italy. Against this contingency the papacy had invited the brother of the king of France to come with an army, offering him as reward the rule of Sicily and of Naples. Charles of Anjou came in 1265. He defeated Manfred decisively in the following year and when the young Conrad, or Corradino as he was affectionately called, arrived in 1268, Charles defeated him also at Tagliacozza. Conrad was captured after the battle and beheaded at Naples. Up in Germany the violent fighting continued until 1273, when a noble of southern Germany, Rudolph of Hapsburg, was recognized as king of Germany and emperor of the Holy Roman Empire on condition that he would not interfere in Italy.

The struggle had been a terrific one, and the wreckage it had caused was just as real as though it were apparent in charred ruins and abandoned towns. In order to gain the victory, the papacy had been forced to the utmost of its resources. It had used its spiritual weapons of excommunication and interdict, of inquisition and crusade, in a cause which few people could view as spiritual in any extensive sense. It was not an edifying spectacle to witness the head of the Church engaged in inflicting such destruction and suffering as these political struggles involved. The final victory had been purchased by the grant of Naples and Sicily to a power just as foreign as the German, a solution which was bound to cause trouble. The Guelf and Ghibelline parties created during the wars caused dissension in Italy for centuries. Although the weakening of Germany removed one source of contention, it also removed a strong element of papal support. For the time being, however, the papacy seemed to be the supreme power in Europe, a position confirmed by its victory over the Hohenstaufens.

The Empire was thoroughly broken. The title continued, but without its former significance. Italy was forbidden ground which might be trod only on the coronation journey. Germany was divided into a vast congeries of principalities and towns. The kingship was purely elective, and the election was becoming fixed in the hands of a few of the leading princes who used their privilege to extract concessions of power or wealth from the candidate. Care was taken not to select a forceful prince inclined to attempt real rule. Germany henceforth was little more than a geographical division in which there were a few large states and many small ones, which tended to become smaller and yet more numerous with the passage of time.

CHAPTER XII

THE RISING POWER OF FRANCE
1180–1270

THE struggle between Frederick II and the papacy had important consequences outside the Empire. As it became embittered both sides needed help. The popes appealed to all Christendom for money and men against Frederick as the foe of Christianity; Frederick in turn appealed to the kings to prevent such subsidies, denouncing the papacy as the enemy of royal government everywhere. While these letters were general, they were addressed particularly to the kings of France and England. The situation presented an opportunity to obtain the leading position in Europe. England, weakened by John's misrule, was scarcely ready for it. Henry III, John's son and successor, was not a ruler of either force or ability. At best his long reign served only to repair some of the damage which John had wrought. He had little energy to spend on distant adventures. Two or three feeble efforts at participation in the quarrel between Frederick and the papacy only made this fact clearer. The great opportunity lay rather with France. Was France strong enough to venture beyond her borders? More important still, was her ruler of sufficient ability to seize the chance?

RECOVERY OF ROYAL POWER BY THE CAPETIANS

These questions can best be answered by a summary review of those antecedent developments in France which have been partially outlined in connection with other events. It will be remembered that in the disruption of Charlemagne's empire the kingdom of West Frankland had suffered most severely. Feudal disorder and independence from royal control had there advanced further than in any other part of Europe. From 987, however, West Frankland, or France as it may henceforth be called, enjoyed one advantage over its neighbors. Its ruling family, the Capetian line, which then acquired the throne, did not fail of a direct heir. The dynastic disputes which tore the other countries apart did not arise in France. For more than a century, though, this was its only advantage. The great feudal nobles had maintained their independence. Until the opening of the twelfth century the French king was ruler only of the country around Paris and was not without opposition even there. Louis VI, who ruled from 1108 to 1137, spent most of that time in the saddle, figuratively speaking, and yet in all that time was seldom ever more than fifty miles from Paris.

It was with Louis VI, however, that the French monarchy began its rise. His able minister, Suger, abbot of St. Denis, was not only a scholar and a churchman but an administrator of rare ability. He saw the value of encouraging towns to seek charters from the king, and he knew, too, how to bring the intangible influence of the Church to the support of the monarchy. He also appreciated the value of alliances in extending the royal domain. He was largely instrumental in arranging the marriage of the king's son with Eleanor of Aquitaine. When Louis VI died, Suger continued as the adviser of the successor, Louis VII.

Under his administration the affairs of the kingdom increased in prosperity, and when Louis VII returned from the Second Crusade he found the royal treasury in better condition than it had been when he left. The death of this minister in 1151 was a serious loss. Eleanor of Aquitaine was separated from Louis the following year and her territory went to his western neighbor, Henry II. Louis VII reigned for many years, from 1137 to 1180, but he was not a man of great personal ability. During the last twenty-five years of his reign he did little more than hold what territory he had. His kingdom lay between the empires of Henry II and Frederick Barbarossa. This was a very dangerous position, but it possessed one advantage: the great nobles on the frontier were driven into closer relations with the king, whose danger was their own.

THE REIGN OF PHILIP II (PHILIP AUGUSTUS)

Philip II, or Philip Augustus as he is usually called, ruled over France exactly as long as his father, but with much greater ability. He very early learned the art of statecraft and, like Suger, pursued the policy of encouraging towns to seek charters from the king. The opportunity of weakening his western neighbor presented by the quarrels between Henry II and his sons was not lost on him. He encouraged Richard and John in their revolt, encouraged John against Richard and encouraged John's barons against John. He was following a consistent policy of strengthening France at the expense of her neighbor. He labored under no illusions of glory. He took the vow to go on the crusade but he went with reluctance, and seized an early opportunity to return. The glory of the Third Crusade fell to Richard; Philip was much more interested in extending the power of France. In return for Normandy he assured John of his support against Richard, and when Richard returned he had almost persuaded John to assume the kingship of England. In 1199 Philip was in a precarious position, for he was not only beset by Richard, but was in difficulties with Innocent III about his marriage with Ingeburga. The death of Richard saved him from the one danger, and his apparent reconciliation with his wife from the other.

About 1200 Philip's position was much improved. Civil war in Germany enabled him to devote his attention chiefly to the western area. He threatened to take up the cause of Prince Arthur, the son of John's older brother Geoffrey. This threat wrung from John a treaty involving certain important concessions and a marriage alliance between Philip's son, Louis, and John's niece, Blanche of Castile. Shortly after this John stole the affianced bride of one of his vassals who protested to Philip as John's overlord. Philip held a court of his chief vassals, cited John to appear, and, upon his failure to do so, declared his fiefs forfeited. In feudal law John was in the wrong and legally condemned, but in feudal practice it was the weakness of John among his own subjects which afforded Philip the opportunity to

sit in judgment upon him.   Henry II had been involved in worse
acts, but his overlord was not in a position to make him suffer
for them.   Philip succeeded in waging a successful war in this
cause of justice, which gave him Normandy and nearly all of
John's possessions north of the Loire.   The unity of the Norman-English Empire was thereby destroyed.

When John was again at odds with Innocent III, Philip took
advantage of the situation to prepare an invasion of England
under the guise of a crusade.   After John's surrender to the pope,
Philip endeavored to acquire grants from the Church to indemnify
him for his crusading expenses.   John's attempt to regain his
lost possessions by making common cause with Otto against
Philip and Frederick II met with disaster at Bouvines in 1214.
The next year saw John in trouble with his barons at Runnymede.   Philip, of course, tried again to capitalize John's difficulties.   He sent his son, who was the husband of John's niece,
to claim the English throne.   Louis actually landed in England
and received the adherence of a large part of the barons, but
the pope, as overlord of England, intervened.   Normandy, Anjou
and Maine, however, remained in Philip's hands.

Owing to Philip's preoccupation in the west and north, he did
not take a very active part in the crusade against the Albigenses.
He kept close watch over the situation, however, and had his
son Louis make an expedition into that region.   Later when
Louis became king, his knowledge of the territory proved very
useful.   In the north Philip made headway partly through his
first marriage but even more because of his participation in
German affairs.   These gains were more real than apparent, consisting, as they did, of a greater control of his vassals in that
region than any former Capetian ruler had enjoyed.   As long as
the Empire had remained strong, these vassals had been in a
position to flirt now with the king of France, now with the
emperor, yet maintaining a high degree of independence all the
while.   Flanders lay at the junction of French, English and German jurisdictions, and some of the counts of Flanders had conducted themselves virtually as kings.   The counts of Champagne
had at times assumed an equally independent air.   This attitude

FRANCE
1154-88

Royal Domain
Possessions of Henry II
Other Tiefs

FRANCE
IN 1328

Royal Domain
Appanages of princes descended from Louis IX
Other fiefs
English possessions before the outbreak of the Hundred Years War
Route of Edward III in France

Scale of Miles
0   50   100   150

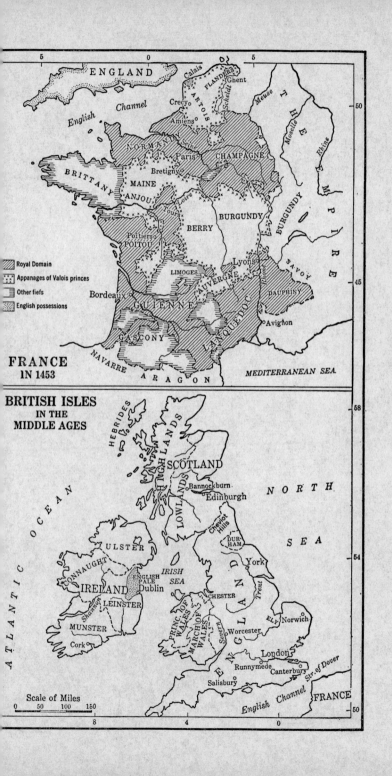

FRANCE IN 1453

ENGLAND

English Channel

Calais
FLANDERS
Ghent
ARTOIS
Scheldt
Crecy
Amiens
Meuse
Moselle
Rhine

NORMANDY
Paris
CHAMPAGNE
Bretigny
Seine
Loire
Tours
MAINE
ANJOU
BRITTANY

BURGUNDY
BERRY
Poitiers
POITOU
LIMOGES
Lyons
AUVERGNE
SAVOY
Rhone
Bordeaux
GUIENNE
LANGUEDOC
DAUPHINY
Avignon
GASCONY

NAVARRE
ARAGON

MEDITERRANEAN SEA.

THE EMPIRE

Royal Domain
Appanages of Valois princes
Other fiefs
English possessions

BRITISH ISLES IN THE MIDDLE AGES

ATLANTIC OCEAN

HEBRIDES
HIGHLANDS
SCOTLAND
Bannockburn
Edinburgh
LOWLANDS
Cheviot Hills

NORTH SEA

ULSTER
CONNAUGHT
IRELAND
ENGLISH PALE
Dublin
IRISH SEA
LEINSTER
Shannon
MUNSTER
Cork

DUR-HAM
York
Trent
CHESTER
PRINC. OF WALES
MARCH OF WALES
Severn
Worcester
ELY
Norwich

ENGLAND

London
Runnymede
Canterbury
Salisbury
Str. of Dover

English Channel
FRANCE

Scale of Miles
0   50   100   150

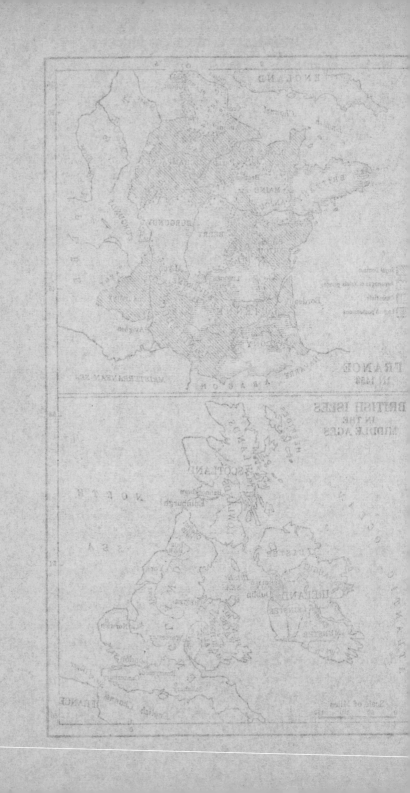

began to change when there ceased to be a strong power to the east to which they could turn when they chose. After the battle of Bouvines, the friendly relationship between Philip and Frederick II made the independent attitude of the nobles less effective.

Philip's sagacity was nowhere better displayed than in his relations with the Church. A story is told of him that, when urged to prohibit the clergy from infringing upon royal jurisdiction, he replied that he was well aware of these encroachments, but when he reflected upon the goodness and favor God had shown him, he preferred to lose something of his rights than to have any dispute with the people of the Holy Church. He managed always to appear as the dutiful son of the Church, even during his controversy with Innocent III over Ingeburga. Thus he made common cause with the papacy against John, against Philip of Hohenstaufen, later against Otto IV, and likewise against the Albigenses. In each instance the alliance brought him increase of territory or of power. For his services to the papacy he was also allowed unusual favors in his dealings with the clergy of his realm. The popes aided him financially and they helped him in the extension of his authority; Philip could well afford to forego a struggle with them about lesser matters of legal jurisdiction.

In the internal administration of the kingdom Philip displayed equally great skill. He incorporated in the royal domain much of the land which he had conquered or acquired in other ways. This territory was now so large that the former domain officials, the provosts, were insufficient for its effective control. He therefore established a new set of officials called bailiffs, who were charged with larger districts, were directly responsible to the king, and met with him at regular intervals to consider the condition of the kingdom. For these offices he freely used men of lesser rank, more confident in their loyalty to him and his kingdom than in that of the greater nobles. He also continued the practice of granting charters to towns, especially those located on the lands of the great nobles, and from time to time he used leading townsmen as counselors. The results of this policy tended to centralize the resources of his enlarged domain and to render the task of ruling the kingdom much easier for his successors.

Philip Augustus was not an heroic figure in European history. Frederick Barbarossa, Richard the Lion-hearted and Innocent III gathered to themselves most of the glory of their age and left Philip to labor in their shadows. He more nearly resembled Henry II of England whose career had undoubtedly furnished him many precepts. Later times, however, have recognized his work as more lasting than that of any of his great contemporaries. His son, Louis VIII, ruled but three years. During that time he waged a crusade against the Albigenses, thus paving the way for the addition of that territory. He pursued the policy of granting large sections of land to his sons, a practice which had caused much trouble in the past and undoubtedly would again. The real fate of Philip's labors was to be decided rather by his grandson, the offspring of Louis and Blanche of Castile by a marriage which Philip had so carefully arranged.

EARLY YEARS OF LOUIS IX

This was Louis IX, or Saint Louis as he came to be known in history, king of France from 1226 to 1270. He was not quite ten when his grandfather died, and less than thirteen years old when his father died. Too young to rule himself, a regency was established for him, but the real management of affairs fell to the queen mother. Queen Blanche was a pious woman and a devoted mother, but she was also an unusually able and strong-willed woman. She took charge of her son's training with gentleness but firmness, and she never relaxed her control over him as long as she lived. It was said that even when Louis was grown up and married, his mother was quite jealous of her daughter-in-law and allowed her to be but little in his company. Years later, when Louis was delaying in the Holy Land after his ill-fated crusade in Egypt, word came to him from France requesting his immediate return because his kingdom was in danger. His counselors advised him to return, but after considering the matter for some time, he decided to remain, "for my lady mother, the queen, has no lack of men to defend it [the kingdom of France]." He was still confident in her power of leadership. Under her care the young king was taught piety and simple living as well as the arts which more directly befitted his position.

The great nobles of the kingdom thought they saw in the combination of boy-king and foreign mother an opportunity to regain some of that independence of which the skillful statesmanship of Philip Augustus had deprived them. In this ambition they were encouraged by the king of England whose power had suffered at the same hands. Accordingly they formed various combinations and broke out in revolt. These revolts were successfully suppressed through the skill of Queen Blanche. The papal legate, acting probably on the theory that a strong France was necessary to the papacy in its struggle with Frederick II, aided her with all the resources at his command. The last and most serious of these revolts was met by Louis himself who in 1242 defeated an English army and nearly captured Henry III. Henry made peace and the other nobles involved with him were forced to accept terms recognizing the power of King Louis. "From this time the barons of France undertook nothing against their anointed lord, seeing that God was with him." Nor did the king of England, this chronicler might have added. The critical period of the reign of Louis IX was now over, and he was free to participate in the affairs of his neighbors.

DECISION OF LOUIS TO GO ON A CRUSADE

A more opportune situation could scarcely have been imagined by an ambitious monarch. At this juncture the struggle between Frederick II and the papacy was at white heat. Innocent IV had just been elected and was meditating his plan of outwitting the emperor by holding the Church council at Lyons. Both were suing for the support of Louis and were apparently willing to pay any price for it. How exasperated his more ambitious followers must have been when Louis, instead of engaging in the quarrel, announced his intention of going on a crusade! He tried their patience almost beyond restraint, as he did again in 1258, when he returned to the king of England the lands acquired by his victory over the latter. On that occasion they protested to him, saying: "It seems to us that if you believe you have no right to it, you do not make fitting restitution to the king of England unless you restore to him all the conquests which you and your predecessors have made; but if you believe that you have a right to it, it seems to us that you are throwing away all that you yield to him." And now he was throwing away even greater opportunities, he, the grandson of Philip Augustus! Was this the result of that pious training which his mother had given him?

Louis was devout and pious. His frequent attendance at mass, his scrupulous observance of Church forms, his numerous gifts to the Church, and his lavish outlay for the purchase of relics left no doubt of it. He was remarkably clean of speech. Joinville claims that he never heard a word of profanity from the mouth of the king during twenty-two years of intimate acquaintance. Instead, he deplored the prevalence of profanity among the people. He was very intimate with the monastic groups, especially the Carthusians, Franciscans and Dominicans. He even attended their chapter or provincial gatherings, and it was his habit when entering a strange town to hunt up the Dominicans or Franciscans there and ask for their prayers. In imitation of the friars, he bathed the feet of the sick and poor and gave food to the poor, sometimes cutting the bread for them himself. Most of his nobles and even his wife would have preferred to have him less pious. They were especially irritated by his resolve to go on the crusade, and most of his followers accompanied him reluctantly indeed.

The occasion for the crusade was several-fold. All western Europe had been thrown into a panic some years before by the invasion of the Mongols or Tartars, another Asiatic horde like the Hungarians, Avars and Huns of earlier days. The empire of the Great Khan, as their leader was called, extended from

China to western Russia. His forces had also made incursions into Poland and Hungary, and it appeared for a time that they might even penetrate western Europe. Fortunately troubles in the far East had weakened the Tartars, and the high tide of their advance into Europe seemed now spent. Indirectly their movement had caused serious disturbances in Persia and the near East, where Jerusalem easily fell a prey to Turcoman rovers. The attempt of the Christian forces in the Holy Land to recover the city in 1244 was met with a disaster almost like that at Hattin in 1187, and the survivors wrote frantic letters to the West. The papacy blamed Frederick II for these calamities, and Frederick blamed the papacy. But Louis, who had been meditating the possibility of the crusade for some time, reached his decision in 1244, partly as a thank-offering for recovery from a severe illness. Once decided, he would not turn back.

He did, however, make careful preparations. Private wars and duels were forbidden for a period of five years, and knights who took the cross were granted a moratorium on their debts for three years. Grain and wine were stored in Cyprus for two years before the expedition actually started, and a fortified port, Aigues Mortes, was built at the mouth of the Rhone as the port of departure.

The crusade itself, which started in 1248, was a failure. Though other rulers had promised to join him, Louis set out alone. His plan was to advance through Egypt. He did capture Damietta, but then attempted an ill-advised invasion deeper into Egypt which resulted in the destruction of his army and his own capture. He was released through ransom and then joined the Christians in the Holy Land with whom he tarried until 1254, vainly hoping somehow to recapture Jerusalem. This crusade of Louis IX has frequently been contrasted with that of Frederick II, who counted little upon military strength but much upon his knowledge of the Moslems. Louis showed little insight into the Mohammedan world. His effort resulted in failure, but the spirit with which he had made the attempt commanded the admiration of pious Christians everywhere.

LOUIS AS A RULER

When Louis IX returned he found his kingdom not any the worse for his absence. Thanks to the careful administration of the merchants, his finances were in excellent shape and, due to the watchful care of his mother, the government, too, was in good condition. There was some trouble in Flanders whose count was receiving sympathy, if not help, from the king of England. Peaceful negotiations with the king of England resulted ultimately in the agreement of 1258 already mentioned, and removed the probability of disturbance from that quarter. Meanwhile Frederick II had died, but the struggle between papacy and Hohenstaufens still continued and the opportunities it offered were still open. Louis, however, exhibited no strong desire to take advantage of them. Instead, he concerned himself with the improvement of government within his realm and with efforts to bring peace among his quarreling neighbors. He made an adjustment with the king of Aragon whereby his title to nearly all the former Albigensian lands of southern France was clearly established.

The improvements which Louis made in the government of his kingdom were partly in machinery, but more in spirit. Under him the lands recently added in the south were given royal officers like those in the north, though they bore somewhat different titles. The local provosts were called bailiffs, while the royal bailiffs in this southern region were called seneschals. "Be careful to have good provosts and bailiffs and make frequent inquiries about them and the people of the household, as to how they conduct themselves and if they are guilty of over-much greed, or of treachery or deceit." This was part of the advice which the dying Louis gave to his son and it well described his own practice. By personal inquiry he had discovered that his representatives were sometimes guilty of grave abuses. For this reason he frequently changed them about in different districts, and he employed regular inquisitors whose task it was to hear complaints against provosts, bailiffs and seneschals. He usually employed friars in this work. Under Louis also the *curia regis,* or body of officials who aided him, tended to become more clearly differentiated. The royal domain was now too large and the routine affairs of government too numerous to be adequately carried on by one body of men. Certain men of the court now concerned themselves with judicial matters alone, others only with financial affairs, while still others devoted themselves entirely to administrative affairs. The change was by no means complete. For much of this work the king employed men of humble birth who were especially skilled or trained, but he also used nobles. The greatest advance, however, which he made was in the spirit of government. The humble, gentle, but persistent way in which he was constantly seeking to make the government serve its purpose to both king and people, however lowly, was of greater value than any machinery in making his rule efficient.

His greatest distinction was in the sphere of justice. He realized, as few kings in history have done, the fundamental importance of this function of government. Doubtless he was moved by the scruples of conscience which his pious training had given him in unusual degree. But it is quite clear that he also appreciated the political value of speedy, fair and exact justice. His reply to the nobles, when they protested his return of some of the conquered land to the English king, might win respect in much more modern times. "Sirs," he said, "I am certain that the king of England's predecessors lost most justly the conquests I hold; and the land which I give up to him I do not give as a thing to which I am bound either towards himself or his heirs, but to create love between his children and mine, who are cousins german. And it seems to me that I am making a good use of what I give to him because he was not before my vassal, but now he has to render homage to me." Five years after this, the barons and king of England gave evidence of their confidence in Louis' sense of justice by submitting their dispute to him in the parley at Amiens. Louis' attitude toward ecclesiastical justice is illustrated by the following incident.[1] At a Church council the prelates of France decided to ask the king for the use of the

[1] Compare this incident with the efforts of Henry II of England to substitute royal for ecclesiastical justice, pages 164*ff*.

royal officials in enforcing bans of excommunication. Their delegation announced to the king that Christianity was perishing in his lands because "no one nowadays has any fear of excommunication," and they therefore asked that the king have his officials force any who had been excommunicated for a year and a day to render satisfaction to the Church. Louis replied that he would be quite willing to do so "provided they would let him know the sentence, to decide if it were just or not." When, after consultation, they refused to grant this request, he replied that he must refuse to lend them his aid, "for if I did so, I should act contrary to God's will and to justice."

Louis dealt with the jurisdiction of the nobles in the same gentle and firm fashion. He dispensed justice among their vassals and encouraged the latter to appeal to the king's court from unjust decisions. By his practice of holding open court at the oak tree in Vincennes, according to legend, or in Paris, he helped to spread the idea that even his humblest subjects might obtain fair and speedy hearing from their king. His reputation for justice became so widespread that people of neighboring lands brought their cases to him. Louis was not unaware that he was thus strengthening the king's power. Happy and enduring is that dynasty or state whose beginnings are associated with the establishment of such even-handed justice among its subjects and between its neighbors!

Another policy especially dear to him was his encouragement of towns and trade. "Above all, keep the good towns and cities of thy kingdom in the condition and liberties in which thy predecessors preserved them; and if there be anything to amend, amend and redress it, and keep all in favour and affection, for, because of the power and riches of thy great cities, thy subjects and foreigners will fear to do anything against thee, especially thy peers and thy barons." This, too, was among his last instructions to his son. In making this statement Louis was voicing what may be described as the royal policy since the days of Louis VI, and one of the important secrets of royal power. He carried this policy out in practice, not only granting charters to towns, but concerning himself with good government in the towns.

Joinville recites a significant instance in connection with the provostship of Paris. This office had customarily been sold to wealthy merchants, probably to the highest bidder, and was frequently used by the purchaser to favor his friends at the expense of others, especially of the poor. Louis corrected this evil practice by appointing to office Stephen Boileau, a merchant highly regarded by his fellows, as one "who would render strict and true justice and would spare the rich man no more than the poor." He was given a handsome salary and did his work so well that "the sales, seizins, purchases and other things were worth double what the king used previously to receive from them." It was probably this Stephen Boileau who drew up the *Book of the Gilds,* an industrial census of Paris at the end of the thirteenth century. The work has been very important in revealing the history of industrial organization. Trade had begun to flourish in France before the time of Louis IX, but under the benign influence of his administration it reached a degree of prosperity never before attained.

RELATIONS OF LOUIS IX WITH OTHER POWERS OF EUROPE

Though his interest was very strongly in the government of his own kingdom during this period, his neighbors were never entirely out of mind. He made marriage alliances calculated to strengthen or protect his successors. He invited the people of the powerful border nobles to seek justice at his court, and he coöperated with the merchants and clergy in those regions to the advantage of the royal power.

His attitude toward the struggle between papacy and Hohenstaufens continued to be neutral and has therefore been much criticized. He was always on friendly terms with the papacy, but despite his well-known piety he refused to be drawn into the quarrel. Even when the whole chapter of Cistercian abbots rushed to meet him and on bended knee implored him to let the pope, Innocent IV, use France as his headquarters in 1245, he assured them of his good will but explained that on a matter of such importance he must consult his barons. He resisted this

appeal to his piety, and he similarly resisted Frederick's appeal
that he act as judge in the dispute, a request which he refused
firmly but gently. Both requests were very flattering, but Louis
was not swayed from his resolve to remain neutral and he
distinctly reserved judgment on the conduct of both parties. In
1262 the papacy offered him Sicily if he would enter the war on
the papal side. Even then Louis refused to accept the offer
either for himself or his heirs, but he did permit his brother
Charles to accept it and allowed Charles to take along many of
his best troops. Perhaps the neutrality of Louis was due to a
feeling of friendship for Frederick, who had gained his position
in Germany with the help of Louis' grandfather. Certainly Frederick had made no efforts to cause trouble in France, though in
1242 the king of England had strongly urged him to do so.
Perhaps, too, Louis did not feel sufficiently safe from English
attack to venture into the papal-imperial struggle until after 1258.

At any rate, the final outcome gave Sicily to France for all
practical purposes, while at the same time Louis was personally
free from the charge of having enriched himself by taking advantage of the misfortunes of his neighbors. The final crusade of
Louis to Tunis may not have been without some bearing on the
Sicilian question, for it certainly placed the main army of France
within easy reach of Charles of Anjou. It was not needed,
however, for Charles had overcome all opposition before his
brother arrived. Louis was able to continue his crusade, on
which he shortly met his death in 1270.

Ambitious politicians of France, in the time of Louis and ever
since, have criticized him for not making the most of his many
opportunities to increase the territory of France. To them his
conduct, particularly the return of lands to Henry III of England,
has seemed little else than the height of pious simplicity. In
their estimation he might be likened to Louis the Pious of
earlier times. And yet France at the end of his reign was the
greatest power in Europe, with fewer political liabilities and
greater royal assets than any state which had occupied that position for many years. Louis had made the kingship so dear to
the affections of all his people that even great nobles thereafter

found it much more difficult to gain support in open defiance of the king. He had outdone the clergy in piety and peaceful justice; he had outdone the nobles in the warmth of his personal solicitude for the welfare of even his humblest subjects. He had caused the rank and file of the people to feel that, though both nobles and clergy might be swerved through self-interest from the paths of justice, they could always find justice with the king. Their interests were his interests and his must, therefore, also be theirs. He had so spread abroad the feeling of a national community of interest between king and people that generations of misrule could scarcely eradicate it. There have been many kings in history who have been ready to wrench lands from afflicted neighbors —few, in fact, who have resisted the temptation—but the kings who have known how to weld the good will of so many of their subjects into a unified force have been few indeed. The Church officially canonized Louis as a saint in 1298, a fitting tribute to his remarkable career, but in the hearts of the French people he had already held that position for nearly half a century.

CHAPTER XIII

COMMERCE AND INDUSTRY IN THE
THIRTEENTH CENTURY

THE religious and political events of the twelfth and thirteenth centuries favored the growth of trade and industry. The increased travel which the crusades, the pilgrimages and the enlarged affairs of the papacy had brought about served to advertise the products of all the regions of Europe and of the Mediterranean world. Travel was necessarily slow, much of it on foot, some of it on horseback, and the traveler was therefore able not only to feast his eyes upon the landscape but also to observe more minute matters of human comfort and personal adornment. In turn, he too was observed, and his clothing, his manner of living, and his tales of his own land's excellencies were doubtless carefully noted. On his return, like the traveler of every age, he was sure to burden himself with souvenirs for his family and friends. At any rate, in thirteenth-century Europe it was an isolated community indeed which did not possess in at least one of its homes silks from the far East, dyed cloth from Italy, spices or drugs from far-off India, woolens from the Netherlands, iron ware from Germany, leather goods from Spain, or linen cloth from Flanders. The actual list of exotic products in almost any region at this time was probably great both in variety and in quantity. The net of commerce was now more widely spread than ever before in history. Far-off Iceland was, in effect, exchanging products with the even more remote islands off the eastern coast of China, though the people of the one were not to see those of the other for centuries yet to come.

Not less important, if less romantic, was the effect of greater centralization of political authority. The growth of states, or the establishment of a central authority in them whether under a king, a prince, or a city government, more and more made war a public matter rather than a private affair of the aristocracy, and peace the rule rather than the exception over a wide range of territory.   Here and there people were able to devote their whole energies to the occupations of peace and were thus encouraged to provide more amply for the comforts of themselves, their children and their children's children.   When the haunting specters of imminent warfare, rapine and devastation which had so long confined the efforts of most men to living for the moment, were laid, the people in many regions looked forward confidently (often too confidently) to the peaceful and indefinite enjoyment of their homes.   Those who had means were building large permanent houses, and others were improving their dwellings to the extent of their ability.   All were eager to add to their comforts and their enjoyment of life, and to find or to exploit new sources of wealth.

Agriculture, which had advanced so greatly in the twelfth century, continued to progress in the thirteenth.   Further inroads were made upon the waste land, and the tendency to use lands for crops especially adapted to them became more marked.   Whole districts turned to the cultivation of vines, grains, or flax, or to sheep-raising.   The former really wasteful practice of seeking from each locality all the necessities of life began to give way to the more profitable, if also more venturesome, specialization of crops.   Such practice would have meant famine in the early age of feudalism, but it seemed now an assurance of prosperity for tillers and owners of land alike.

Equally encouraging was the evidence of more thoughtful attention to the management of estates by their owners.   The earlier practice of seeking higher returns from land by increasing the taxes or dues which the peasantry had to pay was now supplemented by some study of farm management.   Here and there new treatises began to appear, setting forth principles of crop rotation, fertilization of the soil, selection of seed, care of herds, and advising the more accurate keeping of manorial records. Walter of Henley's *Husbandry,* the most famous of these treatises, was written for circulation among the lay nobility.

Probably even more was accomplished by personal visits to well-managed estates, for the nobles were finding more time to interlard their exchanges of feudal gossip with discussions of economic advantage. The results appeared not only in profits and prosperity, but also in social sympathy, a gentle reflection of more widespread peace.

CONTROL OF THE MEDITERRANEAN BY ITALIAN TOWNS

The most profound changes in economic life which the age showed, however, were those involved in the expansion of commerce. This expansion occurred not so much in the necessities of life, such as grain, fish, salt and wood—although this trade likewise increased—as in articles which contributed to the comforts and enjoyment of life. Such were drugs and spices, silks, brocades, velvets and other fine textiles, leather goods and furs of more skillful and artistic workmanship, not to mention jewelry, corals, pearls, ivory and precious stones. These articles were less common, more difficult to obtain, easier to carry, and, as a rule, more profitable. To import them required the linking of three continents, not of a few adjacent feudal states, and was an achievement of human ingenuity rather than of force. No army which could have been mustered at that time would have attempted the task; but under the guise of trade, unarmed or slightly armed relays of merchants equipped with knowledge, ready wit and unusual physical endurance, could assemble and distribute the treasures of Asia, Africa and Europe.

The crusading activities had established the Europeans at the junction of the three continents, the eastern Mediterranean. Since history began the peoples of that region had been masters in the art of trade. Greeks, Armenians and Jews had long held a reputation for skill in trade beyond all others. The most enterprising of these, the Jews, had sent out colonies east and west and north and south. Jews were to be found in the leading centers of Christian, Mohammedan and heathen lands. Through their racial connections some measure of commercial contact had existed since ancient times between fairly remote portions of the three continents, although the actual volume of trade was for long periods very slight. Their ability to procure the luxuries of the far East had been one of the reasons for the protection granted them by leading churchmen and nobles in the otherwise hostile West. With the spread of more favorable conditions in the West they had profited greatly and, despite the crusades, they held the leading position in the commercial and financial affairs of Christian Europe even past the middle of the twelfth century. A learned rabbi, Benjamin of Tudela, made a journey from his home in Spain to Jerusalem and Bagdad about the middle of this century, and his account of the trip has been preserved. In northern Spain, and more especially in southern France, he found large and prosperous colonies of Jews in virtually all the towns. This was true likewise in Italy, where at Rome he found a Jew occupying the post of treasurer to the pope. In the East, of course, the Jews were much more numerous. At Bagdad, the home of the caliph, he found a very large settlement of them living in great prosperity and honor. Had the good rabbi been able to continue his journey farther into and through the Moham-medan lands, he doubtless would have discovered similar settle-ments as far East as India, and perhaps China. These scattered groups maintained some degree of cohesion, as the journey of the rabbi itself illustrates. Everywhere were students of the Law, the Talmud, and through them were maintained the ancient religion, language and traditions. These men also helped to keep Jewish traders of one region in touch with those of another, and thus to form their remarkable organization for the world trade in luxuries.

Before the twelfth century had come to an end, however, the leadership in this trade, at least so far as western Europe was concerned, was passing to the men of the Italian cities. The part which Genoa, Pisa, and Venice had performed in the crusades has already been noted. They had no complete monopoly, of course. For example, Marseilles and Barcelona carried Oriental wares to northern Africa, to southern France and to Spain. And some Eastern goods filtered into the Baltic lands by way of Rus-sia. But by long odds, the great rôle of intermediary was played by the Italians. Unlike the Jews, these Italian townsmen knew how to combine force with trade to their own advantage, and their citizenship in their native town afforded them a bond of organization almost as strong as that enjoyed by the Jews. They operated their fleets in the warfare of the eastern Mediterranean, thereby winning privileges throughout that region. These privileges they turned to commercial advantage as quickly and as fully as possible. Their possession of naval power and their connections with the Christian states of the West served also as diplomatic bases for the extension of their trading privileges into Mohammedan lands. In the thirteenth century they had secured carefully guarded trading rights in nearly all the towns on the eastern Mediterranean islands and shores and all around the Black Sea. These rights usually involved the allotment of a district in the town to their exclusive possession. Here they maintained permanent representatives who acted as traders in exchanging the products of the West for those of the East, as guards for the accumulated stores of goods, and as diplomats in dealing with the local authorities for the maintenance or increase of their privileges. From time to time ships arrived from the home city with news from the West as well as with additional wares for trade, and occasionally with some newcomers to replace the men who had served a long time in the East. These ships then returned, laden with the products of the near and remote East, which were sold either in the home city or farther inland by their own or other merchants.

Recounted in this fashion, the story of these operations seems prosaic enough. The actual story was, however, quite another thing. Each little ship represented, as a rule, the coöperation of several families. Its financing was a joint achievement. The merchant who accompanied the cargo to do the actual trading was but a partner in the undertaking. The cargo represented the thrifty savings of a number of families, and its loss might involve the financial ruin of many of his fellow citizens and relatives. The ships usually did not go singly. Ships similarly laden and circumstanced went out, as did land caravans, twice or thrice a year as a fleet, accompanied by ships primarily built and manned for war. The latter were provided by the home town government. The dangers were many. In addition to the havoc of storms and pestilence, the raids of pirates and the variable tempers of the Eastern potentates, there was usually the possibility of encounter with a hostile fleet from some Eastern land. Yet the greater danger lay probably in the bitter rivalry among the Italian cities themselves. The lust for the large gains which this trade afforded aroused passionate rivalry among them, the more bitter because it occurred at every stage of the trade. There was rivalry in the East for the best bargains; in their own towns for the greatest prosperity, size and splendor; and in the West for the best markets. It was frequently very unfortunate for a single ship or a few ships of one city to meet a greater number of a rival's ships. Sometimes one ship succeeded in escaping to bring the tidings of the disaster home, and often, no doubt, the losses in actual shipwreck were blamed upon the murderous hate of the rivals. Thus the actual trading—the sale of Western goods at the highest possible price and the purchase of Eastern goods as cheaply as possible—the defense of property, the robbery of rivals, all required the highest exercise of wit and skill. Here lay the thrill of a great game, and success in it—for the profits were very large—involved not merely self-satisfaction, but possibly wealth and affluence as well. The successful return of the merchant from an unusually profitable voyage was deservedly an occasion for thanksgiving in which the whole town might join.

The arrival of the cargo of Eastern goods at Pisa, Genoa, or Venice did not end the concern of the Italian merchants. There was still the problem of distribution or disposal. Merchants from the north came down, especially to Venice, to trade for the Eastern goods, but only a portion of the goods was thus disposed of. The Italian merchants for the most part got their Oriental wares directly or indirectly from Venice or Genoa, which cities concentrated on maritime trade. These merchants were interested in carrying Eastern and Mediterranean products as near to the consuming areas as possible. As a result, caravans were formed to carry the goods to the fairs of Europe, of which the chief were to be found in Champagne. This practice also had its dangers, for an extended journey by land was certainly no less hazardous than by sea and always more expensive. Dues had to be paid all along the route. Robbers, whether ordinary highwaymen or more genteel knights, were numerous. Hence the necessity of caravans, whose crew had to be equally ready to beat off the highwaymen or to bargain with the lord of superior might. These crews were usually carefully selected[1] and contained not only men of the Italian towns, but usually also additional men from the regions through which they were about to pass. There was adventure and risk all along the way, but during most of the thirteenth century there was a reasonable probability that a caravan starting, for example, from Genoa for the fairs of Champagne would reach that destination.

THE FAIRS OF CHAMPAGNE

These fairs, already prominent in the twelfth century, continued to grow during the thirteenth, and were beyond question the great international market center of Europe. The business acumen of the counts of Champagne, long apparent in their feudal dealings, was no less evident in their recognition of the financial possibilities of these gatherings. Geographical location, which gave easy access to the merchants of Flanders as well as to those of Italy, to say nothing of the lesser merchants of adjacent regions, also favored the development of the fairs of Champagne. In this region there were six great fairs, so set in time as to cover practically the whole year. They were held at Lagny early in January, then at Bar-sur-Aube just before mid-Lent, with the "May-fair" at Provins, and the midsummer festival at Troyes. Another was held at Provins in harvest-time, and, finally, a second at Troyes during November and early December. The intervals between them were long enough to permit those who desired to move from one to the other. The fairs of Champagne may be regarded as a great wholesale market where the merchants

---

[1] The skill of the Genoese bowmen attained such renown that kings sought them for their armies. Genoese cross-bowmen played an important part in the wars of the fourteenth century.

of all parts of Europe met and the merchandise of the known world was to be seen. This was, in effect, the northern frontier for the full display of goods carried by the Italians, as it was likewise the southern frontier for the exhibition on a large scale of Flemish textiles and the wares of the Hanseatic cities.[1]

The management of the fairs was systematic. A week was allowed for the installation of the goods. Business began in the second week, usually with the sale of cloth, or textiles of all kinds; then occurred the sale of cordovan or leathers and furs of all kinds, and finally the sale of spices, dyes and other small goods. The weights used at the fair of Troyes have left a record in the weight of that name still used by jewelers. Usually each sale lasted a week, and after the three sales a period of two weeks was allowed for the settlement of accounts. The grounds of the fair were excellently policed by the knights and sergeants of the count, and the inevitable disputes between traders were given speedy solution in a commercial court. This court sat during the fair and was often called the "Piepowder Court" (from the French *pied poudré,* the "dusty foot" of the traveling merchant). The simplified procedure of the Piepowder Court, which was to be found at every great fair, furnished a model, too often disregarded, for other courts of State and Church.

The fairs of Champagne, though the greatest, were not the only fairs. If the figure of a tree were used to picture the extent of trade in the thirteenth century, its trunk would rise in the eastern Mediterranean. The greater cities from Constantinople to Alexandria might be likened to the emerging main roots which would extend through the cities of northern Italy up the Rhone Valley to the fairs of Champagne, each of which might be regarded as the beginning of a main branch. Merchandise from these fairs was carried to the next fairs, and so on to the remotest lines of trade, with decreasing volume and variety. Italian merchants seldom carried their goods farther than the greater fairs of England or Germany, less frequently to the former than to the latter. The goods which they brought, however, might be resold from fair to fair, until they reached the

[1] See pages 233*ff.* and also chapter XVII.

most remote regions of Europe, for the branches of the tree of trade reached alike from Spain to northern Russia, Ireland, Scotland and Iceland. In many cases the fairs were chiefly local in importance, and some, such as horse fairs, vintage fairs and even onion fairs, were highly specialized. In practically all cases, however, they involved the same elements—a protecting patron, sometimes a monastery or bishopric; merchants often accompanied by their families; venders of food products; and professional entertainers who moved from fair to fair. All these formed a motley congeries of humanity.

COMMERCIAL ORGANIZATION AND MARITIME RIVALRY

This development required a more or less intricate organization of agents, warehouses, trading privileges and legal provisions, and, while there was still opportunity for individual enterprise, the whole undertaking became closely interwoven with the government of the home town. The scattered colonies in the East were placed under the general direction of an official appointed by the home town. It was his duty to guard the rights of his people in the East, adjudicate quarrels among them, look after the effects of any who died in the East, and in general to keep the home government informed about conditions which might affect trade. To him also was allotted the delicate task of keeping the Eastern governments friendly to his fellow townsmen, and, whenever possible, of advancing the interests of his own townsmen at the expense of their rivals. This required diplomatic skill of the highest type and a fine judgment as to the opportune time for the use of money or force in achieving the desired end. The beginnings of the modern consular, if not also of the diplomatic, service might well be sought here.

The task was not lightened by the intense competition which existed among the three great maritime towns, Pisa, Genoa and Venice. The frequency of desultory warfare on the high seas aroused such ill-feeling that trade was at times interrupted to permit the muster of all naval resources for a decisive war. Pisa and Genoa, both active in the western Mediterranean, had had several such wars during the later twelfth and early thirteenth century. In 1284, however, both cities rallied all their available resources for decisive encounter. The Genoese ships sailed down the coast to the mouth of the Arno, where the Pisans came out to meet them. The fight lasted through the day, ship after ship being destroyed in the encounter. At the end of the conflict the Pisan fleet was destroyed and thousands of Pisans either killed or captured. The bitterness of the rivalry was best shown by the grim resolve of the Genoese authorities to keep their Pisan captives prisoners for life, so that they might not return to Pisa and rear children to endanger the Genoese merchants of the next generation. Many a poet's pen depicted the pathetic efforts of Pisan wives and mothers to locate their lost husbands and sons. This battle of Meloria effectively crippled the wider aspirations of Pisa, which thereafter functioned merely as the leading carrier to and from Tuscany. Henceforth the great rivalry narrowed down to Genoa and Venice.

Their competition did not reach the climax of direct decisive war for another century, but meanwhile it took many forms. The clever tactics of Venice in turning the Fourth Crusade to her own advantage by the capture of Zara and finally of Constantinople had apparently given her control of most of the eastern Mediterranean. She had the lion's share in Constantinople, her citizens had made themselves rulers of many of the eastern islands including Crete and Corfu, and she had extended her control on the Balkan mainland. During the first half of the thirteenth century she also virtually controlled the commerce of the Black Sea. Her supremacy here, however, was brief. The Greeks with good reason hated her, and in 1258, when they were ready to undertake the reconquest of Constantinople, they invited the Genoese to aid them, which the latter did with alacrity. As a result of their joint successes the Genoese gained the position in the Black Sea trade and on the Black Sea coasts formerly held by the Venetians, and maintained and developed it during the latter part of the thirteenth century. The Venetians now improved their trading relations with the Syrian and Egyptian ports, and the rivalry continued.

The main activities of Genoese and Venetians lay in the Mediterranean islands and coasts, where both had veritable commercial empires which their sea power had won and defended. The Venetians brought their Oriental and Levantine imports to Venice, and the northerners came to Venice for these imports and the articles of luxury made in Venice. The Genoese made little for export except ships, and carried most of their imports to other ports of the western Mediterranean. Other Italians, notably the Florentines, went north overland to lend money and to trade. For the shipments of textiles, fish, metals and other wares from the North were, of course, just as much a part of the round of trade as were the shipments of spices, drugs, silks and other costly articles from the South and East.

IMPROVEMENT IN METHODS OF EXCHANGE. BANKING

One further operation must be described to complete the story of the round of trade. When the Italian merchant sold his Eastern wares in Champagne to inland merchants, he received a variety of silver money in payment. Many of the great feudal lords still retained the right to coin money. Many towns exercised the same privilege, and of course the kings practiced it as a sovereign prerogative. The coins varied considerably in their proportions of precious and baser metals and even kings, Philip IV of France for instance, indulged in the art of debasing coinage. Consequently money-changing became somewhat of a science which only experts could practice without danger of serious loss. Even the Genoese and Venetians required help on this problem. The most expert money-changers of the time were the Florentines and Sienese, who had gained their skill in the service of the papal treasury. The flow of money to the religious capital of Christendom from all parts of Europe had early demanded a study of metal composition and value. In the later twelfth and during the thirteenth century the Jews were superseded by the Tuscan townsmen in the conduct of this business for the papacy. The skill which they had acquired made their services desirable at the great fairs as well, and, as a result, when a caravan started it usually included several Sienese or Florentine money-changers with their huge leather wallets.

The desirability of a standard coinage was clear to the merchants, who learned that they lost heavily through the discounts on their doubtful coins, and the Florentines rendered a great service to the commercial world when they began to mint their gold *florin* in 1252. Other communities followed their example, but, unlike the Florentines, they were not always so scrupulous in maintaining the fineness of their coinage at standard. The best of these was the Venetian *ducat* of gold, which shares its reputation with the gold *florin*. The gold *mouton* coined by Louis IX of France was another attempt, but it was early tampered with. The minting of the gold *florin* and *ducat* was also another evidence of the liberation of the West from the commercial domination of the East, as represented by the gold *bezant* of Constantinople and the later Saracen *bezant*. The *florin* and *ducat* soon gained a wide reputation, and it was not long before money-changers everywhere in Europe were employing them as the standards by which all other coins were judged.

This round of trade was so well established by the thirteenth century that it was already assuming a permanent form. The demand for Eastern spices, drugs and art products had become steady or increasing in volume, and the demand of the East for the wares and silver of the West had likewise become firmly established. Instead of the simple venture of a small group which sent the merchant with the cargo to the East, larger companies were formed with merchants permanently located in Eastern towns. Ships plied at regular intervals between the Italian towns and the Mediterranean East, their cargoes being got together for them by their permanent representatives at both ends of the journey.

Not long after this fact became recognized, the merchants resorted to such conveniences of commerce as the opening of accounts, the use of bills payable on demand and of letters of credit. These devices required the existence of strong and reliable associations of merchants and bankers, which had already come into being in twelfth-century Italy. The Italians operating in France were organized with a series of elected officials through whom responsibility was definitely fixed.   The towns of Flanders engaged in the manufacture of textiles also formed a close association of their leading merchants.   Similar associations were formed in other regions, notably in the Baltic, where the Hanseatic League was in process of formation.   Such organizations resembled in some respects the modern chambers of commerce, although their powers were much greater.

Private banks grew up quite naturally in connection with the activities of the money-changers, whose expert knowledge commanded the confidence of merchants and others.   Such banks were first established in the Italian towns, another indication of the economic leadership of medieval Italy.   As the demands for commercial loans increased and opportunities for profit appeared in this business of loans, it was only natural that merchants and others should entrust their savings to the money-changers for investment.   Certain operators and families acquired enviable records for success in banking and trading operations, and thereby attracted investment funds not only from their own towns but from others as well.   Most of the banking business of Europe in the thirteenth century was in the hands of Italians, or Lombards as they were indiscriminately called in trans-Alpine Europe. The money-changing, banking and trading establishments of the Italians took root in all the important towns of the North and served as the agency for the smooth handling of the trunk-line trade.   Great shipments of materials could thus be made from north to south, or in the opposite direction, without the actual transfer of any considerable sums of money.   The northern merchant or his representative could present his bill for goods sold to an Italian, for example, to a northern branch or agent of an Italian bank.   The basis of the transfer was a written promise made by the buyer to pay the seller or his representative.   The Italian bank then instructed its branch or agent to pay the bill. The payment of an equal northern debt in Italy would reverse the procedure and balance the whole matter without the risk of shipping money.   In practice several northern accounts would balance a group of southern accounts.   The wide interests of the bank could take care of any number of such transactions. At the same time these banking and trading houses (usually they were both) served as the most effective means of linking the merchants of one region with those of another, for an Italian house with a branch in a French, Flemish, or English town invariably accepted investment deposits from the local merchants, and usually also took some of them into a kind of partnership.

The banking operations served also to help trade in another way. It was not merely that the bankers were also engaged in exporting and importing goods. Kings, nobles and high ecclesiastics, in whose power it lay to interrupt seriously or to aid greatly the easy flow of trade, were frequently in need of immediate sums of ready money. They were, of course, the chief customers for luxuries, and by the end of the thirteenth century much of the business of government was carried on by means of money. Officials, particularly the lesser officials, were paid in money; soldiers were hired for money; supplies were bought with money; and money, judiciously applied, might be the means of winning an important ally or even of holding a wavering vassal. On the other hand, the income of these authorities came from many different sources, trickling in throughout the year, whereas the expenditures had often to be made suddenly and in large sums. It was here that the banker could help; but such opportunities required the exercise of great judgment. He had to be able to calculate quickly the chances of the repayment of the loan. High ecclesiastics were good risks. Kings and independent feudal lords were, by and large, bad risks from a banker's point of view. What recourse had a Florentine banker if the king of France or England should repudiate a large loan, as sometimes happened? At the same time, could the banker safely refuse such a loan? The trading activities of the bank offered a solution of this dilemma. Such loans were often made on condition that the king or prince grant certain trading privileges, perhaps the exclusive rights to certain kinds of trade in certain towns of the kingdom. Moreover, the Genoese bankers used loans to feudal rulers in southern France as a means of curtailing maritime competition from Narbonne, Montpellier and Marseilles. The Italians likewise used such loans to insure greater military protection along the lines of trade. Under these conditions, the loan, if never repaid, might still be an investment which the banker, through his own trade or his connection with merchants, could in time turn to the profit of his banking house.

The outcome was not always so favorable, especially if heavy loans were made in time of war to a contestant who ultimately lost. Such a calamity brought grief to the household and partisans of the loser, and also carried with it the financial ruin of many other families in their distant Italian town. Bank failures were not uncommon in thirteenth-century Italy. Successful bankers had to keep themselves unusually well informed about current conditions in all the regions in which they did business and to be constantly on the alert. Their own connection with commerce and with other traders whose agents were constantly moving about was, therefore, of great assistance to them. How well they were able to keep themselves informed is illustrated by the fact that Giovanni Villani, a Florentine born at the end of the thirteenth century, when his city had become a leading banking center of Europe, was able to write a remarkably accurate European history of his own times chiefly on the basis of information which he gleaned from his fellow citizens.

GROWTH OF TOWNS.   POLITICAL AND SOCIAL IMPROVEMENT OF MERCHANTS

Such extensive and regular trade could scarcely have existed if the merchants had not possessed certain centers in which they could be reasonably free from outside interference. The walled towns or parts of towns under their control afforded this assurance, though not in equal measure. Venice, which was protected on all sides by water, had never been under the control of feudal nobles. The story of its government reveals changes from time to time in the extent of the participation of its citizens, but control was exercised by the merchants. In the thirteenth century power was passing definitely into the hands of a limited number of the wealthier merchants and Venice became a commer-

cial oligarchy.   Its rivals, Pisa and Genoa, were not so well
situated.   Though protected on one side by water and provided
with strong fleets, they were open to attack by land and never
gained complete freedom from interference by the land powers.
During the twelfth century this interference was one of the chief
problems of these towns.   By the thirteenth century, however,
many of the landed nobility had learned to appreciate the desirability of allying themselves with the new type of wealth.   They
intermarried with the wealthier merchant families, and in Genoa
actually moved into the town and took a share in the administration of the commercial empire.   Noble names were associated
there with banks and large trading companies.   Nobles even participated in the management of Genoese affairs in the East.
Nevertheless, the danger of attack from the land side always
remained.   It was a strong factor in the overthrow of Pisa, and
it was to be a factor in the ultimate defeat of Genoa.

The towns in the other great commercial area of Europe,
around the mouth of the Rhine, were similarly circumstanced.
Some of them, like Amsterdam, Antwerp, and Bruges in the Low
Countries, were almost, although not quite, as well located as
Venice, for by means of canals or the opening of dykes it was an
easy matter for them to draw a water barrier between themselves
and feudal attack.   There, too, the merchants early gained almost
complete control.   Most of the seacoast cities of the north, however, were more nearly in the condition of Pisa and Genoa; that
is, never entirely free from the direct interference of the higher
feudal nobility.   Inland towns, if not quite at the mercy of the
landed nobility, were constantly in danger of attack.   Those whose
location on the main highways of trade had made them prosperous and large were usually able to gain independence from direct
supervision.

Town charters recognizing certain degrees of self-government
had been won during the twelfth and thirteenth centuries.   In almost every case the degree of self-government depended upon the
relative strength of the town and the noble authority from whom
it was won, and consequently town charters varied greatly in
scope.   The towns of northern Italy and of Flanders were espe-

cially fortunate.   In the former region the feudal nobility owed their strength chiefly to the support of the emperor.   When the great struggles between papacy and empire arose these townsmen made common cause with the papacy.   They organized their Lombard League among the towns in the Po valley, first against Frederick Barbarossa in the twelfth century, and again in the struggle with Frederick II in the thirteenth century.   At the battle of Legnano in 1176 the Lombard townsmen won a complete victory by their own efforts.   Their alliance with the papacy probably cost them some of the fruits of their victory, for the resulting Peace of Constance, in which Pope Alexander III gained his recognition from the emperor, involved the loss of some of the rights formerly granted by Frederick I.   In the struggle with Frederick II the partnership between towns and papacy was somewhat more equal, and it would be difficult to determine which contributed most to the failure of the Hohenstaufens.   From about 1250, certainly after 1273, the towns of northern Italy were practically independent of the emperor and of the nobles who had represented him.   A few nobles, like the picturesque Can Grande della Scala, managed to exercise some control over some of the lesser towns, but municipal independence was the rule. Moreover, these towns were now extending their grip over the neighboring countryside, and their chief enemy was no longer the feudal noble but the rival neighboring town.   It was clear, however, before the end of the thirteenth century that Milan, where the great highways from all directions crossed, would dominate the upper Po valley and that Florence would be mistress of Tuscany.   In both the conflict with the lesser nobility of the countryside led to a fusion between feudal nobles and wealthy townsmen, like that which took place in Genoa.   Florence with a democratic constitution was dominated by a commercial oligarchy, while in Milan the merchants were finding it to their advantage to entrust almost absolute political power to an unusually able family, the Visconti.

The peculiarly favorable position of Flanders both politically and commercially has already been noted.   The low, easily-flooded lands lent themselves readily to town organization, and the burghers proved themselves sturdy fighters. The towns early co-operated for trading and military purposes. The lesser nobles were unable to cope with them, and the counts of Flanders, needing much money help, found it wise to let them govern themselves with little interference. This wisdom they had to learn more than once, for the twelfth and thirteenth centuries showed frequent instances of clashes between the two. In those cases the burghers were prepared to negotiate for outside aid with the king of England, or the Hanseatic League, or even with the king of France. Their own league of seventeen cities, which was chiefly interested in the manufacture and sale of textiles, had so thoroughly learned the art of effective coöperation that it must henceforth be regarded as a separate factor in the commercial and, at times, the political affairs of Europe.

The German merchants from the Rhenish and Baltic towns, who traded in northern Europe in the twelfth century and earlier, played in that region a part comparable to that of the Italians in the Mediterranean, but with a significant difference. Instead of fighting each other steadily, they gradually drew together for mutual protection. The towns from which they went forth followed their example in the thirteenth century, and finally in 1358 took over the active direction of the interests of their merchants. Thus was born the Hanseatic League, a model of co-operation in an age of city rivalries. The League fluctuated in its membership from a score to four or five scores of cities around or near the Baltic and the North Sea coasts. It was essentially a North German affair, although outside of Germany it had member cities or factories in Scandinavian, Polish, Lithuanian, Russian, Flemish, Dutch and English lands. Lübeck and Hamburg and Köln were most prominent. Its organization left much to be desired and members constantly had to be whipped into line by a boycott; but it usually succeeded in promoting and defending the trade of the citizens of its member cities. The League as such did not trade; but it had a flag, a common set of regulations, a powerful navy, and sometimes an army. Unlike Venice and Genoa, it operated on land and sea. Its trade extended from London to Nijni Novgorod. In its trading posts its agents were required to observe almost military monastic discipline. It preferred diplomacy to war, but it fought the king of Denmark successfully (1376) and also forced the English government to respect its privileges.

The customs policy of the Hanseatic League resembled that of the Italian cities. In return for gifts and loans to needy rulers, and in consideration of the range of goods it furnished to and purchased from the undeveloped regions of the north, the League, whenever it could, exacted preferential treatment in the form of complete or partial exemption from the regular import and export duties, and thus made competition almost impossible for native or foreign rivals. Its ideal was a complete monopoly.

Elsewhere in Europe the towns were less independent. In England, France and Aragon, for example, the towns established effective coöperation with their rulers. The money which they were able to furnish to the kings permitted them to increase their hold upon their realms, and kings learned that this money could be gained more easily and in larger quantities by respecting the towns. Louis IX of France appreciated their support and profited from his confidence in them when, during his absence on the crusade, he entrusted the management of his affairs to a commission of merchants and lawyers. The English kings were among the first to reduce this coöperation to a system. They invited men from the towns to meet with nobles and clergy in Parliament for consultation on the affairs of the realm. The first instance, perhaps, was in 1265, though the Model Parliament of 1295, called by Edward I, regularized the practice. These commoners cannot be said to have exerted much influence in the period we are studying; nevertheless their importance, which was to grow, was recognized and they had an opportunity to gain consideration for their needs and wants. And of course they contributed more generously to the king's support. Philip IV of France was too shrewd a king not to appreciate the benefits of Edward's scheme, and he too inaugurated the practice of inviting townsmen to advise with him on affairs of state. The Estates which he summoned to meet in 1295 included men of the Third Estate, as the townsmen were called. In Aragon, owing to the growth of Barcelona, the townsmen had gained large privileges as early as the later twelfth century, and as long as Aragon remained a separate kingdom they continued to hold an important position. The towns in Castile and Portugal also acquired greater prominence in the thirteenth century. Towns were neither very numerous nor large in eastern Germany nor in the Slavic countries farther east. Those regions were rather outposts for the merchants from the West, without any large commercial or industrial society of their own.

INFLUENCE OF COMMERCIAL DEVELOPMENT ON LEARNING, LITERATURE AND ART

The commercial and industrial operations conducted by the towns and merchants gave an added impulse to the study and use of law. The contracts between partners in a commercial venture, the rules of conduct governing the associations of merchants, to say nothing of the regulations for the government of the towns, required permanent record and justice in execution to give confidence for the future. Much of this law was different in character from the law hitherto administered by the kings or even by the Church. The commercial law of the Roman Empire, preserved in the laws of Justinian, gave the best guidance in these matters, but the towns developed much of their law out of their own experience. The finest product of their legal achievement was the Maritime Code which the Italian cities built up for the shipping on the Mediterranean. Out of this was to grow the maritime law of modern times.

This extensive use of law led to the development of the occupations of notaries and judges, who wrote up contracts and judged disputes. Every town of any size had some men of these professions, while in Italy some of the towns had many such men, even separate gilds of them. The notaries of Florence became so famous for their proficiency that they were in demand in other places almost as widely as were the Florentine money-changers.   The lawyers of Bologna, a city long famous for its law school, were frequently employed by neighboring towns as well as by kings and Church.   The town notaries constituted one of the first learned professions to break away from the tutelage of the Church.   The essential elements of learning which the merchants needed for the conduct of business were also taught in the towns, at first by churchmen, but later, and especially in the larger towns of the thirteenth century, by school teachers who had no connection with the Church.   In some of the Flemish towns there was considerable friction between the clergy and town authorities about the maintenance of the schools, but in the long run the town authorities had their way and maintained their own schools.

The growth of the towns led also to profound social changes. Most of these, and particularly the influence of town policy upon the development of state economic policy, will be noted in a later chapter.   Here we may remark that the presence of such large numbers of people living so closely together afforded opportunity for the growth of professional entertainments.   Small individual contributions, when added together, made a sum large enough to attract even the best of the itinerant entertainers who had hitherto performed chiefly for the feudal lords.   The entertainment of townspeople became profitable enough to tempt young people to develop their talents and to inspire writers to cater to the approval of this class.

During the thirteenth century the songs and poetry written for the townsmen, usually in the vernacular of the people, came to rival, although they did not equal, the literature of the noble class. Some of this writing was of a satirical type as, for instance, the *Fabliaux* and pseudo-romances like the *Meier-Helmbrecht*, in which the failings of the clergy and nobles were held up to the laughter or scorn of the burghers.   This literature took many forms, and even the later *Decameron* of Boccaccio was not without a strong infusion from this class literature.   The famous *Roman de la Rose*, which was begun in the thirteenth century as a feudal romance, was finished by another writer who used part of his space to teach the townsmen the learning of the schools. Dante, whose family, like so many other noble families, had been drawn into the towns to fuse with the wealthier merchant families, wrote his *Banquet* and also his great poem, the *Divine Comedy,* in the vernacular for the edification of his people. Giovanni Villani, Dante's fellow townsman, also composed his history for the people of Florence in the vernacular.

This great variety in literature of the townsmen was a further reflection of the social differences which had grown up within the towns. In the twelfth century most of the towns had been thoroughly democratic in a social as well as political sense. Gradually, however, certain families rose to prominence through a combination of superior ability and opportunity, and, as the time went on, became a mercantile aristocracy within the towns. It was this class, of course, which intermarried with the feudal nobility of more ancient lineage and thus sought to establish their social leadership more firmly. By the end of the thirteenth century the larger towns probably exhibited more classes than were to be found outside.

The expansion of commerce has been considered in this chapter as a unified activity in which the merchants of all regions were brought together. Of course the great bulk of commerce then, as in much later times, consisted of foodstuffs and fuel, most of which was not transported very far. Fish from the northern seas, wines, fruits and oils from the southern vineyards and orchards, were probably transported to greater distances than any of the other commodities of this class. The merchants engaged in the traffic of foodstuffs and fuel were doubtless more numerous and their interests were primarily local, but they were in close contact with merchants of wider interests. The former operated chiefly in the immediate neighborhood of the towns, the latter ranged over three continents; but their orbits overlapped, and with the exchange of wares went also an exchange of knowledge and opinions. The merchant class contributed in a very real sense to the intellectual life of Europe. They were not limited, like the clergy, to the regions in which their faith was accepted, nor, like the nobility, to regions in which their authority was recognized.

They could traffic with Jew and Infidel, and could become acquainted and exchange ideas with people of distant lands.

Usually their activities did not pass beyond the borders of the Levant, where merchants from the East and West met, but the urge to go to the very sources of Oriental wares was already felt, and younger merchants not infrequently ventured beyond these borders to see the rest of the world. The great Empire of the Khan, with its center in China, which had at first seemed such a menace to the welfare of Europe, facilitated Western travel to the far East. For a while, in the thirteenth century, the Khan entertained the idea of accepting Christianity, and several groups of missionaries were sent to his court. Some of these have left accounts of their journey into the interior of Asia, and one of the interesting items in these accounts is the not infrequent mention of meeting Western merchants in Asiatic towns.

Unfortunately very few of the merchants were writers and there are almost no accounts of their journeys until the very end of the thirteenth century. Then, as a result of the capture of Ser Marco Polo, the Venetian, by the Genoese, the story of his wonderfully romantic journey to India and China was written during the enforced leisure of his captivity. This story was soon widely circulated and helped to give greater definiteness to the tales which had long been circulated by word of mouth. The *Book of Ser Marco Polo* served not only to entertain, but to satisfy more serious curiosity about the world and its ways. The Norman kings of Sicily, in whose court men from all three continents met, had encouraged the compilation of works on geography. Frederick II had especially favored such writings, some of them translations of Arabic treatises on geography, and these were finding their way into the north. How much of this knowledge had been caught up by the learned world of western Europe was illustrated by the writings of Roger Bacon, the English Franciscan (ca. 1214—ca. 1294). Bacon included in them several proofs of the roundness of the earth. The most popular summary of this new geographical lore was written toward the middle of the fourteenth century by a Burgundian physician, who gave as the author of his narrative of travel a certain fictitious Sir John Mandeville.

Along with much fanciful description of the islands beyond China and their inhabitants and many imaginary marvels, his account contained much sober fact and included also detailed proofs of the earth's rotundity. The influence of these travels and tales upon the later geographical discoveries is demonstrable.

CHAPTER XIV

EDUCATION AND LEARNING TO THE CLOSE OF THE THIRTEENTH CENTURY

THE thirteenth century was also characterized by an enormous interest in education, a fact attested by the great
numbers who attended schools. The cumulative effects of the
great reform movement of the tenth and eleventh centuries and
of the expansion of ecclesiastical power in the twelfth and thirteenth centuries were clearly evident. Education was required
to gain positions in the Church, and these positions were not only
very numerous, but they included the highest and most powerful
office in Europe. Both numbers and ability were attracted to seek
at schools the key to advancement. The rapid increase in the
numbers of students had made necessary the establishment of
many teaching positions, which became, in turn, objects of ambition to the abler students. Men were now devoting all of their
time to the teaching of the liberal arts and theology. Such positions had assumed a professional dignity in very many places.
The extension of ecclesiastical justice, which had been so marked
throughout Europe during the eleventh and twelfth centuries, had
created the same respect for the teaching of law at a few places
like Bologna in Italy. This was in marked contrast to the earlier
period when teaching had been little more than an incidental
activity of monks and bishops. Both the professional character
of teaching and the increased number of teachers were symptoms
of the great number of students interested in education.

INCREASING DEMAND FOR LEARNING

During the eleventh and twelfth centuries, the influence of the
growing business of the Church had been felt at educational
centers with increasing force. In the twelfth century other influ-

ences converged upon the same end. Kings and princes, Frederick Barbarossa and Henry II being notable examples, found it desirable to include among their advisers men educated in Roman and canon law. They also employed physicians who had studied medicine. The nobility followed their example especially in the matter of trained physicians, if not always of trained lawyers. The growth of towns and commerce added even greater force to the development of such studies. Merchants needed trained writers to draw up commercial agreements in legal and permanent form. Many of them, too, had sufficient wealth to attract the services of the best physicians. The combination of these influences was enough to send many youths to legal and medical centers where they might educate themselves for profitable careers.

The demand for lawyers and physicians was so great that neither the school at Bologna, which had formerly supplied the lawyers, nor that at Salerno in southern Italy, which had hitherto furnished the physicians, could meet the need. Accordingly, training for these careers was added at a number of places north of the Alps by the opening of the thirteenth century. Yet the demand for well-trained men continued greater than the supply. As early as 1159 John of Salisbury, the scholarly secretary of the archbishop of Canterbury, complained that students no longer stopped to get a thorough education in arts, but, after a mere smattering, dashed into the study of law and medicine. That same complaint was voiced frequently by other eminent scholars for more than a century after John's time.

The existing episcopal and monastic schools were but poorly prepared to meet the needs of the students who were thronging to them. Their chief and almost their sole purpose had been, and of necessity continued to be, the training of priests. For them the seven liberal arts were merely an introduction to the study of theology, the end of education. The training of teachers and the study of law were quite incidental to the main purpose. Bishops and abbots were the responsible authorities in charge of the schools, and though some of them, like John of Salisbury, devoted much, if not most, of their energy to the management of these schools, they could not evade their other responsibilities, and for them, at least, theology remained always the goal of education. Many of the students, on the other hand, had no intention of studying theology. For them the chief end of education was law or medicine or even the teaching of the liberal arts, and a scheme of courses designed to train theologians did not exactly suit their needs.

The difficulties were further multiplied by the natural desire of nearly all the students to obtain the best possible education, which led them to flock to the most famous teachers. Needless to add, the masters encouraged this movement. It flattered their vanity and increased their fame, and later, when they received their income from the fees of the students, it became a matter of material interest to them. Hence it happened that the fame of an Irnerius at Bologna or an Abélard at Paris attracted hundreds and even thousands of students from all parts of Europe. Once such a movement was well started to particular places, it was but natural that able teachers should be attracted to fill the positions left vacant by the death or retirement of the pioneers.

ORGANIZATION OF UNIVERSITIES

Paris and Bologna were the first of the universities. Salerno, though long famous for its medical school, scarcely could be described as a university in the broader sense of the term. During the thirteenth century a number of other universities sprang up. Oxford, Cambridge and Montpellier, which had been important school centers for some time, expanded to the proportions of universities early in the thirteenth century. The universities of Naples, Salamanca and Toulouse were created by charter. Naples was founded by Frederick II in 1224, partly as a means of keeping his able young men at home and away from the other schools where they might become partisans of the pope. Salamanca was founded in 1254 by the king of Castile, but received privileges from the pope soon afterward. These were the most famous of the early universities.[1]

[1] A complete list of the early universities with the dates of their founding, so nearly as those can be ascertained, will be found on the map facing page 244.

Some of the universities possessed charters of privileges from the pope, king and local authorities as well. Classification as a *studium generale,* whose graduates had the right to teach anywhere (*ius ubique docendi*), was a privilege which could be conferred only by the pope. Considerable rights of self-government existed at all of these centers.

Bologna and Paris enjoyed a preëminence, the one for law and the other for arts and theology, which they held for many generations. By 1200 both of these places contained hundreds, Paris even thousands, of students who came from Italy, France, Germany, England and Spain. To judge from an unfavorable description by the great preacher Jacques de Vitry (d. 1240), this motley aggregation of students was such a fixed feature at Paris that each group was reputed to possess recognized (and uncomplimentary) characteristics. "They affirmed that the English were drunkards and had tails; the sons of France proud, effeminate and carefully adorned, like women . . . ; the Germans furious and obscene at their feasts; the Normans vain and boastful; the Poitevins traitors and always adventurers . . . ; the Burgundians . . . vulgar and stupid . . . ; the Bretons . . . fickle and changeable . . . ; the Lombards avaricious, vicious and cowardly; the Romans seditious, turbulent and slanderous; the Sicilians tyrannical and cruel; the natives of Brabant men of blood, incendiaries, brigands and ravishers; the Flemish fickle, prodigal, gluttonous, yielding as butter and slothful." [1] Needless to add, it did not suit the immediate purpose of Jacques to recite the characteristic virtues which each group doubtless displayed on numerous occasions, but the passage well illustrates the cosmopolitan range of students to be found at the leading schools.

DEVELOPMENT OF ORGANIZATION. NATIONS

The overcrowding, the variety of aims, and the wide areas represented by the student body compelled a new type of organization, at least at such centers as Bologna and Paris. Here the problem had reached a stage at which higher education must be undertaken

[1] This passage is found in D. C. Munro's *The Medieval Student,* Penn. Trans. and Reprints Vol. II, No. 3, and in C. H. Haskins' *Rise of the Universities.*

as a business in itself and not as an incidental activity of an otherwise busy bishop or abbot. The mere material needs of such a group of students were too great for the resources or jurisdiction of a bishop or abbot. The students came from outside, expected to remain a year or a few years, and then to leave again. To supply them with food and shelter required the efforts of many townspeople, while couriers journeyed to and fro between the distant homes of the wealthier students and the school. So large a gathering of young men at the most active period of their lives offered endless opportunity for disturbance, as the passage from Jacques de Vitry indicates. And yet, though they were capable of causing great disorder themselves, it should be added that the students were more often the victims of disorder, especially on the highways to or from the schools. They needed protection against attacks and unjust treatment, a protection which a bishop's authority was utterly inadequate to supply. The bishop or abbot was also hampered by his own outlook in providing effectively for the many students who were not concerned with a theological career. He was too ready to assume that a proper training for a prospective priest was the finest kind of education for anybody capable of education, whereas the students, eager to turn their training to financial account as notaries and physicians, did not feel that their efficiency was increased by spending a long time on subjects which had no direct bearing on their professions.

The change in organization which these conditions demanded was a slow growth during the twelfth century and it can scarcely be said to have been completed at the beginning of the thirteenth. Many of the steps which ultimately led to the recognition of higher education as a business in itself were taken first by the students or instructors themselves, or by the two together. To meet their more material needs the students followed the example of the merchants who also traveled far from home, and organized for protection. Young men from the same general regions with similar costumes, customs and language naturally tended to keep together for mutual protection as well as for easier social relationships. They acted together in gaining fair prices for their necessities, in avenging insults and wrongs, and in caring for the

MEDIAEVAL COMMERCE
IN EUROPE
13th CENTURY

Scale of Miles

0   100   200   300

Legend:

— Land routes

- - - Sea routes

— Centers of the Hanseatic League

- - - Foreign offices of the Hanseatic League

-·-·- Mediaeval University founded in the 12th century

········· " " " " " 13th "

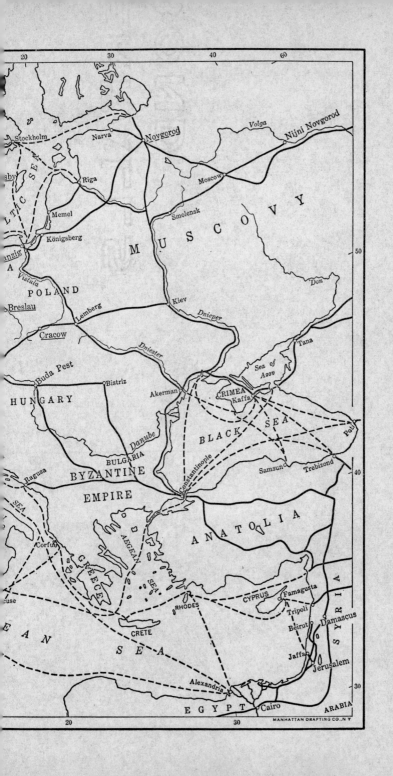

20 30 40 60

Stockholm Narva Novgorod Volga Nijni Novgorod

sby

Riga Moscow

BALTIC SEA

Memel Smolensk MUSCOVY

Königsberg

Danzig 50

A

Vistula Don

POLAND Kiev

Breslau Lemberg Dnieper

Cracow Dniester Tana

Buda Pest Bistriz Sea of Azov

HUNGARY Akerman CRIMEA

Kaffa

Danube BLACK SEA

Ragusa BULGARIA

BYZANTINE Constantinople Samsund Trebizond 40

EMPIRE

SEA ANATOLIA

Corfu

AEGEAN GRÉECE

SEA CYPRUS Famagusta

cuse RHODES Tripoli

Beirut Damascus

CRETE SYRIA

EAN Jaffa

SEA Jerusalem

Alexandria 30

EGYPT Cairo ARABIA

20 30

MANHATTAN DRAFTING CO., N.Y.

sick and needy.   The older students in the group placed their greater experience at the service of the newcomers.   The arrangement inevitably acted also as a restraining force, for local merchants and others who had suffered at the hands of a member were able to gain legal redress from the group, which could not so easily escape.   Hence the officers of these associations found it wise to counsel prevention as a safeguard against such penalties.

Regional associations of students, so advantageous to both students and town, came thus to be recognized as proper organizations at an early period and continued as such in higher education throughout the Middle Ages.   The students at Bologna and at Paris, the one located on the main road to Rome, the other on the edge of the great fairs of Champagne, were the first to form associations on a regional basis.   At Bologna the number of nations, as such organizations were called, was very large, almost as large as that of the separate principalities or states from which the students came; whereas at Paris, though the regions represented were ultimately as many as at Bologna, it early became the practice to distribute all among four nations—French, Norman, English and Picard.   At both institutions the nations developed into recognized governing bodies.

FACULTIES. THE STRUGGLE FOR PRIVILEGES

The nation served the social and material desires of the students, but for professional needs they developed another type of organization.   This was the faculty, which was composed of both students and instructors interested in the same subject or group of subjects.   At Bologna, where the dominant interest during the twelfth and thirteenth centuries was law, the faculty type of organization was slow to develop, while at Paris four faculties existed at an early date.   These were the faculties of arts, medicine, law and theology.   Each faculty sought to determine the subjects of study and the sequence of those subjects in its "course."   It sought also to determine the amount and quality of work necessary for promotion and ultimately for the degree. Naturally it was interested, too, in the qualification of teachers as a safeguard against incompetence. The great number of students at a school like Paris permitted teachers to devote their whole time to the teaching of subjects within a single faculty. Their professional interests were, therefore, more closely identified with those of their students than with those of the episcopal or monastic authorities who administered the school. Instructors and students were thus able to make common cause in winning recognition for their own corporate needs. This was no easy task, but one that had to be advanced slowly by compromise with the views of the established authorities. Then, as now, many a student settled the matter himself by choosing certain courses and leaving to practice his art or profession without completing the prescribed curriculum.

Before the twelfth century had ended another step was taken to strengthen the organization of universities. Students and teachers, nations and faculty learned that they could exert more influence by complete coöperation. Probably the example of the merchants of the period, who were gaining town charters and other privileges from a reluctant feudal nobility, showed the way. At any rate, the students and teachers acted together as a body and used the threat of departure or strike as a weapon to gain their ends. In this they had an advantage over the merchants, who had property which could be seized in case of disagreement with local authorities. Students and instructors had little or nothing. They were not dependent upon buildings, and laboratories were not yet known. There was no common library and the number of books which even a teacher possessed was small and easily transported. Abélard's career had already shown that a school could exist wherever teacher and pupils met.[1] On the other hand, the presence of hundreds of students and teachers added materially to the income of the town in which the school was located. Furthermore, their presence was recognized as giving distinction to the place. Almost any community would welcome such a group. Concerted action by all the students and teachers, especially when they threatened to withdraw, was usually sufficient to bring the town authorities to terms.

[1] See pages 128ff.

The double danger to pride and purse was useful also in bringing pressure to bear on bishops and sometimes on kings. In 1200, as the result of a row between the students and the townspeople of Paris in which a student was killed, the whole body of students and teachers threatened to leave the city. Philip Augustus, then king of France, intervened and pacified the scholars by granting them a definite charter of privileges, righting the particular injustice, and guaranteeing them protection in the future. This charter of 1200 has been generally considered as the first official recognition of students and masters as a corporate body. The term "universitas," hitherto used in addressing gilds of merchants, was now applied to them also, and in the course of time it has come to be restricted to organizations of instructors and students engaged in higher learning.

The privileges granted on this occasion were by no means the first which students and masters had received. The original character of students as prospective priests had insured them the general privileges of the clergy. This status they all retained, even after it was clear that many of them had no intention of becoming priests. Perhaps the first instance of a special grant of privileges was that made by Frederick Barbarossa in 1158. He had employed teachers of law from Bologna to draw up the statement of his rights over the towns of northern Italy. Their report, which was accepted by both towns and king, was quite favorable to the latter, and, perhaps out of gratitude for that service, he issued a decree conferring certain privileges upon students and teachers. "We think it fitting that, during good behavior, those should enjoy our praise and protection by whose learning the world is enlightened to the obedience of God and of us, his ministers, and by whom the life of his subjects is molded." After this royal recognition of the importance of higher learning, the document proceeds to guarantee protection to the students and their servants on the highways, freedom from seizure for debts contracted by a merchant of their native region,[1] and the right to have any suit brought against themselves tried by their teachers

[1] It had become a customary procedure to seize the goods of any other merchant for an unpaid debt contracted by one of his fellow townsmen.

or by the bishop of the city. This document has sometimes been cited as an early charter of the University of Bologna, but, though the students of Bologna were probably uppermost in Frederick's mind, Bologna was not specifically mentioned in the grant, and students anywhere in the Empire might profit from it. After the charter by Philip Augustus, grants of special privileges to scholars by the kings and rulers became more common. These dealt, as a rule, with matters of physical protection and judicial administration, though sometimes they recited privileges of a more professional character. The authorities of the towns in which the universities were located usually accorded students and masters privileges of an economic nature, guaranteeing proper prices for lodging, food and other supplies. Sometimes these were offered voluntarily as an inducement to prospective students, at other times reluctantly to prevent the withdrawal of the students.

It was the popes, however, who were to be the chief patrons of the universities. The supernational scope of papal authority, their natural solicitude for the welfare and the support of the increasing thousands of talented students, together with the traditional opinion that education was primarily a clerical concern, made it certain that the popes would supersede both kings and higher clergy as supreme patrons and directors of the universities. Sometimes the university extracted privileges from the local bishops, but usually recourse was had to the pope. The bishop usually regarded such concessions as infringements of his own rights and authority and frequently opposed the demands of the university bitterly. The popes, as a rule, were friendly to the universities. Such matters as the granting of diplomas and degrees, the selection of instructors and even the determination of courses of study were the causes of frequent disputes between the university and the local bishop. The coveted license to teach anywhere (*ius ubique docendi*) also came with better force from the pope. On several occasions the popes were called upon to interfere in struggles between the university and the bishop. This was notably the case at Paris, where friction occurred so often that the university found it advisable to keep a representative at the papal court during most of the thirteenth century. In 1215

Innocent III, who had been a student at both Paris and Bologna, favored the university with very substantial grants of privileges. Gregory IX, likewise an alumnus of both institutions, also showed the University of Paris great favor, especially by his charter of 1231. Nearly all the universities which sprang up during the thirteenth century obtained grants or confirmations of their charters of privileges from the pope.

There has been preserved a circular letter sent out by the masters of the University of Toulouse in 1229 which contains an excellent summary of the kind of privileges most coveted by the students. The university had just been founded by the pope as an act of grace after the Albigensian crusades which had devastated much of that region. The circular letter which the masters sent out was addressed to masters and students and was designed to make Toulouse seem as attractive as possible. They assured prospective students that "the Moses of our undertaking was the lord cardinal legate in the kingdom of France. . . . He decreed that both masters and students should receive plenary indulgence for all their sins. . . . Lectures and disputations are held more frequently and longer than at Paris." Toulouse they described as a "second land of promise, flowing with milk and honey, where the herds are prolific, trees groan with fruit, Bacchus reigns in the vineyards and Ceres has personal charge of the fields." Here "the theologians instruct the students in the pulpits and the people at the crossroads, logicians instruct Aristotle's recruits in the liberal arts, grammarians fashion the tongues of stammerers into the semblance of speech, masters of music soothe the popular ear with the instrument of the honeyed throat, lawyers extol Justinian, and at their side masters of medicine preach Galen. The books on natural science which have been prohibited at Paris may be here studied by those who desire to scrutinize the innermost secrets of nature's recesses." They further declared that scholastic freedom was here unfettered and that the count of Toulouse guaranteed protection to students or masters and their servants against the malice of the populace, the depredations of robbers, or the tyranny of the prince. Not only was food plentiful, but it was guaranteed to be cheap beyond most generous rumor. In addition, the masters assured prospective students that they would be treated by the people with a courtesy such as was accorded to knights and clergy.

TYPES OF UNIVERSITY GOVERNMENT. BOLOGNA. PARIS

The actual government of the newer universities was fixed after the model of either Bologna or Paris. At Bologna, which was at first largely frequented by older students, priests and often bishops and abbots on leave, much of the government was in the hands of the students. They paid the salaries of the professors and they determined the conditions under which instruction should be given. This was minutely regulated to a degree which sometimes seems absurd. The professors were subject to fine if they lectured too fast or not fast enough, if they absented themselves from class or had too few students, and, finally, even the private lives of the professors were kept under surveillance. The rector of the university was elected and must be a student. Later, when the majority of students were younger, this practice was modified and the town authorities exercised considerable influence in the maintenance of the instructors and the regulation of conduct.

At Paris, on the other hand, where from the beginning the majority of students were youths, the organization of the university included both masters and pupils, and the rector must be a master. The arts faculty was the largest, and was organized into the four nations, each with an elected proctor. The other three faculties were each headed by a dean. Proctors and deans together constituted the regular governing body of the university and elected the rector, who was almost invariably a Master of Arts. Most of the business was of a special type and was usually transacted within the separate faculties, but on ceremonial occasions or at times of crises, the university acted as a whole, with the rector at their head. At Paris during most of the thirteenth century there was also a chancellor appointed by the bishop. His authority was at first very great, but as the century advanced he was shorn of his powers bit by bit, until at the end the office was merely a reminder of former episcopal control. The newer universities usually followed the model of Paris, though the Scots borrowed much from the model of Bologna.

LIFE OF THE STUDENTS

The life of the students at these thirteenth-century universities was none too enviable. Most of the students were very earnest in their desire for learning as a means to a career, but many of them were very poor. The utilitarian motive predominated, for the idea that a gentleman must have the culture of learning as an essential quality of his class was only just appearing. There were some students, however, who were quite wealthy and amply provided with servants and money. These were usually the younger sons of nobles, but the sons of wealthier merchants were already vying with them in splendor. Most of the students were from the middle class and many even from the peasantry. The latter were usually bright boys, discovered either at cathedral schools or by parish priests and then sent on to the universities. The students were of all ages, but at Paris youth predominated. The lodgings in which they lived were of many varieties, none of them very comfortable. Sometimes a wealthy student, or a group of students, rented a whole house. More frequently the students found lodgings where they could and not a few shared stables with horses and cattle. Sanitation was not yet recognized as a public necessity, and there was little provision for adequate protection against cold weather. Disease and death were only too common. Classes were conducted in such halls as the instructors could rent, or quite often out in the open street, a condition which Straw Street in the Latin Quarter of Paris still commemorates. Absence of satisfactory lighting necessitated the full use of daylight and classes began practically with the day's dawn. Books were very expensive and not numerous, which rendered the memorizing of lectures highly desirable.

A wealthy Englishman returning from a pilgrimage passed through Paris and was much moved at the miserable plight of some of the English students. On his return home he arranged for an endowment sufficient to enable several of them to rent a portion of a hospital. This was the beginning of the system of colleges which grew up especially in England, but elsewhere as well. In these a great number of students lived together with one or more instructors. Here they lodged and ate and here also they could learn the fundamental subjects from the resident tutor. Some of them built up excellent libraries as well. The establishment of these colleges did much to improve the lot of the student, but this movement was just beginning in the thirteenth century.

It would be misleading, however, to think of the student's life as all work and no play. Though the great majority were earnest enough, there were always a number of students who carried their burdens very lightly and their escapades furnished much material for such moralists as Jacques de Vitry. These were the students who frequented the taverns, trifled with maidens and disturbed the respectable with their games and brawls. Doubtless many of the more serious had their lighter moments as well, and this side of the student's life has been much more carefully preserved than the stories of their privations and hardships. The statutes of the universities record with considerable frequency breaches of regulations which sometimes involved protracted disputes with authorities. The boys at Paris very much annoyed the monks of St. Germain a mile or so down the river by using their pastures for games. Tavern-keepers had frequent cause to complain of the failure of students to pay for their potations. Sometimes, too, dignified ecclesiastics expressed disapproval of the irreverence frequently displayed by the students who assisted at services. The statutes of the English nation at Paris later specifically forbade the throwing of dice on the altars or their use for any purpose except to divert a sick friend.

The chief source of information about the lighter side of student life is in the student songs which have been preserved and collected. The composition of these songs went on at all of the universities and many of the best of them were brought together into a collection ascribed to Golias, a mythical figure, who was reputed to be the leader of the wandering students. The name Goliardic literature has therefore been applied to the collection of these poems. Many of them are parodies of sacred hymns, often coarse and sometimes vulgar. They deal with all phases of student life and interest except study. The poverty of the students who were often driven to begging, the delights of wine and ale, the varying fortune of dice, love affairs, the open road, and vacations are the usual themes. Such songs afforded a natural outlet for the exuberance of youth living the otherwise restrained lives of students. Along with the more frivolous themes, however, there are some of noble sentiment. That finest of student songs, the *Gaudeamus igitur,* though composed somewhat later, derives much of its spirit from this period. As a rule, these songs were sung and composed in moments of relaxation, but there were some students who indulged their natural inclination toward poetry and abandoned the more serious pursuits of school for careers as wandering minstrels.

THE CURRICULUM

The main business of the student, then as now, was study, and to this end he devoted most of his time. His course of study was not so varied as that of the more modern student. The liberal arts were fundamental. Law and medicine and especially theology required a more or less complete training in the liberal arts before admission. It must not be assumed, however, that the courses were carefully standardized, or that even in the arts all students took the same courses. Students who appeared at the University of Paris had begun their education in various ways. The sons of nobles had received their early instruction from the chaplains of the castles, the merchant's son had probably gone to school in his native town, while bright boys of lower classes had probably started their career of learning as altar boys for the local parish priests. The progress which each had made in the liberal arts before coming to Paris varied equally. A youth who had attended the cathedral school at Chartres had probably received a training in the liberal arts not unlike that afforded by good classical courses of modern secondary schools, whereas some had only the veriest smattering.

Normally the arts course required six years of study for the master's degree. In actual practice its attainment required from two to twelve years, depending upon previous training. The baccalaureate was the first formal step to determine the student's fitness for advanced study. Having passed this test, he was admitted to the disputations which became so marked a feature of twelfth- and thirteenth-century higher education. Usually two years were required before he could become a master. Nominally the liberal arts included the *trivium* and *quadrivium,* for each of which there was a text-book.[1] Actually the emphasis varied greatly. Grammar had undergone many changes. In some places it was still the most important subject in the arts course as late as the beginning of the thirteenth century, and its more advanced study included rather extensive reading of classical authors. At the universities of the later thirteenth century very little place was allotted to it. Rhetoric, too, once very important, had altered. In its original form as a study of the art of correct writing it was largely relegated to the preparatory training. At the universities it tended to take a very practical form, such as the art of drawing up letters and documents, especially legal documents. It therefore appealed especially to those students who expected to become notaries. Logic, on the other hand, had become the favorite subject of the *trivium* and occupied the chief place in the arts course of the universities. The whole body of Aristotle's works on logic, as well as the *Introduction* by Porphyry and the contributions of Boethius, were studied in turn. The *quadrivium* had not been highly developed at any time during the Middle Ages, nor did the universities devote much time to those interests. Music was of practical concern to prospective churchmen, and students so minded took special work in this field. The other three subjects of the *quadrivium*—arithmetic, geometry and astronomy—were not emphasized, and students could attain the master's degree in arts knowing very little of the *quadrivium*. During the thirteenth century Aristotle's books on natural philosophy came into use, and, though sometimes for-

[1] See pages 57*ff*.

bidden, were very popular. These in a certain sense superseded the *quadrivium* for most of the students.

The regular procedure in the conduct of the courses was the slow and clear reading of the text-book by the master, with such comments as he deemed necessary to bring out the meaning. The students took notes on wax tablets. Later in the same day the students were given an opportunity to recite or repeat what they had heard to bachelors selected for that purpose. Once a week disputations were held between the masters, and the bachelors were expected, or even required, to be present. The bachelors were allowed to give "extraordinary" (supplementary) lectures at times during the year, and these usually took place in the afternoons. Such lectures dealt either with review courses or possibly with special works of Aristotle on logic and natural philosophy. The disputations in which the masters debated certain points in philosophy were the great feature of university work. The bachelors were allowed to join in these disputations and thus received their training in matching words and wits with skilled debaters. The emphasis was usually more on the manner and skill of debate than upon the subject discussed, and in this art the excellence attained in the thirteenth century has not since been exceeded. The examination by which the bachelor finally attained the master's degree included a test of his ability to defend a number of propositions in debate. In fact, he gave a sample disputation. The master's degree was not yet strictly differentiated from the doctorate, or even the licentiate. During the thirteenth century they were still practically synonymous, and all three indicated that the recipient was qualified to teach.

The number of students who received the degree of Master of Arts was relatively small. In addition to the many who had found it impossible to continue their studies, either through inability or illness or lack of means, there were many who satisfied their purpose short of this stage. This was especially true of a large number who sought training to become mere notaries or scribes. Others fell by the wayside and were drawn off into less exacting fields of endeavor, seeking careers of adventure on the highways with the merchants, or with bands of minstrels, or in less

laudable ways.   Partly educated vagabonds were not uncommon
in the thirteenth century or afterward.[1]   There was, too, much
wandering of students from school to school, as the lives of
almost any of the leading scholars of the twelfth and thirteenth
century show.   Very few had studied at less than two institutions,
many at more.   This was more easily possible because the language
of learning was everywhere the same, whereas the administration
of the universities was still very lax and varied in requirements.
These various causes brought it about that the proportion of those
who received the degree of Master of Arts to the whole number
of students was much lower than the ratio of those who enter and
those who graduate today.   The Master of Arts from such
institutions as Paris and Bologna or from any other university
privileged by the papacy could teach the liberal arts anywhere.
He was also ready to undertake the study of law or medicine or
theology.

Law had become quite popular and had many devotees among
the students.   As taught at this time, there was already some
distinction between civil and canon law.   The first rested upon the
study of the Justinian Code, which was read entire with commentaries by the teachers.   Bologna, where Irnerius had taught,
continued to hold the leading place among law schools throughout the thirteenth century and even later, though the subject was
also taught elsewhere.   Canon law was taught on the basis of
Gratian's *Decretum*.   Gratian, a monk who had probably studied
with Abélard's pupils, applied his method to the systematiza-
tion of Church law.   Papal bulls and decrees, the decrees of
Church councils and the decisions of Church courts had accumulated in various places and were often contradictory.   By bringing together decisions and pronouncements relating to the same
points he sought to arrive at a common principle, reconciling the
apparent contradictions.   The work was well done by him, and
though never officially adopted as the code of the Church, it was
almost immediately used as the accepted text-book for the study
of the law and became the basis for the official codes of canon law
later drawn up by the popes.   Canon law was studied frequently

[1] See chapter XVIII.

in connection with theology, though it also had an affinity with civil law. Often the prospective lawyer studied both and became a Doctor of Both Laws (J.U.D.). Both opened up a career in the administrative service of either Church or State, for during the thirteenth century the practice of using men trained in law for royal service was well established. Civil law alone was sufficient for the men who transacted the legal business of towns.

Medicine was taught, like law, from books until the student became a Bachelor of Medicine. The writings of Galen and Hippocrates were the foundation. Commentaries on these two, especially by Arabic physicians, were also used.[1] Laboratories were unknown, but there are records of the use of animals and occasionally of human cadavers for demonstration purposes. After the student had become a Bachelor of Medicine he was required to spend some time as assistant to a master in the actual practice of medicine. A certificate of such practice was usually required for the Master's degree. The most famous of the centers for the study of medicine was Salerno in Italy, which was not at this time a university in the wider use of that term. The great universities, however, added the study of medicine to their curricula, and some of them, like Montpellier, became quite famous medical schools. Medicine did not flourish at Paris, though it was included in the curriculum, nor at Bologna, where it was not added until quite late.

Theology continued to be the noblest, if not the most lucrative, of the professions. Paris was the most famous of the schools for the study of theology, a position which it held throughout the Middle Ages. Some theology was taught in nearly every diocese where priests were trained, but both the amount and quality varied considerably. The length of time required to complete the course in theology also varied, but it was longer than for the other professions. The work consisted chiefly of the study of the Scriptures, which were read and expounded with elaborate commentaries. After the student became a Bachelor in Theology he studied the *Sentences* of Peter Lombard, another of Abélard's pupils. Peter Lombard had carried out Abélard's

[1] See chapter XXV.

suggestion contained in the *Sic et Non*. He gathered together the conflicting or divergent views of the Church fathers on certain fundamental doctrines of the Church, and then with the help of reason arrived at a final statement of the doctrine. The *Sentences* continued to be the chief introduction to systematic theology for many years.

The task of establishing and maintaining standards of training for admission to the practice of the professions, including teaching, has never been easy, and was especially difficult when universities first arose. Candidates for teaching positions at universities were required to take oath that they had completed certain years of study. Sometimes an examination of their knowledge was also made. Glib impostors, however, managed from time to time to elude the authorities and gain positions as teachers at universities. As a rule, however, they were detected sooner or later. Away from the universities the chances for fraud and imposition were much greater. Towns, with their strict gild regulations, protected themselves somewhat by investigation, but there were numerous instances in which communities were served by physicians, notaries and teachers who did not have proper training. It was this situation which led to the formal certification of graduates, the conferring of degrees written on sheepskin signed and sealed by the proper authorities.

The universities bore to the world of learning a relation very similar to that which existed between the great fairs and commerce. They were not, however, the only centers of learning, nor even the only centers of higher learning. Monastic and cathedral schools still continued to train priests, and some of them continued to maintain a very high reputation for excellence in certain branches of learning. The cathedral school at Chartres, famous for its instruction in arts in the early twelfth century, continued in the next century as an excellent school for the study of arts, philosophy and theology. In the thirteenth century, likewise, the cathedral school at Cologne was remarkable for its brilliant teachers of philosophy and theology. These are but examples of many schools, not universities, which continued to command the respect of scholars.

THE ADVANCE IN LEARNING

The universities, however, offered a greater variety of subjects, and as a rule had the most distinguished professors of these subjects on their instructional staff. Students frequently numbered thousands, and Paris probably had as many teachers in the thirteenth century as Chartres had students. The presence of so many students and instructors at a university center usually served to attract men of all kinds who were interested in learning, as it also stimulated wider discussions and led to deeper inquiry into intellectual problems. There, too, were to be found the largest collections of books, and it was only natural to expect there the greatest advance in learning. Practically all the leaders in the intellectual life of the thirteenth century were more or less closely connected with the important universities.

The greatest advance occurred in the realm of philosophy and in the application of philosophy to theology, subjects of dominant concern. The books of Aristotle came into general use in the thirteenth century and were eagerly studied. The writings of Arabic commentators on Aristotle, especially those of Averroës and Avicenna, were also extensively used at the universities. Out of this study grew the carefully reasoned attempts to systematize the doctrines of the Church. The Dominican scholars were leaders in this work, and chief among them was Thomas Aquinas (d. 1274).

Thomas was the son of a feudal noble of southern Italy who was a devoted adherent of Emperor Frederick II. He entered the Dominican Order against the wishes of his father and was sent north across the Alps to study at Cologne and Paris. At Cologne he became the favorite pupil of Albertus Magnus, also a Dominican and famous for the boldness of his mind and the vast extent of his learning. Since the days of Augustine of Hippo, no scholar in western Europe had written so much as this erudite German professor, and Augustine did not treat nearly so wide a variety of subjects. In marked contrast to his teacher, Thomas was distinguished for the orderliness of his mind, the ability to arrange the fruits of his erudition in systematic form with penetrating logic. He continued his studies at Paris, where he became Master or Doctor of Theology, and he taught both at Paris and Cologne. The members of his order and the popes came to appreciate his unusual abilities, and he was called upon to deal with some of their most difficult problems. For his order he wrote a work on Christian theology with which the Dominicans could refute the learned arguments of Jews and Moors in Spain or elsewhere and convert them to the Christian faith. He was called by Pope Alexander IV to establish a university at Rome, but little came of this foundation. Thomas, however, was enabled to carry on his scholarly investigations in philosophy and theology. He was asked by the pope and other churchmen to advise them on theological and ecclesiastical affairs. His letters are still a mine from which learned theologians draw solutions for their problems.[1] His greatest work, the *Summa Theologiæ,* which he did not live to finish, placed the capstone on the theological discussions for which the ground had been so brilliantly and recklessly broken by Abélard more than a century before. This work was not completed by Thomas himself, but later scholars, making use of his earlier writings, were able to finish it. Other men of his own time and the generation which immediately followed criticized many of his conclusions. The most brilliant of these critics was a Franciscan, Duns Scotus, who believed that he had found Thomas in logical error. But as time went on the thorough and comprehensive quality of the work became generally recognized, and it has remained an authoritative exposition of Roman Catholic theology to the present day. Dante, who was born before Thomas Aquinas died, showed a thorough familiarity with the *Summa Theologiæ,* and his own *Divine Comedy* has sometimes been characterized, although inadequately, as the *Summa Theologiæ* in verse.

Another critic of Thomas Aquinas was his contemporary, the English Franciscan, Roger Bacon (d. 1284). Bacon had studied at Oxford and Paris and had also been a teacher. He was interested not so much in scholastic philosophy as in the knowledge

---

[1] The writings of Thomas Aquinas were especially recommended for study by Pope Leo XIII.

of nature and natural philosophy. His inclination had led him to read carefully the works on geography, travel and natural philosophy which were circulating in Europe in his time. These included, besides Aristotle's writings, the works of such men as Adelard of Bath and the scholars at the court of Frederick II. Bacon seems also to have derived considerable information from conversations with travelers whom he met at Paris and elsewhere. He learned also from men engaged in various practical arts, and his writings show, too, the results of his own observations and occasionally of something like actual experiment. His three great writings, really three parts of one work, which he wrote for Pope Clement IV, are valuable as the most comprehensive treatise on natural philosophy produced in the thirteenth century. In part this work was an attack upon the educational tendencies of his day, especially the emphasis upon dry logic. Like his fellow country-man of the previous century, John of Salisbury, he believed that a thorough study of language was essential as the foundation of all learning. After this, he urged an equally thorough study of nature in its various forms and phases. He argued that this preparation would be the best approach to theology. Logic and the scholastic philosophy to which it had given rise seemed to him empty without the substance of the other studies. His attitude toward his two great contemporaries, members of the rival order of friars, was rather truculent, somewhat unjustly so in view of the fact that Albertus Magnus had delved rather deeply in natural philosophy himself. This attitude may have lessened Bacon's influence at the time, but his books seem to have been read with approval by later generations. Like John of Salisbury's plea for the study of literature, Roger Bacon's plea for the study of natural philosophy was out of harmony with the spirit of the times in which he lived. Later ages were to prove more sympathetic to both.

During this period so much advance had been made that the old summary of learning which Isidore of Seville had drawn up in the early seventh century was no longer adequate. The most successful attempt to sum up this progress in learning was made by Vincent of Beauvais, a Dominican friar who was in the house-

hold of King Louis IX as tutor of the royal children. Vincent
was probably influential in gathering the library which Louis IX
collected for his palace. At any rate, Vincent acted as librarian
and made the greatest use of it. His chief work, the *Speculum
Maius,* or *Greater Mirror,* appeared about the middle of the thirteenth century. It was a systematic compilation of material from
many sources, ranging all the way from ancient Aristotle to
Albertus Magnus of his own time. He employed assistants to
help him in his task and the result was a huge work, several times
as large as the *Etymologies* of Isidore. It was divided into three
parts, the *Mirror of Nature,* the *Mirror of Doctrine* and the
Mirror of History, all suffused with a pious spirit and purpose.
Like all encyclopædias, its articles were inferior to the sources
from which they were drawn, but it was a very useful work. It
very clearly mirrored the achievements of the preceding six centuries. It drew something from Isidore of Seville, but also
from the sources used by Isidore. The work included excerpts
from many intervening writers and showed the effects of contact
with Arabic learning as well as with pagan classical sources, and
its range of topics was not only richer, but was also wider than
that of Isidore's. Vincent was only a compiler. He did not
understand many of his topics as well as the leading scholars of
his day knew them, and about others he was wholly credulous.
Nevertheless his work constituted a real monument to the advance
of learning.

Although learning naturally centered in the universities, there
was abundant evidence that its use was extending far beyond the
limits of the schools. The *Roman de la Rose,* the second portion
of which was written in the early thirteenth century, has already
been mentioned as an effort to make available to the people the
learning of the schools. The *Divine Comedy* of Dante (1265-
1321) [1] performed a similar service for the reasoned theology of
the great scholastic thinkers, which it carried more lightly on
the wings of poetry to an ever-widening audience. A curious
instance of both the extent and the rapidity of the dissemination
of learning at this time is afforded by the *King's Mirror,* a work

---

[1] See chapter XVIII.

written in old Norse in the thirteenth century. It contained something of the material to be found in Vincent's work and, in addition, some bits of geographical lore of the northern seas.

Existing geographical knowledge, however, was given widest circulation through the Travels of Sir John Mandeville. In this work, along with a lot of romantic nonsense about the peoples and customs of far Eastern isles, there was much accurate information about lands as remote as China and India, and several clear demonstrations of the roundness of the earth and its probable size. To judge from the number of manuscript copies of it still extant, Sir John's Travels quickly found their way into nearly all the castles and towns of Europe.[1]

The importance of learning to' society at large is perhaps best illustrated by the work of Pierre Dubois, a lawyer in the employ of King Philip IV of France at the close of the thirteenth century. He was a man of some consequence and well educated, but he was not primarily a scholar and his chief work was to look after the king's interests in the administration of some of the western provinces, especially in Normandy. Pierre, however, was well read and well informed, and he was anxious to advise the king on some important reforms. The talk about the recovery of the Holy Land which was current at the time furnished him an opportunity, and, under the guise of a plan for its recovery, Pierre published his views on the improvement of society. He would deprive the Church of its lands and properties and turn them over to the secular authorities, whose better management would not only not diminish the income of the Church, but would leave a generous margin to be used for the expedition to the Holy Land. (Secularization of Church lands was by no means an unwelcome idea to Philip IV.) The clergy, especially in the monasteries, were to be much reorganized, and the whole Church stripped of most of its secular functions. Pierre did not intend to interfere with religion but thought thus to give the clergy less distraction in the promotion of religion. In education he proposed that the girls be given much the same education as the boys, though they need not study quite so hard, owing to

[1] See chapter XIII.

the "fragility of their sex," and they were to have separate schools and women teachers. He would revise the text-books so that they could be understood without a teacher. The study of languages was to be emphasized, and at least one of the Eastern tongues—Greek, Arabic, Hebrew and Aramaic—should be studied in addition to Latin. Logic was to be emphasized, while the natural and moral sciences were to be taught in a simplified manner. Mathematics and mechanics were to be taught to some of the students, with emphasis upon the making of instruments such as the burning-glasses touched upon by Friar Roger Bacon. Medicine and surgery should be taught to many; the brightest should study both, the less bright surgery alone. He thought it desirable that the wives of the physicians and surgeons should be likewise trained. There should also be men trained in the civil and canon law and some in theology. The more robust people should have military training, the less bright should be taught mechanical arts such as blacksmithing and carpentry. All education should be accompanied by experience. Pierre anticipated some difficulty from the teachers who naturally wished to keep their students on the study of their subject, which each one of them regarded as sufficient for the regulation of the world! He had an elaborate program for the codification and simplification of law and justice and an equally elaborate scheme for the arbitration of international disputes. Needless to add, Pierre's ideas were not put into immediate practice, but they bring out the extent to which the secular uses of learning had come to be recognized. This secularization was already well under way and in succeeding centuries was to go on with increasing force.

CHAPTER XV

THE DEVELOPMENT OF THE FINE ARTS TO 1300

THE later twelfth and thirteenth centuries are recognized as one of the greatest artistic epochs of Europe. The various events which have been described all seemed to conspire to bring about this result. The leadership of the Church in Europe, the growth of economic prosperity, the concentration of large numbers of people in towns, and the alliance of Church and kings and towns, together with the increased interest in learning, all shared in this achievement. Only at rare intervals in history have so many forces worked together as joined in the building of the great Gothic cathedrals in which centered the art of this period.

The Church had early enlisted art in its service and had continued to do so throughout the Middle Ages. The symbolism in its service, the chalice and the reliquaries, the vestments of its priests, and the veneration of the saints, one and all afforded a constant impulse to the development of the artistic spirit. They likewise assisted in impressing the heathen hordes of the north, in teaching concretely great numbers of people upon whom the learning of books was completely lost, and in attracting to the services many who might otherwise have been indifferent. The Church clung to its art despite the iconoclastic temper of the cultured East and the barbaric fury of the unconverted north. With the approach of greater prosperity and more peaceful times, the artistic development of the Church kept pace with its expansion in other activities of life. Most of its efforts in the earlier period had been directed to the lesser arts, to working in cloth and precious metals, to casting bells, carving images and altar fixtures, and painting crucifixes. These crafts, however, furnished the training which was necessary for the development of the major arts. The monasteries were for a long time the only workshops in which could be found time and opportunity for the uninterrupted cultivation of taste and skill. With the advent of more widespread peace, art burst these narrow bounds and received aid from outside sources.

The first of the greater arts to develop was that of architecture. The religious revival of the tenth and eleventh centuries was accompanied by the building of churches on a more lavish and permanent scale. This was most true in the regions deeply affected by those revival movements. Eastern France, western Germany and northern Italy, and also Normandy and Norman England, shared in the building activities.

ADVANCE IN MASONRY

There was some similarity in the church buildings of the period. Practically all had as their ground plan that of the Roman basilica and used the Roman arch as the chief device for covering open spaces. The ground plan was modified from that of the basilica by the introduction of a transept just before the semicircular apse. Thus it resembled somewhat the Latin cross from which it derived a certain symbolic significance. The term Romanesque has been applied to this style of building because of its borrowed features, however modified. When viewed more closely, important differences appear, to be explained both by variations in local taste and by more advanced skill in building. Regarded as a whole, the style was characterized by very heavy masonry, thick walls and little window space. The masonry, especially of the earlier buildings, was crude, the buildings as a whole appearing as heavy piles of stone intended to resist force. In this they reflected the gloomy, forbidding appearance of the fortresses which frowned down upon them from the hilltop, or countryside. Some of the later buildings in northern Italy, in Germany and in Normandy attained beauty and impressiveness. These, however, all date from the eleventh century.

The development of stone masonry into a highly skilled craft came about with practice. Long before the religious revival had run its full course, the nobility, profiting from its experience and observation in the crusades, had begun its elaborate castle building. Both in church and castle building there was great rivalry, each new structure being designed to outdo its neighbors. The growth of the towns only increased the demand for skilled stone masons. The result was a period of two whole centuries in which they found constant employment. Trained masons had little reason to forget their craft through disuse, and the demand for their services was so great that workmen had to be drawn from other occupations to assist them. As long as the patrons of each new structure demanded larger and better buildings than any others of the same kind, there was real encouragement for the master mason to improve his craft. The rewards were large, and the competition for the best jobs became keen, so that the masons had every incentive to study their trade. This they did in several ways. Successive generations of masons transferred their experience and tricks of skill to the next generation. In addition, the more ambitious masons journeyed far and wide to study buildings already erected or in the process of erection, thus gaining new or improved ideas. Many of them studied mathematics, some of them in the established schools, others no doubt learning it, as they did their trade, during the period of apprenticeship. The mathematical learning of many of the master masons commanded the respect of such scholars as Roger Bacon in their own time, and has won praise from mathematicians of today. Such men ceased to be mere craftsmen and became artists as well, possessing, as they did, a keen sense for the beautiful.

ORIGIN AND DEVELOPMENT OF GOTHIC ARCHITECTURE

The demand for ever larger and finer buildings increased the difficulties of the builders. Two problems especially engaged their attention—a satisfactory roofing arrangement, and, in the north, adequate provision for lighting. A flat roof made of stone was not only difficult to lay, but too often collapsed with tragic consequences; if made of wood, it was liable to burn. Numerous catastrophes of both kinds had long removed this problem from the realm of theory. The use of the Roman arch type of roof promised a solution of the difficulty. Over such arches a roof could be laid more easily and securely, but in large buildings such strong walls were required to hold it in place that there was little space for windows. Even so, the weakening effect of time and weather made these roofs far from secure against collapse. In the south where sunshine was abundant and shade was even more desirable than sunlight, the arch type of roof, with the very heavy walls to support it, continued in favor. The colder, cloudier climate of the north, however, made the introduction of sunlight into the structures almost a necessity. It was the study of this problem of stability and light which led to the discovery of a new principle in building, based upon the pointed arch and the flying buttress which are fundamental in Gothic architecture.

Modern scholars in architecture have been able to trace the gradual development of this principle from the early-eleventh-century buildings of Lombardy to later-eleventh-century buildings in southern France and in Normandy, to its complete discovery in the twelfth and thirteenth centuries. By the use of the Gothic arch and buttress the roof could be both laid and kept in place more satisfactorily, and its weight could be carried on heavy piers of stone so that the space between the piers could be used for windows. At the eastern end of the churches, where light was especially desirable, the use of flying buttresses carried the weight of the roof directly to the ground and left much space available for windows. Thus builders were able to make large structures light and airy in a way that satisfied the demands of both use and beauty. Architects have classed the Gothic cathedral with the Greek temple as the two pure styles in architecture not dependent upon added ornament for their æsthetic qualities.

Abbot Suger of St. Denis, near Paris, was one of the first to appreciate the value of this new style. Suger will be recalled as the scholarly monk with administrative ability who proved so profitable a counselor to Louis VI and Louis VII of France. He was one of the first to appreciate the growing importance of commerce and towns. The growth of the fair at

Lendit had brought added prosperity to the monastery, as the chartering of towns had enriched the kings. He was also instrumental in winning for the kings the steady support of the clergy, and in his day Paris was beginning to assume that position in France which she has since so fully attained. Suger decided to rebuild the church of his monastery, which had grown too small for the crowds on ceremonious occasions. He wanted to make it a beautiful building admired by all, and to this end he employed master masons who understood the new style. That church was by no means a perfect example of Gothic art, but it contained many of the features of that style, including a tall spire to which the Gothic scheme was so well fitted. It was much admired by the people of the time, though Bernard of Clairvaux regarded the spire as an unnecessary vanity. Other communities engaged in rebuilding their churches or erecting new ones saw in it the satisfaction of their desires and demanded buildings like it.

The episcopal city of Chartres, of some importance as an industrial center but more famous for its cathedral school, was rebuilding its cathedral not long afterward. This was to become the first of the famous Gothic churches which are still standing. The building of the edifice extended over a long time, but the twelfth-century portions reveal clearly the simple and severe beauty of the style in its unadorned form. The tall majestic spire so gracefully transformed from its square base to its octagonal pinnacle without the use of any elaborate sculptured devices has always excited admiration. So, too, have the beautiful glass windows, whose insertion the pointed arch allowed.

Archbishop Hugo of Rouen watched the progress at Chartres with interest, and in a letter to Bishop Thierry of Amiens wrote: "The inhabitants of Chartres have combined to aid in the construction of their church by transporting materials; . . . powerful princes of the world, men brought up in honor and in wealth, nobles, men and women, have bent their proud and haughty necks to the harness of carts, and, like beasts of burden, have dragged to the abode of Christ those wagons loaded with wines, grains, oil, stone, wood and all that is necessary for the wants of life or for the construction of the church. . . . Often so great is

the difficulty that a thousand or more are attached to the
carts. . . . When they halt on the road nothing is heard but the
confession of sins, the pure and the suppliant prayer to God to
obtain pardon. . . . When they have reached the church they
arrange the wagons about it, like a spiritual camp, and during the
whole night they celebrate the watch by hymns and canticles.
Our Lord has rewarded their humble zeal by miracles which have
aroused the Normans to imitate the piety of their neighbors. . . . Since then the faithful of our dioceses and other
neighboring regions have formed associations for the same object; they admit no one into their company unless he has been to
confession, has renounced enmities and revenges and has recon-
ciled himself with his enemies. That done, they elect a chief
under whose direction they conduct their wagons in silence and
with humility." The archbishop, we may conjecture, did not
underestimate the piety of the participants. The colored windows
reveal that the contributions of the community were by no means
confined to such humble service as transportation, and the statuary
would probably tell the same story. Some of the windows were
the gift of kings and queens of France; others were donated by
counts; while others were contributed by craft gilds, one of the
most interesting being given by the gild of butchers.

Archbishop Hugo's letter affords striking evidence of the
jealous interest with which the people of neighboring towns
viewed the erection of these cathedrals. The interest was widespread and the desire of the townsmen to have a church which
should excel that of their neighbors was doubtless a powerful
stimulant to the building of these cathedrals. Within a half century from the time when the old spire of Chartres was completed,
or from the reign of Philip Augustus through that of Louis IX,
foundations were laid for practically all the great Gothic churches
of France. Civic pride was probably as strong a factor as episcopal zeal in bringing about this result, and it would be difficult to
imagine the successful completion of these undertakings without
the resources of money and labor which only the populous and
prosperous towns could afford.

To what extremes this rivalry was carried was illustrated most strikingly by the town of Beauvais. The people there were determined that their church should be higher and better than that of the neighboring city, Amiens, which was being constructed on a gorgeous scale. Though the vaulting of the choir, which they built thirteen feet higher than that of Amiens, fell twice within twelve years, they persisted in erecting this wonderfully lighted and beautiful choir which still stands. This church was seriously endangered, however, by another fit of rivalry in the sixteenth century, when the nave was being constructed. Reports of the great height of St. Peter's led the builders to erect a tower over the nave which was nearly five hundred feet high. This collapsed after standing less than a generation, and in falling destroyed much of the church which has never been entirely rebuilt.

ANCILLARY ARTS IN THE GOTHIC CATHEDRALS

The open spaces which the Gothic arch and principle of construction permitted were filled with glass, the manufacture of which had become a fine art in several places. Venice was especially famous for colored glassware, though other localities also contributed varieties of it. This colored glass was fitted together in mosaic form to produce portraits or pictures of symbolic figures. By the later twelfth century the Gothic artists were able to fashion dramatic series of pictures showing scenes from the Old or New Testament. The windows of the thirteenth century were veritable masterpieces, as, for example, those of Rheims. The rose window in the façade and the great window spaces of the choir made possible by the flying buttresses were favorite positions for glass-work, but the windows of the clerestory were often requisitioned for the same purpose and sometimes, also, the windows of the side aisles. Where no story was told, the artist still found room for his skill in devising scroll designs. The colored-glass art of the Gothic window fully rivaled the beautiful illumination of manuscripts which had reached such a high point. It is difficult to say which deserves the greater admiration, the wonderfully colored glass in itself, or the art developed in forming figures from the pieces of colored glass. Both have received unstinted praise.

No less important were the achievements in sculpture with which the exteriors of the buildings were adorned. The protruding skeleton of the Gothic cathedral offered numerous points and corners which called for relief from the jagged effect of plain stone. Buttress piers could be softened by topping with pinnacles or statues. The recessive style of doorway presented a tempting opportunity to break the severe lines with a sculptured border, a temptation which fortunately was almost never resisted. Even the monotony of the tall upright piers and buttresses could be relieved in this fashion. The sculpture of the Gothic cathedral was subsidiary to the architecture. It fitted into the church so fully as to seem an essential part of it. And yet it afforded full opportunity for the sculptor's art. Like the building and the glass, the sculpture also revealed the manifold forces which were responsible for these structures. Along with the members of the Trinity and figures from Scriptural history were statues of kings and lesser personages, ecclesiastical and lay. These statues were carved upon the ground, as though to be inspected from all sides, and were then lifted to their places, sometimes in positions so obscure as to be completely overlooked by the casual spectator. Photographs of some of the statues, especially at Rheims, show an attention to the details of facial expression and bodily gesture seldom equaled or surpassed in the more famous sculpture of the Renaissance period.

The stone carvings with which the lines and spaces of the cathedrals were broken afforded almost endless opportunity for the display of knowledge as well as of artistic skill. There was a tendency to repeat on each successive edifice many of the themes worked out on former buildings, but each statue and relief had to be carved anew and no two cathedrals are exactly alike in their sculpture. The artist furnished the skill, the ideas were the products of the schools. Over one of the doorways was usually found a set of figures to portray the Last Judgment, with Christ enthroned at the top, and, below, the separation of the sheep from the goats. Over the side doorways it became customary to por-

tray the life of the Virgin Mary and that of some local saint.
Even these themes, though often repeated, varied greatly, and the
hundreds and even thousands of figures with which the churches
were adorned included symbols of virtues and vices, scenes from
the Old Testament and the New, reminders of treasured local
lore, and commemorative statues of the pious and the powerful of
contemporary times. The learned resources of ecclesiastics and
scholars, as well as the sentimental stores of local tradition, were
drawn upon and then portrayed in such vivid concreteness as to
challenge the curiosity of all, whether learned or simple. At the
same time that Dante was writing his immortal poem and incidentally expounding the theology of Thomas Aquinas so that
all Italians might read and learn, these unknown sculptors of the
cathedrals were revealing the same lessons to an even wider and
less learned circle. The carvings on the cathedrals were text-
books of theology and learning open to all the world.

The interiors of the churches were not neglected. The awe-
inspiring effect of the lofty naves scarcely possesses the visitor of
today before the thrill of the colored glass, especially in the choir,
grips him in its spell. The windows of the clerestory, the varied
scheme of pillars and recesses below that, and the decorations
within the body of the church next claim attention. Here the lesser arts preside. The choir screen, usually of wood, though
sometimes of stone and even of metal-work, reveals the work of
many hands. Unrelieved flat surfaces find little place. Carvings,
whether of a storied relief or merely fanciful design, hold the
eye and carry it on from point to point to the master altar
adorned with the goldsmith's and needle-worker's art. As on the
outside, so in the interior, there is evidence of the coöperation of
successive generations and centuries, but twelfth- and especially
thirteenth-century ideas predominate. The Church, the State,
learning and art, commerce and industry, piety and pride, the
rich and the humble once coöperated with full will and without
reservation in the achievement of this work of piety and peace.
The Gothic cathedral is not only a masterpiece of art, but is perhaps the greatest social achievement which art has yet attained.

SPREAD OF GOTHIC ARCHITECTURE

While northern France was the early home of Gothic architecture, the region in which it first reached its complete form, neighboring countries took it up and added to it local touches of their own. Virtually all the great French Gothic cathedrals were well under way before the thirteenth century had ended. Additions and modifications were made in later centuries, but the great era of cathedral building was over for France at that time. The Low Countries and the Rhineland had barely begun their building era before 1300. Strasburg, Köln and Antwerp, it is true, had begun their cathedrals by this time, but the great development of the Gothic style for civic as well as for cathedral architecture in these regions belongs to the next three centuries. In that period Gothic architecture was greatly modified in detail, especially in the Low Countries where the so-called flamboyant Gothic arose. In England, too, the Gothic was received with great favor. The rambling lines of the great cathedrals against a sylvan setting are peculiarly English. There, likewise, modifications were made in the details of the style, particularly in the fifteenth and sixteenth centuries, the age of the Tudor Gothic. In Spain the Gothic gained its foothold in the thirteenth century when crusading activities almost doubled the area of the Christian community there. Missionary zeal created the need for new buildings, and the joy of victory found its finest expression in the Gothic cathedrals which subsequently arose. A modern critic has remarked that no one can fully appreciate the Gothic style of architecture without studying the Spanish examples of it.

Italy, on the other hand, was not very hospitable to the Gothic. The cathedral at Milan and the memorial church of St. Francis at Assisi both clearly illustrate the Italian reluctance to accept this style, for neither is genuinely Gothic in spirit. The causes which led to the development of this style in the north, particularly the need for light, were little felt in Italy. There shade and large wall space for painted pictures were more desirable. Besides, the Italians were predisposed to the rounded arch of the Roman and Romanesque styles. To them the points and spires of the Gothic

were too suggestive of restless physical energy and human arrogance. They spoke of it contemptuously as barbarous, and it
was thus that the term Gothic as the designation for this style
was derived. Perhaps their attitude was not altogether free
from envy, for Italians had led in the field of art; but, whatever
the reasons, the Italians did little more than borrow some details
of the Gothic for purely decorative purposes.

Church building was not so active in Italy at this time as it
was in the countries to the north and west. Italy had not yet exhausted its architectural inheritance from ancient Rome, and most
of its building was in the nature of repairs on those structures.
Even where such repairs were quite extensive at this time, the
foundations virtually committed the Italians to following Roman
lines. Few cathedral churches were begun as late as the thirteenth
century. The greatest church building activity in Italy during this period was that of the Franciscans and Dominicans, who
were erecting churches in almost all the larger towns. Most of
these, however, were on Romanesque lines, and Italian artistic
genius displayed itself rather in the decoration applied to these
buildings than in the design of the building itself. In this they
made their great contribution to the ages, the development of
painting, and their most important advance, the achievement of
realism on a flat surface, was made before the close of the century.

ITALIAN PAINTING

Painting was an old art in Italy. Painted crucifixes and pictures of saints had been sent from there to the growing Christian
community north of the Alps as early as the sixth century, and
Italy has continued to furnish such pictures ever since. The
Italians in their travels were very sensitive to new ideas, and
their work in the thirteenth century showed unmistakable evidences of both Byzantine and Gothic influence, the former in
mosaic work and the latter in sculpture. Perhaps the Italian towns
were too engrossed in gaining that political power which strong
kingdoms denied their northern rivals to give their artistic
desires full play at this time. That development was to come

later, but meanwhile the churches of the friars furnished the school in which that later art received its training.

None of the Italian churches was more important than the memorial church of St. Francis at Assisi. St. Francis, himself an Italian, was peculiarly dear to all Italians, and his followers found it impossible to resist the universal desire to rear a fitting monument to his memory. Once this building was begun, the friars were determined to make it worthy of their revered founder. Funds were collected everywhere and no expense was spared to attain their end. The emphasis was laid upon the decoration of the church and the best artists to be found in Italy were engaged to paint its walls. They came from Rome and Pisa and Florence and elsewhere. The presence of so many artists insured keen competition among them, and the purpose of the church itself encouraged a tendency toward realism. It was not sufficient to paint pictures and scenes from the Scriptures, which had long since become conventionalized in standard representations. This church, located in a community which had been the chief abode of St. Francis, called for scenes from his life. The buildings, trees, and even some of the people of that little town had shared in the life of the saint, and all this conspired to win from the artists a supreme effort to make the pictures seem as real as the memory of him.[1]

The results were more than gratifying. The competition between the artists brought out a young Florentine painter, Giotto by name, whose work so far excelled that of the others that he was commissioned not only to do the greatest share of the painting, but even to do over some of the work of his competitors. His fresco pictures of some of the scenes from the life of St. Francis show supreme skill in composition and in the use of background and shading to give the impression of a third dimension. The subjects were undoubtedly furnished by the friars, who may also have suggested the manner of treatment, but the artist showed his genius in making the pictures reveal the desired effects. The fame of this artist spread rapidly, and he was called upon to paint pictures for churches in many Italian towns. When

[1] See chapter XVIII.

he was finally ready to retire from active work and to return to his native city, his fellow citizens cut an entrance for him through the city wall to welcome him in triumph, and further showed their appreciation by electing him architect of the city. His pictures remained the masterpieces of painting for nearly a century, other artists being apparently content to approach his standard as nearly as possible. His apprentices became the leaders in their art throughout all Italy, and from him may be dated the development of the artistic leadership of Florence.

These achievements of the twelfth and thirteenth centuries would have been impossible without the background of the more peaceful political situation and the rising economic prosperity of the period. They also bear evidence to a widespread interest in the fine things of life seldom surpassed at any time. The architecture, the sculpture, the painting and even much of the literature were intended for universal enjoyment, and these arts, in turn, were made possible by the almost universal appreciation of such endeavor. In quality some of this work has since been excelled, but much of it remains unsurpassed, and the age must be ranked, along with the classical periods of Greece and Rome, as one of the greatest cultural epochs of all times.

LOUIS IX had displayed great skill in utilizing the new forces of commerce and learning without losing the support of the older ones represented by the nobility and the Church. He outdid his nobles in quest of adventure, even the more reckless of them having to be dragged on the second of his crusades. He satisfied the highest demands of Christian idealism and excelled most of his clergy in piety and love of justice. Neither class could complain of his lack of zeal. His life illustrated, in fact, the precepts contained in his letter to his son. He also bound to himself the rising strength of the towns and the skilled learning of men trained in the law. In so doing he welded together the most compact political organization which Europe had yet known, all classes of society being held together in direct loyalty to their king. Furthermore, he elevated French influence and power to a commanding position in Italy and he left a heritage such as even the greatest of the medieval emperors might have envied. All this he accomplished in a most unassuming way, apparently always ready to yield to the demands of justice, whether these required unstinting service to Mother Church or the sacrifice of lands and people. His patent idealism and his untiring concern for justice to rival king or humble subject won him the love of all, especially of the rank and file of his subjects. Never had a French king heaped up a greater treasury of good works. It remained to be seen whether the strength of his position would pass away with him, to be remembered only in connection with his name, or whether his descendants would be able to attach his personal prestige to the kingship itself.

Philip III, to whom Louis' farewell letter had been addressed, ruled for fifteen years, during which time he did nothing more than continue the work of his illustrious predecessor, without his skill. His greatest undertaking was a crusade into Aragon to avenge the loss of Sicily. Despite elaborate preparations which yielded taxes from border lands not previously subject to kings of France, and despite the assembling of a larger army than had ever been commanded by a king of France, the venture failed. It was badly planned and poorly executed, but it was in the service of the Church and it gave occupation to the nobility. Philip died before he could renew the venture. His intentions had been good, and apparently the memory of Louis continued to uphold the prestige of the royal office.

THE REIGN OF PHILIP IV, THE FAIR

It was the grandson of Louis, rather than the son, who was to reap most fully the fruits of Louis' labors. This was Philip IV, called the Fair, who ruled from 1285 to 1314. His personality has baffled historians. Some of his devoted admirers and apologists ascribed to him an appearance that was exceedingly handsome and a character that was as saintly as that of his grandfather. His enemies, and these became numerous, saw in him supernatural qualities also, but rather such as are symbolized by horns and cloven feet. He himself left few utterances or written records of the kind that reveal a man's inner self. If he had illusions, he did not indulge them. He appreciated the memory of his grandfather, and it was at his instigation that Joinville wrote those remarkable memoirs which have done so much to keep alive the glorified memory of Louis the Saint. It was in his reign, too, that the official canonization of Louis occurred. That apparently was glory enough of that type for the family and the royal office. Philip the Fair did not pursue any of it himself, at least not very far. He devoted himself to matters of a more material sort and nearer home.

Philip IV continued and expanded the practice of his grandfather in using trained lawyers and administrators in the royal service. The chief of these was Pierre Flotte, whom Boniface

VII was to call "this Belial, one-eyed of body, blind of spirit."
Flotte served his royal master with skill and fidelity and died
fighting for Philip at Courtrai in 1302. Enguerrand de Marigny,
a master of intrigue and finance, succeeded Flotte. But these
were only the leaders of a host of similar servants whose legal or
financial skill was completely at their master's service, and whose
constant activities extended throughout the realm and even beyond,
when necessary. Pierre Dubois, whose memoir on the recovery
of the Holy Land has already been noticed, and William of
Nogaret, so prominent in the tragedy of Anagni,[1] were but members of this host. These "little people," as the nobles contemptuously designated them, or "knights of the king," as Philip
himself styled them, owed their position entirely to the royal
approval and showed their gratitude by loyal and unwavering
service. With their help Philip carried on a tireless campaign
of encroachment upon the lands of his vassals, converting feudal
dependencies into subject territory. Towns continued to seek charters from the king, and vassals were encouraged to appeal their
cases to the king's court. In this way royal authority was nib-
bling its way into Aquitaine and the southwest, into Flanders and
the northeast, and likewise into Dauphiny and Savoy to the
southeast. Less apparently but none the less really, the authority
of the nobility in the center was being undermined in the same
way. The king's officials were constantly on the watch for opportunities, and the policy of encroachment was adding to the king's
authority and power in ever-widening and deepening circles.

Even in the time of Saint Louis some of the more conscientious
nobles had come to appreciate the danger to their own power
which the activities of the royal officials involved. Joinville himself complained bitterly to the king that while he was on the
crusade the king's officials had encroached on his lands and impaired his jurisdiction. Joinville had made his complaint to the
king, confident in the latter's friendship and sense of justice.
Such complaints, however, received little sympathy from Philip
IV, though they were better founded and much more numerous.
Philip, however, was more or less scrupulous in maintaining the

[1] See page 287.

forms of law and in committing no overt acts. The nobility saw
themselves deprived of power and influence bit by bit, without
knowing quite how to prevent it. At most they consoled themselves with an increasing hatred of the "little people" of the king.
Such was the state of affairs within France and on the eastern
border.

In Flanders and Aquitaine Philip's policy met with determined
opposition. The power of the count of Flanders was undermined
successfully enough; the difficulty arose in dealing with the
burghers of the towns. The Flemish towns were more highly
developed than those of France and had acquired a commercial
aristocracy which was becoming burdensome to most of the
people. This was notably the case in Ghent and Bruges, where
a comparatively small group of families had succeeded in usurp-
ing almost absolute control. When appeals were made to the
king's court, royal support was thrown to the side of the commercial aristocracy. Perhaps this policy might have succeeded,
even though the mass of lesser tradesmen and workers were
somewhat embittered thereby, had not their opposition been
sustained by hope of help from England.

RECOVERY OF ENGLAND UNDER EDWARD I

It was the king of England, Philip's vassal in Aquitaine and
other southwestern lands, who proved to be Philip's greatest
obstacle. Henry III had died in 1272 and had been succeeded by
Edward I. Edward, unlike Henry III or John, was popular.
Even as prince he had appealed to the imagination of the English
people, who had looked forward to happier days when the young
man should become king. The fact that he was off on a crusade
to the East when his father died endeared him to his subjects all
the more. When he returned it was to rule over a more united
kingdom than had either of his predecessors. After three-quarters of a century of misrule punctuated by frequent uprisings of
the barons, it would be impossible to account for the power of
Edward's government merely on the basis of his personal popularity or even his personal ability. As A. B. White has pointed

out: "Ninety-one years out of roughly the first century and a quarter after 1066, England was ruled by a William I, a Henry I and a Henry II; and the centennial year of the Conquest brought forth the Assize of Clarendon. Though there was a falling off in the quality of kings during the next century, enough had been done. A standard had been set, traditions had been established, ministers had been trained. No more impressive proof of Henry II's greatness can be desired than to watch generation after generation of ministers perpetuating his ideals and methods under the politically incompetent or abusive Richard I, John and Henry III. . . ." Edward's personal popularity merely gave these latent forces of good government an opportunity to reassert themselves. This advantage Edward managed to hold by the real leadership which he furnished. He addressed himself to the immediate problems of his English subjects. A series of successful wars against the Welsh served to bring peace to his western boundary. His activities on the northern frontier were also crowned with success, the Scots being compelled to cease their depredations upon the cattle folds of the north.

Though Edward's major concern was for the immediate border of England, he was not unmindful of his interests on the Continent. His own advisers were men of the same type as those who served Philip IV so skillfully. They recognized the implications of Philip's policy of encroachment, and while Edward was busy with the Welsh or the Scots, they proceeded to checkmate Philip in Aquitaine. If one group of citizens in a town were in favor of Philip, they stirred up the rest to opposition. In Aquitaine, as in Flanders, the commercial aristocracy was usually for Philip, while the popular party was opposed to him. Edward's officials also found a way of getting into touch with the popular party in Flanders and of stiffening their opposition to Philip. Philip naturally encouraged appeals to the French courts and Edward's agents resorted to various devices to render such appeals uncomfortable for the appellants. The upshot of all this was to make it necessary for Philip to engage in counter tactics, to send money and supplies to the Scots or the Welsh or to stir up the Irish. In the distance there hovered the constant possibility of out-and-out warfare between France and England, whenever either of the kings should feel free enough to undertake it. It must be said, however, that neither Philip nor Edward showed any strong inclination to enter upon such a conflict except as a last resort. The two were chronically on the verge of war, but neither seemed anxious to precipitate it.

Such a policy as Philip was pursuing, in the face of the stout opposition which he was meeting in Flanders and Aquitaine, necessitated the expenditure of great sums of money. While he was supporting armies in the field against Flanders and was providing his agents in other border lands with more than a mere bodyguard, he had also to supply funds to the Scots and Welsh. He was forced also to buy off enemies on the Continent whom Edward's agents were subsidizing to make war upon him. The armies themselves were no longer mere feudal levies, but more largely mercenary troops which cost great quantities of gold. Both Philip and Edward were hard put to it to devise new methods of obtaining additional funds. Both borrowed heavily from Italian bankers. Both resorted to the practice of driving out the Jews and then permitting them to remain or to return upon the payment of large sums of money. Both likewise went as far as custom would permit in levying taxes upon towns and nobles. Frequently, in fact, the ingenuity of their lawyers was almost exhausted in discovering ancient customs which could be used to justify additional taxes upon their subjects. Both used the precedent of the crusading practices in levying income taxes, and both flirted with the idea of taking part in another crusade to the East, largely as a pretext for extra financial aid. Both required money of the clergy in their realms, and Philip, in addition, resorted to such devices as making special levies upon particular Church groups and debasing the royal coinage.

Taxation has never been a very popular activity of government and it was not in these times. There had been grumbling even in the period of the great crusades of the twelfth century, when the clergy had contributed heavily. During the next century, when expeditions in the West against the Albigenses, against Frederick II, and against Aragon were dignified as crusades, the kings had become accustomed to large financial support from the clergy for such military expeditions. It was no great step from that to an outright demand for money from them for any military expedition on which the king might be embarked. Agents skilled in Roman law could have felt little difficulty in advising such a step, and even pious kings could have stayed any qualms of conscience by contrasting their own just aims with the diabolical devices of those who opposed them. But the clergy finally rebelled. In France the Cistercian monks vigorously protested against a levy which Philip was making. Finally the French clergy addressed a protest to the pope against the exactions of their king.

PAPAL INTERFERENCE IN THE RIVALRY OF PHILIP AND EDWARD

Boniface VIII, who received the protest, undertook to aid the clergy against such exactions. In 1296 he issued a bull, *Clericis Laicos,* declaring such taxes illegal. An able lawyer himself, Boniface rested his case upon canon law. The papal bull was addressed to all Christendom, but affected Philip IV and Edward I more directly. Neither of these kings contradicted the papal declaration. Edward merely indicated that, if his clergy were unwilling to support the king, they could not expect any protection from him. Philip discovered that it was unwise to let any gold go out of his kingdom, and therefore forbade its exportation. These tactics also prevented the payment of Church dues from French territory to the papacy. The forms of law were observed carefully, but the use of violence could not have been more effective. Many of the clergy in both countries yielded to the situation and Boniface himself issued another bull under which the clergy were permitted to lend money to the kings at critical periods, though no concession was made in regard to the principle that the clergy could not be taxed. Like most compromises, this arrangement was not entirely satisfactory to either party and trouble soon broke out again. In marked contrast to Innocent III, who also had to deal with several recalcitrant kings, Boniface seems not to have made any great effort to pit one king against the other. Even later, when, under added provocation, Boniface addressed himself chiefly to Philip, he did not secure the support of Edward. The trouble between Philip and Boniface reached its climax in 1302. A bull published in that year, *Unam Sanctam,* set forth the claims of papal power over rulers more explicitly than any writing of Gregory VII or Innocent III. Philip's attitude toward the envoys of Boniface was highly insulting to the pope and drew from him a threatening letter.

The situation now became serious for Philip, and forced him into a series of unusual measures. That year (1302) he invited not only the nobles and the clergy, but representatives of the towns also, to meet with him to consider the welfare of the realm. This was the famous Estates General of 1302 which included the townsmen, or the Third Estate, more fully than the meeting of 1295. Philip's difficulties with the pope were here craftily set forth by Pierre Flotte. It was made to appear that the pope was making unjust demands upon the king which he had no recourse but to resist for the welfare of the country. The king's lawyers were eloquent and persuasive and virtually the whole gathering, including nobles, clergy and townsmen, joined in a protest against the unjust attitude of the pope. Following this meeting, Philip's agents went throughout the kingdom, holding meetings in castle, market-place and highway. They read a doctored copy of the papal bull and pointed out the injustice which it did to the king and the fair realm of France. This was an appeal to popular opinion and national feeling beyond the dreams of Frederick II, and had the effect of giving Philip substantially the united support of all his subjects. The people had decided that in this struggle between the head of their State and the head of their Church the latter was wrong. A new moral force had arisen, the force of national interest. Probably the memory of the saintly Louis IX lingered in the minds of the people as they underwrote the misdeeds of his grandson, but the arguments of Philip's legal agents were very persuasive and the cause of Boniface was not fairly represented. Public opinion then, as now, was capable of being swayed by skillful manipulators of fact.

Though successful in maintaining himself against the papal threats, Philip was not so certain that he could safely weather actual excommunication or interdict. At any rate, he was anxious not to have either issued, and yet he would not yield to the pope's demands. His advisers then planned an attack upon the pope more insidious than any undertaken by Frederick II. Boniface did not occupy so strong and strategic a position as had his predecessors. In the first place, the popes for the past fifty years had been depending upon French aid against their enemies in Italy. The French, established in Naples, had been drawing recruits from France throughout the period. This relationship had built up a strong French party in Rome as well as a strong French state in Italy. Several of the popes had been French and there were a considerable number of French prelates in the college of cardinals. Philip's advisers counted upon these conditions. Boniface, though not a Frenchman, had, on the whole, been favorable to the French in the past, and it was perhaps this feeling which had prevented him so far from singling out Philip as the ruler most offensive in the oppression of the clergy. Circumstances, however, had brought him to the edge of a break with Philip.

Now Philip's advisers made use of their intimate knowledge of papal affairs to attempt the undoing of Boniface. They did not attack the papacy as an office, but they attacked Boniface as an unworthy occupant of the office. The unusual circumstances under which Boniface had been elected were used against him. His predecessor, Celestin V, a simple hermit who found the office of pope overwhelming in its multitude of affairs, had resigned, and Boniface, then a member of the college of cardinals, had been elected. Celestin, after roaming about for some months, had been taken into custody by partisans of Boniface and soon after died. Philip's advisers professed to see in these irregularities evidence of diabolical machination on the part of Boniface. They held that Boniface could not be elected while his predecessor lived, and hinted that Boniface himself was responsible for the death of Celestin. In an effort to prevent his continued attacks upon Philip, they threatened to bring Boniface before a Church council to be held at Lyons. One of these advisers, Nogaret, equipped with a letter of credit on a Florentine banking-house and accom-

panied by a bitter personal enemy of Boniface, went down to Italy
to intimidate the pope. There they hired a thousand ruffians and
found the pope at his summer home, Anagni, where he was preparing a bull of excommunication against the French king. Fearful that the matter had gone beyond possibility of persuasion and
anxious to prevent the launching of the bull, they broke into the
papal palace and took Boniface captive. Stories of what occurred are exaggerated, but it seems clear that the aged pontiff
was rather roughly used. The people of Anagni arose and drove
off the invaders, but Boniface never quite recovered from the
shock. He returned to Rome meditating various rigorous measures against the king of France, but died within little more than a
month after his capture, October 11, 1303.

PHILIP'S EFFORTS TO CONTROL THE PAPACY

The situation of Philip IV was now more critical than it had
been before. A vigorous hostile successor to Boniface might fix
responsibility for the affair of Anagni upon the French king
and denounce him before all Christendom. French interests were
at stake in the election of the next pope, and every effort was
made to rally French influence at Rome to insure a pliable successor. The French king of Naples appeared in person with a
strong force of troops. The cardinals chose one of their number
as pope. He took the title of Benedict XI and proved to be a
very mild, almost timid, old man, who desired peace above all
else. Several of the severe measures which Boniface had enacted
were repealed by him, and the Colonna family, which his predecessor had banished from Rome, was recalled. Philip had little
cause to worry at the conduct of this pope, but Benedict died
within less than a year. The issues which had been so pressing
in 1303 were yet too fresh in people's minds to leave the French
king safe from responsibility for his misdeeds.

The new election proved more difficult than the former and
the college of cardinals was long deadlocked between the French
and non-French factions. Finally a list of candidates was submitted by the latter and from this the former chose Bertrand de

Got, archbishop of Bordeaux, who was duly elected and took the title of Clement V. Various attempts have been made to explain this election, including an unauthenticated rumor that Philip had held a secret conference with the archbishop in which the latter agreed, if chosen pope, to further Philip's plans.

Whatever the truth of the matter, the fact remains that Clement V was very friendly to Philip. He appointed new cardinals who insured a majority for the French party in the college of cardinals, and he remained in the neighborhood of France throughout his pontificate, never going to Rome. The popes after him were French or in sympathy with the French party, and remained at Avignon on the borders of France until 1376. Theoretically, the popes as head of all Christendom might live anywhere in Christendom, and in past times, for one reason or another, popes had lived outside of Rome; but tradition had identified the papacy so closely with Rome and the shrines of Peter and Paul that most Christians regarded the location of the papacy at Avignon with suspicion, and many thought that the French kings had captured the papacy. From the latter point of view Philip IV had accomplished without bloodshed what Frederick II had struggled for in vain. At any rate, Philip had now nothing to fear from the side of the papacy and could devote all of his attention to other problems.

His policy of weakening the nobles continued to be as expensive as before. Philip's schemes for raising money were not yet exhausted, but it was becoming increasingly difficult to discover legitimate devices. The royal coinage which under preceding kings, especially under Louis IX, had come to supplant that of the nobility, was deliberately depreciated and then restored, both processes being to the advantage of the royal treasury. The estates of the financiers of the realm were sequestered upon their death. In 1306 the Jews were ordered expelled from the realm, another device to gain money. Five years later the "Lombards" were similarly treated. And in part, at least, the treatment of the Templars must also be considered as a financial measure.

As long as there were Christian holdings in Syria the Templars had continued their rôle as protectors of the Christian pilgrims.

During the two centuries of their distinguished and heroic service they had received numerous bequests as expressions of gratitude and appreciation from many sources. The accumulation of these bequests had given them extensive holdings throughout Western Christendom, and the administration of these holdings had come to be almost as large a part of their work as the military service in the East. Their massive buildings at the important centers in the West were almost as imposing as their fortresses in the East. It was quite natural that this widespread organization should be entrusted with funds for use in the East or even in the West. In fact, the Templars had developed a very considerable banking business in connection with their organization. When the last Christian stronghold in the East fell in 1291, the Templars seemed almost content with the management of their Western lands and the continuation of their banking business.

The relations of Philip with the Templars had at times been pleasant, at other times irritating. In 1307 he had all the Templars in France arrested on charges of heresy, his agents arranging the attack. To many the spectacle of Philip and his lawyers acting, in effect, as judges of faith and morals must have seemed rather anomalous. They did, however, bring the Templars to trial and by use of torture forced many of them to confessions of preposterous acts of irreverance, confessions which were in many cases denied when the victims were released from torture. In this case, as in his difficulty with Boniface, Philip summoned a meeting of the Estates General to strengthen himself with the support of the nation. Philip's agents took great care to present the case against the Templars without giving the latter a hearing, To clinch matters, Philip and his advisers pressed the papal court to take general action against the Templars. Clement V seems to have acted reluctantly in this affair, but after five years he issued the bull of 1312 which abolished the order. The Knights Hospitallers were entrusted with the administration of the property of the Templars, but they never got possession of all of it. If Philip gained by his mistreatment of the Templars, he was thus prevented from attaining quite all that he might have desired.

Meanwhile Edward I of England had died in 1307, to be succeeded by his less able son, Edward II. The closing years of the great Edward's reign had been troubled by a recurrence of baronial opposition, which was to increase in the next reign. This situation eased the tension in both Flanders and Aquitaine for Philip, who continued his policies there with greater success. To many historians it has been something of a mystery why Philip did not take full advantage of the opportunity to gain all of Aquitaine, Gascony and Flanders. Mere willingness to make such acquisitions, however, was not sufficient, for there was considerable local opposition in each of these regions. Nor was Philip entirely free to devote all of his attention to them. The problem of the Templars, while not exactly a military problem, did, nevertheless, involve expenditure of money and dragged on for several years. There were indications, too, that Philip was not altogether free from some of the ambitious schemes which enthusiastic advisers like Pierre Dubois so eagerly conjured up before his eyes. He was grooming one of his sons for the prospective vacancy on the imperial throne in Germany and actually took the cross himself to go on a crusade. Such schemes, even in prospect, required the outlay of large sums. The decisive factors were signs of growing discontent on the part of his nobles and, more directly, his own death in 1314. He was actually on the point of attacking Flanders in force, having gathered an army for that purpose, when death intervened.

THE LAST CAPETIANS

His oldest son, Louis X, was but twenty-five years of age and, though willing to continue his father's policies, he lacked the insight and ability to succeed. The nobles demanded and received concessions from him, and the expeditions against Flanders failed. What he might have accomplished in time must remain mere conjecture, for he died in 1316.

The forces let loose in these two years gained strength in the succeeding reigns. Their essence was the organized opposition of the great nobles to the power of the king. There was nothing strange in this.   If the border lands had suffered at the hands of the kings, the nobility within the kingdom had suffered no less. Step by step Philip Augustus, Louis IX and Philip IV, with the help of "the little people," had silently and stealthily undermined their power.   The right of private warfare was restricted, and for a time Louis IX had even forbidden duels.   The king's coinage invaded all parts of France and actually supplanted the coinage of many of the nobles.   The "little people"—the king's legists, financial and administrative agents—were scurrying about constantly over the whole kingdom, collecting revenues, recruiting troops and dispensing justice with increasing boldness.   The allegiance of towns was subtracted from the nobles and attached to the king, and the king's justice was substituted for that of the nobles.   At the rate of progress attained by this series of French kings, even the great nobles were on the way to the status of mere landlords, with no governmental functions at all.   These facts had become painfully apparent to most of the nobles.   Joinville's complaint to Louis IX may be taken as typical.   He recognized the tendency of the royal policy and blamed the king's officers rather than the king.   He complained to the king, and urged as his reason for complaint his own obligation to protect his vassals.   Unlike the clergy, the noble class was not organized. Each noble was accustomed to regard himself as a separate ruler within his own domain, subject only to the superior force of his overlord.   Coöperation, therefore, seemed to the nobles, a partial surrender of sovereignty.   This individualism had been their undoing and the great kings had been very careful to prevent much coöperation, Philip IV going so far as to forbid tournaments at which nobles gathered, for fear of their making common cause.   As long as the nobles contented themselves with individual complaints to the king, he could lend a sympathetic ear and dismiss them, satisfied that it was the king's officials and not the king who was to blame, and that all would soon be well.

Now, however, the situation had gone too far to be dealt with in this simple fashion.   The nobles were meeting together in various parts of France.   They took advantage of the youth and inexperience of Louis X to gain the dismissal of some of the royal agents whom they regarded as especially obnoxious. Enguerrand de Marigny and several others were given over to their wrath, Enguerrand being hanged.

The death of Louis X without a son, the first time since 987 that this misfortune had happened to a French king, gave the nobles further opportunity. The two younger brothers of Louis followed him on the throne in succession, neither having a son. In 1328 the throne was again vacant; the direct Capetian line was at an end. There was now a question as to which of the collateral relatives should succeed. Two cousins were living, Philip of Valois, whose father was a brother of Philip the Fair, and Edward III of England, whose mother was the daughter of Philip the Fair. Philip of Valois assumed the crown as Philip VI without any real contest, it being held by the French lawyers that the crown could not be transmitted through the female line, and furthermore Philip of Valois was French. Philip VI obtained the throne through the consent of the nobility, whose class prejudices he thoroughly shared. The nobility felt sure that he would not use the "little people" to their undoing, and likewise felt that they could now recover or reassume many powers which they had formerly lost. In this they were not mistaken, for Philip VI loved the gayer side of the life of the nobility and employed them as his advisers by preference. The advice of the dying St. Louis to his son was quite completely ignored, with results which the future was soon to tell.

Trouble promptly broke out in Flanders, in Aquitaine and on the sea. In Flanders the count had been imprisoned in an uprising of the popular party. He appealed to the French king for aid. The burghers of Bruges took the field, hoping to repeat the success of Courtrai, but they were cut down by the noble cavalry of Philip VI. Shortly afterward an impassioned orator, Jacob van Artevelde, stirred up the people of Flanders. From Ghent his flaming zeal was spread to fan a popular uprising which swept the count of Flanders from his seat and substituted the popular leader in his place. A part of van Artevelde's program was a commercial treaty with the English, upon whose wool much of Flemish industry depended for its prosperity. Such a treaty was made. To protect himself and his people from the retribution which the French king would be sure to exact for the overthrow of the noble count, the Flemish leader asked for the help of Edward III. He maintained that in seeking Edward's aid he was only acting as a loyal feudal subject to the rightful king of France. This was a somewhat strange request of Edward, who had already taken the oath of homage to Philip VI, but Edward decided to entertain it and to lay claim to the French throne.

French aggressions in Aquitaine and Gascony had caused great ill-feeling, and there was danger that Gascony, upon whose wines and grain England was largely dependent, might be completely lost. On the sea also there had been frequent trouble, the merchant sailors of France and England carrying on intermittent warfare and disaffected merchants of both countries complaining to their kings. Causes for war had long existed between these two countries. Other preoccupations had kept Philip IV and Edward I from coming to direct blows. Edward II, easy and pleasure-loving, had become embroiled with factions among his barons and had offered but little opposition to the encroachments of his neighbor and suzerain on the Continent. Edward III, however, though not equal in ability to his grandfather, managed to resume his grandfather's policies.

Wales was no longer a problem, but Scotland was. The Scots had regained their independence at Bannockburn in 1314 and had successfully resisted all further attacks, even venturing on raiding expeditions into England. Edward III brought a deep feeling of relief to his subjects by winning several victories over the Scots. Incidentally he learned valuable lessons on the art of war. He chose not to attempt the reconquest of Scotland, but decided instead to turn his attention to his continental interests. Perhaps the uprising of the Flemish burghers under van Artevelde and their offer of allegiance helped Edward to determine his continental policy. His belated claim to the French throne, which had some strength even if it was not seriously held by Edward himself, was a convenient fiction by which he could hold the Flemish allegiance more firmly and even gain other disaffected subjects of the French king. At any rate, it could do no harm to his interests.

BEGINNING OF THE HUNDRED YEARS' WAR.   ENGLISH VICTORIES

The war which thus broke out between the French and the kings of England has been called The Hundred Years' War. For convenience it may be divided into three periods—1337 to 1360; 1369 to 1386; 1415 to 1453. As a spectacle it left much to be desired. There were few pitched battles, and, though all of these were won by the English, the war was finally won by France. Its importance, however, not only for the two contestants, but for Europe as a whole, can scarcely be overestimated. It absorbed the surplus energy of the two greatest political organizations of the time, and thereby gave the lesser organizations into which the neighboring regions of Europe were at the time divided an opportunity for development.

During the first period (1337-1360) victory lay with the English. After several years of rather desultory warfare, in 1346 Edward III led a large raiding expedition through Normandy toward Paris. The muster of the French forces compelled him to retreat toward Flanders and he was finally overtaken near the village of Crécy. Edward's army was greatly outnumbered, but he had distinct advantages in the position which he had chosen and in the weather. With his knights in the center and his archers extending in semicircular fashion on both flanks, and with a small body of troops in reserve behind the center, he was able to await the enemy's attack. The French army consisted chiefly of knights. A force of Genoese cross-bowmen went ahead to open the way for the cavalry, while a fairly large force of infantry was straggling far behind along the road. Instead of waiting until the next day, or even until all their men could be properly arranged, the impatient knights opened battle almost immediately. The Genoese cross-bowmen were dispersed by the equally accurate and far more rapid fire of the English long-bowmen. As they broke toward the rear the vanguard of the French cavalry dashed impatiently forward, trampling or cutting down the Genoese before them. This caused some confusion, which was soon worse confounded when the French cavalry came within range of the long-bow. Meanwhile the other French battle lines had formed and were marching forward. Those behind pushed on those before, while the latter recoiled before the confusion of the first lines. The few French knights who reached the English center were easily disposed of, and the result was a complete and relatively easy victory for the English army. Among the spoils gathered by the English were hundreds of pairs of golden spurs, reminders of the many distinguished French knights who had that day fought their last battle. These were hung up in a neighboring church as a thank-offering by the victors.

Crécy has often been described as a decisive battle and as marking the rise of the common bowman to a position of equality or even superiority over the heavily armored knight. The strength of the yew of which the long-bows were made and the skill which life-long training had given to the English bowmen were indeed brilliantly displayed. Just as important, however, was the careful organization of the English army, in which bowmen, infantry and knightly cavalry worked together as a harmonious machine. No less important was the lack of discipline displayed by the feudal chivalry of France, whose unbridled pride, individualistic ambitions and contempt for the common soldier led to their undoing. Edward III exemplified the wisdom of combining all elements of his kingdom; his opponent unwisely relied chiefly upon one class, and that the most insubordinate.

The fruits of the victory were few, however, for Edward's army was small and the towns and castles in which his foes concealed themselves were hard to take. The town of Calais, which he now besieged, required nearly a whole year and all the troops he could muster to capture. Its possession was important, for it gave to England a bridgehead opposite Dover, which was to be used both by its armies and by its commerce for over two centuries.

With the capture of Calais the war came to a standstill. A new foe more powerful than either of the contestants had entered the field. This was the plague known as the Black Death, whose ravages were now felt in France and England as they had already been felt in Italy and were to be experienced by virtually all of Europe. Modern physicians have diagnosed the scourge as a form of the bubonic plague, which had traveled westward from China along the trade routes and had entered western Europe through the Italian seaports. It struck Italy in 1347, where its effects are vividly described by Boccaccio in the introduction to his *Decameron*. Transalpine Europe felt its full force in the following year. Apparently no class was spared. It struck with equal force castle and monastery, city and hamlet. In some places whole communities were wiped out. Very few escaped untouched and estimates of its destructive force have been placed at from one-third to one-half of the population of western Europe. Religious frenzy and other emotional disturbances were common. The first attack, which lasted for about two years, was the worst, but it recurred at intervals of several years thereafter, fortunately with diminishing force.

One of the direct results of the plague was a scarcity of laborers. The amount of land to be cultivated remained the same, and consequently the owners entered upon a keen rivalry to procure workers. This situation hastened the substitution of wages for servile tenure, and improved the lot of the peasants. It also led to serious outbreaks among the laborers, especially in England, though somewhat similar outbreaks also occurred in other parts of Europe. Europe recovered slowly from the plague, and its effects on society were long apparent.

Warfare was resumed in 1356 when Prince Edward, the Black Prince as he has been called, led a raiding expedition from Bordeaux in a circle northeastward along the Loire to Tours. His force was short in archers and smaller than the army which his father had commanded at Crécy. The French king, John, assembled an even larger levy of knights and started in pursuit. The armies met near Poitiers. The battle, though more hotly contested than at Crécy, was even more disastrous to the French. Again it was the superior organization of the English army which won the day. There were not so many killed as in the former battle, but many more prisoners were taken, including King John himself. One circumstance of this battle, true also of Crécy, should be mentioned. Both armies included noble mercenaries from Germany, another evidence of the disorganization then prevailing in that country. Four years after the battle (1360) peace was finally arranged at Brétigny, under the terms of which the royal prisoner and his companions were released for a ransom, and England received in full sovereignty a large section of southwestern France, nearly all of which it had held before the reign of Louis IX, together with Calais and other adjacent bits of land. The Treaty of Brétigny was, however, only a truce. It could not bring peace, for all the causes of war which had existed in 1337 were still present, and the terms of Brétigny only aggravated them several fold.

The first period of The Hundred Years' War had revealed in tragic fashion for France the folly of a government dominated by the feudal nobility. The Valois kings with their noble, not royal, background had attempted to continue the policy of their Capetian predecessors, but without understanding the secret of the latter's success. The earlier kings for almost an unbroken century had been utilizing the business acumen and organization of commerce and the legal skill of lawyers, without sacrificing the support of the nobility. The Valois kings apparently hoped to gain the same ends by relying mainly upon the nobility and not upon the lesser classes. Crécy, Calais, Poitiers and Brétigny all showed the futility of such a policy. At the rate of progress toward the achievement of national boundaries maintained by the Capetians in the thirteenth century, only another long reign like that of Philip IV seemed requisite to gain their ends and to complete the expulsion of the English. Instead, almost half a century had passed since the death of Philip IV, and now the English held even more land than before. The Valois kings aspired to pursue the same end as Philip IV, and so, too, did all the peoples of France who were imbued with national pride, but the Valois kings had not known how to accomplish it. On the other hand, Edward III, with fewer resources than those of his opponent, was able to win victory after victory because he did utilize all the elements in his country's population and was not ashamed to rely heavily upon the military, as well as the financial, strength of the middle classes. Much now depended upon the attitude of the French kings, and even kings can learn from experience. It was certain that the war would be continued, but the outcome was still unpredictable.

RECOVERY OF FRANCE UNDER CHARLES V

In a formal fashion the war was not resumed until 1369. The embers of the earlier warfare, however, were scattered over western France and adjacent regions. These flared up into actual fighting in Brittany, in Gascony and in Spain. As a result English and French soldiers had been fighting one another for some time before their respective governments became openly arrayed against each other.

The king of France was now Charles V. It was a fortunate accident for France which had caused the captured King John to set aside Louis of Anjou for conduct unbecoming a knight and to designate Charles as next King. Charles had experience of the feelings of other classes regarding the disasters of the earlier period of the war. He had seen the merchants of Paris rise up in protest and he was able to view critically the attitude of the court and to share somewhat the opinion of its incompetence voiced by the middle and lower classes. He seems also to have possessed more ability than Louis, his brother; this, with his broader point of view, augured well for France.

The most significant act of Charles V was to appoint Bertrand du Guesclin constable of France, or commander of the French armies. Du Guesclin was a younger son of a relatively unimportant Breton nobleman. His only claim to consideration, therefore, was that he had displayed marked ability and courage as a soldier. He showed no social prejudices in his selection of lieutenants. Competence and demonstrated ability were sufficient to bring preferment and promotion. King and constable supported each other in full sympathy and loyalty. The result was a war which failed to satisfy the chivalrous requirements of the nobility, but proved very successful for France.

There were no pitched battles such as those of Crécy and Poitiers. Relying upon his superior knowledge of the country, the French sympathies of the inhabitants in most of the territory held by the English, and upon the swiftness and unexpectedness of his movements, du Guesclin took one castle or fortress after another away from the English. Time and again the king of England sent expeditions to France to stem the steady losses of territory. One or two of these expeditions, notably the expedition of John of Gaunt in 1373 and that of the duke of Buckingham in 1380, were larger than either of those which figured so brilliantly at Crécy and Poitiers. Each time, however, du Guesclin, with the full support of Charles V, allowed these expeditions to journey afar without a battle. He moved along parallel to them, harrying their flanks, interrupting their supplies and wearing them down until what remained of the expedition was quite content to return home without having accomplished anything to stop the French gains.

Edward III had died in 1377 and now the troubled reign of Richard II was begun. The kings found it increasingly difficult to obtain money from a parliament which grew more and more insistent upon a larger share in the business of conducting the kingdom. Undoubtedly the repeated failure of the expeditions sent to France, which involved great expenditures without any return to either purse or pride, afforded undeniable support to Parliament in its demand for improvement in the manner of conducting the nation's business. Whether or not du Guesclin deserves any credit for contributing thus indirectly to the growth of parliamentary power in England, he does deserve the place which France has accorded him as one of its great national heroes. The net results of his tactics, for which he must share credit with "the Wise King," Charles V, was the recovery of most of the lands yielded to the English in 1360.

Unfortunately for France, both du Guesclin and Charles V died in 1380. The war continued successfully for France until 1386, when with mistaken zeal those in power led the French to prepare an invasion of England. Nothing came of this except the wreck and destruction of a portion of the French fleet. This marks the high point in French recovery during the second phase of the war. Internal affairs of both countries were to prevent any serious further undertakings until 1415.

The war between England and France occupied the center of the European stage during the fourteenth century. The preoccupation of these two countries had exerted a powerful influence on affairs, and was not now without its effect on Europe. A glance over the political happenings in the rest of Europe during these years would seem to indicate that the example of these two states was setting a fashion. The Spanish peninsula was torn by the rivalries of its feudal states (Castile, Aragon, Navarre and Portugal) or by dynastic struggles within the separate states, notably in Castile. To the north the Scandinavian kingdoms were in a similar chaotic state, the Hanseatic League being apparently the strongest single force in that region. In the Empire the lack of strong neighbors to the west probably hastened the crystallization of "particularism" which occurred in the Golden Bull of 1356.[1] The seven electors, the great princes and many lesser ones, as well as individual towns or leagues of towns, were guarding their own independence jealously, so that there was little prospect of united action. In Italy the absence of both emperors and popes afforded the numerous city states an opportunity to develop and work out their relationships. Military companies trained by the war in France found Italy as well as Spain a fruitful region for employment. The rising states of east central and eastern Europe were still too much concerned with driving back the Tartar or resisting the Turk to play important parts in the affairs of Europe. The most promising development during this period was the growth of commerce and trade in the more favored or less distracted regions. This will be discussed in a later chapter.

[1] See above.

CHAPTER XVII

POLITICS AND RELIGION IN THE FIFTEENTH CENTURY

ANYONE who compares the course of events in the thirteenth century with the first part of the Hundred Years' War will be conscious of a great change in European affairs. In the earlier period no war of any consequence had progressed very far without papal intervention. In the later period the two strongest states in Christendom had been engaged in war for twenty-three years without any marked evidence of papal influence. Where Philip IV and Edward I had been prevailed upon to check their open hostilities, lesser kings, Edward III and his Valois opponents, had continued their warfare unabated until they themselves were ready to sign a treaty. Closer examination shows that the later popes were not uninterested and that they sent legates from time to time to bring about peace. The difference lay rather in the fact that these missions had little effect. By following the history of the papacy during these critical years we shall learn how this decline in papal influence came about.

THE PAPACY AT AVIGNON (1309-1376)

Clement V resided at first in France and then settled in Avignon, and the six popes who followed him there were French. The cardinals whom they selected were mostly of the same race. Once located at Avignon, it was quite natural for the papal court to remain there. During this epoch (1309-1376) Avignon was not yet French territory, but it was on the Rhone River, among French people, and in an atmosphere congenial to most of the papal court. The Italians were naturally displeased at the absence of the papacy from Rome and they exaggerated the influence of the French monarchy over these seven popes, of whom only the

first, Clement V, had displayed really compromising friendliness
for the French king. They spoke of the seventy years' stay at,
or near, Avignon as the "Babylonian Captivity," a characteriza-
tion which was soon spread all over Europe and has ever since remained the title for this period of papal history. The effect of
the papal residence at Avignon on the English has already been
noted. Other regions of lesser importance tended also to condition their attitude toward the papacy upon their own relations
with France. Actually the kings of France did not control the
papacy throughout this period, and some of the popes at Avignon,
notably John XXII, conceived of their office in as high terms as
any previous popes. But the mere fact that they stayed at Avignon and that most of the *curia* were French was alone sufficient
to weaken papal influence in Europe.

The stay of the popes at Avignon is also noteworthy for the
systematic way in which papal taxation was increased. The
erection of all the buildings at Avignon was an additional expense,
while disorder in the Papal States and disrespect in Italy, England
and elsewhere noticeably decreased the normal papal income. At
the same time the ordinary expenses of the papal court were not
diminishing. This combination of circumstances led to the increase of papal taxation. The chief means adopted was to increase the taxes upon bishops and abbots. These clergymen were
in a rather difficult position, with both the lay rulers and the popes
seeking a part of their incomes. The principal taxes which they
had to pay to the popes were the *tithes* and the *annates*. The first
was a ten-per-cent tax on their incomes; the latter represented the
whole or a large part of the first year's incomes after they assumed
office. Not all bishops and abbots had to pay these taxes, but
the number of those who did was steadily increasing. The popes,
too, now extended their practice of making direct appointments
to benefices by means of letters, or bulls, commanding local authorities to elect the papal nominee. Such incidents as the virtual
selection of Stephen Langton for the archbishopric of Canterbury
by Innocent III no doubt served as precedents. At any rate, the
fees received by the papal secretaries for writing and sealing bulls

of this kind were by no means a negligible part of the income of the papal *curia.*

The use of these papal letters or *provisions* by the popes at Avignon provoked serious opposition. The cathedral and other chapters and the higher clergy, who had formerly elected or appointed many important ecclesiastics, naturally disliked their loss of power. Leading laymen in several countries objected to having rich benefices pass into the hands of foreigners named by the popes, not a few of them nonresidents who valued the benefices principally for their revenues. The Italian writer Petrarch, for example, was supported in his literary labors by the income of several such benefices. The English House of Commons spoke bitterly on the subject and in 1351 Parliament passed the Statute of Provisors, which, under severe penalties, forbade anyone to secure an English benefice through papal provision. This law reflected the attitude of the local clergy and people of the realm. Kings, in England as well as elsewhere, found the letters of provision a convenient device for securing rewards for their high officials, and made no objection when, in return for such accommodation, the popes issued other letters of provision to men of their own choice. The popes, of course, never admitted the legality of the Statute of Provisors and pointed out that the use of provisions, which were legal according to canon law, enabled them to find places for worthy candidates who otherwise would have had to go without. Nevertheless, the extension of papal taxation and direct appointment was causing rather widespread grumbling and dissatisfaction.

During the Babylonian Captivity the criticism of the papacy was loudest and most persistent in Italy and England, the two regions which felt the situation most deeply. At Rome there was almost constant disorder and the outbreak headed by the "tribune" Rienzo [1] in 1347 was in part directed against the papal claim to

---

[1] Rienzo, the son of a tavern-keeper in Rome, grew up amid the factional strife in which the Roman nobles engaged during the absence of the papacy. Mystical by nature, he acquired some education and developed ability as an orator. In 1342 he was sent on an embassy to Avignon to invite the pope to Rome. His oration won him some favor at the papal court and he received appointment as a papal notary in Rome. In this capacity he became acquainted with the political forces in the city and in 1347 he seized an opportunity to

rule Rome from Avignon. Petrarch, though enjoying benefices from the popes at Avignon, was very sympathetic with Rienzo and, as time went on, became increasingly critical of the papacy for its absence from Rome. St. Catherine of Siena, the most talented and pious woman of the fourteenth century, wrote to the pope imploring him to return to Rome and to purify the Church. "Do you uproot in the garden of Holy Church the malodorous flowers . . . , that is, the bad priests and rulers who poison and rot that garden. . . . Plant in this garden fragrant flowers, pastors and governors who will be true servants of Jesus Christ, who will attend to naught else save the honor of God and the salvation of souls and who will be fathers of the poor." Added impulse was given other critics by occasional outbursts of men like Pelayo, a prominent official at Avignon: "If one compares the present with the past, one sees that the pope and the cardinals have increased in honors, dignities and riches, but they have proportionately lost in virtues." In England, where the news of loans made by the popes to the kings of France during the early part of the Hundred Years' War caused deep resentment, criticism was at times very bitter. The Statute of Provisors was shortly followed by the Statute of Præmunire, which forbade appeals of cases from England to the papal court. The resentment, though very bitter at times, was directed only at practices, and few men even dreamed that the attack might pass to questions of doctrine. It was, so far, rather a protest of loyal and orthodox Catholics who wished to correct abuses.

RETURN TO ROME. THE PAPAL SCHISM

The long "Captivity" was ended in 1376 by Pope Gregory XI. It was his realization of the dangers in the situation, as well as the pleas of such persons as Catherine of Siena, which led him

lead an uprising of the people against the nobles. Success turned his head. Claiming originally to establish order on behalf of the papacy, he was so intoxicated by his success as "Tribune of the People" as to defy both pope and emperor and to summon them to prove their right to rule over Rome. His friends fell away from him and his enemies were able to drive him out before the end of the year. Because he sought vaguely to form some sort of Italian state, his name is especially dear to Italian Nationalists today.

to leave Avignon. One or two of his predecessors had come to recognize that if they were to reëstablish the papal reputation for international impartiality, to combat the worldliness of the clergy, and to regain possession of Italian Church territories, the papacy would have to return to Rome. It was doubtless with some such thought that Urban V went to Rome in 1368, only to find conditions there so inhospitable that he returned to Avignon. Gregory XI, however, finally in 1376 broke loose from the bonds of habit by which he and his cardinals were tied to the French frontier. What a contrast the appearance of Rome, abandoned for seventy-two years, must have presented to the members of his *curia,* fresh from the new well-built palaces of Avignon! The ordinary wear and tear of time had been fearfully augmented by civil strife and poverty, so that few of the great papal buildings afforded adequate shelter and all were in disrepair. Perhaps even Gregory weakened in his resolution to stay in Rome. It was reported that he planned to return to Avignon, as so many of his followers urged him to do. A serious illness, however, prevented his moving, if such really was his plan, and he died at Rome in 1378.

The death of Gregory necessitated an election at Rome. The people of Rome, already fearful that the new pope might take the papal court back to Avignon, crowded around the cardinals with great tumult which reached the proportions of a riot. The shouts of "Give us a Roman pope; at least an Italian," drifted into the conclave hall along with threats and imprecations. The cardinals chose an archbishop from the Neapolitan territory as a compromise candidate, hoping no doubt that, though an Italian, his association with the ruling house of Naples would make him acceptable to them. This election took place in April, 1378. The new pope took the title of Urban VI. He was zealous for reform and harsh in manner to such a degree that he was soon quarreling with most of the cardinals who had elected him. Within a few weeks they deserted him, withdrew from Rome, and at Anagni proclaimed the election of Urban VI invalid. They afterward defended their action on the plea that they had been intimidated into electing Urban at Rome and that his election was therefore void. In September they proceeded to a new election. Their choice now fell upon a Frenchman, a distant relative of the French king, who took the title of Clement VII. To protect themselves, Clement and his followers engaged Italian mercenaries but these were defeated in battle, and he then withdrew to Avignon, taking most of the cardinals with him. Urban, however, stiffly maintained that he was rightful pope, created a new college of cardinals, and remained at Rome. Each pope denounced the other as a usurper and appealed to Europe for support.

France in 1378 was again ruled by Charles V. Charles supported Clement VII. England in 1378, under the adverse fortunes of war, was less disposed to favor a French pope than in earlier and happier days of the war and decided to support Urban VI in Rome. Scotland, naturally hostile to England and friendly toward France, favored Clement. Most of the principalities of Spain also favored Clement. In Germany, though there were important exceptions, most of the divisions supported Urban. This was likewise true of Italy. On the whole their adherence to one or the other of the two popes coincided with the political relations of the states, but individuals within those states, professionally or otherwise closely concerned with Church matters, sometimes held other views. The border lands between the two obediences, like Flanders, found the conflict a matter of daily concern in the struggle of rival claimants for the same offices.

The Schism, thus begun in 1378, lasted almost forty years. The evils which it caused were very serious. The respect for the headship of the Church, which had been much impaired during the Babylonian Captivity, was now further weakened. The power which the papacy had exercised in the thirteenth century to restrain warfare and to maintain justice had still been exerted during the "Captivity," if only feebly. Now, however, the political influence of the papacy outside of Italy, which had been built up through centuries of effort, virtually vanished. Perhaps the chief evil arising from the Schism was the distress of thoughtful Catholics who could not know with absolute certainty which of the rivals was true pope. One of them was the false pope; the bishops whom he confirmed were not bishops, and the priests these bishops ordained were not priests, and the sacraments these priests administered were vain; and adherence to these priests carried with it excommunication and everlasting condemnation. But which was the false pope? The weight of modern opinion is against Clement VII and his successors, but the question is probably insoluble, and it was certainly obscure at the time. In any case, practically half of Catholic Christendom lived in error, the monastic and mendicant orders were split in twain, and a generation grew up which had a declining respect for worship and for the authority of the Church.

GROWING DISCONTENT AMONG CHRISTIANS. WYCLIFFE

This absence of authority made heresy inevitable. If the leaders of the Church could not settle so fundamental a problem, who could? The spectacle of two rivals, each supported by a college of cardinals and half of Europe, each claiming to be the sole representative of God on earth, and each excommunicating all his opponents from the Church, was enough to drive many thinkers into repudiation of the doctrines professed by the rivals. Was it necessary to have a pope at all? What were the doctrines which made possible this scandalous situation? Must they be respected? Every thoughtful Catholic was almost compelled to speculate on such questions. Within little more than a century after the *Summa Theologiæ* of Thomas Aquinas, in which men thought all practical questions of theology had been settled for all time, the whole problem was reopened by the Schism. Once started, such speculation was bound to lead far.

Such was the situation when the Englishman, Wycliffe (1320-1384), withdrew from his small pastorate to devote himself chiefly to writing and agitating. He had been for many years a priest and a prominent lecturer in theology at the University of Oxford. His eloquence, his earnest and sincere interest in the welfare of his fellowmen and his deep learning had won him many friends, some of them leading figures in the political life of England. During the Babylonian Captivity his services had been invoked to resist the papal claims for taxation. With the outbreak of the Schism he had begun to criticize quite fully and freely the political and financial abuses of the Church. If he had hoped for improvement through Gregory's return to Rome, those hopes were rudely shattered by the Schism which had followed. Despairing of reform from the head of the Church, he bravely undertook the task himself.

He believed and taught that the wealth of the clergy was at the root of their worldliness. Like St. Francis, he believed that they should own nothing. He also believed that the State had the right to take possession of the property of worldly clerics. He was opposed to pilgrimages, to the veneration of images and relics, and to monastic vows. Now that the Church was divided by two papal claimants warring against each other, he repudiated the supreme authority of the popes and councils in religion. He was a pronounced pacifist, declaring that Christ's teaching forbade the use of force. For him, as for Luther generations later, the Bible became the final authority in matters of faith, and he desired to make it accessible to all. To this end he planned and took part in the making of a complete English translation from the great Latin version of St. Jerome. Wycliffe's Bible became his chief literary monument, as it is also one of the first great monuments of English prose. The circulation of this Bible was naturally limited, since only the well-to-do could afford it. To overcome this difficulty and at the same time to give an object lesson to the clergy, Wycliffe organized his "poor preachers." They were usually men who had been regularly ordained, and they went about clad in russet gowns, living on alms. They appear also to have done something to spread Wycliffe's philosophic opinion that all men possess what they have only on condition that they behave righteously. The peasants seem to have got from this the idea that people may justly rebel against wicked rulers.

Wycliffe represented the extreme to which earnest churchmen had gone in their reaction against a papacy which they could not respect. At first indignant that the head of his Church should continue apparently in subjection to the leading enemy of his country, he had moved on to examine the foundations of the faith. In so doing he had convinced himself that many of the doctrines upon which the papal supremacy rested were wrong. He went so far as to question the fundamental doctrine of transubstantiation. This was heresy, but so deep was the resentment at the condition of the papacy and the Church that more than half of the English, hitherto renowned for their orthodoxy, are thought within a generation after his death to have become his followers. His views were kept alive for years after his death by his "poor preachers," who were not always as moderate as their master had been. The Lollards, as his followers were called, ultimately came under the ban of both government and Church, many of them being burned as heretics. Wycliffe, however, died a natural death when the Schism was four years old. He was the first great scholarly opponent of the medieval Church, and his many writings, sermons, pamphlets and books exerted a broad influence for a long time, while his memory is revered today by many Protestants. A statue of Wycliffe forms part of the monument to Luther at Worms.

A distinction must be drawn, however, between the attitude of such men as Wycliffe and that of the political leaders in the state. As long as the state was suffering from the apparent alliance of the papacy with France, Wycliffe was applauded by nearly all. That situation, however, was changed when the Babylonian Captivity came to an end. Even the election of two popes was not regarded as an unmitigated calamity by those whose primary interest was politics. What if the pope at Avignon were friendly to the king of France? There was the pope at Rome to whom the English could turn. Henceforth no English money was to find its way into the hands of the French king through a papal loan, and the French could not cripple the English with papal intervention. From a political point of view the Schism indeed afforded decided advantages to the kings. The strife between the rival popes made it far easier for the kings to extend their inroads upon ecclesiastical jurisdiction and to use the Church for their own purposes. The more conservative elements in England gradually joined the king in giving their full allegiance to the Roman pope, so that ultimately the followers of Wycliffe were to be found chiefly among the more radical elements.

EFFORTS TO HEAL THE SCHISM. COUNCILS

In this period of uncertainty most people clung to the hope that neither their religion nor its unity would be destroyed. The theological faculty of the University of Paris undertook to gather the advice of leaders all over Christendom on the best way to end the Schism. Questionnaires were sent out asking for solutions, and thousands of replies were received. As a result of this study several plans were suggested and tried in vain, but finally it was agreed that a General Council could most authoritatively settle the matter. Even this plan had its difficulties, for it was established Church law that a General Council could be called only by the pope. This was now impossible, since the rival popes would not issue a joint summons and a council called by only one would be useless. But this difficulty was met when most of the cardinals, pleading necessity (*salus populi suprema lex*), abandoned their popes and in their own names summoned a council to meet at Pisa in 1409.

The Council of Pisa was well attended, though not all regions were represented. It acted too hastily and too arbitrarily, however, to obtain the complete success for which all had hoped. The two popes were summoned before it and, after a very short interval when neither had appeared, both were declared deposed. The cardinals in attendance then elected as pope an Italian cardinal of Greek extraction who had no relatives to favor or national interest to serve. The questions of heresy and abuses were left for the future, and the council adjourned.

The new pope, Alexander V, was recognized by all the great states and the States of the Church; but Gregory XII, a successor of Urban, retained the allegiance of parts of Italy, and Benedict XIII, a successor of Clement VII, that of Aragon and Scotland. The double Schism had become a triple Schism and another council had to be summoned. This was the Council of Constance, which sat from 1414 to 1418. It was called by Pope John XXIII, the successor of Alexander V, who was most widely recognized. He was induced to call it for personal reasons. In order to return to Rome, from which he had been expelled by the Romans, he needed outside help. This the German king Sigismund, who wanted to increase his own fame, offered to give him if he would call the council. Constance in Switzerland was the place selected.

The attendance was enormous. In addition to the thousand followers of Sigismund, there were present thirty-three cardinals, about three hundred bishops and archbishops, five hundred heads of religious houses, about sixteen hundred nobles, besides ambassadors from nearly all the principalities of Europe. Many hundreds of interested knights and their numerous followers also attended, as well as thousands of other visitors, together with minstrels, peddlers, beggars, and adventurers of all sorts. One can well believe that sixty thousand people were entertained in the old imperial city. As its ordinary population was not much more than five thousand, it is doubtful if any modern world's fair has ever made proportionate demands upon a city.

The depth of interest which all Europe felt in this religious dilemma was evidenced by the number and the dignity of the participants in the council and by the wide area of Europe which they represented. The fact that Sigismund, his knights, and representatives of other important rulers were present indicated likewise that the problem was not exclusively of religious concern. The early decision of the council to organize, like the Council of Pisa, on the basis of nations in a sense also reflects its recognition of both the religious and the political factors involved. One reason for this form of organization, more effective at Pisa than at Constance, was to avoid the undue influence of a single region, Italy in particular, which might result from its greater nearness. The suggestion probably arose from the organization of students at the universities where most of the clergy present had been educated. But it likewise found support in the development of political nations like France and England. At first four nations were recognized—Italy, Germany, France and England. Each of these had one vote in all matters acted upon by the council as such. These councils, therefore, are significant not only for their part in the history of the Church, but also as the first instance in which European nations, as such, met to settle matters of general concern by peaceful discussion.

EFFORTS OF SIGISMUND TO GAIN SUPPORT OF SPAIN, FRANCE AND ENGLAND

The assembling of such a council was an achievement in itself. The task of holding it together until it should accomplish at least the major portion of its work was another. In the first place, the absence of recognized delegates from the Spanish peninsula, to which the Avignonese pope had withdrawn, was a serious defect whose correction was essential to the complete success of the council. Just as serious, however, was the danger that political and other rivalries of the countries represented would produce such friction at Constance as to make coöperation impossible. The most intense rivalry was that between France and England. Sigismund directed his energies to meeting these circumstances. It was largely his pressure which had compelled John XXIII to call the council, and he was loath to have it fail.

Sigismund first addressed himself to the Spanish problem. Accompanied by religious representatives as well as by his own retinue, he visited Aragon and some of the other Spanish principalities. Spain was much divided and the negotiations required great care. Fortunately aid came from several quarters. Benedict XIII, now an old man, had alienated many by his unreasonable acts. Probably more important was the fact that many high-minded Spaniards recognized the necessity of working for the common good. The example and efforts of Vincent Ferrier, renowned through all Spain for his sanctity, were most helpful. He had been a follower of Benedict XIII. For the welfare of all he now broke away and in an energetic campaign of persuasion through Castile, Navarre and Aragon, he won those regions to the support of the council. The delegates from Spain were hailed with great joy at Constance and were recognized as a fifth nation.

The problem of the antagonisms between France and England

offered greater difficulties, though both countries were represented at the council from its beginning. The Hundred Years'
War was renewed while the council was in session and under
circumstances widely different from those of the earlier period.
The "Wise King," Charles V, had been succeeded by his son,
Charles VI. Charles VI was an infant king and after he grew
up was often insane. Both conditions necessitated a regency.
This afforded his ambitious uncles an opportunity for bitter
rivalry, and France became divided between the leading claimants
for the regency. Most of the south adhered to the house of
Armagnac, while the north and east supported the claims of
Burgundy. The murder in 1407 of the duke of Orléans, whom
the Armagnacs supported, intensified this rivalry to the point of
warfare between the factions. Meanwhile England, much dis-
traught by troubles between king and Parliament as well as by
disputes over the succession, had finally become somewhat stabi-
lized. The first of its Lancastrian kings, Henry IV (1399-1413),
had weathered the storms of disturbed political conditions sufficiently to pass his crown to his son, Henry V, in 1413. For Henry
V the divided condition of France afforded an opportunity to enhance the prestige of his house, and he early began his preparations for the renewal of the war. His first campaign in the fall
of 1415 had ended gloriously in the victory at Agincourt, where
the French army under the leadership of its nobility repeated most
of the mistakes of Crécy and Poitiers.

It was after Henry's return from this successful campaign that
Sigismund reached England to urge peace. A delegation of
Armagnacs accompanied him. Negotiation for peace, however,
proved fruitless, for Henry V demanded more territory and rights
than the Armagnacs were willing to concede. Sigismund thereupon decided to ensure the support of the stronger of the contestants. He made a secret treaty with Henry V recognizing the
latter's claims, and on his return journey he used his influence
with the duke of Burgundy, who had remained practically neutral
during the campaign of Agincourt, to bring him over to the
side of the English. The duke of Burgundy was not yet ready
for this advanced step. That was taken, however, when in 1419

Duke John of Burgundy was murdered by the Orléanists. His followers thereupon made common cause with Henry V. Meanwhile Sigismund returned to Constance, assured of the support of the English king and confident also of at least Burgundian support in France.

ACTIONS TAKEN BY THE COUNCIL OF CONSTANCE

The first and foremost object of the council, the ending of the Great Schism, was gained in 1417, after many months of varied labors. Gregory XII resigned and John XXIII and Benedict XIII were deposed. Only Benedict, with a negligible following, refused to submit. Cardinals and council then elected Martin V, an Italian, as head of the reunited Church. The termination of the Schism was celebrated with devout thanksgivings.

John XXIII had at first planned to retain his papacy by dissolving the council before it should depose him. In order to checkmate him, the council in 1415 passed the famous decree *Sacrosancta,* by which it declared that it had its authority directly from Christ and that everybody, including the pope, was bound to obey it in matters pertaining to the faith, the ending of the Schism, and the reformation of the Church in head and members. In 1417 the council passed another decree, *Frequens,* that a council should meet regularly every ten years. These two decrees grew out of the immediate situation, no doubt, but they summarized the developments which had taken place since the death of Boniface VIII in 1303.

If carried out, these two decrees, reënforced as they were by the success of the council in settling the Schism, meant that the government of the Church was changed from an absolute monarchy to a representative government in which the important nations possessed an equal voice. Such an outcome was probably agreeable to rulers of states who could thus nullify practically any unpleasant interference from a pope by appealing to the council. It was agreeable also to many bishops and other prelates of the Church, for it gave them a hope of securing a much larger share in the government of the whole Church than they had for long enjoyed. It was looked upon with favor, too, by many of the ordinary clergy who saw in it a chance to redress their grievances which had increased during the disordered period of the Schism. Unfortunately for the reformers, these decrees did not include a systematic revision of canon law which had been built upon the theory of an absolute monarchy. Nor did they wipe out all memory of past tradition. The papacy, once freed from the immediate control of the council, might therefore be expected to oppose these decrees and to exhibit the utmost reluctance to convene further councils. On the other hand, if it took such an attitude it would encounter hostility not only from disgruntled rulers but also from many churchmen. The Council of Constance in settling the Schism had in fact opened up another constitutional question which might prove even more serious.

As to the second problem, the reform of abuses, little was done. Measures were passed which limited the pope's power over taxation and seriously threatened papal finances. After lengthy consideration the council was able also to agree on legislation designed to reform the cardinals. Beyond this point, however, it was difficult to go. Abuses varied in different regions. They varied also among the different ranks of the clergy. Laymen too had certain reforms to urge. Amid the clamor of so many voices and with such wide differences existing, there was little hope for early action if that action must be taken in common. Now that the Schism was ended by the election of a recognized pope, the long stay at Constance began to wear on the delegates and most of them were anxious to return home. The suggestion of Martin V that the pope be left to deal separately with each nation regarding its most crying abuses was adopted. But such a course was full of danger for the adherents of representative control of the Church. Actually little of value was accomplished by the pope's separate negotiations.

The third problem of the council, the extirpation of heresy, seemed more simple. The more extreme doctrinal differences which the wide discussions of the last forty years had brought forth threatened to disrupt the unity of the Church. This was particularly true of the ideas of Wycliffe and Hus. The opinions of Wycliffe were condemned, his body was ordered to be dug up and burned, and a systematic effort was made by Church and State in England to wipe out the Lollards, his followers. As these were now largely confined to the more radical and humble classes, most of the upper classes joined in the movement of repression. Though apparently successful, the persecution left many smoldering embers which were to be fanned into a new flame in the next century. The repression of the Hussites proved to be a more difficult problem.

John Hus (1373-1415) was a learned priest and lecturer at the University of Prague. He criticized the Church in Bohemia as Wycliffe had criticized it in England. His views found all the more favor among his fellow Bohemians because the higher ecclesiastical offices in Bohemia were held by Germans. The books of Hus show clear evidence of the influence of Wycliffe whom Hus respected highly, though it is quite possible that he arrived at his opinions independently. Hus was invited to lay his views before the council and went to Constance under a safe-conduct from Sigismund. The council condemned Hus for heresy, and Sigismund, to his everlasting disgrace, allowed the great Bohemian to be burned at the stake. The same fate was meted out to Jerome of Prague, a dashing, adventurous knight who had espoused the ideas of Hus and boldly accompanied him to Constance. Many persons in attendance at Constance were moved to deep sympathy and admiration at the heroic way in which these two men met their deaths. In Bohemia the news of Sigismund's betrayal of Hus aroused the people to great indignation. They asserted that Hus was a saint and that the Germans had brought about his death as an insult to the Bohemians. Instead of checking the spread of heresy in Bohemia the effect of Hus's martyrdom was to increase his following among many who had hitherto held aloof.

The Council of Constance, formally ended April 22, 1418, furnished the highest example of voluntary coöperation in a great cause which Europe had witnessed. But a sober review of its achievements must always raise the question whether it did not create more problems than it settled. Its members, to be sure, had departed in the thought that they had set up machinery to deal with those. The pope, Martin V, found many serious problems of his own in Italy. The restoration of Rome, only partially accomplished during the Schism, and the regulation of the Papal States, always a distracting problem, now engrossed his immediate attention. To the more distant problems he could give only occasional consideration. Even Martin V, sympathetic though he was with the enactments of the Council of Constance, found it difficult to carry on his work under the conflicting guidance of tradition and canon law on the one hand, and the decrees of the council on the other. In accordance with the decree *Frequens,* he called a council to meet at Pavia. It was hastily called. The place of meeting was changed to Siena, and after several months of ineffectual discussion it was adjourned. The preoccupation of Europe with its immediate local difficulties was so great that there was little protest against this perfunctory compliance with the decree *Frequens.*

THE NEED FOR FURTHER COUNCILS. BASEL

Events in Bohemia and Germany prevented the second scheduled council from repeating the experience of the first. The burning of Hus had united Bohemia into a solid force. When Sigismund, who had given safe-conduct to Hus in 1415, sought to make himself king of Bohemia on the death of his brother in 1419, the Bohemians rose in revolt. Sigismund appealed to the Church for help. A crusade was preached against these heretics and Sigismund received aid in both men and money. At least six different expeditions called crusades were led against the Bohemians, some by Sigismund, others by cardinals of the Church like Henry Beaufort, bishop of Winchester, and Cardinal Cesarini, but the stubborn, resolute resistance of the Bohemians, led first by John Ziska and later by the priest Procopius, brought all these attempts to naught. The Bohemians protected themselves with their heavy wagons tied together with chains, and by their skillful use of pikes they wrought such havoc among their foes that later expeditions melted away when they heard the rumbling of those wagons and the battle hymn of the Czechs. Not only did the Bohemians demoralize the crusading armies, but they were spreading heretical ideas into neighboring lands. The situation was one which required serious attention from the Church. Cardinal Cesarini, leader on one of the expeditions, became convinced that a Church council could accomplish what the crusades had failed to do, and he found the Bohemians willing to submit their case to a full and fair hearing.

The next council met at Basel in 1431. Martin V, who called it, had died. Eugenius IV, who had been elected his successor by the cardinals, did not attend. Instead, he was represented by Cardinal Cesarini who presided, and by several other cardinals. It was quite clear that Eugenius was loath to have the council remain in session long, a feeling which increased as the council continued. This council, however, was almost as fully attended as that of Constance, and many of the leaders at Constance were present at Basel.

Sigismund journeyed to Rome in 1432 to be crowned emperor by the pope, and though the latter sought to turn him against the council, Sigismund remained firm, realizing, no doubt, that only the council could settle his Bohemian difficulties. Reluctantly, therefore, Eugenius was compelled to withdraw his dissolution of the council. The Bohemians were allowed to present their case fully and freely early in 1433, and their safe-conduct was respected. Then a delegation from the council went to Bohemia and a compromise was arranged which granted certain of the demands while refusing others. This proved acceptable to the more conservative Bohemians and effectively divided these from the more radical Bohemians. War broke out between the two groups, and the conservatives won the victory in 1434, Procopius who led the radicals being killed in the decisive battle.

OBSTACLES TO SUCCESS AT BASEL. HUNDRED YEARS' WAR. THE TURKS

The further work of the Council of Basel was hampered somewhat by the lack of adequate delegations from France and England. Commissions from the council were again sent to bring about peace between these two countries. Circumstances aided them materially. As we have seen, the murder of Duke John of Burgundy had thrown his followers on the side of Henry V of England. In 1420 a treaty was made between Henry V and the insane Charles VI whereby the daughter of the French king was given in marriage to Henry; the Dauphin, the son of Charles, was disinherited; and Henry was recognized as regent, and as king of France upon the death of Charles. This treaty had the approval of the Burgundians, and its provisions were carried out. But war did not stop, for the Armagnacs still held much of southern France and they rallied around the disinherited Dauphin as their king, Charles VII. Orléans, almost their last stronghold, was being besieged by the English and Burgundians in 1428 when the tide of war turned.

Several times the two factions in France had attempted to reunite. Sentiment and tradition exerted their influence in this direction, but each time some tragic incident occurred to drive them back into hostility. There was felt to be something un-natural in the alliance of the north of France with the English against the south—so far had nationalism progressed. The nearer the English were to complete success, the greater must have been this feeling of resentment among the French of the north. It is against such a background that the career of Jeanne d'Arc stands out.

The history of Catherine of Siena (d.1380) was too recent for the visions of this robust peasant girl of Domrémy to require explanation, and the people willingly believed in them. She was sixteen years old when her "voices" commanded her to seek the Dauphin. Admitted finally to his presence at the castle of Chinon, she won him to faith in her mission, as she already had converted others on her way. At her request she was given a military outfit and was commissioned a captain, though not until she had been examined by four bishops at Poitiers to determine that she was not a witch or an impostor. Her presence, example and encouragement inspired the beleaguered garrison of Orléans. With new courage they attacked and forced the English to give up the siege; then they followed up their victory by destroying one of the English armies, and finally they carried through the mission of the Maid by conducting Charles through northern France to be crowned at Rheims (July, 1429).

From this time on French national feeling was thoroughly aroused. The capture of Jeanne d'Arc by the Burgundians who turned her over to the English, and her trial for witchcraft by the clergy of English France did not alter this fact. The burning of the Maid at Rouen (May 29, 1431) only strengthened her influence as a national force and caused Frenchmen to overlook the fact that Charles VII had shamelessly failed to attempt her rescue. The French of the north looked only for an opportunity to release themselves from their unhappy alliance with the English. The duke of Burgundy concluded a private truce with Charles VII in 1434. Only the great influence of the duke of Bedford, who was looking after English affairs in France, prevented the Burgundians from taking the field against their former allies. The duke of Bedford had been entrusted with the English interests in France when Henry V died in 1422. He had managed these with rare skill and success during the minority of Henry VI until the coming of Jeanne d'Arc. Even then his personal influence prevented a more rapid disintegration of English rule in France. He died in 1435 and was buried in Rouen, the city in which Jeanne, largely through his influence, had been burned.

The envoys from the Council of Basel brought English and French representatives together at Arras in 1435, but the duke of Bedford was too ill to take part in the final negotiations. The English representatives refused to accept the terms offered by the French and insisted on demanding more than the military situation justified. The net result was to alienate the sympathies of the envoys of the council from the English and to prompt them to use their influence to hasten the union of France. Another consequence was that the French delegation at Basel was able to present a united front and to exert great influence on the deliberations there.

Failure to establish peace between England and France was

not to be the only failure of the council. Word was received from Constantinople that the Greeks realized their precarious position and were sending an important embassy to the West for aid. The Turks, who had been advancing for many years, had established themselves in Europe as well as in Asia, and Constantinople was threatened on all sides.[1] In this extremity the Greek emperor, accompanied by leading Greek churchmen, decided to seek aid in the West. Such an embassy raised hopes of union of the Greek and Latin Churches, and the Council of Basel sent envoys to invite the Greeks to come to it. Eugenius IV, however, seized this opportunity to defeat the council. He ordered the council to adjourn from Basel to Ferrara in Italy and prevailed upon the Greek embassy to come to Ferrara. The more radical members of the council saw in this move an effort of Eugenius to destroy the council, and refused to move. The more conservative members, including most of the Italians, obeyed the pope's instructions. The papal council, as we may call it, met at Ferrara where the Greek envoys were received, and then it moved to Florence. It was at Florence in 1439 that the Greeks were won to sign a paper union with the Latin Church under the headship of the pope. It remained only a paper union, for the Greek representatives were badly treated on their return home and the agreement was not ratified. It was, however, announced with great joy throughout the West and did much to help Eugenius in his struggle with the council at Basel, which finally went so far as to elect another pope.

FAILURE OF THE COUNCIL OF BASEL

The transfer of most of the Italians from Basel to Ferrara in 1438 was followed by other signs of disintegration. Reunited France took advantage of the opportunity to hold a national assembly of its clergy at Bourges, where, under the presidency of Charles VII, a number of the radical reforms already passed at Basel were officially adopted for France. These were promulgated as the *Pragmatic Sanction of Bourges* in 1438. Some German

[1] See Chapter XXVI.

princes held a similar meeting at Mainz in the following year. The outcome was to draw away more and more representatives from Basel, leaving only the most radical and irresponsible elements there. These continued to sit with dwindling numbers until they were driven out in 1449 by Emperor Frederic III, who had come to an understanding with the pope. The reforms of the Council of Basel had become increasingly radical as its numbers decreased, and distrust of it weakened the idea of a Church governed by councils. Europe had had enough of schism and the anti-pope elected by the council had few followers and no success. The cause of reform suffered from the excesses of this remnant of a council.

The unity of the Church was far from being restored in actual fact. Many of the lesser clergy and some of the prelates, especially north of the Alps, were strongly committed to the idea that the council was supreme in the Church and that the needed reforms could only be accomplished through a council. The papacy, naturally reluctant to surrender to the supervision of a council, was made doubly so by its experience with the Council of Basel. As a result it seemed doubtful that a pope would again call a council except under conditions which promised to leave him in control of the situation. This was a very unwholesome state of affairs, for it meant that the head of the Church and many of its members were in a condition of more or less real alienation from one another. In such a situation the powerful laity were in a position to throw their influence to one side or another, as circumstances dictated. France, by the Pragmatic Sanction of Bourges, was virtually settling its own Church problems almost as if it had a national Church. And the Concordat which Frederic III had procured from the papacy has sometimes been described as a bargain by which emperor and pope agreed to support each other at the expense of the clergy in Germany.

THE PAPACY IMMERSED IN ITALIAN AFFAIRS

After Basel the papacy became deeply immersed in Italian affairs, to the neglect of those outside. Possibly it counted upon time to remove the feeling of hostility among so many of the churchmen north of the Alps. On the other hand, the Italy of the last half of the fifteenth century was well calculated to keep the papacy occupied. The city states, originally predominantly economic units, had become amalgamated into a few states of political as well as economic significance. Florence had extended its influence until it dominated all of Tuscany, and its policies were now directed by the family of the Medici. First come to notice as bankers, the Medici under their ablest member, Cosimo, who dominated the city from 1434 to 1464, had combined political power with financial prestige. His grandson, Lorenzo, known as the Magnificent, was virtually ruler of Florence from 1469 until his death in 1492. North of the Apennines, Lombardy was controlled by Milan, over which the house of Sforza now ruled. Milan's dominion over eastern Lombardy was disputed by Venice, a state under the rule of a powerful commercial oligarchy. These three states had widespread interests and ambitions and had developed the arts of diplomacy and political intrigue beyond anything known to statecraft since Roman days. The northern portion of the Papal States bordered on all three of these states. To the south of the Papal States lay Naples, theoretically a fief of the papacy, but actually an independent state under the rather somnolent control of a house related to the ruling family of Aragon.

The ambitions of these states involved the Papal States, partly because the latter possessed important economic resources like the banking business of the papacy and the alum mines, partly because certain regions like the Romagna had furnished many of the mercenary companies of soldiers employed by the other states, and partly because the political influence of the papacy might prove a decisive aid or an obstacle to the particular hopes of the other states. And, finally, the location of the Papal States, a diagonal across the peninsula, placed them in actual contact with every one of these rival states. Every one of the five—with the possible exception of Naples—was eager to grow. The type of politics and diplomacy practiced by them furnished Machiavelli with most of the illustrations in his book, *The Prince*. They were ready to use almost any means, including bribery and other forms of corruption as well as murder, to gain their ends. Even humanism and art, the finer side of Italian development, were likewise employed as devices in the diplomatic game. The restored papacy had found itself immediately embroiled in Italian politics, and without outside aid it was soon engulfed. The fact that the papal office was filled by election and that the election was in the hands of cardinals appointed by the popes, afforded an easy opening for the designs of the neighbor states. Prospective candidates for the papal office were carefully cultivated, their candidacy was advanced with powerful influence, and, once elected, they were importuned to appoint as cardinals persons favorable to their promoters. Under such conditions, it cannot be a matter of surprise that the composition of the college of cardinals was soon altered to include fewer leading theologians from Europe at large and more members who were primarily interested in the political affairs of Italy. Nor is it difficult to understand why the popes of the latter half of the fifteenth century seem more like leaders in Italian politics than heads of the universal Church.

Affairs outside of Italy were not of a nature to improve the status of the papacy. The war between England and France had dragged on in the direction so clearly indicated when the envoys of Basel had sought to bring about peace. When the war finally petered out in 1453, only Calais remained to the English. But the close of the war did not bring much respite to either country. In England Henry VI, grandson through his mother of the insane Charles VI of France, developed insanity, and England was torn by civil war due to the rivalries of its nobles. This was the War of the Roses which ended in the battle of Bosworth Field in 1485, when a new line of kings, that of the Tudors, was inaugurated with Henry VII.

In France the great nobles who had been so independent during the wars were reluctant to surrender their powers to the king. The dukes of Burgundy were most troublesome. Charles the Bold even desired to create an independent kingdom out of the French and German fiefs which had come into the possession of his family. Such problems engaged most of the energy of the French kings, especially of Louis XI, whose shrewd tactics of close coöperation with the bourgeoisie and of unscrupulous dealings with the nobles ultimately led to the recovery of royal control over France. In the course of his difficulties Louis XI sought to gain the favor of Pope Pius II by undertaking to abolish the Pragmatic Sanction of Bourges. But the abolition was not put through until 1516 (*Concordat of Bologna*).

In Germany the separate states, following their own interests, were frequently at war with one another. Frederick III, who held the honored title of emperor over this region, was not an individual of great force or power. He was quite content to throw his influence to the side of the papacy in return for certain privileges over the clergy of Austria. His quarrel with Hungary over the crown was more helpful to the Turks, who were advancing up the Danube, than it was to himself. Bohemia was still a problem to the Church as well as to its neighbors in the Empire, the concessions made by the Council of Basel never having been sanctioned by the papacy.

The war against the Turks was a project to which the papacy had been committed by the agreement with the Greek envoys at the Council of Florence. Some effort was made by Eugenius IV and by the popes who followed him to arouse interest in this war, but without success, though the Turks captured Constantinople in 1453 and continued their advance into the Danube Valley. The pope most zealous for this crusade was Pius II. He even ventured to call a council of rulers to meet at Mantua in Italy for the specific purpose of considering war with the Turks. Few rulers appeared, but Pius II took advantage of the occasion to promulgate the bull *Execrabilis* (1460) declaring heretical the theory that the councils were supreme over the pope and automatically excommunicating anyone who should appeal to such a council. The crusade came to naught, even though Pius II agreed to lead the expedition himself and actually died on his way to join a fleet gathered for this purpose (1464).

After Pius II the popes paid relatively little attention to matters outside of Italy except as these were forced upon their attention. During this last half of the fifteenth century the best of the popes were distinguished as patrons of art and learning, the worst of them by their scandalous lives. Alexander VI (1492-1503), of the Spanish Borgia family, who sought to provide principalities for his children, has usually been regarded as the least reputable of them. He was very severely criticized by the great Dominican preacher of Florence, Savonarola. Julius II (1503-1513), his successor, who undertook to subjugate the turbulent elements of the Papal States in person, is famous as a successful warrior and as the patron of Michelangelo, Raphael and Bramante. Leo X (1513-1521), a son of Lorenzo de' Medici, who was made cardinal while yet a boy, is distinguised for his patronage of art and learning and for his help in restoring the Medici family to power in Florence. We shall meet him again, confronted by a plain German friar named Martin Luther.

During the half century which passed after the Council of Basel the progress in the affairs of the Church was more apparent than real. The city of Rome had been restored and beautified to a degree which recalled the days of its ancient glory. Some order too had been established in the Papal States, though that task still required much of the papal energy. But north of the Alps agitation still continued. The separate compacts which the popes had made with leading rulers involved concessions which were a heavy price to pay for their acquiescence in papal control of the Church. Abuses of various kinds remained uncorrected, and in some instances the privileges which had been granted to the rulers by the papacy had added to such abuses. The lesser clergy and, indeed, some of the bishops and other ecclesiastical leaders were still much disaffected. There was dissension within the Church quite as real, though much less evident, as when there were still two rival popes. It was still undetermined whether time and changing circumstances would allay the discontent or cause it to burst forth in open revolt.

CHAPTER XVIII

COMMERCE, INDUSTRY AND TOWN LIFE
1300-1500

D URING the later Middle Ages commerce and industry and the towns in which they had their roots became increasingly important factors in the development of civilization. Even etymologically, *civilization* is derived from *town*. The exile of the papacy at Avignon, and the Great Schism which followed it, hampered the Church in its religious and educational work and lowered its effectiveness. The Hundred Years' War antagonized the governing classes and, in a measure, the peoples of France and England, and lesser wars had similar effects elsewhere. But commerce continued and spread in spite of all obstacles; for the love of gain and the desire for the material products, especially the luxury goods, of other lands were undiminished. These desires steadily promoted those contacts, habits and institutions which have been so important, for good and for evil, in the development of our Western-European type of civilization.

In this commercial and industrial expansion the Italian cities maintained the leadership which they had secured in the preceding period. Indeed, in the accumulation and employment of capital; in the creation of commercial, industrial and banking organizations; in the invention of double-entry bookkeeping (praised by Sombart as of epochal importance to modern business, "born of the same spirit as the discoveries of Galileo and Newton"); in the management of colonies and the advancement of navigation, as well as in the fine arts and the revival of learning, the Italian cities were the schoolmasters of modern Europe.

EVOLUTION OF INTERREGIONAL COMMERCE

The main lines of the picture of European commerce from 1300 to 1500 show no important changes from those of the thirteenth century. The Italian cities still dominated the Mediterranean and the traffic in Oriental and Mediterranean products, and their bankers and merchant princes continued to be the chief lenders of money to kings, great nobles and prelates. Similarly in the North, the traders of the Hanseatic League of cities had the upper hand. They enjoyed their greatest prosperity during the century 1350-1450. The organization and maintenance of this league of natural rivals was a really remarkable achievement of urban statecraft. The peculiar sphere of the Hansa cities was in the North. But they pushed their trade down the coasts of France beyond the mouth of the Loire where they loaded salt, and even at times to Bordeaux where they secured wine for their northern clients.

Northern wares and southern wares still passed each other, so to speak, especially on the roads and rivers between Italy and the region around the mouths of the Rhine and Scheldt. In the course of the fourteenth century the routes through southern Germany and down the Rhine gained the preference over those running northward through southern France. This choice was made partly because of the prevalence of warfare in France. The cities of southern Germany—Augsburg, Nürnberg, Ulm and others on this North-South route—flourished. Land traffic was still borne chiefly on horseback. The crossing of the Alps was difficult, but the dwellers in the passes were organized, from the thirteenth century, to aid transport at so much per pound. Judged by modern standards, the traffic over the Alps was not large. It has been calculated, for example, that two freight trains now carry through the St. Gothard Tunnel as much goods as were carried through the pass in an entire year in the later Middle Ages. But it is to be remembered that the medieval wares of the overland trade were of slight bulk in proportion to their value.

Land and river traffic was hampered by dues, tolls and various customs to an extent almost unbelievable today. Every feudal lord of any importance, every city on the route, collected from the merchants. Maritime traffic, adequately protected from pirates and rivals by armed galleys, escaped these vexatious levies. Hence it is not surprising that the chief commerce of the Middle Ages was maritime. In the early years of the fourteenth century a supplementary line of regular traffic between North and South was opened by both Venice and Genoa. After some trial trips in the thirteenth century, each of them established an annual service of galleys from the home port through the Straits of Gibraltar to Flanders. The Italian merchants on the galleys traded at intermediate ports, of which Lisbon and Southampton were the most prominent, and unloaded the bulk of their Oriental and southern products at Bruges, taking back as their principal freight English wool and Flemish textiles. The vessels in these fleets, like all medieval ships, were quite small, ranging from one to three hundred tons, though ships of 480 tons have been noted in the records. According to Sombart, even the very largest East Indiamen of the seventeenth century did not exceed 800 tons. Poor harbor facilities partly explain this small tonnage. It has been calculated that a modern Atlantic liner could easily carry all the goods freighted by a medieval trading fleet.

The importance of this annual maritime connection with the North is shown by the fact that when the Barbary pirates temporarily blocked the Gibraltar straits about the end of the fourteenth century, the products of Damascus, Cairo, Alexandria, Venice and Genoa became scarce in the markets of Flanders, and the cost of spices rose enormously. But the growth of commerce on and along the overland routes from Italy to the Netherlands was such that the annual fleets did not so much diminish as supplement the use of these routes.

One striking result of commercial expansion was the growth of Bruges, already an important weaving city, which early in the fourteenth century replaced the fairs of Champagne as the chief center for the exchange of northern and southern goods. The decline of these fairs—those more to the east continued to

function for centuries—was due in part to political disturbances
in France and the neighboring Netherlands, and in part to some
unwise extortions attempted by the count of Champagne. At
any rate, the Italian merchants and bankers shifted to Bruges
shortly after 1300, a clear indication that the fairs of Champagne
were done for. The Hanseatic merchants followed the example
of the Italians, and Bruges became a city of perpetual fairs, a
true world market, resorted to by Italians, Germans, English,
Spanish, Portuguese and French. Bruges held its position of
commercial and financial leadership until the later fifteenth century. Then, in consequence of the silting up of its ports, which
could have been prevented, and of the political troubles which
centered in the city after the death of Charles the Bold, most of
the international merchants shifted their interests again to Antwerp near by, a more peaceful and a better port. But the Hanseatic merchants, who were stubbornly becoming unduly conservative, clung to Bruges until well into the sixteenth century.

The fierce commercial rivalry between Genoa and Venice, which
had been marked by a long series of wars in which the honors
had on the whole rested with Genoa, came to a head in the War
of Chioggia, which lasted from 1378 to 1380, when Genoa made
her supreme effort to "bit and bridle the horses of St. Mark."
This time a Genoese fleet blockaded Venice and, with some aid
from land forces, captured Chioggia, one of the Venetian outpost island towns. The Venetians fought doggedly, blocking the
Genoese advance through the lagoons until the main Venetian
fleet, operating against the Genoese possessions on the Black
Sea, could get back and, as it happened, turn the Genoese block-
ade into a surrender. Genoa was not able to make an effective
counter-stroke and had to accept unfavorable terms. She still
remained a naval and commercial power to be reckoned with, and
an important factor in the money market; but she was never again
strong enough, single-handed, to challenge "the bride of the
Adriatic."

This ultimate inferiority of Genoa is to be ascribed in part
to the decline of her trade in the western Mediterranean. This
resulted from the decay of the Mohammedan states in North

Africa and Spain, and in part to the spirit of faction within the city itself, which spirit was in sharp contrast with the solidarity of the commercial aristocracy that governed Venice. Probably the decisive factor was Venice's superior geographical location, at the center of the shortest line between the Near East and Western Europe and at the head of the Adriatic which she absolutely controlled. This gave her an economic advantage which was bound to tell in the long run. Genoa could be attacked on the land side, and insensibly gravitated into the orbit of Milan; while Venice, protected by her lagoons, maintained her independence until the wars of the French Revolution.

The ruthlessness which marked commercial rivalry in Italy is even more fully shown in the crushing of Pisa by Florence. Florence had grown steadily in industrial, banking and political power during the later thirteenth and the fourteenth century, and then found it intolerable that her weaker neighbor, Pisa, by virtue of her location on the Arno between Florence and the sea, was able to levy toll on Florentine commerce. In 1406 Florence captured and annexed Pisa and, although it was now Florentine territory, in effect made it a dead city by narrowly restricting its industry in favor of that of Florence and by making Livorno its seaport. Thus Florence at length secured free access to the Mediterranean. She pushed her commerce under her own flag, demanded and secured Pisa's former privileges in Constantinople, and must hereafter be reckoned as one of the great trading, as well as industrial and banking cities of medieval Europe.

The picture of interregional commerce in central and western Europe, sketched in the chapter on the thirteenth century and brought down into the later Middle Ages in the foregoing pages, is by no means complete. The energetic efforts of Marseilles, Montpellier, and especially of Barcelona, in the western Mediterranean, to hold and build up their share in the maritime trade of the South would repay special study. So, too, would the trade between Bordeaux and Bayonne and England, which was founded on the export of wine, and which grew after the English got possession of southwestern France. The weaving cities of

Flanders—Brabant, Hainault, and the other provinces in the great triangle formed by the Rhine, the Seine, and the sea—were not led to take up navigation even though they were on or near salt water. They contented themselves with their industrial successes and allowed the foreigners to come and get their products. But the Dutch, their neighbors to the north who had few industries, early embarked upon the carrying trade and gradually worked their way, in the teeth of Hanseatic jealousy, into the Baltic and back as far as Spain.

The English also began to awake from their passive attitude toward commerce. Their wool was the finest grown in Europe and formed their chief export. From the late thirteenth century onward the English government established a *staple*—*i.e.,* an exclusive place of sale for English wool in foreign parts—at one or another town in the Netherlands. Several times the staple was located at Bruges and finally at Calais after that city became English. The merchants engaged in this part of the export trade in wool were organized, with a charter from the king, as an association or gild of *merchant staplers*. Of course foreigners, notably the Italians and the Hanseatic traders, still bought wool in England itself. A further step was taken early in the fifteenth century, when another gild organized by London merchants and chartered by the king, the *merchant adventurers,* was formed to push the sale of English woolen cloth on the Continent. They located at Antwerp in 1407, since Bruges, itself a great cloth-making center, would not tolerate their presence. This English cloth was as yet coarse and crude, but it boded ill for Flanders and Italy if the English, who controlled the production of the best wool, should develop the skill required for the weaving of the finer wool fabrics. The way in which the English in their own first export ventures clung to the Netherlands, is another indication of the economic importance of that part of northern Europe. Soon they were to push into the Baltic itself, and later into the Mediterranean.

These illustrations of the subsidiary and developing aspects of interregional commerce could be much increased, but they are enough to suggest to the reader that the completed picture of large-scale commerce in the later Middle Ages would require the inclusion of much additional detail. And if national or intra-state commerce were added, the canvas would have to be greatly enlarged.

ORIGINS AND ACTIVITIES OF THE CRAFT GILDS

Commerce promoted industry and industry promoted commerce and both centered in the towns. According to Pirenne's rigid argument,[1] which has not escaped critical challenge, the early medieval towns were the creation of traveling merchants who settled down after a time at conveniently located *burgs* or epis-copal residences, and secured from the local lord or bishop the privilege of trading. Other towns gradually grew up at cross-roads, fords, or landing-places. When large-scale commerce had developed, the towns on the established route or line of traffic were likely to develop industries if they had, or could easily get, the materials for the making of goods in wide demand. For the traders naturally preferred to carry goods a shorter rather than a longer distance, and were fairly quick to seize the chance to make a profit. For example, Venice, centrally located on the long line from the Near East to the West and North, started its brilliant career in commerce and industry with fish and salt. It imported and exported Oriental wares, the true basis of its sur-prising commerce. It added trade in grain and slaves. Then it took up the manufacture of colored-glass articles, mosaics, jewelry, metal goods, silk and cotton fabrics, gold and silver thread. Other towns became renowned for their special products, Dinant for its copper wares, Nürnberg for its wooden wares, Liége for its iron goods, Valenciennes for its lace. In short, the river of European commerce which took its rise in the Medi-terranean was fed by many tributaries, small and large.

The medieval towns or cities were not large. Constantinople, Venice, Palermo and Paris, with over 100,000 inhabitants, were regarded as world cities. Florence, Milan, Genoa, Barcelona, and perhaps Cologne and London, each with about 50,000 inhabi-

[1] Pirenne: *Medieval Cities.*

tants, were considered large cities. Bologna, Padua, Rouen, Brussels, Nürnberg, Strasburg, Prague and other cities which boasted populations of 20,000 to 40,000 or thereabouts, as well as Ypres, Antwerp, Louvain, Rheims, York, Bristol, Plymouth, Zürich, Basel, Geneva and other towns whose inhabitants numbered 6,000 to 20,000, were thought of as medium-sized. It is in these cities of medium size that the characteristics of normal, urban economic life can best be found. Smaller cities than these were too agricultural; larger ones, too far-flung in their activities.

In all the medieval cities there was a noticeable surplus of women. Wars, feuds and perhaps the long hours of manual labor killed off the men faster than the women. For both sexes, however, city life was less healthful than it is today. The death rate always exceeded the birth rate, and immigration from the country was essential to the maintenance, to say nothing of the growth, of the population.

The most striking feature of the industry of a medieval city was the manner in which it was organized into many separate handicrafts or trades. The men in each of these were associated together in an art, craft, gild, mistery (French, *métier*), brotherhood, fraternity, or company. This list of synonyms is not exhaustive. We shall use the name commonly employed today, gild or craft gild. The ruling principle was that there should be a separate gild for every handicraft or trade that made a complete article which could be sold direct by its maker to a purchaser (*an ultimate consumer*) for his own use. A village would have a miller and a blacksmith; a small town would have perhaps a dozen gilds; a medium-sized city might well have a hundred gilds. Karl Bücher has made a list of forty-five separate crafts in one city of the latter type which grew out of the work of the blacksmith.

The members of each gild were the masters, who had learned the trade or handicraft and had gone into business each for himself. They carried it on alone or with the help of one or two journeymen, who had likewise learned the trade but worked by the day for a master, and with the aid of one or two apprentices, who "washed the dishes and swept the floor" and served three, seven, or ten years, as the case might be, before they might become journeymen or masters. The members of each gild had a monopoly in the city and its environs; no one outside the gild could make or sell the article it fabricated. But as each master could have only one or two journeymen and two or three apprentices (the exact number was fixed in each gild's regulations), no one master could by reason of superior capacity and enterprise build up a dominant business and squeeze out his fellow masters.

Each gild had its own warden or overseer and other officers. Its members lived and worked in a separate street or streets. Each master's workshop was usually connected with the living quarters in which he resided with his journeymen and apprentices as part of his household. The members of the gild usually attended church as a group, contributed to sick and funeral benefits, participated in feasts, and took part in simple plays called *mistery plays,* which were connected directly or fancifully with the craft and which were performed in the church enclosure or the streets. Clearly the gild scheme embraced not only the work but much of the play of its members, and wrapped its tentacles around hearts as well as brains and muscles.

Quality of the article, weights, measures, working time, holidays, wages and prices were regulated by the gild, subject to the authority of the town government and usually, in the later Middle Ages (and especially in England and France), to the terms of the charter from the crown and to the legislation of the State. The town governments concerned themselves particularly with the quality and prices of food and drink, so immediately important for the whole population of the town. But prices of all articles made and sold in a town tended to fluctuate only slightly, because of the sway of the idea of the "just price" taught by the theologians which in practice came close to the customary price. It was only in the later Middle Ages that they began to recognize the legitimacy, within limits, of the rôle of supply and demand in the fixing of prices.

The gild system originated and worked very well in towns which had only a local trade, where the town craftsmen supplied the other citizens and the people of the adjoining country with the wares they needed. It did not work for those types of trade that produced goods on a large scale for export. Here obviously the scheme could not function. For the merchant who conducted an export or wholesale trade in wool or cloth or iron or copper wares inevitably had the upper hand, and the masters who worked for him fell into the position of employees, dependent for better or for worse on his capital and initiative. And it must be said that his initiative exceeded that of the gild brothers whose output enjoyed purely local consumption.

The origins of the craft gilds are still hotly debated by the specialists. Some of them argue that the gilds originated in grants or charters issued by a lord to economically free workers plying their crafts in a town growing up on his land. Others claim that they are an outgrowth from the organization of the unfree artisans working on the manor. And there are several other theories. In any case the important point is that free craftsmen, organized in groups according to handicrafts, in one way or another secured the right to buy and sell in the town market or in the town.

This "market right" had been given, in still earlier times, to the traveling merchants congregating and then settling in or near the burg or other fortified place. Here and there, especially in the North, these merchants had organized by the eleventh century into merchant associations or merchant gilds, and had secured from the lord the exclusive right of trading in his town. It is clear that the subsequent grant to a group of crafts of a right to share in this monopoly would pretty effectually break it, unless the merchants happened to deal exclusively in wares that the newly licensed craftsmen did not make; and this could not have been frequently the case. The whole subject of the relations between merchant gilds and craft gilds is full of unsolved problems.

In northern Europe where there had been merchant gilds, and in southern Europe where the primitive stage of urban development when such gilds might have been useful was quickly outgrown, the situation as it developed in the twelfth and thirteenth centuries was, broadly speaking, the same: the craft-gild scheme of organization was substantially universal. The merchants and even the members of the professions organized as if they were crafts. So did craftsmen who did not make a completed article, such as the dyers and the cobblers. All bowed to the sway of the craft-gild idea. And if some types of untrained workers were not so organized, that was due chiefly to the opposition of interested parties.

The list of the gilds of Florence in the later thirteenth century, which is only one-sixth as long as that for Paris, will make clear how inclusive the craft gilds were. The greater gilds, which for a long time substantially ran the city government, were: judges and notaries, dressers of foreign cloth, wool weavers, silk weavers, bankers, doctors and druggists, furriers. The lesser gilds, engaged mainly in local trade, were: linen-makers and mercers, shoemakers, smiths, salt dealers, butchers, wine-merchants, inn-keepers, harness-makers, leather-dressers, armorers, iron-mongers, masons, carpenters, bakers.

The relations between the gilds and the town governments will require closer scrutiny a little later. Here it will suffice to note that by and large, in the thirteenth century, the more powerful gilds were dominated by the people who controlled the town. In many cases it is impossible to say whether these gilds ran the town, or *vice versa*. In Florence the priors of the greater gilds in the later thirteenth century formed the council which governed the city. At the same period the merchant aristocracy of Venice took complete possession of the government. The larger the city and the more extensive its industry or commerce, the greater the probability that the economic leaders controlled the city government. Smaller towns with little trade more easily preserved something approaching a democratic type of government.

THE GROWTH OF CAPITAL AND OF CAPITALISM

In all these developments money played an important part. Where did Europe, overwhelmingly agricultural and virtually self-sufficient on its manors before the time of the crusades, secure the necessary funds? And how did the Italian banker-merchants gain such a dominant position in the medieval money market? These are two related questions which the economists are not as yet able to answer satisfactorily. But partial answers can be given.

A prerequisite to the establishment of a money economy was the growth of supplies of silver and gold. These were forthcoming, even before America was discovered or the invention of the quicksilver process made the Spanish silver mines so productive. New mines were opened. Germany furnished most of the new silver and Hungary most of the new gold. It is possible that the Mohammedan countries around the coasts of the Mediterranean contributed some gold and silver to the European stocks of which we are speaking.

The accumulation of fluid capital by the merchants is perhaps the most notable feature of the establishment of the reign of money. Mercantile gains were high, and individual initiative and family pride had a much freer field in commerce than they had in handicraft. Commerce favored the man of daring and initiative. The accumulation of money or savings from handicraft was on the whole small, although some rich men came from the crafts. Next in importance to commerce, in all probability, in explaining the rise of capital, come ground rents. The topic deserves a paragraph.

Sombart [1] and his socialistic followers consider ground rents the chief source of medieval capital. In the rising towns where the growth of population and business made the land increasingly valuable, the owners enjoyed the fruits of the unearned increment. They need not sell the land; they could rent it or use it as security for loans or for purchases of raw materials or finished products. The importance of ground rents in the building up of Italian capital seems definitely proven.

Another source for Italian capital was the papacy. The papacy employed the skilled banking houses of Siena and, toward the close of the thirteenth century, of Florence, in the collection and disbursement of its growing funds which were drawn from its Italian lands and from all of Christian Europe. In times of ex-

[1] Sombart, *Der Moderne Kapitalismus,* 2d ed.

traordinary expenditures the popes borrowed from the bankers, and at other times they enjoyed the use of the papacy's unemployed funds. The bankers received money for their services as financial agents and interest on their advances and loans.

It is well known that the canon law declared the taking of interest by Christians immoral and illegal. But the canonical prohibition dated from early times, when money was scarce and when it was usually employed only in nonproductive undertakings. The situation changed from the crusading era onward and, although the canon law against interest was not repealed, its application was altered so as to permit what it literally forbade. The scholastic doctors and judges of the later Middle Ages realized that money had become the nerve of business, and that a lender was entitled to remuneration for letting another have the use of money which could have been used gainfully in business enterprises. It is not always easy to repeal a law.

From a modern point of view the medieval interest rates were high. They ranged from fifteen to fifty per cent and above. Furthermore, the lenders received securities in the form of lands, mines, customs duties, from which they drew the income to be applied on the loan, and of which they usually became the owners, after the almost inevitable foreclosure occurred. The growth of the capital of the Medici in the fourteenth and fifteenth centuries, and of that of the Fugger family in the fifteenth and sixteenth centuries, shows what money lending on such a basis could produce.

Italy led in commerce, industry and capital accumulations; in short, Italy was the earliest home of medieval, and consequently of modern, capitalism. But capitalism, with its spirit of enterprise and its command of money, was alien to the gild system. How did these two mutually hostile children of medieval business get along together? Italy should furnish some good answers to this question.

As we have incidentally noticed, the craft-gild ideal of equality of the masters broke down when the raw materials had to be imported and when the finished goods were largely made for export. The Florentine gild of dressers of foreign cloth (*calimala* gild) was the creation of the city merchants who imported foreign cloth for Italian consumption. This cloth did not exactly suit Italian taste and consequently the importing merchants undertook, during the twelfth century, to refine it. They bought up cloth in Flanders and elsewhere, shipped it to Florence, and there had it fulled, dyed, clipped and otherwise transformed into a more luxurious product. The individual workmen who fulled, dyed, sheared, clipped and prepared it for sale were not in a position to watch the foreign markets for purchase and sale. The banker-merchants and their agents, who did know the foreign field, therefore assumed the direction of the industry and controlled it through their capital. Some of the workmen, who carried on some of the more difficult processes of dressing, occupied a quasi-independent position. Substantially all the workers carried on their labors at home, or in quite small workrooms accommodating six or eight of them; there were no factories in the modern sense of the word. In general the artisans were the hired workmen of the merchants who supplied the capital, bought the unfinished cloth, directed the processes of dressing it, and disposed of the finished goods.

The situation was much the same in the Florentine gild of wool-weavers. The merchants who controlled the dressing of foreign cloth realized in the thirteenth century that they could have and sell still finer fabrics if they could also do the weaving. They therefore imported the higher grades of wool from England and Spain, and had them woven in Florence. Thus arose the powerful gild of wool-weavers, embracing the necessary handicrafts, which carded, spun, wove, dyed and completely finished their own product. This gild, as is noted above, was really an offshoot from that of the wool-dressers, and the merchants who imported the wool and exported the cloths were at least in part the same individuals and firms who directed the gild of dressers of foreign cloth. The gild of wool-weavers flourished and gained great wealth until the fifteenth century, when the English government began to shut off the export of English wool. But by this time the production of silk fabrics in Italy—in Lucca, Bologna, Milan, Venice and Florence, to mention only a few centers—had reached such a point that the wool-weavers of Florence could be shifted to silk manufacture and thus their skill could be utilized at home.

It is obvious that the situation of the craftsmen in the gilds of dressers of foreign cloth and of wool-weavers in Florence bore little resemblance to that of the independent, equal and self-governing masters of the gilds already described. The more skilled bleachers, dyers and fullers had some measure of independence, but the rank and file of the workers, especially the wool-beaters, carders and combers, were laborers working for a daily or a piece wage, with maximum wages fixed by law, with no right to organize, and with poverty and misery for their portion. And what was true of them was similarly true of the weavers in the great industrial centers of the Netherlands and in the larger cities elsewhere. In the preamble to a statute of Philip and Mary, we read: "the rich clothiers do oppress the weavers . . . by engrossing of looms into their hands and letting them out at such unreasonable rents as the poor artificers are not able to maintain themselves by and much less their wives and families." [1] A similar situation developed almost contemporaneously in Germany in the mining industry, which now required extensive pumping machinery, and in iron-smelting, where a newly-invented and superior smelting furnace called for expenditures far beyond the financial capacity of a craftsman or his gild.

CONFLICTS BETWEEN LABORERS AND CAPITALISTS

The capitalists, the managers of export businesses, the great cloth merchants, the makers of metal wares for export were growing wealthy, in spite of the economic crises and stoppages which threatened their ill-paid artisans with penury and starvation. And yet the ideals of the equality of masters, of the restraint of the strong for the protection of the weak, which had been stressed by the gilds, were still living forces. And the friars, the brothers of the poor, and Wycliffe's "poor preachers," who emulated their example, taught the brotherhood of man and denounced the rich for their selfishness and greed. Even the

[1] Sombart.

peasants throughout western Europe were caught up by the current of opposition to the heavy burdens resting upon the poor. The fourteenth century was specially full of democratic unrest, in which misery and praiseworthy ambition and keen insight joined hands with envy and hatred and ignorance in scores of efforts to redress the balance. We must examine a few of the more representative of these conflicts between laborers and early capitalists.

By the beginning of the thirteenth century each of the industrial cities of the Netherlands, notably the Flemish towns of Ghent, Bruges and Ypres, was ruled by the richer merchants or patricians. Theoretically the governments were broadly democratic; actually the patricians were in control and were governing with a shrewd eye to their own advantage. The craftsmen and day laborers who worked for the patrician capitalists resented their poverty and misery and blamed it upon their rich employers. Even the crafts not connected with the larger export industries shared the resentment of their less favored brethren, and felt that the town regulations restricting their activities were made in the interests of the rich rather than for the welfare of all. The result was a long series of bloody revolts in which the weavers usually took the lead. They fought the city governments in many a sanguinary battle, and in 1302 at the battle of Courtrai they even inflicted a crushing defeat on Philip IV of France when he came to the aid of the patricians. The net result was that in every large city the artisans in one way or another secured control of the government. They did not exclude the patricians entirely from civic affairs; they were too wise for that. But, like the patricians before them, they did govern primarily in their own interests, and made more stringent the regulations protecting their own local crafts from outside competition. They would have liked to curb the great industries engaged in the export trade, upon which the prosperity of the land so largely depended. But they did not know how to do it without "killing the goose," and perforce left these industries in the hands of capitalists, with the necessary result that the economic lot of their artisans was little better than before.

It was the misfortune or the fault of the artisan governments of the Netherland cities that they were not able to develop a broad, democratic temper, recognizing the equal rights of all men as men. They governed, however wisely, in the interests of their own class. Hence they were not able to throw the united strength of their populations against the efforts of the dukes of Burgundy to make themselves effective masters of the Netherlands, and in the fifteenth century they had to accept the ducal control. But they retained wide rights of self-government in their cities, and in the centuries to come they learned, through bitter experience, the necessity of widening the base of their democracy to include the whole population. The modern democratic governments of Belgium and Holland owe a real debt to the turbulent weavers and coppersmiths of the fourteenth century.

The lot of the poorer Italian artisans was not so happy. The story of the *Ciompi* revolt in Florence will serve to illustrate their fortunes. The *Ciompi* were the hardest worked and poorest paid of the workmen who toiled for the great industrialists. They numbered over 10,000 men, most of them day laborers, and had no voice in the government which, in the fourteenth century, was largely in the hands of the greater gilds. The members of the lesser gilds, who composed the middle class and were mainly engaged in local industry, secretly encouraged the *Ciompi* in 1378 to agitate, petition, stop work and riot for a share in the government. The lesser gilds, in short, stirred up the "lower classes" to help them against the "upper class." The scheme had worked before in 1293, when the middle class controlled the government for a couple of years, only to lose it to the major gilds. As in the Netherlands, economic purposes underlay the struggle for political control: the government determined the incidence of taxation and fixed maximum wages for the artisans.

The *Ciompi* riots of 1378 were successful. The government recognized the organization of the poorer workmen into three new gilds and gave them a share in the government which would have enabled the lesser gilds, with the aid of the three new ones, to hold the upper hand. But the new gilds, misled by their momentary success, and nursing plans for taking control of industry in the interests of the poorer artisans, steadily increased their demands upon the government and ended by insisting that their representatives should have a veto upon the decisions of the regular branches of the government. They backed up their latest demands with arson, plunder and some murders. The lesser gilds now swung over to the side of the greater gilds, and the combination used the militia of the city to crush the *Ciompi* and then to disfranchise them anew. For a few years the lesser gilds controlled the government. Then in 1382 the greater gilds regained control and they retained it until in 1434 Cosimo de Medici, the great banker and merchant, championing the cause of the poor and holding out to greater and lesser gilds the hope of orderly progress and a cessation of class struggles and of fears for the future, was invited to become "boss" of the government. This momentous event turned out to be the beginning of the despotism of his family over Florence. If the *Ciompi,* when beaten in 1378, had been given some slight voice in the government and the heartening sense of personal dignity which citizenship confers, then Florence, the city of talent and intellect, might have developed beyond the stage of class government. But the more prosperous of the gilds, blinded by the sense of their own superiority and fearful of the economic program of the *Ciompi* which involved the fixing of wages by themselves and the state, took the other tack. The chance was lost and class government was restored, to end in a despotism which, like other dictatorships, gave internal peace at the price of liberty. The other cities of north and central Italy had already taken or soon took the same road to despotism.

PEASANT RISINGS

The discontent of the peasants of Western Europe with their lot became aggravated in the second half of the fourteenth century. They were treated with disdain by the upper classes, as if they were not fellow countrymen and Christians. The Black Death, which made the circuit of Europe in 1347-1351, caused

the services of the surviving peasants to be more valuable.   The
different national governments, however, turned against them
the doctrine of the "just price," and passed statutes fixing wages
at the old rates current before the great pestilence.   The statutes
were largely futile, but none the less aggravating.   In addition,
warfare bore heaviest on the open lands of the peasants, whether,
as in France, they were ravaged by the troops or, as in England,
they were heavily taxed to pay military expenses.   The causes
of the actual revolts varied widely, but through them all ran the
common motive of improving the economic position of the tillers
of the soil.

The *Jacquerie*[1] is the most celebrated of the many local revolts
of the French peasantry.   Its center was the province of Champagne and the region near Paris.   These parts had been most bitterly ravaged in the war with the English and their supporters, and
in the early summer of 1358 the peasants, who had been authorized
by the king to defend themselves against brigand lords and roving
mercenaries, took the aggressive against the landholding nobility.
Under the leadership of William Karle, a giant of a man, they
organized themselves into a rough army, armed with scythes and
flails and other improvised weapons, and slew some thirty offensive nobles.   They also attempted to capture three hundred noble
ladies who had gone to a small town near Paris for safety.   This
attack was foiled by a handful of knights, and after Karle had
been killed in a parley, the peasant army was scattered by the
nobles who took a bloody revenge for the fear they had endured,
slaughtering twenty thousand peasants.   The revolt itself lasted
less than a month.   Étienne Marcel, the provost of the merchants
of Paris, who was trying to reform the miserable government of
France, endeavored to link up with the peasant army, but failed
to do so and suffered Karle's fate.

A much more serious insurrection was the Peasants' Revolt
which broke out in the southeastern half of England in the summer of 1381.   The working people of the towns and of London

[1] From Jacques, the nickname given to the French peasants in the fourteenth
century.

shared the discontent of the peasants. There was wide dissatisfaction with the bad government of Richard II, and unrest was
aggravated by the weight of the taxes and by lawlessness bred by
the troops returning from France, as well as by the doctrines of
personal equality preached by busy agitators. The most interesting of these agitators was the ex-priest, John Ball, who popular-
ized the couplet, never since forgotten:

> When Adam delved and Evë span
> Who was then the gentleman?

The rebels murdered the most obnoxious of the landlords, lay and
clerical, and were admitted to London by their sympathizers. For
several days they held the young Richard II and his advisers
blockaded in the Tower. They wreaked vengeance on the law
courts and the palaces and persons of the hated advisers of the
king, killing the lord treasurer and the archbishop of Canterbury.

The leaders of the English revolt had an intelligent program.
They demanded the complete abolition of serfdom, a uniform
land rent of fourpence per acre, and a close reliance of the king
upon the working classes. They had little respect for Parliament,
which to them represented their masters.

Wat Tyler, the chief of the rebels, was slain at a parley with
the king, and the rebels dispersed under the protection of royal
promises to grant their demands, which were violated as soon as
the upper classes recovered from their panic. Thousands of
the peasantry and their town supporters were executed. The
revolt was unsuccessful, but it was a warning to those in power.

The German risings resembled those of the Netherlands rather
than those of Italy, although with inevitable variations. The
struggles will be passed over in favor of their outcome. First, in
a considerable number of important German towns the patricians
were overthrown and governments were set up by the victorious
crafts. Occasionally the latter allowed the patricians to have some
voice in affairs, on condition that they enroll in one of the gilds.
Augsburg, Brunswick and Constance will serve as examples of
this first group. Secondly, in many places the patricians remained
in control, making slight concessions to the crafts. Nürnberg,

Frankfurt and the chief Hanseatic cities are examples of this group. The general tendency was in the direction of the reëstablishment of an aristocratic type of town government by a fusion of the patricians and the upper portion of the crafts, with the usual result in the fifteenth century, namely, renewed and generally unsuccessful revolts.

The one successful rising of the combined lower classes of town and country was that of the Hussites of Bohemia in the fifteenth century. Here the revolt was not only economic, but also racial and religious. The rebels withstood the upper classes of Bohemia and also the crusades of Church and Empire.[1]

ALIENATION OF TOWN AND COUNTRY

The relations of town and country in the Middle Ages left much to be desired. To be sure, the towns broke down the partial isolation of the manors or feudal estates by offering their inhabitants necessary wares produced by specialists, and by furnishing a market for, and a motive for producing, surplus food and other raw materials. Moreover, the use of money and the opportunity to find work in a neighboring town undermined villainage and made inevitable the liberation of the peasants of western Europe, which was substantially accomplished by the close of the Middle Ages. These results were not willed by the townsmen. Their chief desire was that the surrounding countryside should furnish steady supplies of food and form a secure market for town wares. Indeed, in Italy, the Netherlands and parts of Germany—wherever a strong monarchy did not intervene—the country around an important city was forcibly annexed and its inhabitants treated as subjects, not as fellow citizens. As a consequence there was little sympathy between town and country as such. There was some solidarity between the oppressed peasants and the oppressed part of the craftsmen, and between the city aristocracy and their kindred outside; but, as a rule, effective coöperation· was lacking. The townsmen treated the country

[1] See pages 316-317.

districts with harshness, as if they were overseas colonies, existing for the benefit of the mother country. There is one brilliant exception to this rule, that of Switzerland.

The Swiss Confederation started out in 1291 as a league of self-defense of the three rural cantons of Uri, Schwyz and Unterwalden to which little by little were added other rural cantons and cities of upper Germany, bound together to defend their freedom against the attacks of the Hapsburgs. Their success was phenomenal and steady, culminating in the recognition of their virtual independence by the Hapsburg emperor, Maximilian, in 1499. On several occasions alienation between the democratic rural cantons and the patrician governments of the cities seemed certain to lead to ruinous civil war and the destruction of the Confederation; but in every case better counsels prevailed. "The strength of the Confederation consisted mainly in the union of opposites, a combination of the food supply of the country with the markets and superior knowledge of the towns." The explosive force of the Reformation, it is true, did lead to a brief civil war, but it was quickly settled on the basis of local (cantonal) option, and Switzerland continued to give its object lesson to the rest of the Continent.

Inspired in part by the example of the Swiss, the fourteen imperial cities of South Germany (Swabia) formed the Swabian League in 1376, and five years later the Rhenish cities from Mainz to Strasburg united in a similar League of Rhenish Cities. Their enemies were robbers, neighboring princes and the intermittently threatening emperor. The two leagues immediately joined hands and linked up with the Swiss. But when war with Leopold of Hapsburg faced them, the two city leagues, fearful for their commerce, retreated. Although the Swiss, single-handed, defeated Leopold at Sempach (1386), the city leagues had lost their opportunity. They were separately defeated by the allied neighboring princes in 1388, and the leagues dissolved. The princes were satisfied and did not annex the cities. They continued to enjoy their measure of independence; but henceforth they had but a subordinate rôle in German political history.

POLITICAL INADEQUACY OF THE HANSEATIC LEAGUE

It is conceivable that the Hanseatic League, whose beginnings have been sketched in an earlier chapter, might have succeeded in organizing northern Germany into a stable federation. The member cities had wealth, sea power, wide experience in diplomacy, and a successful record in warfare, not only against Waldemar of Denmark but also against the formidable "forage brethren" or *Vitalien-Brüder,* a veritable pirate state on the sea. Nevertheless, the Hanseatic League failed without even trying to organize Germany on the Baltic.

The inexplicable decision of the herring, in 1425, to substitute the coasts of the North Sea for those of the Baltic as a spawning-ground, undoubtedly hurt the Hanseatic cities economically. But the true causes of failure were not economic but political. The League was a loose organization, comparable in structure to the ineffective Empire of its day. Moreover, the patrician oligarchies which governed in the cities of the League were more keenly concerned with maintaining themselves in power against the revolts of the crafts and the proletariat than with making far-reaching plans for political consolidation.

The Hansa had prospered among peoples of slight political maturity, and it declined when they developed internal stability and external power. The union of the three Scandinavian kingdoms at Kalmar in 1397, although it was not permanent, took place in the teeth of futile Hanseatic opposition. Similarly, the establishment of the power of the Burgundian house in the Netherlands, the recovery of Poland, the revival of Russia after the expulsion of the Golden Horde, the pacification of England by the Tudors, the rise of Sweden under the House of Vasa, and the emergence of Brandenburg-Prussia, each and all whittled down the membership of the League by the incorporation of its member cities. The League lived on for centuries as a purely North German affair, but its vigor from the sixteenth century onward was little more than the strength of Lübeck, Hamburg and Bremen. These cities proudly perpetuated its name into the nineteenth century, and even now, as states within the German *Reich,* recall the days when the League represented the Fatherland, not unworthily, in the northern seas. The Hanseatic cities had to throw in their lot with the countries of which they had been, at least nominally, a part from the beginning. The prince, not the patrician oligarchies, gained control.

THE CITY DESPOTISMS OF ITALY

The fate of the Italian city states was far different. They passed, for centuries, under the yoke of the foreigner. The steps which led them to this bitter outcome can be traced with some certainty.

The fundamental cause of the failure of the Italian communes was class selfishness. The narrow, mercantile aristocracies were not able to reconcile their fellow townsmen to exclusion from a share in the government. Moreover, the aristocracies themselves, with the notable exception of Venice, were split into factions, each of which feared the other as well as the subject population. The outcome, as revealed above in the case of Florence, was the concession of supreme power to a tyrant or lord. Under him all classes were in the same boat and he, it was thought, would maintain peace and prosperity. Once he was in firm control, however, the citizens found that they were subject to his caprices. And so the age of the communes, approximately covering the period 1100-1300, gave way to the age of the tyrannies, which extended roughly from 1300 to 1500.

The origins of the tyrants were varied. But whether a feudal lord, a nobleman, the military or judicial chief of a commune, a captain of mercenaries, the nephew of a pope, or a merchant prince, the tyrant ruled on the basis of capacity. No divine right, no ancient lineage, hallowed his rule. Force, craft and sleepless vigilance alone preserved him from his enemies. He kept order by destroying his opponents. He flattered his subjects by adorning the city with palaces and other sumptuous buildings, by giving lavish entertainments and spectacles, by patronizing artists and men of letters, and by letting his hands fall lightly on the common people.

The chief assistants of the tyrants were the mercenary captains, known in Italy as *condottieri*. The earliest of these adventurers were foreigners, but before the tyrannies were a century old Italian captains monopolized the business of warfare. They fought for pay in money, lands, or cities, and changed employers as often as they thought it profitable. Their troops were chiefly cavalry, in contrast with the armies which won such fame in the Hundred Years' War. Their battles were rarely bloody affairs, since every *condottiere's* troops were his capital which he must not seriously impair.

The wars carried on by the tyrants with the aid of the *condottieri,* like the more sanguinary conflicts among the communes, were primarily wars of aggression. Each state still strove to expand at the expense of its neighbors. Experimental combinations, so to speak, of different states into one were almost endless. Gradually, however, the number of Italian states diminished as the stronger absorbed the weaker, and in the second half of the fifteenth century there was relative stability in the peninsula as a result of the balanced antagonisms of the five greater states— Venice, Milan, Florence, the Papal States and Naples. A few minor states like Siena, Modena and Ferrara, also maintained a precarious existence.

Venice was the most wealthy and the most feared of the five. Shortly after the wars of Chioggia, Venice turned her attention to the Italian mainland and gradually built up a domain which gave her command of passes over the Alps and a source, although an inadequate one, for food supplies. By stepping on the mainland Venice became more vulnerable, but she governed the conquered cities with such moderation that in time of need she could withdraw to her islands and, when the storm passed, regain their allegiance. Thus she pushed her land frontier westward to the Adda and the Po.

Milan, the great rival of Venice in the north, fell under the control of the Visconti family in the early fourteenth century, and by 1350 they ruled over all Lombardy, a rich and fertile region whose prosperity rested on agriculture, industry and commerce. The most cunning, cruel and successful Visconti was

Gian Galeazzo (1385-1402), whose conquests and ill deeds have given him a sinister renown. When the last male Visconti died in 1447 the succession was momentarily in doubt, but it was soon seized (1450) by his son-in-law, Francesco Sforza, the great *condottiere,* and remained in his family until the foreigner came.

Florence seemed content under the veiled sway of Cosimo de' Medici (1434-1464), a rich patron of art and letters who shunned ostentation and public office, but manipulated elections with finished skill. His grandson, Lorenzo the Magnificent (1469-1492), was more talented and less retiring. On his death the descendants of the old liberty-loving Florentines looked to his feeble son, Piero, for guidance. Cosimo and Lorenzo were the real founders of the triple alliance of Florence, Milan and Naples, which checkmated the ambitions of Venice and the Papal States.

The Papal States were infested with tyrants until after the Great Schism. Pope Alexander VI (1492-1503) was a strong ruler. However, he appears to have allowed his son, Cæsar Borgia, to attempt to establish a tyranny in the center of the Papal States. But the fruit of his labors really fell to the papacy when the warlike Julius II (1503-1513) became pope.

Naples, the large southern kingdom, never enjoyed a true communal era, and consequently its baronage was not submerged. After 1443 it passed into the masterful hands of Alfonso V of Aragon and was by him transmitted to his illegitimate son. Its history is related elsewhere.[1]

Such, briefly, was the organization of Italy, in the later fifteenth century, into five independent states, with a successful balance of power and skillful captains of mercenary troops. Were the subjects of these five autocratic states, untrained in arms as well as in government, as capable of defending themselves against the foreigner as the liberty-loving, turbulent citizens of the Lombard communes had been in the face of Frederick Barbarossa? And would the rulers of the five states sink their differences and close their ranks in a new and larger Lombard League? Was there a genuine Italian patriotism? Was the ancient valor still alive in the Italy of the tyrants?

[1] See pages 378 *ff.*

These questions are only rhetorical. The independence, the wealth, luxury, art and literature of Italy, we know, existed only on sufferance. The preoccupations of France and Spain, not yet organized, gave the petty Italian States an illusion of power and adequacy in the fifteenth century. The danger to which Italy was exposed did not escape the prophetic sight of Savonarola, the great friar of Florence, one of the most remarkable preachers of righteousness that Catholicism ever produced. True, he regarded the danger as due to the sinfulness of the Italians, especially of the Florentines. But that was natural in a preacher of religion. In a remarkable series of sermons upon the Flood, delivered in 1492, Savonarola "foretold the coming of a new Cyrus, who would march through Italy in triumph, without encountering any obstacles, and without breaking a single lance." Returning later to the same general topic, Savonarola concluded a second series of sermons on September 21, 1494, with a discourse on the text, and announced with a terrible voice, "Behold, I bring a flood of waters upon the earth!" The sensation was tremendous, for that very morning the Florentines had learned that the army of Charles VIII of France had crossed the Alps. With the invasion of 1494 [1] we reach the beginning of the end of Italian independence. As Cipolla has pointed out, the age of the tyrannies was a bridge between the age of the communes and the age of foreign domination. Only Venice with her millennium of experience, entrenched behind the waters of the Adriatic, escaped.

SERVICES OF THE TOWNS

The kings of western Europe and the princes in the Netherlands and Germany, who at the close of the fifteenth century had taken the center of the economic stage from the towns, were not without a real appreciation of what they could learn from them. Many a time in the past, the towns had aided the kings against their common foes, the nobles, and had furnished both money and financial advisers to them. Most of the economic policies fol-

[1] See pages 387 ff.

lowed by the monarchs in the sixteenth and seventeenth centuries
were nothing but applications on a larger scale of the practices
of the towns. The so-called mercantile system of national economics, which the rulers followed from about 1650 to 1800 and
which sought to sell much to the foreigner, to buy little from him,
and to accumulate a stock of money; which strove to regiment
and direct the economic activities of the kingdom to higher
productivity in the interest of national self-sufficiency and
strength—all this was only town policy writ large. The maintenance of colonies overseas for the benefit of the home land was
but an enlarged application of the treatment accorded by the
greater city states to their subject country districts. And so on.
Our riper wisdom condemns many of these policies as mistaken.
They none the less demonstrate the economic leadership of the
towns. Indeed capital, which had been accumulated chiefly in
and by the towns, entered the service of Charles V, Francis I,
the Tudors, and other rulers of the sixteenth century. Even the
story of the geographical discoveries will have something to say
on this topic.

CHAPTER XIX

EDUCATION. REVIVAL OF LEARNING. THE FINE ARTS

1300-1500

THE zeal for education which was so strong in the thirteenth century did not decline in the following period. It showed itself in the rise of gild and city schools and even more clearly in the establishment of new universities made necessary by the swarms of students and possible by local pride. In Germany alone fourteen universities were founded in the later Middle Ages.

All the universities were still cosmopolitan in theory or practice. Latin being universally used as the speech of instruction, there was no language barrier to prevent students and professors from migrating. Another international bond was the unity of Christendom; all the universities were Catholic and theology was the highest subject of study.

STUDENT LIFE AND LEARNING

The methods of instruction underwent little change. The lecturers still dictated and commented upon authoritative texts in arts, medicine, law and theology, and the students tested their knowledge by holding formal and informal disputations, or debates, upon the content of the lectures. Great value was still attached to skill in disputation, and enthusiasm still ran strong for the arts courses in dialectics—that is, in the art of disputation. The devotion of the medieval student to dialectics has often been derided, but there is no doubt that it did much to develop his reasoning power and his skill in classification.

The idea that practice should accompany theory was not unknown. In the later thirteenth century Robert of Sorbonne required the theological students in his "endowed boarding-house" at the University of Paris to preach in the parishes while they were pursuing their courses. In 1309 Pope Clement V ordained that candidates for the medical degree at Montpellier should have eight months of practical experience. Pierre Dubois, a few years later, stressed the importance of practice accompanying precept in substantially all fields of study.

The life of the university students was still free and relatively unsupervised. The rise of *colleges*—endowed boarding-houses, especially favored by the friars, with a resident master to help the students get up their studies—in the thirteenth century tended to steady them somewhat, but many students selected their own boarding-places. On the whole they were still a boisterous lot, with a well-earned reputation for turbulence and brutality in hazing which modern students have almost completely outgrown. Many of them were desperately poor and had to live on alms. But begging was not dishonorable. The friars were mendicants. The students were much given to moving from one university to another, seeking renowned professors and the excitement of life on the road. Friars and pilgrims made wandering respectable.

It is certain that the reputation of the students as thieves, especially of food, was not quite deserved, for many light-hearted and light-fingered vagabonds pretended to be students. It was not unusual for older students and for tramps masquerading as students to take with them on their travels younger boys whom they promised to teach and valued chiefly as unpaid servants. Thomas Platter, a young Swiss with a hunger for learning, tells us of his experiences on the road in the early sixteenth century, when "wandering scholars" were still common. He was trained to bring down a goose with a stone, to pilfer vegetables, beg beer, and gather other provisions. At Ulm he was sent around with a piece of cloth, begging money to have it made into a coat. Later he and his "student" went to Munich, and after a year there they returned to Ulm where Thomas went out again with the identical piece of cloth. "Zounds!" said one man, "isn't the coat made yet? I believe you are going around tricking people." Thomas afterward escaped from his "student," whom he had supported for years, got a real chance to study, and became a respected school-master.

The growth of universities was accompanied by and dependent upon an increase in the number of schools. It is impossible to tell what percentage of boys had a chance to go to school in the later Middle Ages since statistics were not kept. But a German scholar has calculated that there were six thousand attending the German universities in the later years of the fifteenth century, while a careful English scholar thinks that there was a higher average of school attendance in England in the fifteenth century than in the nineteenth. We do not know. And yet, considering also the large reading public which the early printers found for their books, and much other evidence, it is clear that those who argue for the existence of schools in most villages of any size, to say nothing of the towns, have the probabilities on their side.

There was a wide variety in these schools, which ranged from the small ones, taught by a country or chantry priest, to the larger schools in the cities with a dozen or more teachers. In the very smallest, located in out-of-the-way places, singing and reading (sometimes in the mother tongue), and occasionally simple arithmetic and writing, were taught; in the largest, located in big cities, the teachers sometimes carried the boys through the equivalent of the earlier part of the university course in arts. Music received much attention, since it was so important in the Church service and such a valued accomplishment. Religious instruction was given in all the schools, but not so much emphasis was placed on doctrine as after the Reformation.

In all the schools, except some of the most elementary—we are not using this word in a technical sense since there were no *grades* in the Middle Ages—the basic job was the learning of Latin, the universal language of scholarship and the professions. A man with any pretence to education knew Latin. And the boys started to learn it as soon as they went to school. After they had learned it passably, they would proceed to rhetoric and dialectics and then possibly to the mathematical and scientific branches of the *quadrivium*.

The medieval schools had been founded originally for the education of the clergy, but for generations before 1500 a considerable and probably increasing number of laymen attended them and also the universities. Boys and girls were not allowed to attend school together except in the most rudimentary type of schools and in their very early years. There may have been other exceptions. Froissart, at any rate, speaks of being bothered in school by the presence of "ravishing little girls." Women were not admitted to the universities, and what schooling girls got had almost always to be obtained from private tutors or, possibly, in convent schools. Occasionally we read of schoolmistresses and of schools for girls in the fifteenth century, for example at Frankfurt-on-Main, but they were unusual.

School discipline was very strict. Solomon's admonition, "Spare the rod and spoil the child," was better heeded than any other Scriptural precept in the Middle Ages. Martin Luther relates that he was whipped fifteen times in one morning—because the teacher was mixed in his grammar! The pictures of medieval schoolrooms almost invariably show the master with a switch in his hand. In some regions it was the custom for the pupils to make a holiday excursion into the woods to cut a store of birches for future use.

The schoolmasters usually derived at least a part of their living from fees paid by the pupils. But pious and public-spirited laymen and clergymen endowed schools to give free instruction in whole or in part, and the brightest boys could often get scholarships for the universities.

Moreover from the thirteenth century onward, here and there, notably in industrial centers, the gilds founded and maintained schools for the education of the sons of their members. These schools at first taught the regular branches in Latin; then instruction in simple business and in "the three R's" was added or substituted. The cities themselves more and more took a hand in this sort of instruction and also in the standard type of school work, providing the school buildings and contributing to the support of the teachers. The teachers, with rare exceptions, continued to be clerics, and the bishop of the diocese retained his ancient supervision over these schools. But the cities, which "paid the piper," began to "call the tune," and we note occasional grumblings that the studies were not "practical" enough. In 1510-1512, John Colet, the great and also rich English divine, founded St. Paul's School, London, with the mercers' gild as trustee. Cities and gilds, in the later Middle Ages, were clearly taking a hand in education. The beginnings of the secular control of education may well be sought here. The Revival of Learning may be regarded as another indication of the growth of secularism.

MEDIEVAL LITERATURE AND THE REVIVAL OF LEARNING

Medieval literature, whether in Latin or in the vernacular, dealt with the lives of saints, the mighty deeds of historical, Biblical and legendary heroes, the romantic adventures of errant knights, the sweetness and sadness of love, and the careless joys and ribaldries of wandering minstrels and students. This literature, taking it as a whole, is rich in imaginative power and is saturated with medieval Christianity and its hopes, fears, ecstasies, superstitions, miracles and interventions of angels and devils. In this literature the clergy are treated with respect and with disrespect, in accordance with their behavior. There is much frank criticism of clerical weaknesses, especially from the twelfth century onward; but it is, on the whole, the criticism of a friend by a friend.

Medieval literature has its roll of great names. Although the list is shorter than antiquity and modern times can boast, it is worthy of note that the Middle Ages produced one of the three writers whom men have agreed to place above all others—Homer, Dante and Shakespeare.

Dante (1265-1321) was a Florentine noble and a genius of the first order. He saw much of life, was an official of the government of Florence and spent the last twenty years of his short span as a political exile from the city of his birth. He wrote a number of books, some in Latin and others in Italian. Among the latter are the *New Life,* one of the world's great, although not simple, love stories; and the *Divine Comedy,* one of the world's deathless epics. The *Divine Comedy* is rich in imagination and in vivid insight into character; it is permeated with Catholic theology and love of God, and is almost matchless in style. It is the literary masterpiece of the Middle Ages.

In the *Divine Comedy* and in his other writings Dante shows a deep veneration for and a real familiarity with the great authors of pagan antiquity, so far as they were accessible in Latin. In these respects he exemplifies, only more perfectly, the position of many medieval writers. But Dante was at the same time loyal to his mother tongue which he did much to perfect, and to the great interests of medieval civilization, especially vernacular literature in French and Italian, philosophy and theology. Not so Petrarch and Boccaccio, who were born in Dante's lifetime. To them, who inaugurated the so-called *Revival of Classical Learning* (usually abbreviated into *Revival of Learning*), and to their followers, the Middle Ages were nothing and antiquity was everything.

Petrarch (1304-1374) was another Florentine. He grew up in Avignon and was sent by his father to study law at Montpellier and Bologna, the great law schools of the age. But the bias of young Francis was invincibly toward Latin classical literature, and to this he devoted his great powers from his student days onward. He was an accomplished writer of little Latin biographies of ancient worthies and carried on a voluminous and polished correspondence in Latin with the scholars and rulers of his time. He was a highly capable essayist and an interesting autobiographer, as we can see in his *Secret*. As a historian he lacked critical power. Yet his desire to understand antiquity as it really was led him to employ classical Latin sources, both good and bad, exclusively for his authorities. As a consequence, he ruled out supernatural explanations of historical events (a besetting medieval vice), and thus helped to *laicize* history. His most ambitious Latin work was his *Africa,* a laborious imitation of the *Æneid*. His most successful work was his *Canzoniere,* a collection of Italian poems mostly in praise of the mistress of his poetical affections, Laura, a Provençal lady. The laudation of Roman civilization, of Roman wisdom, of classical Latin literature, was constant with him. He hated medieval law, dialectics, philosophy, theology and medicine. Indeed, he knew little about them. His political theories leaned toward ancient Roman republicanism, and his practice countenanced contemporary despotisms. He was a bundle of contradictions. He was introspective, morbid, and in his later years devout and, of course, strictly orthodox.

It is impossible to explain exactly why Petrarch, Boccaccio (1313-1375) his disciple, and the other *Humanists,*[1] their followers, felt such scorn for the civilization of the Middle Ages to which they were so deeply indebted, and concentrated their attention and their praise upon the great literatures of pagan Rome and Greece. Dante, Petrarch and Boccaccio were all Florentines. Petrarch must be classified as a cleric, since he had taken minor orders (he may have been a priest) to the end that he might draw an income from Church benefices; Dante assuredly was a layman. Florence was rich and self-reliant in Dante's time as well as in Petrarch's. And yet we probably draw near the real explanation when we say that the middle class and the commercial aristocracy, developed by town life and growing in wealth and intelligence, welcomed a more secular treatment of our mundane existence than clerically-minded writers furnished. The specialized study of the masterpieces of pagan Rome and Greece fitted into the scheme of these secular interests.

The Revival of (classical) Learning may be defined as an increased interest in, and a heightened appreciation and knowledge of, the literatures of pagan Rome and Greece—the classical literatures of the past. It involved, among other results, a restoration of classical Latin to honor and to use. Petrarch and the other Humanists, whose "spiritual" father he was, were particularly charmed by the beauty of the Latin of Cicero, Virgil and others of the great writers who had lived at the height of Roman civilization. The Humanists regarded medieval Latin as barbarous and shuddered, or pretended to shudder, at the strange, although often very useful, words and unclassical constructions employed by the

[1] A name later given to the supporters of the study of the ancient classical literatures as the best foundation for a cultivated personality. *Human,* as opposed to theological or *other-worldly.*

medieval Latin writers. They might have found much to praise in the stately music of the medieval Latin hymns, in the learned letters of Gerbert, or in the impassioned sermons of St. Bernard, but they chose to identify medieval Latin with the dry and technical verbiage of the medieval theologians of their time. The style of a modern scientific treatise might with equal justice be taken as representative of English prose.

As one Humanist said in writing to another, Pico della Mirandola, who was also familiar with medieval philosophy: "But is it not a polished and elegant, at least a classical and chaste, style, which confers immortal reputation on an author?" Pico replied, speaking for the medieval philosophers: "If Pythagoras could have communicated his thoughts by looks, or otherwise than by discourse, he would not have spoken at all; much less was he inclined to study elegance of language. . . . We are solicitous what, and not how, we write."

The retort put into the mouth of the medieval philosophers by the great Pico had some point to it, for the Humanists did underestimate the value of having something important to say. But their worship of classical Latin style won the day, and as a result scholars gradually abandoned medieval Latin for classical Latin. The Revival of Learning killed medieval Latin.

A second feature of the Revival was the collection of manuscripts of the authors of Roman antiquity. The Middle Ages had been familiar with many of their writings, but not with all of them. The Humanists set to work with passionate zeal to *recollect* them from monastic and other libraries, and their labors were crowned with abundant success, although they left many discoveries for modern scholars to make.

The Humanists also undertook to edit the writings of the great Latin authors and purified them from many errors made by copyists. Their editorial work was very useful, although it does not satisfy the requirements of modern scholarship, since their method was to make the authors intelligible rather than to discover, by critical comparison of texts, what the authors had really written.

A third feature of the Revival of Learning was the virtual reintroduction of the study of classical Greek authors into western Europe. Some of these, notably the whole of Aristotle, had been known in Latin translations, but the knowledge of classical Greek itself had pretty completely died out in the West. Vernacular Greek, spoken in Greece and southern Italy and Sicily, was, of course, known. Petrarch knew no Greek and Boccaccio was acquainted with little more than the Greek alphabet. But from the closing years of the fourteenth century a growing number of Humanists learned the language and the literature of ancient Greece and extended their work of collecting and editing to include Greek manuscripts.

At first the Humanists devoted much energy to turning the Greek classics into Latin or to polishing up medieval Latin translations of them, but they got over this idea at the close of the fifteenth century, and soon good working editions of the Greek classics were in print. Few Italian Humanists, however, excelled in Greek, and early in the sixteenth century leadership in Greek scholarship passed north of the Alps, where the new Latin scholarship had already taken root.

The veneration of the Italian Humanists for the Latin classics was for a long time carried beyond reason. Petrarch went so far as to assert—in the face of Dante's achievement—that poetry, to be poetry, must be written in classical Latin. Nevertheless, Petrarch wrote Italian verses, and by the irony of fate it is to these and not to his *Africa* (first printed in 1874) that he owes his solid reputation as a poet. Similarly, Boccaccio's Latin writings rest in the dust of neglect, while his *Decameron,* an artistic collection of stories, is still read and admired, in spite of its immoralities, as a model of early Italian prose. The Italian followers of Petrarch, Boccaccio excepted, lacked his genius and only too faithfully observed his precept; but they wrote nothing in Latin that is now highly regarded. Only from the close of the fifteenth century did Italian writers of universal importance reappear and renew the production of masterpieces of Italian literature in prose and verse. We shall consider them in the chapter on the sixteenth century.

The Revival of Learning has been called the third gift of Italy to European civilization, the other two being the Roman Empire and the papacy. The list could be extended. By the middle of the fifteenth century the zeal of the Italian Humanists began to spread to France, Germany, England and the other countries of Europe, and in the sixteenth the Revival was in full swing. Indeed, it even succeeded in the North in producing some real literature in Latin; for example, the *Colloquies* of Erasmus and the *Utopia* of Thomas More. The *Letters of Obscure Men* are also genuine literature, but they are written in intentionally *medievalized* (George Saintsbury says *caninized*) Latin, although the authors are German Humanists.

REVIVAL OF LEARNING AND "RENAISSANCE"

Our debt to Italy for the Revival of Learning is real; but its size and nature must not be misunderstood. The Revival did not affect agriculture, industry, commerce, law, medicine, government, national and international politics, religion, invention or exploration. It did not directly touch the lives of ordinary men and women, but only of the literary and scholarly few. In the second place, it did not introduce Greek and Roman ideas into the medieval world. That had been done from the beginning of the Middle Ages. The classical heritage and Christianity, as everyone knows, were the great molding and transforming elements in medieval civilization. Neither did the Revival introduce classical Latin literature to medieval scholars. They had loved it for centuries, although the shifts of fashion in scholarship and especially the vogue of dialectics and philosophy had well-nigh eliminated the masterpieces of Latin literature from the arts curriculum of the universities. We are familiar with a comparable situation today.

It was only in the last half of the nineteenth century that a small group of writers and scholars, enamored of the classical literatures and inadequately acquainted with the Middle Ages— and also forgetful of the useful historical doctrine of "plurality of causes"—came to a startling conclusion. This was, that the Revival of Learning had caused all, or nearly all, the marvelous advances and changes which had taken place in the fifteenth and sixteenth centuries. Lumping all these advances together, they gave them the old name, *Renaissance* (rebirth). Hence their simple formula was: the Revival of Learning produced the Renaissance. But as Taylor had cogently observed, the word Renaissance thus employed, "carries more false notions than can be contradicted in a summer's day." We have attempted, in this chapter, to present the Revival in its proper perspective, and shall now sum up its genuine services.

The Revival of Learning strengthened the fertilizing influence of the classical literatures upon medieval and modern civilization —increased our debt to Greece and Rome—with the fruits of specialization. The Humanists were the first medieval specialists in Latin and Greek literature. They had the virtues and also the vices of specialists. Their later representatives, the great classical scholars of the eighteenth and the subsequent centuries, understand antiquity much better than the Humanists did.

More specifically, the Revival of Learning strengthened and made more flexible and expressive the vernacular languages in which our modern literatures are written. The classics supplied many terms of art, letters, philosophy and science, which color our modern languages and enable them to express a wider range of ideas and sentiments.

The Revival of Learning enriched the vernacular literatures by affording additional and often superior models of verse and prose, as well as a heightened appreciation of literary style. The vernacular writers drew easily upon the life of their time and of all time, which is the very substance of all great literature. But they did need a more sensitive feeling for form or style, a keener appreciation of the values of ordered beauty. Geniuses like Dante could secure this for themselves. Others could and did acquire it from the study of the masterpieces of antiquity. Ultimately the mature vernacular literatures themselves became qualified to afford much of this training in formal beauty to our modern writers.

The Revival of Learning altered the content of the arts course. The interest in dialectics and in scholastic philosophy, which in the later Middle Ages had lost its vitality and become barren, waned before the desire to gain a writing and speaking knowledge of classical Latin, and in the sixteenth century the universities surrendered to the change. The preparatory schools were even quicker in making the shift.   Thus the study of classical Latin and, to a lesser extent, of Greek authors became the central feature of academic or nonprofessional education from preparatory school to university.   Latin and Greek held the place, thus won, until the advent of experimental science in the nineteenth century forced them to give ground.   The debate between the supporters of the classical and the scientific types of education is not yet concluded.   Each has valuable elements to contribute to the all-round man.

It is barely possible that the Revival of Learning made scholars more critically-minded, more apt to challenge tradition.   But if one tests the question by comparing the demonstrations of the spuriousness of the Donation of Constantine, made independently by the Humanist, Lorenzo Valla, in the fifteenth century, and by his contemporary, Bishop Reginald Pecock, the scholastic doctor, one will not be too sure.   For the only advantage the Humanist has is the possession of a tool—a knowledge of the historical evolution of the Latin language—which enables him to detect anachronisms in the language of the Donation.   In other respects Pecock easily holds his own.   Critical-mindedness, emancipation from deference to authority or tradition, and reliance upon tested evidence are plants of slow growth which draw their nourishment from a very wide variety of sources.   Classical scholars are not always more critical than lawyers, doctors, or merchants.

THE INVENTION OF PRINTING

The spread of copies of the ancient classics, of the writings of the Middle Ages and above all of the Bible, was made possible on a large scale by a great medieval invention, the discovery of a method of casting type, commonly called the invention of printing. The Chinese had printed from engraved blocks and type as early as the tenth century, and Europe had learned this sort of printing in the fourteenth century. But John Gutenberg's invention about 1455 of a way of casting metal type was revolutionary. For by his method a letter needed to be cut by hand only once; then, by means of molds, it could be reproduced in quantities and with uniformity. Exactly the same was true of books. Once set up, a book could be reproduced in quantities and with uniformity. Careful preparation of copy, careful revision of proofs, ensured a thousand, any number of thousands of identically accurate copies. Exact scholarship was now possible in a sense never before conceivable.

Gutenberg's invention marks an epoch in the intellectual life of mankind. It gave wings to knowledge which had hitherto been compelled to plod laboriously along, since the copying of books was so slow, inaccurate and expensive. Gutenberg's invention, Germany's greatest gift to civilization, so cheapened books that by the close of the fifteenth century a printer could sell for a florin or two a book which a copyist would take months to reproduce by hand. The art of printing opened wide the doors of knowledge to all, peasant and peer, layman and cleric; it rendered government by the people not only possible, but inevitable. Frederic Harrison said: "We place Gutenberg amongst the small list of the unique and special benefactors of mankind, in the sacred choir of those whose work transformed the conditions of life, whose work, once done, could never be repeated."

The circumstance that the Revival of Learning began in Italy was almost an accident. If the humanistic movement of twelfth-century France, with which the name of John of Salisbury is so closely associated, had not been arrested by the onset of practical "bread-and-butter" studies as law, medicine and, above all, dialectics, France might have had the glory of beginning the specialization in the classics of Rome and Greece which Petrarch and his followers gave to Italy in the fourteenth century.

Looking back—hindsight is so much easier than foresight—it now seems to have been inevitable that the development of painting and sculpture should owe most to the artistic endowment of the Italians of the Middle Ages and particularly to the Florentines, their most talented representatives.   But the Northerners, especially the Flemings, were real rivals, and it was not until the second half of the fifteenth century that the Italians drew ahead.

It was the Gothic sculptors of France and Germany who began the realistic movement which emancipated art from Byzantine stiffness and formality.   The style of the Byzantine artists, whose work in mosaic is characteristic, was rigid and hieratic, but probably this very rigidity was helpful in preserving a minimum of the ideals and technical processes of antiquity amid the flux of the barbarism of the millennium after the birth of Christ.   The development of Gothic architecture in the twelfth and thirteenth centuries was the first great assertion of creative artistic genius in the Middle Ages.   And it was Gothic sculpture, notably displayed, for example, in the cathedrals of Amiens, Rheims, Chartres and Naumburg, which led the way toward the abandonment of Byzantine formulas in favor of the study, the imitation, of nature.   The Northern artists who created the plants, leaves, fruits, animals, patriarchs, prophets, angels, saints, donors and patrons of these cathedrals were clear-eyed and capable individuals.   And the painters who decorated the Church of St. Francis at Assisi show that the Northern lesson was not lost on them.[1]

For various reasons, financial and political, Northern art in the fourteenth and fifteenth centuries was at its best in the rich cities of Flanders.   The genius of the Flemish painters led them to prefer the small painting, derived probably from the illuminations of manuscripts, on panels to the larger paintings on walls—frescoes—which were the vogue in Italy.   The Flemish artists developed marvelous skill in copying what they saw, and no consideration of labor kept them from depicting it in almost micro-

[1] See Chapter XV.

scopic detail and with enamel-like colors. Moreover, they made
a discovery without which the art of painting would have been
shackled; they invented or rather greatly improved painting in
oils. Throughout the fourteenth century the Flemish, the French,
and also the German paintings were done usually in *tempera*—that
is, the vehicle for the colors was the white of an egg or a similar
substance. Tradition, with its customary simplification, ascribes
the invention of oil painting to the brothers Hubert and Jan Van
Eyck, whose masterpiece, the Adoration of the Lamb, was executed about 1420-1432. Vasari says it was "a most beautiful
invention" and "lit up the colors so powerfully that it gave a gloss
of itself." [1] Later the Venetian artists carried the "invention" to
great perfection. It lies at the basis of modern painting.

The art of Flanders did not stand still with the brothers Van
Eyck, but was carried to greater heights of expressiveness by such
talented painters as Roger Van der Weyden (d. 1464) and Hans
Memlinc (d. 1494). Under them it reached its goal—to equal
nature; "their force, their inspiration, reside altogether in the
tenderness, the assiduity, the skill with which they view things
and reproduce them." But unfortunately for fifteenth-century
Flemish art, "nature does not compose," and Italy stepped in and
assumed the leadership.

It is not possible to explain fully the superiority of the Italian
genius for painting and sculpture. There is an enigma, an insoluble problem, in every work of genius. It is God-given,
miraculous, inexplicable. But, clearly, circumstances had some
part. The wall spaces of the Italian Romanesque churches called
for decoration in the large. The vogue of the fresco was the
result. The fresco is water color brushed on to lime plaster before
it is dry. The lime water diffuses into the wet pigments, takes up
carbonic acid from the air, and produces carbonate of lime, which
acts as the binding material. The ancients knew the process.

The Flemish painter in *tempera* or in oil had, so to say, his
model under his eyes. The Italian frescoist, with vast surfaces
to be covered—and covered quickly, before the plaster dried—had

[1] Vasari's *Lives*.

to call upon memory and imagination; he required the constant collaboration of thought.

The first great Italian painter, Giotto (1276-1336), possessed this gift; his realism was midway between the world of ideas and the world of nature. Under his followers imitation of the master led to sterility, but Masaccio (1402-1429) again placed Florentine painting on the true road. Nor can it be doubted that Masaccio's goal was in part pointed out by the reliefs of the bronze doors or gates of Ghiberti (1378-1455), which Michelangelo a century later declared worthy to be the gates of Paradise. That goal was the conquest of the third dimension. "The first requisite of painting," says Leonardo da Vinci, "is that the bodies which it represents should appear in relief, and that the scenes which surround them with effects of distance should seem to enter into the plane in which the picture is produced by means of the three parts of perspective, namely: the diminution in the distinctness of the forms of bodies, the diminution in their size, and the diminution in their color." "This art," he also says, "resides in the play of shadows and lights, that is to say, in *chiaroscuro*."

The study of perspective and of anatomy engrossed the best minds of the Florentine artists. Leonardo da Vinci (1452-1519), the universal genius, was the theorist or expositor of this work of research, and Michelangelo (1475-1564), poet, sculptor, architect and painter, was its greatest practitioner.

Parallel with this work of scientific investigation, which is primarily intellectual, there went a steady growth of power in composition, which is primarily a matter of taste. As Burckhardt says, Italian painting "possessed, as an original gift from heaven, the tact to follow out external reality into every detail, but only so far as that the higher poetic truth should not suffer from it." The art of the Florentines—the allusion is to the fresco—"born of a decorative necessity, was, from one end of its history to the other, dominated by elegance of design and rhythm of composition" (Hourticq). The relation of the position of the part to the whole was regarded with close and separate attention, and there was developed a union of the parts, an "inevitability of arrangement," which caused earlier work to appear incoherent and arbitrary (Wölfflin). Simplification, equilibrium and expressiveness characterize Italian art at its highest point in the early sixteenth century, while reticence, dignity, distinction and beauty accompanied them hand in hand. Leonardo, Michelangelo and Raphael were the chieftains of the new art; Titian of Venice, close in spirit to the Flemish masters, stands near to the three Florentines.

Italian genius for painting, armed with science, had mastered composition and perspective, and Flemish painting, the best in northern Europe, had to adopt the Italian ways. On the other hand, the Flemish oil technique had won its victory over *tempera* and the fresco, and Flemish delicacy of perception left its mark on Italian painting. The victory of the Italians was not without its drawback, for their "superhuman humanity" impoverished the world by taking away, for a time, pleasure in the simple things of everyday life. In the restoration of that pleasure, as well as in portraiture, Northern art was to render distinguished service. That, however, lay in the future (Van Dyck, Rembrandt). In the meantime the North set to work to learn from Italy, and Albrecht Dürer (1471-1528) and Hans Holbein (1497-1543) showed how the North could learn.

The name commonly used to indicate fifteenth-century Italian art is "Early Renaissance," and for that of the succeeding early sixteenth century—the period of Leonardo, Raphael, Michelangelo and Titian—the name is "Late Renaissance." These names were bestowed long ago when scholars ignorantly thought that the blossoming of Italian sculpture and painting, in the epoch we have just considered, was due to the imitation of antique models. Of course, the antique was always a factor in medieval civilization. But Italian art like Flemish art—which had no antique remains before its eyes—was a hardy, natural growth, based on the laborious study of nature. "The painter," says Leonardo, "will produce pictures of little merit if he takes the works of others as his standard; but if he will apply himself to learn from the objects of nature he will produce good results." The names "Early Renaissance" and "Late Renaissance" are unfortunate, but they will probably stick. They will be employed to identify and not to describe. It is rare nowadays for Mr. Fletcher to be a maker of arrows; but Fletcher is his name.

RENAISSANCE ARCHITECTURE

Italy, however, did develop one art for which the adjective Renaissance is not inapt, namely, architecture. It is rather difficult for lovers of Gothic architecture, that type which stresses construction as the foundation for decoration and which flowered in Amiens, Chartres and Cologne, to do justice to the merits of Renaissance architecture. For the Italian architects of the fifteenth century, led off by Brunelleschi, turned back to the architecture of imperial Rome for inspiration and deliberately subordinated constructional frankness to esthetic results. They viewed architecture as primarily a matter of appearances, as something essentially pictorial. In this they were true to the Italian genius, for their predecessors who had attempted to domesticate Gothic architecture in the peninsula had done the same thing, and Italian Gothic is little more than a scheme of decoration. A comparison of the Gothic cathedral of Milan with that of Chartres or Paris, or of a Gothic spire with an Italian Gothic campanile, will clinch this point.

The creation of the Renaissance style of architecture came through the development of archeological interest in antiquity, and this was an outgrowth of the Revival of Learning. Brunelleschi studied the ancient monuments of Rome and in 1420 began the dome of the cathedral of Florence. This dome is the first great monument of the new style; it is the "ancestor" of the greater dome of St. Peter's which Michelangelo planned, and of the thousands of domes of modern times. The Florentine dome is higher, more majestic, more beautiful, than any antique Roman dome. Its erection was soon followed by the abandonment of Italian Gothic and by the construction of countless churches, city halls and palaces in the new style. Balance, equipoise, symmetry mark Early Renaissance architecture; dignity, majesty, power, grandeur, the Later Renaissance architecture. The Roman "orders" replaced the Gothic piers, the barrel vault the Gothic vault, the round arch the pointed arch; and columns, entablatures and pediments served for interior and exterior decoration.

Renaissance architecture underwent successive changes in Italy and the other countries of Europe—which promptly adopted it— but it holds its own today, even with revived Greek architecture, for public and private buildings. It represents order, form, symmetry, dignity and repose; and these will always be valued by a section of mankind, for they correspond to human needs.

CHAPTER XX

THE AGE OF CHARLES V
EUROPE 1500-1559

THE dominant monarch of Europe during the forty years ending in 1559 was the Hapsburg emperor, Charles V. His dominance was not based on genius, although he was talented and industrious, but rested rather on the circumstance that the accident of birth had given him sway over three groups of territories which otherwise had little in common. These were: Spain and its dependencies in Italy and the New World; the Netherlands, Luxembourg and the Free County of Burgundy; and the Hapsburg lands in Germany. Moreover, he was elected in 1519 head of Germany, that loose aggregation of many states technically known as the Holy Roman Empire. We shall survey these three groups of territories in order and then study the attempts to operate them as a unit. The survey will take some time, especially in the case of Spain, but it will be worth while.

SPAIN, TO THE UNION OF FERDINAND AND ISABELLA

Until near the close of the fifteenth century the Spanish peninsula was a relatively unobtrusive part of Christendom. It was separated from the central region by the Pyrenees and was deeply engaged in the struggle with the so-called Moors within its gates. Its chief services to the rest of Christendom had been to block the Mohammedan invasion of western Europe and to transmit the learning which had been amassed by Jewish and Moorish scholars in the Mohammedan section of the peninsula.

Ever since the early eighth century the Spaniards had warred with the Moors and, from the fastnesses of the peninsula in the northwest (the Asturias) in which the stubborn remnants of the

Visigothic population had found a refuge, they had slowly fought their way southward and organized little but growing states. They had fought one another too, but the great victory of Las Navas de Tolosa (1212), which broke the power of the Moors, was the achievement of their united strength. Almost at once, however, the Christian Spanish states reverted to their normal state of intermittent hostility among themselves, and the prosecution of the war against the Infidel ceased. But it was resumed again by the king of Castile in 1224, and a little later by the king of Aragon, and by 1266 the Moors retained only the little kingdom of Granada in the south. Granada paid tribute to Castile, and inner strife in Castile permitted the Moslem state to survive until 1492. This long period did not pass without warfare, in which the Moorish states of North Africa took a hand, sometimes against, but often with, Granada. Religious animosities, so useful in warfare, quickly died down as they had done in the Holy Land. Indeed, toward the close of the thirteenth century we find Christian legions, recruited in Aragon and many other parts of Europe, fighting in the armies of the North African Moslems, while Moorish cavalry similarly served the Christian kings in Spain, as they had served Frederick II in Italy, earlier in the same century.

The states of Christian Spain in 1266 were four—Castile and Leon, hereafter called Castile, Portugal, Aragon and Navarre. None of them was firmly united within. Aragon itself was composed of three semi-independent states. In all of them feudal turbulence and excessive local pride were the rule. It is not surprising that, with the removal of real danger from the Moslem foe, the Christian states indulged in recurrent civil and dynastic wars.

The Church in the peninsula was in a somewhat better position. Its bishops and priests had shared in the work of reconquest, strengthening the confidence of the people in divine aid and favor. As a reward the Church received large possessions. Monks and soon friars were numerous, and the strong crusading orders, of which that of Santiago (St. James) was the greatest, had broad lands and veritable armies of their own.

A peculiar inheritance which Christian Spain took over from Moorish Spain during the period of reconquest was a large population of Jews and Moors. They and their religions were tolerated—the Christian people were used to them—and their skill and industry were very important in healing the economic ravages of the wars. Each alien group lived apart in its own quarters in the towns and on the estates of the nobles and the military orders. The Jews continued to display their racial gifts in medicine, banking and commerce. The Moors excelled in agriculture and the manual trades. Save for a short outburst in the late fourteenth century, they were immune from religious persecution. To be sure, their Christian competitors disliked them for their industrious habits and their lower standards of living, but that was as far as it went until the days of Ferdinand and Isabella.

The history of Castile from the year 1266 to the accession of Queen Isabella in 1474 is a confused and melancholy chronicle of selfish baronial anarchy and civil war in which crown and Church lost dignity, worth and strength. It is a familiar story, varying only in persons and incidents from that of England and France and Germany in the later Middle Ages. One illustration must serve. In the fourteenth century Peter the Cruel and his half-brother, Henry, fought each other for the crown of Castile. Each got help from abroad, and as a result the country was ravaged by both English and French troops. The strength of the throne was further weakened by the loss of lands and governing rights with which Henry bought the support of the nobles; the higher clergy became embroiled in intrigues for one or the other claimant; and the towns were forced to form private leagues, called *brotherhoods,* to protect themselves, in part at least, from the nobles and other robbers. Similar conditions reappeared in the generation prior to the accession of Isabella. Let us leave Castile out of the picture and turn to Aragon.

Aragon after 1266 was composed of the three subkingdoms of Aragon, Catalonia and Valencia. These little kingdoms differed in their laws and institutions—indeed, the speech of Catalonia is a variation of Provençal—but they were each marked by a strong

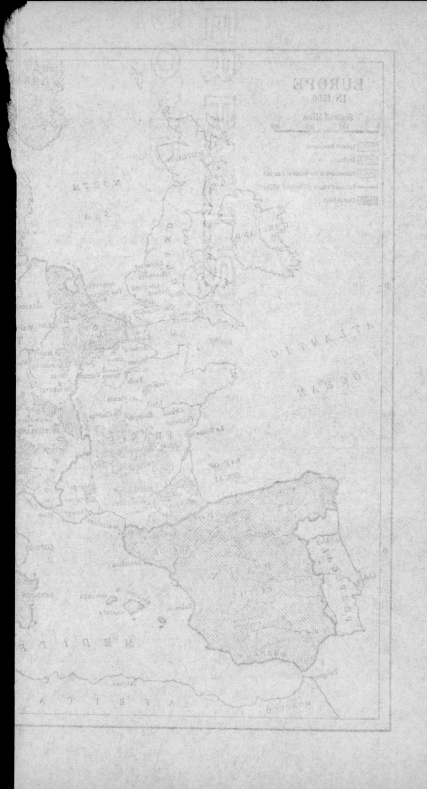

EUROPE
IN 1560

Scale of Miles

0   100   200   300

Spanish Dominions
Austrian   "
Possessions of the House of Bourbon
European empire of Charles V (1526)
Church lands

10   0

NORW

SCOTLAND

NORTH

SEA

SCHLESW

HOL

Hambu

IRELAND

Dublin

Amsterdam
The Hague
Brill
Münster

GELDERN
LAND

ENGLAND

Leicester
Bosworth
Bedford
Oxford
London
Canterbury
Winchester

Calais
Antwerp
Köln   Wart

FLANDERS
NETHER

Köln

BRABANT

ATLANTIC

English   Channel

Agincourt
Creci
Cambrai
Amiens
Crepy
Rouen
St.Denis
Paris
Vendôme

Chateau
Arras
Guise
Vervins
Reims
Chateau
Thierry
Verdun

Trier   Mainz

Luxemburg   Wor

Metz
Toul
Strasburg

Rhine

OCEAN

Chinon
Poitiers
La Rochelle
Cognac

Loire
Bourges
La Charite

Orleans

Basel

UNTERWALDEN
URI

Berne

SWITZERLAND

FRANCE

BOURBON

BURGUNDY

Geneva

BAY OF
BISCAY

SAVOY

ASTURIUS
Leon

ARMAGNAC

Montauban
Montpelier
Toulouse

Orange

Avignon

PROVENCE

Genoa

Nice

NAVARRE

Duero
Ebro

CERDAGNE

ARAGON

ROUSILLON
Marseilles

CORSICA

Alva

PORTUGAL

Lisbon

Tagus

Madrid

SPAIN

CASTILE

Las Navas
de Tolosa

Seville

Granada

GRANADA

Barcelona

CATALONIA

Valencia

BALEARIC IS.

MAJORCA

MINORCA

SARDINIA

MEDITE

Tangier

MOROCCO

Algiers

AFRICA

0

50

40

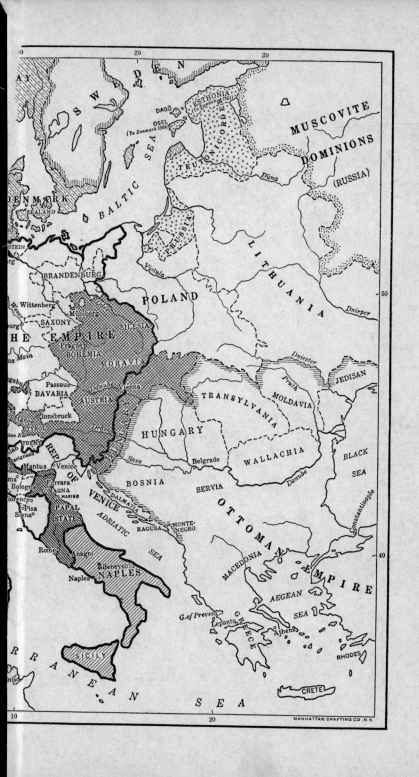

love of liberty and by a sense of the solidarity of the interests of nobles and commoners which was far beyond that to be found in Castile. At times the Aragonese kings were almost deprived of power, but long before the end of the later Middle Ages their position became strong, although by no means despotic, for the *Cortes* retained a real share in lawmaking and taxation. The most enterprising of the three subkingdoms was Catalonia. Its capital city, Barcelona, was one of the great ports of the Mediterranean, and its merchants and fleets carried on commerce on all shores of that sea. It was the Catalans who led in the expansion which must now be sketched, and they had almost to drag Valencia and Aragon along with them.

The Balearic Islands were wrenched from the Moors in the thirteenth century. Almost at once they were given to a younger son of the Aragonese king as a partly independent realm called, after the name of the largest island, the kingdom of the Majorcas. This collateral royal line, after many shiftings, petered out by the middle of the fourteenth century, and thereafter the islands were governed directly by the king of Aragon through a viceroy.

In 1282 Sicily revolted from the Angevin dynasty in a rising and massacre known as the Sicilian Vespers. Peter, king of Aragon, was then invited to assume the Sicilian crown and defend the Sicilians against the ousted Charles of Anjou, king of Naples, who was backed by the papacy. Peter had married Constance, granddaughter of Frederick II, the Hohenstaufen. Moreover, Peter brought with him a strong Aragonese fleet. The Angevin, even with papal aid, could not dislodge Peter or the younger son who succeeded him in Sicily, the elder son becoming king of Aragon. The Sicilians were jealous of their independence and, chiefly out of deference to their wishes, they were allowed a collateral Aragonese dynasty of their own from 1295 to 1409. They then passed directly under the king of Aragon and were governed by his viceroy, although the Sicilian parliament retained a share in the government of the island.

Sardinia came for a few years under the control of Aragon in 1326, when the Pisans and Genoese, who had expelled the Saracen

ruling class in the eleventh century, were in turn displaced. But
the grip of Aragon was soon relaxed and the natives and the
Italians divided control between them. In 1421, however,
Alfonso the Magnanimous (1416-1458), one of the greatest
kings of Aragon, regained the island which was thereafter governed by a viceroy, while a parliament was set up to represent the
people and facilitate the voting of taxes.

The events which enabled Alfonso the Magnanimous to add
the kingdom of Naples to his other possessions are involved and
can be sketched only in a very simplified form. The Angevin
dynasty of Naples had steadily degenerated and was now represented by Queen Joanna II. She was much married but childless, and, in order to gain Alfonso's aid against rivals, she adopted
him as her heir shortly after he had gained Sardinia. He came
to Naples, drove off the rival claimants and—the queen revoked
the adoption! It was renewed and the queen died in 1435 after
again revoking it. Nevertheless, Alfonso claimed the throne.
But the Genoese fleet defeated his fleet and carried him captive
to Filippo Maria Visconti, tyrant of Milan and overlord of Genoa.
Shrewd politician that he was, Filippo came to the conclusion that
it would be better to have Alfonso on the throne of Naples than
his French rival, René of Anjou, another of Joanna's "adopted"
heirs, since the French would be marching their troops through
Milanese territory to reach Naples, while Alfonso's fleets would
enable him to send troops from Aragon to Naples by sea. Accordingly, Filippo released Alfonso, who by 1443 won complete possession of Naples. Filippo, dying in 1447, appointed Alfonso his
principal successor, but Alfonso did not accept the dangerous be-
quest. Alfonso, enamoured of life in southern Italy, did not go
back to Aragon but ruled it and the rest of his empire, as it may
be fairly called, from Naples and Sicily. He died in 1458, leaving
Naples as a separate kingdom to his illegitimate son Ferrante
(1458-1494). The remainder of the Aragonese dominions—
Aragon, the Balearic Islands, Sardinia and Sicily—passed to
Alfonso's brother John.

The financial strain imposed upon the homeland in winning and
defending these extensive territories was severe. Concurrently

there were wars in Spain as well. In 1452 the *Cortes* of Aragon protested to Alfonso: "Aragon, during these seven years, has expended four hundred thousand florins in the ransom of prisoners alone; all industry, all commerce is at a standstill. . . . For such manifold evils, the country can find but one remedy—and that is the presence of its king." [1] But it is more difficult to stop territorial expansion than to start it, as Spain was subsequently to learn.

THE DEVELOPMENT OF ABSOLUTISM UNDER FERDINAND AND ISABELLA

The conspiracies, wars and revolts which immediately preceded the marriage of Isabella of Castile to Ferdinand of Aragon in 1469 will be passed over. Isabella was queen of Castile (1474-1504) and Ferdinand was king of Aragon (1479-1516). Their kingdoms were, and remained, as independent of each other as are Norway and Sweden today. Each retained its own laws, finances, tariffs, *Cortes,* and other institutions. The marriage, however, paved the way for a somewhat closer union of the two countries when the two crowns passed to Charles, their grandson, and his successors. For although the kingdoms were not united, Ferdinand and Isabella were.

The two young rulers supplemented each other almost perfectly. Isabella was pious, resolute, courageous, generous and intolerant. Ferdinand was worldly, persistent, parsimonious and crafty. Isabella was especially devoted to internal affairs; Ferdinand, to foreign affairs.

Their first task was to restore order in Castile, the larger and more disorganized of the two kingdoms. Here the nobility were, as so often, the chief offenders. The towns of Castile had possessed wide powers of self-government ever since the early wars against the Moor, and to them Isabella turned. The *Cortes* of Castile, to which nobles and clergy were now summoned for almost the last time (since they paid no taxes), except on ceremonious occasions, was called together in 1476 and voted that

[1] See R. B. Merriman, *Rise of the Spanish Empire.*

the old league of the towns should be revived and put under royal direction. It was given the name of *The Holy Brotherhood* and at the expense of everyone, lay and clerical, it raised strong bodies of archers in each district, whose business it was to run down in successive "waves" all brigands throughout Castile. Once captured, the bandits were given swift and terrifying punishment in "courts" of the Brotherhood. Isabella herself, at the head of an army, rode through the land and leveled hostile castles. From the city of Seville alone four thousand malefactors are said to have taken flight as Isabella drew near. The severities of the Brotherhood and the queen helped to restore order, and within a few years the ordinary courts were able to preserve the peace. The Aragonese Brotherhood functioned in a similar fashion, from 1488 to 1510.

Another important step in establishing order and strengthening the royal power—kings usually believed that these were the same thing—was the gaining of control over the Castilian crusading orders with their wealth and their troops. Isabella daringly succeeded in this by persuading the pope to allow King Ferdinand to be elected to the grand-masterships as they fell vacant. Henceforth, instead of being sources of strength to the nobility, these military orders augmented the power and revenues of the crown. Of course the crusading orders of Aragon maintained their independence to a much later time.

Isabella also took measures to cleanse the clergy from the consequences of the period of anarchy. During the old wars against the Moors, the crown of Castile had enjoyed wide power of nomination to Church offices, and these powers were now revived and extended, with the acquiescence of the papacy and with the counsel of the learned but inflexible Cardinal Ximenes. Isabella nominated good and learned men, and the morality, learning and zeal of the Spanish clergy were gradually established, for a similar plan was later adopted in Aragon. The Spanish Reformation, as this improvement was called, also enhanced the authority of the monarchs.

In reforming the clergy, policy and religion joined hands. Isabella was most devout. And she realized that to reawaken "in the breasts of all Spaniards the mystic exaltation and spiritual pride that gave strength to their arms against the Moor in the heroic days of old" would help to weld the people together. Accordingly, she resolved to reorganize the machinery for checking heresy among the Christian population. There were many Christians of Jewish and Moorish extraction whose fidelity to their new faith left much to be desired.

The medieval Inquisition had entered Spain in the thirteenth century. It was under episcopal control, and the bishops were closely connected with the nobility. In 1481 the monarchs set up for both kingdoms the more efficient Spanish Inquisition, which was under royal control in all its secular aspects. It employed torture, as did most medieval courts, ecclesiastical and lay. It conducted its trials in secret and thus added the horror of the unknown. The property of the convicted heretic went to the royal treasury. The ruling of the Inquisition that his property was forfeited, not from the date of his conviction, but from the time when he had become a heretic, was logical but unwise, for no one could be sure that the contracts he entered into might not be invalidated by the subsequent conviction of the other party.

The new Inquisition was at first unpopular. It was also more aggressive in Castile than in Aragon, where nobles and merchants stood up for the supremacy of their own courts. Its earliest prosecutions were directed against those converted Jews whose Christianity was suspected. Professed Jews and Moors were of course free from molestation by the Inquisition. In the long run it exercised surveillance over every Christian Spaniard, including even the highest of the nobility, and that probably pleased the middle class. Its popularity grew rapidly after the renewal of the war against Granada when racial and religious differences were deliberately stressed, and it was soon established in Sicily and Sardinia, and later in America. Its activities promoted—perhaps created—Spanish religious pride and intolerance. These were a heavy price to pay for a sense of national solidarity and the growth of the royal power, even were the terrible fate of thousands who perished in the flames left out of the reckoning.

The independence of the little Moslem kingdom of Granada

was now to end. Its population did not exceed half a million. Its agriculture, industry, art and learning were still at a high level compared with Christian Spain, and its mountain defenses were strong. Queen Isabella was determined that the power and prestige of the monarchy should be displayed and enhanced by completing the age-long "Christian Recovery" of Spain. The war against Granada lasted ten years (1482-1492). The Moors got some help from Africa, but the Castilian fleet barred extensive aid, while Christian volunteers flocked to the Spanish army from all parts of Europe. The war was shortened by the revolt of the son of the king of Granada and by the offer of very liberal terms of surrender. The Moors were guaranteed possession of their property and the enjoyment of their religion, language, laws and customs, and laid down their arms. The conquest of Granada created a considerable sensation in Europe. It was some compensation for the loss of Constantinople to the Turks (1453).

The chances that Isabella would keep her promise to her new Moorish subjects cannot have looked bright in March, 1492. For then, a short three months after the surrender of Granada, a royal decree was issued giving every unconverted Jew four months to be baptized or quit the land. The Inquisition could be trusted to look after the converted Jews. The expulsions were carried out with incalculable suffering and much loss of life, and they deprived Spain of about 200,000 industrious people,[1] whom she could ill afford, economically, to lose. It was a terrible deed. The survivors took refuge in Africa, Italy, and especially in Turkey, where some Jewish settlements speak Castilian until this day. It cannot be doubted that Isabella was responsible for the cruel deed, that Ferdinand did not favor it, and that the anti-Semitism of the Christian competitors of the more industrious and successful Jews made it easier for the government to put its program through. What it cost Spain economically cannot be reckoned.

Heaven's favor, however, seemed to rest upon Queen Isabella. In October, 1492, Columbus, her agent, discovered the new lands beyond the Atlantic and thus opened up extensive regions to

[1] The expulsions from Sardinia and Sicily are left out of this reckoning.

Spanish exploitation, missionary zeal and settlement. In 1494 Pope Alexander VI, who was of Spanish extraction, conferred upon Ferdinand and Isabella the high title of "the Catholic Kings," which they and their successors proudly bore.

The turn of the Moors of Granada soon came. For eight years they enjoyed toleration, and gentleness won over many of them to Christianity. Then the great Cardinal Ximenes went to Granada and employed terrorism to hasten conversions. This provoked revolts which were put down by the army, and Isabella was persuaded that the Moors, by rebelling, had forfeited the toleration which she had already violated, thus precipitating the revolts! In 1502 a royal decree gave the Moors of Castile two months and a half to accept Christianity or leave the land of their birth. Most of them were tillers of the soil and were therefore less exposed to popular hostility than the more urban Jews had been. As the Moors could not possibly get out within the allotted time, the specified ports of departure being too far away, they turned Christian to save their lives. And the Inquisition, of course, had jurisdiction over them after they underwent baptism. The Moors of Aragon enjoyed toleration until 1525.

The other measures which Ferdinand and Isabella took for increasing the power of the monarchy and laying the foundations for absolute control may be briefly summarized. First, as to Castile. A comprehensive act of resumption was passed by the *Cortes* in 1480, restoring to the crown the immense estates which had been given to, or taken by, the nobility during the period of disorder. The royal council was reorganized and other councils were created in which men of humble birth were given the controlling places. The share of the *Cortes* in the government was reduced virtually to the voting of taxes, while its subservience was augmented by bringing the cities, which appointed the members other than the nobles and clergy, under the direction of royal agents. In Aragon the plans were similar, but they were put through very slowly, time and the example of the larger kingdom being relied upon to bring the stubborn people into line. The royal council of Aragon had some members who also sat in the

Castilian council, so that the two kingdoms might after a fashion march together.

In spite of the vast improvement in the economic life of Spain which resulted from the measures taken by "the Catholic Kings," the kingdoms were not in a position to finance, without a heavy strain, an aggressive foreign policy. Spain had a population of about seven millions, but there was little manufacturing. The crown tried to develop the weaving of wool and silk fabrics which had flourished in the hands of the Jews and Moors, but even with the aid of royal favor the country did not weave enough to supply its own needs. Its exports were almost exclusively raw materials—iron, copper, wool, silk, wine, oil and fruits. Except in favorable seasons, considerable grain had to be imported for food. Fortunately Sicily produced a large surplus of it, and as long as Spain held Sicily her food supply was safe. The prosperity of the sheep-grazers, who were organized in a great gild, was some offset to this state of affairs, especially as their contributions to the royal income were heavy. Moreover, the great upland region of Castile was better suited to pasturage than to agriculture, so that the damage inflicted on agriculture by enclosures was not nearly so great as it was in England. The royal income from taxes, export and import tariffs, feudal dues, and the *alcabala* (a ten-per-cent tax on sales) was very much larger in the latter part of the reigns of "the Catholic Kings" than it had been in the first part. The product of the American mines, on which the government levied the royal *fifth* (a share of twenty per cent), did not figure in the receipts until the succeeding reign. Wars could be financed by Spain—as by other countries—only by means of loans. It is estimated that the interest on the Spanish debt at the accession of Charles V (1516) amounted to half the royal income. What the state of the finances of Spain would be under the ever-warring Charles must be left for the present to the imagination.

On the other hand, Ferdinand and Isabella had certain important assets, after the reduction of Granada, in addition to improved finances. First, they enjoyed a growing national consciousness and solidarity, based in part upon recent successes and a strong belief in the special favor of God. Secondly, their country supplied excellent material for foot soldiers. There was a large element of the Spanish population that was accustomed to a hardy open-air life in the changeable climate of the pastoral uplands and, as a consequence, was gifted with a special capacity for enduring the hardships of war. As there were no rapidly-growing manufactures to absorb their energies and as the Moors and Jews had placed a certain stigma on labor in field and workshop, many of these Christians were available and willing to serve as infantrymen. The Spanish infantry was not, in 1492, the equal of the Swiss, which was the finest in Europe; but by the close of Ferdinand's reign (1516) the Spanish had learned the new Swiss infantry tactics and were at least as good as their teachers. Ten years later, just before the Reformation broke the unity of Switzerland and curtailed the availability of its surplus population for foreign service, the Spanish infantry probably ranked first. But this is anticipating. A third important asset of "the Catholic kings," especially valuable in case of war in Italy, was the possession of the Balearic Islands, Sardinia and Sicily. Some money could be raised in each of them, and Sicily afforded a superior base for operations in the peninsula.

THE FOREIGN POLICY OF FERDINAND AND ISABELLA

In turning to the foreign policy of Ferdinand and Isabella it is advisable for the reader to bear in mind that in their day and long afterward kings and other rulers were still in a state of free competition, unembarrassed by any effective public opinion that one prince ought to respect the rights or possessions of a neighbor or that peoples have the right to choose their rulers. Moreover, states still passed, together with their populations, in the same way as a piece of land or other property—that is, by transfer from one ruler to another, or in accordance with the laws of descent. The consequences for the people might be very distasteful, but acquiescence was the rule. By the close of the fifteenth century the kings of France and England, as well as of Spain, had got the better of their feudal nobility and consequently were able to embark on much more extensive undertakings—especially wars—than their predecessors. Their states were now monarchical rather than feudal, and at the same time the growth of trade and industry made it more easy for them through loans or taxation to finance these undertakings. Of course there was honor among kings as well as among thieves, but at best treaties were fragile things in the period we are now to review. Perhaps that is why so many of them were made. As fortune willed it, France and not Spain opened the series of great wars which began in 1494. If France had held back, Spain would probably have had the responsibility.

In foreign affairs Ferdinand was the senior partner, while Isabella dominated in domestic and colonial affairs. When she died in 1504, Ferdinand controlled in all these spheres. Their foreign policies ranged all over Europe, searching for helpful alliances by marriages or otherwise, which would bring gain or ward off danger. Actually the policies, alliances and marriages formed a very complex fabric; but it will be easier for the reader (and the authors) to tear it apart and study separately what "the Catholic Kings" wanted, how they gained their ends, and how they married off their children.

Ferdinand and Isabella, having established their power at home, desired to gain (Ferdinand would have said *to recover*) Navarre, Cerdagne and Roussillon, and Naples. Navarre, the little kingdom astride the Pyrenees, but mostly on the Spanish side of these mountains, commanded the important western passes or gateways into Spain or France. In the thirteenth century Navarre had fallen to a French dynasty. In the fifteenth century King John, the father of Ferdinand, ruled Navarre in the name of his French wife and, after her death, in the name of their children. When King John died (1479), his son Ferdinand, the offspring of a second marriage, succeeded him in the territories of Aragon but not in Navarre, which went to a daughter of the first marriage, who had become the wife of a French prince. Cerdagne and Roussillon, ancient outposts of Aragon, protected the weak spot between the eastern end of the Pyrenees and the sea, through which so many invaders had passed. Ferdinand's father had transferred these two provinces in mortgage to the ambitious Louis XI of France, to cover the cost of French aid in repressing a fierce and prolonged revolt of the Catalans. Naples had been won by Alfonso the Magnanimous, whose principal heir had been the father of Ferdinand. Neither he nor his father had ever been satisfied that the transfer of Naples to the illegitimate Ferrante had been fair to them. The strength of the claims of Ferdinand to these three territories may be figured out by the reader. Probably "the Catholic Kings" would have been wiser if they had kept out of the Italian peninsula, but the same is true of many others before and after Ferdinand. There was work for them to do in the Spanish peninsula and in America, not to mention North Africa with its Moslem states and pirates. But they decided otherwise.

THE INVASIONS OF ITALY BY FRANCE AND SPAIN

The recovery of Cerdagne and Roussillon came as a gift. Charles VIII of France, being head of a strongly-organized and wealthy state and being romantic rather than realistic, resolved (1492-1493) to seize Naples as heir to the Angevin claimant. His native country had unsettled frontiers with Spain and with the Netherlands and the Germanies. But Italy lured him on. So he bought the acquiescence of Spain in his Italian adventure by giving back Cerdagne and Roussillon without so much as mentioning the mortgage money. He similarly secured the acquiescence of Maximilian of Austria (later emperor) and his son, Archduke Philip, heir to the Burgundian lands and therefore lord of several provinces of the Netherlands, by restoring the Free County of Burgundy and parts of the Netherlands seized by Louis XI in 1477. The neutrality of Henry VII of England was likewise purchased with 745,000 gold crowns. Did Ferdinand of Spain really intend that Charles VIII should get Naples or was it his idea that Charles should shatter the dynasty of Ferrante, to the subsequent advantage of Spain? We suspect, but we do not know.

Charles VIII's artillery was the best in Europe; his cavalry was also the best, and the bulk of his infantry was Swiss, also the best. Ludovico Sforza, duke of Milan, had reasons of his own for fearing Ferrante of Naples and his son. So he agreed to let Charles VIII pass through Milan and have the services of the powerful Genoese fleet, the French fleet in the Mediterranean being almost nonexistent. Charles VIII led his army across the Alps in the autumn of 1494. All went according to plan. Florence gave him fortresses and money, Pope Alexander VI became his friend, the Neapolitan frontier was crossed, and by March 22, 1495, the last fortresses had been reduced by the French artillery. It was a striking revelation of French efficiency to all Europe.

In the meantime, during the winter of 1494-1495, Spanish diplomacy was at work building up a league to expel the French from Naples, and Ferdinand was making ready heavy reënforcements for Sicily. On March 31, 1495, the league was constituted at Venice. The signatory powers were the pope, Maximilian, Spain, Ludovico of Milan, and Venice. The latter ally was particularly useful since its war fleet was very strong. Before this formidable combination could get going, Charles VIII hurried home with part of his troops to carry him through (summer of 1495). Since the forces he had left behind could not get reënforcements or supplies by land or by sea, they had finally to surrender to the Spanish-Sicilian troops and the Venetians. The dynasty of Ferrante (he himself had died, 1494) was restored, but only nominally, for Venice held the ports on the Adriatic and Ferdinand many of the other strongholds in the Neapolitan kingdom.

In 1499-1500 the history of 1494 was repeated with variations. Louis XII of France, with the aid of Venice and the acquiescence of the other powers, seized the duchy of Milan, Venice receiving a share. In 1501-1502 Louis XII and Ferdinand of Spain overran Naples with the exception of the ports held by Venice, and divided it between them. But there was "trouble in delimiting the frontier" between their shares and in a new war Ferdinand expelled the French and thus *recovered* Naples (1504). It constituted one more in his string of kingdoms and was governed by a viceroy without a parliament.

In 1508-1509 Pope Julius II organized a league including Maximilian, the French (ensconced in Milan), himself and others, and attacked Venice. Venetian expansion on the mainland during the fifteenth century had been carried out largely at the expense of Milan and the Papal States. It had been due primarily to Venice's efforts to get a secure food supply. As it was, Venice was still compelled to import much grain, chiefly from Sicily and the Turkish lands, but there was always the danger that these supplies might be shut off by the governments of these countries. The attack of 1508-1509 was very serious but the capital was safe since the fleet protected it, and Venice bought off her enemies with territorial concessions and turned over the Adriatic ports of Naples to Ferdinand.

In 1511 Pope Julius II, Spain, Venice, the Swiss, Maximilian and England joined in a war against France. England and the Burgundians attacked in the region of the Netherlands, Spain overran Navarre (*recovered* 1512), and the Swiss occupied the duchy of Milan (1513).

In 1515 the French and the Venetians combined against the Swiss in Milan. King Francis I of France with his hired German infantry, or *Landsknechts,* defeated a Swiss army at Marignano and about the same time the Swiss governments concluded, very wisely, that they would give up the idea of further expansion into Italy and rest content with the gains they had made in Ticino and elsewhere in 1510 and 1512. The French got Milan, save parts given to Venice, and peace was made all around.

The details—much simplified—of the wars that raged from 1494 to 1516 have been given, not to bore, but to instruct the reader. They are designed to suggest the faithlessness, opportunism, greed and lack of well-considered policy which characterized most of the rulers of the time. They furnish part of the material employed by Machiavelli in *The Prince.* The major net results of all these wars are very simple, if we disregard the destruction of life and treasure. Spain got Cerdagne and Roussillon, Naples and Navarre; the Hapsburgs recovered the Free County of Burgundy; France secured Milan. In Italy, Venice, through her sea power and her commercial wealth, and the Papal States, through the spiritual prestige of the papacy, maintained their independence; but the other states existed only on sufferance. Of all the participants the only one that had experienced no set-back was the shrewd, calculating, unscrupulous Ferdinand of Spain. He had rounded out the home territory of Spain and had established her dominion in the southern half of Italy. The matter of the succession to his crowns and that of Isabella must now be taken up, for he died in 1516.

THE ACCESSION OF THE BURGUNDIAN, CHARLES V

The marriages which Ferdinand and Isabella arranged for their five children, like most royal marriages, were part and parcel of the diplomatic efforts of the parents to secure allies or neutral friends in war and peace. The diplomatic plans must be omitted,[1] which is a pity. Ferdinand and Isabella married their only son John, and their second daughter Joanna, respectively, to Margaret and Philip, children of Maximilian of Austria and his wife, Mary of Burgundy. Isabella, the eldest of the daughters, and, after her death, Maria, the third daughter, married King Emmanuel of Portugal. Finally Catherine, the youngest child, wedded Arthur, Prince of Wales, and some years after his death became the wife of his brother, Henry VIII of England.

Unfortunately for the hopes of Ferdinand and Isabella, their son John died in 1497 without offspring, and the only child of Isabella of Portugal followed his mother to the grave in 1500. These were staggering blows for they left Joanna's eldest son, Charles, next in the succession after his mother. The son of Isabella of Portugal, if he had lived, could have been given the Spanish point of view; but a Hapsburg, a foreigner, to get the thrones of Spain! That was gall and wormwood to Ferdinand and Isabella. But there was no help for it. The grand old queen died in 1504; the son-in-law, Philip, took over the administration

[1] See R. B. Merriman, *Rise of the Spanish Empire,* ii, chapters XIX, XX, for details.

of Castile jointly with his father-in-law, on behalf of Queen
Joanna, for a few months; but, to Ferdinand's relief, Philip died
in 1506 and Joanna lost her reason almost entirely,[1] so that the
old king ruled Castile as well as his Aragonese dominions until
his death in 1516. He was succeeded by Charles, eldest son of
Joanna and Philip, born in 1500.

With the accession of Charles V—to give him his later imperial
title—Spanish policy ceased to have an independent existence.
His Spanish grandparents had rounded out the homelands of
Spain and had brought it to an international position where it
might follow its own foreign and domestic interests. All that was
now done with. For Charles had also other grandparents, other
lands, and other interests. His policy included Spain; but it was
not—at least for many years—a Spanish policy.

THE BURGUNDIAN DOMINIONS OF CHARLES V

As grandson of Mary of Burgundy, Charles was lord of the
Free County of Burgundy and of Luxembourg and many other
provinces of the Netherlands. These Burgundian lands, as they
were all called, had a population of about three and a quarter
millions. Flanders and Brabant drew much wealth from industry, especially from weaving, and the city of Antwerp was just
beginning its astonishing growth as the center of the spice trade
and of banking in the North. Holland also was gaining increased
wealth, especially from the carrying trade in which her fleets
were soon to be the best and most flourishing in Northern waters.
Each province of the Burgundian lands had its own Estates or
parliamentary bodies of a medieval type, and its own rights to
some voice in its own government. But in practice Charles, like
his predecessors, was able to get a large revenue from the rich
provinces of the Netherlands and to use it about as he chose.
The desire of the Netherlanders was for peace and prosperity,
especially for peace with France, one of their best customers.
Toward England they were not so friendly, for the English were

[1] She lived until 1555.

attempting to build up a weaving industry of their own which would curtail the export of the fine English wools to Flanders and Brabant.

THE AUSTRIAN DOMINIONS OF CHARLES V

The third group of Charles's possessions was the Austrian territories, which descended to him and his brother Ferdinand jointly on the death of their grandfather, Maximilian, in 1519. In 1522 Charles transferred his share in the administration of these lands to Ferdinand, but Ferdinand had to play in the main to Charles's hand. In 1526, after the battle of Mohacz, Ferdinand secured Bohemia, Moravia and Silesia. These gains brought the total population of the Austrian lands up to something over five millions. There was little commerce or industry in them, however, and it was hard to get their Estates to vote money and harder to get them to pay it. The "hereditary enemies" of the Austrian government were the Turks and the Venetians, the former advancing up the valley of the Danube, and the latter seeking to push the Austrians away from the northeastern shores of the Adriatic.

The election of Charles to the throne of Germany in 1519 increased his prestige, if it did not enlarge his territories. The candidacy of Charles had been urged upon the German electors by Maximilian in his last days, and he had informed his grandson that it would cost him 450,000 gold florins to secure the votes of the electors. The rival candidacy of the young Francis I of France (king, 1515-1547), however, raised the price so that Charles had to borrow over 845,000 gold florins from German and Italian bankers and use armed pressure upon the electors [1] before he could gain the election. The Hapsburgs were notoriously poor, but Charles's credit as ruler of Spain and the Burgundian lands was good. The powers which went with the imperial office (the actual title of emperor was conferred by the papacy in 1530) were chiefly latent. But something might be made out of them and, as Germany had a population of twenty millions

[1] See *American Historical Review,* January, 1926, pages 307-309.

with over sixty wealthy cities and much foot-soldier material (*Landsknechts*), the position of emperor was not to be despised.

THE POLICIES OF CHARLES V, TO THE PEACE OF CAMBRAY

The attempt to characterize Charles's policy will be made at the close of this chapter. The interests of his diverse realms could not be brought under a single program, except that of peace, and that was not a sixteenth-century program., The Spaniards wanted to crush the North African pirate states and desired friendship with England as a protection against France. The Netherlanders favored peace with France and stiff measures against the English. The Burgundian politicians were resolved to regain the duchy of Burgundy, and that meant war with France. These simple illustrations suggest that Charles would have difficulty in getting team-work out of his heterogeneous dominions. Each major member strove to set the direction of his policy. It is well to remember, too, that he was born in 1500 and had never been out of the Netherlands till he went to Spain in the autumn of 1517 to take over the actual government of the Spanish realms.

On his first visit Charles made a poor impression on his Spanish subjects. He was a gawky boy, not yet sure of himself, and his train of extravagant Burgundian nobles, eager for rich offices and pensions which Charles gave them, strengthened the Spaniards in their hearty dislike of foreigners. This dislike included Charles himself, who as yet spoke no Spanish. The various *Cortes* acknowledged him as king, to be sure, but grudgingly and only jointly with his mother Joanna, who lived in Spain and might, they hoped, recover her reason. Charles's urgent pressure for votes of money aroused the opposition of the *Cortes,* who complained that their rights were not recognized, and when he left in the spring of 1520 to be crowned as king of the Romans and future emperor, revolts broke out in Castile, Aragon and Majorca. There was similar trouble in Navarre and Sicily.

The revolt of the *comuneros,* or burghers, in Castile (1520-1522) was led by the great cities, and the regent whom Charles had left in charge was powerless against it. The rebels protested against foreigners and arbitrary taxation and sought to regularize their control of affairs by securing the approval of Queen Joanna. They got possession of her but she was sane, or insane, enough to refuse to sign any papers. Moreover, the rebel program was vague and the leaders fell out with one another when they got the ascendency. Gradually the nobles who were faithful to Charles recovered their courage and secured arms, and after a number of sanguinary battles the government of the absent king was reëstablished. It was a narrow squeak.

The risings in Aragon, Majorca and Sicily were not linked up with the revolt in Castile. They rested in part upon dislike of the foreigner, and in part upon the desire of the unprivileged classes to get control of the governments. The risings were stubborn but not very intelligent, and in the end the regents and the nobility regained the upper hand. The trouble in Navarre was caused by the effort of the ousted French dynasty, the Albrets, to regain their kingdom. The people of Navarre disliked their Spanish governor, and when the French king, although tardily, gave Henri d'Albret an army of some 12,000 men, he overran the whole of the little kingdom in the space of three weeks (May, 1521). Unfortunately for him, the invasion was not made until the *comuneros* were on their last legs, and when their revolt was over the Spanish troops pushed on into Navarre and drove the Albrets back into France with a crushing defeat (July, 1521).

The attack of Henri d'Albret on Navarre had been preceded by a somewhat similar raid, countenanced by the French king, upon Luxembourg (March, 1521). These aggressions were soon countered by an invasion of Milan, from the south, by Spanish and Italian troops in the service of Charles V. Thus began the first war between Francis I and Charles V, on "three fronts." It is easy to tell "what they fought each other for." The two young kings had been rival candidates for the imperial crown and Charles had won the election; Charles was determined to regain the lost duchy of Burgundy; Francis desired to "recover" Navarre. The inherited rivalry in Italy and the belligerent spirit of the youthful monarchs did the rest. The results of the attack on Navarre have already been noted. The war on the frontiers

of the Netherlands was a seesaw.   In short, Italy was the main
theater of the struggle.   It would be useless to follow the Italian
campaigns in detail or to cite the reasons which led the Italian
states, including the Papal States, and also King Henry VIII of
England, to take one side and then to switch to the other.   Nor
would it be worth while to learn how Milan changed hands over
half a dozen times in about as many years.   It will be more
profitable to notice some of the high lights of the struggle.

In 1525 the French army, led by Francis I in person, was be-
sieging Pavia.   Francis had hired Swiss and German infantry,
and Charles's forces were augmented by heavy drafts of German
infantry sent down by his brother Ferdinand.   When these armies
clashed, the French were overwhelmingly defeated and their king
was captured (battle of Pavia).   It was a great shock to European opinion, which had expected Francis to win another Marignano.   The captive Francis was taken to Spain, where Charles
resided continuously from 1522 to 1529, and he secured his
freedom only by signing the treaty of Madrid (1526), in which
he promised to surrender the duchy of Burgundy to Charles and
renounced his claims to Milan and Naples.   Once free, Francis
repudiated the treaty and renewed the war.

The Italian princes, including the pope, swung over to the
French side; and Charles's troops, which included a strong contingent of German Lutheran *Landsknechts,* sacked Rome with
somewhat more than the customary barbarity (1527).   Encouraged by the resulting outcry throughout most of Europe outside
of Spain, French troops mastered Milan and overran most of
Naples.   But the capital city, Naples, held out although it was
besieged on the land side and blockaded at sea by the Genoese
fleet.   There was no hope of saving Naples; and then, almost
in a trice, the tables were turned, for the Genoese fleet swung
over to the imperial side and shut off French reënforcements and
supplies so completely that the French army in Naples had to
surrender.   It was Andrea Doria, the Genoese admiral, who thus
decided the war.   He was well paid in money and rank, and the
independence of his native land, Genoa, was guaranteed him by
Charles.   He remained faithful to his new employers until the

day of his death (1560) and assured to Spain the mastery of the Mediterranean, at least so far as the Christian powers were concerned. After their defeat in Naples, the French made another fierce attack on Milan, and when it failed they were ready for a settlement, which was embodied in the Peace of Cambray (1529).

By this treaty France gave up her claims in Italy and her feudal rights over Flanders and Artois, while Charles renounced his claims to the duchy of Burgundy. The peace left Charles in control of Milan and in effect master of Italy.

To Italy he now came (1529), and next year he was crowned emperor by the pope he had beaten so completely. He then proceeded to Germany, where, at the Diet of Augsburg (1530), he laid down the law to the Lutheran princes and set a date for their return to the mother Church. The Lutheran princes organized a league of defense and joined hands with the enemies of the Hapsburgs in Hungary, but before battle could be joined Charles hastened to make a peaceful settlement with them so that he might have their aid in stemming the advance of Solyman, the Turkish sultan, against Vienna (1532). The Turk had saved the Lutherans.

THE WARS OF CHARLES AGAINST FRENCH AND TURKS
(1529-1544)

It was one of the misfortunes of Charles V that his reign coincided with that of Solyman the Magnificent, the most talented and aggressive of the sultans of Turkey (1520-1566). Selim, his predecessor, had conquered Syria and Egypt. Solyman directed his arms against Persia and also against Hungary. His empire was lacking in the technical, mechanical skill required for the production of efficient artillery, but he got some of it from Christian renegades who appreciated high and regular pay, for he had ample revenues derived in part from the sale of Anatolian grain to the Venetians. His armies were not the equals of those of the West, man for man; his artillery was inferior, and his navy had to have superior numbers before it would clash with the Christian armadas.

Solyman's advance into Hungary synchronized with the opening of the first struggle between Charles V and Francis I. The Turk captured Belgrade in 1521 and destroyed King Louis II of Bohemia and Hungary at the battle of Mohacz (1526). By previous agreement, Charles V's brother Ferdinand, who ruled the Austrian dominions of the Hapsburgs, succeeded to the crowns of King Louis, but in Hungary he got little more than a disputed royal title, for Solyman took under his protection as a vassal the Hungarian noble, John Zapolya, who was set up by the majority of the Hungarian magnates as their prince. As patron and over-lord of Zapolya, Solyman advanced against Vienna in 1529 and again in 1532. He was now the direct foe of the Hapsburgs.

To lessen the pressure upon Vienna, in 1532 Charles V sent Andrea Doria to ravage the coasts of Greece. Doria won a great victory over the Turkish fleet, although he did not follow it up. The victory did, indeed, make matters worse for Charles since it led Solyman to find a resourceful admiral. The man he chose was a Christian renegade, Kheireddin Barbarossa, the great Al-gerian freebooter, who now linked the fortunes of his pirate Moslem state with those of the sultan, whose grand admiral he became in 1533. In all the later wars of Charles, Kheireddin proved a worthy foe of Doria. He could be defeated but he could not be vanquished.

The emergence of Kheireddin Barbarossa was indirectly to be credited to the Spaniards, who had overthrown his brother in a well-fought action in North Africa (1518). In the period 1521-1529, when the energies of Spain were engrossed with the war against France, the Spanish posts in North Africa were on the defensive, and Kheireddin built up his naval strength. When Charles V, out of gratitude to God after the battle of Pavia, re-voked the toleration of the Moors in Aragon, Kheireddin ravaged the coasts of Spain and succored groups of his co-religionists. And now, in 1533, he had taken over the command of the Turkish navy. The next year he celebrated his accession by giving the Italian coasts a thorough ravaging and by taking Tunis from a smaller Moslem rival. The new port established him within striking distance of Sicily. In 1535 Charles V led an inter-national armada—from which France, however, held aloof—

against Tunis and captured it. It was a notable victory. But the pirate chief escaped to Algiers.

His defeat had a less satisfactory side. For it led Solyman at last to consent to the proposal of the king of France for joint operations against the emperor. The Turk and the Most Christian King now united (February, 1536) against their common enemy, the Holy Roman Emperor. France now had in Kheireddin a counterweight for Andrea Doria, and the sultan's grand admiral had the Mediterranean harbors of France for revictualing and for refuge. It is obvious that the alliance of France and the Turk presaged a renewal of the war which had been ended in the Peace of Cambray (1529).

The renewed war with France (1536-1538) was not desired by the emperor. His finances were in bad shape. They would have been even worse if gold had not begun to trickle in from Mexico and Peru. He wanted no war with any Christian ruler. His capture of Tunis inclined him, rather, to push the war against the Moslems. But the king of France had again set his heart on gaining Milan. It was an obsession. This time, instructed by experience, he first made sure of his line of communications by taking possession of Savoy with the help of the Swiss canton of Bern. The duke of Savoy had allowed the French to pass through in the past, but he was now an ally of the emperor's. Charles resolved to sicken the French of warfare. He arranged for attacks on all fronts and himself led an army into Provence, while Doria harried its coasts. The emperor, however, found the strongly-fortified Marseilles too hard a nut to crack and had to retire into Italy, followed by a strong French army. It is unnecessary to narrate the events on the other fronts or to outline the campaigns of 1537, which were a repetition of those of the preceding year with one significant modification: Doria ravaged no coasts, but Kheireddin Barbarossa made a descent on Naples, expecting to coöperate with a French invading force. And so the fairly equal war petered out in a series of truces (1537-1538). The net result, disregarding the destruction of life and treasure, was that France held on to two-thirds of Savoy until the final settlement of 1559.

The breathing space which Charles had thus been vouchsafed by France lasted until 1542. He used it to attack the Turk. He got the pope and Venice to join him in a counter raid in the eastern Mediterranean. The joint naval and military force found Kheireddin waiting for them in the Gulf of Prevesa. The allied Christian commanders did not coöperate loyally and the honors of the battle fell to the Turk. Thereafter, until the battle of Lepanto, the Turkish navy had the edge in the Mediterranean. The Venetians, who were loath to fight the Turk, since to do so interfered with their commerce, made peace in 1540. Charles kept up the struggle, which now shifted to the western Mediterranean. His motive was to make that part of the sea safer for Spanish commerce and also to lessen Turkish pressure upon his brother Ferdinand in Hungary. The chief event in this naval contest was a formidable attack on Algiers (1541). The precedent of Tunis was to be followed. Charles's forces were 12,000 sailors and 24,000 soldiers, with Doria commanding the fleet. The cost of bringing this armada together from Germany, Italy and Spain was staggering. The attack began auspiciously, but an October tempest broke and the result was the complete failure of the enterprise. The blow to the emperor's prestige was heavy, and the western sea was more subject than ever to the piratical activities of the Moslem corsairs. But the emperor could not devote his strength to repairing the loss, for France again renewed the war in 1542.

The ramifications of this war (1542-1544) were wide. France again linked up with Scotland—to hold England's attention—and with Denmark, Sweden, the sultan, and the duke of Gelderland, whose resources were small but whose affiliations with the Schmalkaldic League of Lutheran princes were expected to drag them into the struggle. No attempt will be made to outline the war. It was another seesaw, with the emperor slightly the superior. The French, supported by Kheireddin Barbarossa, captured Nice, the last bit of independent Savoy; the sultan took the fortress of Grans in Hungary; the emperor seized Gelderland, while the Schmalkaldic princes aided Ferdinand against the Turks. The emperor brought the French to terms by invading France from the Netherlands and getting as near to Paris as Château-Thierry. In the Peace of Crespy (1544), France's obsession for Milan was met by the emperor, who agreed that if the duke of Orléans (a younger son of King Francis I) should marry a niece or daughter of the emperor, she should have an unfortified Milan for a dowry and Savoy should then be given back to its duke. It was part of the emperor's luck or strategy to escape from the war, while England and France remained embroiled until 1550, and from the danger of French intervention in German affairs.

FROM THE PEACE OF CRESPY TO THE PEACE OF CÂTEAU-CAMBRÉSIS

For Charles now saw a chance, at long last, to iron out the German situation, and to that end he made brilliant diplomatic arrangements. Ferdinand, in return for tribute, got a truce with Solyman (1545); Pope Paul III agreed to furnish 12,000 men to help crush Lutheranism; the Catholic duke of Bavaria—usually an opponent of the Hapsburgs—was brought into line by the promise of an electoral hat; and two Protestant princes, Maurice of Saxony and the margrave of Brandenburg, joined up for similar prospective gains, plus a promise of religious toleration for their lands. The emperor gathered troops from Spain, Hungary, Italy, the Netherlands and Germany (1546-1547). The duke of Alva was his military adviser. The battle with the Lutheran princes at Mühlberg in April, 1547, was a walkover for Charles, and Germany was for once in his hands. Indeed, he had several years to solve the German problem, undistracted by foreign complications. But the pope could not coöperate with him in authorizing the religious changes which he regarded as necessary to a solution of the religious issue. Nor could the emperor reëstablish the Swabian League, so useful to the Hapsburgs in the past, because of the religious antipathies of the Lutheran states of the southwest. Above all, the presence and bearing of the Spanish detachments, distributed throughout Germany, few though they were in the aggregate, led Germans of all classes to feel that it was a foreigner, rather than their own emperor, who was regulating their affairs, and convinced the German princes that their ancient independence was threatened with extinction.

As time passed the diplomatic constellations became unfavorable. The Turks, stirred up by Doria's attack upon the pirate Dragut, another Christian renegade operating in the western Mediterranean, renewed the war with Ferdinand in Hungary (1551); the French began to move in Italy late in the same year; and Maurice of Saxony secretly won over the Lutheran princes to recognize his gains and to join with him in securing French money and military help in exchange for Metz, Toul and Verdun, German border fortress cities which were not German in speech. The emperor, confident that a little more pressure would bring the Lutherans into line with his views and thus free him to settle finally with France, ignored all warnings, and the swift advance of Maurice forced him to flee to the Tyrol (1552). He decided to temporize. He agreed to settle the religious issue to the satisfaction of the Lutherans (Truce of Passau, 1552) and thus detached them from France; and he persuaded Maurice to help Ferdinand hold the Turks in Hungary. Then, in the autumn of 1552, he made a supreme effort to reconquer Metz. He assembled an army three times as large as the one which had given him the victory of Mühlberg; but the French had fortified Metz too well and the duke of Alva had lost his cunning, and Charles had to raise the siege (January, 1553).

The war with France and the Turks continued. The main theaters were the Netherlands, Italy and the Italian waters. Charles, after his failure at Metz, retired to the Netherlands. He was worn out and fearful for the safety of the Netherlands. But the marriage he arranged between his son Philip and his cousin, Queen Mary of England (a glorious recompense for the "divorce" of Queen Catherine!), restored his optimism and confirmed his decision to give the Netherlands to Philip rather than to Ferdinand. It was a perilous gift for the future king of Spain, for its safe retention required secure sea connections with Spain through the English Channel. This the new relations with England would provide. Queen Mary was not old. The emperor was now exhausted and Philip must shoulder the burdens. Naples and

Milan were given over to him in 1554, the Netherlands in 1555, and Spain and the other Spanish possessions in Italy and the New World in 1556. Ferdinand, emperor in all but name since 1553, became emperor in fact when Charles resigned in 1556. Ferdinand had already settled affairs with the Lutherans at the Peace of Augsburg (1555), which reëstablished the old independence of the German principalities under the leadership, but not the domination, of the emperor and left to the secular princes the right to establish either Lutheranism or Roman Catholicism in their respective states.

Meanwhile the war with France and the Turks and smaller Italian states ran its tortuous and expensive course. Philip made no innovations in its conduct, for he was guided by the old advisers and generals of his father. And so, in spite of the death of Charles in 1558, we may regard the Peace of Câteau-Cambrésis, which was signed in 1559, as winding up the wars between him and France.

The peace of 1559 shows, by its terms, that the Hapsburgs had won the contest but that France had a defensive power that could not be overcome. France gave up the Italian dreams which had recurrently beguiled her since 1494. Spain kept Milan, and the duke of Savoy got back his land and married a French princess; Corsica was returned to Genoa and central Italy was regulated as Spain desired. The Spaniard's word was to be law in Italy for generations. Charles's gains in the Netherlands were not disturbed. France, on the other hand, recovered long-lost Calais (the price Queen Mary of England had to pay for helping her husband in the war) and acquired Metz, Toul and Verdun, in fact, if not yet in full sovereignty. The war was meant to be over. And so, Mary having died in 1558, Philip of Spain married Elizabeth, eldest daughter of King Henry II of France.

AN ESTIMATE OF THE REIGN OF CHARLES V

The war was over. But its cost in lives, money, debt and wasted opportunities for promoting the arts of peace cannot be calculated. France, with her fertile soil, had greater powers of recuperation than Spain. True, the mines of America were now pouring a steady and increasing stream of gold and silver into the royal Spanish coffers, and the Netherlands, whose commerce was to reach the zenith in the future, were a reservoir of wealth. But when all is said, it was Spain that had to bear the chief burden of financing the foreign policy of Charles and of Philip after him. At the close of his reign Spain was paying Charles three times the taxes she paid at its start. And the country was less prosperous and the state debt incredibly higher. That was part of the price Spain paid for the dizzy eminence to which Charles had raised her. And the price mounted under Philip, even though in 1580 he secured the rich domains of Portugal and her colonies.

Another part of the price, paid before Charles died, was the decline in individual initiative and self-reliance among the Spaniards. These had been displayed in the revolt of the *comuneros,* in the commercial versatility of Catalonia, in feats of arms, and in the marvelous exploits of the *conquistadores.* Magellan (a naturalized Spaniard) had circled the earth under the banner of Charles V, 1519-1522. Cortes had conquered Mexico after burning his ships behind him (1521), and Pizarro had taken possession of the empire of the Incas (1532), laying the foundations for the Spanish type of civilization which flourishes today from the Rio Grande to the straits of Tierra del Fuego. This is the true glory of the reign of Charles V. This spirit of self-reliance and daring, marred though it was with deeds of cruelty, now declined at home and in Spain beyond the seas. The growth in royal absolutism and paternalism of government at home and in the colonies may be traced in large part to the necessity of centralized control and heavy revenues in time of war. And Charles V was nearly always fighting or preparing for it.

Charles V has been praised for favoring municipal self-government in the Spanish colonies and for his efforts to prevent the exploitation of the Indians by the colonists. He and his successors controlled the Church in the colonies as to patronage and revenues. Yet the Church did not really succeed in protecting the Indians. If Charles had not been so preoccupied with wars in Europe he might have praise for more than good intentions and efforts which were not successful.

The ends which Charles V pursued cannot be summarized in a telling phrase. They changed as he grew older and more experienced. The old charge brought against him, that he sought to become the master of Europe, is no longer made. His position was essentially a defensive one. He had inherited so much! He desired, like other rich men, to keep what he had inherited, to recover what was owing to him, and to organize his dominions better. This formula must be stretched a little to allow room for the conquest of incidental bits of territory which were needed to consolidate this or that group of possessions. By 1529 his "education" had progressed far enough to lead him to give up the idea of recovering the duchy of Burgundy, which France had taken from his grandmother, Mary of Burgundy. Why? Because he now realized that Europe was afraid of him, afraid that he might weaken France too much for the safety of non-Hapsburg Europe. Certainly if his policy was not soundly defensive before, it was after 1529. On the other hand, it looks as if his victory over the Lutherans in 1547 momentarily turned his head and caused him to dream for a time of getting into his own hands the control of Germany and German resources. It is certain that Europe would not have endured this increase of his power. As it was, the French and the German princes prevented it.

Viewing the reign of Charles V as a whole, certain other conclusions stand out. It seems clear that the union in his hands of so many diverse regions was hurtful to them and to him. He had too much to do, and the difficulties of one region interfered with, or prevented, any effective attempts to clear up the difficulties of the other regions. Spain and her Italian dominions and her colonies would have furnished an ample task for Charles. The addition of the Netherlands and of the imperial crown proved in the long run an impossible burden for Spain. They brought Charles into a conflict with Protestantism which, as a ruler of the Latin peoples of Spain and of her Italian dominions alone, he would

have escaped, and which exhausted the Spain of Philip II. For
the chief burden-bearer of these conflicts—despite the treasure
fleets from America—was Spain, especially Castile. It may be
argued with show of reason that Spain continued for centuries
to pay, and has not even yet liquidated, the costs of the inherit-
ances which came to Charles V from his ancestors.

CHAPTER XXI

THE REFORMATIONS: PROTESTANT AND CATHOLIC

THE most impressive event of the sixteenth century was the Protestant Revolt. It is still impossible to explain, in a really satisfactory way, what brought this about, but some of the general causes can be indicated.

THE CAUSES OF THE PROTESTANT REVOLT

The most important cause was the worldliness which still cursed the Church. There were many men, especially among the higher clergy, who had entered the Church from the desire for wealth and power or a comfortable living. They did not behave as if religion were a vital force, transforming their lives after the pattern of Jesus, but rather acted as if it were a mere matter of ceremonies. They celebrated the magnificent rites of the Church, led gorgeous processions, favored pilgrimages, exposed relics to the veneration of the multitude—and themselves led worldly and frequently profligate lives. The scandalous conduct of Pope Alexander VI (1493-1503), against which Savonarola vainly thundered, is the most striking case in point. The behavior of these clerics tended to divorce religion from morality and to alienate pious souls from the Church.

The weight of Church taxation—borne directly and indirectly by the laity in tithes, tenths, annates, money dues for marriages and burials and fees for "dispensations" of various sorts—would hardly have been the serious cause of complaint it was if the clergy had been pious and devoted, for "the laborer is worthy of his hire." Nor would the expense and delays of justice in the ecclesiastical courts have been very serious grievances, considering the venal character of the lay courts, if only the Church's income had been used consistently for religious ends.

A second cause of the Revolt, which operated in many countries, was the desire of lay rulers to increase their power. By the close of the fifteenth century the stronger of these rulers had quite generally subdued their lay nobility; the cities were submissive; and the only class which was still largely independent was the clergy, or, in other words, the ecclesiastical nobility. Now, if the independence of the clergy were overthrown and the wealth of the Church seized, the absolutism of the lay ruler would be measurably nearer.

A third cause, none the less real because indirect, was the rise of the laity in education and influence. As has been shown in earlier pages, the laity in the later Middle Ages were overtaking the clergy in many spheres. The Church's control of education was declining, its virtual monopoly of learning was gone, and the classical literatures of pagan antiquity were held in high esteem; the invention of printing had made books accessible to the poorer layman; and the geographical discoveries, the work of laymen, had opened up new lands and realms of thought and had made men more hospitable to new ideas. Was it strange, then, that some of the laity should lend a willing ear to Protestant teachings, which denied to the clergy the last element of their superiority to the laity, namely, their control of religion? For while the Catholic Church teaches that it has an exclusive commission from God to interpret the Bible and to supplement its teachings, and that the clergy are, by divine appointment, indispensable mediators between the individual and God, the underlying principle of Protestantism is "the priesthood of the believer": (1) that the Bible is the exclusive source of divine revelation and can be adequately interpreted by every believer for himself; (2) that the individual, by faith in Christ's promise to forgive the repentant, can obtain salvation directly without the aid of the priest.

A fourth cause, which is probable rather than certain, is the individualism of the northern people of Europe, that quality which Tacitus remarks among the primitive Teutons as exalting the independence of the individual. Is it not probable that "the priesthood of the believer" would have an especial attraction for them? At any rate, this is the only single explanation for this remarkable fact: the Revolt began in northern Germany and in the end succeeded, with rare exceptions, only in the countries of the North, namely, in North Germany, the Scandinavian kingdoms, the Dutch Netherlands, England, Scotland and Switzerland.

The first of the four causes of the Protestant Revolt, the inveterate worldliness, was the most important cause. It had attracted the attention of worthy clergymen for hundreds of years. The great councils of the fifteenth century had made some attempts to secure reformation. Pious leaders like Saint Catherine of Siena, prominent preachers of righteousness of whom perhaps Savonarola is the chief, reforming prelates like Cardinal Nicholas of Cusa of whom it was said: "the glory of God and the bettering of mankind were the object of all his wisdom," had all striven earnestly within the Church to stem the tide of worldliness. Equally symptomatic was the revival which improved several of the orders of monks and friars during the closing years of the fifteenth century, among which may be mentioned the Augustinian Friars, whom Luther was to join.

A prominent place among the laborers for reform within the Church must be given to several Humanists. John Colet, an English priest, was a zealous promoter of Christian education, simple piety, and personal religion. Cardinal Ximenes, a Spaniard, strove to vitalize Catholic theology by bringing out a scholarly edition of the entire Bible with the original Hebrew and Greek. This was completed in 1517 and published a little later. Others, like Sebastian Brant, a German, held up the vices of clergy and laity to public scorn [1] in the hope that the erring ones would see and forsake their faults. The most renowned Humanist, the Dutch cleric Erasmus (1476-1536), issued improved editions of the writings of the Fathers, an edition of the Greek Testament (published 1516), and a number of Latin books,[2] in which he satirized the religious formalism of the age and urged more attention to simple religion and less to forms and ceremonies.

---

[1] In his *Narrenschiff* (*Ship of Fools*).
[2] Notably his *Encomium Moriae* (*Praise of Folly*).

The effectiveness of the work of these and other Humanists for reform within the Church was much weakened by the antagonism which sprang up between them and the majority of the Catholic theologians. Many of the Humanists, who loved the classical style and usually disdained things medieval, frequently spoke with scorn of Catholic theology and philosophy, calling them uncouth jargon and foolish hair-splitting. Most of the theologians returned scorn with scorn, saying that the Humanists were pagan in morals and at heart hostile or indifferent to the Church. This, it must be said, was true of many Humanists, but probably not of the majority. For when the time for decision came, after the outbreak of the Protestant Revolt, the majority remained loyal to the Roman Catholic Church.[1]

There was, however, a fatal defect in the efforts of the councils, evangelists and other groups of workers for a peaceful reformation: they were neither led nor supported by the papacy—the responsible head of the Church. If the popes from Alexander VI (1493) to Leo X (1521) had been men of piety and insight and had devoted their mighty authority to a thorough reformation of admitted abuses, it is not likely that there would have been a Protestant Revolt in the sixteenth century. But the papacy lagged behind, and revolutionary reformers came to the front and led northern Europe into Protestantism.

THE LUTHERAN REVOLT, TO THE EDICT OF WORMS

The chief of these reformers was the peasant's son, Martin Luther (1483-1546), a friar, priest, Master of Arts, Doctor of Theology, and professor of theology in the University of Wittenberg since 1512. As a friar in his convent he had been much troubled by the thought of his sinfulness and the impossibility of winning salvation by anything that he could do. Then, through the study of the Bible and the counsel of his superior in the convent, Brother Martin attained religious peace and certitude by having faith in God's promise of forgiveness to the contrite sinner. As professor of theology and university preacher he empha-

[1] Erasmus, More and Reuchlin are well-known examples.

sized the supreme importance of faith and won a large following. Indeed, the elector of Saxony regarded Brother Martin as the leading light in his university. In 1517 Luther was driven by his conception of the Gospel to attack the theory and practice of in- dulgences, and this attack proved to be the definite beginning of the Protestant movement.

To understand the controversy over indulgences it is necessary to recall the doctrine of the sacrament of penance. In Luther's day it was—and it still is—the teaching of the Catholic Church that a contrite sinner who confesses his sin and is absolved by the priest is required by God's law to do something, imposed or specified by the priest, to emphasize or demonstrate the sincerity of his repentance, and this *thing* is called *penance* or *satisfaction*. And if such penance is not performed before death, then the sinner, although forgiven, must undergo a period of purification in Purgatory in lieu of such penance; and so for all forgiven sins and their penances. In other words, every sin, *after* forgiveness, involves penance *or* purgatorial pains.[1] The reader of the second part of Dante's *Divine Comedy* will understand this perfectly.

Furthermore, it was and is Catholic teaching that the pope or his representative is authorized by God to remit all or part of the *penance,* and the document in which this remission is set forth is known as an *indulgence.* In the days of Luther it had long been the custom to raise money for the Church by the sale of indulgences. It is clear that an indulgence would be of no effect if the sinner who bought it had not truly repented of his sin, since in that case the absolution itself would be null. But in Luther's day many uneducated laymen who purchased indulgences were quite unable to distinguish clearly between the forgiveness of the sin and the remission of the penance. And it must also be said that the authorized venders occasionally made use of lan- guage which the ordinary church-goer might easily misunderstand as an offer to sell salvation.[2] In 1517 a vender of this type began work near Wittenberg, and Luther made a public and comprehen- sive protest.

[1] Gibbons, *Faith of Our Fathers.*
[2] See Penn. *Trans. and Reprints,* vol. ii, no. 6, pages 4-11.

Luther's protest consisted of ninety-five theses, or propositions, on the use and abuse of indulgences.[1] It was in Latin, since that was the language of scholars, but it attracted such attention that it was promptly translated and scattered over western Europe in the vernaculars. The theses show that Luther had already given much thought to the subject, although it was not until 1520 that he repudiated indulgences completely. He attacked the sordid aspects of the sale, declared that "Christians should be taught that he who gives to a poor man, or lends to a needy man, does better than if he bought indulgences" (No. 43), and he developed the idea that the truly repentant sinner has God's forgiveness and needs no indulgence. Particularly significant, indeed, is the thirty-sixth thesis: "Every Christian who truly repents of his sins has complete remission of penance and guilt even without an indulgence." Indeed, reading between the lines, one can see that Luther already viewed religion as a matter between the individual sinner and God, and that he was on the way to a rejection of the clergy as necessary mediators. After three years of study, negotiation and debate, Luther himself realized that in denying the value attached by the Church to indulgences he was really repudiating the supreme authority of the Church in religion. Then he said: "I have hitherto taught and held all the opinions of John Hus unawares; . . . in short, we are all Hussites without knowing it."

It was toward the close of this three-year period, namely in 1520, that Luther published three German works,[2] which are fundamental in the exposition of his views. (All told, Luther's voluminous writings number four hundred books and pamphlets.) In the *Address to the Christian Nobility of the German Nation* he pointed out the financial abuses in the Church and appealed to the lay authorities to correct them. In the *Babylonian Captivity of the Church* he sharply criticized the Church's teaching on the seven sacraments and declared that the Bible lays down definitely only the sacraments of baptism and the Lord's Supper. He also repudiated, as unscriptural, monastic vows and the celibacy of the

---

[1] English translation in Penn. *Trans. and Reprints,* vol. ii, no. 6, pages 11-18.
[2] Translated in Wace and Buchheim, *Luther's Primary Works.*

clergy, and asserted emphatically the "priesthood of the believer" —"that we are all equally priests, that is, that we have the same power in the Word, and in any sacrament whatever, although it is not lawful for anyone to use this power, except with the consent of the community or at the call of a superior." In his pamphlet, *The Freedom of a Christian Man,* Luther explained in simple language his conception of Christianity, pointing out the supreme importance of faith and the relative unimportance of ceremonies. "The work of God," he says, "cannot be received or honored by any works, but by faith alone." "It is not by working, but by believing, that we glorify God and confess Him to be true." "A Christian, being consecrated by his faith, does good works; but he is not by these works made a more sacred person, or more of a Christian. That is the effect of faith alone." "Whatsoever work is not directed to the sole end either of keeping the body under, or of doing service to our neighbor—provided he require nothing contrary to the will of God—is no good or Christian work."

That Luther's teachings were acceptable to millions of his countrymen by the end of 1520 seems certain. Aleander, sent by the pope to Germany as papal nuncio in 1520, reported—doubtless with exaggeration—: "Nine-tenths of the Germans shout 'Long live Luther,' and the other tenth, 'Death to Rome.'" When Aleander urged Charles V, elected king of Germany and "future emperor" (1519), to do his duty and declare Luther an outlaw, Charles decided that Luther must have a hearing before the German Diet, or legislature, since to condemn him without a chance to defend himself might cause popular revolts.

Charles opened his first German Diet in January, 1521—the same month and year in which Luther was declared a heretic by the pope. Much important business came before the Diet, but the absorbing question was Luther. Provided with an imperial safe-conduct guaranteeing his safe return to Wittenberg, he entered Worms in April amid the acclaims of the populace. Here, in the presence of Charles V, the Diet and many ambassadors and courtiers, he expounded his views, making a powerful address in Latin and repeating it immediately in German. The imperial official chided him for calling in question what had been officially decided by general councils and asked him flatly whether he would recant his opinions or not. Luther replied: "Unless I am convicted by Scripture or by right reasons (for I trust neither in popes nor in councils, since they have often erred and contradicted themselves)—unless I am thus convinced, I am bound by the texts of the Bible, my conscience is captive to the Word of God, I neither can nor will recant anything, since it is neither right nor safe to act against conscience. God help me. Amen."

A few weeks later, after Luther had had plenty of time to get back safely to Wittenberg, Charles V signed the Edict of Worms, which, in the name of the Diet, declared Luther an outlaw, forbade anyone to have or read his writings, and commanded that he be surrendered to the authorities.

In the meantime Luther had failed to reach Wittenberg. Stories circulated that he had been killed, but actually his powerful elector, Frederick of Saxony, whose protection had saved Luther ever since 1517, had caused him to be "seized" and hidden in his castle of the Wartburg on a hilltop deep in the Thuringian forests, where Luther spent eight or nine happy months writing books and beginning his new German translation of the Bible, which was to help so much in promoting the Lutheran cause and in developing the modern German language. Luther was hidden away, of course, in order that Elector Frederick might have an opportunity to find out whether he could safely continue to disobey the papal bull and the Edict of Worms. This he finally did, even permitting Luther to resume his university teaching.

Luther left the Wartburg—without his elector's permission—and returned to Wittenberg, when he heard that "prophets," claiming divine guidance, had got the upper hand in the university town and were imperiling the Lutheran cause by mob violence against the Catholic clergy, and by fantastic interpretations of the Bible. For example, they were closing the schools as useless on the ground that God's truth is concealed from the wise and prudent, but is revealed unto babes. Luther was indignant. He was opposed to the use of force to win converts, and he knew that his movement would fail if it were identified in the minds of

decent people with extravagances and absurdities. His return to
Wittenberg and his sermons soon caused the fanatics to flee, but
they, and others less sincere, caused much trouble and reproach
elsewhere.[1]

A far greater threat to the Lutheran cause was the Peasants'
Revolt (1524-1525). The hard lot of the German peasants in the
later Middle Ages has already been pointed out.[2] Their condition
did not improve, and now, for the seventh time in fifty years,
they rose against their masters. The revolt began in the southwest—near Switzerland—and spread over most of Germany.
The insurgents appealed to the Bible in justification of their demands,[3] looked confidently to Luther, a peasant's son, for support,
and were urged by frenzied religious demagogues to exterminate
their masters. They slaughtered many nobles, sacked castles and
monasteries, and threw the princes into a panic. Finally, as in the
past, the disciplined troops of the princes crushed the revolt with
dreadful bloodshed, killing about one hundred thousand of the ill-
armed peasantry. Their emancipation from galling burdens was
delayed for three weary centuries.

The Peasants' Revolt checked the rapid progress of the Lutheran movement because the two were, rightly or wrongly, connected by Luther's opponents. "There," they in effect said, "you
see what revolt from the Church leads to." The cause of the
peasant rising was of course economic, but it is likely that Luther,
by repudiating the authority of the Church, had encouraged others
to attempt to throw off the yokes which oppressed them.

The Peasants' Revolt had other consequences. Luther was a
firm believer in the authority of the State, of "the powers that be."
As early as 1523 he had declared that the State was necessary "to
keep the unruly in order," and when the insurgents asked his help

[1] For the wild proceedings in Münster, for example, see Lindsay, *Hist. of the
Reformation,* ii. pages 452-469.

[2] See pages 346 *ff.*

[3] The most influential statement of these demands is the *Twelve Articles.*
See Penn. *Trans. and Reprints,* vol. ii, no. 6, pages 25-30.

he told them that "even if princes are wicked and unjust it does not excuse rebellion." The rising made Luther more distrustful of the "common man" and more inclined than ever to rely, for earthly support, upon the territorial rulers of Germany. In so doing he swam with the current of German political development. In truth, it was the decentralization of Germany and the weakness of its central government which gave his movement its opportunity.

LUTHERANISM'S WAR OF INDEPENDENCE TO 1555

The only serious danger was that Charles V might extricate himself from his wars with the French, the Turks and opponents in North Africa, Italy and elsewhere, and concentrate his strength against his Lutheran foes. The danger seemed imminent in 1529-1532, when Charles was temporarily at peace and ordered that the Edict of Worms be enforced, but Lutheran princes and cities organized the *League of Schmalkald* and the Turks advanced against Vienna, so that Charles found it necessary, in order to get the aid of the League, to agree not to enforce the edict. Sixteen years were to pass before he had another opportunity, and thus Lutheranism had a quarter-century to develop and intrench itself in a territory which may be "roughly described as a great triangle, whose base was the shores of the Baltic Sea from the Netherlands in the west to the eastern limits of East Prussia, and whose apex was Switzerland" (Lindsay).

The Lutheran churches, which grew up in the different states of this region, were guided rather than controlled by the conservative statesmanship of Luther. The services were conducted in the vernacular, preaching was emphasized, German hymns were sung, and the Lord's Supper was administered "in both kinds." The altar, vestments, candles, and most of the holy days of the old Church were retained although, as Luther explained, they were not essential. There was considerable variation in the services as well as in the systems of Church government. There were, however, two features common to all: the government of the Church in each state was vested in officials appointed by the territorial ruler; and the Church of each state had to be content with such fragments of the property of the old Church as the ruler was willing to surrender. As will be shown later, this growth of princely influence over the Church was not confined to Protestant lands, but appeared also even in such strongly Catholic states as Spain and France.

The Lutheran states of Germany, grouped within their great triangle, were at length challenged in 1546 by Emperor Charles V.[1] He was now, after many arduous campaigns, at peace with France and the Turks and enjoyed the support of the pope. But he was able to bring only a few thousand Spanish troops with him to Germany. These, with contingents from the Netherlands and Germany and the Italian lands, made up his motley army, which was directed by the duke of Alva. The Schmalkaldic League was revived by the Lutherans, and their forces overtopped those of the emperor. However, he reduced them to something approaching equality by securing the neutrality of the elector of Brandenburg and the active support of Maurice, duke of Saxony. To both he guaranteed, for themselves and their subjects, a large measure of religious toleration—expecting, no doubt, to withdraw it later. He also promised them territorial gains, in particular agreeing to transfer to Maurice the office of elector and the bulk of the territory which belonged to his relative, the elector of Saxony. The offers were accepted. With the aid of Maurice and his troops, the emperor overthrew what was left of the Schmalkaldic League, and then took up the religious problem.

Charles's leading idea in solving this was to have the Council of Trent, which began work in 1545, make such reforms that the Lutherans could be brought to return to the Catholic fold without too much pressure from himself. He was averse to a rough, wholesale application of force because his troops were too few and because there was danger that the German princes, Catholic and Protestant, might become fearful for their independence and combine against him. Unfortunately for Charles, the Council of Trent felt it to be impossible, consistently with Catholic principles, to make the changes necessary to satisfy the Protestants.

[1] See pages 400 ff.

Then Charles attempted for some years, with small detachments of Spanish troops, to force the German Protestants to accept certain religious reforms—the so-called *Interim*—which he contrived for them. He was successful in this for the time being, but how he expected to get a permanent settlement out of it we cannot tell, for his enemies again combined against him. In 1552 the newly-made elector, Maurice of Saxony, renewed relations with the other Protestant princes, who were now thoroughly alarmed for their liberties, and with them formed an alliance with King Henry II of France, who was given possession of Metz, Toul and Verdun as the price of his support against Charles. Maurice then advanced swiftly against the emperor, who was unprepared for the new combination, and Charles had to flee from Innsbruck to a temporary refuge in the Austrian lands. From there he summoned such forces as he could collect and in the winter of 1552-1553 he attempted, Alva again acting as his military adviser, to recapture Metz from the French. If he had succeeded in this he would probably have made another effort to put through his plans in Germany. But he failed and he told his brother Ferdinand to make the best settlement he could with the German princes. The emperor himself turned to other problems.

The German princes, both Catholic and Protestant, insisted upon a permanent peace—they now had a chance to avert Spanish and also imperial domination—and this was arranged at the Diet of Augsburg (1555). The Peace of Augsburg provided: (1) that each of the lay rulers in Germany might choose between the Catholic and Lutheran faiths, and compel his subjects, on penalty of exile, to accept his choice—the so-called principle of *cujus regio, ejus religio;* (2) that if a ruler of an ecclesiastical principality [1] in Germany should turn Lutheran, he was bound to resign and allow another Catholic ruler to be chosen as his successor— the so-called *ecclesiastical reservation;* (3) that Church property already (1552) seized, or *secularized,* by Lutheran rulers should remain in the possession of these rulers, but that no further secularizations should be made. The second provision was designed

[1] That is, those bishops and abbots who were also the temporal rulers of German states.

particularly to keep the three ecclesiastical electorates [1] in Catholic hands and thus help to maintain the Hapsburg monopoly of the imperial crown. There were seeds of future trouble in this and also in the third provision, but the Peace of Augsburg gave Germany relief from serious "religious" struggles for two generations.

Luther had not lived to witness either the humiliation of the Schmalkaldic League or the definite recognition of Lutheranism as one of the two official creeds of Germany, for he had passed away in February, 1546. In the face of Church and emperor and the general opinion of Europe, he had attacked the principle of a mediating priestly class and had asserted the direct responsibility and access of the individual to God. A revolutionist, he had striven to confine the revolution to the religious sphere; a conservative, clinging to much of the old, he still put aside all compromise with the old Church, for he saw that the two conceptions of Christianity were irreconcilable. He was harsh in controversy and opinionated, but also courageous, conscientious and human. He was a lover of music, birds and the prattle of his children. He was truly of heroic mold, and Germany has not produced a greater man than Martin Luther, the peasant's son.

The influence of Luther was not confined to Germany but passed, although with diminished force, into neighboring lands, originating or promoting religious discontent with the old Church. At the time of his death his views had won many adherents among the peoples of southern Germany, Bohemia, Poland and the Netherlands; the three Scandinavian kingdoms were Lutheran; almost half the Swiss cantons were Protestant; and England under Henry VIII had repudiated the authority of the pope over its Church.

THE SWISS REVOLT. ZWINGLI AND CALVIN

Switzerland, like Germany, was no more than a loose league of states. The Swiss league was founded for mutual defense in 1291 by three cantons, and by 1513 it had increased its member-

[1] Mainz, Trier and Cologne.

ship to thirteen. In theory these thirteen Alpine republics were a part of the empire, but in fact they were as good as independent. The confederates had been brave and inaccessible enough from 1291 onward to throw off the overlordship of Hapsburg counts and other nobles, and in 1499 had compelled Maximilian I, the talented Hapsburg emperor, to admit their contention that they were exempt from the laws of the empire.[1] The thirteen cantons were almost entirely German in population, but they had as allies, especially to the south, a fringe of small provinces inhabited by Frenchmen, Italians and Germans. After the French Revolution these were admitted to full membership in the Confederation, and thus brought up the number of cantons to twenty-two, at which it remains today.

The leader of the Protestant Revolt in Switzerland was Ulrich Zwingli (1484-1531), a native Swiss. Like Luther, a well-educated university graduate, he entered the priesthood and became the leading preacher in Zürich in 1518. In theology he was in substantial agreement with Luther, except in his philosophy of the Lord's Supper.[2] In the matter of Church practices Zwingli's rule was to reject those practices of the old Church which he believed to be unauthorized by the Bible, while Luther's was to retain those which, in his judgment, were not forbidden by the Bible. Thus Zwingli did away, for example, with candles, pictures and vestments in the churches, and with nearly all the Church holidays. Zwingli's repeated assertion that he arrived at his religious opinions through an independent study of the Bible is worthy of respect, although it is doubtful whether he could have accomplished what he did if the progress of the Lutheran movement had not paved the way.

A peculiar feature of the Swiss Reformation was the public disputation. This was a debate, usually one-sided, held under government auspices, in which Protestant champions presented their views to the people and invited defenders of the old Church to meet their arguments. As the Protestants always insisted that

[1] The international recognition of Swiss independence came in 1648.

[2] The views of Luther, Zwingli, and Calvin on this subject are briefly explained in Lindsay's *History of the Reformation,* ii, pages 52-60.

all arguments be based on the Bible alone, the Catholic champions
were handicapped. The disputations were a recognition that the
people were the real rulers in the Swiss cantons. When the people were favorable, the government of the canton took possession
of the property of the Church, reformed it along Zwinglian lines,
and in general exercised full control over it. Thus in Switzerland, as in Germany, the Protestant Reformation increased the
authority of the State, but obviously it did not decrease the power
of the Swiss peoples.

The Zwinglian Reformation triumphed first in Zürich (1525),
then in Bern, and by 1529 in four other cantons. Seven cantons,
including Uri, Schwyz and Unterwalden, remained Catholic. In
contrast with Luther, Zwingli favored forcible conversion, and
desired to compel the opposing cantons to permit their citizens
to become Protestants. He wished also to change the constitution of the Swiss Diet, in which each canton had two votes, so that
the great city cantons of Zürich and Bern might have increased
representation and greater influence. The result was a civil war
ending in the battle of Cappel (1531), in which Zürich was defeated and Zwingli slain. Peace was then made on the basis that
each canton should be free to choose between the old faith and the
new, and this arrangement lasted until recently when the growth
of toleration made it of little importance.

The death of Zwingli left the Protestant cause in Switzerland
without any great leader and with diminished prestige. But a
greater man than Zwingli soon stepped into the breach. That
man was John Calvin.

John Calvin (1509-1564) was a Frenchman. He was thoroughly educated in several universities for the priesthood, then
for the law, then in the ancient classics and Hebrew, and finally
he found his vocation as a Protestant reformer. His conversion
to Protestantism took place about 1533. Its beginnings go back
some years to a reform movement, led by some of the French
clergy who desired to spiritualize religion along the lines favored
by Erasmus, and its completion may be found largely in the influence of Luther's writings.

The French government already enjoyed, by an arrangement

made with the pope in 1516 known as the *Concordat of Bologna,* a very large control over the French clergy and, when it realized the nature of the reform movement just mentioned, the government began persecutions which drove some of the French reformers into submission and others into open revolt. To the latter class belonged Calvin, who fled for refuge to the liberal Swiss city of Basel.

The most notable event in Calvin's stay at Basel was the publication in March, 1536, of his famous *Institutes of the Christian Religion.* The book is a clear exposition of Protestant doctrine and a forceful refutation of the opposing Catholic views; it also lays down the lines of Church government later known by the general name of *Presbyterian.* Four months after publishing this book Calvin set out for Strasburg by the southern route, since the direct road was barred by the war between France and Charles V, and came to Geneva. Here, as it happened, his help was demanded in the name of God by a sorely-tried Zwinglian leader named Farel, and here Calvin, obeying the call, stayed to do his life-work.

The adoption of Protestantism in Geneva—the city was not a part of Switzerland proper—which had taken place in May, 1536, was largely a political affair. The citizens of this old, French-speaking city of the empire had undertaken some years before to break the tightening grasp of their feudal superiors, the duke of Savoy and his tool, the prince-bishop of Geneva. This task the little city of 16,000 inhabitants accomplished in 1536 with the aid of the great Swiss canton of Bern. Meanwhile, before the final campaign, Bern used her position as indispensable ally to secure the admission of Protestant evangelists, notably Farel, into Geneva. The result of their preaching, of Bernese pressure, and of the political advantage which the Genevans saw in repudiating the religious as well as the political authority of their prince-bishop, was the legal adoption of Protestantism. Henceforward Geneva was in close alliance with Bern and in intimate relations with Protestant Switzerland.

The task which Calvin was induced by Farel to undertake was to make the more or less nominal Protestantism of the Genevans real. In performing this task, to which he gave most of his strength for the remainder of his life, Calvin laid emphasis upon the Church's duty not only to preach the Gospel and administer the sacraments—to Luther these were the whole duty of the Church—but also to discipline its members and thus make them more effective soldiers of Christ.[1] Moreover, while Luther characteristically regarded Church and State as simply two aspects of one and the same society, Calvin was profoundly convinced that the Church was an organization of Christians entirely distinct from the State, owing obedience in matters of religion only to God and His Word and subject to no secular control. Hence the activity of the Genevan *Consistory,* a committee of ministers and lay members of the Church, which watched over the behavior of all, and by counsel, reproof and exclusion from the Lord's Supper, constrained wrong-doers or frivolous folk to repent or to leave the Church. Such enforced withdrawal was known as excommunication, and it was the severest penalty the Church could inflict. But the State, that is, the secular government of Geneva, punished offenses—some of them very trivial from our point of view—against morals or religion by fines, imprisonment, banishment and death.

In practice, the relations between Church and State in Geneva were much the same as in Zürich or, for that matter, in Wittenberg. And yet Calvin's view of the independent spheres of Church and State—so strangely similar to the Catholic view—was of enduring importance. It promoted the active interest of the Church members in the affairs of the Church, caused them to look to the Bible and not to the State for the standards of conduct and to be critical of the secular government. In the long run it contributed greatly to that separation of Church and State which is now the rule rather than the exception.

In doctrines Calvin differed seriously from the other Protestant leaders only in the theory of the Lord's Supper, although he laid greater emphasis than did any other Protestant or Catholic theologian of the sixteenth century upon the idea that sinful man can do nothing by himself to win God's favor, and is saved only by

[1] On Calvinistic "discipline," see also page 491.

the deliberate choice of God. This is the so-called doctrine of predestination. Calvin's theory of the Lord's Supper separated him for a time from communion and coöperation with the Protestant churches of Switzerland, but in 1549 they agreed on a method of stating the theory of the Lord's Supper which satisfied both parties and enabled the Calvinist ideas to take root in Protestant Switzerland. In the matter of Church *practices* Calvin was in agreement with Zwingli.[1]

The success of Calvin in transforming the loose-living and pleasure-loving city of Geneva into a sober, industrious, prosperous, God-fearing commonwealth was prodigious. The change was due, in part, to the immigration of energetic Protestant refugees from other lands, and especially from France, and the city became the model for the rest of the Protestant world. Its schools were renowned and its academy—later known as the University of Geneva—was a famous educational foundation. In Geneva, especially while Calvin lived, were trained the iron leaders of the militant Protestantism of the second half of the sixteenth century —the leaders of the Huguenots of France, of the Dutch who defied Philip II, of the Covenanters of Scotland, and of the Puritans of both England and New England.

THE ENGLISH BREACH WITH ROME

The history of the English Revolt lacks the unity and interest which flow from the dominant leadership of a great religious champion. It was led by the Tudors, who were masterful rulers and adroit politicians, and their activity obscures the part played by religious sentiments among the people at large. And yet, after the turnings and twistings of the Tudor monarchs during twenty-five years (1534-1559), the religious problem was solved along Protestant lines in a settlement which has substantially endured to this day. It is therefore not unreasonable to think—especially when one recalls the strong following which Wycliffe's views obtained, despite the heresy laws, in the fourteenth century—that the majority of English people accepted the reformed faith which

[1] See page 419.

Queen Elizabeth imposed on them, not only because they had to, but because they were prepared to accept it.

King Henry VIII (1509-1547) "broke the bonds of Rome" and made the clergy of England dependent on himself. There were still some embers of Lollardy in England when Henry's rule was young, and reformers—witness John Colet—who hoped for a peaceful reformation of Church abuses. Luther's opinions also attracted considerable attention. But the *cause* of Henry's attack upon the Church was the desire to round out his authority by mastering the clergy and seizing Church property. The *occasion* of Henry's attack was his sordid matrimonial desires.

Henry's marriage with Catherine of Aragon, the aunt of Charles V, became displeasing to him. They had a daughter, Mary, but no son who lived, and after some eighteen years of married life Catherine's place in his affections—never a strong one—was given to Anne Boleyn, an unscrupulous maid-of-honor to Queen Catherine. Henry's dishonorable desires were cloaked, but not concealed, by his alleged distress of conscience. His royal conscience argued that his marriage with Catherine was no marriage at all, because Pope Julius II had had no right to grant the dispensation necessary for Henry's marriage with Catherine, his brother Arthur's widow. Henry asked Pope Clement VII (1523-1534) to accept this view of the matter, and backed up his demand with threats and then with a series of laws, passed by the compliant Parliament, which cut off the papal revenues in England and compelled the English clergy to acknowledge that they could do nothing without the king's consent (*Submission of the Clergy*). Clement VII, however, was unwilling to declare Julius II's dispensation invalid since it was valid, or to offend Catherine's nephew, Charles V, who had much power in Italy. Thereupon the headstrong English king had Parliament pass laws which cut off the English Church entirely from the papacy and established it as a national Church under his own headship. The pope excommunicated Henry, but the rivalry between Charles V and Francis I of France was so bitter that there was no one to support with war the papal excommunication and the bull of deposition which followed it. The English Church had to accept

Henry's view of the nullity of his union with Queen Catherine and the legality of his marriage to Anne Boleyn, who became the mother of Queen Elizabeth.

The breach with the papacy was made complete by the Act of Supremacy (1534). The Act declared that the king, his heirs and successors, should be "taken, accepted, and reputed the only supreme head in earth of the Church of England, called *Anglicana Ecclesia,*" should have and enjoy the revenues belonging to the said dignity, and should have full authority to reform, restrain, and amend every sort of "errors, heresies, abuses, offenses, contempts, and enormities." Thus was the Church of England completely separated from the papacy and transferred to the autocratic control of Henry VIII.

It was no doubt the intention of Henry VIII to keep the Church of England unchanged in doctrine, ceremonial and organization, except in regard to the headship, which had been transferred to himself. To be sure, he destroyed "superstitiously venerated" images, placed for a time a vernacular Bible in every church, and confiscated monastic lands and goods. The latter proceeding provoked a serious rising in the conservative and rural north of England, the so-called "Pilgrimage of Grace" (1536-1537), but it was put down by craft and force, and in the Six Articles Act (1539) belief in the essential Roman Catholic doctrines was made obligatory.

But Henry's breach with Rome really opened wide the door to Protestant opinions. The clergy were no longer an independent power in the land, possessing the prestige of immemorial spiritual authority and the overshadowing protection of the papacy; they were now officials—somewhat shaken and discredited officials—of King Henry VIII, Supreme Head of the Church of England, and their opposition to Protestant teachings no longer carried its former weight with the people. Moreover, Protestant teachers now crept into England more than before, naturally considering it fertile soil, and knit connections with surviving elements of Lollardy. Hostility to Catholic doctrines grew apace, as is shown by the very first Act of Parliament of Henry VIII's successor. This Act was directed against revilers of the traditional conception of the Lord's Supper, who "not only disputed and reasoned unreverently and ungodly of that most high mystery, but also, in their sermons, preachings, readings, lectures, communications, arguments, talks, rhymes, songs, plays, or jests, name or call it by such vile and unseemly words as Christian ears do abhor to hear rehearsed." In truth, "Henrian Catholicism" could not endure; it had to pass into Protestantism or Roman Catholicism.

The short reign of Edward VI (1547-1553), who was only fifteen when he died, witnessed the establishment of Protestantism as the official faith of the English. This was mainly the work of the King's Council, which, under the leadership of two successive regents, exercised the royal authority and enjoyed the support of Parliament. Under the first regent, the Protector Somerset, a cautious advance was made in protestantizing the Church, which is well indicated by the service book, prepared chiefly by the learned and broad-minded Cranmer, and known as the *First Prayer Book of King Edward VI* (1549). But Somerset's growing arrogance and incompetence, and his good-hearted but unskillful efforts to protect the peasantry against the "enclosing" of pastures, commons and arable lands by the landholders for the more profitable sheep-grazing, brought about his fall and, a little later, his execution. His successor in the regency, the duke of Northumberland, was more incompetent and was unprincipled to boot. But he threw in his fortunes with the more advanced reformers who had flocked over to England and won an increased following for reform after the death of Henry VIII. One notable result was the revision of the service book and the drawing up of a creed for the English Church. The *Second Prayer Book of King Edward VI* (1552) and the *Forty-Two Articles of Religion* (1553) show a distinct advance in the direction of Geneva and Wittenberg, although the changes in the Prayer Book were comparatively few.[1] It still retained the noble dignity and felicity of language which Cranmer gave it, and in the days of Elizabeth it was easily altered to serve the uses of both the liberals and the conservatives who supported her Church establishment.

---

[1] The two prayer-books are published in a single volume in *Everyman's Library* (Dutton).

The reign of the unhappy Queen Mary (1553-1558), daughter of Henry VIII and Catherine of Aragon, arrested the progress of Protestantism. She was a sincere Roman Catholic and a true Tudor, and the power of the sixteenth-century monarch was never better exhibited than in the restoration of the Church of England to the papal obedience at her behest. The restoration was made by a papal legate, Cardinal Pole, an Englishman, and was enacted by Parliament (1553-1554) with one significant reservation, namely, that the titles of ownership of those who had received monastic lands should not be disturbed.

The restoration of England to the papal obedience appears to have been accepted by the great mass of the people as a pledge of settled conditions and quietude. The religious changes of Northumberland had outrun the capacity of the people to follow and were associated by them with his treasonable effort to keep Mary off the throne. But Mary's marriage with her cousin Philip, son of Charles V, alarmed many, since it tended to subordinate England's interests to Spanish policy, and at the end of the reign it involved England in Philip's war with France and humbled the pride of the island people by the loss of their last possession in France—Calais (1558). Furthermore, Mary's ruthless executions of some three hundred Protestants, both high and low in station, although conscientiously designed by the queen to cleanse the kingdom of heresy as by a surgical operation, helped to swing English opinion away from Rome. The executions were few, judged by continental standards, but the English, unaccustomed to them, dubbed the queen "Bloody Mary." The chief cause, however, of Mary's failure was the shortness of her reign, which gave her resettlement of religion no chance to take root.

THE ELIZABETHAN SETTLEMENT

The most notable achievement of the long and successful reign of Elizabeth (1558-1603) was her settlement of the religious problem. It is not necessary or possible to unravel the tangle of personal and political motives which inclined the daughter of Anne Boleyn to a settlement which was not widely removed from that of Edward VI's reign. A new Act of Supremacy (1559) extinguished the "usurped foreign power" of the papacy and "restored" the control over the Church to Elizabeth with the title of "Supreme Governor." A new edition of the *Second Prayer Book of Edward VI,* less radically Protestant and no longer anti-Lutheran, was imposed as the manual of public worship (1559). The creed of the Church of England was drawn up by Convocation—the assembly of the clergy—in thirty-nine articles, and confirmed by the queen in 1563. The Thirty-Nine Articles are a revision of the Forty-Two Articles of Edward's reign, a revision made in the spirit which characterized the changes in the Prayer Book. The Articles and Prayer Book of Elizabeth's reign, with slight modifications, are still in use today.

The Church thus established by law was worthy to stand by the side of the Lutheran Church as the embodiment of a conservative reformation. "Beyond all the other Reformed Churches, the Anglican and the Lutheran clung to every reputable relic of Roman Catholic tradition and custom. If in its articles the former Church went further apart than the latter from the parent Romanism, in its ritual and its government and its tone it was more conservative" (Curtis).

It was the hope of the queen and of her talented, life-long adviser, William Cecil, later Lord Burleigh, that the religion thus established by law would gradually grip the affections of the great mass of the people, and that Roman Catholics and extreme Protestants might thus be safely coerced and the country spared the wars and weakness which religious divisions had helped to produce in Germany and other lands. This hope was realized. The long and prosperous reign of Elizabeth allowed time for a generation to grow up in the faith she had established, which viewed her Church as part of the natural order of things, "allied with honest money, cheap and capable government, national independence, and a reviving national pride" (Maitland). The support of the bulk of the influential classes and its own vigilance enabled the government without excessive severities to detect and to crush Roman Catholic plots and to repress those Protestant laymen and clergymen who wanted the Church "purified from all taint of popery"—the so-called Puritans. We shall, however, hear of both of these dissident groups later. Another factor of tremendous importance was the preoccupation of Elizabeth's continental rivals with civil and international conflicts. Still another cause for Elizabeth's success was the outcome of the Scottish Reformation.

THE SCOTTISH REFORMATION, TO THE DEATH OF MARY QUEEN OF SCOTS

Scottish Protestantism was largely the work of John Knox (1515-1572), a disciple, and a man after the heart, of Calvin. Calvinism quickly gripped many nobles and townsmen; its uncompromising appeal to logic and to duty seems to have touched a kindred chord in the hearts of the Scots. In 1557 a league of nobles, later called *Lords of the Congregation,* swore to protect and spread the new teaching, saying: "We do promesse befoir the Majestie of God, and his congregation, thet we (be his grace) shall with all diligence continually apply our hole power, substance, and our verray lyves, to manteane, sett fordward, and establish the most blessed Word of God and his Congregatioun."

The Scottish government found the movement very embarrassing. The regent, Mary of Guise—mother of Mary, the child queen of Scots and widow of King James V—was endeavoring to strengthen the monarchy and lessen the power of the everturbulent nobility. She was also striving, in the interests of her native France, to transform the traditional French alliance into a French protectorate. Her daughter, Queen Mary, was educated at the French court and was married to the Dauphin Francis in 1558. The Protestant movement threatened the regent's plans, for it gave to the Scottish lords another motive for opposing her, and to England a fulcrum for lifting Scotland away from France.

The interest which the English felt in Scottish affairs soon became intense. It had come to open and unequal war between Mary of Guise, supported by disciplined French troops, and the poorly-equipped Protestant lords. Should Elizabeth stand idle and allow the regent to crush Protestantism and make Scotland

French and Roman Catholic, or should she interfere and, what was abhorrent to her, support rebels against their lawful ruler? Elizabeth's answer to this question turned upon the claim of her cousin, Mary Queen of Scots, to the English throne.

As the table shows,[1] if Elizabeth was rightful queen of England and heredity alone counted, then Mary was her heir; but if, as many Roman Catholics asserted, Elizabeth was debarred from ruling by illegitimacy and heresy, then—such was their conclusion—Mary was by right queen of England and Elizabeth was a usurper who should be deposed by true Roman Catholics. The probability that Mary Queen of Scots, with a centralized and Roman Catholic Scotland behind her, would join hands with the English Roman Catholics and overthrow Elizabeth led the latter to send troops and a small fleet to Scotland.

The English forces and the troops of the Scottish nobles soon checkmated the French, and in the Treaty of Edinburgh (1560) it was agreed that both the English and the French should evacuate Scotland. This was equivalent to the victory of the Protestant lords, and in a few weeks the Presbyterian Kirk was set up by the Scottish Parliament (1560). It is not too much to say that Elizabeth's intervention laid the foundation for the future union of the English and the Scottish peoples.

But Mary Queen of Scots was still to be reckoned with. The death of her young husband, King Francis II of France (1559-1560), led her to return to Scotland, and here the nineteen-year-old widow took up the struggle which to all appearance had already been decided against her. She did not openly attempt to overthrow Presbyterianism, but, without concealing her allegiance to Rome, she strove to build up a party loyal to herself. She pitted her keen intellect, youth, beauty and magnetism against the suspicions of the Scottish nobles, the distrust of the redoubtable John Knox, and the money and intrigues of Elizabeth, and she won again and again. But the murder of her despicable second husband, Lord Darnley, and her prompt marriage with Earl Bothwell, the probable author of the murder, filled the cup of Scottish opposition to the brim, and in the rising which fol-

[1] See page 490 for genealogical table.

lowed she was deposed and imprisoned and replaced by her infant son James (1567).

The scene now shifts to England. Mary escaped from her prison, fled over the border, and threw herself upon the mercy of her cousin Elizabeth. The moving story of her stay in England, of the conspiracies against Elizabeth which sprang up around her—some of them instigated by Philip II—of her tightening imprisonment, and of her execution in 1587 by Elizabeth's command, is told in many an absorbing volume.[1] Her death was demanded by English opinion, for her existence and her faith rendered Elizabeth insecure and threatened English peace, should she survive the English queen. Her mortal remains repose, near the body of Elizabeth, in Westminster Abbey, whither they were removed by her son James, after he became king of England.

THE CATHOLIC REFORMATION

The Catholic Reformation,[2] which had been so long desired and despaired of, at last became a reality. Like its rival, the Protestant Reformation, it sprang out of the religious soil of the later Middle Ages. St. Catherine, Savonarola, and others had voiced its hopes, and asked, not for change of doctrine, but for renewed religious fervor. The spread of the Protestant movement almost certainly hastened the coming of the Catholic Reformation with its "exalted devotion," its "unquenchable religious hope," and a "tenacity which no reversal could wear out." Its outstanding features were the Society of Jesus and the Council of Trent.

The Society of Jesus was the most influential of the monastic associations which set to work in the first half of the sixteenth century to renew Catholic faith and zeal. Its founder and first general was Ignatius Loyola (1491-1556), a Spanish nobleman and brilliant army officer, who was converted at the age of thirty and abandoned a worldly career for evangelistic labors. Finding his education inadequate for the new career, he started to school

---

[1] See, for example, R. S. Rait, *Mary Queen of Scots* (*Scottish History by Contemporary Writers*).

[2] Also called the Counter Reformation; more accurately the Roman Catholic Reformation.

again with the little boys, and, though his educational progress was slow because interrupted by religious meditations, street preaching and the like, he persevered and, at the age of forty-three, he secured his M.A. at the University of Paris (1534).

Ignatius was deeply religious and had perfect trust in God's guidance. He found great spiritual comfort in the services of the Church and regarded implicit obedience to her teachings as the very foundation of righteousness. His little book, the *Spiritual Exercises*,[1] is a manual of religious drill designed to lead the sinner to concentrate all his faculties upon the task of realizing his sinfulness and God's abounding grace. "Did they not show you monsters and devils?" asked a scoffer of one who had gone through the *Exercises*. "Worse than that," was the answer; "they showed me myself." In truth, the book is to the Catholic Reformation what Luther's *The Freedom of a Christian Man* is to Protestantism.

It was the cherished plan of Loyola, all through these years of preparation, to lead a mission to the Mohammedans of Palestine, and to this end he enrolled a small band of fellow students at the University of Paris. But a year of evangelistic work in Italy opened their eyes to the wider needs of their Church, and they broadened their plans to include also the pagans beyond the seas, heretics, schismatics and the faithful. Their plans were approved and their order established by Pope Paul III in 1540.

The Jesuits were an order of a new sort. They took the ordinary monastic vows, and those of the highest rank took also a special vow of unquestioning obedience to the commands of the pope in everything pertaining to the salvation of souls and the propagation of the Roman Catholic faith. The early name they gave themselves—the Company of Jesus—indicates their military ideal: they were to be the holy *condottieri* of Christ and his vicar. As such they were freed from wearing a special costume, from routine Church services, and from all control save that of their general and the papacy.[2]

The success of the new order was astounding. The Jesuits

[1] English translation by Father Mullan is the best.

[2] Of course this did not prevent the various secular governments from interfering.

were men of action. As preachers of simple religion in pulpit or on street corner, they brought about a widespread revival and stirred the parish clergy to emulation. Their efforts to lift up the poor and the fallen have been likened to the work of the Salvation Army. Their missionary labors carried Francis Xavier to India and Japan, and North and South America were soon familiar with the dauntless Jesuit fathers. In the field of education they probably won their greenest laurels. Their belief in education may be seen in the fact that the ten "charter members" of the order were all Masters of Arts of the University of Paris. They opened schools and colleges for the clergy and the laity and developed an educational system which embraced the ancient classics as well as the medieval subjects. When Loyola died (1556), the order already had one hundred colleges and houses in Portugal, Spain, Italy, Sicily, Germany, France, Brazil, and the East Indies. Their successful efforts to attract to their schools young men of promise and worldly position have been adversely criticized, but the order gloried in depriving "the world" of its leaders.

The charges of excessive political activity, spiritual pride and casuistry, made against the order in later centuries may be true or not;[1] its invaluable services to Roman Catholicism in the sixteenth century are indubitable. The society inspired the Church with its faith, its fervor, its ideals; it made monasticism again respected and feared; it may be said to have held southern Europe loyal to the papacy, to have disputed parts of Teutonic Europe with the Protestants, and to have given Catholicism compensation in the New World for its losses in the Old. Even the Council of Trent was, in a way, a triumph for the order founded by Loyola.

The Council of Trent was called together by Paul III in 1545 at the urgent demand of Charles V. The emperor hoped that it would reform the abuses which had been criticized and thus cause the German Protestants to cease their opposition to Roman Catholicism and to himself. But the council promptly declared that its work was to be the extirpation of heresies and the refor-

[1] The order was suppressed by the papacy from 1773 to 1814.

mation of abuses.　Moreover, it gave formal notice in its first business session that "in confirming dogmas and in restoring morals in the Church," it would be guided by the Bible *and* unwritten tradition—that is, the supplementary decisions of the Church; and it also decreed that no one should "presume to interpret the said sacred Scripture contrary to that sense which holy mother Church—whose [right] it is to judge of the true sense and interpretation of the holy Scriptures—hath held and doth hold. . . ." Obviously the Protestants had nothing to expect from the council.

The council was in session with several long interruptions from 1545 to 1563 and carried out its program.　Nine-tenths of its members came from Italy, Spain and France, and the Italian prelates alone formed an overwhelming majority.　Teutonic Europe was virtually unrepresented.

The Council of Trent defined, in a broad and inclusive spirit, the leading doctrines of the medieval Church, especially those which had been attacked by the Protestants, and anathematized the opposing and usually Protestant doctrines.　It caused to be drawn up a new and comprehensive list of heretical and immoral books which the faithful were forbidden to read or possess, the so-called *Index Librorum Prohibitorum*.　This superseded the various local indexes and, with subsequent revisions made by papal authority, it has remained an essential feature in the protective system of the Church.

The council reformed the more serious abuses in the Church at large, but left to the papacy the reform of its own court; it put an end to many financial scandals and superstitious practices; and in a way it outlined the further reforms which the papacy would need to make.　Most important of all, the council provided for the selection of better and more thoroughly educated men for the higher and lower offices of the Church.　The scandal of worldly ecclesiastics was to cease.

From the very beginning of its labors, although not without some heated debates, the council deferred to papal leadership and guidance.　The opposition to the papacy, which had been so marked at Constance and Basel, now came to an end in the face of the Protestant foe.[1]

In all the work of the council the Jesuits had a distinguished part. They were the learned and zealous advocates of medieval doctrine, of an educated and devoted clergy, of papal supremacy, and of "no terms to heretics."

The Council of Trent marks the decisive acceptance of reform by the papacy and the Church. "For the whole Roman Catholic Church of the sixteenth century its consequences are of an importance which can scarcely be exaggerated: it showed that Church as a living institution, capable of work and achievement; it strengthened the confidence both of her members and herself, and it was a powerful factor in heightening her efficiency as a competitor with Protestantism and in restoring and reinforcing her imperiled unity."

RESULTS OF THE REFORMATION

That the Reformation (Protestant and Catholic) was vitally important is admitted by all, but why it was important is still a question of doubt or of controversy. Looking at the question from the standpoint of the present, some of the least debatable results seem to be as follows:

(1) The Reformation involved an increased interest in religion. (2) It contributed to religious toleration. In the sixteenth century each Church and government felt that it was right and necessary to constrain heretics by fire, sword, or exile. But the successful claim of the Protestant to hold views which the Catholic Church regarded as heretical was logically an admission that others might disagree with them, and in the long run toleration was established in practice and accepted in theory. (3) Similarly, the Reformation placed Church membership upon a voluntary basis instead of leaving it compulsory as it was in the Middle Ages. (4) The successful assertion by the Protestants of a right to reach religious conclusions at variance with the teachings

[1] The declaration of the supremacy of the pope over the Church—of *papal infallibility*—was explicitly made at the Vatican Council in 1870.

of the Catholic Church laid the foundation for complete freedom of investigation. Scholars may now make researches in all the fields of human knowledge or curiosity, and may maintain their conclusions or inferences, however they may impinge upon, or clash with, religious dogmas. To be sure, Roman Catholicism will strictly, and some Protestant Churches less strictly, discipline or expel a man or woman, especially a clergyman, whose conclusions seem to contradict their tenets; but expulsion from a Church no longer involves secular penalties.

Broadly speaking, the modern state tends to maintain neutrality among the different faiths which men may choose to profess. It was not so in the sixteenth or seventeenth century. Indeed, civil wars and international wars were fought at least ostensibly for religious reasons. Actually, the so-called religious wars were waged primarily for secular purposes, and it will therefore be most instructive to treat of them below as part of the ordinary history of mankind in the period we are considering.

CHAPTER XXII

HAPSBURG AND VALOIS. THE AGE OF PHILIP II
EUROPE 1559-1610

"THE sixteenth was the century of Spain, the seventeenth the century of France, and the eighteenth the century of England." This broad generalization has considerable truth behind it. We shall provisionally accept its validity by calling the second half of the sixteenth century the Age of Philip II, leaving the reader free to choose a better title if he can find it. But since, in this chapter, we continue to deal chiefly with international affairs, it will be convenient to adjust chronology to diplomatic events. Accordingly we shall regard the half-century after the Peace of Câteau-Cambrésis (1559-1609) as the Age of Philip II. True, Philip died in 1598; but the chief problems with which he dealt received their solution around 1609.

Philip II possessed real talent. He had not the dash and fire of his half-brother, Don John of Austria, or the statesmanship of his half-sister, Margaret, duchess of Parma, or the military genius of Margaret's son, Alexander Farnese, later duke of Parma. These, no doubt, inherited talent from Charles V. But Philip had a prodigious capacity for hard work, a wonderful tenacity in clinging to his plans, and a long reign in which to realize them. His detailed information about the various governments of Europe and the strong and weak points of their leading men was worthy of a super-detective. But he was often incredibly tardy in reaching a decision when speed was essential to success. "If death were coming from Spain," a Spanish viceroy of Naples said, "I would be sure of living a long time." Philip was a thorough Spaniard. He was more Iberian than Charles, for his mother was Portuguese. Moreover, he had grown up in Spain and had the typical aristocratic Spaniard's scrupulous religious orthodoxy, austerity, pride of country and hauteur. To many of his contemporaries and to most non-Spaniards since his time he appears as a somber, bigoted tyrant. Yet there was a vein of poetry and art in the man that hints at gentler gifts.

THE INTERNATIONAL SITUATION DURING THE EARLY YEARS OF PHILIP II'S REIGN

Spain was impoverished at his accession. But people can, and often do, fight on until their country economically is but a shell. And the treasure fleets from America brought home a yearly harvest of silver and gold. It was not enough to save Spain from exhaustion, but it was enough to help finance her wars. Furthermore, Philip was able to enlist Spanish backing for most of his campaigns because of the "unquestioning crusading orthodoxy" of his people. Usually he was in a position to pose as the defender of the Faith, as we shall see in the survey of his career.

But the position which Philip II occupied in his time was not so much due to these factors or the prestige of his father as to the circumstance that his great rivals were more hampered by events than he was. A brief survey of the international situation will make this clear.

The Austrian Hapsburgs—Ferdinand I and his immediate successors—had withdrawn from general European affairs after the Peace of Augsburg (1555) and were devoting their attention to the immediate problems of their lands—the Austrian territories, Bohemia and Hungary. In France the accidental death of King Henry II in the celebration of the peace of 1559 left the crown to three ineffective and sterile sons in succession (1559-1589) and brought on a crop of intrigues and revolts which well-nigh paralyzed the international influence of the kingdom. In England the accession of Elizabeth (1558) placed on the throne a ruler who at the beginning of her long reign had neither army nor navy. Moreover, her heir was Mary, Queen of Scots since 1542, who was bred in France and was queen of that country during the short reign of her husband, Francis II (1559-1560). Elizabeth had to walk warily for many years because of her domestic problems, especially the establishment of peace in the dangerous sphere of religion. In Turkey power passed on the death of Solyman the Magnificent (1566) to his less competent successor, Selim II. In 1571 a great international force commanded by Don John of Austria inflicted an overwhelming defeat on the Turkish fleet at the battle of Lepanto. The victory enhanced the prestige of Spain, although it did not abate the Barbary pirates in the western Mediterranean.

Of all the rivals of Spain, England was in the happiest position. She was protected by the seas and by the statesmanship and luck of Queen Elizabeth. It was part of England's good fortune, and of Philip's too, that Elizabeth abhorred war and continental complications and sought to win support for her precarious throne by maintaining a policy of peace and royal parsimony which permitted her people to grow in wealth and in contentment with their queen. She might have taken a leading part in the affairs of France and of the Spanish Empire; the revolts in France and the Netherlands, to be discussed below, gave her ample opportunity. She played only a very minor part in them. When the Huguenots or the Calvinists of the Netherlands seemed likely to be crushed, she lent them a little money or a handful of troops or encouraged her subjects to bear them private aid to the end that they might not be overborne. She did not afford them enough assistance to win. The giving of this aid, and the piracies she permitted English sea captains to indulge in at the expense of the Spanish or French governments, might have been treated by them as acts of war, but each country was more afraid of throwing her on the side of the other than of enduring her pin-pricks, and they contented themselves with reprisals of the same sort. Besides, each of the royal families was opportunely encouraged, as need arose, to think that Elizabeth might marry into it. Elizabeth's methods, it is clear, were thoroughly tricky and selfish. But not more so than those of her opponents. And Elizabeth's methods involved no great expense and promoted the growth of English wealth and well-being while her rivals were exhausting themselves. She "kept her people out of the war." And even when she did finally intervene, she soon reverted to her earlier practice of letting her subjects fight on their own hook. It may again be said that Elizabeth's bias toward peace was a relative advantage to Philip and helps to account for the prolonged ascendency of Spain.

THE CIVIL AND RELIGIOUS WARS IN FRANCE, 1562-1592

The effacement of France from international affairs after 1559 was due to a series of civil wars. It has been said of the long religious wars in France (the civil wars) that in "one-fifth of them religion was the cause, in four-fifths it was only the pretext."

The weakness of Francis II, Charles IX and Henry III, who reigned but did not rule in France from 1559 to 1589, is the primary explanation of these wars. Their weakness encouraged many great nobles and cities to attempt to throw off the royal authority which Francis I and Henry II had asserted. These efforts at decentralization were aided by the three-cornered struggle among Henry II's widow, Catherine de' Medici, and the princely families of Guise and Bourbon for the valuable privilege of ruling in the king's name. This struggle was complicated by two other factors: first, the head of the Bourbon family was next in succession to the throne after the sons of Henry II; secondly, some of the Bourbons were Calvinists and the French Calvinists were a force to be reckoned with.

Calvinism, the militant form of Protestantism, had spread into France from Geneva, had absorbed the earlier French Protestantism, and had won over many Frenchmen of the middle class, a large number of the lesser nobles, and some of the high nobility. A few of the nobles had been attracted by Calvin's doctrine; others had been won over by its spirit of independence and by the fresh excuse it gave them for opposing the royal government. The French Calvinists, who are known as Huguenots—a word probably derived from the *Eidgenossen* (Swiss)—increased rapidly after the death of Henry II, and by 1562 they numbered about one million out of a total population of about twelve millions. They were to be found in all parts of the country, but especially in the southwest—that is, in the territory bounded by the Loire, the Bay of Biscay, the Pyrenees and the Rhone, where the Bourbons had their principal possessions including their microscopic kingdom of Navarre on the French side of the Pyrenees. The Huguenots were formidable by reason of their spirit and their organization. But the mass of the French people was and remained faithful to the ancient Church.

During the reign of the boy king Francis II (1559-1560), the Guises, who were uncles of Francis II's wife, Mary Queen of Scots, were all-powerful, and, resolute Catholics that they were, they continued Henry II's policy of persecuting the Huguenots. When, however, Charles IX (1560-1574) came to the throne at the age of ten, Catherine de' Medici, his mother, secured the regency. She was a relative of Pope Clement VII, who had bowed to the force of Charles V and had crowned him. A little later Clement had arranged the marriage with the future Henry II in one of his spasmodic efforts to get a counterweight to the power of the emperor. And now the Italian princess was regent in France. She was "a true Medici in her taste for the arts, for magnificence and for luxury, as well as in her intelligence" (Lavisse). But she was also a stranger to generosity, enthusiasm, or fanaticism. Her master passion was the desire for power. She accordingly sought to free herself from dependence on the Guises by securing the support of the Bourbons. That meant that she must favor the Huguenots. Accordingly a royal edict was issued in January, 1562, granting the Huguenots the right of public worship outside of the cities and walled villages.

This large measure of toleration was displeasing to many Catholics, and the young duke of Guise gained instant popularity when his escort picked a quarrel with an unarmed congregation of Huguenots at the walled village of Vassy and slew twenty-three of them (March, 1562). The Massacre of Vassy turned out to be the opening of prolonged civil war.

The mutual hate of Catholics and Huguenots now combined with political discontent, mob passions and the lust of plunder to produce massacres, ravagings and sanguinary battles. The Huguenot forces were usually beaten, but they hung on, with some help from Elizabeth and from Germany. Queen Catherine was struck with their power of recuperation and, after two unsuccessful efforts to satisfy them with a more limited degree of toleration, she announced most generous terms. By the edict of 1570 she granted the Huguenots the right of public worship in two cities in each province, in the residences of great nobles, and in all places where it had been enjoyed before the wars began. Furthermore, the edict declared the Huguenots eligible for all offices and careers equally with the Catholics and, as security for the observance of the new decree, allowed the Huguenots to hold four fortified cities—La Rochelle, Montauban, La Charité and Cognac. The location of these cities is significant.

The queen mother's efforts to make the peace of 1570 permanent did not stop here. She made the leading Huguenot general, Coligny, whose military title was Admiral of France, a member of the royal council and presented him with a fortune. Finally, she negotiated a marriage between her daughter Marguerite and the young Huguenot chief of the Bourbons, King Henry of Navarre. The marriage took place in Notre Dame, Paris, August 18, 1572, in the presence of a great concourse, which included the leading Huguenots who had flocked to Paris to witness it.

Nine days after the marriage most of these Huguenot "wedding guests" were dead, massacred by Guise troops and the populace of Paris. The Massacre of St. Bartholomew began on the eve of the feast of St. Bartholomew, which falls on August 24. It lasted three days in Paris and ten days in other cities, to which it was extended by royal command. Ten thousand Huguenots perished in the massacres and Henry of Navarre barely escaped by turning Catholic. Protestant Europe thrilled with horror. Philip II of Spain had several reasons for satisfaction.

The responsibility for the massacre rests on Catherine de' Medici. Admiral Coligny, it seems, had won over the young Charles IX to a plan for declaring war on Spain and driving Spain out of the Netherlands. To Coligny this meant the liberation of the Calvinists of the Low Countries; to the king it meant glory and freedom from his mother's tutelage. To Catherine it looked like a war of defeat. But the king stood firm and she had a thug hired to murder Coligny. The attempt on the admiral's life merely wounded him (August 22). The Huguenots traced the attempted murder to the Guises, whence the trail would have led to the door of the queen. She accordingly resolved to destroy her pursuers and their avengers by wiping out all the Huguenot leaders. Charles IX was browbeaten into consenting to the massacre, and the Guises arranged the details. The plan was worthy of an Italian despot.

The massacres weakened the Huguenots by depriving them of many valuable leaders, including Coligny. But the queen found that they were not ruined. They still had La Rochelle, and courage, and Henry of Navarre, who promptly reverted to his former faith, and they now gained the support of a growing group of French Catholics.

This group had already been convinced that it would cost France too much in blood and treasure to crush the Huguenots, and they were now persuaded by the massacres that they must, as patriots, help the Huguenots to secure toleration as quickly as possible. These Catholics were dubbed *Politiques* ("politicians") by their more fanatical coreligionists. There was another class of *Politiques* with motives less honorable, who thought that they could extort more from the government by aiding than by fighting the Huguenots. The chief of these mercenary *Politiques* was for a time no less a personage than the king's own brother, the duke of Anjou, who died before his turn came for the crown.

The combination of Huguenots and *Politiques,* led by the duke of Anjou and supported by 20,000 hired German troops, forced Henry III, who came to the throne in 1574, to buy off the duke and issue another and very liberal edict of toleration (1576). The edict, however, suffered the fate of its predecessors.

The union of *Politiques* and Huguenots brought about a counter-organization of Catholic nobles and cities, whose members swore to obey the head of the association and to establish the supremacy of the old faith and the "ancient liberties" of the provinces of France. The League, as it called itself, pleased the Catholic populace, whose religious devotion had now been increasing for some years under the inspiration of the Catholic Reformation, but it alarmed Catherine de' Medici, especially when the duke of Guise, the idol of the Catholic populace, became its head. Henry III was therefore persuaded to declare himself the head of the League. He used its backing to whittle down the last edict of toleration and then declared the League dissolved (1577).

For the next seven years the civil war degenerated into small raids, plunderings, revolts and sieges, with no large-scale operations. Henry III's government steadily lost popular favor, because of economic distress due to disorder and maladministration. King Henry of Navarre's stock at the same time was rising. He knew how to court popularity. The restless duke of Anjou coquetted with various plans. In 1581-1583 he was in the Netherlands on his own account, hoping to become the head of the insurgent state. Henry III gave him only secret and grudging aid, and the Netherlands, disappointed in their hopes, saw him depart for home with feelings of relief. In 1584 he died.

The death of the duke of Anjou was the most momentous act of his life. For it left Henry of Navarre as heir to the throne of the childless Henry III. This infuriated the ardent Catholic majority, and the ambitious duke of Guise revived the League on a popular basis. The people of the capital joined it almost *en masse*. Its published program declared for the wiping out of Huguenotism, the exclusion of Henry of Navarre from the throne, and the "restoration of good government" throughout the country. Philip II of Spain was accepted as a member of the League and supported it with money and troops.

King Henry III thought it prudent again to join the League and to order the Huguenots to return to Catholicism. But his orders were ignored. The struggle was now on between the League headed by the duke of Guise, and Henry of Navarre supported by *Politiques* and aided by funds supplied by Queen Elizabeth. German and Swiss troops were hired to come to the assistance of the Huguenots. The struggle engrossed all France and gave Philip II an opportunity to prepare his Armada against Elizabeth in order to sweep her from his path and then to crush the rebel Netherlanders. How this plan fared will be shown later.

Henry of Navarre scored the first great victory of the Huguenots in October, 1587, but the next month the duke of Guise evened the score by defeating and then feloniously massacring a Huguenot army of German-Swiss mercenaries. All Catholic France rang with the fame of the duke of Guise, who cast the discredited Henry III into the shade and bore himself as the master of the State. The king therefore came to the desperate decision to have the duke murdered. The murder (December, 1588) merely made matters worse for King Henry, for the duke of Mayenne, the younger brother of the duke of Guise, became head of the now embittered League and assumed the government of Catholic France with the title of Lieutenant-General of the Kingdom.

King Henry III thereupon threw himself into the arms of Henry of Navarre, who for his part announced that he would never deny public worship to the Catholics. The two Henrys now decided to attack Paris, the center of the League, and laid siege to it with Huguenot, royal and hired foreign troops. But the ardent Catholic population of the city stood firm. Ceaseless processions passed from church to church, imploring the aid of Heaven. One young man, urged on by visions, decided to come to the aid of Heaven and murdered Henry III, August 1, 1589. This raised the siege of Paris, but it extinguished the race of the Valois and made Henry of Navarre king of France—unless, as the League declared, his heresy excluded him from the throne.

King Henry of Navarre was well fitted by nature and training to defend his claims to the throne. He was now thirty-five, dashing, hearty and of winning manners; he was, it must be said, very dissolute, but of superabundant vitality, shrewdness and soldierly qualities. Huguenot hopes rose high.

Trusting in the strength of his legal right to the crown, his devoted followers and the aid of Queen Elizabeth and other interested foreigners, Henry of Navarre set to work to overthrow the League. But the League, supported by French Catholic feeling and openly aided by Philip of Spain, could not be overthrown. Twice, in 1590 and 1592, Alexander of Parma, the Spanish general, led his disciplined troops over the frontiers of the Netherlands and checkmated the army of Navarre. A Spanish force garrisoned Paris in 1591, and other Spanish troops occupied strategic places in Brittany and the South. It was risky to suspend Parma's promising operations against the Dutch, but Philip believed the outcome would justify the risk.

To understand what was involved we must now (1592) leave French affairs in suspense and bring the situation in the Netherlands up to date.

THE REVOLT OF THE NETHERLANDS, TO 1590

The revolt of the Burgundian dominions—it will be convenient henceforth to speak of them as the Netherlands or Low Countries—from the government of Philip II as that of a foreigner is not surprising. Had not the Spaniards risen against Charles V at the beginning of his reign for a similar reason? Charles was a Netherlander-born. He was suave and conciliatory, knew how to humor the people among whom he had grown up, and kept the nobles in his employ. He recognized the charters of the different provinces and cities, although in practice he largely governed as if they did not exist. And Charles had made it harder for his successor by heightening the self-consciousness of the Netherlands. He had freed some of their provinces from the suzerainty of France and the others from any real jurisdiction of Germany; he had honored the Estates-General in order to lessen the separation of the provinces. But Philip II was of a different type. He was Spanish-bred, less tactful, more autocratic, more peremptory, more bigoted. Moreover, he was an absentee ruler, governing through a succession of governors-general.

The leading nobles, including William of Orange on whose arm Charles had leaned in that touching abdication ceremony in Brussels (1555), protested to Philip that Margaret of Parma (governor-general, 1559-1567) ignored their advice, and they re-

monstrated—although they were all Catholics—against the fierce
persecution of the Protestants as hurtful to the country. (Northern Europe never took kindly to the burning of heretics.) They
also petitioned that the Estates-General should be called to consider the situation. Philip ignored their representations. Then
some two hundred lesser nobles, a few of them Protestants, met
and pledged themselves to work for the relaxation of the persecutions and the calling of the Estates-General. An opponent
dubbed them *"Beggars"* and they boldly adopted the name (1566).

The Protestants were as yet only a minority. The Calvinists,
as was natural, were in the South and the Lutherans in the
North. The Calvinists, who were mostly artisans, erroneously
interpreted the demands of the *Beggars* for less persecutions as a
promise of support. They defied the regent by worshiping openly,
while some of the bolder spirits among them, with the gleeful
aid of the riffraff of the cities, wrecked and pillaged a number of
churches (1566). These "iconoclastic riots" alarmed the leading
nobles with the prospect of mob rule, and they aided Margaret in
crushing the opposition.

But Philip resolved to teach the Netherlands a lesson. He
accordingly dispatched the old duke of Alva overland from Italy
with an army of 10,000 veterans. Margaret vainly advised
moderation and then resigned; whereupon Alva replaced her as
governor-general (1567-1573). Thousands—Protestants and
Catholics—fled at his approach and Orange himself discreetly
withdrew to his German estates. Alva opened a reign of terror.
He set up an arbitrary tribunal, the "Council of Blood," which
executed hundreds, including the great Catholic nobles, Egmont
and Horn. Orange and his brother Louis led private armies into
the land, but they were defeated. Alva was triumphant master
(1568) and Philip announced an amnesty. But the revolt was
to be renewed and was to last officially for eighty years (1568-
1648).

Alva's army was invincible, but how was he to pay it? Legally
the provincial estates voted the taxes. Charles had cajoled them.
Alva would force them, and he proposed, along with other plans,
a perpetual tax of ten per cent on all sales. He would exempt

raw materials and goods for export, but he turned a deaf ear to
the cry of the merchants that such a tax—called the *alcabala* in
Spain—would ruin a commercial people. Philip backed up the
regent and ordered the collection of the "Tenth Penny" (February, 1572). This decision piled financial grievances upon constitutional and religious ones.

In 1569 the indefatigable William of Orange, in his capacity
as sovereign prince of the tiny state of Orange (located in the
heart of France), had issued letters of marque to his Nether-
lander seafaring friends, to give them some sort of legal position
in privateering against Spanish vessels in the Channel and on the
coasts of the Netherlands. Orange had no seacoast, and the
privateers were at best patriotic pirates whose deeds were often
barbarous. Having no home port, these "Sea Beggars," as they
called themselves, were hampered in their work. In April, 1572,
however, they captured Brill, a home port, and the capture kindled
a flame of revolt which Alva could not extinguish. He could
and did defeat William of Orange and his brother Louis, who
had raised an army in France, and drove them from the South.
But in the meantime Holland and Zealand, the wealthy states of
the North, had revolted and chosen William as their stadtholder
or governor, under the nominal sovereignty of Philip II. If Alva
had been supplied with money he could have ended the rebellion.
As it was, he could not quite finish the task. And his successors
were to be in the same boat.

The long story of the war, with its tales of heroism and
ferocity, of Catholic bigotry matched by Calvinistic bigotry, of
racial antagonisms, of foreign intrigue and domestic treachery,
of the deathless spirit of liberty ever rising from crushing blows,
can be told here only in broad outline.

Recalling Alva and appointing the conciliatory Requescens as
regent or governor-general (1573-1576), Philip attempted to
break up the opposition by withdrawing the "Tenth Penny" and
by granting an amnesty to all save the leaders of the revolt. The
concessions were welcomed, but they could not satisfy the Calvinists or the opponents of absolutism, who could expect nothing
but the worst from Philip of Spain. Indeed, in the very month

that Alva left, the prince of Orange made a close alliance with the Calvinists by adopting their form of faith. It was to be a finish fight.

Prince William of Orange, or William the Silent (he knew when to keep his mouth shut), was by birth and baptism a German Lutheran. From a relative he inherited rich possessions in the Netherlands and also the independent principality of Orange. He was brought up a Catholic at the court of Charles V and served him and Philip II as general, diplomat and administrator. When Alva's approach led him to flee, he returned to his German estates and his Lutheran faith. When he got his foothold at last in Holland (1573), he became a Calvinist. He was not bigoted; his religion was broader than the creeds of his age. He went over to Calvinism because he had at length realized that the Netherland Calvinists were, in fervor and unwillingness to compromise, the backbone of the resistance to Spain. Most of the Dutch Lutherans followed his example. But it must not be forgotten that there were not a few Catholics who stood shoulder to shoulder with their Protestant compatriots in the battle for freedom from Spain.

Requescens could not end the revolt. The spirit of the patriots was shown in their heroic, year-long defense of Leyden. Requescens had the troops but no money to pay them, and they organized themselves into independent bands which ravaged the lands of friend and foe. The people of the South turned to Orange for protection against the lawless soldiery and went over to his side when Antwerp was sacked and almost ruined by them (1576). Requescens had died some months before and his death facilitated the coalescence of North and South.

By the *Pacification of Ghent* (1576) all seventeen of the provinces of the Netherlands, Walloon, Flemish and Dutch in race, Catholic and Protestant in religion, leagued themselves together to compel the withdrawal of the Spanish troops, the cessation of persecution of Protestants, and the establishment of constitutional government. Don John of Austria, the hero of Lepanto, had to swear to observe the terms of the Pacification before he was accepted as the successor of Requescens (1576-

1578). He soon found that his authority was empty and that William of Orange was the one to whom all local authorities looked for guidance.

The Pacification of Ghent did not prove to be a lasting settlement. The Dutch provinces intended that Philip II's rule should be merely nominal. The Calvinists of the North were hostile to the Catholics. The South, rendered more Catholic by the emigration of Calvinists to the North, was inclined to concede that Philip's representative should have real authority. This inclination was strengthened by the jealousy of Orange felt by a group of leading nobles in the South. This jealousy was skillfully fomented by Alexander of Parma, son of the former regent Margaret, who was sent to the Netherlands with reënforcements, for Don John toward the end of 1577. Parma proved to be probably the greatest soldier of the period, and as a statesman the equal of the prince of Orange. In January, 1579, he organized the nobles of the South to support the cause of King Philip. This compelled the other provinces to close their ranks in opposition. This they did in the *Union of Utrecht,* 1579.

By the Union of Utrecht the people of the seven Dutch provinces dedicated their lives and property to the cause of freedom and drew up a framework of government. As a constitutional arrangement it conceded too few powers to the central government which it created, but the recognition of the quasi-monarchical leadership of the prince of Orange and his successors supplemented it adequately for generations.

The Union of Utrecht was achieved none too soon. For the cause of King Philip was now in the ascendant again. This was due in part to the genius of Parma, who became governor-general in 1578, and in part to Philip's improved financial position which resulted from his acquisition in 1580 of the crown and dominions of Portugal.

Sebastian, king of Portugal, perished in a rash campaign against Morocco in 1578, and his heir, Cardinal Henry, was king for only two years. The earlier intermarriages of the royal families of the peninsula now at last bore their inevitable fruit, and Philip II of Spain plucked it. He was a near heir, if not the nearest, and the support of the Jesuits and the argument which the duke of Alva furnished with a Spanish army led to the acceptance of the claims of his master, who was crowned in 1581. The new king was pledged to keep Portugal and her colonies for the Portuguese. Of course he did not do so. Portugal's resources went into the Spanish pot, and the Portuguese colonies were opened to the raids of the open and secret foes of King Philip, especially the Dutch. But these raids did not begin at once, while Philip's fresh support for Parma in the Netherlands was soon forthcoming.

Parma gained ground steadily in the southern Netherlands, and in 1585 he had possession of the last part of it when he reconquered Antwerp from the Orange partisans and expelled all the Protestants from the city. Long before this stroke, however, the prince of Orange was convinced that without extensive foreign aid the revolt would collapse. It was his opinion that the ancient foe to Spain, namely, France, was the natural liberator, and to France he appealed.

In 1581 Philip's authority was formally renounced by the Dutch in the noble and stirring "Declaration of Independence," and the duke of Anjou was set up as "prince and seigneur" of the Netherlands, with the prince of Orange as his lieutenant-general. Anjou, as has been noted above, proved quite unsatisfactory. Not only did he lack judgment, but he brought the insurgents only a modest amount of help, for the very good reason that the French monarch was afraid and unable to give him open support. He turned his back on the Netherlands after two years of mutual disappointment.

In 1584 the Dutch fortunes sank to their lowest point. Parma was steadily gaining, foreign support was lacking, and to crown all, the prince of Orange was assassinated (July). The murder was instigated by King Philip, who in 1580 had published his *Ban and Edict in Form of Proscription* in which he promised a title of nobility to the one who should kill the prince. Orange's notable *Apology* answered Philip's aspersions (1580).

"Such was the end," says Blok, "of the great prince to whom the Netherland nation owes her independence. His distinguished statesmanship, his indomitable energy, his unbroken courage and firm confidence in the justice of the cause, his broad views on the so narrowly understood ideas of religion and of conscience, his unstinted zeal for popular liberty and self-government, give him title to the admiring homage of posterity." [1]

The Dutch patriots now turned to Queen Elizabeth for aid, since French help was out of the question. Elizabeth's caution led her to refuse to accept the sovereignty of the Netherlands, but she sent some money and men and allowed her favorite, the earl of Leicester, to take office as "governor-general," a more or less fictitious office which he held from 1585 to 1587.

THE INVINCIBLE ARMADA

Leicester's direct assistance was of only moderate value, but indirectly it was of importance, for it convinced Philip that he must sweep the English from his path before he could complete the subjugation of the Dutch. Don John and other advisers had urged this for years, and Philip now adopted their views. The situation seemed favorable. France was paralyzed by civil war; Mary Queen of Scots, who as queen of England might have gravitated to the side of France, was executed in 1587. And so the preparation of the "Invincible Armada" went on apace. Philip had been very patient. Drake, Hawkins and other marauding English freebooters and traders had been pillaging the Spanish colonies for upwards of twenty years and capturing Spanish vessels in European waters. Elizabeth had shared the plunder and had secretly and openly aided the Dutch. Philip's retaliations became marked from 1585 on. A crisis was clearly approaching.[2]

Elizabeth's preparations for meeting the great Spanish Armada were largely improvised. The English freebooting and trading captains contributed the bulk of the defending force, which had a contingent of royal vessels and was placed under the supreme command of Lord Howard, a Catholic nobleman.

[1] *History of the People of the Netherlands,* iii, pages 178-179. Translation revised.
[2] See pages 572-573.

The Spanish plan contemplated the destruction of the English fleet by the Armada, which was then to convoy Parma and an army across from the Netherlands, who, with the aid of a spontaneous rising of English Catholics, would replace Elizabeth with a Catholic sovereign. This might conceivably be Philip himself, for Mary Queen of Scots had bequeathed her claims to him.

The decisive sea battle took place in July, 1588. The outcome was a brilliant success for the English. Their vessels were smaller but they were easier to maneuver, sailed closer to the wind, and were better armed. The battle was in a way a contest between two systems. The one was that of self-reliance and daring, cultivated by years of unchecked and unsupervised privateering and piracy on all the seas. The other was a system of ponderous mass tactics, which had worked well in the Mediterranean, but was unfitted to grapple with the elusive strategy of the English sea-dogs. No doubt Parma would have made short work of the green English troops that Elizabeth assembled and harangued so magnificently. But Drake, Hawkins, Howard and Frobisher gave him no opportunity to bring an army across the Channel.

The defeat of the Armada was a tonic as well as a decisive battle victory. In the crisis Englishmen of both religions had stood together. Their troubled and gloomy temperament, bred of the executions, confiscations and miseries of the preceding reigns and of fears for the future, had been steadily mellowing under the scepter of Elizabeth, and now it "gave place to a sanguine self-confidence, a robust and boisterous national pride, which . . . broke out in a national poetry, which in Shakespeare overflows with jubilant patriotism" (Seeley). The English Protestant state had "won its spurs." The English colonies in America were to be one of the results.

The failure of his great fleet was a bitter disappointment to Philip, but it did not dishearten him. Parma's veteran army was intact and the French situation continued to favor him. Elizabeth's great Armada, sent in 1589 to provoke a rising of the Portuguese, failed of its object, and Elizabeth reverted in the main to her earlier policy of letting her sea-dogs follow their own devices and of giving modest subsidies to the Dutch and the Huguenots. Philip's confidence that all would yet be well remained unshaken. He would "carry on."

The interaction of events in France and the Dutch Netherlands, to which we now turn, comes out most closely in the years 1590-1593, which were crucial both for the French and for the Dutch.

THE REVOLT OF THE NETHERLANDS AND THE CIVIL WAR IN FRANCE AFTER 1590

In 1590 Alexander of Parma had the upper hand in the Netherlands; despite the lack of funds, his veterans, living mainly on plunder, pushed on. But in France Henry IV was gaining. And so Philip, as we have seen, ordered Parma to assume the defensive in the Netherlands and to lead an army into France to the support of the League (1590). Parma obeyed, and in his absence the Dutch took the aggressive. For they had now found a worthy successor to William the Silent in his young son Maurice (the eldest son was a Catholic, in Spain), and Maurice had military talents of the highest order. Parma occupied Paris (1591) and then returned to the Netherlands to resume his original task. Again he was called upon to help in France (1592) and on his second return journey to the Netherlands he died and his command passed into less competent hands.

In 1593 Philip II played his last card against the heretic Henry of Navarre by urging the Estates-General of Catholic France to recognize his (Philip's) daughter, Isabella, as queen. Isabella's mother was a daughter of Henry II of France and Catherine de' Medici. The League would probably have accepted Isabella if the duke of Mayenne, its head, had not himself aspired to the crown. At this critical juncture Henry IV announced his conversion to Catholicism.

The ceremony of reconciliation was staged at the church of St. Denis just outside Paris, which was garrisoned by Spanish troops. Brilliantly attired, Henry and his suite drew near the portals of the historic church, where sat the archbishop of

Bourges with a group of clergy. "Who are you?" asked the archbishop. "I am the king." "What do you want?" "I ask to be received into the bosom of the Catholic, Apostolic and Roman Church." The king knelt, swore to live and die in the ancient faith and renounced all the heresies. The archbishop heard his confession, gave him absolution, admitted him to the Lord's Supper. In the evening Henry rode to a neighboring height and gazed upon the silhouette of the great city. "Paris," he remarked, "is well worth a mass."

The Huguenots were bitter at his desertion, and the pope and Philip of Spain refused for some years to recognize the reality or validity of his conversion. But the king's change of faith gradually clarified the situation. Paris welcomed him in 1594 and the noble members of the League began to come over. Henry IV saw to it that their support was made profitable, saying that it was cheaper to buy them than to crush them. Yet in 1595 he still had most of his kingdom to regain. In that year he formally declared war on Spain with the aim of bringing his French opponents over to his side on patriotic grounds. In 1596 he made treaties with Elizabeth and the Dutch providing for united action against the Spanish foe. The war went on as before.

THE EDICT OF NANTES AND THE PEACE OF FRANCE WITH SPAIN (1598)

In 1598 King Henry took the momentous step, essential to national union, of granting toleration to his old comrades, the Huguenots, who, as he said, "had guarded his cradle and borne him to power on their shoulders." The Edict of Nantes (1598) gave the Huguenots *freedom of conscience* throughout France and the *right of public worship* in all places where it had been celebrated in 1597, and also in one town in every bailiwick and in the residences of great nobles; but this right of public worship was not to be exercised in Paris. The Huguenots were declared eligible to all state employments and to the schools and universities. In cases at law affecting Huguenots, judges of both religions were to sit. As a guaranty of the observance of the Edict, the Huguenots were authorized to retain and to garrison, at the expense of the government, some hundred fortified places, including the strong cities of La Rochelle, Montpellier, and Montauban.[1]

The Edict of Nantes was not the fruit of the spirit of toleration, but of statesmanship; it was cheaper and safer to tolerate the Huguenots than to conquer them. To be sure, it raised serious problems, for it established a state within the State. But in the meantime it gave France internal peace and a chance to rebuild her shattered strength.

A few weeks after issuing the Edict of Nantes, Henry IV deserted his Dutch and English allies and signed a peace with Spain. The Peace of Vervins (1598) restored the frontiers of 1559 and Henry promised not to help the Dutch. This was the outcome of Philip's intervention in France, which had cost him much treasure and had also cancelled Parma's gains in the Dutch Provinces. It was some compensation to Philip to believe that he had restored the French monarchy to the Catholic fold.

Philip II died in 1598. Spain was much weakened inwardly. She was almost a shell, but she held her head high. Her armies were still superior to others. Philip died, as he had lived, the most powerful ruler of his time.

The details of the "campaigns" of the English and the Dutch against the Spaniards from 1595 on will be passed over. They did best at sea. In 1598 Elizabeth tried to get peace with Spain, but the Spanish terms were too high. Philip III knew that Elizabeth had a serious revolt on her hands in Ireland and, tit for tat, he hoped to profit by it. But the small army that he sent to extend the revolt was captured by the English lord-deputy at Kinsale and was shipped back to Spain in English transports. King James I, who succeeded Elizabeth in 1603, had better luck. He was advised by Elizabeth's minister, Robert Cecil, son of Burleigh. He made peace with Spain in 1604, but he refused to admit that English trade with Spanish America was illegal or to agree to exclude Dutch goods from English vessels. Spain

[1] Compare the edict of 1570, above.

nevertheless made peace hoping, not without reason, that the son
of Mary Queen of Scots might serve Spanish plans later.

THE DUTCH TRUCE WITH SPAIN (1609)

The Dutch continued the war, Henry IV, despite his promises
at Vervins, giving them substantial aid after, as before, 1598.
Elizabeth also helped them for a consideration. The Dutch
hoped to win over the southern Netherlands, but the people there
had had their chief grievances redressed and the defensive
strength of the Spanish army was too great. Yet the Dutch
wanted to continue the war. Maurice, William the Silent's great
son, realized that peace would weaken his position in the state.
Above all, the Dutch sailors desired the war to go on, for the
Spanish territories were on the defensive and the Dutch colonial
empire, formed mainly at the expense of Portugal, was already
founded.[1]

But Henry IV, the principal backer of the Dutch, wanted the
war to stop. He was already nursing far-reaching plans which
contemplated an attack upon the Austrian Hapsburg, and he
desired peace in order to mature them. And Spain was willing
to make a truce. A truce affords a breathing space. And so the
great truce of 1609 was signed. It provided for a twelve-year
cessation of war, during which time the Dutch were to be treated
as if they were independent, both in Europe and in their colonies.
The peace stopped most of their depredations on Spain's commerce and on her colonies. Much might happen in twelve years.

The prosperity of the Dutch in 1609 was marvelous. It was
based on the sea and on the enterprise and resourcefulness which
necessity breeds in a richly endowed people. They had perhaps
ten thousand ships engaged in the carrying trade and in fishing,
probably twice or three times as many as the English. They
were prospering in the midst of war. The greatness of soul
which had been developed in half a century of struggle for liberty
now flowered in literature, scholarship, architecture, and painting.
Even the rise of bitter theological quarrels was not to quench

[1] See chapter XXVI.

utterly the ideas of toleration which the great William had
cherished, for the Dutch never withheld freedom of conscience
from their Catholic fellow citizens.

The English genius for colonization and commerce was not
yet disclosed. Unlike the Dutch, they could live on the products
of their country. Unlike the Dutch, also, their island was unas-
sailable, an asset whose value was only later to be fully realized.
The practical temper of the English, their self-reliance and initiative, their willingness to expatriate themselves for wealth and for
religion, were soon to be displayed on a wide scale. (Virginia
was founded in 1607.) Meanwhile they pushed their trade and
contended with their trade rivals, frequently to the shedding of
blood, on all the seas.[1]

The purposes for which Henry IV imposed the truce of 1609
upon the Dutch are not fully known. It does not matter. For
he had to pay a legacy from the French civil wars which he
had brought to a close. In 1610 he was struck down by an
assassin. But, until Richelieu appeared, France found no one to
take up the work of this most genial and talented descendant
of St. Louis.

[1] See chapter XXVI.

CHAPTER XXIII

THE EPOCH OF THE THIRTY YEARS' WAR
EUROPE 1610-1660

GERMANY FROM 1555 TO THE OUTBREAK OF THE THIRTY YEARS' WAR

EXPERIENCE of the horrors of war inclines men to peace and lends vital meaning to the ancient supplication, "Give peace in our time, O Lord!" The Peace of Augsburg (1555) was the fruit of such experience and Germany had rest from all but local clashes for almost two generations (1555-1618). This period of German history was on the whole marked by economic well-being. Wealth was eagerly sought and, despite the decline of the Hanseatic League and the growth of Dutch commerce in the Baltic, the German cities and landowners were prosperous. Some of their wealth went into luxurious living and ostentatious display, but a part of it was used to advance the arts and education. The age, however, was not one of achievement in arts and letters in Germany. Morals were relatively low. In a word, Germany was well-to-do and rather materialistic.

In the political sphere it is to be noted that the German princes continued to strengthen themselves at the expense of the central imperial power. The failure of Charles V in Germany explains that. Still, the ambitions of the princes did not fly very high; they were, in the main, content to lessen the influence of their "territorial" diets and to organize their states somewhat more effectively. There were no serious wars among them, and the war-loving among their subjects found employment and pay in the Baltic lands, the Netherlands and France.

In the sphere of religion the outstanding fact was the revival of Roman Catholicism. In 1555 it had been on the defensive, for North Germany then was overwhelmingly Protestant and South Germany was either Protestant—as in the Palatinate—or honeycombed with Protestantism, as in Bavaria and the Austrian lands. The revival of Catholic zeal and aggressiveness and the resulting change in the balance of religious parties, must be credited largely to the Jesuits and the Council of Trent. The Jesuits set to work promptly in Germany, as elsewhere, preaching, founding schools, colleges and seminaries, and strengthening the fervor of Catholic rulers and their heirs. Results appeared from 1575 on, and about 1600 Protestantism was on the defensive. In the South the dukes of Bavaria, for example, suppressed Protestantism, and in the northwest a majority of the bishoprics Protestant in all but name, were re-Catholicized. In 1585, when Archbishop Gebhard, elector of Cologne turned Protestant and refused to resign, he was expelled and his Catholic successor was installed by Spanish and Bavarian troops.

The Protestant princes were still strong enough, if united, to oppose the current, but they were divided by theological disputes and were loath to break the peace. In truth, their own skirts were not exactly clean, for they had secularized Church lands contrary to the terms of the Peace of Augsburg. The imperial city of Donauwörth was occupied (1607) by the troops of its powerful neighbor, Duke Maximilian of Bavaria, at the behest of the emperor, because the city had unlawfully refused to permit Catholic processions. Elector Frederick IV of the neighboring Palatinate then organized a league known as the *Protestant Union* (1608). Frederick was a Calvinist, his faith was not authorized by the Peace of Augsburg, and the religious weather looked stormy.

The Protestant Union was composed of Elector Frederick, Christian of Anhalt and a number of neighboring princes and cities. It entered into relations with Henry IV of France and, if that enterprising ruler had not been murdered in 1610, there is no telling what the consequence might have been. But the great Lutheran princes of the North, Saxony and Brandenburg, kept aloof. The Catholic answer to the *Union* was the *League,* which was organized in 1609 by Maximilian of Bavaria, the three ecclesiastical electors and other bishops. These two organizations were ominous, for there had been no such confederations since the days of the Schmalkaldic League. But the cloud of war did not break, although it did not disappear, and in the meantime both organizations increased their memberships.

THE BOHEMIAN PHASE OF THE WAR

The Thirty Years' War (1618-1648), which was ultimately to involve most of Europe, began as a civil war in the dominions of the Austrian Hapsburgs. These lands may be roughly classified as the Austrian territories, the Bohemian kingdom and the kingdom of Hungary.[1] In all three Protestantism[2] was rife, and the nobles were strong. This was particularly true of Bohemia. As a consequence, the Hapsburgs, who were loyal but unenergetic Catholics and who steadily secured the imperial crown,[3] had little power in proportion to the extent of their territories. Their international rôle was almost *nil*. Indeed, in Bohemia the Czech spirit was so strong and the Protestant nobles were so influential that Rudolf II had been constrained to concede full liberty of worship to the Protestants.

In 1617 a change took place in the prospects of the Hapsburgs, for in that year Ferdinand, the most talented and ardently Catholic member of the family, was selected by the members of the House as their next head, and Matthias, emperor and king, beguiled the Diet of Bohemia into recognizing Ferdinand as his successor in the kingship. The Bohemians soon had cause to repent, for Matthias, egged on by Ferdinand, began to encroach on the chartered liberties of the Protestant Bohemians. Thereupon the nobles rebelled, threw the representatives of Matthias out of a window, and established a provisional government for

[1] *I.e.*, that fragment of Hungary which recognized Ferdinand I after the battle of Mohacz (1526) and the wars which followed it.

[2] Including in the term *Protestant*, Lutherans, Bohemian Brethren and those Hussites who were known as Utraquists.

[3] The Hapsburg emperors immediately following Charles V were Ferdinand I, 1558-1564; Maximilian II, 1564-1576; Rudolf II, 1576-1612; Matthias, 1612-1619.

their country (1618). Such was the *Defenstration of Prague* and the beginning of the Thirty Years' War.

In 1619 Matthias passed away and the Bohemian Diet declared Ferdinand deposed, and in his place (August 26) chose the young Elector Frederick V of the Palatinate as their king, believing that as head of the Protestant Union, grandson of the great William the Silent, and son-in-law of James I of England, he would be able to maintain their independence of the Hapsburgs. A few days later Ferdinand was elected emperor.[1]

Ferdinand II accepted the challenge of the Bohemians with grim joy. His own military resources were slight—barely enough to hold in check the Austrian nobles who had followed the example of the Czechs by rising against their Catholic master. But the Protestant Union and James I had both declined to support Frederick in his Bohemian adventure, whereas Maximilian of Bavaria, who had a fair-sized army of his own and was head of the League, and the foolish Philip III of Spain had both promised military aid to Ferdinand—aid which was promptly forthcoming in the summer of 1620. The Czechs played Ferdinand's game by failing to raise taxes for an adequate army of their own, and Frederick weakened their unanimity by attempting to establish Calvinism in Bohemia.

A few days after his coronation in Prague, Frederick was completely defeated by the troops of Ferdinand and the League in the battle of the White Hill, just outside Prague, 1620. Meanwhile the Spaniards under Spinola were reducing the Palatinate. Frederick, dubbed the *Winter King,* took refuge in Holland. The Bohemian nobles were replaced by German Catholics, Bohemian Protestantism was suppressed, and force and Jesuit zeal established the authority both of the Hapsburgs and of Catholicism. The battle of the White Hill marks an epoch in the history of Bohemia.

A few years later Ferdinand found an opportunity, again with Bavarian help, to deal similarly with the Protestantism of the Austrian lands, while in Hapsburg Hungary Jesuit fervor and Jesuit schools succeeded in restoring the Magyars (Hungarians)

[1] Emperor Ferdinand II, 1619-1637.

to the Catholic fold (1601-1637). Thus, before the death of Ferdinand II, the Austrian Hapsburgs were again a great European power.

By 1623 the troops of Spain and the League had completed the subjugation of the Palatinate, the Protestant Union had dissolved, and the emperor had recompensed Maximilian for his services by transferring to him Frederick's office of elector, together with the upper Palatinate (1623). Maximilian's reward was well earned. He was a cousin of the emperor, was educated with him at the Jesuit university of Ingolstadt, equaled him in devotion to the Catholic faith, and surpassed him in statesmanship and organizing ability. He knew where he wanted to go and he knew how to get there. Maximilian was the hero of the Catholic cause in Germany.

THE DANISH PHASE OF THE WAR

The war might have stopped in 1623, but the chances were against such an outcome. For the twelve-year truce of 1609 had expired and Spain and the Dutch were again at war. Moreover, the Spanish and the Austrian Hapsburgs were now in close accord, and one good turn deserves another. If England had had a ruler like Elizabeth or France a king like Henry IV, surely they would have resumed the old game! But England had Charles I, and France was now pro-Spanish.

The war did not end in 1623. For Mansfeld and Christian of Brunswick, two soldiers of fortune who had attempted to hold the Palatinate for Frederick, fled after their overthrow to the Dutch territories and, enrolling fresh mercenary troops, led them into the Catholic bishoprics of northwest Germany. Charles I sent some thousands of English conscripts to help, but they starved in Holland. The army of the League went to the rescue and defeated Mansfeld and Christian (1623-1625). This victory awakened the fears of the possessors of Protestant "bishoprics" (illegally secularized) in the northwest. The most redoubtable of these was Christian IV of Denmark. Thus the war, like a fire once lighted, had eaten its way to the northern frontier.

Christian IV was a Lutheran and a headstrong and ambitious ruler. He was king of Denmark and Norway—Sweden had been independent since the revolt of Gustavus Vasa in 1523— and duke of Schleswig and Holstein. He aspired to the domination of the Baltic (he already controlled the Sound, its entrance), and his ambitions in Germany are further shown by the fact that his Lutheran son was "bishop-administrator" of Verden and of Bremen, little German city-states which controlled the mouths of the Weser and the Elbe. Christian IV's ambitions were threatened by the presence of the army of the League in his neighborhood. Charles I of England, whose mother was Danish, thought to use Christian to help restore Frederick to the Palatinate, and promised him heavy subsidies to intervene. Christian accepted the promise, which was not fulfilled, and made war on the League.

The emperor, however, had prepared for such a contingency and for even more serious ones by obtaining a substantial army of his own. This was raised by Wallenstein, a Czech ex-Protestant, who had made a huge fortune out of speculation in confiscated Protestant estates in Bohemia. The new army was composed of adventurers professing any faith or none, but it differed from other mercenary armies—for example, Mansfeld's and Christian of Brunswick's scourges—in two particulars: it was held under strict discipline, and it was maintained, at least in the early period, not by wasteful, promiscuous plundering, but by a system of requisitions upon opponents of the emperor. The imperial army, as it was called, made the emperor an independent power beside the League.

King Christian IV's invasion of northwest Germany proved disastrous. He got the support of the duke of Mecklenburg and some other lesser German princes, and had some successes; but the armies of the emperor under Wallenstein and of the League under Count Tilly gradually gained possession of the lands on the northern coast and ended by driving Christian out of Germany and then out of Jutland (1625-1629). Christian took refuge in his islands, leaving the foe master of the coastal territories from Danzig to Lübeck, with the sole exception of Stralsund. Wallenstein was given the forfeited duchy of Mecklenburg and was created Admiral of the Baltic by the grateful emperor. Christian was allowed to withdraw from the war with the loss of Bremen and Verden alone. This show of generosity was dictated by prudence, for it was known that the king of Sweden was contemplating intervention.

Shortly before making peace with Christian, the emperor crowned his work for his Church by issuing the Edict of Restitution (1629). It declared that Calvinism was still illegal in Germany and ordered that the Church lands which had been seized by Protestant rulers since 1552 should be restored to the Catholic authorities. This would involve the return of two great archbishoprics, ten bishoprics, and over one hundred smaller foundations. Legally and morally the edict was sound, but politically it was perilous, for it threatened to bring into the war Saxony and Brandenburg, the strong Lutheran states which had hitherto stoutly maintained their neutrality. It came, too, just after the collapse of the Huguenot political power in France, which left Cardinal Richelieu free to enter the lists against a Germany dominated by the Hapsburgs.

Could the emperor enforce the edict if Saxony and Brandenburg, notorious secularizers of Church lands, joined against him, and if Gustavus Adolphus should place his disciplined Swedes on German soil, and if France should settle her home troubles and strike at the Spanish-Austrian combination which controlled the Rhine frontier? These were dangerous possibilities. Perhaps the armies of League and emperor could handle these dangers as they took form. But a new (and old) factor had been forgotten.

The emperor's strength was also his weakness, for it now alarmed the German princes, as Charles V's strength after Mühlberg had alarmed them, for their political independence. The Catholic princes, led by Maximilian of Bavaria together with the Lutheran electors of Saxony and Brandenburg, united in a protest against Wallenstein, and the League notified the emperor that he must choose between League support and Wallenstein.

The emperor bowed to the ultimatum and dismissed Wallenstein (August, 1630), and transferred the command of the imperial army to Tilly, the chief general of the League. But the imperial army shrunk over one-half when its creator returned to his estates. It was the first serious check in the emperor's fortunes, which had prospered marvelously for ten years. It was a very serious matter; for Gustavus Adolphus had landed with 16,000 veterans near Stralsund in June, 1630.

THE SWEDISH PHASE OF THE WAR

Gustavus Adolphus (b. 1594) had become king of Sweden in 1611. He was most learned, was devoutly Lutheran, and waged war brilliantly and incessantly. His father had gained the throne of Sweden in 1600 after a successful revolt against the foreign and catholicizing policy of his nephew Sigismund, king of Poland and of Sweden. Sweden's standing army was established in the same year. It was employed against Denmark, Russia and, of course, Poland, and gained renown and territory for the homeland. Gustavus Adolphus brought these wars to a close, securing from Russia and Poland the entire coastal region of the eastern Baltic from Riga up to Finland. The river tolls in the former Polish territories equaled the funds Gustavus received from the Swedish Diet and formed an essential element in his war finance.

It had not been easy for Gustavus to make a profitable peace with Poland, for the Poles latterly had more than held their own against him. But Richelieu, first minister of France, had placed French diplomacy at his service in order to set him free for intervention in Germany. Richelieu helped to finance this intervention. The situation grew darker for the emperor.

The motives which drew Gustavus Adolphus into the German war were in the main two. First, his determination to build Swedish strength on the control of the Baltic and its trade caused him to view Wallenstein's progress in North Germany with grave concern. Wallenstein had Mecklenburg and Pomerania and was planning a war fleet. Secondly, Gustavus was an ardent Lutheran, and the success of the emperor's policy would spell destruction for Lutheranism. In short, Gustavus, from the standpoints of commerce, national greatness and religion, must be hammer or anvil, and he chose to be hammer.

The coming of Gustavus Adolphus to the rescue of the Protestants and his occupation of Pomerania, were not at first pleasing to Saxony and Brandenburg. They did not wish to attack the emperor and they feared that Gustavus was just another foreign adventurer seeking his own profit in troubled Germany. The great Swede could not move south unless Saxony and Brandenburg were friendly; his communications would not be secure. It took about a year's persuasion and pressure, aided by the emperor's foolish attempt to make Saxony disarm, to bring them round. Gustavus Adolphus was now free to begin his real operations. In a brilliant battle, revealing a marked advance in the art of war,[1] he crushed Tilly at Breitenfeld (September, 1631) and thus freed North Germany from the imperial grasp. He then swung over to the region of the Rhine and Main, and by occupying the Palatinate broke the land connection of Spain between the Netherlands and Italy. The Dutch controlled the sea. In the spring of 1632, overthrowing the inferior force which Tilly had collected behind the Danube, he occupied Bavaria, and in May he rode into Munich with Elector Frederick of the Palatinate at his side, while the Saxon elector took possession of Bohemia.

Already, by Christmas, 1631, the emperor had realized his peril. In his desperation he had turned again to Wallenstein, offering him the powers of a dictator. Wallenstein had accepted, had sent his call over Europe, and by May, 1632, his army, equipped and eager, stood ready in the Austrian lands. Indeed, while Gustavus was entering Munich Wallenstein was clearing the Saxons out of Bohemia. A battle of giants impended.

In the strategic duel between the two armies Wallenstein had the best of it. But Gustavus forced a battle—at Lützen, November, 1632. Victory rested, by a narrow margin, on the Swedish banners, but Gustavus was killed. His death more than out-

[1] See T. A. Dodge, *Gustavus Adolphus.*

weighed the victory in a military sense, and in addition deprived the Protestant cause of that outstanding embodiment of religious devotion which was so well represented on the other side by Maximilian of Bavaria.

Wallenstein survived Gustavus little more than a year. After Lützen he felt that he was master and he entered into a tangled maze of negotiations with the Swedes and the elector of Saxony designed to realize, on the basis of religious toleration, his own policy for the pacification of Germany and for his own aggrandizement. But neither side trusted him, and the emperor, rightly or wrongly believing in his treachery, had him murdered (February, 1634). Wallenstein was the most enigmatic personality in the war.

The emperor's good fortune held. In September, 1634, his son (later Ferdinand III), in command of Wallenstein's old army and supported by a strong Spanish force *en route* from Italy to the Spanish Netherlands, crushed the Swedes at Nördlingen and restored to the emperor and Maximilian the control of most of southern Germany.

A few months later the emperor took a leaf out of the astute Wallenstein's book and offered peace to the Lutheran princes. Nördlingen had balanced Breitenfeld. Why not clear up the religious-economic issue and unite Catholics and Lutherans in defense of the Fatherland against the foreigner? The emperor offered peace on the basis of a modification of the Edict of Restitution which changed the test date from 1552 to 1627—*i.e.*, secularizations in effect in 1627 would stand. This was almost equivalent to a withdrawal of the edict. The elector of Saxony was the first to accept the olive branch (Peace of Prague, May, 1635), and Brandenburg and the other leading Lutheran states soon fell into line. The peace bade fair to end the war, even though the Calvinists were excluded from its terms—unless France should join wholeheartedly with the Swedes.

The Swedes refused to withdraw unless they got the Baltic coasts of Germany. Gustavus Adolphus had fixed upon that recompense and nothing less would content them. Their position was not foolhardy. France had just agreed to back them with

money and men and had signalized her resolution by declaring
war on Spain (1635). Allied with the Swedes and the Dutch,
France proposed to settle scores with both branches of the House
of Hapsburg. The Peace of Prague was therefore only a pre-
lude to more terrible conflicts. Before considering them it will
be helpful to bring the history of France down to 1635.

THE POLITICAL HISTORY OF FRANCE, 1610-1635

The death of Henry IV of France (1610) gave the crown to
his son Louis XIII (b. 1601), and the government to his
widow, Mary de' Medici, a Florentine. Mary had neither the
capacity nor the authority to pursue Henry's adventurous plans
and promptly reversed his foreign policy. She wanted peace and
enjoyment and, to insure them, she married Louis XIII to Anne,
daughter of King Philip III of Spain (1615). Mary's government was lax. Italian favorites were enriched and the leading
nobles resumed their old game of acting independently and flirting
with the foreigner. The League seemed about to arise from the
grave.

The queen mother's rule was cut short in 1617 by the abrupt
seizure of power by her young son and his favorite. Louis XIII
ruled and, though he restored his mother to favor now and then,
he did not trust her. In the end she found a refuge with the
Spaniards in their Netherlands. She had served them well. Perhaps she has a claim upon French gratitude because of the favor
which she extended in the days of her power and of her adversity to a young and ambitious nobleman and bishop, Richelieu
(1585-1642).

Richelieu had originally prepared for a military career, but the
finances of the family, which had been given the patronage of
a bishopric by Henry III, compelled him to enter the Church.
However, his heart was set on a political career. He served the
queen mother and the child queen, and curried favor with Louis
after he began to rule. But it was not until 1624 that Louis admitted the brilliant and forceful ecclesiastic, who had secured a
cardinal's hat in 1622, to the royal council. The advent of Riche-

lieu marks an epoch in the history of France comparable to that of Bismarck in modern Prussia. Louis XIII gave Richelieu his confidence, albeit grudgingly, and Richelieu gave the monarchy a brain and a will. His career shows the importance of talent. He was not benevolent or kindly. He used spies freely and skillfully, even upon the king himself. He punished his own enemies as enemies of the State. He built lavishly and entertained royally. He was not active in promoting agriculture and manufacturing which Henry IV had nourished. But the fertility of France and the thrift of the people were adequate to the needs of the time. In all that he did, worthily and unworthily, Richelieu sought the greatness of France; a strong monarchy in a strong country was his goal.

In his political testament Richelieu notes that when he took office France was suffering from two evils—heresy and liberty. By the first he meant the political and military powers granted the Huguenots by the Edict of Nantes; by the second, the rebelliousness of the Catholic nobility. France could not take a strong position in foreign affairs until these "evils" were abated or at least reduced. The Huguenots relied on foreign aid, especially on that of the English; the nobles, upon Spain. The civil wars had indeed left their mark on France.

Richelieu settled the Huguenot problem in five years. When in 1626 he took a hand against Spain by weakening the connection between Milan and the Austrian lands (affair of the Valtelline pass) the Huguenots again rose. Richelieu promptly settled the Valtelline issue with Spain and turned upon the Huguenots. In spite of the English, he captured La Rochelle (1628) and then crushed Huguenot resistance in the South. The Huguenots accepted his terms. The Peace of Alais (1629) took away from them their cities of refuge and their exceptional political privileges, but left them (despite the clamors of extreme Catholics) the religious rights granted them by the Edict of Nantes. Richelieu wanted—and got—their support in his foreign undertakings.

The Catholic nobles were a tougher problem. Even the heir to the throne, Gaston, brother of King Louis, supported their pretensions to feudal independence and took aid from Spain. The birth of the future Louis XIV in 1638, however, lessened Gaston's importance. Richelieu let the nobles and the people see that the monarchy regarded itself as master by issuing and enforcing edicts forbidding dueling and ordering the destruction of private castles away from the frontiers. Revolting nobles even of the highest rank were condemned for treason and beheaded. The importance and power of the provincial governors, who were nobles, were undermined by the very general appointment of *intendants,* royal officials of humble rank who acted as deputies of the king throughout the provinces and left the governors little but their dignity. Nevertheless, the nobles were loath to give up their dream and it was not until Louis XIV transformed them into courtiers that they really abandoned their factiousness. In the meantime Richelieu terrorized them and diverted their energies into the foreign wars.

THE FRANCO-SWEDISH PHASE OF THE WAR

Richelieu saw his opportunity to strengthen France by weakening the Hapsburg powers. Spain, which supported the rebellious French nobles, was the chief and most contiguous enemy, and the emperor's alliance with Spain made her more dangerous. When the struggle with the Huguenots was about over, Richelieu, as it were, sparred for another opening. He tried Italy, going to the aid of the French heir to the little duchy of Mantua-Monferrat (1629-1631), but withdrew and made peace with Spain when his immediate object was achieved. Then for some time he fell back upon the policy of subsidizing the Dutch and the Swedes and gradually edging in on the Rhine. When Gustavus died Richelieu got the fortress of Ehrenbreitstein opposite Coblenz. He had already expelled the pro-Spanish duke of Lorraine from his lands. Even after Nördlingen, when the Swedes turned over certain Alsatian fortresses to the French, France was not officially in the war. In 1635, as we have seen, when the emperor and the Lutherans were getting together, France entered the war as a principal and strengthened the Dutch and Swedes with subsidies. The Dutch and the French would help each other to realize their ambitions in Germany. The conflict, of course, embraced Spain, Italy, the Netherlands and the Spanish-Portuguese colonies. But we shall simplify matters and handle the Franco-Swedish section of the Thirty Years' War (1635-1648) as if it were isolated. Later we shall consider the French-Spanish-Portuguese conflict.

The alert reader must have noticed that the religious motive was evaporating from the war in 1635 when the Peace of Prague was made. The alignment of the antagonists after 1635 supports the observation. Catholic France directed by a cardinal, Lutheran Sweden, and German principalities mainly Calvinist, confront the Catholic emperor and the bulk of the Catholic and Lutheran states of Germany. The political-economic motive is nakedly disclosed.

The details of the war cannot be set forth here. Let us look at the matter broadly. From 1635 to 1639 France's chief service was to finance the Protestant German, Bernhard of Weimar, a general of great talent who was to get Alsace for his reward. It would have been a German Alsace. But when Bernhard died (1639), France inherited his army and occupied Alsace. Moreover, by this date the French armies had experience and had developed talent. Sweden had a succession of brilliant generals. Austria fought doggedly and with occasional striking successes. France in the main stuck to the vicinity of the Rhine. Sweden operated in the North, of course, with invasions of Bohemia and the Austrian lands. Brandenburg, with the Great Elector at the helm since 1640, bought a truce with the Swedes and retired from the struggle. King Christian IV of Denmark now threw in his lot with the emperor against the Swedes and was again driven to his islands and forced to make a very unfavorable peace by his victorious Scandinavian rival (the war of 1642-1645). Saxony followed the example of Brandenburg in 1645. In the remaining years the emperor [1] and Maximilian were forced by the united French and Swedish armies to accept the terms which the diplomatists had been working out for three years at Osnabrück and Münster, both in Westphalia. The last clash of the war took place where the first blow had been struck—in

[1] Ferdinand III, 1637-1658.

Prague—and on the day the Peace of Westphalia was signed, October 24, 1648. Richelieu had died in 1642, but his successor, Mazarin, was his pupil, and the French annexations carried out the ideas of the Iron Cardinal.

THE PEACE OF WESTPHALIA

In several respects the Peace of Westphalia supplemented the Peace of Augsburg (1555). It put Calvinism on a par with Lutheranism and Catholicism as legal faiths in Germany. The principle of *cujus regio ejus religio* ("the prince determines the religion of his subjects") was reaffirmed; but it cut no real figure after 1648, for no state, in the impoverished conditions of German life, could afford to exile its subjects. The *Ecclesiastical Reservation* was unequivocally accepted by all; the test date for secularizations was changed from 1552 to 1624 (a compromise between 1618 and 1630). This date left the Protestant states of the North in substantial possession of the Church lands they had formerly secularized. On the other hand, it guaranteed to Catholicism the gains which the emperor and Maximilian had made in the South.

The territorial adjustments were more difficult and details will be omitted. Sweden was given western Pomerania with Stralsund, together with Bremen and Verden, and thus secured the mouths of the Oder, Elbe and Weser, with their remunerative tolls. Gustavus had not fixed on so much. These lands were received by Sweden as "fiefs of the Empire"—that is, they remained German territory and the Swedish ruler (Christina, daughter of Gustavus) became, by virtue of these possessions, a German princess as well.

France got Alsace, Strasburg excepted, and received a legal title to Metz, Toul and Verdun, which she had occupied in 1552. These lands France received in full sovereignty; they ceased to be German territory. France's annexations strengthened her eastern frontier greatly, removing it also farther from Paris, and opened up further prospects for the future, for they thrust a wedge between the Free County of Burgundy and Spain's other dominions in the Spanish Netherlands.

Brandenburg made gains somewhat out of proportion to her sacrifices in the war, but not out of relation to her military importance in 1648. The shrewd elector had built up his army in East Prussia after 1642. He received eastern Pomerania and the secularized lands—Magdeburg, Halberstadt and Minden. These were contiguous to Brandenburg and made this section of the Hohenzollern dominions quite imposing. And when one notes that the elector still had East Prussia and now secured possession of Cleves, Mark and Ravensberg, which his father had inherited in 1609, one can perceive that Brandenburg-Prussia will have to be reckoned with later.

Bavaria's reward was more justly earned. Maximilian was confirmed in his possession of the upper Palatinate and the rank of seventh elector given him by the emperor a quarter century earlier. The Rhenish Palatinate was restored to the son of the ill-starred Frederick, and an eighth electorate was created for him. Saxony retained Lausitz.

The emperor received no territorial gains as such. But his grasp on catholicized Bohemia was not loosened, nor was the establishment of his authority in the Austrian lands and royal Hungary undone. The Austrian Hapsburg was now a power of the first rank, or nearly so, in Europe, and such he was to remain for 270 years longer.

The independence of the Dutch (agreed to by Spain in January, 1648) and of the Swiss was acknowledged in the Peace of Westphalia, and thus the last tenuous legal bonds connecting them with Germany were severed.

Constitutionally, the Peace of Westphalia merely records and rounds out a German situation which was discernible four hundred years earlier. Germany possesses no central government worthy of the name. The separate states of which Germany is made up in 1648 are now recognized to be substantially independent and they are given the legal right to make alliances with foreign powers—a thing they had done for centuries. The machinery of the central government still exists; it is even made more complex by various new devices for balancing Protestants against Catholics. But it will not work. It can only creak and rust. And even if it were workable, what strictly German interests could be achieved through it, with France and Sweden appointed by the treaty as joint guarantors of the maintenance of its terms? Germany, after 1648, exists in loyal hearts here and there; and patriotism, localized, takes refuge and is nourished in the separate states, Austria, Saxony, Brandenburg-Prussia. But *Germany* as an effective political force is done for until the days of Bismarck. And even then, in order to live and flourish, she will dismember herself by excluding Austria (1866).

The disastrous consequences of the Thirty Years' War for Germany alone—disregarding the other countries—can be only approximately estimated. The population declined about one-half. In Bohemia it shrank from three millions to three-quarters of a million. Whole towns and villages were blotted out and agricultural lands reverted to wilderness. Cities dwindled. Trade and commerce dried up to a trickle or passed to England, France, or the Netherlands. The Hanseatic cities were reduced to three— Hamburg, Lübeck and Bremen. Only Leipzig and Frankfurt had any surviving trade connections worth mentioning. Art and literature fell and resorted to slavish imitation of the foreigner, especially of France. Manners roughened, morals declined, dogmatism encroached further on religion, superstition flourished anew. When one contrasts the prosperous Germany of 1618 with the Germany of 1648, one marvels again at the evils wrought by cupidity and stupidity. Fortunately each generation accepts what it inherits almost as if it were inevitable, and sets to work to remold it into more satisfactory forms. But even a century and a half after the great peace the scars of the thirty years of conflict were still visible on the face of the land.

THE FRANCO-SPANISH WAR, 1635-1659

We turn to the Franco-Spanish war of 1635-1659, which was a pendant to the Thirty Years' War. Spain, too, might have secured peace in 1648 if she had been willing to make some modest sacrifices of territory. Instead, being freed from war with the Dutch, she dreamed of victory over France, or of a draw at least. To understand this we must go back to the situation as it stood at the time of the truce with the Dutch in 1609.

The truce of 1609 had given Spain a breathing space for recuperation and rededication to useful labor. Instead, her government utilized it almost immediately (1610) to expel from Aragon a half million of Moriscos, the ablest and only industrious cultivators of the soil, because, Christians though they were, in name at least, they had sought help abroad against the ravages of the Inquisition. A due calculation of consequences or the exercise of intelligent judgment would have prevented the infliction of such a blow to the well-being of the only unexhausted portion of Spain. The Aragonese constitution still protected the people from taxation at will.

It was part of the misfortune of Spain that the kings who succeeded Philip II were progressively inferior in capacity. Philip III (1598-1620) was pious, proud and pleasure-loving. Philip IV (1620-1665), his son, was more pious and more dissolute. Charles II (1665-1700), son of the fourth Philip, was a scrofulous moron. The inbreeding practiced by the Spanish Hapsburgs, as well as by their Spanish predecessors, was cumulatively terrible in its consequences, because the growing despotism of the government steadily threw increasing responsibility for initiative upon the monarchs themselves. Seldom has outraged heredity taken such revenge upon a dynasty and the country it ruled.

The Spanish upper classes cannot be freed from responsibility for what happened. They still believed that Spain was the greatest power in the world, that it was her job to crush the heretic and exalt the Faith. They did not perceive what secular ambitions sheltered themselves under that great name. And they trusted that God in His own time would give them the victory. Neither kings nor nobles lived the moral lives which would at least have given dignity to such extraordinary hopes.

The peninsula could have done better if it had been unified. But Aragon and Portugal clung to their constitutional privileges. Castile was submissive but poverty-stricken. The "wealth of the

Indies" might have helped to heal the wounds of war after 1609, but the extravagance of the court, the debts, and the vicious incidence of taxation upon industry made it of little avail. The state debt grew even in time of peace. Only a miracle could save the land, and no miracle was vouchsafed.

A keen sense of reality would have kept the Spanish government from helping the emperor in Germany from 1620 on. Spain had nothing to gain in comparison with the risk of stirring up France. France made peace with Spain in 1631, and Spain helped the emperor, Ferdinand II, to his victory at Nördlingen (1634). In 1635 Richelieu declared war anew and vitalized the Dutch and the Swedes with gold. It was to be war on all fronts.

French armies invaded Aragon (1638-1640). The defensive *élan* of the Aragonese repelled these invasions. But victory here could not repair the damage wrought by the Dutch navy in 1639, when it destroyed Spain's last great fleet, got together with terrible sacrifices, and finally shut off Spanish access to the Netherlands by sea.

In 1640 Portugal and Catalonia (one of the constituent kingdoms of Aragon) revolted. The Catalans, who were conscious of their vigor and jealous of their right to a real voice in their own government, resented the efforts of the central government to impose its will upon them. They rose in June, 1640, and called in France to aid them. The garrisons in Portugal were withdrawn for service against the Catalans, and the Portuguese nobility, fearful for their lands and goods—for the wars had to be financed somehow—proclaimed the independence of Portugal under their greatest noble, John of Braganza, and took complete possession of the government in a few hours. Two other wars!

In 1642 Cerdagne and Roussillon passed back into the armed possession of France, never to return. In 1643 the prestige of the matchless Spanish infantry was wrecked on the Netherlandish front by the defeat of Rocroy, administered by the French under the twenty-two-year-old prince of Condé. The war went on. Spanish nobles and clergy gave up more and more of their wealth. Yet Spanish hopes and pride refused a settlement in 1648. Then came a ray of sunshine. France now had her rebellion, the *Fronde*.

The *Fronde* began in 1648 in an effort made by the *parlement* of Paris, the chief law court of France, to check the autocratic and unpopular government of Mazarin, the supple successor of Richelieu, who had ruled France in the name of the queen mother, Anne, since the death of Louis XIII in 1643. The *parlement,* inspired by the example of England, demanded the suppression of the *intendants,* the reduction of taxation, *habeas corpus,* and the recognition of the right of the *parlement* to authorize or refuse taxation. The Estates-General had not met since 1614, and this gave the *parlement* its opportunity to step into the breach as champion of the *rights of the people.* Mazarin temporized until the troops came home from Germany. And when they arrived he was shocked to find that most of them, with their leaders, adopted the cause of the *parlement.* But the adoption was not genuine; they saw and seized the chance to weaken the central government. Gaston of Orléans, uncle of the boy king, and Condé, the victor of Rocroy, joined the other noble rebels in waging feudalism's last great fight against the monarchy. The struggle lasted four years. The Spanish of the Netherlands linked arms with Condé; the Spanish of the homeland backed another revolt in southern France. French patriotism awoke and rallied round the boy king —Mazarin shrewdly effacing himself for a brief period—and in 1652 the *Fronde* had burned itself out. But Condé became a Spanish general and fought against his country until the peace of 1659.

The *Fronde* inevitably prolonged the war with Spain. Both contestants were so exhausted that neither could administer the knockout blow, and each maneuvered for the aid of Cromwell. That doughty Protestant decided to attack Spain, and the moral effect of Cromwell's entrance into the war was probably more important than the valor of the redcoats at the battle of the Dunes (1658) in persuading the Spanish that it was useless to continue the war.

By the Peace of the Pyrenees (1659) Roussillon and Cerdagne became French again. Catalonia had returned to her Spanish allegiance in 1652, so that the line of the Pyrenees thus became (and remains) the frontier.   In the northeast, France gained Artois and part of Flanders.   They had been French long ago. England kept Dunkirk, and France secretly promised not to give any more aid to Portugal.   The treaty was sealed by the marriage of young Louis XIV with the daughter of Philip IV.   At the marriage festivities Philip had a short and poignant interview with his sister Anne, mother of Louis XIV.   It was their first meeting in forty years.

Spain now took up the task of conquering Portugal.   Spain was virtually bankrupt in morale and resources.   But her people had flashes of their old brilliancy, and it is likely that European Portugal would have had to succumb if she had not got foreign aid.   American Portugal—that is, Brazil—had shaken off the Dutch yoke by about 1655.   It is scarcely possible that vigorous Brazil would have accepted Spanish control again.   France was *openly* pledged to free Portugal and *secretly* pledged not to aid her.   The solution of France's dilemma was found in persuading Charles II of England to marry Catherine of Braganza and hire out Cromwellian veterans to the Portuguese.   The aid of a few thousand men, during four years or more, was enough to enable the Portuguese to maintain their independence, and Spain acknowledged it in 1668.   The story of Spain's national revival after 1700 can be read elsewhere.

THE SETTLEMENT OF THE BALTIC WARS, 1660-1661

The second pendant to the Peace of Westphalia is found in the group of treaties (1660-1661) winding up the Baltic rivalries. These rivalries, as we have seen, became enmeshed in the Thirty Years' War with the interventions of Christian of Denmark and of Gustavus Adolphus.   The hostility between Denmark and Sweden had flamed up again in 1642-1645 when Christian, now in alliance with the emperor, attacked the Swedes.   The peace which closed this special war within a war transferred Halland, on the Swedish side of the Sound, to Sweden and freed Sweden from the payment of dues on her ships passing through the Sound.

That meant that Denmark could not thereafter hamper or throttle Swedish commerce by raising the Sound dues.

The king of Poland had his own grievances against the Swedes, but these will be passed over in favor of a brief study of the appearance of a new and stronger rival to the Baltic predominance of Sweden. This was Frederick William of Brandenburg, the Great Elector, the same who had got out of the war against the Swedes in 1641. His territories, East Prussia, Brandenburg and the Rhenish duchies, were each separated from the other, but he handled them as a unit soon after the great Peace of 1648 made that possible. He threw them open to immigrants, fostered agriculture and industry and "placed above the provincial estates and the privileges of each of the countries a central administration which represented the Prussian Fatherland" (Lavisse). He built up a strong little army, uniformed alike in all three sections of his unrelated dominions. Prudence dictated this, for each of the three was exposed and accustomed to attack. The Great Elector was, in truth, the man who established arms as a national industry in Prussia. He was thrifty, shrewd and not very scrupulous. His rivals, however, were no better than he was. With him the stream of Prussian history becomes navigable. We shall observe his conduct.

In 1654 Christina, the cultivated and eccentric daughter of Gustavus Adolphus, resigned the crown of Sweden to her cousin, Charles X (1654-1660). He promptly decided to resume the quarrel with Poland. With a very large army he overran Great Poland and set himself up as king. But he found it difficult to arrive at a settlement with the Polish people, who fought a guerrilla war and then rose in a mighty insurrection against him. In his need he turned to the Great Elector, coerced and cajoled him into rendering aid, and finally reimbursed him by freeing him in 1656 from his vassalage to the king of Poland (himself). But as Gustavus Adolphus had found, it was not possible for the Swedes to do more than barely hold the risen Poles in check.

Denmark, thereupon, declared war against Charles X (June, 1657). The persistence of the Danes is remarkable. The appearance of this additional foe was most welcome to Charles X as offering an excuse to leave Poland. He led his troops through northern Germany into Jutland. That territory promptly reduced, he proposed to capture insular Denmark. His fleet was checked by the Danish. No matter. The winter came to his aid. From Sweden he led his army, infantry and cavalry, over the ice to triumph. It was an astounding feat. The Danes were forced to make a bitter peace (July, 1658).

Meanwhile Poland, Austria and the Great Elector joined forces against the Swedes. The Prussian exacted his price from the Polish king—recognition of his sovereignty over East Prussia (September, 1657). An Austrian-Prussian-Polish army invaded Swedish Pomerania, Schleswig and Holstein (1658-1659).

But the other German states were now afraid of another great war engulfing them all. Holland and England, too, feared for their Baltic commerce if Charles X should gain control of the Sound, and intervened to impose peace. This was the more easy to secure because of the sudden death of Charles X in 1660. The Baltic region was "pacified" in three treaties—Oliva, Copenhagen and Kardis (1660-1661). Sweden rounded out her home territory at the expense of Denmark, but Denmark remained a state; Poland and Sweden agreed to forget their feud, Russia reappeared, and the Great Elector became an independent sovereign in his duchy of East Prussia. He had relinquished western Pomerania reluctantly, but he had acquired patience. The outlines of the Prussian eagle are now discernible. Brandenburg forms the body, the Rhenish duchies and East Prussia are the tips of the wings. The outlines will be filled in, during the next two centuries, with "etching tools" of steel.

The Europe of the treaties of Westphalia, the Pyrenees, and Oliva-Copenhagen-Kardis is much changed from the Europe of Câteau-Cambrésis (1559). Spain has yielded the first place to France, and England under Charles II is now subordinate to French, instead of to Spanish, policy. Holland has appeared, wrought marvels, and soon will have to assume a defensive attitude in the world which she has done so much to alter. Sweden is still to be reckoned with, but Brandenburg-Prussia is gathering strength. Austria has recovered and faces southeast and east.

Roman Catholicism has enjoyed a mighty revival, although the papacy has lost in international importance.

Almost everywhere on the Continent the absolute monarchy is ready for its great career, shaking off the control of noble, burgher and cleric.   Spain already exhibits some of its worst sides, but the glamour of the success of the French monarchy, nursed to triumph by Richelieu and Mazarin, and now (1661) visibly embodied in the young Louis XIV, causes the states of the Continent to regard the absolute monarchy (French model) as the last word in statecraft.   It transforms the nobles into supple courtiers, holds the Church in check, and knits the towns into the fabric of the State.   Efficiency, dispatch, large-scale operations, resistless strength are its earmarks.   It is "big business" in its political incarnation, before the phrase was invented.

But will the absolute monarchy remember popular liberties or will it identify and confuse the welfare of the people with the whims of the monarch, who is to claim that "I and the state are one" (Louis XIV)?   Will it, seeking more and more to direct the entire life of the nation, discourage and blight the productive forces of intellectual and moral daring, initiative and self-reliance, and thus ultimately cripple progress and impoverish the life of the individual and of the people as a whole?   A study of the conditions in Spain in 1661 throws some light on the probable answers to these questions.

The English system of constitutional or limited monarchy, which Charles II had to accept in 1660, looks awkward and ineffective in comparison with that of the absolute monarchy of the Continent.   The future was to determine which scheme afforded the best basis for national and individual happiness.[1]

[1] See also pages 523-524.

CHAPTER XXIV

ENGLAND, IRELAND AND SCOTLAND
1603-1660

THE English Channel, that narrow strip of ocean separating England from the Continent, facilitated the growth of significant differences between the English and the kindred peoples of mainland Europe. Diversity of racial mixture and of physical environment no doubt played a part; but the outstanding cause of difference was the insularity of England. The Channel slowed up the infiltration of continental ideas and practices and protected the English from those recurrent military invasions which forcibly shaped the evolution of the continental peoples; the Channel gave the islanders a chance to develop certain qualities and institutions —which in turn mold qualities—of their own. The English were Europeans, but Europeans with a difference.

Since the Norman Conquest the English had repeatedly surrendered the advantages of their location to participate in exhausting continental campaigns; but the Tudor sovereigns substantially withdrew from the Continent. Their policy of abstention was the more easy to follow because of the engrossment of their continental rivals in the protracted series of wars which began, say, in 1494. The joint results of insularity, ocean ventures and a century of freedom from extensive wars were institutions, habits and points of view which in large part determined the solutions of the chief problems of the Stuart period. A brief survey of these institutions, qualities and tempers, as they stood at the close of the Tudor epoch, will form a helpful introduction to this chapter.

THE TUDOR SYSTEM OF GOVERNMENT UNDER ELIZABETH

England was no longer a land of feudal loyalties where fealty to class outranked allegiance to the commonwealth. It had attained national solidarity. The last Parliament of Elizabeth's reign expressed this idea with real eloquence: "Forasmuch as we do seriously consider that your Majesty and we your faithful and obedient subjects are but one body politic, and that your Highness is the head and we the members, and that no good or felicity, peril or adversity can come to the one but the other shall partake thereof . . ." (Prothero). The nobles did not form a caste as they did on the Continent. Only the eldest son of a noble inherited "nobility"; the younger sons and the daughters were, in law, commoners; young and often older sons intermarried with the merchants, entered commerce, took to sheep-farming and even to piracy. The younger sons of "gentlemen" frequently migrated to the cities, became apprentices, entered business, and merged into the city population without losing touch with the manorhouse. Successful merchants frequently were ennobled. No sharp line divided the middle from the upper class. The cities and boroughs which possessed wide, although varying, rights of self-government and were ruled by elected mayors, aldermen and bailiffs, or officers of a similar type, usually elected neighboring country gentlemen to represent them in the House of Commons along with their own merchants and a sprinkling of lawyers. Hence the existence of a real degree of solidarity between country and town; hence the absence of that hostility between burghers and nobles which on the Continent was marked by the exploits of robber barons and by class wars against leagued cities. Hence, too, the care for commerce and the commercial interests which made the Tudor government unique among the monarchies.

Outside the cities, which had similar officials of their own, the administration of the criminal law throughout England and Wales was vested in the main in the *justices of the peace,* unpaid magistrates chosen by the central government in every shire from among the more influential of the gentlemen of the county. They averaged about fifty to the shire and owed their selection and much of their influence to their family importance. With exceptions to be mentioned in a moment, they enforced all the criminal laws "for the conservation of the peace," and meted out, with the aid of the jury, the whole range of punishments from hanging to whipping and fines. The justice of the peace helped to enforce (and sometimes to leave unenforced) the laws against Catholics and other nonconformists, fixed the rates of wages for the year, kept an eye on prices and quality of food, and saw to the observance of the great Statute of Apprentices (1563). To them also fell the arduous task of enforcing the Poor Law of 1597, which required each parish to raise funds for binding out poor children as apprentices, for providing work for the unemployed and support for the impotent poor. This statute and the kindred laws against begging and vagabondage gradually cut down the thefts and pillagings of wastrel bands and helped to reduce to the status of a nursery rhyme the ancient warning, "Hark, hark, the dogs do bark, the tinkers are coming to town."

The justices of the peace were supervised—at long range—by the Privy Council. In addition, they were reported on by the twelve *justices of assize,* who left their seats in the high courts at Westminster twice a year to go on circuit, in pairs, through the shires or counties of England and Wales. These expert judges, in the course of a couple of days at each county town, tried civil suits, handled cases of treason, forgery and a few other high crimes which were not given over to those amateurs, the justices of the peace, and lectured the assembled leaders of the shire on the needs and desires of the central government.

And yet, when all is said, it was chiefly the justices of the peace who carried on the work of the government in the shires, and incidentally gained from it a political training which in the Stuart period was to make them particularly useful members of the House of Commons. "The policy of the Crown depended for its execution on the active consent of magistrates, who again depended for their own social position on the good will of the neighboring squires, and were on such friendly terms with the middle class in town and country, that magisterial resistance to the Crown might at moments become one with the resistance of the whole nation" (Trevelyan). The parsimony of the Tudors and perhaps their insight into English characteristics prevented them from attempting to set up *intendants* throughout England.

There was no standing army in England. Elizabeth regularized the appointment of lord lieutenants who were usually nobles, one to a shire or a convenient group of shires, whose duty it was with the aid of "muster masters" to see to the training of the county militia or "trained bands," and to the giving of some little drill to the other able-bodied men. The more important cities had their own trained bands under their own control. All these were foot soldiers or infantry. For horsemen or cavalry the government depended on the nobles and squires, who were required to furnish and equip one or more when needed, in accordance with their wealth. For service in Ireland, the Netherlands, or France, volunteering, the draft, and the press gang were employed. The cost of this plan of military "preparedness" was borne very largely by the counties and cities themselves.

From the military standpoint this English system of local armament left much to be desired. From the point of view of self-government it was admirably suited to the end of restraining the government from clearly unpopular courses. For a revolt or invasion in one section could be suppressed only by means of the assembled forces of the rest of the country. If the government became seriously unpopular it would be helpless in the face of general apathy or active opposition. That situation did not arise under the Tudor kings.

The autocratic temper and structure of the Tudor government stand out clearly under Elizabeth. She chose her own ministers and ruled with the aid of the Privy Council, to which they and others belonged. She appointed, and could at will remove, the judges of the high courts of justice which sat at Westminster. For the punishment of powerful offenders, who theoretically might be too strong for the regular courts, she had the Court of Star Chamber, founded by Henry VII. It was made up of her Privy Council and two of the high-court justices, and it was not bound so closely by existing laws and previously decided cases as were the regular courts. It could be an instrument of injustice. As supreme governor of the Church of England she appointed the higher Church officials, and she controlled them directly or through her Court of High Commission, made up of laymen and clergymen chosen by herself. In all these her will was supreme

THE BRITISH ISLES
1603-1660

Scale of Miles
0 25 50 75 100

SHETLAND IS.

ORKNEY IS.

NORTH

SEA

H E B R I D E S

H I G H L A N D S

Aberdeen
Dee

Dundee

S C O T L A N D

Clyde
Glasgow   Edinburgh   Dunbar

L O W L A N D S
Tweed

CHEVIOT HILLS   Newcastle

Londonderry
ULSTER   ANTRIM

I. OF
MAN

LANCASHIRE   *Swale*

CONNAUGHT
I R E L A N D   Drogheda
LEINSTER   Dublin

Preston   Marston   York
Moor

IRISH SEA

ANGLESEA

Shannon

MUNSTER

Cork

St. George's Channel

W A L E S

Trent

E N G L A N D

Naseby   *Ouse*
Severn
Worcester

Buckingham
London   Stratford
Thames
Westminster   Canterbury

CORNWALL

E N G L I S H   C H A N N E L

FRANCE

- - - Line of division between Royalists
      & Parliamentarians in 1642
····· Line of division between highlands &
      lowlands in Scotland
▒▒ The English Pale in 1641
▨▨ Scottish Settlements
▧▧ Area assigned to Irish proprietors
      loyal to Parliament in 1653

MANHATTAN DRAFTING CO.,N.Y

whenever she chose to express it. Nor did she hesitate to order the judges at Westminster not to try this or that case, if she wished to have it settled elsewhere.

Elizabeth's Parliaments were very deferential and submissive. They met irregularly, sat as a rule for only a few weeks, and were scarcely regarded as having a regular share in the conduct of national business. England was governed by queen and council. To be sure, Parliaments had certain rights and powers, especially in the matter of taxation and of general legislation, which came down from the Lancastrian era and which might well be regarded by a political scientist as limiting the queen's despotism. These rights were not dormant. From Henry VII on, it had been the policy of the Tudors to use Parliament as "shield and buckler," and sometimes as accomplice. For example, it strengthened the royal hand at home and abroad to have the representatives of the people break the power of the old Church and set up the Church of England. Moreover, the old reason for establishing Parliaments—to make it more easy for the king to get money from the people—was still a good reason. The Tudors kept up the use of Parliaments for their own convenience.

Elizabeth had a fair regular income of her own from crown lands, feudal rights, "first-fruits" and other sources, and she husbanded it thriftily, but it was not enough to pay the increasing costs of government, especially those of her foreign policy. Every four years or so she was driven to call a Parliament to vote her taxes. The members of both Houses, carefully shepherded by Elizabeth's privy councilors who were elected to the House of Commons or sat in the House of Lords, busied themselves with matters of legislation, as they had done for many generations. Very frequently Elizabeth had to chide the members—usually with very great tact—for discussing matters or proposing legislation which she regarded as unwise or outside the scope of the powers of Parliament; on rare occasions she emphasized her disapproval by sending the overzealous member to cool his fervor with a few weeks or months in the Tower. She would not allow Parliament to press marriage upon her; she would not allow it to "meddle" with ecclesiastical laws or the Church after she and

Parliament and Convocation had reëstablished it; she kept foreign policy away from Parliament—that was a matter for her and her Council; she even declined to allow it to pass laws restraining the monopolies she had granted, on the ground that the royal *prerogative* (reserved powers belonging to the Crown) gave her control over such matters.   Some of the subjects on which Parliament was allowed to legislate have been spoken of in preceding paragraphs.

Elizabeth's Parliaments, broadly speaking, respected her wishes. Apart from the awe inspired in them by royalty, they realized that the country was exposed to many dangers, especially from the uncertainties of the succession to the throne if Elizabeth should die.   Moreover, the people had a continuing memory of the miseries of the past from which, as they believed, the Tudors had rescued them.   After the execution of Mary Queen of Scots, however, and the defeat of the Spanish Armada and of the other efforts of Spain to bring Elizabeth low, there is evidence of a gradual change of temper.   The country was safe, confidence in England was high, foreign trade was increasing, capital was going into mining and weaving as well as into agriculture, and London was modestly preparing for its career as a great money market. The need for royal tutelage was passing at the very time that it was becoming irksome to capitalistic enterprise.   But the habit of deference toward their "dread sovereign" maintained its sway until Elizabeth's death.

Cogent arguments have been advanced to prove that the growth of Protestantism in Elizabethan England increased the self-reliance and assertiveness of the English.[1]   It may or may not be so.   Certainly the Puritans, who disagreed with the queen's religion established by law, would find it easier to disagree with other features of her government.   We know from various sources that their discontent with conditions in the Church was actually increasing; we also know that in Elizabeth's later Parliaments they were quiescent on religious affairs.   It is interesting to reflect that the attack upon monopolies may have had some

[1] G. P. Gooch, *English Democratic Ideas in the Seventeenth Century.*

Puritan animus behind it; London and the industrial towns were
largely Puritan in religious sentiment.

Monopolies were royal grants made through "letters patent"
by Elizabeth and her immediate predecessors, giving certain individuals, in return for money or services, an exclusive right for a
period of years to make or import or sell, as the case might be,
such and such an article or ware.   In some cases these royal
grants conflicted with the laws of the land, but the Privy Council
did not permit the courts to interfere.   Most of the monopolies
were of the nature of true patents or copyrights, as we know these
words, and entirely unobjectionable.[1] Some of them, however,
were mere permits to monopolize the sale of certain forms of
common wares, as salt, soap, starch. Naturally prices were raised
far beyond the gain accruing to the crown, and quality was frequently impaired; and trade was injured by the extortions practiced in enforcing the monopolies.   There was a sense of injustice
which constantly grew.   In the Parliament of 1601 matters came
to a head and various bills were introduced to secure relief.   The
resulting discussion was lively, although not always intelligent.
The wise old queen was tactfulness itself.   She thanked the Commons for "bringing the matter to her attention" and issued a
proclamation revoking the most vicious of the grants.   She did
not admit that Parliament had any right to legislate on the matter.
She merely met their wishes very largely and received their effu-
sive thanks.   The whole affair was significant.   But the significance escaped the attention of the learned Scottish king, the
son of Mary Queen of Scots, who was proclaimed king of England by the royal council when Elizabeth passed away in 1603.

The proclamation of King James VI of Scotland as King
James I of England met with general approval throughout England. He was welcomed by all, including Catholics and Puritans,
both of whom hoped that he would ameliorate their lot.   James
was the nearest heir to Elizabeth, according to the general rules
of inheritance. To be sure, the will of Henry VIII, which had

[1] W. R. Scott, *The Constitution and Finance of English, Scottish and Irish
Joint Stock Companies* (3 vols., Cambridge, 1910-12).

been given statutory force by one of his Parliaments, gave the succession after Elizabeth to Catherine Grey.[1] But Elizabeth's Council, in her later years, realized that the acceptance of James VI, king of Protestant Scotland, would prevent disputes, perhaps civil war. Robert Cecil, who had followed his father, Lord Burleigh, as Elizabeth's leading minister, corresponded secretly with King James for some time prior to Elizabeth's death, advising him how to behave so as to improve his chances. Cheyney conjectures that Cecil may have let Elizabeth see the letters that passed between them. Elizabeth on her death bed indicated that James was her choice. And so he was proclaimed and crowned as successor to her who had put his mother to death.

WHAT KING JAMES I OF ENGLAND HAD LEARNED IN SCOTLAND

King James I (b. 1566) entered upon his English heritage with certain strong convictions, which were based primarily upon his experience in Scotland where he had reigned since 1567. He had grown up in a country of little wealth, among turbulent and rapacious nobles who had kidnapped him more than once and in his name as well as on their own hook had killed their rivals and seized their property. He was a Calvinist in theology but his relations with the Scottish Kirk, which had been founded under the inspiration of John Knox, had been most unhappy. What this meant to him and ultimately to the English Puritans will be clearer if we bring the history of the Kirk down to date.

[1] Genealogy of descendants of Henry VII:

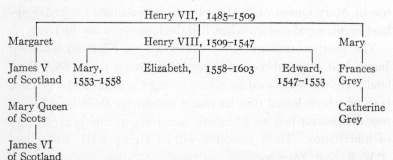

Henry VII, 1485-1509

Margaret   Henry VIII, 1509-1547   Mary

James V   Mary,   Elizabeth,   1558-1603   Edward,   Frances
of Scotland   1553-1558   1547-1553   Grey

Mary Queen   Catherine
of Scots   Grey

James VI
of Scotland

Knox's *First Book of Discipline* (1560) had sketched the organization and functions of the Kirk. The sketch was filled in by Andrew Melville, his learned and fiery successor, likewise trained in Geneva, in the *Second Book of Discipline,* which was adopted by the general assembly of the Kirk in 1577. It embodies the Calvinistic principle of the independence of the Church from control by the State. The minister (presbyter) derives his authority under God from the congregation and is assisted in ruling the congregation by other presbyters, the elders. All the ruling bodies of the Church are made up of ministers and elders. All ministers are equal; there is no hierarchy. At the top is the general assembly, the supreme legislature and court of the Kirk, which is to meet when it chooses. Between the Kirk session (minister and elders) of the individual church or congregation and the general assembly, room is left for intermediate assemblies; for example, the presbytery, which is composed of ministers and chosen elders from the congregations of a certain region which corresponds roughly to the medieval diocese. The whole Kirk is thus to rule herself, subject to no secular authority, be it king or Parliament.

But the Kirk, being Calvinistic, will not be satisfied in the sixteenth century and even later unless the Scots in all their affairs—economic, social and political, as well as religious—form a true "Kingdom of Christ." Hence the importance of enforcing *discipline*—that is, the surveillance of the behavior and the regimentation of all the members of the Church. They must, of course, know the Scriptures and the catechism; they must also be moral in all their conduct, fair in business transactions, seemly in their pleasures. If they err, they will be admonished, reproved, corrected, disciplined; if incorrigible, they will be cut off—excommunicated—from the Kirk. And in the Kirk princes and kings are, of course, simple members. Such is the ideal of the *Second Book of Discipline.*

The Scottish Kirk soon covered the land, outside of the inaccessible parts of the Highlands, with its ministrations, and won the ardent loyalty of the great majority of its members. The services were austere, but so were the land and the people. The Kirk gave its members a real voice and a genuine political training in its various assemblies. The ministers were looked up to as leaders rather than as rulers imposed from above. To outsiders, to opponents, the "new presbyter" might well seem "old priest writ large"—that is, a more efficient and domineering cleric; to the members of the Kirk, he was the authentic exponent of their dearest beliefs, their highest hopes, the teacher of morality, duty and human equality. The Kirk bade fair to become the most powerful force in Scotland.

The regents who ruled Scotland during the minority of James did not venture to challenge the pretensions of the Kirk, but they did appoint bishops of a sort to draw the ancient revenues of the former dioceses. James himself went further, for he early realized that a strong Kirk meant a weak kingship unless he was prepared to accept its guidance. Accordingly, in 1584, he had the Scottish Parliament pass laws declaring that the king was supreme over all causes and persons and giving the bishops the powers claimed by the presbyteries and the general assembly. Nevertheless, James had the old Church endowments transferred to the Crown. Then a Catholic rising frightened him into seeking the favor of the Kirk, and so the *Second Book of Discipline* was accepted by Parliament in 1592. It was not long, however, before the outspoken criticisms of the ministers and the opposition of the general assembly to some of his political plans led him to retrace his steps. The ministers were again subordinated to bishops, and the general assembly was packed and coerced into accepting something resembling the English system of royal and episcopal control over the Kirk.

By the end of the century James had also reduced the nobles to some sort of submission. He could thus fancy himself to be master of Scotland. His *Basilicon Doron,* published in 1599, reveals his conviction that monarchs derive their power from God and are responsible to Him alone for the manner in which they rule their peoples. This divine-right theory, expounded by James, links him with the continental despots of the seventeenth century.

Such had been the experience, such was the temper, of James, when he made his triumphant progress from Edinburgh to London in 1603. As the successor of the Tudors, who had subdued the nobility, established the Church of England under their own headship, and founded traditions of autocratic rule which they had sanctified by a century of internal peace, James's new prospects, by contrast with those of poor and turbulent Scotland, appeared dazzling. And the English Parliament, in making formal recognition of his title, seemed to subscribe to his divine-right theory. For it passed an Act, "being bounden thereto both by the laws of God and man," that, upon the death of Elizabeth, the crown of England "did, by inherent birthright and lawful and undoubted succession, descend and come to your most excellent Majesty, as being lineally, justly and lawfully next and sole heir of the blood royal."

James was learned and witty, but he lacked gumption. He did not understand the art of management by a mixture of concession and firmness in which Elizabeth had excelled; he was no judge of men; he talked too much. On the other hand, he disliked war; and his termination of the slackened conflict with Spain, in 1604, brought domestic problems to the front and gave opportunity for the threshing out of those questions of religion, taxation and the constitutional rights of Parliament whose settlement was to involve the ruin of his dynasty.

ATTITUDE OF KING JAMES TOWARD RELIGIOUS DISSIDENTS AND PARLIAMENTARIANS

James's skill in handling the Puritan and Roman Catholic problems of England was soon put to the test. Even before he reached London he received a petition from hundreds of Puritan clergymen of the Church of England, who were afraid that their Church might drift back to the parent Romanism unless it were "purified from all taint of popery." They were not extreme Puritans of the Presbyterian or Independent type. They petitioned that the sign of the cross in baptism, bowing at the name of Jesus, and the wearing of the surplice should be abolished. They asked that candidates for the ministry should not be compelled to declare their approval of all the Thirty-Nine Articles (this requirement kept many Puritan recruits out of the ministry of the Church), but only of those, required under Elizabeth, relating to the faith and sacraments; they requested that certain oppressive practices of the Court of High Commission should be reformed.

The petitioners received a hearing at the Hampton Court conference. James rebuked them and uttered his famous aphorisms: "If you aim at a Scottish Presbytery, I tell you it agreeth as well with a monarchy as God with the devil," and "No bishop, no king!" He closed the conference by telling these moderate Puritans that he would make them conform or "harry them out of the land." When his first Parliament met, the House of Commons, broadly representative of influential English opinion, promptly supported the petition. James was adamant and the archbishop of Canterbury, appointed by him, ejected three hundred of the Puritan ministers whom Elizabeth had tolerated in the Church, because they would not acquiesce in the stricter tests. Yet, despite his blustering, James did nothing more to the Puritans. The laws were enforced rather more strictly; dissident religious gatherings—conventicles—were broken up; a few who would not acquiesce emigrated to the more tolerant Holland. Puritanism continued to develop through the practice of family worship which was not forbidden. Puritanism bided its time.

Toward the Roman Catholics James showed a softer heart. Elizabeth's penal laws, although never steadily enforced, hung heavy over their heads. Recusants—those refusing to conform— were compelled to stay in the neighborhood of their estates, were excluded from the professions and from office under the government and were subject to ruinous and repeated fines as long as they stayed away from church; their priests were forbidden the land on pain of death. James now relaxed the enforcement of these laws; but the number of avowals of Catholic opinions soon frightened him into reversing his position.

The consequence of this disappointment of their hopes was that half a dozen Catholic gentlemen, with the reluctant acquiescence of the secret Jesuit organization in England, formed the Gunpowder Plot to blow up James and both Houses of Parliament together on the 5th of November, 1605. A series of Catholic risings were to be set off simultaneously, and in the resulting confusion the Catholics were to seize control of the government. The plot was discovered in the nick of time. But Protestant fears of Catholic and Jesuit conspiracies with Spain—the hereditary enemy—grew apace, and for generations the celebration of Guy Fawkes' Day—the 5th of November—served to keep active an unreasoning fear of the creed of the Roman Catholics and to foster suspicion of the motives of anyone who strove to ease their lot.

While Puritans and Catholics were having these experiences, James undertook to instruct his first Parliament on the amplitude of his royal power. Elizabeth had talked guardedly about her prerogative, for she was one to "let sleeping dogs lie." James said that "Kings are not only God's lieutenants upon earth and sit upon God's throne, but even by God Himself they are called gods." "As to dispute what God may do is blasphemy, so it is sedition in subjects to dispute what a King may do in the height of his power. I will not be content that my power be disputed on." James was here expounding the theory of the divine right of kings.[1] Originally invented as a weapon against the papal claim to depose kings, it was now being used by the continental rulers against their peoples. The English members of Parliament knew what James was driving at. "England is the last monarchy that yet retains her liberties," said one of them. They knew their *Magna Carta* and the other rights extorted from reluctant kings in past centuries, especially through the "power of the purse."

The king's address really served to put his Parliament on its guard. And when James sought to have a disputed election to the House of Commons settled by the judges, the Commons deferentially but firmly maintained that it was their privilege to determine such contests. To the king's remark that they derived all their privileges from him—a hint that their "privileges" were revocable —a member answered that the king was misinformed, and that the royal plan for settling disputed elections would mean that "none shall be chosen but such as shall please the king and council." King James gave way on the issue. And it is broadly true that, when it came to the scratch, neither he nor his son and grand-

[1] J. N. Figgis, *Theory of the Divine Right of Kings.*

sons were able to make use of the divine-right theory. Both kings and Parliaments in their contests relied upon the precedents of the past; the kings upon those of Tudor times and the Parliaments chiefly upon those of the preceding epoch. James's excursion into the divine-right theory served chiefly to lessen the royal bargaining power since his Parliaments were now afraid to make concessions.

In their efforts to secure the king's consent to legislation which he disliked, one of the most effective weapons in the armory of Parliament was the power of the purse; Parliament must vote the taxes. In 1606 the judges decided (Bates's case) that, as the law stood, the king had a right to increase a very considerable range of customs duties, called *impositions,* without the consent of Parliament. In 1610 Parliament awoke to the danger that, with the growth of trade, the king might use the product of increased impositions to dispense with its meetings. One member remarked in the course of a long argument, "Considering what is the greatest use they [our kings] make of assembling of parliaments, which is the supply of money, I do not see any likelihood to hope for often meetings in that kind, because they would provide themselves by that other means" (impositions). The parliamentary leaders tried to get the king to surrender his claim to the impositions and to his irritating but unproductive feudal rights (wardship, marriage, etc.) in return for a *fixed* annual income, but the negotiations broke down because James resented parliamentary criticisms of the clergy. James dissolved Parliament and decided to get along without it. The experiment lasted ten years (1611-1621).

THE FOREIGN POLICY OF KING JAMES

James's conduct of affairs did not enhance his reputation. His court was dissolute and horrified the Puritans, and he followed the advice of upstart and spendthrift favorites, of whom the duke of Buckingham is the most notorious. There was no war, but James ran heavily into debt, and his unsuccessful efforts to raise forced "loans" served chiefly to increase discontent. The thing which enraged most of his subjects, however, was his determination to marry his son Charles to a Spanish princess. Was it merely a desire for the reflected glory of an alliance with the most haughty monarchy of the Continent that led him on, or was it his idea that as "father-in-law of Spain" he would be able to play the part of peacemaker of Europe? We do not know.

Certainly Europe in general and James's own son-in-law, the Elector Palatine Frederick, in particular needed a peacemaker. The Austrian and Spanish Hapsburgs had driven Frederick out of Bohemia and the Rhenish Palatinate, and were forcibly converting the populations to Roman Catholicism, to the terror of the Protestant English who still feared that their turn would yet come. The English were clamoring for war with Spain—and James was still pushing the Spanish match, encouraged thereto by the intelligent Spanish ambassador. James thought that, through fear of war with England, he might bluff Spain into the marriage and into restoring the Palatinate to Frederick, and so, to the great joy of his naïve people, James called Parliament in 1621.

Parliament took advantage of the situation to crush a new, Jacobean crop of monopolists and to pass a law forbidding, with certain advisable exceptions, grants of monopolies to individuals, and also to impeach, not the favorite, but a high-placed client of the favorite, Lord Chancellor Bacon. The successful revival, after an interval of a century and a half, of this method of attack, in which the Commons serve as prosecutors and the Lords as judges, was a real gain for Parliament. But when the members of the House of Commons proceeded to rage against Spain, James ordered them, à la Elizabeth, to leave foreign affairs alone as beyond their capacity. The Commons replied with a formal protest that it was their birthright, as representatives of the people, freely to debate all matters whatsoever "concerning the king . . . , the defence of the realm, and of the Church of England." James lectured them and dissolved Parliament. The Spanish ambassador had reason for his jubilation.

Then ensued the "romantic" (to the Puritans, tragic) spectacle of Prince Charles, accompanied by Buckingham, going to Spain to woo the Infanta in the best troubadour fashion. These ambassadors offered to have the penal laws repealed (James had stopped enforcing them) ; they promised that the children of the marriage should be Catholics. The Spaniards could not bring themselves to consent to the match *before* the first of these promises was fulfilled. It could not be fulfilled; and Buckingham and Charles returned home, now immensely popular, with war against Spain on their lips. Parliament was called and voted funds; James declared war, left its management to Buckingham, and soon died (March, 1625).

THE EARLY POLICIES OF KING CHARLES I

The war went badly from the start. The English had been at peace for twenty years and Buckingham was incompetent, although brave. After the first year Parliament refused to vote more money unless Buckingham were removed; but Charles was even fonder of him than James had been. Buckingham tried to play the Elizabethan statesman by allying England with France through the marriage of Charles with Henrietta Maria, daughter of Henry IV and sister of Louis XIII (1624). Richelieu, of course, had engineered the match so as to keep England friendly. But he was not ready for open war with Spain since he had not yet "drawn the teeth" of the Huguenots. And so, because of minor disputes, Buckingham had Charles declare war against France also (1627). It was a silly deed, considering the object of the war against Spain (recovery of the Palatinate) and the refusal of money by Parliament.

Charles had attempted to raise money by forced loans (1626-1627), backed up by the imprisonment of those refusing to "aid their country." The attempt failed because scores of men of prominence set the example by going to prison rather than pay. They feared for the liberties of their country; they were afraid, too, that forced loans might be linked with the extension of martial law from the troops, which were already collected by press-gangs and billeted on private citizens, to the citizens themselves, and might thus be used as the basis for a regular system of despotic government. The fear was most lively in the centers of Puritanism. Elizabeth had done these very things, but her motives were considered to be patriotic.

Without funds Charles could not get his revenge on France. So he called Parliament again in 1628. Most of the prominent men who had recently suffered imprisonment rather than "lend" were returned as members of the House of Commons. Parliament promptly passed a measure declaring the king's recent practices illegal and offered him a heavy vote of money for its acceptance. Charles finally agreed. The measure, known as the *Petition of Right,* thus made law, ranks with *Magna Carta* as one of the bulwarks of English freedom. It covers four points and declares illegal trials by martial law, billeting of soldiers on private houses, imprisonment without a specific charge of violation of law, and the exaction of loans or taxes not imposed by Parliament.

The war continued to go badly. Even when Buckingham, denounced in Parliament and protected by Charles, was murdered (August, 1628), there was no improvement; and the English fleet, far from raising the siege of La Rochelle, merely witnessed the capture of that Protestant stronghold by Richelieu. The English would not back Buckingham's war—especially against France, the old ally. So Charles, perforce, in 1629 and 1630 made peace with France and with Spain and turned his attention to purely English affairs.

For the House of Commons, whose insistence had secured the Petition of Right, was not disposed to rest on that achievement. It proposed a timely assertion of parliamentary control over the king's peace-time revenues, which control might be employed to ease off the increasing pressure on the Puritans. For, as it happened, Parliament had not yet voted Charles the tonnage and poundage duties [1] which a new king was customarily granted for life at the opening of his reign. These duties made up about a quarter of the royal income. The Commons offered to vote

[1] These were ancient import and export duties on wine, wool, sheepskins and leather. The impositions covered a wider range of goods.

Charles the tonnage and poundage for one year. He refused to accept anything but the life-grant.

The Puritan grievances were now injected into the controversy. The House of Commons was not so much wrought up by the support which the Anglican bishops were giving to Charles all along the line—the Commons were used to that relation of mutual helpfulness under James—as by the support which Charles was giving to a new (or very old) ritualistic or high-church movement now led by Bishop Laud. The group of bishops following Laud was not only exalting episcopal prerogatives and forcing ritualistic ceremonial on unwilling congregations; it was also attacking the Calvinistic theology which had long held the upper hand in the Church of England, questioning in particular predestination, the cornerstone of that theology, and exalting the new doctrine of Arminianism (free will) which nowadays is widely accepted. The Puritans of 1628 erroneously regarded the new doctrine as a device for making the Church of England ready for "the return to Rome."

Charles was outraged at the maneuvers of the House of Commons and decided to prorogue Parliament. But the House of Commons locked the door against his message of prorogation until it could pass, amid tumultuous scenes, three memorable resolutions of defiance. The resolutions declared that anyone seeking "to extend or introduce Popery or Arminianism," or endorsing the levy of "tonnage and poundage, not being granted by Parliament," should be regarded as "a capital enemy to the Kingdom and Commonwealth"; and that anyone voluntarily paying such tonnage and poundage should likewise "be reputed a betrayer of the liberties of England, and an enemy of the same."

THE ARBITRARY GOVERNMENT OF CHARLES I, 1629-1640

Charles now announced that he would not call any more Parliaments until his opponents should come to their senses. He kept his word for eleven years, 1629-1640. He had no standing army, no *intendants,* no masterful and statesman-like minister such as Louis XIII had in Richelieu. His chief adviser, in State as well as in Church, was the con...entious and pedantic Laud, whom he made archbishop of Canterbury in 1633. Charles relied upon the traditional loyalty of the English and his confidence was justified, for there were no revolts. He had his chance to demonstrate the virtues of Stuart autocracy.

It is time to consider what manner of man Charles I was. He was not so shrewd as his father. But he was dignified, artistic, tenacious of his royal "rights." He was entirely loyal to the Church of England and devotedly attached to his wife, Henrietta Maria, and their children. His wife's encouragement of autocratic practices, based upon the despotic powers of her brother Louis XIII, did Charles harm; and the favors he showed the English Roman Catholics, out of courtesy to the faith of his wife, erroneously led the suspicious Puritans to view him, as well as Laud, as preparing for the triumph of "popery." Charles's chief defect, as yet undisclosed, was not his inability to fathom the English mind—James had the same defect—but rather his untrustworthiness. He could not be relied on to keep his promises.

The personal government of Charles I (1629-1640) was marked by ecclesiastical and secular coercion. As to the former, Charles acted as if his father's aphorism, "No bishop, no king!" was to be replaced with the positive precept, "Up bishop, up king!" And so Laud systematically and forcefully brought to an end the "working system of local variations in religion" which had enabled many Puritan-minded clergymen and very many Puritan laymen to remain in the Established Church. The parishes were gone over one by one and clergy combed out and replaced by men in sympathy with Laud, while the laymen who attempted to secede and worship in conventicles were fined and imprisoned. Puritan towns which had supplemented the ministrations of the regular clergy with the discourses of Puritan "lecturers," and Puritan gentry who had similarly installed Puritan chaplains were compelled to relinquish them. Strict episcopal censorship put an end to the legal expression of Puritan opinions, and persons assailing the bishops or their jurisdiction were punished barbarously by the Court of Star Chamber. "The only legal form of worship, beautiful and orderly as it had now become, appeared an intolerable triviality to many of the most imaginative and intellectual, and as it proved the most forcible men of every class" (Trevelyan). Between 1628 and 1640 twenty thousand Englishmen fled from Laud's persecutions to New England, whither in 1620 the *Mayflower* had brought its first shipload of Puritans.

The secular coercion practiced by Charles (1629-1640) was dictated by the need of money. His measures were all the more irritating because, being professedly legal, they seemed to show that the Englishman's bulwark of law, so slowly built during past centuries, afforded him no real protection against the Crown. The chief promoters of the Three Resolutions of 1629, often called Eliot's Resolutions, were sentenced by servile judges, under charges of sedition, to imprisonment "during the king's pleasure," thus evading the Petition of Right. Tonnage and poundage and of course, the impositions were collected as usual, as properly belonging to the Crown and wrongfully left ungranted by Parliament. The growth of commerce made this source of revenue increasingly productive. Obsolete royal rights were revived to permit the king to levy heavy fines on well-to-do citizens who had neglected to secure knighthood and on nobles and other landholders whose ancestors had encroached on the ancient limits of the royal forests. Trading monopolies were sold to corporations, thus evading the Act of 1624 forbidding monopolies. But the most productive device, and the one which provoked the most vehement constitutional opposition, was *ship-money*.

The germ of *ship-money* was found in Plantagenet times, when the monarchs had occasionally called upon the seaports to turn over their merchant vessels for naval warfare. Elizabeth had done something similar in fighting the Armada. Between 1634 and 1637 Charles's lawyers had developed the germ into a ravenous levy of money upon all the shires of England, ostensibly (and partly) for the protection of the nation at sea. To the charge that *ship-money* violated the Petition of Right, Charles answered that it was not a tax but a mere commutation of the service which every man owed in time of war. And when sturdy John Hampden refused to pay, the full bench of judges, after listening to elaborate argument (1637-1638) which let everyone with eyes see what cat was in the bag, decided, seven to five, that the king was right.

Charles's oppression, his use of constitutional weapons for monarchical instead of for national interests, forced into a common opposition Puritans who placed their religion foremost, constitutionalists and lawyers who put the law above the king, and people of property who thought of income first of all. These groups had supported Elizabeth who was assuredly, although more cleverly, as autocratic as Charles. Would they likewise stand by Charles in a national crisis? The test soon came.

The crisis was created by Charles. In 1637 he and Laud undertook to bring the Scottish Kirk finally into line with the English Church. It may well have been Charles's idea that this step would lead to the unification of the kingdoms. King James had imposed bishops on the Kirk and had restrained its general assembly in order to bridle its political activity; but he "had taken care to leave it consistent with Calvinist doctrine and ritual, and with democratic government of the village kirks" (Trevelyan). Charles had gone a bit further and now, without adequate preparation of Scottish opinion, Laud added the capstone by ordering the Kirk to substitute a modified Anglican Prayer Book, conveniently shipped from London, for Knox's beloved *Book of Common Order*. The Scottish nobles, fearful of the loss of the Church lands they had gained, and the devout Presbyterians, alarmed for their faith, joined in armed covenant to defend their religion. A general assembly of the Kirk, the first to meet in forty years, met and restored the complete Presbyterian system of Andrew Melville (1628). This was virtual revolt. Charles, having no army, called out the trained bands of northern England and summoned his reluctant nobles to lead them against the embattled Scots (1639). But the disparity between the two forces (the Scots were mostly veterans of the wars in Germany) was so patent that Charles withdrew the new book and temporized. The Scots organized a government, and Charles, finding Laud inadequate and discredited, sent for Thomas, Viscount Wentworth, lord-deputy of Ireland since 1633.

Wentworth had won a great reputation in Ireland. He put down revolts and piracy. He managed—with promises and brow-beatings—the Irish Parliament (founded by Edward I in 1297) with its Protestant majority and its strong Roman Catholic minority. With the funds it voted and the customs duties which doubled under his fostering of commerce he maintained a small Protestant army. He had no real sympathy with the native Irish. He maintained justice in ordinary cases; but he carried on the newer English policy of despoiling the great Irish and Anglo-Norman landowners of their extensive estates by partisan applications of English law and the verdicts of coerced native juries. The scheme involved the destruction of the rights of the peasants as well as of the landowners, but it was profitable for the English land jobbers and strengthened the grip of the English on the country.

The first large-scale operation of this type had been carried out some twenty-five years prior to Wentworth's appointment, when six Ulster counties were confiscated and "planted" in part with Protestant Scots and English. Some of the dispossessed Irish cultivators were allowed to remain as "hewers of wood." Wentworth was putting through similar confiscations and *plantations* (the word then used by the joint-stock companies for their locations of groups of people on lands taken from aborigines or from the Irish), when Charles called him home for advice. Wentworth's government of Ireland was Protestant, effective, masterful; it made use of parliaments; it rested on an adequate army employed with decision; it was solvent and produced a surplus. Wentworth was the man for the crisis in England and Scotland. If he succeeded, then Charles would be master of the three kingdoms!

The plan Charles and the earl of Strafford (Wentworth's new title) agreed upon was this. The king should "press" a new army in southern England and stir up the old hostility against the Scots; Strafford should raise an army of 8,000 in Ireland and bring it over as soon as it was trained. Strafford went to Ireland in March, 1640, and got the Irish Parliament to vote the funds for the new army. He had the equipment all ready in Dublin Castle. The army was to have been Protestant, but the Scots in Ulster were cold and haste was essential. So he enlisted a Protestant nucleus of 1,000, together with 7,000 Catholic Irish, had their training started, and then hurried over to England to help Charles to a similar success.

Charles had called an English Parliament, usually called the *Short Parliament,* for April, 1640. But, to Strafford's chagrin, it refused to be coerced or cajoled into voting the needed funds, was rather sympathetic with the Scots, and talked about English grievances. It was accordingly dissolved after an abortive session of three weeks.

Strafford now made a tremendous effort to raise the money necessary to maintain the army Charles was levying in southern England. The great viceroy believed in strong government and was of the opinion that, legally and historically, Parliament was now attempting to subvert the ancient system of monarchical rule in England,[1] and that, as a consequence, Charles was free to do anything that would help him to uphold the royal authority. Strafford did not succeed. "Though he knew that failure meant ruin, Strafford was unable, by all the efforts of his will and genius, to extort enough money to pay for one army" (Trevelyan).

Nevertheless the new army, suspicious and unreliable though it was, was got together and led north by dependable nobles to confront the armed Scots. They for their part advanced into England and settled down around Newcastle. Strafford's Irish army was drilling in Ireland. To attack the Scots would be suicide. Not to attack them would be defeat. Charles negotiated. But the Scots would not budge, for all Charles's concessions, until their expenses were paid, and so Charles had to summon another Parliament to supply the money. The jig was up. The Scots would stay until their money was forthcoming, and Parliament would not vote the indemnity until it got satisfaction from the king. And the Englishmen made no complaint at the size of the bill the Scots presented.

[1] Weighty opinions support him. See F. W. Maitland, *Constitutional History of England,* pages 297-301.

THE ACHIEVEMENTS OF THE LONG PARLIAMENT PRIOR TO THE CIVIL WAR

The *Long Parliament,* which met in November, 1640, was no ordinary choice of the English electorate. For Pym and Hampden, proved champions of the popular cause, had made a tour of the constituencies, discreetly explaining the momentousness of the coming session and urging the election of tried and true Puritans. Nor was their leadership of the parliamentary cause allowed to lapse when the session opened; for they, with other influential members of Lords and Commons, met regularly for concerted action.

The impeachment of Charles's agents in the late tyrannies was drastic and effective. But the simplest chart of the development of opinion, down to the opening of the war, as to the measures needful to prevent the kings from renewing despotic government, will be found in the legislation Charles accepted before August, 1641. The laws follow in order of date. The Triennial Act provided that Parliament should meet at least every three years. The Act for the Attainder of Strafford declared his life forfeit. He was too capable and too dangerous a champion of monarchy to be allowed to live, and his execution would help to deter anyone from attempting to follow in his footsteps. Laud was allowed to live four years longer. The Act against Dissolving the Long Parliament without its own consent, approved the same day as the law destroying Strafford, was designed to prevent Charles from cutting short the projected reforms of the constitution. The Tonnage and Poundage Act declared illegal all customs duties whatsoever without grant by Parliament. The Act for the abolition of the Court of Star Chamber, and the kindred one abolishing the Court of High Commission and other similar "courts," wiped out the arbitrary councils which had enabled the monarchy to override the common law. The Acts declaring ship-money illegal, for the limitation of forests, and against the exaction of knighthood "fines," passed in August, 1641, made an end of the financial expedients of Charles's lawyers and left the monarchy dependent entirely on Parliament for its income.

In February, 1642, the Clerical Disabilities Act took away the seats of the bishops in the House of Lords and forbade the clergy to exercise any secular jurisdiction.

The interval of six months separating the last-mentioned Act from the preceding group is significant of much. The last measure deals with the clergy. And yet the question of religion was foremost in the thoughts of the members from the first day of the Parliament. In December, 1640, a monster petition had been presented to the House of Commons by citizens of London, asking for the "abolition of episcopacy with all its roots and branches." The petition was well received, for the opinion was general in both Houses that the royal nominees (the bishops) were teaching subservience to autocracy in the State and near-Catholicism in the Church. It was easy for all to agree that the episcopacy needed an overhauling. But agreement stopped there.

There were three competing ideas as to the proper type of reform. Under the first, the existing Anglican Church would be "Puritanized" and its government transferred from the bishops to a board of laymen appointed by Parliament. Under the second, the Anglican Church, still comprising all the people, would be "Presbyterianized" along the well-known Scottish lines. Under the third, there would be liberty of belief and worship on the basis of a Congregational system; in a word, Protestant nonconformists would be free. But the ruling opinions were still hostile to liberty of worship, and genuine adherents of Presbyterian discipline were relatively few; the majority wanted no more clerical domination.

But men soon perceived that the elimination of the bishops would probably involve the abolition of the Anglican Prayer Book, and it had many warm supporters, even if the friends of the bishops were few. Moreover, when the moderate Anglicans actually faced the prospect of having their Church "purified" by the Puritan majority of the Parliament, their affection for the existing Church reasserted itself, especially as the king was now curbed and might well consent to go back to the Elizabethan type of Church government and worship.

While opinions were thus crystallizing, Charles went to Scotland (November, 1641), hoping to get Scottish support. While he was away, the Puritan majority led by Pym registered their fear of the drift of moderate sentiment by making an appeal to public opinion. This took the form of the *Grand Remonstrance,* a lengthy but well-organized document outlining the grievances of forty years, the remedial legislation already passed, and the needs and dangers of the hour. The promoters of all the "mischief," denounced as "the malignant party," are said to be the "Jesuitical Papists," the "Bishops and corrupt part of the Clergy," and evil "Councillors and Courtiers." In essence the *Grand Remonstrance* contains only two demands. First, that parliamentary government should replace royal government; secondly, that the system under which Charles could appoint coercive, anti-Puritan bishops should somehow be reformed.[1]

Some of the effect of this notable piece of propaganda was due to the massacre of some thousands of Ulster Protestants by revolting native Irish seeking to recover their lands, their religion and their freedom. They were led by former officers of Strafford's army of 8,000 men, which had been disbanded by Charles in May, 1641, in an unsuccessful effort to placate Strafford's foes. News of the massacre, which lost nothing in the telling, circulated on Guy Fawkes Day, 1641, and stirred the passions of Protestant England. The facts were terrible enough; but the attribution of the massacre to the machinations of the "malignant party" (*Remonstrance,* Sec. 176), can be explained only by ignorance or the propagandist temper.[2]

The *Grand Remonstrance* passed the Commons November 22, 1641, by the narrow majority of eleven. The split among the reformers was completed by the debates over the command of the army which all agreed must be raised to subdue the Irish revolt. If Charles's appointees officered the army, it might be used against Parliament or at least the Puritan majority; if Parliament named the officers, it might be employed to settle the religious issue as the Puritan majority of the Commons might wish

[1] For text of the Remonstrance, see S. R. Gardiner, *Constitutional Documents,* pages 202-232.

[2] For a judicious account of the events in Ireland, see Stephen Gwynn, *History of Ireland* (N. Y., 1923), chapter XXV.

it settled. The moderates now felt that Charles was adequately chastened and that he, balanced by Parliament, would be safer than the Puritan majority. Under the existing law the king had the right to name the officers; but the two Houses finally issued orders on their own authority for the officering of the new troops. Neither Charles nor the two Houses would give way. But the Houses could wait, and Charles, lacking funds, would have to yield.

Charles decided to snatch at victory by robbing Parliament of its leaders. On January 3, 1642, the attorney-general rose in the House of Lords and "impeached" Pym, Hampden and three others. The step was clearly illegal; only the House of Commons could use this weapon. The Lords declined to order the arrests until they could "study the law." Next day Charles with a following of swashbucklers went to the Commons house to seize the five members. But his plan had "leaked" and the five were already safe in the city; and the king was guilty of a grave breach of the privileges of Parliament and was now suspected of a design to murder the members. It was this that led the Lords to agree to the Commons' plan to give the control of the army for Ireland to parliamentary commissioners. The city of London, foremost in zeal for Puritanism and for Parliament, called out its well-drilled, trained bands and undertook the easy task of defending Parliament. A few days later Charles fled to York. He still temporized, as is shown by his approval of the Clerical Disabilities Act in February. But the die was cast for war. The king was determined to rule as well as reign.

As one studies the whole situation, it seems clear that if Parliament had not attacked the Church, the king could have got neither a party nor an army. It is equally clear that the attack on the Church was inevitable. After the breach was open, the king's partisans in Lords and Commons, moved by religious sentiments, feudal loyalty, reverence for kingship, self-interest, fear of the mob, and all the other motives by which men explain their actions, slipped away to join Charles at York. "Mr. Firth calculates that thirty peers supported Parliament, eighty the king, and twenty remained neutral, while 300 of the Lower House were for Parliament, 175 for the King" (Trevelyan).

THE FIRST CIVIL WAR, 1642-1646

The first civil war lasted four years (1642-1646). It was a peculiar sort of civil war. It was not a war of classes, for all classes were represented on each side. Although most of the nobles were for the king and most of the middle class were for Parliament, the bulk of the population was indifferent. Nor was it a war of geographical sections for, though South and East were the centers of parliamentary strength, and North and West of the king's strength, there were supporters and regions adhering to each in the territories most favorable to the other. In one sense it was a war of religion; but, although the Catholics naturally supported the king against the more ultra-Protestant Parliament, it was primarily a war of Protestant against Protestant, and therefore of diminished religious ferocity. In a similar sense it was a war for popular liberty; and yet, even if the victory of the king would almost certainly have led to royal absolutism, it by no means follows that the royal supporters were insincere who said that they were championing a kingship subordinate to the constitution and the laws against parliamentary absolutism.

As the parties stood in 1642 the balance of forces leaned strongly to the parliamentary side. London, the island's center of ready money, was overwhelmingly Puritan; the navy, faithful to its traditions of a breezy Puritanism, at once declared for Parliament and thus guaranteed the control of all the ports and the customs revenue, and easy importation of artillery and munitions. Parliament also had a superior taxing power since its right to vote the taxes had long been accepted. It held the more urbanized and "civilized" parts of the country. It had behind it the Calvinistic constancy and fervor which had won in Holland and Scotland against heavy odds. And finally, the great wars raging on the Continent down to the Peace of the Pyrenees (1659) made foreign intervention on behalf of the king impossible.

The king's assets were the bulk of the nobility, with the ardor

of the cavalier and his greater aptitude for war; the deep sentiment of loyalty to the Crown—"Fear God and honor the King!"
—which held many faithful to him despite their better judgment
and caused them to give their income and their plate to the royal
cause; a unified command; and Prince Rupert, his nephew from
the Palatinate, a dashing cavalry leader who bade fair to win
against odds.

The parliamentary chiefs, not unnaturally, expected to "win in
a walk." As a matter of fact, Charles had the best of the war
for two years. His strategy was superior and the parliamentary
generals, the nobles Essex and Manchester, consciously or unconsciously shrank from beating the king to his knees and fought
as if they were seeking a compromise settlement. The outlook
was so dubious indeed that Parliament appealed to the Scots for
help and accepted their terms—that the Church of England should
be "Presbyterianized" (*Solemn League and Covenant,* 1643).
The Scots believed that only a parliamentary victory would safeguard their own Kirk.

With a Scottish army in England the tide began to turn. Marston Moor (July, 1644) delivered the North into the hands of
Parliament and revealed the striking talents of Oliver Cromwell,
whose troopers scattered Prince Rupert's gallant cavalry. Within
three months, however, the tide was arrested, for Essex lost
his army to the royalists of Cornwall, and Manchester failed to
exploit a marked advantage he had over the king—to the disgust
of Cromwell, who commanded Manchester's cavalry.

At this juncture Cromwell pushed through Parliament a plan
for a reorganized army and for new commanders who would
fight to a finish. A polite method for shelving Essex and Manchester was found in a Self-Denying Ordinance, and young Sir
Thomas Fairfax became commander of the new "national" parliamentary force, known as the "New Model" army, with Cromwell
as his chief of cavalry.

It was with considerable hesitation that Parliament sanctioned
the formation of the New Model. For the agreement with the
Scots required that the Church of England should become Presbyterian and Parliament already had the *Westminster Assembly* of

divines at work on the necessary revisions of the Thirty-Nine Articles and of the Service Book. Moreover, the growth of non-conformist religious sects, so marked since 1641, was disquieting to the parliamentary majority, who still regarded an all-inclusive Church as essential to national safety. The New Model, however, was to be organized on the principle which had proved so success-ful in the local army which Cromwell had raised in and for the Eastern Association of shires, and that was that any God-fearing Puritan, whether Independent, Baptist, or "Presbyterian," was welcome in the force. For Parliament to reject that principle would be to dispense with Cromwell's veterans and many like them. The dilemma was real. Parliament finally decided that the first necessity was to win the war, and that the practical estab-lishment of an inclusive Presbyterian Church of England would have to wait. And that is why the New Model was authorized. At the start, half its cavalry were Independents, but the infantry were pressed men. As time passed the Independents in the New Model steadily increased and by the time of the execution of Charles they formed an overwhelming majority.

The high efficiency of the New Model was proven in the battle of Naseby (June, 1645), which ruined the royal cause. Another year was spent in reducing isolated royalist posts. In May, 1646, Charles surrendered to the Scottish army in northern England. In January, 1647, the Scots traded the king to the English Parlia-ment for the £400,000 due them. Clearly the king was still valuable.

A month after Charles surrendered to the Scots, the English Parliament ordered the new Presbyterian system to be set up in the Anglican churches. A beginning was made by replacing 2,000 Anglican clergymen, expelled on small pensions, with Pres-byterian ministers, and by prohibiting the use of the Anglican Prayer Book. The new Presbyterianism, controlled, however, by a Parliamentary committee of laymen, took root in London and Lancashire. Elsewhere it failed to please. Nonconformist con-gregations existed and multiplied, with none to interfere.

Almost contemporaneously Parliament attempted to arrange its disordered finances by shifting a large part of its war debt on to the backs of royalist landowners. They were required to pay heavy "fines" which were equivalent to a capital levy.

Anglicanism and royalism were thus crowned with martyrdoms of their own and given a sense of community of interest through common sufferings.

In December, 1646, Parliament passed an ordinance providing for the suppression of all nonconformist worship. Everyone knew that the ordinance could not be enforced so long as the New Model was in existence. In May, 1647, Parliament ordered the New Model to disband. The order pleased many, perhaps most, Englishmen. The army was a heavy burden. But those armed Independents were not even offered their back pay, and the ordinance of December told them what to expect in the matter of religious toleration. If that had been offered them, the story might have been different! They therefore declined to disband and, to improve their bargaining power, they seized the king (June, 1647), occupied Presbyterian London (August), and drove the eleven leaders of the Presbyterian majority from Parliament.

EFFORTS TO MAKE A FINAL SETTLEMENT, 1646-1648

It is not feasible to review the many plans and negotiations for an enduring settlement which were vigorously pressed after the king's surrender to the Scots. All, however, agreed that the legislation passed by the Long Parliament down to August, 1641, should form the basis of the relation of the restored monarchy to Parliament. The general idea of the English Parliament and of the Scots comes out in their offer of the summer of 1646. Parliament was to command the army and navy for twenty years; royalists who had fought for the king should be excluded from office, civil and military; episcopacy should be abolished, Presbyterianism established in its place, and the sectaries compelled to conform.

A much superior plan was that evolved by the New Model dur-

ing its period of military inactivity (1646-1647) and presented
to the king in the late summer of 1647 by Cromwell and Ireton.
The wealth of reform ideas that came out of that strange
forcing-house is truly remarkable.   The plan is known as the
Heads of the Proposals.[1]   "The protection of Cavalier estates
from ruinous sequestration, the retention of the Episcopate shorn
of all coercive power, and the use of the Prayer-Book in Church
by those who wished, stood to reconcile one-half of England;
while religious toleration for all, equal electoral districts, large
security for the control of royal power by Parliament, should have
satisfied the democrats" (Trevelyan).

THE SECOND CIVIL WAR AND THE BEHEADING OF KING CHARLES

Charles toyed with all the proposals, promising contradictory
things and keeping up negotiations, hoping and expecting that his
enemies would fall out and destroy one another. He was loyal to
nothing but the Anglican Church. That, however, was much. It
made the royal cause respectable. He was willing to accept the
establishment of Presbyterianism for three years. He fomented
a division in Scotland between the royalists, who hated the English
Parliament and army, and the true-blue Covenanters, who feared
the king more than the Parliament. The hostility between the
New Model and the Parliament filled him with glee. "You cannot
do without me—you are lost if I do not support you," he told
Ireton, one of the New Model's negotiators. He spent the winter
of 1647-1648 promoting a conspiracy of Cavaliers and discontented Presbyterian royalists in Scotland and England, and of
men who feared the army more than the defeated king. These
strange allies were to overthrow the New Model and then secure
their (incompatible) hearts' desires. The result was the second
civil war, 1648.

It was a short war. The New Model, commanded by Cromwell, suppressed the scattered risings in England before they could
fuse into an insurrection, and then swiftly crushed the army of

[1] Text in S. R. Gardiner, *Constitutional Documents,* pages 316-326.

royalist Scots, which invaded England too late to help its confederates (battle of Preston, August, 1648). The Scottish Kirk
rejoiced.

The New Model was now out of patience. Learning that the
English Parliament was again negotiating with Charles for the
establishment of Presbyterianism and the coercion of noncon-
formists, it drove out the Presbyterian majority from Parlia-
ment (Pride's Purge, December, 1648). The remnant, number-
ing somewhat under a hundred and popularly known as the
Rump, assumed to speak for the people and declared that the
House of Commons "have the supreme power in this nation"
(January, 1649). In February they abolished the House of
Lords as useless and dangerous.

A week earlier King Charles was beheaded. The Rump
brought him to trial before a special commission for treason to
the nation. In his speech from the scaffold he made the dying
declaration of the divine-right monarchy in England. "For the
people, truly I desire their liberty and freedom as much as anybody whatsoever; but . . . their liberty and freedom consist in
having government. . . . It is not their having a share in the
government; that is nothing appertaining to them." He died
January 30, 1649. A few months before, Philip IV of Spain
acknowledged the independence of the Dutch. The significance
of the two events is worthy of thought.

THE REDUCTION OF IRELAND AND SCOTLAND BY CROMWELL

The execution of the king raised a host of problems for the
Commonwealth—the new title given by the Rump to the people
of England and the dominions in May, 1649. All of Ireland,
outside of Dublin and Londonderry, acknowledged Charles II as
king. Scotland did likewise. The Irish wanted protection for
religion and lands; the Scots desired freedom from coercion by
the English Independents. Half the colonies adhered to Charles.
The Dutch, whose great citizen, Prince William II of Orange,
was married to Charles's sister, recognized Charles and gave

asylum to that fragment of the parliamentary navy which had turned royalist in 1648. The remainder of Europe execrated the "regicides." Clearly the Commonwealth must bestir itself or be destroyed.

A beginning was made with Ireland. The Ulster massacre was still to be "avenged." Cromwell landed in Dublin with a strong army in August, 1649. The island, weakened by nine years of warfare and isolated by the environing sea, was in no condition to resist him. Native Irish and Anglo-Irish Catholics had fought against the Protestants of Ulster and other centers and against the small reënforcements sent over from Scotland and England. But they had also fought against each other, and some of them for local reasons had joined with the Protestants. There was no comprehensive plan and organization to reach the goal of security for religion and lands. Charles I had served as a will-o'-the-wisp. He promised—not too definitely—to meet Irish wishes. He wanted peace in Ireland so that he might draw reënforcements from it. His lord lieutenant, Lord Ormonde, had finally succeeded in winning over all the Catholic and some of the Protestant organizations to support the Stuarts and achieve the goal, only to find the Stuarts a liability rather than an asset, and Cromwell at the gate.

Cromwell's first exploit was to storm Drogheda and massacre its garrison of 3,000 men, most of them English royalists (September, 1649). In nine months he subdued all the island but the western portion. His methods of warfare exhibited the worst features of the religious wars plus those of the repression of the German Peasants' Revolt of 1525. When he left for Scotland in May, 1650, Ireton, his son-in-law, finished the job. The "Cromwellian Settlement," enacted by the Rump in 1652 and left in large part intact at the Restoration, followed the lines of the Ulster Plantation scheme. It took from the Catholic Irish and Anglo-Irish who survived the twelve years of war three-fourths of the soil and gave it in the main to English Protestant landlords, separated in faith from their tenants and alien for the most part from their sympathies. To England Cromwell left a legacy of civil and religious liberty. To Ireland he left a curse. The twelve years of warfare cost the lives of half a million Irish, of whom one-fifth were of English extraction, and left the island population below a million.[1] This staggering price Ireland paid for England's security.

Charles II reached Scotland in June, 1650. To win the support of the Kirk faction, the stronger element since Preston, he swore to the Covenants of 1638 and 1643. That meant that he would maintain an independent Kirk in Scotland and establish Presbyterianism in England. A month later Cromwell, now lord general, crossed the border. The army of the true-blue Presbyterians soon had its experience with the Independent general. It was crushed at Dunbar (September 3, 1650) and its conqueror occupied Edinburgh. The Kirk now relented enough to accept the aid of the Scottish royalists, and another army was organized in the North. Cromwell found he could not attack it advantageously, and so stepped aside in order that it might take Charles into England. The Rump was alarmed. But few English royalists joined the army of the northern Presbyterians, although it got as far south as Worcester before Cromwell caught up with it. He destroyed it on the anniversary of Dunbar (September 3, 1651). Charles made a thrilling escape from the rout and resumed his "travels" on the Continent. Scotland was soon subdued and was treated with great consideration, although the general assembly was suppressed.

Meanwhile the English war vessels which had found a refuge in Holland were refitted by royalist exiles and sent to sea under Prince Rupert to prey on regicide commerce. The Rump doubled its fleet and put it under the command of Blake, another soldier turned sailor. Blake chased Rupert away from the Irish coasts into Portuguese waters, thence into the Mediterranean. Rupert escaped and fled to the American colonies. But the long sea arm of the Rump followed him, and by 1652 the royalist navy was no more and the American colonies all acknowledged the Commonwealth.

[1] On all this see Stephen Gwynn, *History of Ireland,* chapters XXV-XXIX.

THE WAR WITH THE DUTCH, 1652-1654

The Rump had fostered the navy partly out of jealousy of Cromwell and the army. It had a fair grievance against the pro-Stuart Dutch. Moreover, the growth of the Dutch carrying trade, which had profited from the English troubles, hurt English pride and pocket. One result was the Navigation Act of 1651, designed to build up an English merchant navy by forbidding the Dutch and other foreigners from carrying any wares except those of their own growth or manufacture to any English territories. The principle was old, but Cromwell actually enforced it. Another result was a war picked with the Dutch and lasting from 1652 to 1654. The Dutch put up a stubborn but not a whole-hearted fight. They induced Denmark (controller of the Sound) to close the Baltic, whence came essential ship supplies, to the English. Cromwell countered by negotiating for an alliance with Denmark's great rival, Sweden. Prodigies of valor were performed by the English and Dutch fleets. But the English had better cannon and a unified command, and since the sea-borne commerce of the Dutch had virtually to pass through the Channel if their country was to prosper, the Dutch made peace and furnished Denmark with much of the money required to pay damages to the English republic. But the English navy was kept at full strength by its Puritan rulers.

CROMWELL'S DOMESTIC LEGISLATION AND CONSTITUTION MAKING

Supreme in the three kingdoms and victorious over the Dutch, while France and Spain were still at death grips, the triumphant Independents were now free to usher in the millennium—that is, to mold English institutions into the forms they desired. The "Rule of the Saints" was primarily in the hands of Cromwell, the head of the New Model.

The transformation of the government had begun in 1653, when the army, weary of the Rump and anxious for a new Parliament, turned the Rump out-of-doors. Thus was the last remnant of the Long Parliament cast aside. The army chiefs then changed the Commonwealth into the *Protectorate* (1653). Cromwell was made lord protector with a single-chamber parliament for legislature. The Constitution of 1657 added an "Other House"—a substitute for the old House of Lords—and only the army's republican sentiments prevented Cromwell from accepting the title of king. The drift toward the older type of constitution is obvious and significant of the general desire to get away from arbitrary government and back to the old, understood type.

Under the Protectorate a new electoral law was passed, establishing a uniform qualification—£200 in property—for voters, disfranchising rotten boroughs,[1] increasing the number of county representatives, and calling in 30 members each from Scotland and Ireland to sit with 400 English members. But Catholics and former royalists were excluded from the franchise, and the members chosen by the electors were regularly purged of not a few objectionable ones before they were allowed to take up their parliamentary duties.

The religious legislation was remarkably sane. As early as 1652 all the laws imposing penalties on those absenting themselves from church were repealed. The Established Church remained established. Tithes were still collected as of yore. Patrons retained their right to "present to livings," but with this difference: they could name only Puritan ministers, that is, Independents, Baptists and Presbyterians. State commissioners—"Triers and Ejectors"—dismissed incompetent pastors and certified suitable candidates. They did their work conscientiously and fairly. So much for the establishment. Outside of the parish organizations were many free congregations of other "dissenters," notably the Quakers. The Anglicans, although the Prayer Book service was proscribed, were bothered little. Catholics had freedom of conscience but not of worship. The Jews, after three and a half centuries, were readmitted to the country (their money was needed).

These changes and many other salutary reforms suffered from one decisive defect: the government that made them did not rest on the consent of the governed. The Independents, an effective

---

[1] Constituencies whose voting population had declined to almost nothing.

minority because of the army, did not consult the people because the majority was against them. The Constitutions of 1653 and 1657 were not submitted to the people. Here was a real dilemma. The Independents, who defeated Charles, were more concerned to have their type of Puritanism protected than to have representative parliamentary government established. They were Puritans first and parliamentarians second. They hoped to have the people come around to their views, but in the meantime they ruled.

In addition to the loyalty of the Cavaliers and Anglicans to the old system, now doubly venerated because of their sufferings, there were three major reasons why Cromwell's government failed to take root. First, the taxes were crushing. The cost of an army of 57,000 men maintained to hold down Scotland and Ireland and England, and of a large navy made heavy taxes inevitable. In 1635 Charles I had a revenue of £618,000. In 1654 the Commonwealth's expenditures amounted to £2,670,000.[1] Secondly, the people resented government by the army. Under the Stuarts, at their worst, the people had been governed by civilians. The civilian temper of the English made them increasingly hostile to the Cromwellian system. Finally, the "Rule of the Saints" keyed life too high for the average mundane Englishman. Horse-racing, cock-fighting, bear-baiting, theatrical performances, the village revel and even the Maypole dances were forbidden. Merrie England was forced to be austere.

The success of Cromwell's foreign policy could not sweeten his domestic tyranny. He did not understand the foreign situation. He still thought of Spain as the enemy and failed to realize that France was taking her place. Moreover, he needed money and Spanish galleons still carried treasure to Spain. And so, in the Elizabethan vein, without a declaration of war he sent a fleet to seize San Domingo and pick up a Spanish treasure fleet or so. It failed miserably, although it took Jamaica on the voyage home. This casual conquest was permanent. Spain wrathfully declared war. Admiral Blake performed some valorous feats, but commerce languished and the London merchants ceased to bet on Oliver. Yet his luck held, and when Mazarin, the great minister

[1] See S. R. Gardiner, *Cromwell's Place in History*, page 97.

of France, beguiled him in 1657 into sending 6,000 redcoats for service in Flanders, they vindicated their reputation by helping to defeat the Spanish under the interested eyes of Charles II, who was enjoying Spanish hospitality and support at the time. Dunkirk passed into the possession of the English, and the victory hastened the end of the Franco-Spanish war which came in 1659. Nevertheless, Cromwell's foreign policy was mistaken. Queen Elizabeth would not have approved of it.

THE CRUMBLING OF CROMWELLIAN GOVERNMENT

But Cromwell's life was now drawing to its close. He was not old as we count age—he was born in 1599—but the hardships of war and the burdens and anxieties of government in an era of upheaval had worn him out. He was one of the great masters of the art of war. He was conservative in temper and simple in his tastes and in intercourse with his fellow men; but circumstances forced him to follow in the paths of autocracy and to reproduce—with greater success—the very despotism in government which he had drawn the sword to overthrow. To be sure, his motive was religious—to defend "the people of God." Indeed, he had a divine-right theory of his own, averring that God inspired his actions and hallowed his power with unbroken victories. The tragedy of his career was his failure to establish civil government in place of the rule of the sword. He was not a constructive statesman. His ignorance of the social history of Ireland and of foreign affairs worked woe. In these respects he represented the Puritanism of his era, writ large. The consideration of his services or influence may therefore be postponed until we attempt to assess its accomplishments. He died in 1658, on the anniversary of Dunbar and Worcester, with a prayer upon his lips. "Thou hast made me," he once prayed, near the end, "though very unworthy, a mean instrument to do Thy people some good and Thee service. . . . Pardon such as desire to trample upon the dust of a poor worm, for they are Thy people too; and pardon the folly of this short prayer, even for Jesus Christ's sake, and give us a good night, if it be Thy pleasure. Amen." The statue of Oliver Cromwell fittingly stands, the Bible in one hand, the sword in the other, outside the walls of Parliament. For he was its strange champion, even unto autocracy.

The Protectorate did not long survive him. His son, Richard, succeeded him as lord protector but, lacking capacity to ride the storm, he wisely abdicated and was rewarded with the sobriquet of "Tumbledown Dick." The chiefs of the army did not pull together but they did avoid civil war. Amidst general cries for "a free Parliament" the Rump was recalled; then those rejected by Pride's Purge came back and the Long Parliament, after ordering new elections, dissolved itself.

THE RESTORATION OF 1660 AND THE REVOLUTION OF 1688

The new "Parliament" declared for the restoration of the ancient system of government by king, lords, and commons, and took up with the impatient Charles II the terms on which he might return. But its negotiations were supplanted by those secretly initiated by General Monk, the dominant figure among the New Model's chiefs. There was no alternative to the Restoration. Cromwell had found no way out, and lesser men could not do more. English and Scottish opinion recalled Charles, who had responded to Monk's proposals with the Declaration of Breda (April, 1660) in which he promised a general pardon and a government of law.[1] In the formal welcome which greeted him in May, 1660, the New Model took a decorous part. The "Rule of the Saints" was over.

The Cavalier Parliament (1661-1679) gave the Puritans a heavy dose of persecution which did much to even the score. It drove the Puritan gentry back into the Anglican Church, but the middle- and lower-class Puritans remained faithful to nonconformity, and purged their ranks of the hypocrites who had joined them in prosperous days. The persecution was not royal or ecclesiastical but parliamentary, and public opinion would in time cor-

[1] For text of the declaration, see S. R. Gardiner, *Constitutional Documents*, pages 465-467.

rect mistakes. It remains to estimate the enduring results of the Puritan regime.

Despite the Restoration, royal absolutism had fallen forever in England. The legislation of the Long Parliament down to August, 1641, was not repealed and it bound the king captive to parliamentary grants of money and to all that these implied. Neither king nor lords ever regained their ancient political ascendancy, and the predominance of the House of Commons was never lost. Even George III's effort at tyranny, a century later, was based on the purchased support of the House of Commons. The control of the Anglican Church passed from the Crown to Parliament. Another legacy of moment was an intense parliamentary and national antipathy to a standing army. The monarchy had been recalled; it had not been imposed by foreign or domestic armies upon an unwilling people. It was, after 1660, a chastened element in the English constitutional system. "This government has a monarchical appearance because there is a king, but at bottom it is very far from being a monarchy." Thus wrote the French ambassador in England to his master, Louis XIV, in 1664. It was even so. Judged by continental standards, Charles II was no true monarch.

"During the seventeenth century a despotic scheme of society and government was so firmly established in Europe, that but for the course of events in England it would have been the sole successor of the medieval system. Everywhere on the ruins of the old privileges and powers of city, Church and baronage, arose the [absolute] monarchy, firmly based on a standing army and a service of bureaucrats. . . . Military despotism was the price to be paid for national unity and power. Thus the white races of Europe and America, in whom the hope of mankind lay, were developing a political structure and a fashion of public sentiment akin to those of modern [Czaristic] Russia. But at this moment the English, unaware of their destiny and of their service, . . . evolved a system of government which differed as completely from the new continental model as it did from the chartered anarchy of the Middle Ages. This system . . . was proved, in the final struggle of Marlborough with Louis, to combine freedom with

efficiency, and local rights with national union. It showed the
world . . . how liberty could mean not weakness, but strength"
(Trevelyan).

Nor were the moral labors of the Puritans sterile. Their ideals
of hard work, simplicity, and sound Christian conduct remained
potent long after the revelers of Charles II's court had done their
worst. Conduct is not the whole of religion, but the English
Church of Laud needed the reminder that conduct reflects religion.
The majority of Englishmen long remained "what Puritanism
had made them, serious, earnest, sober in life and conduct, firm in
their love of Protestantism and freedom" (Green). There are
other types of creed and worship and of Christian morals more
attractive to many. But Puritanism in its day bestowed benefits
which are not yet exhausted.

Puritanism and the English system of limited monarchy soon
had to undergo another test. For James II renewed the endeavor
(1685-1688) to ensnare and coerce the English into accepting the
benefits of absolutism. The attempt left him with no party
supporting him, and his flight and supersession were the comple-
ment to the civil war and its true and satisfactory culmination.
The "Glorious Revolution" of 1688 which enthroned William and
Mary reëstablished the limited monarchy on a firmer foundation.
And the Toleration Act of 1689 ended the persecution of the nonconformists. The surviving authors of the "Heads of the Proposals" must have been gratified.

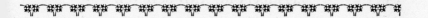

CHAPTER XXV

LITERATURE AND SCIENCE IN THE SIXTEENTH CENTURY AND AFTER

THE exuberant vitality of the sixteenth century is amazing. It was shown in the political organization of states, in devastating wars, in geographical exploration, in extended commerce by land and sea, in religious revolutions and reformations, in art, literature and science. No previous century since the birth of Jesus, save the thirteenth, will bear comparison with it.

The history of religious reforms brings us closest to our European ancestors at moments of tension, when their powers were strained to the uttermost. But to get near them in their everyday littlenesses and greatnesses, hopes and fears, we must turn to literature. It is not a perfect mirror since it is distorted by ideals, by the willfulness of literary characters, the compulsions of artistic creation, and the bias and limitations of the writers. Nevertheless, taking it by and large, it is adequately faithful to reality.

The literary history of the later Middle Ages records the names of only four men of high rank—Dante, Petrarch, Boccaccio and Chaucer. Of these Dante was the brightest star. But the last of them had passed away before the fifteenth century dawned, and no successors of comparable power appeared for over one hundred years.

THE REVIVAL OF ITALIAN VERNACULAR LITERATURE: PULCI AND BOIARDO

In Italy the vernacular writings of Dante, Petrarch and Boccaccio, which have already been dealt with, stimulated lesser men. Broadly speaking, it must be confessed that the century following the death of Boccaccio (d.1375) was one of literary barrenness. This may be explained, although only in part, by the "cult of antiquity" which led young men of talent to devote themselves to classical learning rather than to creative writing in their mother tongue. Then two writers appeared, with whom Italian literature resumed its march.

Pulci (1432-1484), a courtier-buffoon to Lorenzo de' Medici, the political boss of Florence, wrote for Lorenzo's mother a chivalrous romance which he called *Morgante Maggiore,* or *Morgante the Giant.* The poem is built around two Italian versions of old French romances, but Pulci introduces grotesqueries and jovial marvels of his own. Pulci was not a Humanist but he was something of an artist, and he outdistanced, while imitating, his humbler rival story-tellers, whose audiences were the common people.

Boiardo (*ca.* 1430-1494) was a nobleman, a courtier and an official of the duke of Ferrara. Without knowing anything of Pulci's work, he undertook to entertain his patron with a similar tale also derived from French romances, to which he gave the immortal name of Roland—*Orlando Inamorato* or *Orlando in Love.* Chivalry was still a living ideal at the court of Ferrara, and so Boiardo's work, unlike Pulci's, never parodies knightly ideals, although Boiardo occasionally smiles at his heroes. Furthermore, Boiardo, possibly because of his greater familiarity with the classics, had a real feeling for literary style, and his poem, although it will be surpassed in the sixteenth century by the work of Ariosto and Tasso, is a worthy culmination of the medieval romances of chivalry. It is interesting to reflect that the resumption of creative writing in Italy, after the Revival of Learning, involved a return to the chivalrous literature of the Middle Ages.

FRENCH LITERATURE: FROISSART, COMMINES AND VILLON

In France the period 1300-1500 saw nothing so significant of progress as the work of Pulci and Boiardo, although imitations of the *Romance of the Rose* and other interminable poems were produced by second- and third-rate writers. In Froissart (*ca.* 1337-

1410), however, France had a high-class writer of French historical prose. His *Chronicles,* which embrace the whole of Europe for the years 1326-1400, are valuable for their fluent prose style and for their brilliant picture of the vacuous life of the nobility of his time. He was nominally a cleric but actually a mundane story-teller. He did not understand, any more than the nobles did, the underlying causes of the wars he described. He shared their sentiments and, like them, had no sympathy to spare for the sufferings of the down-trodden peasantry. But what a story-teller he is! His *Chronicles* "unroll themselves like some long tapestry, gorgeously inwoven with scenes of adventure and chivalry, with flags and spears and chargers, and the faces of high-born ladies and the mail-clad figures of knights."

Far different was the calculating Commines (*ca.* 1447-1511), who despised chivalry and all its conceits. His *Memoirs* cover the periods 1464-1483 and 1494-1495. The high point of the book is the exposition of the diplomatic duel between the hot-headed Charles the Bold of Burgundy and the crafty king of France, Louis XI. Commines was well equipped to analyze this by special knowledge as well as by temperament, for he was at first an adviser of Charles, whom he left for the service of Louis XI who was a better paymaster and a more canny ruler. It was an age when princes gave retainers, or pensions, to the advisers of other princes, a policy which Commines commends. He is not interested in battles, but in their causes and results, and prefers diplomatic combinations and chicanery, mining and countermining, to warfare. Commines writes a clear French prose, but he rarely stirs the blood. He was no Humanist but a "practical" politician. His view of European problems excluded some essential factors, but within the range of his knowledge he was profound. There was some honesty of sentiment in him, and his religion was not so superstitious as that of Louis XI. With Froissart, history attempted to entertain; with Commines, to instruct.

Neither Froissart nor Commines was a writer of pure literature. Their time was one of poetic sterility. But France had one poet in the later Middle Ages whom mankind will not forget. François Villon (1431- ?) was an ex-student of the University of Paris, a guttersnipe, thief, murderer and jailbird, who wrote wonderful verse. Gautier says that good poets are rarer than honest folk. Villon depicts his fellow wastrels, his own sufferings and cravings with a poignancy, realism and lyric beauty that touch us to the quick. "He was not a simple character; his melancholy was shot with irony and laughter; sensuality and sentimentality both mingled with his finest imaginations and his profoundest visions; and all these qualities are reflected, shifting and iridescent, in the magic web of his verse." Villon "restored the exhausted literary language of his time to youth and health by infusing into it the healing poisons, the revivifying acids and bitters of the popular speech, disdaining no materials that served his purpose."

THE ERA OF MIDDLE ENGLISH GREATNESS: CHAUCER AND LANGLAND

In England shortly after the middle of the fourteenth century, Anglo-Saxons, Celts, Danes and Normans had completed their fusion, and Parliament, law courts and literature were content to express themselves in the Middle English of the royal court. It was precisely at this time that Geoffrey Chaucer (1340-1400) began to write, a poet whose temper, talents and experience with men and affairs, at home and abroad, equipped him to paint in enduring verse a picture of the "merrie England" of his time. He began, naturally enough, by imitating, largely in translations, French poetry of the type of the *Romance of the Rose;* but after two diplomatic journeys to Italy, which he made a short time before the deaths of Petrarch and Boccaccio, he attained independent mastery and the first place among the poets of his time. The final fruit of this culminating period of productiveness was his *Canterbury Tales.*

Chaucer's *Canterbury Tales* have been likened to Boccaccio's *Decameron,* but they have fewer and less coarse episodes and, in addition, the men and women who make the pilgrimage from London to Canterbury are quite as interesting as the tales they tell to lessen the tedium of the road. They include representatives of every class, from the nobility, lawyers and merchants, priests, friars and nuns, to tradesmen and tillers of the soil.   These pilgrims talk, behave, joke and quarrel, each in his own appropriate way, in such fashion that we know the England of the time with its wit, broad humor, common sense, stubbornness, greed, fraud, coarseness, religion and superstition.   Chaucer's own words may be applied to him: "And gladly wolde he lerne, and gladly teche." The *Canterbury Tales* is an immortal work.

And yet the picture it affords is not complete.   Chaucer gives us the individual Englishman of every sort, painted from the life; but his art or temperament or worldly prosperity does not permit him to reveal the sorrows and deeper sentiments of the poor of his day.   This task was performed, during his lifetime, by another great poet, who has come down to us under the name of William Langland and whose grand poem is called *The Vision of Piers the Plowman.*[1]   Unlike Chaucer, who used rhyme, Langland wrote in the alliterative verse which had been dear to the Anglo-Saxon heart since *Beowulf,* and probably was still most pleasing to the common people.   Probably he reflects popular sentiment about the vices of Church, State and society.   Langland pictures an England of luxury, poverty and greed, vice and oppression.

> A fair field full of folk
> Found I there between
> Of all manner of men
> The mean and the rich,
> Working and wandering
> As the world asketh.

His poem has been well called the Divine Comedy of the Poor. His religion is real, his morals austere.   Chaucer was not deeply religious and at the end of the *Canterbury Tales* he asks, "for many a song and many a lecherous lay that Crist for his grete mercy foryeve me the synne."   Langland was a stern, puritanical denouncer of sin in high and low, rich and poor.   He preached the gospel of honest work to all classes, and his hero and example is

[1] It is now contended, by some excellent authorities, that the poem is the work of several hands.

not a noble nor yet a cleric, but Piers the Plowman who ends by being Jesus himself.

The fourteenth century was a great epoch in the history of English literature with the old verse of Langland, the new of Chaucer, and the prose of Wycliffe's translation of the Bible. After them came a century of comparative silence, broken chiefly by the clear voice of Bishop Reginald Pecock, the opponent of the Lollards, a master of controversial prose.

THE LITERARY RICHNESS OF THE SIXTEENTH CENTURY

With the sixteenth century we enter an era of literary riches, when the vernaculars are ready and the writers appear for the production of masterpieces. It is as if the languages were exuberant with the strength of youth, for there is a virility, a meatiness, in their words and often a sonorous, rolling, wave-like majesty in their periods, which subsequent ages have lost. These qualities appear in the religious as well as in the secular writings, although naturally in varying degrees. Luther's translation of the Bible from the original Hebrew and Greek was a most remarkable achievement, and with his vigorous pamphlets and stirring hymns, such as "Ein' feste Burg ist unser Gott" (Psalm 46), did much to make the language of the Saxon court, which he took as his basis, the literary language of Germany, for he enriched it with skillfully chosen drafts from the speech of the people. In like manner, although not to the same degree, the French version of Calvin's *Institutes,* which was given to the world in 1541, proved a powerful stimulus to the displacement of Latin by French for learned writings, and it won for Calvin, in some authoritative quarters, the title of "father of French prose." In England William Tyndale translated the New Testament (1525) and part of the Old Testament from the original tongues, but his execution by fire left his work to be completed by others. The "authorized version" of 1611, which J. R. Green so nobly eulogizes in his *Short History,* is very largely in the very words of Tyndale. "The mingled tenderness and majesty, the Saxon simplicity, and præternatural grandeur . . . all are here, and bear the impress of the mind of one man—William Tyndale" (Froude). A similar although a lesser tribute is due to the share of Cranmer in the composition—largely from older service books—of the Book of Common Prayer, whose beauty of diction and unassuming dignity have in a measure shaped the devotions of most Protestants who worship in the English tongue. If all other evidence of the literary capacity of the sixteenth century were lost, these writings of the first half of it, done by Luther, Calvin, Tyndale and Cranmer, would suffice to prove its greatness. But Italy, France, England, Spain and Portugal produced other works which furnish ample corroboration.

THE ITALIANS: ARIOSTO AND TASSO; MACHIAVELLI

In Italy the great imaginative poems of the sixteenth century are the romantic epics of Ariosto and Tasso. Ariosto (1474-1533), like Boiardo, was a client of the Este of Ferrara, and his *Orlando Furioso* or *The Insane Orlando* (he was not insane for long) is nominally a continuation of Boiardo's unfinished masterpiece. It takes up the war between the Saracens and the Christians at the crisis where Boiardo left it and concludes it, but it is essentially an independent poem. It is superior to its predecessor in unity, variety of episodes and humor. It is probable that Ariosto's literary power, his superior feeling for form and his refinement of phrasing—his exquisite sense of humor was a gift from Heaven—owe something to his greater familiarity with classical Latin literature. "The *Orlando Furioso* had a Latin mother." Familiarity with the ancient masterpieces did not make Ariosto a great poet, but it did enrich and purify his style. And this is probably the great service that the Revival of Learning rendered to modern writers.

The *Jerusalem Delivered* of Tasso (1544-1596) is a less complicated romance-epic, without the intricacy and multiplicity of digressions which make such a scintillating medieval tapestry of the *Orlando Furioso*. It is more the epic and less the romance. Yet the romantic episodes, which to many give the poem its chief charm, always contribute to the march of events. The framework of the story is the siege and capture of Jerusalem in the First Crusade—a timely topic in that era of the Turkish peril. The love element is marked by a more tender and delicate sentiment than Boiardo knew, the religious tone is more sincere, and the grosser scenes which occasionally disfigure the *Orlando Furioso* are noticeably absent. The style is noble and dignified. Its opening lines intentionally recall Virgil's "Arms and the man I sing" and its central topic has reminiscences of the siege of Troy. It would be rash to assert that Tasso has surpassed Ariosto; but the *Jerusalem Delivered* is undoubtedly the most popular Italian masterpiece.

The most renowned, or notorious, work of the Italian sixteenth century is, of course, *The Prince* of Machiavelli (1469-1527). This treatise on the art of government is the work of a traveled and experienced political thinker, who helped to govern Florence in the perilous and depressing years after France and Spain had upset the equilibrium of Italy. Its illustrations are frequently drawn from ancient history, but its terrible realism is based on a keen analysis of the contemporary practices of the Italian, French and Spanish princes. The end justifies the means; faith ought to be kept unless its breach will be more profitable; fear is superior to love; states are not bound to observe the moral principles which should govern individuals; these are some of the maxims laid down in *The Prince*. It has been well described as a handbook for tyrants, and its sinister renown has not been purified by the proof that Machiavelli was an Italian patriot or by the argument that he was merely describing politics as they really were. The book is a most striking revelation of the secularism of the sixteenth century, and the diplomacy preceding modern wars has only too often shown how little the world has advanced since it was penned. Machiavelli's style, which is shown in his histories and other writings as well, is simple, direct and vivid. It owes little, if anything, to classical studies, for Machiavelli was no Humanist but rather a talented man of affairs who wrote directly what he thought and thought as he wrote.

A century after Machiavelli, Hugo Grotius, a grand Dutch scholar, published his *De jure belli et pacis,* in which he argues that mankind should be regarded as a family of nations living together on terms of mutual respect and obligation in accordance with natural law. The tercentenary of the publication of the book was celebrated throughout the world in 1925. The "cold and individualistic nationalism" of Machiavelli will pass away.

THE FRENCHMEN: CALVIN, RABELAIS AND MONTAIGNE

In French literature the sixteenth century reveals its sharpest contrasts in the writings of two contemporaries, Calvin and Rabelais. Calvin, in his *Institutes,* teaches, as the basis of his theology, the total depravity of man's nature. Rabelais (*ca.* 1494-1553), in his *Gargantua and Pantagruel,* asserts the divinely established wholesomeness of every natural appetite. Calvin, a layman—for he was never ordained—represents theology and religious devotion; Rabelais, a physician, a friar, then a monk, champions the secular spirit of his and every age.

In form *Gargantua and Pantagruel* is a prose romance of chivalry; but it is a burlesque romance. Gargantua and Pantagruel are giants; but they and their fellow characters talk, in the main, like ordinary worldlings who happen to be endowed with huge appetites and passions, colossal laughter, rollicking satire, uproarious buffoonery, jovial obscenity, classical scholarship, tender sympathies and wisdom. This list may be taken as a catalogue of the protean characteristics of Rabelais himself. His masterpiece is not a tract; but, making due allowance for the spirit of burlesque, it seems evident that he was really hostile to the medieval type of education, to the restraints of monasticism, and to anything that "runs counter to nature." A monk who had performed prodigies of valor in warfare against a tyrant was rewarded by Gargantua with the gift of a new type of monastery, the "Abbey of Theleme." In it all the monastic regulations of old are reversed: no walls, required services or vows; no rule but this, "Do what thou wilt." Why this freedom? "Because persons that are free, well born, well educated and accustomed to good company have by nature an instinct and spur which prompts them to virtuous acts and withdraws them from vice." Nevertheless—such are the contradictions of the man—in his letter to his son setting forth a program for a liberal education, Gargantua concluded wth this admonition: "But since, as the wise Solomon says, wisdom entereth not into an evil mind, and knowledge without conscience is but the ruin of the soul, it behooves thee to serve, love, and fear God, and in Him place all thy thoughts and all thy hope. . . ."

The *Essays* of Montaigne (1533-1592) are the second great secular work of the French sixteenth century. Montaigne lacks the optimism, exuberance and coarse hilarity of Rabelais, but he shares many of his opinions, notably his belief in the adequacy of nature's guidance: "Nature has seen to it as a mother that the actions which she has enjoined for our needs are also pleasurable." "The more simply one commits oneself to nature, the more wisely he commits himself." And he concludes, after some hesitation, that the important thing is not to die happily but to live happily; it is that which makes human felicity. This is the secular, not the Christian, point of view.

Montaigne was a man of thought rather than of action, and before he was forty he retired from judicial business and with the ample wealth inherited from his father built a study—his "tower of refuge"—separate from his house, whither he retired to read, reflect and write his essays. He studied the writings of the ancients, notably Plutarch's *Lives* which Amyot had recently translated into French and from which North was soon to make his magnificent English translation; he studied Latin, Italian and French literature; above all, he studied himself. In his *Essays,* as he tells us in the preface, he gives us a picture of himself:—"*C'est moy que je peins.*" And in doing this he paints universal human nature.

Montaigne's style has not the clarity of Descartes (1516-1650), a champion of the sole authority of reason, or the persuasive eloquence of Pascal (1623-1662) who, in his *Provincial Letters,* will incidentally disagree with his master, Montaigne, on the adequacy of reason. Montaigne's style is his own and yet of the sixteenth century, a beautiful, meaty, flexible, not too orderly French, enriched with many phrases and turns of expression of his own coinage. His style has been superseded, but not his thought, which was drawn upon by Bacon and later by Emerson for their *Essays,* and by many other students of prudential morals.

THE ENGLISH: WYATT, SURREY, SIDNEY AND SPENSER

In the secular literature of early sixteenth century England there is little indication of approaching greatness. To be sure, Sir Thomas Wyatt (1503-1542) and the Earl of Surrey (1516-1547), both of them classical scholars and students of French, Italian and Spanish literatures, wrote love verses after the manner of Petrarch and his continental imitators. And Wyatt domesticated the sonnet in England while Surrey did the same for blank verse, which Shakespeare was to employ so magnificently. After them came Sir Philip Sidney (1554-1586), another scion of the nobility trained in the classics and in French and Italian literatures. Learned, traveled, serious and of extraordinary personal charm, he vainly sought a career in politics. His fame rests in part on his *Arcadia,* a confused pastoral romance in prose of mingled refinement and coarseness—much appreciated in its day—and on his sonnets, *Astrophel and Stella,* which surpass those of his English predecessors. He suffered an early death from a bullet wound received at Zutphen, where he had quixotically laid aside his thigh armor because a comrade had forgotten his. His noble gesture when, stricken to death, he gave his water bottle to a dying soldier, saying, "Thy necessity is greater than mine," has outlived the memory of his sonnets. He was, in fact, the perfect type of Elizabethan gentleman—poetic, chivalrous, rash, charming. The older ideals of chivalry still lived in him.

With Edmund Spenser (1552-1609) the great era of Elizabethan literature arrived. Although the son of a poor London tradesman, he enjoyed, thanks to scholarships open to poor boys of talent, an excellent classical education in school and university. To this training he added an intimate familiarity with French, Italian and older English literature. He secured the backing of Leicester and then of Essex,—and perhaps for that reason the opposition of Burleigh,—but despite his poetical successes and the adulation which he lavished on Elizabeth and her friends in his writings, he failed to secure a remunerative post at court.

> I was promised on a time
> To have reason for my rhyme.

But all the "reason" he received was minor offices in Ireland. Before he left England, however, the reception of his first verses encouraged him to attempt to give his country an extended poem, worthy of comparison with the masterpieces of Homer, Virgil and Ariosto. The result was the *Faerie Queene*. The first part of it was published in 1590, the second in 1596. Each part was acclaimed, as it appeared, by the aristocracy for whom it was written.

The *Faerie Queene* is a romance, conceived on a most impressive scale, planned to entertain the nobility with chivalrous adventures of love and fighting, especially love. "Fierce warres and faithful loves, Shall moralize my song." Ariosto's *Orlando Furioso* is the chief model, and the classical literatures, medieval tales of adventure, and later English, French and Italian writings, especially those of Tasso, are all brought under contribution. Furthermore, the poem was designed to instruct, to educate, the nobility as well as to entertain them, and to this end an elaborate allegory of the principal virtues is set up and in part carried out. "For all that faire is, is by nature good, That is a signe to know the gentle blood." The romantic subject matter and the allegory are interesting tributes to the Middle Ages. Contemporary ideals and manners inevitably, and also intentionally, appear and we find reflected, for example, the current flattery of Elizabeth, the vaunting patriotism of the Elizabethans, their elegant worldliness, their interest in dubious amatory adventures, their hostility to Roman Catholicism, and their indifference to the common people.

The *Faerie Queene* is deficient in action. Its creator lacked Ariosto's skill as a story-teller and as a painter of thrilling combats. But there are large compensations. The music of the verse is marvelous; the author is a master of noble harmonies and gives us innumerable passages of extraordinary vigor and beauty. The

Spenserian stanza, in which the poem is written, is "one of the most memorable creations of English poetry," and Burns, Byron, Keats and Shelley paid it the tribute of employing it for some of their finest works. The moral tone of the *Faerie Queene* has been widely praised, but some there are who prefer the robust coarseness which occasionally marks *The Canterbury Tales* to the indelicacies which Spenser relates at length and then briefly condemns. Be that as it may, Spenser's masterpiece ranks him with Chaucer, by whose side he sleeps in the Abbey. He is the "poet's poet," and his admirers defend him with ardor and sincerity.

SHAKESPEARE

The Elizabethan age reached its noblest and fullest secular expression with the dramas of Shakespeare (1564-1616). They began to appear upon the stage about the time when Spenser published the first part of the *Faerie Queene* and they continued until about 1611. The might of Shakespeare's genius so far surpasses that of his predecessors, rivals and successors that it is difficult to regard him as a creature of his time. Nevertheless, he is of his age and reflects it in a thousand ways.

His formal education was obtained in the grammar school of Stratford, a town of about fourteen hundred inhabitants. The teacher—it was a one-teacher school—gave him a school-boy's familiarity with the commoner Latin authors, but, judging from the allusions to schoolmasters in his dramatic works, he did not enjoy his school days. His education continued throughout his life, with French literature, with the many English translations from the classics and the writings of other countries, with the historical chronicles of England, with the poems and plays of his predecessors and contemporaries, and with "the study of mankind." He was not an "exact scholar," he was not a Humanist by education. But his powers of assimilation were unsurpassed and his dramatic talent, marching forward to perfection, enabled him to portray virtually all aspects of mundane life.

The Shakespeare revealed in *Venus and Adonis, Lucrece* and

the *Sonnets,* which were written, all three, before his thirtieth year, is a poet who chooses to obtain recognition as a master of "amourist" verse of the Italian type, and a man who is interested in earthly and even irregular love. His successes as a dramatist had already begun, but an Italianate poet was then esteemed more highly than a dramatist.

When Shakespeare began to write his plays the English drama was already flourishing. It had outgrown the mystery, miracle and "morality" plays and had incorporated interludes and masques. Marlowe (1564-1593), like Shakespeare a man of humble birth, was one of a group of university-trained playwrights who were writing for the London stage, and his *Tamburlaine, Faustus,* and especially his *Edward II* helped to shape Shakespeare's dramatic powers. Marlowe was the first to employ a flexible blank verse for the public stage and Shakespeare followed him in this and in other ways. But Marlowe was killed in a lewd brawl before his talent had reached its prime.

Shakespeare's dramas were shaped also, and more decisively, by the demands of the London play-goers. The theaters were located just outside the city limits for the reason that the city authorities did not regard them with a kindly eye. In the same region, indeed often in the same building, were held the bear and the bull baitings and the dog fights, and near at hand were the taverns and disreputable places. The theater had to compete with these rivals. The theater-goers were of two classes, in the main: —the pleasure-loving nobles chiefly of the court, and the keen-witted groundlings, the "great unwashed," who frequented the pit. "Thus it came about that the success of authors, managers and players depended on their ability to interest two kinds of audiences in one play. An unlettered crowd paid the bulk of the gate money; but court lords and Temple gallants [lawyers], proud of their taste and learning, shielded the theatres from invectives of the clergy and the official action of the respectable middle classes. . . . It is possible to trace the effects of this dual patronage in the very various kinds of drama introduced into one play and even into one scene . . ." (Trevelyan).

Shakespeare accepted the limitations thus placed upon him as did most of the other playwrights of England, for he wished his plays to succeed and to procure him a fortune, which they did. He accepted the limitations and triumphed over them. He expressed sentiments that outran the intelligence of most if not all of his audiences, and profundities that escaped them and entrance us (if we are wise), but he saw to it that they had plenty to interest them, and Elizabeth also, and King James in turn.

Shakespeare wrote thirty-seven plays in whole or in part. His full powers are first shown to perfection in *Romeo and Juliet,* which was written about 1594. The best of his other plays, with their approximate dates, are—let us be rash and state our own preferences—*The Merchant of Venice* (1596), *Henry IV* (1597-1598), *Henry V* (1599), *The Merry Wives of Windsor* (1600), *Hamlet* (1601), *Othello* (1604), *Anthony and Cleopatra* (1606), and *The Tempest* (1611). The majority of his plots are borrowed and glorified. The persons of the dramas may be English, Roman, Greek, Italian, French, or Danish. It matters not; they are living individuals, stamped with their own vital characteristics. They amuse, shock, delight and instruct. They reveal humanity at its best, its average, its worst. They express the eternal sentiments of mankind with ever-living and life-giving vitality. They are immortal.

Shakespeare was a genius of the very first rank, and it is not possible to determine from his writings precisely the manner of man he was. It is more feasible to say, with some approach to accuracy, what manner of folk his Elizabethan and Jacobean audiences were, for he acted before them, studied their likes and dislikes, and wrote to please them. Judged by his plays, they liked action, sharp, even violent contrasts, such as tragedy with comic interludes, word-play and "verbal slap-stick," jokes, jests both coarse and refined, love at its most idyllic extreme, indecorous but comic scenes, marvels, drinking, fights, poking fun at enemy foreigners, the glorification of England, noble sentiments, heroic deeds, magnificently rolling English, noise, music and songs. They were less refined and thicker skinned than we, but robust and sturdy, with their feet on the ground (sometimes in the mud) and their eyes (frequently) on the stars.

In London also, and outside of London especially in the towns, dwelt the self-reliant Puritan English, a minority of the population, studying their Bibles, conducting family prayers, discussing predestination, Anglican orders, the use of the surplice, the profanation of the Lord's Day by afternoon sports and games, and doing their duty as they saw it. To them the theater was godless and lewd. They were not entirely wrong, especially when the successors of Shakespeare, who was himself not altogether without spot, produced their bloody plays of lust and murder. And when Charles I, debonair and devout, provoked the Commons to war, the Puritans closed the theaters (1642) and kept them closed until the Restoration (1660). The Puritans were too serious to depict the human comedy. Their masterpieces were to be Milton's *Paradise Lost* (1663) written, like Shakespeare's dramas, in blank verse, and Bunyan's *Pilgrim's Progress* (1673), a prose tale surpassing, as an allegory, the *Faerie Queene,* and surpassing it, too, in readers and influence. The Puritans were extremists, but it may well be that they were a salutary corrective to their more mundane opponents.

FRENCH CRITICISM OF THE SHAKESPEAREAN DRAMA

Across the Channel, the French drama developed along different lines from the Elizabethan drama. To the orderly, logical French mind, which naturally yielded more ready allegiance than the English to the classical ideas of dignity and restraint which had been recalled by the Revival of Learning, the practice of the Elizabethan dramatists, notably of Shakespeare, in mingling comedy with tragedy and the ignoble with the exalted, and in depicting the fullness, waywardness and inconsequence of real life upon the stage, in one and the self-same play, was puzzling when it was not laughable or absurd. Had not the ancient classical drama laid down as authoritative the "three unities" of time, place and action—that is, that the play must deal with events transpiring in not to exceed twenty-four hours, in one place, and with all irrelevancies or distracting episodes pruned away from the action? Ben Jonson, a learned, witty, classically trained English competitor of Shakespeare's, might have replied: "Yes, you are right; and I have offered the Londoners plays of the sort you have in mind; for example, *Every Man in His Humor;* but they don't care for them." It was even so, and the drama of the two countries diverged more and more. The French "ideal of reticence and simplification" reached its first adequate expression in Corneille's *Le Cid* (1636), and attained its heights in the plays of Molière (1622-1673) and of Racine (1639-1699).

Tastes change; above all, capacities differ; and so it came about that modern playwrights follow more closely the practice of Racine than the example of Shakespeare. "Who shall draw the bow of Ulysses?" The modern representative of the Shakespearean play is the novel.

THE PORTUGUESE: CAMOENS

The sixteenth century gave Portugal her greatest epic, *The Lusiads* of Camoens (1524-1580), a poem which expresses the buoyant and adventurous spirit of the age. Camoens' humanistic education and intimate familiarity with the romantic literatures of Italy, Spain and his own land were of importance, but the realism of his masterpiece came from the experiences of his sea voyage to and from India and of his prolonged residence in the East. The form of the story is reminiscent of Virgil and of Ariosto; the story itself is built around Vasco da Gama's historic voyage to India in 1497. It is a relatively simple story, with even less intricacy than Tasso's *Jerusalem,* which was written shortly after *The Lusiads.* It is not a veritable romance, although it has its romantic episodes, notably the entertainment of the weary sailors, homeward bound, on the enchanted island by Venus and her nymphs (Canto IX), in which the superior delicacy of the treatment is marked. *The Lusiads* is the great epic of geographical discovery. It is also a monument to Portuguese patriotism and to Portugal's great days of old.

THE SPANIARDS: CERVANTES

Spain's chief contribution to the literature of the world, *Don Quixote,* was not written in the sixteenth century, but it followed closely on its heels (Part I, 1605; Part II, 1615) and is true to its genius. Cervantes (1547-1616), who wrote it, had a very slender formal education. He knew a little Latin and had picked up some Italian, but his experience of life was very broad. He fought with distinction at Lepanto (1571) with Don John of Austria, was a slave to Barbary pirates for five years—filled with efforts at escape—helped to outfit the Armada, served as a tax collector in Castile where he gained an intimate knowledge of all classes, and strove to earn his living as a dramatist. The theater was flourishing in Spain, but Cervantes could not hit the popular taste. However, he knew life and the popular litera-ture of his country, especially the romances of chivalry which the Spanish writers were spinning out voluminously. To Cer-vantes these revampings of the literature of knight-errantry, which had passed away, appeared to be not only out-of-date but actually pestiferous. Hence *Don Quixote.*

Don Quixote is not a tract, but a burlesque romance of chivalry. Its hero, who gives his name to the story, has lost his wits— although he recovers them in large part—from reading and pon-dering over too many romances. The book presents, with un-smiling gravity, the standard events of the typical romance with its jousts, stratagems, exalted cult of love, damsels in distress, enchantments. The fun ranges from broad farce to subtle comedy, and with it we are given countless pictures of human nature exhibited by all classes of Cervantes' countrymen. The range of characters is indeed immense, surpassing by far that of Chaucer's pilgrims, and every one stands out with unforget-able individuality.

Don Quixote is one of the great books of the world. It has been printed oftener than any other book, the Bible alone ex-cepted, and its popularity does not abate. It is still true that "children turn its leaves, young people read it, grown men under-stand it, old folks praise it."

SIXTEENTH-CENTURY SCIENCE: VESALIUS AND COPERNICUS

As the foregoing survey has shown, the sixteenth century produced a rich harvest of works of the poetical imagination. If it be true, as some great critics aver, that the scientific imagination, which is of the intellect rather than of the emotions, flourishes in an atmosphere that is unfavorable to poetry and religion, then the sixteenth century must be an exception to the rule for it also witnessed the undoubted beginnings of modern science.

Science, Charles Singer has well said, is inadequately described as "accurate and organized knowledge." He defines science as "the process which makes knowledge." It is the systematic interrogation of nature by means of experiment or research that constitutes science. Accepting this definition, it may be said that modern science was born in 1543 when two momentous books were published: one on human anatomy, by the Fleming, Vesalius; the other on astronomy, by the Pole, Copernicus.

Vesalius (1514-1564) studied arts at Louvain and anatomy at Paris and in Italy, especially at Padua, where he became professor of anatomy in 1537. The accepted method of teaching human anatomy in his youth was to expound the anatomical writings of Galen, the learned and versatile Greek scientist of the second century after Christ, and to illustrate the exposition with parts of the bodies of animals. Vesalius's own irresistible bent was to study the human structure directly and to illustrate his lectures with dissections of the human body. He found Galen's information defective at many points and incidentally discovered that Galen's descriptions of human anatomy were drawn from dissections of the bodies of apes. In 1543 Vesalius published the results of his research in a huge work of seven hundred folio pages, entitled *De fabrica humani corporis.* It was a convincing demonstration of superior anatomical knowledge together with a criticism of Galen's errors. The book encountered the most serious opposition from champions of the ancient authority, but it triumphed and placed the study of anatomy upon a truly scientific foundation.

It is not feasible in this book to continue the story, even in

outline, of the subsequent development of the science of anatomy.
But one illustration from the kindred science of physiology must
be given. Vesalius did not understand, any more than any of
his predecessors, that the blood is pumped through the body. He
thought, as did Galen, that there was one sort of blood in the
arteries and another in the veins. Other hypotheses were advanced, however, and in the second edition of his book Vesalius
expressed a doubt as to the correctness of the ancient opinion.
The true solution of the matter was discovered by Harvey half
a century after the death of Vesalius. Harvey (1578-1657)
took his arts degree at Cambridge and his medical degree at
Padua in Italy; he taught and practiced his profession in London.
After laborious investigations, involving much vivisection, he discovered the truth, that the blood circulates "from the left side
of the heart by the aorta and its subdivisions, to the right side by
the veins." He imparted his discovery to his students as early
as 1619 and published it to the world in 1628. The title of the
treatise is long, although the book is hardly more than a pamphlet:
Exercitatio anatomica de motu cordis et sanguinis in animalibus.
It is one of the capital books in the history of medicine.

Copernicus (1473-1543) enjoyed a very broad education, but
concentrated on mathematics and astronomy, which he studied at
the greatest Italian universities. Soon after his return home
from Italy he was appointed a canon of Frauenburg, but his
energies were given to the movements of the heavenly bodies.
The accepted astronomical theory was that of Ptolemy, a contemporary of Galen, which made the earth the center of the universe. The idea that the earth rotated on its axis had been
broached in ancient times and again in the fifteenth century.
Copernicus took up the actual investigation along mathematical
lines. His calculations convinced him of the correctness of the
hypothesis and about 1530 he communicated his conclusions to
various friends in a brief manuscript. In 1539 they were given
to the world by a disciple in a summary printed form. In 1543
Copernicus published them *in extenso* under the title, *De revo-
lutionibus orbium cælestium,* or *The Revolutions of the Celestial
Bodies.* The new theory made its way but slowly for it met with

opposition from teachers of the Ptolemaic theory and from theologians as well. Moreover, there were errors which had to be cleared away. Nevertheless, the great Pole had discovered that our world system is heliocentric.

The rounding out of the work of Copernicus involved the labors of a brilliant series of investigators. Among these must be named Tycho Brahe (1546-1601), a Dane, Kepler (1571-1629), a German who was a pupil of Tycho's, and Galileo (1564-1642), an Italian. Galileo probably surpassed these others in the breadth and brilliance of his talents, but it was his utilization of the telescope, invented by a contemporary, which enabled him to clinch the proofs of the correctness of the heliocentric theory. To Sir Isaac Newton (1643-1727), an English investigator who was an even greater prodigy than Galileo, it was given to place the capstone upon the astronomical discoveries of this brilliant group by his discovery of the law of gravitation.

The work of these scientists afforded convincing evidence that the path to an enlarged knowledge of nature's forces passes through hypothesis, experiment and calculation. It was their work which furnished the proof and also the suggestions for the further advance which is still going on with increasing speed. Yet it is a remarkable fact, and a tribute to the power of eloquence and intellect, that the first great popularizer of the idea of research, Francis Bacon, was not himself a scientist in the technical sense, and did not accept the new astronomy of Copernicus. Yet he stands to this day, as he stood to Voltaire and the Encyclopedists in the eighteenth century, as the prophet of science Bacon (1561-1626) was by profession a lawyer and judge and attained the position of Lord High Chancellor of England. His literary style is Elizabethan; it is apt, dignified, rich, compendious, exuberant, aphoristic. He wrote in English and Latin with equal ease. His *Essays,* compact of worldly wisdom, are still read. His *Advancement of Learning* is an English classic. The *Novum Organum* is his most ambitious work; its title indicates that he regards Aristotle, the embodiment of the principle of authority, as the foe. He argues for the establishment of science on the solid foundation of experiment and induction, as against the deductive procedure of the scholastic doctors. Yet there is a scholastic flavor about the book. In the *New Atlantis* he sketches an ideal commonwealth, in which coöperative scientific research is carried on with ample endowments and on a very large scale in the interest of human betterment. It is a fascinating picture, which was realized, after a fashion, in the establishment of the English Royal Society in 1660 and the French Academy of Sciences in 1666. Bacon was a cold-blooded, ungrateful calculator, but his heart actually warms as he contemplates the future victories of science. All in all, he is one of the great representatives of the spirit of the sixteenth century.

THE GEOGRAPHICAL DISCOVERIES: THE PARTITION OF THE NEW WORLD AND THE ANCIENT EAST TO 1660

IT IS difficult, indeed it is impossible, to determine what achievement of the Middle Ages was the most important for the future of mankind. But it is hardly likely that we, dwellers in the "lands beyond the seas," will ever fail to assign a high place to the discovery of America and of the sea route to the East. It may even be that these discoveries, in the light of their ultimate consequences, will be regarded by Europeans as the most significant event in their recorded history.

Looking back on the conditions in Europe in the fifteenth century, it seems as if the discoveries were inevitable. Western Europe was now organized into large states, with central governments able to tax their subjects in large amounts, with youthful national patriotisms which have always been potent stimulants to high, and sometimes to low, deeds, and with nobles and middle classes habituated to the use of Oriental products and able and willing to purchase them in increasing quantities. Moreover, in the arts of navigation the Europeans of the fifteenth century were far in advance of the Romans. They had sailing ships of from one to two hundred tons, which were able to stand the buffetings of the seas; they had the compass (known since the twelfth century) for determining directions, and the St. James's staff, the precursor of the quadrant, and timepieces for determining location. Above all, they had inventiveness, courage, stamina and daring unsurpassed, perhaps unequaled, since Alexander the Great. Finally, the commercial spirit was widely diffused among them—that spirit which seeks and risks because it believes in the possibility of great gains.

And yet it is perfectly clear, and it will be shown, that the actual discoveries of America and of the sea route to the Far East were the achievements of a few individuals, and that the wealth and strength of the national states were employed only for the exploitation of the discoveries. These states utilized but did not, as such, initiate the discoveries.

MEDIEVAL TRADE ROUTES BETWEEN EUROPE AND THE ORIENT

The old medieval and ancient routes between Europe and Asia, over which passed the Oriental wares so much prized by Europeans, and the silver, gold, woolens, copper, lead, tin and coral so highly valued by the Asiatic peoples, continued to serve and serve adequately the needs of West and East until after the discovery of the route around the Cape of Good Hope. The particular route or routes favored at any particular epoch depended primarily on political conditions in or near the areas traversed by the routes. Sometimes the northern land route—from Tana on the Sea of Azov, thence north of the Caspian Sea and onward to distant China—was most feasible as, for example, in the best days of the great Mongol Empire, say 1240-1340. Sometimes, perhaps usually, the southernmost routes—one of them from Alexandria, down the Nile, thence across to the head of the Red Sea and onward by ship to India and the Fast East, and the other from Beirut in Syria to the Persian Gulf and thence by sea to the East—were the cheapest and best. At still other periods the more central routes were the safest. It depended largely on political conditions along the routes. Strong governments favored and helped trade since it brought them revenues; weak ones could not put down banditry and piracy, which throttled or tended to throttle it. Warfare inevitably interrupted it. Nevertheless, it can be said that the East-West routes which were open were adequate to the needs of the later Middle Ages. This is easily proven for the fifteenth century: the cost of spices in Europe remained steady throughout the whole of it.

THE OTTOMAN TURKS TO 1516

The rise and progress of the Ottoman Turks may have contributed something to the increasing employment of the southernmost routes, *via* Alexandria and Beirut. The point will be made clear in considering the growth of the Ottoman power.

The Ottoman Turks appear on the stage of the thirteenth century as one of several small tribes or bands of Turks fleeing westward into Asia Minor ahead of the bloodthirsty Mongols. They and many other of the Turkish refugees settled down where they could among the discordant Seljuk principalities or emirates of Asia Minor. The little group we are considering settled, under a chief named Othman or Osman (hence *Ottoman* Turks), in the region southeast of, and at a short distance from, the Sea of Marmora, and close to the end of the thirteenth century they accepted Islam as their faith. Near their settlements were some of the outlying cities of the Byzantine Empire, which still acknowledged its sovereignty—for example, Brusa, Nicæa, and Nicomedia. These cities clung to the inefficient Empire as long as they had hope of aid from it. But their trade languished, and one by one they opened their gates to the environing and ambitious Osmanlis, Nicomedia in 1337 or 1338 being the last to do so. In the main the dwellers in these cities accepted Islam, for that made them full citizens, or rather subjects, freed them from taxes, and made them eligible for grants of land and positions in the army. With the annexation of Nicomedia the Osmanlis were in possession of the southern shores of the Sea of Marmora.

It was not long before they were invited to cross the Dardanelles into Europe. The imperial dynasty was not united, and the Serbs and Bulgarians were each threatening to take Constantinople. In 1345 Orkhan, the son and successor of Osman, lent six thousand soldiers to the emperor in return for his daughter's hand in marriage. Soon other troops were asked for and they were sent or brought. In the emperor's service they traversed the land and saw that it was good, and then they spread along the European side of the straits. They occupied Gallipoli, brought settlers across, seized Adrianople (about 1361), and had effective possession of Thrace. Again the Christian population, especially in the country districts, became Osmanlis. In 1371-1372 the same things took place in Macedonia. The Osmanlis as yet made no real effort to occupy Constantinople; they had no navy, which was necessary to hold the city, and they did not want to provoke a great crusade from the West.

Undoubtedly the Christians of western Europe could have blocked the advance of the Ottoman Turks into Europe if they had tried. But the Black Death, which was endemic in the Levant, helped to keep the West at home; the Great Schism occupied the Western Church with its own troubles; the Venetians and the Genoese, suspicious of one another's plans, each made commercial treaties with the rising Osmanlis; and it seems as if the rank and file of the Byzantine Christians feared the papal West more than they dreaded the, as yet, tolerant Turk.

In the last decade of the fourteenth century the Osmanlis, firmly rooted in Europe, began to expand southward from their territory in northern Asia Minor. Their numbers had grown materially since they had crossed the Dardanelles. "From first to last, the extension of Ottoman sovereignty over the Moslems of Asia was [accomplished] by means of a soldiery gathered and war-hardened in Europe, themselves Christian or of Christian ancestry, in whose veins ran the blood of Greek and Roman, of Goth and Hun, of Albanian and Slav" (H. A. Gibbons). Their progress southward was, however, interrupted for a time, in the early years of the fifteenth century, by the terrible Tartar raid led by the redoubtable Timur, who overran their Asiatic province, captured their sultan, Bayezid I, and drove their troops back to the Dardanelles. The Venetian and Genoese vessels ferried the Ottoman troops across to Europe. The Tartar storm soon passed, and under Solyman I and his successors the Osmanlis resumed their advance in Europe and Asia. They took Constantinople in 1453, drove the Venetians and the Genoese out of their possessions on the Black Sea, and in effect made it a Turkish lake. Their first efforts to take Syria from the Mameluke sultans, who had reigned in Egypt since about 1250, failed and were not renewed until about 1516 when both Syria and Egypt were quickly overrun and annexed.

In the course of their progress southward the Osmanlis took over the profitable trade agreements, originally made by the rulers they displaced, with Venice, Genoa, Florence and the other trading cities of the western Mediterranean. But when they annexed Syria and Egypt and thus secured control of the western termini of the southern trade routes, including Beirut and Alexandria which had borne the bulk of the East-West traffic under the Mamelukes in the fifteenth century, they found the trade had virtually dried up. The Portuguese had diverted it to their vessels![1]

PORTUGUESE EXPANSION; PRINCE HENRY THE NAVIGATOR

The beginnings of Portuguese expansion overseas may be dated from the conquest of Ceuta in Morocco in 1415. Thirty years before this event a new dynasty had been set up by the Portuguese people in the person of King John I. He vindicated their choice of himself by successfully maintaining Portuguese independence against a powerful invasion from Castile. He won the great victory of Aljubarrota (1385) and clinched its results by an alliance with England, in connection with which he married Philippa, sister of the later king, Henry IV. The Portuguese were confident of their future and anxious to advance. In the thirteenth century they had expelled the Moor from the region south of the Tagus and thus had rounded out the home territories; they had established their independence against Castile, but could not expect to expand eastward at her expense. What more natural than to cross the narrow stretch of water between Portugal and Africa and attack the hereditary enemy of their land and their religion? Hence the capture of Ceuta in 1415. And what more natural than to continue that attack, so to say, by getting into touch with the peoples south of Morocco? The

[1] On the rise of the Turks, sketched above, see H. A. Gibbons, *The Foundation of the Ottoman Empire*. The charge that the Turks made the discovery of the sea route necessary by blocking the old trade routes is disposed of by A. H. Lybyer, in *Eng. Hist. Review,* xxx (1915), pages 577-588.

explorations down the west coast of Africa developed naturally from the conquest of Ceuta.

These explorations, however, might not have taken place but for Prince Henry "the Navigator." He was the third of the capable sons of King John and Philippa. All three had fought at the capture of Ceuta. Henry was rich, unmarried, head of the Portuguese crusading Order of Christ, persistent, practical, studious, scientific. He became the initiator, patron and director of southward exploration, using his own money and that of the Order of Christ. He made his explorations "by deputy"; he stayed at home, assembled books, maps and cosmographers, studied, planned, enlisted sailors and captains, including many Italians, promoted improvements in ship-building and the like. In Morocco he had heard of trade routes to a fertile region in Central Africa. It is said that he had in mind to push down the African coast to the "western branch of the Nile" (really the Senegal), to link forces, via this river, with the traditional Christian "Kingdom of Prester John" (Abyssinia?), and then to recapture the Holy Places from the Moslems. This plan, if Prince Henry entertained it, was an attractive embroidery on the explorations he directed. The explorations offered adventure, battle against the African Moslems, and prospects of settlements and trade. Venetian galleys landed Oriental wares at Lisbon annually. Why not African wares in Portuguese vessels? The idea of reaching the Far East by sea probably never was entertained by Prince Henry; but it took shape with the continuance of exploration southward after his death, and thus, in a very real sense, was an outgrowth of his life-work.

The tangible achievements of Prince Henry's labors may be readily summarized. He rediscovered and colonized the Madeiras and the Azores and discovered the Cape Verde Islands. It should be recalled that Frenchmen were already in the Canaries under the authority of Castile. He pushed his coastal explorations down past Cape Verde to the neighborhood of the modern Sierra Leone, and opened up a profitable trade in gold, ivory and negro slaves on the Guinea coast. The trade was so promising that it apparently retarded the progress southward. More than that, the

slaves were sold chiefly to the owners of plantations in Portugal
south of the Tagus and, while the owners profited from their
toil, their use discouraged white labor and paved the way for
greater importations of negroes in the future.

THE ESTABLISHMENT OF THE PORTUGUESE IN THE FAR EAST

With the death of Prince Henry in 1460 progress southward
slackened. The kings who now in succession took over his tasks
turned their attention to attacks on Morocco, and even when
the goal was in sight—after the rounding of the Cape of Good
Hope—other projects received the preference. None the less,
the impulse given by Prince Henry was only weakened, not lost.
In 1487-1488 Bartholomew Diaz pushed on and rounded the
Cape of Good Hope. He was sure that the way to India had
been found. Almost at the same time a Portuguese mission *via*
Egypt went down the Red Sea and followed the east coast of
Africa down to the neighborhood of Zanzibar; and when the
reports of both expeditions were checked up it was perfectly
clear that the sea route to the East was an actuality. Next to
Prince Henry the glory of the discovery belongs to Bartholomew
Diaz. But for some reason King Manuel sent another, Vasco
da Gama, to make the complete voyage.

In 1497-1498 da Gama followed the West African coast southward, rounded the Cape, followed the east coast up to about
Zanzibar, took on a Moslem pilot, and was by him conducted
across the Indian Ocean to Calicut, India. He had four ships
and 170 men. The Mohammedan traders at Calicut gave him
a very cool reception. But he observed the wealth of the region,
learned of its trade connections and returned home with his report. Almost immediately a large and well-armed fleet was dispatched to the East under Cabral, who *en route* involuntarily
swung too far to the west and discovered Brazil, and it brought
home a rich cargo. Thereafter yearly fleets of a dozen ships or
so became the rule. In 1502 the Venetian galleys found few
spices at Alexandria and Beirut; two years later they found none
at all: the Portuguese had bought up the supplies in the East.

The Arab traders, who for centuries had grown rich on the transportation of the spices, drugs and other Oriental wares to Egypt, Persia and Syria, and the Mameluke sultan of Egypt and Syria, whose profits had also been large, were enraged. Urged on by the Venetians, the sultan dispatched a strong fleet from the Red Sea to join forces with ships assembled on the west coast of India. But the Portuguese got wind of their plans and sent out a specially strong squadron, which in 1509 defeated the combined war fleets off Diu. When the Ottoman Turks took Egypt they made a similar effort to crush the Portuguese in the East, and with equally disastrous results for themselves. After the victory of 1509 the Portuguese systematically set to work to exclude the Arabs from all share in the East-West trade by sea. They took possession of the entrance to the Persian Gulf and by naval patrols almost closed the Red Sea to Arab traders; they tightened their grasp on the Arab ports of East Africa; they occupied Malacca (1511), thus gaining control of the "bottle neck" through which passed the bulk of that part of the sea-borne commerce of the Spice Islands—the Moluccas—which sought India and the West. From Malacca they established posts in the Spice Islands and opened up trade with China and Japan. Other expeditions, a little earlier and later than that which secured Malacca, took possession of Ceylon and of Goa, Diu, and other key places on the coast of India. As a result the Portuguese had almost a century of uninterrupted control of the Eastern seas.

The Arabs were the chief although not the only sufferers. Their ancient heritage of maritime trade with the West was seized by Portugal. In Europe, likewise, the center of the trade in Oriental wares was automatically transferred from Venice to Lisbon, and the proud Venetians were invited to come to Lisbon and buy. In effect the Portuguese had nearly all the profits in the East-West trade which the Arabs, the Mamelukes and other intermediaries of the Near East, and the Venetians had formerly shared. Such was the outcome of the circumnavigation of the Cape of Good Hope by Bartholomew Diaz.

In the ten-year interval between Diaz's feat and da Gama's

voyage to India, two other explorers attempted short cuts to the East. These were Christopher Columbus and John Cabot, both of them Genoese by birth and early training.

THE VOYAGES OF COLUMBUS AND CABOT

Columbus (*ca.* 1451-1506) had sailed the seas for many years, from Chios, in the Levant, to Iceland, the Madeiras, the Gold Coast. In Iceland—if he actually visited it—he may well have heard of the discovery of Vinland (Nova Scotia?) in the year 1000 by Leif Ericsson, one of the adventurous sons of Norway who were, all in all, the best sailors of the Middle Ages. Columbus settled in Portugal, married the daughter of one of the captains who had been in the service of Henry the Navigator, made maps and sailed in the employ of the Portuguese crown. No doubt he had many conversations with the mariners of Portugal regarding the continents and seas. We do not know just when his plan for reaching the Far East took shape in his mind. He is said to have corresponded with Toscanelli, the Florentine geographer, on the subject as early as 1474.

Two misconceptions shared by Columbus with the geographers of his time entered into his calculations. First, the size of the earth was estimated to be smaller, by about one-quarter, than it actually is. Secondly, Asia was thought to be much wider than it is in reality, so that Japan, for example, was figured out to be where Mexico in fact is. These misconceptions made the plan of Columbus seem reasonable to him and his friends.

Shortly after a voyage to the Gold Coast in 1481-1482, Columbus sought the modest patronage necessary for his project from the king of Portugal. But that monarch had his money on the other horse. Then Columbus turned to the rulers of France, England and Spain. The experts consulted by all these kings advised against the project as hare-brained. Ferdinand and Isabella, although in the midst of their war against Granada, nevertheless encouraged Columbus to look for favor after they had finished fighting. That happened early in 1492, and it was not long, although it took considerable urging from his friends, before Queen Isabella, on behalf of her kingdom of Castile, undertook to finance the voyage. It cost only about $100,000 in our pre-war money, reckoning the dollar as it was valued before the Great War. It was not an expensive bit of speculation.

The epoch-making expedition consisted of three small vessels of one hundred, fifty, and forty tons, respectively, with a personnel of eighty-eight men, including one Englishman and one Irishman. The little fleet left Spain August 3, 1492, refitted in the Canaries, and sailed thence September 6. America (Watling's Island) was discovered on October 12, and the natives were dubbed Indians, since Columbus believed he had reached the distant East. Only thirty-six days out from the well-known Canaries! Nevertheless, it was an intrepid feat. The Portuguese, even though swept out of their course by storms, had followed the coast; Columbus boldly set sail for the heart of the unknown.

Unfortunately for Columbus's immediate happiness he had, in fact, stumbled upon an unknown continent, when he thought to reach Japan, China and India. But the weight of his misfortune is lightened by the consideration that, if he had not done so, if America had not been there, he would not have succeeded in his project of reaching the Far East for the simple reason that neither his sailors nor his supplies would have held out. The Portuguese route to central and eastern Asia was, we know, the shortest route after all.

But Columbus was certain that he had arrived at an outlying part of the East, and that, with some further efforts, he would pierce through to the glowing cities of wealth and refinement described by Marco Polo. To this end he made three other voyages. On the second one he had a personnel of 1,500 men, so high were the expectations raised by his brightly-painted account of the wonders he had found. The reality, to be sure, was simple and prosaic enough. Five ships filled with West Indian natives were sent home by this expedition to be sold as slaves. That was not auspicious, although modeled upon Portuguese practice, and Queen Isabella frowned upon and stopped it. In the course of his voyages Columbus discovered many islands, including San Domingo, Cuba and Jamaica, skirted the coasts of Central and

northeastern South America, and established a colony on Hispaniola (San Domingo) where profitable but short-lived gold-mining
was carried on with forced Indian labor. The settlers were proud,
intractable and averse to labor. They wanted what they had
been led to expect—gold, silver, jewels, spices; in short, riches.
Columbus died, we are told, in the firm conviction that he had
reached eastern Asia. But there were already some who were
certain that he had found a new world.

The conquest of Mexico (1519-1521) by Cortes was more in
keeping with the earlier expectations. He set out from Cuba,
recently occupied, with six or seven hundred men, eighteen horses
(a fearful novelty to the natives), and a few small cannon. With
the coöperation of a discontented tribe of the natives and by deeds
of incredible daring and of great cruelty, when cruelty would
serve, Cortes, the foremost and most statesmanlike of the *conquistadores,* overthrew the Aztec emperor and took firm control
of the entire country. Great accumulations of gold and silver
were seized and, in large part, sent home to the needy Charles V,
and the mines were worked zealously with forced Indian labor.

An even more astounding feat, accompanied by greater cruel-
ties and less wisdom, was the overthrow of the highly developed
Empire of the Incas in Peru by Pizarro, 1531-1532. He set out
from Panama and captured the Empire with one hundred and
eighty men and twenty-seven horses. Once again hoards of the
precious metals were seized and in part distributed, in part sent
to Charles V, while the mines were feverishly worked and a
steady stream of metallic wealth was directed homeward. In both
Mexico and Peru the home government soon took over control
from the *conquistadores* and their lieutenants—sometimes their
rivals; separated civil and military authority; sent out priests and
other clergy; and by and by initiated the measures which, in spite
of serious and only partly inevitable defects, gradually built up a
higher and more humane civilization than either country had
known.

The huge plunder secured in Mexico and Peru encouraged
many other adventurers, some of them men of noble gifts, to
make far-flung and most arduous explorations. These brought

knowledge rather than gold and jewels, and resulted in additional settlements of small numbers of Spaniards at strategic points in the newly found regions.   The chief of these were in New Granada between Panama and Peru, in Chile, in the region of the river La Plata (Argentina), and in the territory on the north between Panama and the island of Trinidad, which forms the southern shore of the Caribbean Sea and was known to the sixteenth century by the glamorous title of the Spanish Main.   The unattractive stretch of coast between Trinidad and Brazil was left to itself by the Spaniards.   Adding in the larger West India islands and Florida, and omitting the outer crescent of the islands called the Lesser Antilles—let alone by the Spaniards mainly because of the fierceness of the Caribs who inhabited them—one may easily form a picture of the extensive Spanish empire in America which took shape so quickly after the discoveries of Columbus.

The second sailor to seek the East by sailing westward, in the interval between the voyages of Diaz and da Gama, was the English explorer, John Cabot, Genoese by birth and Venetian by naturalization.   His voyage was stimulated by the news of Columbus's feat, although Cabot says that the idea came to him as a result of a visit to Mecca where he saw dazzling quantities of precious Oriental wares.   Such a visit, however, would have been very difficult indeed for a Christian.   Cabot settled his family in London about 1484 and explored the Atlantic waters westward from Ireland in the service of Bristol merchants who had for some time been fishing off Iceland.   In 1496 the thrifty English king, Henry VII, authorized Cabot and his sons "upon their own proper costs and charges" to seek lands of "the heathen and infidels."   The Bristol merchants financed the expedition, which consisted of one ship with a crew of eighteen.   In June, 1497, after a voyage of fifty-two days, Cabot reached Cape Breton (or Labrador?) and "took possession" of the land in the name of the English king.   To Cabot the land was obviously northeastern China.   On the way home he discovered the fishing-banks of Newfoundland, which soon yielded great wealth to the mariners of all the seafaring nations of western Europe.   For the second time—if we accept evidence that is somewhat shaky—in 1498, with a considerable fleet, equipped in part by King Henry, Cabot sailed to East Greenland and then turned southward to seek Japan. He is said to have followed the coasts of Nova Scotia and New England, down perhaps to the thirty-eighth parallel, and then to have returned home. He was, it would seem, the discoverer of North America and the first of many to try to reach the East by way of the Northwest.

THE DEMARCATION LINE OF 1494

The suspension of Portugal's advance eastward for almost ten years after Diaz had rounded the Cape seemed, in 1493, likely to cost her dear. For then, shortly after Columbus got home, Spain secured from Pope Alexander VI, a Spaniard by birth, four bulls progressively more favorable, granting to her rulers all the pagan lands they should discover to the west of a line drawn, from pole to pole, one hundred leagues west of the Cape Verde Islands, provided such lands were not in the possession of any other Christian power (meaning Portugal) by Christmas, 1493. The bulls forbade all others even to seek for such lands without the permission of Spain. These bulls, it would seem, superseded the papal bulls of much earlier dates in favor of Portugal, notably that one which granted to her the right to make discoveries southward from Cape Bojador even to the Indies. The "international law" of the later Middle Ages conceded, or at least did not deny, the ancient right of the papacy to dispose of the lands of infidels.

The Portuguese, however, stood upon their earlier rights, and the Spanish rulers met them halfway in the treaty of Tordesillas, 1494. This provided that a meridian should be drawn in the Atlantic from pole to pole at a distance of 370 leagues west of the Cape Verde Islands, and that the Spaniards should have all the lands they discovered to the west of this line and the Portuguese all that they discovered to the east of it; and this treaty, confirmed by Julius II in 1506, was regarded for centuries by both Spain and Portugal as furnishing the real basis of their rights.[1] The treaty does not determine what is to happen if the two powers, exploring in opposite directions, should meet or overlap. Presumably prior occupation or a fresh treaty or bull would settle the difficulty. Spain pursued her explorations in America, and Portugal hers in the East and in Brazil. The line of 1494 passes through the mouth of the Amazon.

In 1517 Ferdinand Magellan (ca. 1480-1521), a Portuguese captain who had distinguished himself in the service of his country in Malacca and farther East but was now at outs with his king, went to Spain and offered, by sailing westward and therefore in accordance with the treaty of 1494, to reach and secure the Moluccas—the Spice Islands—for Spain. And he made an interesting argument to the effect that the Moluccas were on the Spanish side of the line of 1494 *when it was continued around the world*. Charles V must have known that the Portuguese had been in the Spice Islands, at least off and on, since 1512, but he asserted that these islands were unoccupied and accepted Magellan's offer. Charles also bore three-quarters of the expense of equipping the little fleet of five ships and its crew of about 275 men, which were put under Magellan's command. The total cost was about $250,000 in our pre-war money.

In the early autumn of 1519 Magellan sailed to the coast of South America, sought long and ultimately found an opening far south in the straits which bear his name, entered the Pacific (first seen by Balboa, near Panama, in 1513), and in March, 1521, after incredible hardships, on short and decayed rations, reached the Ladrones and, shortly after, the Philippines. Here he was killed in an unnecessary battle with natives in April, 1521. The survivors then went on to the Moluccas, made a treaty with the natives of one or two of the islands, and started for home with a cargo of spices by way of the Cape of Good Hope. In September, 1522, one surviving ship, bearing the auspicious name of *Victory* and with a crew of thirty-one men, arrived home after touching at a Cape Verde port.

[1] For bulls and treaties, in English translation, see *The Philippine Islands,* Blair and Robertson, ed., vol. i.

Magellan has unanimously been accorded the glory of the first circumnavigation of the globe. The voyage demonstrated conclusively that America lay between Europe and Asia. And Magellan may be said to have done what Columbus had first set out to do.

Charles V promptly claimed the Moluccas as his by right of occupation and by the terms of the treaty of 1494. The Portuguese resisted his claim, asserting their earlier possession and declaring that the islands were located on the Portuguese side of the line of 1494 prolonged around the world. The king of Portugal and the emperor tried to settle the question through a joint board of judges, but the two sides were forty-six degrees apart in estimating, mainly by dead reckoning, where the line would fall. Finally in 1529, the impecunious emperor sold his "rights" in the Moluccas to Portugal for the sum of 350,000 gold ducats (about $3,275,000 in our money, pre-war value). The voyage of Magellan was indeed very profitable to Charles V. Charles also agreed that the location of what should be taken as the 1494 line in the East should be made at a specified distance *east* of the Moluccas.[1]

The interesting history of the line of 1494 in South America cannot be pursued here, except to note that it guaranteed to Portugal, at least as against Spain, possession of a large part of Brazil. As to the eastern "line of 1494," it may be added that the occupation of the Philippines, which are west of the Moluccas, by command of Philip II early in the second half of the sixteenth century was a violation of that line as agreed upon in 1529. The islands were taken possession of by a fleet built in and sent out from Spanish America. They did not at that time produce spices, and therefore had not been occupied by Portugal, who made no serious objections to Philip's act. Their progress in population, well-being and contentment under Spanish control, down to the nineteenth century, forms one of the brighter chapters in the somber colonial history of Spain.

The line of 1494 was not recognized by the other nations of

[1] Text of the treaty in Blair and Robertson, *The Philippine Islands.*

Europe as debarring them from making settlements or establishing factories or posts in unoccupied parts of America or the East.
The papal bulls and the treaty of 1494 were not satisfactory to
them, and they fell back upon the common law that discovery must
be followed by effective occupation to give a valid title. But a
consideration of their efforts to profit from discovery and exploration may well be postponed until we have surveyed the more
immediate effects of the Portuguese and Spanish acquisitions
upon Europe.

DISTRIBUTION AND EFFECTS OF THE NEW WEALTH OF SPAIN
AND PORTUGAL

The great geographical discoveries gave to the Iberian kingdoms a large and regular income. Gold and silver poured into
Spain from the accumulations and the yearly product of the mines
of America in an annual stream. Spices and drugs and other
precious wares were brought to Lisbon yearly by the Portuguese
fleets and were there disposed of to the traders of Europe mainly
for cash. Another "ware" of at least equal value in the long run
was the African negro. The possessions of Portugal on the
Guinea coast and farther south furnished supplies of negro slaves,
who were seized or bought for trifles from African chiefs. These
were not only imported by the tens of thousands to cultivate the
large estates of southern Portugal, incidentally further discredit-
ing white manual labor and inflicting a serious wound on the
racial integrity of the Portuguese people, but they were also exported, in increasing numbers, to America. For the Spaniards in
the West Indies and in parts of South America, finding that the
Indians died out under the hardships of forced labor, turned
early in the reign of Charles V to the more docile and rugged
negroes imported from Portuguese Africa. The colonies established in tropical America in the first half of the seventeenth
century by France and England and the Dutch furnished an additional market. The traffic in negroes became enormous and was
very lucrative.

Weighed in the scales of eternal justice, which knows no privilege of race or religion, the new wealth of Spain and Portugal and of their later rivals was largely plunder—plunder extorted from, or purchased for trifles from, the defenseless natives of America, the Far East and Africa. These natives had their own bad qualities and evil habits. Cogent arguments can be made on behalf of the stronger-handed Europeans—our own ancestors among them—who exploited their weaker fellowmen, but these arguments need not be presented here.

The large and relatively steady income derived by Spain and Portugal from overseas did not have a good effect upon their peoples. The new wealth might have been employed productively in developing industry, agriculture and banking. It was employed to some extent in promoting literature and the fine arts. But Spain used her income primarily, in the sixteenth and seventeenth centuries, in the waging of incessant wars under Charles V and the Philips, and Portugal spent hers in luxury for the few and their many dependents and in the building of stately edifices. Indeed, one clear and decisive result of the easily acquired wealth was that labor—the chief mine of true wealth—became distasteful among increasing circles of the leisurely Iberians. And although Spanish industries were stimulated for a time under Charles V by the demand for goods required by the Spanish colonists in America, the rise of prices in Spain, resulting—at least in part—from the influx of the precious metals, made it cheaper for the Spanish dealers to import these goods from other countries. Prices rose throughout Europe during the sixteenth century but not so high as in Spain, which received the first impact of the new supplies of bullion. European prices were comparatively steady in the seventeenth century.

In Portugal the new wealth might have served to make Lisbon the banking center of Europe. For the Portuguese Jews were very talented and had wide connections as well as great financial capacity. They began to arrange for the widespread employment of money in productive ways. But royal politics and popular fanaticism drove them out in the first quarter of the sixteenth

century.   Many of them went to Holland, taking with them
their wealth and their wisdom.

Who, then, profited from the new wealth that flowed into the
Iberian peninsula?   Let us first trace some of the paths it took.
The Spanish funds went directly, or in the form of taxes, to state
creditors (*e.g.* to the German bankers, the Fuggers, and to the
Genoese bankers) to be borrowed again and again, finally to remain unpaid.   They passed also to the hordes of favorites and
their hangers-on in Madrid, to the foreign traders and carriers
who supplied goods, including ship materials, arms and munitions,
and to the Spanish troops fighting in Europe and Africa and on
the seas.   In the end much of the money seeped through to the
peoples of Europe who knew how to put money to work in agriculture and industry.   Among these the Dutch begin to attract
special attention as the sixteenth century wears on.

Portuguese wealth emigrated in similar ways, although none
of it went directly into warfare in Europe until after Spain
"annexed" Portugal in 1580.   Partly out of a crafty desire to
encourage the commercial peoples of northern Europe to refrain
from efforts to break the Portuguese monopoly, the Portuguese
soon gave up carrying their Oriental wares beyond Lisbon.   As
a result the French, English, Netherlanders, Baltic Germans and
others came to Lisbon to buy.   Their trading fleets grew and
their naval skill increased, for the Bay of Biscay is a tricky stretch
of water to navigate.   Each of them profited, the Dutch most of
all.   It was they who did so much to make Antwerp the main
center for the distribution of Portuguese wares in the North
and southwards into Germany.   When, in the course of the
Revolt of the Netherlands, the Spanish troops sacked Antwerp
(1576), Amsterdam, the metropolis of Holland, began to share
honors with Antwerp and after 1585 superseded it as the "Lisbon" of the North.   In fact, then, the Dutch were the chief
beneficiaries of the Portuguese monopoly in the East.   Their
commerce, shipping, industry and banking absorbed and made
productive much of the wealth that Portugal drew from the
Orient.

THE GROWTH OF COMMERCE IN THE SIXTEENTH CENTURY
LEADERSHIP OF THE DUTCH

In a survey of the commercial expansion of the sixteenth century the Dutch must be given the leading place. Their numbers were under a million. They were the soul of the Revolt against Spain, and after 1579 they alone of the Netherlanders kept up the fight, which lasted, with an intermission (1609-1621), until 1648. They fought Spain on land and sea,[1] and at the same time, in the very midst of the war, they extended their carrying trade, almost monopolized the lucrative herring fisheries of the North Sea ("Amsterdam is built on herring bones," runs the proverb), and developed manufacturing, with the aid of emigrants from the southern Netherlands. By the close of the sixteenth century their ships engaged in the Baltic trade at least equaled in number those of all their competitors put together. Their services in carrying grain, flax, hemp and, in general, materials for the building and equipment of ships, from the Baltic lands, together with cured herring and their own and German wares, to the western and southern ports of Europe, especially to Spain, Portugal and Italy, were well-nigh indispensable. Indeed, the trade with Spain was so essential to the Spanish and so profitable to the Dutch that, in spite of the Revolt, it was kept up on a large scale with only short interruptions down to 1595, when Philip II's government suddenly seized the four to five hundred Dutch ships then in Iberian harbors. In fact, the English were again complaining in 1597-1598 at the extent of the clandestine Dutch trade with Spain. No more complete proof of the enterprise of the Dutch and of the dire situation of Spain can be offered than this astounding spectacle of their extensive commerce with the power they were at the same time fighting to the death.

In the sixteenth century the English were not yet a great manufacturing people. Their chief export was still, and long remained, woolen cloth which they carried, along with miscellaneous materials, in their own vessels to the Netherlands,

[1] See chapter XXII, especially pages 446 ff.

Germany (*staple* located at Hamburg), Spain, Russia (Muscovy Co., 1555), Turkey (Levant Co., 1581) and other lands. They no longer depended on the foreigner to carry their goods abroad. But their industry still lacked the technical skill and inventive talent which immigrant Flemings, quitting their war-torn country in the sixteenth century, and immigrant Huguenots, escaping from France before and after the Revocation of the Edict of Nantes (1685), were to awaken and fructify. The English were at home on the sea and possessed a wealth of individual self-reliance and enterprise which they displayed, in the sixteenth century, in explorations and privateering enterprises, rather than in the carrying trade and commerce, in both of which the Dutch surpassed them.

The share of France in the development of European commerce in the sixteenth century was not so great as it should have been. She had taste and technical skill as well as excellent sailors in the Bretons and Normans. But the wars with Charles V and Philip II, and the civil and religious wars which ended only with the Edict of Nantes (1598), gave her little opportunity. With the establishment of peace under Henry IV, France again began to reach out in commerce and exploration.

It would be a mistake to assume that, in the sixteenth century, the prosperity of the German cities, north and south, was struck with a blight as a result of the discovery of the sea route to the East. Their productive powers were too strong, their industry, including mining, too firmly established, their functions as bankers too fully developed, to permit of any sudden fall. In fact, the German cities made progress economically, and the ships of the Hanseatic cities, especially of Hamburg and Danzig, continued to ply northern waters in increasing numbers, even though the League was crumbling. But the shipping of the Dutch and the English in the Baltic increased much faster. If the central government of Germany had been effective in the sixteenth century and able to protect German shipping in the nearer and more distant seas, the story of the commercial expansion and explorations of the sixteenth century might include what it lacks —a striking chapter relating to Germany.

The situation of the Italian cities, especially of Venice, in the sixteenth century, was similar to that of the German cities. They did not decline immediately. True, the great wars which carried foreign armies over Italian soil after 1494 injured Italian industry severely. But they did not seriously interrupt Venice's activities in manufacturing and commerce. Her artisans still fabricated their luxurious products; her islands in the Levant still produced their wine and their currants, even if the Venetian galleys ceased after 1560 to carry them through the Straits of Gibraltar. Venice still secured, by hook or by crook, over the land routes from the Far East, a limited supply of spices, drugs and other wares for herself and for the South German merchants who had for generations resorted to her for such goods. Venice had hopes that, in some way, her old leadership might be regained. She continued to be great and wealthy throughout the sixteenth century, and only little by little lost her strength. In truth the ultimate economic and political results of the great discoveries revealed themselves very slowly.

The remarkable development of industry and commerce in sixteenth-century Europe owed much to the tripling of the European stock of gold and silver in the course of that century. This came, in part, from augmented production in Europe, but more largely from the metallic flood from America. The development in question owed not a little, also, to the appearance of a new type of business organization in Germany, Holland, England and elsewhere, which was destined to become almost supreme in our day. This was the joint-stock company. It grew out of medieval business organizations and maybe simply, but not completely, described as the offspring of a cross of the medieval partnership with the "regulated company." The former needs no explanation. The latter—the regulated company—was composed of a number of merchants, each of whom traded with his own goods, but did so in association with his fellows under common regulations. The English *Merchant Adventurers* [1] were such a regulated company. The joint-stock company, on the other hand, secured its capital by subscriptions from all sorts of persons—merchants or

[1] See page 332.

not—who were willing to entrust their money or goods to the management of the officers of the company. The new type of organization was not only useful for bringing together small surpluses into a really serviceable sum-total, and for interesting many who were not merchants in commercial enterprises; it was also specially well adapted to ventures in new, semi-barbarous, or otherwise dangerous regions where the chances of loss and of gain were great. Failure would not spell ruin to the participants, since the risks were spread widely among the shareholders and loss in one venture might be more than offset by gain in the next one. The sixteenth century was peculiarly a period of risky enterprises, and that accounts in part for the growing vogue of the joint-stock company and for the gradual decline of the regulated company. The two best-known joint-stock companies were formed at the close of the century: the Dutch and English East India companies. But the new type of company was useful for simpler and often more dubious enterprises, and these must be considered in any adequate survey of the sixteenth century.

SIXTEENTH-CENTURY EFFORTS TO BREAK DOWN THE MONOPOLIES OF SPAIN AND PORTUGAL

The medieval merchants, whether on land or on sea, were keen in their search for profits and not squeamish about mishandling rivals; and brigands and pirates kept them pretty steadily on guard. Peaceful commerce hardly existed. But the quick wealth and the huge gains which poured in on Spain and Portugal after the discoveries, kindled a greed and a get-rich-quick spirit among the other seafaring peoples of Europe as well, which made the sixteenth century very different indeed from its predecessor in enterprise, daring and ruthlessness. Surely further explorations, these rivals thought, would reveal other lands of ready metallic wealth or new sea paths to the Far East. Hence feverish voyages of discovery. And while these voyages were in progress, could not the Spaniard be forced to share his gains with his envious rivals? Hence privateering and piracy at the expense of Spain. Let us consider the latter first.

We are not at present concerned with the wars against Spain, but with plunder and attack upon her commerce in time of peace. It must be remembered that, broadly speaking, there was "no peace beyond the line"—that is, outside of European waters armed attacks upon ships or settlements were occurrences which produced protests and claims for redress but did not usually involve the "mother countries" in war. It must further be recalled that the public opinion of the time (one hesitates to speak of international law) permitted self-help—that is, an individual who had suffered loss at the hands of a foreigner might recoup himself at the expense of a fellow countryman of that foreigner. It was advisable, but not absolutely necessary, before resorting to such self-help on the sea, to secure "letters of marque" from one's own government. Such letters authorized privateering—that is, the virtual waging of private war on the sea. Theoretically they restricted the holder to recovering only as much as he had lost. Actually such restriction was impossible of enforcement. Indeed, the original loss might be fictitious or the claim resulting from it might be assigned to another. The line separating privateering from piracy was a narrow one.

In the second half of the sixteenth century such privateering became almost a regular industry. Joint-stock associations were organized in Elizabethan England to finance such enterprises. The French Huguenots played the same game against Spanish shipping. It is almost certain that Queen Elizabeth had shares of this type. Certainly she received the lion's share of the booty, estimated to be worth £600,000 in Elizabethan money, which Sir Francis Drake secured in his peace-time raid against Spanish America in 1577-1580. The cost of outfitting his fleet was about £5,000. The hope of such gains kept the business going; but on the whole the losses exceeded the winnings, so that the chief advantage which the English, for example, derived was in seamanship, familiarity with American waters and a conviction of naval superiority over the Spaniards. The defeat of the Armada may be credited in part to English privateering.

The privateers were versatile. A man like Sir Walter Raleigh would set out on a voyage to explore, or to make a settlement in

Virginia, or to trade with the natives, or to seize Spanish treasure ships, according as opportunity offered. In 1562-1563 Sir John Hawkins, financed by a joint-stock group, introduced a new feature. He seized three hundred negroes on the Portuguese Guinea coast and disposed of them in the Spanish West Indies at a great profit. The trade was illegal at both ends. Sometimes this type of trader used force to compel the Spanish in America to buy his wares; sometimes the use of force was fictitious—that is, it was employed in order to afford the American Spanish an excuse for illicit trade with the foreigner.

The Spanish in America numbered perhaps 15,000 in 1550. By 1600, largely through births in America, the numbers had risen to about 175,000. They were in the main town-dwellers, depending for labor on the Indians or imported negroes. Cattle and horses, introduced from Europe, were raised. Sugar and tobacco—the former introduced from the East—were grown and became important toward the close of the sixteenth century. America had few indigenous products of value for Europe. The potato, however, was found in Peru by Pizarro and was soon carried to the Old World; and the Jesuits of South America, a century later, gave quinine to European medicine.

In accordance with the economic theory of the age, trade with Spanish America was a monopoly reserved for Spaniards. Charles V started out with liberal ideas as to emigration and trade, but a decade before he turned over the reins to Philip II these liberal ideas were abandoned in favor of strict supervision and monopoly. Under Philip control was stiffened to the point of rigidity, and foreigners were absolutely excluded from trading with the colonies. All goods destined for America had to be shipped from Seville. The business of supplying the export goods passed into the hands of a few corporations in Seville licensed by the Spanish crown. This made the collection of taxes easy. When the ships of Philip's rivals began to hover around his coasts, Philip definitely established the fleet system, which Charles V had experimented with. Under this system all commerce to and from the whole of Spanish America was restricted to two fleets of twenty to thirty vessels each per year. One went to Vera

Cruz, Mexico; the other to Porto Bello on the Isthmus of Panama. The round trip, back to Seville, consumed a year. Return cargoes for Spain, which included the precious metals, were made up only at Vera Cruz and Porto Bello. Chile and the region of La Plata (later, Argentina) could trade with Spain only via Lima, thence to Panama and Porto Bello. Corporations favored by the Spanish crown got control of the business at the American ends, where the imported goods were disposed of at annual fairs. Here again it was easy to tax the trade. Prices were very high and selections very limited, and stagnation set in after the fairs were over. The facilities for export were so slight that the Spanish colonists in America had little encouragement to develop production.

Under these discouraging circumstances the colonists—at first in outlying regions like Buenos Aires, and a little later in the more central regions—welcomed, more or less warmly, the contraband vessels of the Dutch, English and French, which furnished them the goods they needed in exchange for surplus products which were otherwise a loss. Occasional raids, like those of Drake, checked this illicit commercial intercourse. But in the long run it increased and grew, and it contributed far more to the economic progress of Spanish America than did the two annual fleets from home. Indeed, it is not fanciful to see, in the trade sympathies which originated in this contraband trade, the beginnings of intimacies which brought European aid to the Spanish-American colonies in their revolts against their mother country in the early nineteenth century. It is certain that the efforts made by the English, French and Dutch, at the close of the sixteenth century, to establish settlements in the West Indies and in Guiana—that unoccupied coastal region between Brazil and Trinidad—were largely due to a desire to have convenient bases for the contraband trade.

The efforts of the European rivals of Spain to find the precious metals in unoccupied parts of America or to discover a new waterway to the Far East form a part of the story of exploration and discovery in the sixteenth century. The French and the English —the Dutch were busy in Europe until near the close of the century—sailed up the bays, rivers, and straits of North America, seeking for the short cut to the Orient. The English devoted special attention to the search for the Northwest Passage. Their efforts to discover it are commemorated in North American waters with the names of Frobisher, Davis, Hudson, Baffin and James. Some of the settlements which the English tried to plant, largely in the hope of finding precious metals, were Sir Humphrey Gilbert's in Newfoundland (1583) and Raleigh's in Virginia (1584) and Guiana (1595). Of course, none of these reached Cathay or yielded any profit to its joint-stock backers. The French, mostly in the rare intervals of peace at home, made similar attempts. For example, in 1524 the Italian Verrazano, who was commissioned by Francis I under the stimulus of Magellan's feat, sought a westward passage to the Indies along the Atlantic coast of North America; in 1534-1536 Jacques Cartier discovered the Gulf of St. Lawrence and then pushed up the river itself, and in 1542-1543 Roberval, following his lead, made a short-lived settlement near the future Quebec. These French enterprises did not open a way to the Orient, but they did open up a profitable trade in furs which, added to codfishing on the Banks, kept the French interested in the St. Lawrence region. Probably the most single-minded efforts to establish genuine colonies of settlement and permanent homes overseas, which were made by the rivals of Spain in the sixteenth century, were due to the religious motive. These were Coligny's Huguenot settlements on an island in the bay of Rio de Janeiro, 1555, and in Florida, 1562-1564. The Portuguese soon destroyed the former, and the Spanish the latter. When the sixteenth century ended, neither the English, the Dutch, nor the French had any permanent settlement or post in America.[1]

The commercial and industrial expansion of Europe in the sixteenth century, the raiding of Spanish shipping and colonies in time of peace, the contraband trade with Spanish America, and the explorations and attempted settlements in America made by the competitors of Spain during this century, have been treated

---

[1] The very numerous efforts to reach the Far East by way of the West are set forth in Nellis M. Crouse, *In Quest of the Western Ocean* (New York, 1928).

separately for the purpose of easy exposition. They were not really separate. On the contrary, they were consciously and unconsciously parts of a larger enterprise, which also embraces the French, Dutch and English wars against Spain in the sixteenth century. The central purpose of this larger enterprise, we can now see, was to break the Spanish and Portuguese monopolies. The turning point in this Titanic effort was the defeat of the Armada in 1588, which broke, or at least revealed the inadequacy of, the united sea power of Spain and Portugal. It was, so to speak, the signal that unleashed the colonizing and maritime activities of the seventeenth century. The century of Spain was drawing to its close.

The attacks upon the Spanish-Portuguese monopolies, East and West, in the seventeenth century were made contemporaneously. It will be convenient, however, to treat them separately.

SEVENTEENTH-CENTURY ATTACKS UPON THE PORTUGUESE MONOPOLY IN THE FAR EAST

It was the Dutch and the English who undertook to smash the monopoly in the East. In 1591 an Englishman who had been sent East for the purpose, and in 1592 an experienced Dutch traveler, reported independently on conditions in the Orient. The reports indicated that the natives hated their Portuguese masters and that the Portuguese control was slack. The virtual absorption of the Portuguese Empire by Philip II in 1580 had helped Philip, but it had not increased the defensive strength of the Portuguese East. The next steps of the Dutch and the English, which were taken independently, were to dispatch what we may call test expeditions by way of the Cape of Good Hope. English merchants clubbed together. Their fleet went out in 1591, made a treaty with a sultan in Sumatra, and returned with a profitable cargo. The Dutch expedition went out in 1595, secured a treaty with a sultan in Java and brought home a very profitable cargo. Other fleets were almost immediately sent out by associated merchants. The English sent one and the Dutch many. The latter had great success. The next step was to organize aggression

systematically.   The English East India Company was chartered
in 1600, the Dutch rival company in 1602.

There were significant differences between the two companies.
The English one, a joint-stock affair, was organized by some
scores of London merchants with a total capital for the first
voyage of some £68,000.   The company was chartered by Elizabeth, but the Stuarts gave it such dubious support that it had to
be ready to wind up its affairs on short notice; and it could not
safely embark on an ambitious program involving, for example,
the costly erection of fortified posts in the East.   It located "factories" in the Moluccas—the Spice Islands—but its first fortifications were erected at Madras, India, in 1639, and they were built
for protection against European rivals, not against the natives.
The English East India Company, although not averse to using
force or to capturing stray Portuguese merchantmen, was as
purely a trading affair operating in distant regions as the early
seventeenth century knew.

The Dutch East India Company was a much stronger and more
resolute organization.   Its initial capital was at least tenfold that
of the English company.   Its management was interlocked with a
majority of the provincial governments and with the States-
General itself.   The best mercantile talent of the age was behind it.   It was regarded by the Dutch as a veritable arm of the
state, designed for the purpose of replacing the Portuguese in
the East.   The Dutch were already the chief commercial people
of Europe.   They were—or had been until very recently—the
chief distributors of Oriental wares in Europe.   They were resolved to remain such and to be, in addition, the chief importers
of those wares from the East.   Hitherto they had financed their
war against Spain largely at the expense of Spain; now Portugal
was to be levied upon as well.

The Dutch East India Company went out to the East to stay,
and from the start its agents established fortified posts, or seized
them from the Portuguese.   It does not detract from the enterprise, daring and glory of the Portuguese pioneers in the East to
say that their less virile successors were no match for the Dutch.
The Dutch in the early years of the seventeenth century, fighting

for independence and for wealth, with the tide of battle turning in their favor in the Netherlands, were virtually irresistible. In 1605 the Dutch company took Amboyna from the Portuguese and in the ensuing year it decisively defeated their naval power in the Straits of Malacca. Then bit by bit it seized the Banda group and, finally, the Spice Islands. Malacca itself held out until 1641. Ceylon was overrun by 1656, and a "factory" or two were located in India itself. Meanwhile, in 1619 the Dutch company built a fortified post at Batavia in Java, thus securing control of the southern gateway from the West into the Spice Islands. When Malacca was captured the Dutch held the Spice Islands in a tighter grip than the Portuguese ever had. The Dutch reached out to China and Japan in the pursuit of trade. The names, New Holland, New Zealand, Tasmania, and Van Diemensland, down in Australasian waters, indicate how, in the first half of the seventeenth century, they were reaching out their hands over the distant seas. In 1652 they seized the future Cape Town from the Portuguese as a revictualing station for their fleets. The spice production of the Moluccas, which they regulated most stringently, became the very heart of their Oriental trade. The Moluccas and Java are Dutch possessions to this day.

For some time the English East India Company competed for trade with its Dutch rival in and near the Moluccas. But after the Dutch had made peace in Europe by the truce of 1609, the relations of the two companies grew cold and then hostile. In 1623 the Dutch company arrested the English in Amboyna on a charge of treason and executed half a score of them ("Massacre of Amboyna"). Thereupon the English company, not getting any effective backing from the Stuart kings, withdrew from the islands and concentrated its energies upon trade in India proper. It had secured a "factory" at Surat in 1613, in spite of the armed opposition of the Portuguese fleet at Goa. After transferring its attention to India, the English company got additional "factories" at Madras, Hughli (above the future Calcutta), and elsewhere. The company paid good dividends to its shareholders at about the same rate as its Dutch rival, but on a much smaller capital and volume of business. In 1660 it was a solvent, cautious concern, without as yet any hint of ambitions for territorial power in India. The collapse of the great Mogul empire in the early eighteenth century opened political vistas which could not be disregarded.

The French did not enter seriously into the competition for the Eastern trade until shortly after 1660. Even earlier, King Henry IV, freed from war within and without in 1598, promptly embarked on colonizing and commercial ventures in both West and East. He organized a French East India Company in 1601. By 1615 it and three other similar efforts had failed. Richelieu chartered another company in 1642, but it spent its strength in a premature attempt to occupy Madagascar. It was Colbert, Louis XIV's great minister of finance, who organized the first successful East India Company for France in 1664. It established a factory in Surat four years later and started on the long rivalry with the English company that was to reach its culmination in the middle decades of the eighteenth century.

The Portuguese in 1660 retained Goa and Calicut in India, Maçao in China, and a few other unimportant and somnolent places in the East. The chief possessions remaining to them were, and are to this day, in East and West Africa, if we leave Brazil out of the reckoning. In effect the Dutch, and to a slight extent the English, had expropriated the Portuguese in the Orient. In America the Dutch did not do so well; in that region both the English and the French surpassed them.

SEVENTEENTH-CENTURY ATTACKS UPON THE IBERIAN MONOPOLIES IN THE WEST

The seventeenth-century attacks upon the Spanish-Portuguese monopoly in the West fell into two geographical divisions :—those in and near the West Indies and those on the mainland of North America.

It was a tribute of respect for the defensive strength of the Spanish colonies and for the prestige of Spain that the earlier aggressions of her rivals in the region of the West Indies were directed against the unoccupied Guiana coast and the unoccupied islands of the Lesser Antilles. The French and the English were first in the field. The Dutch became active after the organization of their West India Company in 1621, when their war with Spain reopened.

Only a few of the islands occupied by the rivals can be named here. Barbados, with a fertile soil and no fierce Carib inhabitants, became the prize of the English in 1605. St. Kitts was divided between the English and the French in 1628. Curaçao was taken by the Dutch in 1634. Martinique and Guadaloupe were occupied by the French about 1635. A little later, French buccaneers got a footing in Hispaniola and Richelieu took over their gains, which ultimately developed into the French colony of Hayti. In 1655 Cromwell's fleet captured Jamaica from the Spanish. These two attacks upon occupied islands of the Greater Antilles mark a decline in respect for the power of Spain. But the efforts of the English and the Dutch to plant colonies in the delta of the Amazon (1610-1633) were defeated by the Portuguese. Defeat also marked the courageous and sustained effort of the Dutch to gain and keep possession of all Brazil.[1]

By 1660 the Dutch, English and French had settlements in Guiana and, together with the Danes, were firmly established in the smaller West India islands. The growth of tobacco and, after about 1640, of sugar, cultivated by thousands of imported negroes, gave them a solid economic footing. Their commerce, in the aggregate, far exceeded that of all Spanish America and contributed largely to the upbuilding of their home countries.

If the rivals of Spain ignored the line of 1494 in the Caribbean region, they showed even less regard for it along the Atlantic coast of North America where, save in Florida, no Spaniard dwelt.

Early in the seventeenth century Henry IV's French Company of Acadia and Canada, chartered in 1599, turned to the St. Lawrence region. Under the intrepid leadership of the great Champlain, Port Royal was founded in 1605 and three years later Quebec was established. Champlain nursed the hope that he might find a short cut to the Pacific by exploring westward.

[1] See page 479.

Quebec became the headquarters for the fur trade and a center for the remarkable explorations upon which France in the next century was to base her claim to the whole Mississippi Valley. In 1627 Richelieu turned over the control of the young colony to another company and laid down the principle that no heretic could be admitted to it. A few years later the Jesuits came over and entered upon their notable careers as civilizers of the Indians.

The growth of French Canada was slow. In 1660 there were not over three thousand whites in it, although France itself was the most populous country of western Europe. Perhaps the reluctance of the Frenchman to leave his beautiful land is a partial explanation. Certainly the exclusion of heretics kept out of Canada thousands of industrious Huguenots who, after 1661, were becoming uncomfortable at home. Furthermore, the autocratic and aristocratic character of the government of the colony, the stiff monopoly of trade, and the lack of substantial inducements to settlers who would cultivate the soil, brought it about that the colony grew from the top and was more given to hunting, fishing, exploring and "ranging the woods," than to building up a compact, self-sufficient population. Notwithstanding these drawbacks, the colony was a promising one and offered France an opportunity to develop an empire equal to that of Spain.

The story of English colonization in North America is less romantic and more important. It began in what may be called the usual way, with a royal charter incorporating a group of merchants, some of whom were stockholders in the English East India Company, who hoped to make money out of founding a colony in Virginia. The charter, granted in 1606, promised the settlers—indeed the English common law guaranteed to them— all the rights of native-born Englishmen. That meant, in the final analysis, a voice in their own government and, ultimately, self-government. The company hoped to find gold and silver and to discover a short route to the Pacific. The subscribers under the first, as under subsequent charters, lost money; but the first settlers, who founded Jamestown in 1607—a year before Champlain founded Quebec—and their successors, although suffering terrible losses of life due to inadequate knowledge of how to live in a strange land, hung on, took root and ultimately prospered. Tobacco was the basis of their commerce, probably of their existence as a colony. The neighboring Bermudas, occupied in 1612 as an appendage to Virginia, prospered on tobacco almost from the start.

Farther north, in a less fertile region, the Pilgrim Fathers settled Plymouth, 1620. They were English Puritans who had resided for some years in the more tolerant Holland, and now sought a home in the West where they might preserve their language, institutions and nationality. If they remained in Holland, absorption into the Dutch people would be their lot unless, perchance, Spain, in the war which was to reopen in 1621, should destroy them.

In 1630 began the "Great Emigration" of Puritans from England to Massachusetts Bay, seeking escape from political and religious tyranny at home.[1] By 1643 there were more than 16,000 of them in this colony, not counting the offshoots which developed later into Connecticut and Rhode Island.

The New England colonists occupied a less fertile region than the Virginians. But they supplemented the returns from a less generous soil with fishing and manufacturing.

Maryland was founded in 1633 under a charter secured by Lord Baltimore. This charter enabled or at least permitted him to establish a colony in which adherents of the Roman Catholic faith—his faith—should be tolerated. In it Protestant and Catholic lived and prospered side by side.

In 1660 the English colonies in North America had a white population of over 75,000 and were growing steadily. Their people were self-reliant to an unusual degree and were developing effective, democratic, parliamentary institutions. The home government had done little for them beyond permitting them to emigrate at their own, or their chartered company's, expense. Disagreement with the faith professed in the homeland excluded settlers from the Spanish and French colonies; it brought English dissidents overseas by the thousands. The fiscal control of the home government was loose and intermittent. In short, the Eng-

---

[1] See pages 501-502.

lish colonies were the best demonstration of the importance of self-reliance, religious toleration (of a sort), self-government, and dependence upon agriculture and industry which was to be found anywhere in the colonial world.

Two other colonial ventures in North America demand consideration. The Swedes, whose disciplined valor had been revealed by Gustavus Adolphus, founded a West India Company which established a little colony on the Delaware in 1638. Seventeen years later the neighboring Dutch colony of New Netherland pounced upon and annexed it.

The Dutch colony had been established by the Dutch West India Company. Henry Hudson, the English navigator, sailing for a short time in the Dutch service, had sought in 1609 to find the hoped-for passage to the Pacific up the river which bears his name. Thereafter individual Dutch fur traders had frequented the region, with their headquarters on Manhattan Island. In 1623 the West India Company undertook to develop the fur trade up the river and to bring in settlers. In spite of its admirable location the colony grew slowly, for the company was primarily interested in its profits and settlers did not increase them. Nevertheless it grew, and it was governed despotically by an appointee of the company. In 1660 New Netherland with its capital, New Amsterdam, had a population of six or seven thousand; but almost half of them were immigrants from the neighboring New England colonies. These colonies were not well disposed toward the Dutch province which cramped their trade and the expansion of their settlements and, as we realize, also separated them from the colonies to the south. In the Anglo-Dutch war of 1652-1654 New Netherland barely escaped invasion. Ten years later, the war being resumed in Europe, an English fleet appeared before New Amsterdam and New Netherland became New York. At the peace the Dutch received West Indian territory in exchange for it. The loss of its only North American colony did not signify that the Dutch nation was in decline. Its commercial and financial position was never stronger. The misguided territorial ambitions of France under Louis XIV involved the Dutch in a protracted series of land wars, which fact best explains the gradual decline of Dutch economic leadership in the course of the eighteenth century.

THE CONSEQUENCES OF EUROPEAN EXPANSION

The story of the great geographical discoveries and of the beginnings of the exploitation of the outlying regions of the earth by Europe has now been told. The foundations for subsequent explorations and exploitations have been examined. A brief rehearsal may be helpful. Portugal and Spain had sponsored the epoch-making voyages of discovery and, with the aid of papal bulls, had attempted to monopolize the results. The other European states which fronted on the Atlantic, the ocean which gave Europeans easy access to the lands overseas, declined to accept exclusion from a share in the new wealth-bringing enterprises. In the sixteenth century the Dutch, the English and the French hammered at, or tried to turn the flank of, the Iberian monopolies. In the first half of the seventeenth century they broke them and ranged themselves by the side of Spain and ahead of Portugal, as rivals in the race for colonial and commercial wealth and power.

The results of the geographical discoveries cannot be finally catalogued here or elsewhere, for the forces they let loose are still molding life over the entire globe. Let us be content to touch upon a few of the less debatable consequences.

The discoveries introduced larger quantities of luxury products and many commodities new to Europeans, including foods, beverages, narcotics and medicines. They increased Europe's money and capital, with all that these imply for business, art and letters, but they also increased Europe's aggressiveness, self-confidence and greed of gain. They decreased contentment with simpler and less costly modes of life, but they also weakened the strength of tradition and made men more hospitable to new ideas. They furthermore aroused a spirit of exploration and research which would not limit its investigations to the outer material world. It is probable that the growing secularization of life owed something to the great discoveries. It is even possible that the decline in religious antipathies, so marked after 1660, may be due in some measure to the intensification of economic rivalries.

The new wealth brought to Europe by the discoveries also augmented the social and political power of the mercantile classes at the expense of the more ancient landed aristocracies. (The shift in power was obscured by the passing of merchant families into the ranks of the nobility and of nobles into the field of business. This was peculiarly the case in France and England.) Hence it may be argued with cogency that the discoveries hastened the advent of democratic government.   And, finally, the overseas discoveries helped, perhaps decisively, to transfer international leadership for some centuries to one or other of the European states fronting on the Atlantic.   The Mediterranean and the Baltic were the important seas of Europe in the Middle Ages. The Atlantic has been the dominant ocean of the modern epoch.   Its western shores now rival its eastern in world importance. Is the Pacific about to take over oceanic ascendency? That question raises the problem of the effects of the geographical discoveries upon the native peoples of the outlying parts of the earth.   It is a problem which thoughtful men of good will are now considering with anxiety.

BIBLIOGRAPHY

This period of history is unusually well equipped with bibliographical aids for the student, teacher, and scholar. The bibliographies listed below furnish not only fairly complete, but likewise carefully classified, lists of readings and other aids, and should serve as the chief bibliographical guide for both students and teachers. The books listed under the separate chapters are supplementary and represent a selection of works deemed especially valuable for differing points of view, more extended treatment, or because they appeared too recently to be included in the published bibliographies. Titles are given in full when first cited.

BIBLIOGRAPHIES AND ATLASES

DAHLMAN-WAITZ. *Quellenkunde der deutschen Geschichte*. Eighth edition. Leipzig, 1912.

Dow, E. W. *Atlas of European History*. New York, 1907.

FUETER, EDUARD. *Geschichte der neueren Historiographie*.

GOOCH, G. P. *History and Historians in the Nineteenth Century*.

GROSS, C. *The Sources and Literature of English History from the Earliest Times to about 1485*. Second edition. 1915.

Meyers' Historischer Handatlas. Leipzig, 1911.

MOLINIER, A. *Les sources de l'histoire de France*. Paris, 1901–1906.

MUIR, R. *Hammond's New Historical Atlas for Students*. Fourth edition. New York, 1921.

MUNRO, D. C., and SELLERY, G. C. *A Syllabus of Medieval History*. Rev. ed. New York, 1919.

PAETOW, L. J. *Guide to the Study of Medieval History*. University of California Press, 1917.

Philip's Historical Atlas, edited by R. Muir and G. Philip in collaboration with R. M. McElroy. London, 1927.

POOLE, R. L. *Historical Atlas of Modern Europe from the Decline of the Roman Empire*. Oxford, 1902.

POTTHAST, A. *Bibliotheca Historica Medii Ævi: Wegweiser durch die Geschichtswerke des europaischen Mittelalters biz 1500*. Second edition, 2 vols. Berlin, 1896.

PUTZGER, F. W. *Historischer Schulatlas*. Thirty-fifth edition. 1911. (American ed. 1903.)

SHEPHERD, W. R. *Historical Atlas*. New York, 1911.

THOMPSON, J. W. *Reference Studies in Medieval History*. In three parts. The University of Chicago Press, 1924.

Church and ecclesiastical affairs played a part throughout this period. For convenience the following works on this phase of history are grouped

583

together here, though they may be consulted in connection with most of the chapters of the book.

ALZOG, J. *Manual of Universal Church History*, 4 vols. Trans. from ninth German edition. 1889–1902.

Catholic Encyclopedia. 15 vols. 1908–1914.

CREIGHTON, M. *A History of the Papacy during the Period of the Reformation.* 6 vols. 1897.

Encyclopedia of Religion and Ethics, edited by J. Hastings and others. 1908 ff.

FISHER, G. P. *History of the Christian Church.* 1888.

FLICK, A. C. *The Rise of the Medieval Church.* 1909.

HAUCK, A. *Kirchengeschichte Deutschlands.* 5 vols. 1887–1911.

LAGARDE, A. *The Latin Church in the Middle Ages.* 1915.

MANN, H. K. *The Lives of the Popes in the Early Middle Ages.* 1902 ff.

PASTOR, L. *Geschichte der Päpste seit dem ausgang des Mittelalters.* 10 vols. Vols. I–XII, 1884–1927. Trans. by Antrobus.

SCHAFF, P. *History of the Christian Church.* New ed. in 7 vols. 1882–1910.

SCHAFF-HERZOG. *Encyclopedia of Religious Knowledge*, edited by S. M. Jackson and others. 1908–1912.

WALKER, W. *A History of the Christian Church.* 1918.

CHAPTER I

THE BACKGROUND OF MEDIEVAL HISTORY

GEOGRAPHY AND HISTORY

FREEMAN, E. A. *The Historical Geography of Europe*, 2 vols. Third edition by J. B. Bury. 1903.

GEORGE, H. B. *The Relation of Geography and History.* 1907.

HUNTINGTON, E. *Civilization and Climate.* 1915.

PLAYFAIR, R. L. *The Mediterranean, Physical and Historical.* 1890.

SEMPLE, E. C. *The Influences of Geographical Environment.* 1911.

THE BARBARIANS BEFORE THE MIGRATIONS

BURY, J. B. *The History of the Later Roman Empire.* 1923.

CÆSAR. *Gallic War.*

Cambridge Medieval History, Vols. I, II.

DAHN, F. *Die Könige der Germanen.* Latest edition. 1911.

DILL, S. *Roman Society in the Last Century of the Western Empire.* 1899.

EMERTON, E. *Introduction to the Study of the Middle Ages.* 1888.

GIBBON, E. *Decline and Fall of the Roman Empire.* 1896–1900.

GUMMERE, F. B. *Germanic Origins.* 1892.

HODGKIN, T. *Italy and her Invaders.* 8 vols. 1880–1899; Vols. V–VI, 1916.
———— *Theodoric the Goth.* 1891.

LAVISSE et RAMBAUD. *Histoire Générale*, Vol. I.

MUNRO, D. C. *The Middle Ages.* 1921.

RICHARD, E. *German Civilization.* 1913.

SCHMIDT, L. *Geschichte der Deutschen Stämme bis zum Ausgang der Völkerwanderung.* 1904.

GERMANIC LAW

EMERTON, E. *Introduction.* 1888.

GUMMERE, F. B. *Germanic Origins.* 1892.

HENDERSON, E. F. *Select Historical Documents of the Middle Ages.* 1892.

LEA, H. C. *Superstition and Force.* 1878.

POLLOCK, F., and MAITLAND, F. W. *The History of English Law*, Vol. I. 1895.

RICHARD, E. *History of German Civilization.* 1911.

THE ROMAN EMPIRE BEFORE THE MIGRATIONS

ADAMS, G. B. *Civilization during the Middle Ages.* New ed. 1914.

BOAK, A. E. R. *History of Rome.* 1925.

BRYCE, J. *Holy Roman Empire.* New ed. 1919.

BURY, J. B. *The Later Roman Empire.* 1923.

Cambridge Medieval History, Vol. I.

DILL, S. *Roman Society.* 1899.

FIRTH, J. B. *Constantine.* 1905.

GLOVER, T. R. *Life and Letters in the Fourth Century.* 1901.

HODGKIN, T. *Italy and her Invaders.* 1885–1899.

——— *The Dynasty of Theodosius.* 1889.

JONES, H. *The Roman Empire.* 1908.

LAVISSE et RAMBAUD. *Histoire Générale*, Vol. I.

LOT, F. *Fin du monde antique et début du moyen age.* 1927.

MUNRO and SELLERY. *Medieval Civilization.* 1907.

ROSTOVTZEFF, M. I. *Social and Economic History of the Roman Empire.* 1926.

CHRISTIANITY AND ITS INFLUENCE

ADAMS, G. B. *Civilization.* 1914.

BURY, J. B. *The Later Roman Empire.* 1923.

Cambridge Medieval History, Vol. I.

CARR, A. *The Church and the Roman Empire.* 1902.

COLEMAN, C. B. *Constantine the Great and Christianity.* 1914.

DILL, S. *Roman Society.* 1899.

FIRTH, J. B. *Constantine.* 1905.

GIBBON, E. *Decline and Fall.* 1896–1900.

HARNACK, A. *Expansion of Christianity.* 1904–1905.

HATCH, E. *Organization of the Early Christian Churches.* 1909.

LECKY, W. E. H. *History of European Morals.* 1870.

MCCABE, J. *St. Augustine.* 1903.

RAMSAY, W. M. *The Church in the Roman Empire.* 1894.

CHAPTER II

ROMAN OR TEUTON

376–565

TEUTONS WITHIN THE EMPIRE

BRYCE, J. *Holy Roman Empire.* 1919.

Cambridge Medieval History, Vol. I.

DALTON, O. M.   *The Letters of Sidonius.*   1914.
DILL, S.   *Roman Society.*   1899.
EMERTON, E.   *Introduction.*   1888.
GLOVER, T.   *Life and Letters in the Fourth Century.*   1901.
HADDON, A. C.   *The Wanderings of Peoples.*   1911.
HODGKIN, T.   *Italy and her Invaders.*   1885–1899.
HUTTON, E.   *Attila and his Huns.*   1915.
PETRIE, W. M. F.   *Migrations.*   1906.
TAYLOR, H. O.   *The Medieval Mind,* Vol. I.   1914.

JUSTINIAN

BÉMONT and MONOD.   *Medieval Europe.*
BRYCE, J.   "Justinian" in *Encyclopedia Britannica.*
BURY, J. B.   *The Later Roman Empire.*   1923.
Cambridge Medieval History, Vol. II.
DIEHL, C.   *Justinian, et la civilisation byzantine au VI⁰ siècle.*   1901.
FREEMAN, E. A.   *The Goths at Ravenna.*   In essays, Series III.   1871.
GIBBON, E.   *Decline and Fall.*   1896–1900.
HODGKIN, T.   *Italy and her Invaders,* Vols. IV, V.   1885–1899.
HOLMES, W. G.   *The Age of Justinian and Theodora.*   1905–1907.
LANCIANI, R.   *Destruction of Ancient Rome.*   1899.
LAVISSE et RAMBAUD.   *Histoire Générale,* Vol. I.
OMAN, C.   *Story of the Byzantine Empire.*   1892.

ROMAN LAW

BURY, J. B.   *Later Roman Empire.*   1923.
COLLINET, P.   *Etudes Historiques sur le droit de Justinien.*   1912.
GIBBON, E.   *Decline and Fall.*   1896–1900.
HADLEY, J.   *Introduction to Roman Law.*   1873.
MILMAN, H. H.   *History of Latin Christianity.*   1903.
"Roman Law" in *Encyclopedia Britannica.*
SOHM, R.   *The Institutes.*   Trans. into English by J. C. Ledlie.   Third edition.   1907.

CHAPTER III

THE SEPARATION OF EAST AND WEST:

THE EAST TO 718.   MOHAMMED

THE EASTERN EMPIRE AND THE RISE OF MOHAMMEDANISM

Arabian Nights.
BÉMONT and MONOD.   *Medieval Europe.*
BURKE, U. R.   *A History of Spain,* Vol. I.   Second edition.   1900.
BURY, J. B.   *The Later Roman Empire,* Vol. II.   1923.
Cambridge Medieval History, Vol. II.
DAVIS, W. S.   *Short History of the Near East.*   1923.
DOUGHTY, C. M.   *Travels in Arabia Deserta.*   1926.

Dozy, R. P. A. *Spanish Islam.* 1913.

Draycott, G. M. *Mahomet: founder of Islam.* 1916.

Freeman, E. A. *The History and Conquests of the Saracens.* Third edition. 1876.

Gibbon, E. *Decline and Fall.* 1896–1900.

Goldhizer, I. *Mohammed and Islam.* Trans. by K. C. Seelye. 1916.

Grimme, H. *Mohammed: die weltgeschichtliche Bedeutung Arabiens.* 1904.

Hogarth, D. G. *Arabia: the penetration of Arabia.* 1922.

Huart, C. *Histoire des Arabes.* 2 vols. 1912–1913.

Hume, M. A. S. *The Spanish People.* 1901.

Hurgronje, C. S. *Mohammedanism; lectures on its origin, its religious and political growth, and its present state.* 1916.

Lane, E. W. *Arabian Society in the Middle Ages.* 1883.

Lavisse et Rambaud. *Histoire Générale,* Vol. I.

Lawrence, T. E. *Revolt in the Desert.* 1927.

Margoliouth, D. S. *The Early Development of Mohammedanism.* 1914.

——— *Mohammed and the Rise of Islam.* 1905.

Muir, W. *The Caliphate: its rise, decline and fall.* New edition. 1915.

——— *The Life of Mohammed.* New edition. 1912.

Munro and Sellery. *Medieval Civilization.* 1907.

Palmer, E. H. *Haroun-al-Raschid.* 1881.

——— *Koran.* 2 vols. 1880. (In *Sacred Books of the East,* Vols. VI, IX.)

Poole, L. *Moors in Spain.* 1903.

Rodwell, J. M. *El-Kor'an: or Koran.* 1876.

Sale, G. *Koran, commonly called the Alcoran of Mohammed.* 4 vols., 1896.

Sykes, P. M. *History of Persia,* Vol. I. 1921.

CHAPTER IV

The Separation of East and West:

The West to 700. The Monks

ORGANIZATION OF THE CHURCH

Barry, W. *The Papal Monarchy.* 1902.

Bury, J. B. *The Later Roman Empire.* 1923.

Cambridge Medieval History, Vols. I, II.

Dudden, F. H. *Gregory the Great.* 1905.

Gardner, E. G. *The Dialogues of St. Gregory.* 1911.

Gregorovius, F. *History of the City of Rome in the Middle Ages,* Vol. II. 1894–1902.

Gregory's *Pastoral Rule and Select Letters.* Translated in the Select Library of Nicene and Post-Nicene Fathers. Second series, Vols. XII, XIII.

Hatch, E. *Organization of the Early Christian Churches.*

Hodgkin, T. *Italy and her Invaders,* Vol. V. 1885–1899.

Lavisse et Rambaud. *Histoire Générale,* Vol. I.

Montalembert, Ct. de. *The Monks of the West,* Vol. II. Edition by Gasquet. 6 vols. 1896.

Taylor, H. O. *The Medieval Mind,* Vol. I. 1914.

MONASTICISM

BUTLER, E. C.   *Sancti Benedicti regula Monachorum.   Editio critico-practica.*
   1911.
Cambridge Medieval History, Vol. I.
DUDDEN, F. H.   *Gregory the Great.*   1905.
ECKENSTEIN, LINA.   *Women under Monasticism.*   1896.
GARDNER, E. G.   *The Dialogues of St. Gregory* (Legends about St. Benedict).
GASQUET, F. A.   *Rule of St. Benedict.*   1908.
────── *English Monastic Life.*   1905.
HANNAY, J. O.   *The Spirit and Origin of Christian Monasticism.*   1903.
HARNACK, A.   *Monasticism: its ideals and history and the confessions of St.
   Augustine.*   1901.   Trans. by E. E. Kellett and F. H. Marseille.
HENDERSON, E. F.   *Documents.*   1892.
LEA, H. C.   *An Historical Sketch of Sacerdotal Celibacy in the Christian
   Church.*   Third edition.   1907.
LECHNER, P. P.   *St. Benedict and his Times.*   1900.
LECKY, W. E. H.   *European Morals.*   1870.
MARECHAUX, D. B.   *Saint Benoit: Sa vie, sa règle, sa doctrine spirituelle.*
   1911.
MONTALEMBERT, CT. DE.   *Monks of the West*, Vol. I.   Trans. by F. Gasquet.
   1896.
TAYLOR, H. O.   *The Classical Heritage of the Middle Ages.*   Third edition.
   1911.
WISHART, A. W.   *Short History of Monks and Monasteries.*   1902.
WORKMAN, H. B.   *The Evolution of the Monastic Ideal.*   1913.

CHRISTIANITY IN THE BRITISH ISLES

BEARD, C. A.   *Introduction to the English Historians.*   1906.
Bede's Ecclesiastical History of England.   Trans. by A. M. Sellar.   1912.
BROWNE, G. F.   *Boniface of Crediton.*   1910.
BURY, J. B.   *The Life of St. Patrick.*   1905.
Cambridge Medieval History, Vol. II.
CUTTS, E. L.   *St. Augustine of Canterbury.*   1895.
DUDDEN, F. H.   *Gregory the Great*, Vol. II.   1905.
HOLMES, T. S.   *The Origin and Development of the Christian Church in Gaul
   during the First Six Centuries of the Christian Era.*   1911.
HOWORTH, H. H.   *Saint Augustine of Canterbury.*   1913.
HUNT, W.   *The English Church, 597–1066.*   1901.
KURTH, G.   *Saint Boniface.*   Fourth edition.   1913.
LAVISSE et RAMBAUD.   *Histoire Générale*, Vol. I.
Life of St. Boniface by Willibald.   Trans. by Robinson.   1916.
Life of St. Columban by the Monk Jonas.   In *Translations and Reprints, Uni-
   versity of Pennsylvania*, II, No. 7.
MASON, A. J.   *The Mission of St. Augustine to England.*   1897.
MONTALEMBERT.   *Monks of the West.*
MUNRO and SELLERY.   *Medieval Civilization.*
TAYLOR, H. O.   *Medieval Mind*, Vol. I.
ZIMMER, H.   *The Celtic Church in Britain and Ireland.*   1912.

CHAPTER V

The Rise of the Frankish Empire to 850

THE FRANKS BEFORE CHARLEMAGNE

Bémont and Monod. *Medieval Europe.*
Bryce, J. *Holy Roman Empire.*
Cambridge Medieval History, Vol. II.
Caspar, E. *Pippin und die römische Kirche.* 1914.
Dahn, F. *Die Könige der Germanen.* 1911.
Emerton, E. *Introduction.*
History of the Franks by Gregory, Bishop of Tours. Selections translated with notes by E. Brehaut. 1916.
Hodgkin, T. *Charles the Great.* 1897.
—— *Italy and her Invaders.*
Kitchin, G. W. *A History of France*, Vol. I. 1899.
Kurth, G. *Clovis.* Second edition. 1901.
Lavisse, E. *Histoire de France*, Vol. II.
Lavisse et Rambaud. *Histoire Générale*, Vol. I.
Sergeant, L. *The Franks.* 1898.

THE FRANKS UNDER CHARLEMAGNE

Cambridge Medieval History, Vol. II.
Davis, H. W. C. *Charlemagne: the hero of two nations.* 1899.
Duchesne, L. *The Beginnings of the Temporal Sovereignty of the Popes, 754–1073.* 1908.
Emerton, E. *Introduction.*
Gibbon, E. *Decline and Fall.*
Grant, A. J. *Early Life of Charlemagne.* 1907.
Gregorovius, F. *Rome in the Middle Ages*, Vol. II.
Henderson, E. F. *Documents.*
Hodgkin, T. *Charles the Great.* 1897.
—— *Italy and her Invaders.*
Kitchin, G. W. *History of France*, Vol. I. 1899.
Lavisse, E. *Histoire de France*, Vol. II.
Lavisse et Rambaud. *Histoire Générale*, Vol. I.
Lea, H. C. *Studies in Church History.* 1883.
Mombert, J. I. *Charles the Great.* 1888.
Oman, C. W. C. *The Dark Ages.* 1894.
Sergeant, L. *The Franks.*
Villari, P. *The Barbarian Invasions of Italy.* 1902.

ECONOMIC LIFE AND POLICY

Blanqui, J. A. *History of Political Economy.* 1880.
Cunningham, W. *Western Civilization in Its Economic Aspects.* 1900.
Day, Cline. *A History of Commerce.* 1907.
Richard, E. *German Civilization.*
Translations and Reprints from Original Sources in European History, University of Pennsylvania, Vol. III, No. 2.

REVIVAL OF THE IMPERIAL T.TLE IN THE WEST, 800 A.D.

BRYCE, J. *Holy Roman Empire.*
Cambridge Medieval History, Vol. II.
DUNCALF and KREY. *Parallel Source Problems in Medieval History.*
EMERTON, E. *Introduction.*
FISHER, H. *The Medieval Empire.* 1898.
HODGKIN, T. *Charles the Great.* 1897.

REVIVAL OF LEARNING AT THE COURT OF CHARLES

BROWNE, G. F. *Alcuin of York.* 1908.
GASKOIN, C. J. B. *Alcuin: his life and his work.* 1904.
KER, W. P. *The Dark Ages.* 1904.
MANITIUS, M. *Geschichte der lateinischen Literatur*, Vol. I. 1911.
MULLINGER, J. B. *The Schools of Charles the Great.* 1877.
POOLE, R. L. *Illustrations of the History of Medieval Thought.* 1884.
SANDYS, J. E. *A History of Classical Scholarship*, Vol. I. 1903–1906.
TAYLOR, H. O. *Medieval Mind.*
THORNDIKE, L. *History of Magic and Experimental Science in the Middle Ages.* 1923.
WEST, A. F. *Alcuin and the Rise of the Christian Schools.* 1892.

CHAPTER VI

The Beginnings of Feudalism
Europe 850–1050

THE NORTHMEN

BEAZLEY, C. R. *The Dawn of Modern Geography*, Vol. II. 3 vols. 1897–1906.
Cambridge Medieval History, Vol. III.
DU CHAILLU, P. B. *Viking Age.* 2 vols. 1889.
GJERSET, K. *History of the Norwegian People.* 1915.
HASKINS, C. H. *The Normans in European History.* 1915.
KEARY, C. F. *The Vikings in Western Christendom.* 1891.
LARSON, L. M. *Canute the Great.* 1912.
LAVISSE et RAMBAUD. *Histoire Générale*, Vol. II.
MAWER, A. *The Vikings.* 1913.
PLUMMER, C. *The Life and Times of Alfred the Great.* 1902.
THORNDIKE, L. *History of Medieval Europe.* 1917.
VOGEL, W. *Die Normannen und das fränkische Reich bis zur Gründung der Normandie.* 1906.

ORIGINS OF FEUDALISM

ADAMS, G. B. *Civilization during the Middle Ages.* 1914.
ASHLEY, T. W. *Surveys, historic and economic.* 1900.

Cambridge Medieval History, Vols. II, III.

CHADWICK, H. M. *The Origin of the English Nation.* 1907.

EMERTON, E. *Medieval Europe.* 1894.

FLACH, J. *Les Origines de l'ancienne France.* 1886–1904.

FUSTEL DE COULANGES, N.D. *Histoire des Institutions politiques de l'ancienne France.* Reëdited and revised by E. C. Jullian. 1914.

GUILHIERMOZ, P. *Essai sur l'origine de la noblesse en France au moyen âge.* 1902.

KOVALEWSKY, M. *Die Ökonomische Entwicklung Europas bis zum Beginn der Kapitalistischen Wirtschaftsform.* Trans. from Russian by L. Motzkin and others. 1901–1914.

LAVISSE, E. *Histoire de France*, Vol. II.

LEA, H. C. *Studies in Church History.* 1883.

MAITLAND, F. W. *Domesday Book and Beyond.* 1897.

MEITZEN, A. *Siedelung und Agrarwesen.* 3 vols. 1895.

MUNRO and SELLERY. *Medieval Civilization.*

SEE, H. *Les classes rurales et la régime domanial en France au moyen âge.* 1901.

SEIGNOBOS, C. *The Feudal Régime.* Trans. by E. W. Dow. 1902.

THOMPSON, J. W. *Feudal Germany.* 1927.

Translations and Reprints, University of Pennsylvania, Vol. IV, No. 3.

WAITZ, G. *Deutsche Verfassungsgeschichte.* 6 vols. Second and third editions. 1880–1896.

THE RISE OF GERMANY IN THE TENTH AND ELEVENTH CENTURIES

BARRY, W. *The Papal Monarchy.*

BRYCE, J. *Holy Roman Empire.*

EMERTON, E. *Medieval Europe.*

FISHER, H. *The Medieval Empire.* 1898.

HENDERSON, E. F. *A Short History of Germany.* New edition. 2 vols. 1916.

KLEINCLAUSZ, A. *L'empire carolingien.* 1902.

MANITIUS, M. *Deutsche Geschichte unter den sächsichen und salischen Kaisern, 911–1125.* 1889.

THOMPSON, J. W. *Feudal Germany.*

TOUT, T. F. *The Empire and Papacy, 918–1273.* 1898.

THE REFORM MOVEMENT IN THE CHURCH

BARRY, W. *The Papal Monarchy.*

Cambridge Medieval History, Vol. V.

CHAUMONT, L. *Histoire de Cluny depuis les origines jusqu'à la ruine de l'abbaye.* Second edition. 1911.

EMERTON, E. *Medieval Europe.*

HENDERSON, E. F. *Documents.*

KREY, A. C. "The International State of the Middle Ages." *American Historical Review*, XXVIII, pp. 1–12.

LAVISSE, E. *Histoire de France*, Vol. II.

LEA, H. C. *Studies in Church History.*

MUNRO and SELLERY. *Medieval Civilization.*

SACKUR, E. *Die Cluniacenser in ihrer kirchlichen und allgemeir geschichtlichen Wirksamkeit bis zur Mitte des elften Jahrhunderts.* 2 vols. 1892–1894.

THOMPSON, J. W. *Feudal Germany.* 1927.

TOUT, T. F. *The Empire and Papacy.*

Translations and Reprints, University of Pennsylvania, Vol. IV, No. 4.

ENCOURAGEMENT OF LEARNING BY THE GERMAN KINGS

Cambridge Medieval History, Vol. III.

DRANE, A. T. *Christian Schools and Scholars.* 1909.

KER, W. P. *The Dark Ages.* 1904.

MANITIUS, M. *Geschichte der lateinischen Literatur,* Vol. I.

MUNRO and SELLERY. *Medieval Civilization.*

PICAVET, F. J. *Gerbert, un pape philosophe.* 1897.

SANDYS, J. E. *A History of Classical Scholarship,* Vol. I. 1906.

TAYLOR, H. O. *The Medieval Mind.*

WELCH, ALICE K. *Of Six Medieval Women.* 1913.

WULF, M. DE. *History of Medieval Philosophy.* 1912.

CHAPTER VII

THE RISING POWER OF THE CHURCH
EUROPE 1050–1150

HENRY IV AND GREGORY VII

BARRY, W. *The Papal Monarchy.* 1902.

BERNHEIM, E. *Das Wormser Konkordat und seine Vorurkunden.* 1906.

BRYCE, J. *Holy Roman Empire.*

Cambridge Medieval History, Vol. V.

DELARC, O. L'ABBÉ. *Saint Gregoire VII et la reforme de l'église au XIe siècle.* 3 vols. 1889–1890.

DUFF, NORA. *Matilda of Tuscany.* 1912.

DUNCALF and KREY. *Parallel Source Problems.*

EMERTON, E. *Medieval Europe.*

GREGOROVIUS, F. *Rome in the Middle Ages.*

HENDERSON, E. F. *Documents.*

LAVISSE et RAMBAUD. *Histoire Générale,* Vol. II.

MANITIUS, M. *Deutsche Geschichte.*

MARTENS, W. *Gregor VII: sein Leben und Wirken.* 2 vols. 1894.

MATHEW, A. H. *The Life and Times of Hildebrand, Pope Gregory VII.* 1910.

MEDLEY, D. J. *The Church and the Empire, 1003–1304.* 1910.

MILLER, W. *Medieval Rome.* 1902.

THOMPSON, J. W. *Feudal Germany.* 1927.

VILLARI, P. *Medieval Italy from Charlemagne to Henry VII.* 1910.

BIBLIOGRAPHY

THE EARLY CRUSADES

ARCHER, T. A., and KINGSFORD, C. L.   *The Crusades.*   1895.
BARKER, E.   *History of the Crusades.*   1925.
BREHIER, L.   *L'église et l'orient au moyen age: les croisades.*   1907.
Cambridge Medieval History, Vol. V.
CONDER, C. R.   *The Latin Kingdom of Jerusalem, 1099–1291.*   1897.
KREY, A. C.   *The First Crusade.*   1921.
MUNRO, D. C.   For essays on nearly all phases of the history of the Crusades, cf. bibliographies of Paetow and J. W. Thompson.   It is hoped that these scattered essays will soon be collected in a single work.
———   *The Crusades and other Historical Essays.*   Presented to D. C. Munro.   1927.
MUNRO, D. C., PRUTZ, H., and DIEHL, C.   *Essays on the Crusades.*   1903.
NEWHALL, R.   *The Crusades.*   1926.
OMAN, C. W. C.   *Byzantine Empire: a history of the art of war.*   1898.
PRUTZ, H.   *Die geistlichen Ritterorden.*   1908.
RÖHRICHT, R.   *Geschichte des Konigreichs Jerusalem.*   1898.
STEVENSON, W. B.   *The Crusaders in the East.*   1907.
SYBEL, H. VON.   *Geschichte des ersten Kreuzzuges.*   Third edition.   1881.
TAYLOR, H. O.   *Medieval Mind,* Vol. I.   1914.
TOUT, T. F.   *The Empire and Papacy.*   1898.
WOODHOUSE, F. C.   *The Military and Religious Orders.*   1879.

BERNARD OF CLAIRVAUX

BREWER, J. S.   Preface to Vol. IV of Opera of *Giraldus Cambrensis.*   No. 21 of the Rolls Series.
COULTON, G. G.   *Five Centuries of Religion,* Vol. I.
LAVISSE, E.   *Histoire de France,* Vol. II.
MORISON, J. C.   *The Life and Times of St. Bernard, Abbot of Clairvaux.*   1884.   Second edition.   1901.
MUNRO and SELLERY.   *Medieval Civilization.*   1907.
STORRS, R. S.   *Bernard of Clairvaux.*   1892.
TAYLOR, H. O.   *Medieval Mind.*
VACANDARD, E.   *Vie de St. Bernard.*   Fourth edition.   2 vols.   1910.

CHAPTER VIII

EUROPEAN SOCIETY IN THE TWELFTH CENTURY
THE CLERGY

BATESON, MARY.   *Medieval England.*   1904.
BÉMONT and MONOD.   *Medieval Europe.*
BLATCHFORD, A. N.   *Church Councils and Their Decrees.*   1907.
COULTON, G. G.   *A Medieval Garner.*   1910.
CUTTS, E. L.   *Parish Priests and their People in the Middle Ages in England.*   1891.
———   *Scenes and Characters of the Middle Ages.*   Third Edition.   1911.

DODD, J. *History of Canon Law.* 1884.

ECKENSTEIN, L. *Women under Monasticism.* 1896.

EMERTON, E. *Medieval Europe.*

GASQUET, F. A. *Parish Life in Medieval England.* 1907.

HEATH, S. *Pilgrim Life in the Middle Ages.* 1912.

HEFELE, C. J. *Conciliengeschichte.* Second edition. 6 vols. 1873–1890.

HENDERSON, E. F. *Documents.* 1892.

HIRN, Y. *The Sacred Shrine: a study in the poetry and art of the Christian Church.* 1912.

JUSSERAND, J. J. *English Wayfaring Life in the Middle Ages.* Eighth edition. 1905.

KREHBIEL, E. B. *The Interdict: its history and its operation, with especial attention to the time of Pope Innocent III.* 1909.

LAVISSE et RAMBAUD. *Histoire Générale*, Vol. II.

LEA, H. C. *A History of the Inquisition of the Middle Ages.* 1888.

—— *A History of Auricular Confession and Indulgences in the Latin Church.* 3 vols. 1896.

—— *Studies in Church History.* 1883.

LUCHAIRE, A. *Social France at the Time of Philip Augustus.* 1912.

—— *Manuel des institutions françaises.* 1892.

MCCABE, J. *Peter Abelard.* 1901.

MEDLEY, D. J. *The Church and the Empire, 1003–1304.* 1910.

MONTALEMBERT. *Monks of the West.*

POLLOCK, F., and MAITLAND, F. W. *The History of English Law before the Time of Edward I.* Second edition. 1898.

POOLE, R. L. *Lectures on the History of the Papal Chancery down to the Time of Innocent III.* 1915.

—— *Illustrations of the History of Medieval Thought.* 1884.

POWER, EILEEN. *Medieval English Nunneries c. 1275–1535.* 1922.

RASHDALL, H. *The Universities of Europe in the Middle Ages.* 1895.

TAYLOR, H. O. *The Medieval Mind.*

Translations and Reprints, University of Pennsylvania, Vols. II, IV.

VACANDARD, E. *The Inquisition.* Trans. by P. L. Conway. 1908.

VINOGRADOFF, P. *Roman Law in Medieval Europe.* 1909.

THE NOBILITY

ASHTON, J. *Romances of Chivalry.* 1887.

Aucassin et Nicolette. Trans. by A. Lang. 1887. Also in Everyman's Library.

BATESON, M. *Medieval England.*

BURY, J. B. *Romances of Chivalry on Greek Soil.* 1911.

CHAYTOR, H. J. *The Troubadours.* 1912.

CORNISH, F. W. *Chivalry.* 1901.

CUTTS, E. L. *Scenes and Characters.* Third edition. 1911.

DAVIS, W. S. *Life on a Medieval Barony.* 1923.

DELBRUCK, H. *Geschichte der Kriegskunst*, Vol. III. 1902.

BIBLIOGRAPHY 595

EMERTON, E. *Medieval Europe.*

GAUTIER, L. *La Chevalerie.* Third edition. 1895.

HASKINS, C. H. *Studies in Norman Institutions.* 1917.

JUSSERAND, J. J. *English Wayfaring Life.* 1905.

LANGLOIS, C. V. *La Société française au XIIIe siècle d'après dix Romans d'aventure.* Third edition. 1911.

LAVISSE, E. *Histoire de France,* Vols. II, IV.

LINTON, E. L. "The Women of Chivalry." In *Fortnightly Review,* Vol. XLVIII; pp. 559–579.

LUCHAIRE, A. *Social France.*

MUNRO and SELLERY. *Medieval Civilization.*

OMAN, C. W. C. *A History of the Art of War.* 1898.

SEIGNOBOS, C. *The Feudal Régime.* Trans. by E. W. Dow. 1902.

SMITH, J. H. *The Troubadours at Home.* 2 vols. 1899.

Song of Roland. Trans. by L. Bacon.

Tales from Old French. Trans. by Isabel Butler. 1910.

TAYLOR, H. O. *Medieval Mind,* Vol. I.

TILLEY, A. A. *Medieval France.* 1922.

Translations and Reprints, University of Pennsylvania, Vol. IV, No. 3.

VIOLLET-LE-DUC, E. *Annals of a Fortress.* 1875.

WRIGHT, T. *Homes of Other Days.* 1871.

THE CULTIVATORS OF THE SOIL

ASHLEY, W. J. *An Introduction to English Economic History and Theory,* Vol. I. 1888–1893.

BATESON, M. *Medieval England.*

CHEYNEY, E. P. *An Introduction to the Industrial and Social History of England.* 1901.

COULTON, G. *The Medieval Village.*

DAVENPORT, F. G. *Economic Development of a Norfolk Manor.* 1906.

DAVIS, W. S. *Life on a Medieval Barony.*

DELISLE, L. *Etudes sur la condition de la classe agricola et sur l'état de l'agriculture en Normandie pendant le moyen age.* 1851.

GRAS, N. S. B. *A History of Agriculture.* 1925.

INAMA-STERNEGG, K. T. VON. *Deutsche Wirtschaftsgeschichte.* 3 vols in 4. Fifth edition. 1879–1901.

JESSOP, A. *The Coming of the Friars.* 1889.

LAMPRECHT, K. *Deutsches Wirtschaftsleben im Mittelalter.* 3 vols in 4. 1885–1886.

LIPSON, E. *Introduction to the Economic History of England.* 1915.

LUCHAIRE, A. *Social France.* Trans. by E. B. Krehbiel. 1912.

POWER, EILEEN. *Medieval People.* 1901.

SEE, H. *Les Classes rurales.*

SEEBOHM, F. *The English Village Community.* Fourth edition. 1890.

SEIGNOBOS, C. *The Feudal Régime.*

Translations and Reprints, University of Pennsylvania, Vol. III.

Walter of Henley's Husbandry. Edited by Elizabeth Lamond. 1890.

CHAPTER IX

THE AGE OF THE CHIVALROUS KINGS
EUROPE 1150–1200

FREDERICK BARBAROSSA

BALZANI, U. *The Popes and the Hohenstaufen.* 1888.
BARRY, W. *The Papal Monarchy.*
BRYCE, J. *Holy Roman Empire.*
BUTLER, W. F. *The Lombard Communes.* 1906.
Cambridge Medieval History, Vol. V.
COULTON, G. G. *From Francis to Dante:* translations from the chronicle of the Franciscan, Salimbene (1221–1288). 1907.
EMERTON, E. *Medieval Europe.*
FISHER, H. A. L. *The Medieval Empire.*
HAMPE, K. *Deutsche Kaisergeschichte in der Zeit der Salier und Staufer.* Second edition. 1912.
HENDERSON, E. F. *A Short History of Germany.* 1916.
MEDLEY, D. J. *The Church and the Empire.* 1910.
POOLE, A. *Henry the Lion.* 1912.
SEDGWICK, H. D. *Italy in the Thirteenth Century,* Vol. I. 1912.
TOUT, T. F. *The Empire and Papacy.*

THE THIRD CRUSADE

ARCHER, T. A. *The Crusade of Richard I.* 1889.
CARTELLIERI, A. *Philipp II Augustus.* 3 vols. 1899–1910.
Chronicles of the Crusades. 1848.
NORGATE, K. *Richard the Lion Heart.* 1924.
POOLE, S. L. *Saladin and the Fall of the Kingdom of Jerusalem.* 1898.

HENRY II

ADAMS, G. B. *History of England, 1066–1216.* 1905.
ADAMS, G. B. *The Origin of the English Constitution.* 1920.
BIGELOW, M. M. *History of Procedure in England, 1066–1204.* 1880.
BÖHMER, H. *Kirche und Staat in England und in der Normandie im XI und XII Jahrhundert.* 1899.
BRUNNER, H. *Die Entstehung der Schwurgerichte.* 1872.
DAVIS, H. W. C. *England under the Normans and Angevins.* 1905.
GREEN, MRS. J. R. *Henry II.* 1888.
MAITLAND, F. W. *Roman Canon Law in the Church of England.* 1898.
MORRIS, JOHN. *The Life and Martyrdom of St. Becket.* 1885.
NORGATE, KATE. *England under the Angevin Kings.* 1887.
RAMSAY, J. H. *The Angevin Empire.* 1903.
SALZMAN, L. F. *Henry II.* 1914.
STEPHENS. *The English Church from the Norman Conquest to the Time of Edward I.*
STUBBS, W. *Early Plantagenets.* 1891.
STUBBS, W. *Historical Introductions to the Rolls Series.* 1902.
WHITE, A. B. *Making of the English Constitution.* New edition. 1925.

CHAPTER X

The Age of Innocent III
1198–1216

INNOCENT III AND THE CRUSADES

Cambridge Medieval History, Vol. IV.

GERLAND, E. *Geschichte des lateinischen Kaiserreiches von Konstantinopel.* 1905.

GRAY, G. E. *The Crusade of the Children in the Thirteenth Century.* 1870.

LUCHAIRE, A. *Innocent III.* 6 vols. 1905–1908.

MUNRO. "The Children's Crusade." *American Historical Review*, XIX, 516–524.

OMAN, C. *Byzantine Empire.* 1892.

PEARS, E. *The Fall of Constantinople.* 1886.

Translations and Reprints, University of Pennsylvania, Vol. III, No. 1.

Villehardouin's Chronicle of the Fourth Crusade. (In *Everyman's Library* and other editions.)

INNOCENT III AND THE STATES OF EUROPE

BARRY, W. *The Papal Monarchy.*

EMERTON, E. *Medieval Europe.*

LUCHAIRE, A. *Innocent III.*

PACKARD, S. R. *Europe and the Church under Innocent III.* 1927.

THATCHER and McNEAL. *A Source Book of Medieval History.* 1905.

TOUT, T. F. *The Empire and Papacy.*

HERESIES AND THE INQUISITION

BARRY, W. *The Papal Monarchy.*

COMBA, E. *History of the Waldenses.* 1889.

EMERTON, E. *Medieval Europe.*

HOLLAND, F. M. *Rise of Intellectual Liberty.* 1885.

LAVISSE, E. *Histoire de France*, Vol. III.

LAVISSE et RAMBAUD. *Histoire Générale*, Vol. II.

LEA, H. C. *A History of the Inquisition.* 1888.

LUCHAIRE, A. *Innocent III*, Vol. II.

MUNRO and SELLERY. *Medieval Civilization.*

POOLE, R. L. *Illustrations of the History of Medieval Thought.* 1884.

TRENCH, R. C. *Lectures on Medieval Church History.* 1878.

VANCANDARD, E. *The Inquisition.* Trans. by L. Conway. 1908.

FRANCISCANS AND DOMINICANS

BARRY, W. *The Papal Monarchy.*

BREWER, J. S. *Monumenta Franciscana*, Vol. I, Preface. No. 4 Rolls Series. 1858.

Brother Leo's Mirror of Perfection. 1903. (Temple Classics.)
COULTON, G. G. *From St. Francis to Dante.* 1907.
CUTHBERT, FATHER. *Life of St. Francis of Assisi.* 1912.
GUIRAUD, J. *Saint Dominic.* 1901.
HENDERSON, E. F. *Documents.* 1892.
JESSOP, A. *The Coming of the Friars.*
JÖRGENSON, J. *St. Francis of Assisi.* 1912.
LEA, H. C. *A History of the Inquisition.* 1888.
SABATIER, P. *Life of St. Francis of Assisi.* 1894.
TAYLOR, H. O. *Medieval Mind,* Vol. I.
The Little Flowers, and the Life of St. Francis, with the Mirror of Perfection. 1910. (Everyman's Library.)

CHAPTER XI

FREDERICK II AND THE COLLAPSE OF THE EMPIRE
1215–1273

FREDERICK II

ALLSHORN, L. *Stupor Mundi: the life and times of Frederick II.* 1912.
BALZANI, U. *The Popes and the Hohenstaufen.* 1888.
BARRY, W. *The Papal Monarchy.*
BRYCE, J. *Holy Roman Empire.*
BUTLER, W. F. *The Lombard Communes.*
COULTON, G. G. *From Francis to Dante.* 1907.
EMERTON, E. *Medieval Europe.*
FISHER, H. *The Medieval Empire.*
FREEMAN, E. A. *Historical Essays.* First Series. 1871 ff.
HAMPE, K. "Kaiser Friedrich II." *Historische Zeitschrift.* LXXXIII. 1899.
—— *Deutsche Kaisergeschichte.* 1912.
HASKINS, C. H. *The Normans in European History.* 1915.
HUILLARD-BREHOLLES, J. L. A. Introduction, *Historia diplomatica Friderici Secundi.* 12 vols. 1852–1861.
KINGTON, T. L. *History of Frederick,* Vol. II. 1862.
MEDLEY, D. J. *The Church and the Empire.*
SEDGWICK, H. D. *Italy in the Thirteenth Century.* 1912.
TOUT, T. F. *The Empire and Papacy.*

CHAPTER XII

THE RISING POWER OF FRANCE
1180–1270

FRANCE IN THE TWELFTH AND THE THIRTEENTH CENTURIES

ADAMS, G. B. *The Growth of the French Nation.* 1896.
Cambridge Medieval History, Vol. V.
CARTELLIERI, A. *Philip II Augustus, König von Frankreich.* 1899–1910.

CARTELLIERI, O. *Abt Suger von Saint-Denis, 1081–1115.* 1898.
Chronicles of the Crusades (de Joinville's Life of St. Louis).
DAVIS. E. J. *The Invasion of Egypt in A.D. 1249 by Louis IX of France.*
    1898.
HUTTON, J. *Memoirs of the Sieur de Joinville.*
HUTTON, W. H. *Philip Augustus.* 1896.
KITCHIN, G. W. *A History of France,* Vol. I. Fourth edition, revised. 1899.
KNOX, W. F. *The Court of a Saint.* 1909.
LANGLOIS, C. V. *Saint Louis.* 1886.
LAVISSE, E. *Histoire de France,* Vols. II, III.
LAVISSE et RAMBAUD. *Histoire Générale,* Vol. II.
LECOY, DE LA MARCHE. *France sous St. Louis et sous Phillippe le Hardi.*
    1894.
LUCHAIRE, A. *Histoire des institutions monarchiques de la France (987–1180).*
    2 vols. Second edition. 1891.
——— *Louis VI le Gros.* 1890.
——— *Social France.* 1912.
MACKINNON, J. *The Growth and Decline of the French Monarchy.* 1902.
MASSON, G. *The Story of Medieval France.* 1888.
MUNRO and SELLERY. *Medieval Civilization.*
PERRY, F. *Saint Louis, the Most Christian King.* 1901.
PETIT-DUTAILLIS, C. *Étude sur la vie et le regne de Louis VIII.* 1894.
POWICKE, F. M. *The Loss of Normandy.* 1913.
THOMPSON, J. W. *The Development of the French Monarchy under Louis VI,*
    le Gros. 1895.
TILLEY, A. A. *Medieval France.*
TOUT, T. F. *The Empire and Papacy.*
WALKER, W. *On the Increase of the Royal Power in France under Philip*
    Augustus. 1888.

CHAPTER XIII

COMMERCE AND INDUSTRY IN THE THIRTEENTH CENTURY

COMMERCE AND BANKING

ADAMS, G. B. *Civilization.*
ALENGRY, C. *Les Foires de Champagne.* 1915.
BEAZLEY, C. R. *The Dawn of Modern Geography,* Vols. II, III.
BROWN, H. *The Venetian Republic.* 1902.
BROWN, R. *Introduction to Calendar of State Papers, Venetian,* Vol. I. 1864.
BYRNE, E. For scattered articles on Genoese Commerce see Thompson's
    Reference Studies.
CARLILE, W. W. *Evolution of Modern Money.* 1901.
CHEYNEY, E. P. *European Background of American History.* 1904.
DAY, C. *A History of Commerce.* 1907.
GIRY, A., and REVILLE, A. *Medieval Commerce and Industry.* Trans. by
    Bates and Titsworth. 1908. Cf. Ch. IX in Lavisse et Rambaud, Vol. II.
HEYD, W. *Geschichte des Levantehandels im Mittelalter.* 2 vols. 1879.
    Trans. into French by F. Raynaud. 1885–1886.

LEA, H. C. "Ecclesiastical Treatment of Usury." *Yale Review*, II. 1893–1894.

LIPSON, E. *Introduction to the Economic History of England*, Vol. I. 1915.

NOEL, O. *Histoire du commerce du monde depuis les temps les plus recules.* 3 vols. 1891–1906.

PIRENNE, H. *Medieval Cities.* 1925.

―――― *Belgian Democracy.* 1915.

―――― "Villes marches et marchands au moyen age." *Revue historique,* LXVII. 1898.

SCHOENHOF, J. *History of Money and Prices.* Second edition. 1897.

TILLEY, A. A. *Medieval France.*

WALFORD. *Fairs, Past and Present.* 1883.

WRIGHT, J. K. *The Geographical Lore of the Time of the Crusades.* 1925.

TOWNS: GENERAL ACCOUNTS

Ancient Cities. Edited by B. C. A. Windle. 8 vols. 1903–1908.

EMERTON, E. *Medieval Europe.*

European History Studies. Edited by Fling, Vol. II, No. 8.

GIRY and REVILLE. *Emancipation of Medieval Towns.*

Historic Towns. Edited by E. A. Freeman and W. Hunt. 9 vols. 1887–1893.

LAVISSE et RAMBAUD. *Histoire Générale*, Vol. II.

Medieval Towns. Dent. 1898 ff.

Translations and Reprints, University of Pennsylvania, Vol. II, No. 2.

NORTH-ITALIAN TOWNS

BUTLER, W. F. *The Lombard Communes.* 1906.

NOYES, ELLA. *The Story of Milan.* 1908.

SEDGWICK, H. D. *Italy in the Thirteenth Century*, Vol. I. 1912.

TUSCAN TOWNS

BROWN, J. W. *The Builders of Florence.* 1907.

―――― *Florence, Past and Present.* 1911.

DAVIDSOHN, R. *Geschichte von Florenz*, Vols. I-III (to about 1330). 1896–1912.

DUFFY, BELLA. *The Tuscan Republics: Florence, Siena, Pisa, Lucca.* 1892.

GARDNER, E. G. *The Story of Florence.* 1901.

HYETT, F. A. *Florence: her history and art to the fall of the republic.* 1903.

ROSS, J. A., and BRICHSEN, NELLY. *The Story of Pisa.* 1909.

SCHEVILL, F. *Siena: the story of a medieval commune.* 1909.

VILLARI, P. *The Two First Centuries of Florentine History.* 2 vols. 1894–1895.

VENICE

BROWN, H. *Venice: An Historical sketch of the Republic.* Second edition. 1895.

―――― *The Venetian Republic.* 1902.

DIEHL, C. *Une république patricienne: Venise.* 1915.

HAZLITT, W. C. *The Venetian Republic.* 2 vols. Fourth edition. 1915.

MOLMENTI, P. G. *La Storia di Venezia nella vita privata.* Third edition, 3 vols., 1903–1908. Trans. by H. F. Brown, 6 vols., 1906–1908.
THAYER, W. R. *A Short History of Venice.* 1905.

FLEMISH TOWNS

BLOK, P. J. *History of the People of the Netherlands,* Vol. I. 5 vols. 1898–1912.
PIRENNE, H. *Belgian Democracy.* 1915.

FRENCH TOWNS

Cambridge Medieval History, Vol. V.
LUCHAIRE, A. *Social France.*
——— *Les communes françaises a l'époque des Capetiens directs.* 1890. New edition by L. Halphen, 1911.
MASSON, G. *The Story of Medieval France.*

GERMAN TOWNS

HEGEL, K. *Städte und Gilden der Germanischen Völker im Mittelalter.* 2 vols. 1891.
——— *Die Entstehung des deutschen Städtewesens.* 1898.
KING, W. *Chronicles of Three Free Cities, Hamburg, Bremen, Lübeck.* 1914.
MUNRO and SELLERY. *Medieval Civilization.*
VINCENT, J. M. *Municipal Problems in Medieval Switzerland.* 1905. (Johns Hopkins University Studies, Series XXIII.)
ZIMMER, HELEN. *The Hansa Towns.* 1889.

CHAPTER XIV

EDUCATION AND LEARNING
TO THE CLOSE OF THE THIRTEENTH CENTURY

THE UNIVERSITIES

Cambridge Medieval History, Vol. V.
DENIFLE, H. *Die Entstehung der Universitäten des Mittelalters bis 1400,* Vol. I. 1885.
DUNCALF and KREY. *Parallel Source Problems.*
HASKINS, C. H. *The Rise of the Universities.* 1923.
JESSOP, A. *Coming of the Friars.*
LAVISSE, E. *Histoire de France,* Vol. III.
LUCHAIRE, A. *Social France.*
——— *L'université de Paris sous Philippe-August.* 1889.
MUNRO and SELLERY. *Medieval Civilization.*
NORTON, A. O. *Readings in the History of Education: Medieval Universities.* 1909.
PAETOW, L. J. *The Arts Course at the Medieval Universities.* 1910.
POOLE, R. L. *Illustrations of the History of Medieval Thought.*

RAIT, R. S.   *Life in the Medieval University.*   1912.

RASHDALL, H.   *The Universities of Europe in the Middle Ages.*   2 vols. in 3. 1895.

SYMONDS, J. A.   *Wine, Women and Song.*   1884.

TAYLOR, H. O.   *Medieval Mind.*

TILLEY, A. A.   *Medieval France.*

Translations and Reprints, University of Pennsylvania, Vol. II, No. 3.

ADVANCEMENT IN LEARNING: PHILOSOPHY AND THEOLOGY

ALLBUTT, T. C.   *Science and Medieval Thought.*   1901.

Cambridge Medieval History, Vol. V.

CHARLES, E.   *Roger Bacon: Sa vie, ses ouvrages, ses doctrines.*   1861.

CONWAY, P.   *St. Thomas Aquinas, of the Order of Preachers.*   1911.

GHELLINCK, J. DE.   *Le Mouvement theologique du XIIᵉ siècle.*   1914.

GRABMANN, M.   *Thomas von Aquin: eine Einführung in seine Persönlichkeit und Gedankenwelt.*   1912.

HASKINS, C. H.   *The Renaissance of the Twelfth Century.*   1927.

———   *Studies in the History of Medieval Science.*   1924.

Introduction to Alexander Neckam, De naturis rerum.   Edited by T. Wright. Rolls Series.   1863.

LAVISSE et RAMBAUD.   *Histoire Générale,* Vol. II.

MUNRO and SELLERY.   *Medieval Civilization.*

PICAVET, F.   *Essais sur l'histoire générale et comparée des theologies et des philosophies medievales.*   1913.

Roger Bacon Essays.   Edited by A. G. Little.   1914.

SEDGWICK, H. D.   *Italy in the Thirteenth Century,* Vol. II.

SERTILLANGES, A. D.   *Saint Thomas d'Aquin.*   2 vols.   1910.

SORTAIS, G.   *Histoire de la philosophie ancienne.*   1912.

TAYLOR, H. O.   *Medieval Mind,* Vol. II.

THORNDIKE, L.   *A History of Magic and Experimental Science during the first Thirteen Centuries of our Era.*   2 vols.   1923.

TOWNSEND, W. J.   *The Great Schoolmen.*   1881.

VAUGHN, R. W. B.   *The Life and Labours of St. Thomas of Aquin.*   1871–1872.

WEBB, C. C. J.   *Studies in the History of Natural Theology,* part III.   No. 4. 1915.

WRIGHT, J. K.   *The Geographical Lore of the Time of the Crusades.*   1925.

WULF, M. DE.   *History of Medieval Philosophy.*   Trans. by P. Coffey.   1909.

CHAPTER XV

THE DEVELOPMENT OF THE FINE ARTS TO 1300

ADAMS, HENRY.   *Mont-Saint-Michel and Chartres.*   1913.

ARNOLD, H.   *Stained Glass of the Middle Ages in England and France.*   1913.

BERENSON, B.   *Florentine Painters of the Renaissance.*   Third edition.   1909.

BURCKHARDT, J.   *The Cicerone: or Art Guide to Painting in Italy.*   New impression, 1908.   Trans. by Mrs. A. H. Clough.   1873.

CRAM, R. A.   *Six Lectures on Architecture.*   1917.

—— *The Substance of Gothic.* 1917.

CROWE, J. A., and CAVALCASELLE, G. B. *A New History of Painting in Italy.* 3 vols. 1908–1909.

FAURE, E. *History of Art.* Trans. by W. Pach. 4 vols. 1922.

GARDNER, A. *French Sculpture of the Thirteenth Century.* 1915.

JACKSON, T. G. *Byzantine and Romanesque Architecture.* 2 vols. 1913.

—— *Gothic Architecture in France, England and Italy.* 2 vols. 1915.

MALE, E. *L'art religieux du XIIIᵉ siècle en France.* Trans. by Dora Nussey. Third edition, revised. 1910.

MARQUAND, A., and FROTHINGHAM, A. *A Text-book of the History of Sculpture.* 1896.

MOORE, C. H. *The Development and Character of Gothic Architecture.* 1890. Second edition, enlarged, 1899. Reprint, 1904.

—— *The Medieval Church Architecture of England.* 1912.

MUTHER. *History of Painting.* 1907.

NORTON, C. E. *Historical Studies of Church-building in the Middle Ages.* 1880.

NUSSEY, DORA. *Religious Art in France.* 1913.

PERKINS, F. M. *Giotto.* 1902.

PORTER, A. K. *Medieval Architecture.* 2 vols. 1909. New edition, 1912.

PRIOR, E. S. *History of the Gothic Art in England.* 1900.

REINACH, S. *Apollo: an illustrated manual of the history of art.* New edition. 1914.

RUSKIN, J. *Mornings in Florence.* 1876.

SEDGWICK, H. D. *Italy in the Thirteenth Century.*

STURGIS, R., and FROTHINGHAM, A. L. *A History of Architecture*, Vols. I-IV. 1906–1915.

TILLEY, A. A. *Medieval France.*

VASARI, G. *Lives of Seventy of the Most Eminent Painters, Sculptors and Architects.* Edited by E. W. Blashfield and A. A. Hopkins. 4 vols. Temple Classics. 1902.

ZIMMERMAN, M. G. *Giotto und die Kunst italiens im Mittelalter*, Vol. I. 1899.

CHAPTER XVI

ENGLAND, FRANCE AND THE PAPACY
EUROPE 1300–1386

FRANCE AND ENGLAND

ADAMS, G. B. *Growth of the French Nation;* also *Origin of the English Constitution.* 1920.

EMERTON, EPHRAIM. *Beginnings of Modern Europe (1250–1450).* 1917.

KITCHIN, G. W. *History of France*, Vol. I.

*LAVISSE, ERNEST. *Histoire de France*, Vols. III, IV.

*MAITLAND, F. W. *Constitutional History of England.*

*OMAN, C. W. C. *History of the Art of War.*

STODDARD, E. V. *Bertrand du Guesclin.* 1897.

TERRY, S. B. *Financing of the Hundred Years' War, 1337–1369.* 1914.

TOUT, T. F. *History of England, 1216–1377.* 1905.

WHITE, A. B. *Making of the English Constitution.*

PAPAL POLICIES

BARRY, WILLIAM F. *Papal Monarchy.*

*CARLYLE, R. W. and A. J. *History of Medieval Political Theory*, Vol. V, 1928.

DÖLLINGER, J. J. I. ("Janus"), and HUBER, JOHANNES. *The Pope and the Council.* Trans. by Roberts Bros. 1870.

*FINKE, H. *Papstthum und Untergang Templerordens.* 1907.

GREGOROVIUS, FERDINAND. *A History of Rome*, Vol. V. 1900.

HERGENROTHER, JOSEPH VON. *Anti-Janus.* 1870.

*HOLTZMANN, R. *Wilhelm von Nogaret.* 1898.

*LEA, H. C. *History of the Inquisition in the Middle Ages*, Vol. III.

*SCHOLZ, RICHARD. *Die Publizistik zur Zeit Philipps des Schönen und Bonifaz VIII.* 1903.

CHAPTER XVII

POLITICS AND RELIGION IN THE FIFTEENTH CENTURY

THE PAPACY AT AVIGNON, THE SCHISM, THE COUNCILS, AND CONTEMPORARY POLITICS

Consult additional references for Chapter XVI, above, and also:

BARRY, WILLIAM. *Papacy and Modern Times.*

BRYCE, JAMES. *Holy Roman Empire.*

DUNNING, W. A. *History of Political Theories, Ancient and Medieval.*

EMERTON, EPHRAIM. *The Defensor Pacis of Marsiglio of Padua.* 1920.

*FIGGIS, J. N. *Theory of the Divine Right of Kings.* 1896.

—— *From Gerson to Grotius.* 1907.

FISHER, H. A. L. *Mediæval Empire.*

FRANCE, ANATOLE. *Life of Joan of Arc.* Cf. Andrew Lang, below.

GAIRDNER, JAMES. *Lollardy and the Reformation in England.* 1908.

GARDNER, E. G. *Saint Catherine of Siena.* 1907.

GEBHARDT, H. *Handbuch der deutschen Geschichte.* 1891.

*GREGOROVIUS, F. *History of Rome.*

HANOTAUX, G. *Jeanne d'Arc.* 1911.

HARE, C. *Life of Louis XI.* 1907.

HENDERSON, E. F. *Short History of Germany.*

*KASER, KURT. *Das späte Mittelalter.* 1921.

KRAUS, V. VON. *Deutsche Geschichte im Ausgange des Mittelalters.* 1905–1912.

LANG, ANDREW. *The Maid of France.* Cf. France, Anatole, above.

*LAVISSE, E. *Histoire de France*, Vols. III, IV.

LEA, H. C. *History of the Inquisition of the Middle Ages*, Vol. II.

LINDNER, T.   *Deutsche Geschichte unter den Habsburgern und Luxemburgern.*
   1890–1893.
LÜTZOW, COUNT F.   *Life and Times of Master John Hus;* also *Hussite Wars.*
   1909.
*MOLLAT, G.   *Les papes d'Avignon.*   1912.
POOLE, R. L.   *Illustrations of the History of Medieval Thought and Learning.*
PUTNAM, RUTH.   *Charles the Bold.*   1908.
*RIEZLER, S.   *Die literarischen Widersacher der Päpste zur Zeit Ludwig des
   Baiers.*   1874.
SCHAFF, D. S.   *John Huss.*   1915.
*SMITH, A. L.   *Church and State in the Middle Ages.*   1913.
TREVELYAN, G. M.   *England in the Age of Wycliffe.*   1899.
*VALOIS, N.   *La France et le Grand Schisme d'Occident.*   1896–1902.
WYLIE, J. H.   *Council of Constance.*   1900.
———   *The Reign of Henry V.*   1914.

CHAPTER XVIII

COMMERCE, INDUSTRY AND TOWN LIFE
1300–1500

ABRAHAMS, ISRAEL.   *Jewish Life in the Middle Ages.*   1896.
ADY, C. M.   *History of Milan under the Sforza.*   1907.
*ARMSTRONG, EDWARD.   *Lorenzo de' Medici and Florence in the Fifteenth
   Century.*   1896.
*BLOK, P. J.   *History of the People of the Netherlands.*   Trans. by Ruth
   Putnam.   1898–1907.
BROWN, H. R. F.   *Studies in the History of Venice.*   1907.
CLARKE, M. V.   *The Medieval City State.*   1926.
CRUMP, C. G., and JACOB, E. F., editors.   *Legacy of the Middle Ages.*   Essay
   by N. S. B. Gras.   1926.
*CUNNINGHAM, WILLIAM.   *Growth of English Industry and Commerce.*
*DAENELL, E. R.   *Die Blütezeit der deutschen Hanse.*   1905–1906.
DÄNDLIKER, KARL.   *Short History of Switzerland.*   Trans. by E. Salisbury.
   1899.
*DAVIDSOHN, R.   *Geschichte von Florenz.*   1896.
DOREN, A.   *Das Florentiner Zunftwesen vom 14-16 Jahrhundert.*   1908.
*GROSS, CHARLES.   *Gild Merchant.*
HEGEL, KARL.   *Städte und Gilden der germanischen Völker im Mittelalter.*
   1891.
*HELMOLT, H. F., ed.   *History of the World,* Vol. VII.   1902.
*HEYD, W.   *Histoire du commerce du Levant au moyen-âge.*   New edition.
   1885–1886.
KASER, KURT.   *Das späte Mittelalter.*   1921.
*KOTZSCHKE, RUDOLF.   *Allgemeine Wirtschaftsgeschichte des Mittelalters.*
   1924.
*LEVASSEUR, P. E.   *Histoire du Commerce de la France.*
———   *Histoire des Classes Ouvrières et de l'Industrie en France avant 1789.*
   1900–1901.

LIPSON, E. *Introduction to the Economic History of England.*
*LUZZATTO, G. *Storia del Commercio.* 1914.
PAGE, T. W. *End of Villainage in England.* 1900.
PERRENS, F. T. *Histoire de Florence . . . 1434–1531.* 1893.
*PIRENNE, HENRI. *Medieval Cities.*
SALZMANN, L. F. *English Industries of the Middle Ages.* New edition. 1923.
SCHÄFER, DIETRICH. *Die deutsche Hanse.* 1903.
*SOMBART, WERNER. *Der moderne Kapitalismus.* Revised edition. 1924.
UNWIN, GEORGE. *The Gilds and Companies of London.* 1908.
VILLARI, PASQUALE. *Two First Centuries of Florentine History.*
—————— *Savonarola.*

CHAPTER XIX

EDUCATION, REVIVAL OF LEARNING, THE FINE ARTS
1300–1500

EDUCATION

CRUMP, C. G., and JACOB, E. F., editors. *Legacy of the Middle Ages.* Essay by Adamson. 1926.
*LEACH, A. F. *Schools of Medieval England.* 1915.
PARRY, A. W. *Education in England in the Middle Ages.* 1920.
PAULSEN, FRIEDRICH. *Geschichte des Gelehrten Unterrichts.* 1885.
RAIT, R. S. *Life in the Mediæval University.*
*RASHDALL, HASTINGS. *Universities of Europe in the Middle Ages.*
SANDYS, J. E. *History of Classical Scholarship.*
*WATSON, FOSTER. *English Grammar Schools to 1660.* 1908.
WOODWARD, W. H. *Vittorino da Feltre and other Humanist Educators.* 1897.

REVIVAL OF LEARNING AND THE RENAISSANCE

In addition to the translations of the writings of Dante, Petrarch, Boccaccio, Machiavelli, Cellini, Castiglione, etc., the following are of value:

*BRANDI, K. "Das Werden der Renaissance," in *Deutsche Rundschau*, March, 1908, pp. 416–430. Cf. Goetz, below.
*BURCKHARDT, JAKOB. *Civilization of the Renaissance in Italy.* Still a classic, although his interpretation has to be modified.
BURDACH, KONRAD. *Reformation, Renaissance und Humanismus.* 1918.
*DE SANCTIS, FRANCESCO. *Storia della Letteratura Italiana.* Croce's edition. Vol. I. 1925.
*DE WULF, M. M. *History of Medieval Philosophy.* 1900.
EMERTON, EPHRAIM. *Beginnings of Modern Europe (1250–1450).*
GARDNER, E. G. *Dante* (Temple Primer). 1913.
GEIGER, L. *Renaissance und Humanismus.* 1882.
*GOETZ, WALTER. *König Robert von Neapel (1309–1343).*
—————— "Mittelalter und Renaissance," in *Historische Zeitschrift*, Vol. 98 (1906–1907), pp. 30–54. Cf. Brandi, above.

*HOLLWAY-CALTHROP, H. C. *Petrarch.* Probably the best life in English. 1907.

HUTTON, EDWARD. *Giovanni Boccaccio.* 1910.

LOOMIS, LOUISE R. *Medieval Hellenism.*

—— "The Greek Renaissance in Italy," in *American Historical Review*, Vol. XIII (1908), pp. 246–258.

*MONNIER, PHILIPPE. *Le Quattrocento.* (In French.) Brilliant book. 1912.

MUNRO, D. C., and SELLERY, G. C. *Medieval Civilization.* (Articles by Graf, Voigt and Neumann.)

NOLHAC, P. *Petrarch and the Ancient World.* 1907.

OZANAM, A. F. *Dante and Catholic Philosophy.*

PECOCK, REGINALD. *The Repressor.* Rolls Series.

ROBINSON, J. H., and ROLFE, W. H., editors. *Petrarch.* 1914. This quite supersedes the first edition.

SYMONDS, J. A. *The Renaissance in Italy.* 7 vols. To be used with caution. 1882.

*TAYLOR, H. O. *Thought and Expression in the Sixteenth Century.* 1920. Surveys the earlier epoch.

VALLA, LORENZO. *Treatise on the Donation of Constantine.* Text and translation by C. B. Coleman. 1922.

*VILLARI, PASQUALE. *Machiavelli.* 1898.

—— *Savonarola.*

VOIGT, G. *Die Wiederbelebung des classischen Alterthums.* 1893.

THE FINE ARTS

In addition to the biographies of the artists, the following are suggested:

BALCARRES, D. A. E. L. *Evolution of Italian Sculpture.* 1909.

*BERENSON, BERNHARD. *Central Italian Painters of the Renaissance*, 1897; *Florentine Painters of the Renaissance*, 1909; *North Italian Painters of the Renaissance*, 1907; *Venetian Painters of the Renaissance*, 1894.

BURCKHARDT, JAKOB. *Cicerone.* Much revised by other hands.

*CROWE, J. A., and CAVALCASELLE, G. B. *History of Painting in Italy.*

HAGEN, OSCAR. *Art Epochs and their Leaders.* 1927.

HOURTICQ, LOUIS. *La Peinture des Origines au XVIe siècle.* 1908.

HUIZINGA, J. *Waning of the Middle Ages.* 1924.

JACKSON, T. G. *Renaissance of Roman Architecture*, Part I, Italy. 1921.

KLACZKO, JULIAN. *Rome and the Renaissance.* Trans. by J. Dennie, 1926.

Leonardo da Vinci's Note Books. Edited by Edward McCurdy. 1923.

MOORE, C. H. *Character of Renaissance Architecture.* 1905.

MUTHER, RICHARD. *History of Painting.* Trans. by Geo. Kriehn. 1907.

REINACH, SALOMON. *Apollo.* New edition. 1924.

*ROBINSON, J. B. *Architectural Composition.*

*SCOTT, GEOFFREY. *Architecture of Humanism.* Second edition. 1924.

*THODE, HENRY. *Franz von Assisi und die Anfänge der Kunst der Renaissance in Italien.* Second edition. Impressive study. 1885.

WEALE, W. H. J. *The Van Eycks and their Art.* 1912.

*WÖLFFLIN, HEINRICH. *Art of the Italian Renaissance.* 1913.

PRINTING

Cambridge History of English Literature, Vol. II.
*CARTER, T. F. *The Invention of Printing in China and its Spread Westward.* 1925.
PUTNAM, G. H. *Books and Their Makers in the Middle Ages.* 1896.

CHAPTER XX

THE AGE OF CHARLES V
EUROPE 1500–1559

The *Cambridge Modern History* now becomes available and should be consulted for succinct accounts, often of great value. The standard national histories of the various countries can also be drawn upon with steady profit. Additional bibliography:

*ARMSTRONG, EDWARD. *Charles V.* Second edition. 1902.
*BLOK, P. J. *History of the People of the Netherlands.*
BRIDGE, J. S. C. *History of France from the Death of Louis XI.* Two volumes already published. 1921.
CHAPMAN, C. E. *History of Spain.* 1918.
CHEYNEY, E. P. *European Background of American History.* 1904.
*FUETER, EDUARD. *Geschichte des Europäischen Staatensystems von 1492–1559.* 1919.
GEBHARDT, H. *Handbuch der deutschen Geschichte.* 1891.
*GOSSART, E. *Charles V et Philippe II.* 1910.
GRANT, A. J. *French Monarchy, 1483–1789.* 1900.
HEFELE, K. J. VON. *Cardinal Ximenez.* 1885.
HENDERSON, E. F. *Short History of Germany.*
HUME, M. A. S. *Spanish People.* 1901.
——— *Queens of Old Spain* and other works relating to Spanish history.
KITCHIN, G. W. *History of France.*
LANE-POOLE, S. *Turkey.* 1899.
*LAVISSE, ERNEST. *Histoire de France*, Vol. V.
*LEA, H. C. *History of the Inquisition of Spain.*
——— *Moriscos of Spain.* 1901.
LYBYER, A. H. *Government of the Ottoman Empire in the Time of Suleiman the Magnificent.* 1913.
*MENTZ, G. *Deutsche Geschichte, 1493–1648.*
*MERRIMAN, R. B. *Rise of Spanish Empire.* Three volumes already published. A masterly work. 1918.
*PIRENNE, H. *Histoire de Belgique.*
RANKE, L. *Latin and Teutonic Nations, 1494–1514.* 1824.

CHAPTER XXI

THE REFORMATIONS: PROTESTANT AND CATHOLIC
HISTORICAL SETTING; GENERAL ACCOUNTS

BARRY, WILLIAM. *The Papacy and Modern Times.* 1911.
*BEARD, CHARLES. Hibbert Lectures on *The Reformation.* 1927.

BRIEGER, THEODOR. *Das Wesen des Ablasses am Ausgang des Mittelalters.* 1897.

Cambridge Modern History, Vols. I-III. Note especially Maitland's remarkable chapter in the second volume on the Elizabethan Settlement.

CURTIS, W. A. *History of Creeds and Confessions of Faith.* 1911.

ERASMUS, DESIDERIUS. *Praise of Folly.* Trans. by John Wilson, 1668. 1913.

*FRIEDENSBURG, W. "Fortschritte in Kenntnis und Verstandnis der Reformationsgeschichte seit Begründung des Vereins," in *Schriften des Vereins für Reformationsgeschichte*, Vol. 100 (1910).

HEUSSI, K., and MULERT, H. *Atlas zur Kirchengeschichte.* 1905.

HULME, E. M. *Renaissance and Reformation.* 1914.

HUMBERT, A. *Les origines de la théologie moderne.*

*IMBART DE LA TOUR, PIERRE. *Les Origines de la Reforme.* 1905-1914.

KIDD, B. J., editor. *Documents Illustrative of the Continental Reformation.* 1911.

LAVISSE et RAMBAUD. *Histoire Générale.* Vols. IV, V, VI.

Letters of Obscure Men. English trans. by F. G. Stokes. 1909.

LINDSAY, T. M. *History of the Reformation.* 1906-1907.

*McGIFFERT, A. C. *Protestant Thought before Kant.* 1911.

MONNIER, MARC. *La Reforme de Luther à Shakespeare.* 1899.

MORE, THOMAS. *Utopia.*

*SCHAFF, PHILIP. *Creeds of Christendom.* Invaluable translations of the official creeds. 1877.

SCHAPIRO, J. S. *Social Reform and the Reformation.* 1909.

*SMITH, PRESERVED. *Age of the Reformation.* 1920.

——— *Erasmus.* 1923.

*TAYLOR, H. O. *Thought and Expression in the Sixteenth Century.*

Translations and Reprints, University of Pennsylvania. Volume on the Reformation.

TROELTSCH, E. *Protestantism and Progress.* 1912.

THE LUTHERAN REVOLT

In addition to the above, consult the national histories and also:

BAX, E. B. *The Peasants' War.* 1889.

——— *Rise and Fall of the Anabaptists.* 1903.

Corpus Schwenkfeldianorum. Edited by Hartranft.

*EGELHAAF, GOTTLOB. *Deutsche Geschichte*, Vols. I, II. 1889-1892.

GRISAR, H. *Luther.* English translation in six volumes. 1913-1917.

HARNACK, A. *History of Dogma*, Vol. VI. 1914.

HAUSRATH, A. *Luthers Leben.* 1914 edition.

*JANSSEN, JOHANNES. *History of the German People.* Trans. by M. A. Mitchell and A. M. Christie. 1910-1915.

JONES, R. M. *Spiritual Reformers in the Sixteenth and Seventeenth Centuries.* 1914.

*KASER, K. *Bewegungen im deutschen Burgertum zu Beginn des XVI Jahrhunderts.* 1899.

Luther's Primary Works. Edited by Wace and Buchheim.

McGiffert, A. C. *Martin Luther.* 1911.

*Rieker, Karl. *Die rechtliche Stellung der evangelischen Kirche Deutschlands.*

*Sehling, E. *Die evangelischen Kirchenordnungen des XVI Jahrhunderts.*

Smith, Preserved. *Life and Letters of Martin Luther.* 1914.

Stolze, W. *Der deutsche Bauernkrieg.* 1908.

Vedder, H. C. *Balthasar Hübmaier.* 1905.

*Wolf, G. *Deutsche Geschichte im Zeitalter der Gegenreformation*, Vol. I. 1908.

Zimmermann, W. *Geschichte des Bauernkriegs.* 1856.

SWITZERLAND: ZWINGLI AND CALVIN

See general works, above, and also:

Baird, H. M. *History of the Rise of the Huguenots in France.* 1879.

*Calvin, John. *Institutes of the Christian Religion.* Trans. by J. Allen. 1909.

Emerton, E. "Calvin," in *The Nation* (U. S. A.), July 8, 1909.

Foster, H. D. "Geneva before Calvin," in *American Historical Review*, VIII (1903), pp. 217 ff.

——— *Calvin's Programme for a Puritan State in Geneva.* 1908.

Jackson, S. M. *Huldreich Zwingli.* 1900.

*Lavisse, E. *Histoire de France*, Vol. V. (Calvinism in France.) 1904.

*Rieker, Karl. *Grundsätze reformierter Kirchenverfassung.*

Walker, W. *John Calvin.* 1906.

ENGLAND

See general works, above, the national histories, and also:

Bayne, C. G. *Anglo-Roman Relations, 1558–1565.* 1913.

Burrage, C. *Early English Dissenters.* 1912.

First and Second Prayer-Books of King Edward VI (Everyman's).

Gairdner, James. *Lollardy and the Reformation in England.* 1908.

*Gasquet, F. A., Cardinal. *Eve of the Reformation in England.* 1905.

——— *Henry VIII and the English Monasteries.*

*Gee, Henry, and Hardy, W. J., editors. *Documents Illustrative of English Church History.* 1909.

Innes, A. D. *England under the Tudors.* 1905.

Jacobs, H. E. *Lutheran Movement in England.* 1894.

*Maitland, F. W. *Roman Canon Law in the Church of England.* 1898.

*Makower, Felix. *Constitutional History and Constitution of the Church of England.* 1895.

Ogle, A. *Canon Law in Medieval England.* 1912.

Stephens, W. R. W., and Hunt, W., editors. *A History of the English Church.* 1901.

Summers, W. H. *Lollards of the Chiltern Hills.* 1906.

SCOTLAND

In addition to the general works listed above, see:

Blennerhassett, Lady. *Maria Stuart, Königin von Schottland.*

Brown, P. H. *History of Scotland.* 1899–1909.

———— *John Knox.* 1895.

*FLEMING, D. H. *Reformation in Scotland.* 1910.

———— *Mary Queen of Scots.*

LANG, A. *John Knox and the Reformation.* 1905.

———— *The Mystery of Mary Stuart.* 1902.

*RAIT, R. S. *Mary Queen of Scots.* 1900.

CATHOLIC REFORMATION

See lists, above, church and national histories, and also:

BOEHMER, H. *Les Jésuites.* Trans. by Monod. 1910.

Canons and Decrees of the Council of Trent. Trans. by Waterworth. The introduction gives the best account of the Council of Trent in English.

FROUDE, J. A. *Lectures on the Council of Trent.* New impression. 1905.

GOTHEIN, E. *Ignatius Loyola und die Gegenreformation.* 1905.

*HUGHES, THOMAS. *Educational System of the Jesuits.* 1892.

JOURDAN, G. V. *Movement towards Catholic Reform in the Early XVI Century.* 1914.

LOYOLA, ST. IGNATIUS. *Autobiography*, edited by O'Conor. 1900.

———— *Spiritual Exercises.* Trans. by Mullan. 1914.

*REUSCH, F. H. *Der Index verbotener Bücher.* 1883.

RODOCANACHI, E. "La Reformation en Italie," in *Revue des Deux Mondes*, March, 1915.

*THOMPSON, FRANCIS. *St. Ignatius Loyola.* 1913.

VAN DYKE, PAUL. *Ignatius Loyola.* 1926.

*WHITNEY, J. P. *Catholic Reformation.* 1907.

CHAPTER XXII

HAPSBURG AND VALOIS. THE AGE OF PHILIP II
EUROPE 1559–1610

Many of the references for Chapter XX apply here. See especially Blok and Pirenne, there cited, and also:

*ARMSTRONG, E. *The French Wars of Religion.* 1892.

BAIRD, H. M. *The Huguenots and Henry of Navarre.* 1886.

HERRE, P. *Papsttum und Papstwahl im Zeitalter Philipps II.* 1907.

HUME, M. A. S. *Philip II of Spain.* 1897.

———— *Spain, Its Greatness and Decay, 1479–1788.* 1898.

*LAVISSE, E. *Histoire de France*, Vols. V, VI.

MARCKS, ERICH. *Gaspard von Coligny.* 1892.

PUTNAM, RUTH. *William the Silent* (Heroes of the Nations). 1911.

RACHFAHL, F. *Wilhelm von Oranien.* 1906–1908.

*ROMIER, L. *Les origines politiques des guerres de religion.* 1911–1913.

SEELEY, J. R. *Growth of British Policy.* 1922.

SICHEL, E. *Catherine de' Medici and the French Reformation.*

———— *Later Years of Catherine de' Medici.* 1908.

THOMPSON, J. W. *The Wars of Religion in France, 1559–1576.* 1909.

*VAN DYKE, PAUL. *Catherine de' Medici.* 1922.

WHITEHEAD, A. M.   *Gaspard de Coligny.*   1904.
WILLERT, P. F.   *Henry of Navarre.*   1893.

CHAPTER XXIII

THE EPOCH OF THE THIRTY YEARS WAR
EUROPE 1610–1660

See additional items in lists for Chapters XX and XXII, above.

BAIN, R. N.   *Scandinavia.*   1905.
*BLOK, P. J.   *History of the People of the Netherlands.*   1898–1912.
*BOURGEOIS, E   *Manuel historique de la politique étrangère,* Vol. I.   1901.
Cambridge Modern History, Vol. IV.
*D'AVENEL, GEORGES.   *Richelieu et la monarchie absolue.*   4 vols.
*DENIS, E.   *Fin de l'indépendance Bohême.*   1890.
——— *La Bohême depuis la Montagne-Blanche.*   1903.
FLETCHER, C. R. L.   *Gustavus Adolphus.*   1890.
*GARDINER, S. R.   *Thirty Years' War.*   1903.
GEBHARDT, H.   *Handbuch der deutschen Geschichte.*   1891.
GRANT, A. J.   *The French Monarchy, 1483–1789.*   1900.
*HAIMANT, E.   *La guerre du Nord et la paix d'Oliva, 1655–1660.*
HANOTAUX, G.   *La France en 1614.*   1914.
HENDERSON, E. F.   *Short History of Germany.*   1916.
*HUME, M. A. S.   *Court of Philip IV.*   1927 edition.
KITCHIN, G. W.   *History of France,* Vol. III.   1896–1903.
*LAVISSE, E.   *Histoire de France,* Vols. VI, VII.
*MOREL-FATIO, A.   *L'Espagne au XVIe et XVIIe siècles.*
——— *Etudes sur l'Espagne.*   1878.
PERKINS, J. B.   *Richelieu and the Growth of French Power.*   1900.
——— *France under Mazarin.*   1886.
*PIRENNE, H.   *Histoire de Belgique,* Vol. IV.
*RITTER, M.   *Deutsche Geschichte im Zeitalter der Gegenreformation und des dreissigjährigen Krieges, 1555–1648.*
WAKEMAN, H. O.   *Europe, 1598–1715.*   1894.
*WINTER, G.   *Geschichte des dreissigjährigen Krieges.*   1893.
YOUNG, GEORGE.   *Portugal Old and Young.*   1917.

CHAPTER XXIV

ENGLAND, IRELAND, AND SCOTLAND, 1603–1660

See list for Chapter XXI, above, especially for Scotland, and also:

*CHEYNEY, E. P.   *History of England from the Defeat of the Armada to the Death of Elizabeth.*   2 vols.   1914, 1926.
*CREIGHTON, M.   *Queen Elizabeth.*   1920.
CROMWELL, OLIVER.   Biographies by C. H. Firth, S. R. Gardiner, F. Harrison, John Morley.
FIGGIS, J. N.   *The Divine Right of Kings.*

FIRTH, C. H. *Cromwell's Army.* Second edition. 1912.

*GARDINER, S. R., editor. *Constitutional Documents of the Puritan Revolution, 1625–1660.* Has a remarkable introduction. Cf. Prothero, below.

GOOCH, G. P. *English Democratic Ideas in the Seventeenth Century.* 1927.

*GWYNN, STEPHEN. *History of Ireland.* 1923.

HUME, M. A. S. *The Great Lord Burghley.* 1898.

INNES, A. D. *England under the Tudors.* 1905.

*JENKS, E. *Constitutional Experiments of the Commonwealth.* 1890.

*McILWAIN, C. H. *High Court of Parliament.* 1910.

*MAITLAND, F. W. *Constitutional History of England.*

MONTAGUE, F. C. *The History of England from the Accession of James I to the Restoration, 1603–1660.* 1907.

POLLARD, A. F. *Political History of England, 1547–1603.* 1910.

*PROTHERO, G. W., editor. *Select Statutes and other Constitutional Documents, 1558–1625.* 1913. Has a very useful introduction.

RANKE, L. VON. *History of England.* Valuable for foreign relations. 1875.

*READ, CONYERS. *Mr. Secretary Walsingham.* 1925.

*SCOTT, W. R. *Constitution and Finance of English, Scottish and Irish Joint-Stock Companies.* 3 vols. 1910–1912.

SEELEY, J. R. *Growth of British Policy.* 1922.

SHAW, W. A. *History of the English Church, 1640–1660.* 1900.

TASWELL-LANGMEAD, T. B. *English Constitutional History.* Eighth edition. 1919.

TATHAM, G. B. *The Puritans in Power: a Study of the English Church, 1640–1660.* 1913.

*TREVELYAN, G. M. *England under the Stuarts.* Twelfth edition, revised. 1925.

CHAPTER XXV

LITERATURE AND SCIENCE IN THE SIXTEENTH CENTURY AND AFTER

LITERATURE

The best reading for this chapter will be found in the masterpieces discussed in the text. Virtually all of them can be obtained in English. The national histories and the great encyclopedias all devote attention to the literature of the different countries. See also:

Cambridge History of English Literature. Edited by A. W. Ward and A. R. Waller. Vols. II-VII.

CHAUCER. *The College Chaucer.* Edited by H. N. McCracken. 1913.

*DE SANCTIS, FRANCESCO. *Storia della letteratura italiana.* Croce's edition. Vol. I. 1925.

DITCHFIELD, P. H. *England of Shakespeare.* 1917.

EVERETT, W. *Italian Poets since Dante.* 1904.

*FAGUET, ÉMILE. *Literary History of France.* 1907.

*FRANCKE, KUNO. *History of German Literature.* 1901.

GARNETT, RICHARD. *History of Italian Literature.* 1898.

*HALLAM, H. *Introduction to the Literature of Europe in the 15th, 16th and 17th Centuries.* Antiquated in part but still useful. 1882.

HAUVETTE, H. *Littérature Italienne.* 1906.
JUSSERAND, J. J. *Literary History of the English People.* 1926.
KUHNS, O. *Great Poets of Italy.* 1903.
LANSON, G. *Histoire de la littérature française.* 1908.
SAINTSBURY, GEORGE. *History of Criticism.* 1900–1904.
Shakespeare's England. A coöperative work in two volumes. 1916.
STRACHEY, G. L. *Landmarks in French Literature.* 1923.
*TAYLOR, H. O. *Thought and Expression in the Sixteenth Century.*
THOMAS, CALVIN. *History of German Literature.* 1909.
TICKNOR, GEORGE. *History of Spanish Literature.* Rather old. 1891.
TILLEY, A. *From Montaigne to Molière.* Second edition, 1923.

SCIENCE

Here again the works listed in the text form the most important reading list. See also:

BRYANT, W. W. *History of Astronomy.* 1907.
Cambridge Modern History, Vol. IV, Chap. XXVII; Vol. V, Chap. XXIII.
CURRY, W. C. *Chaucer and the Medieval Sciences.* 1926.
HEARNSHAW, F. J. C., editor. *Medieval Contributions to Modern Civilisation.* Essay by Charles Singer. 1921.
LAVISSE et RAMBAUD. *Histoire Générale,* Vol. V, Chap. XI. 1895.
Newton, Sir Isaac, 1727–1927. A bicentenary evaluation of his work, prepared under the auspices of the History of Science Society (of America). 1928.
SINGER, CHARLES. *A Short History of Medicine.* 1928.
STIMSON, D. *Gradual Acceptance of the Copernican Theory of the Universe.* 1917.
WOLF, RUDOLF. *Geschichte der Astronomie.* 1877.

CHAPTER XXVI

THE GEOGRAPHICAL DISCOVERIES

THE PARTITION OF THE NEW WORLD AND THE ANCIENT EAST TO 1660

DISCOVERIES, EXPLORATIONS, SETTLEMENTS

ABBOTT, W. C. *Expansion of Europe,* Vol. I. 1924.
*AZURARA, G. E. DE. *Chronicle of the Discovery and Conquest of Guinea.* With valuable introduction by Beazley.
BEAZLEY, C. R. *Dawn of Modern Geography,* Vol. III. 1903–1906.
——— *Prince Henry the Navigator.* 1895.
BLOK, P. J. *History of the People of the Netherlands.* 1898–1912.
*BOURNE, E. G. *Spain in America.* 1904.
*CHANNING, EDWARD. *A History of the United States,* Vol. I. 1926.
CHEYNEY, E. P. *European Background of American History.*
CORBETT, J. S. *Drake and the Tudor Navy.* 1899.
——— *Successors of Drake.* 1900.
CROUSE, N. M. *In Quest of the Western Ocean.* 1928.

DANVERS, F. C. *The Portuguese in India.* 1894.

*DE LANNOY, C., and VANDER LINDEN, H. *L'Expansion coloniale des peuples Européens.* 1907.

EDMUNDSON, G. *Holland.* 1922.

——— *Anglo-Dutch Rivalry, 1600–1654.* 1911.

*GIBBONS, H. A. *Foundation of the Ottoman Empire, 1300–1403.* 1916.

HILDEBRAND, A. S. *Magellan.* 1924.

JAYNE, K. G. *Vasco da Gama and his Successors.* 1910.

KELLER, A. G. *Colonization.* 1908.

LANE-POOLE, S. *Turkey.*

*LEROY-BEAULIEU, P. *La Colonization chez les peuples modernes.* Sixth edition. 1908.

LUCAS, C. P. *Beginnings of English Overseas Enterprise.* 1917.

MARKHAM, C. R. *Incas of Peru.* 1910.

*MERRIMAN, R. B. *Rise of the Spanish Empire.* 3 vols. to date. 1918.

MORRIS, H. C. *History of Colonization.* 1900.

NEWTON, A. P. *Colonizing Activities of the English Puritans.* 1914.

NUNN, GEORGE E. *Geographical Conceptions of Columbus.* 1924.

OLSON, J. E., and BOURNE, E. G., editors. *The Northmen, Columbus and Cabot.*

ROSCHER, W. *Spanish Colonial System.* 1904.

*RUGE, S. *Geschichte des Zeitalters der Entdeckungen.* 1881.

SCHÄFER, DIETRICH. *Die Neuzeit,* Vol. I.

*SHEPHERD, W. R. "The Expansion of Europe," in *Political Science Quarterly,* 1919.

STEPHENS, H. M. *Albuquerque and the Portuguese Settlements in India.* 1897.

*VAN LOON, H. W. *Golden Book of the Dutch Navigators.* 1916.

VIGNAUD, H. *Le vrai Christophe Colomb et la Légende.* 1921.

WOODWARD, W. H. *Short History of the Expansion of the British Empire.* 1924.

ZINKEISEN, J. W. *Geschichte des osmanischen Reiches in Europa.* Old but still useful. 1840–1863.

NEW FORMS OF ECONOMIC ORGANIZATION: AGRICULTURE

See bibliography for Chapter XVII. See also:

BONASSIEUX, P. *Les Grandes Compagnies de Commerce.*

CARR, C. T. *Select Charters of Trading Companies.* 1913.

CAWSTON, G., and KEANE, A. H. *Early Chartered Companies, 1296–1858.* 1896.

*CHEYNEY, E. P. *History of England from the Defeat of the Armada to the Death of Elizabeth.* 1914–1926.

COTTA, J. G. *Zur Entstehung des Kapitalismus in Venedig.* 1905.

D'AVENEL, G. *Paysans et Ouvriers depuis sept cent ans.*

EHRENBERG, R. *Das Zeitalter der Fugger.* 1922.

Fugger News-Letters. Selections of unpublished letters from correspondents of the House of Fugger, 1568–1605. Edited by V. von Klarwill and translated into English. 2 vols. 1924, 1926.

*GORIS, J. A.   *Etude sur les colonies marchandes meridionales . . . à Anvers de 1488 à 1567.*   1925.

GRAS, N. S. B.   *History of Agriculture in Europe and America.*   1925.

HABLER, K.   *Die wirtschaftliche Blüte Spaniens im XVI Jahrhundert und ihr Verfall.*

HANNAY, D.   *Great Chartered Companies.*   1926.

HELMOLT, H. F., editor.   *History of the World,* Vol. VII.   1902–1907.

PROTHERO, R. E.   *English Farming, Past and Present.*

ROOSEBOOM, M. P.   *Scottish Staple in the Netherlands, 1292–1676.*   1910.

SCHAPIRO, J. S.   *Social Reform and the Reformation.*   1909.

SCHÖNEBAUM, H.   "Antwerpens Blütezeit im XVI Jahrhundert," in *Archiv für Kulturgeschichte,* Vol. XIII.   1917.

*SCOTT, W. R.   *Constitution and Finance of English, Scottish and Irish Joint-Stock Companies.*   1910–1912.

*SÉE, HENRI.   *Les Origines du Capitalisme moderne.*   1926.

SMITH, P.   *Age of the Reformation.*   1920.

*SOMBART, WERNER.   *Der moderne Kapitalismus.*   1924.

*STRIEDER, J.   *Studien zur Geschichte Kapitalistischer Organisationsformen im Mittelalter und zu Begin der Neuzeit.*   New edition.   1925.

*TAWNEY, R. H.   *Religion and the Rise of Capitalism.*   1926.

UNWIN, G.   *Industrial Organization of England in the Sixteenth and Seventeenth Centuries.*   1904.

INDEX

Consult maps for ecclesiastical and economic centers not otherwise noted
For early history of modern nations see name of country

THE HOUSE OF HARPER

NEW YORK
Publishers of BOOKS and of
HARPER'S MAGAZINE
—
Established 1817